Human Relations for Career and Personal Success

Human Relations for Career and Personal Success

Concepts, Applications, and Skills

Ninth Edition

Andrew J. DuBrin
Rochester Institute of Technology

Prentice Hall

Boston   Columbus   Indianapolis   New York   San Francisco   Upper Saddle River   Amsterdam   Cape Town
Dubai   London   Madrid   Milan   Munich   Paris   Montreal   Toronto   Delhi   Mexico City   Sao Paulo
Sydney   Hong Kong   Seoul   Singapore   Taipei   Tokyo

Editor in Chief: Vernon Anthony
Senior Acquisitions Editor: Gary Bauer
Development Editor: Linda Cupp
Editorial Assistant: Megan Heintz
Director of Marketing: David Gesell
Marketing Manager: Leigh Ann Sims
Marketing Assistant: Les Roberts
Senior Managing Editor: JoEllen Gohr
Project Manager: Christina Taylor
Operations Specialist: Laura Messerly
Image Interior Permission Coordinator:
    Nancy Seiese

Senior Art Director: Diane Ernsberger
Cover Designer: Kellyn E. Donnelly
Cover Photo: Jupiter Images
Full-Service Project Management:
    Jogender Taneja, Aptara® Inc.
Composition: Aptara® Inc.
Printer/Binder: Webcrafters
Cover Printer: Coral Graphics
Text Font: Utopia

Photo Credits: Skjold Photographs/The Image Works, p. 2; Getty Images, pp. 34, 62; Image Source/Corbis RF, p. 92; PhotoDisc/Getty Images, p. 120; Todd Wright/Getty Images, Inc.—Blend Images, p. 150, Image Source/Getty Images Inc.—Image Source Royalty Free, p. 182; Image Source/Getty Images Inc.—Image Source Royalty Free, p. 216; Anderson Ross/Getty Images/Digital Vision, p. 244; © Jim Craigmyle/CORBIS All Rights Reserved, p. 278; Photo Alto/Eric Audras/Getty Images Royalty Free—PhotoAlto, p. 310; Chris Windsor/Getty Images —Photodisc-Royalty Free, p. 344; Image Source/Corbis RF, p. 372; PhotoDisc/Getty Images, p. 402; Tomas Rodriguez/Corbis RF, p. 432; Todd Warnock/Getty Images Inc. RF, p. 466; Stockbyte/Getty Images, Inc—Stockbyte Royalty Free, p. 494.

Library of Congress Cataloging-in-Publication Data
DuBrin, Andrew J.
    Human relations for career and personal success : concepts, applications,
and skills / Andrew J. DuBrin.—9th ed.
        p. cm.
    ISBN-13: 978-0-13-506390-3
    ISBN-10: 0-13-506390-6
    1. Success in business. 2. Organizational behavior. 3. Psychology, Industrial. 4. Interpersonal relations.   I. Title.
    HF5386.D768 2011
    650.1'3—dc22   2009041552

10 9 8 7 6 5 4 3 2 1

Prentice Hall
is an imprint of

www.pearsonhighered.com

ISBN 10:   0-13-506390-6
ISBN 13: 978-0-13-506390-3

To Rosie—and her sparkle

To Clare—and her spirit

To Camila—and her spontaneity

To Sofia—and her self-confidence

To Eliana—and her sweetness

To Carson—and his smiles

Brief Contents

Preface   xiii

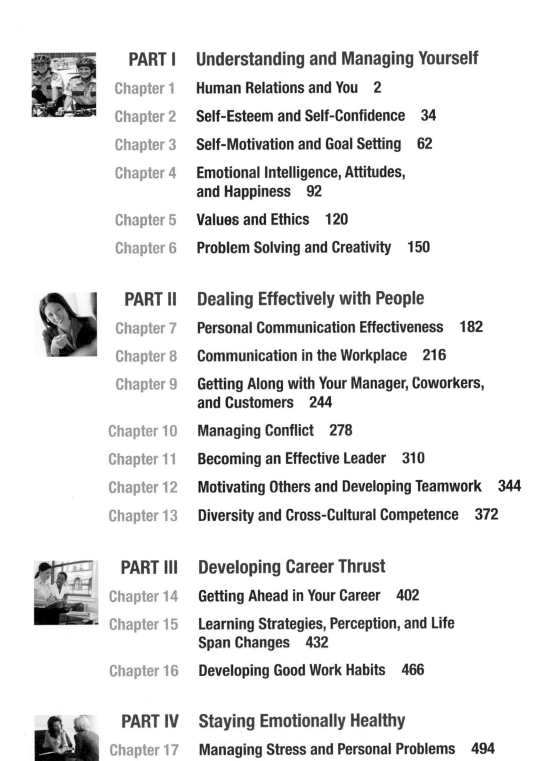

PART I   Understanding and Managing Yourself

Chapter 1   Human Relations and You   2

Chapter 2   Self-Esteem and Self-Confidence   34

Chapter 3   Self-Motivation and Goal Setting   62

Chapter 4   Emotional Intelligence, Attitudes, and Happiness   92

Chapter 5   Values and Ethics   120

Chapter 6   Problem Solving and Creativity   150

PART II   Dealing Effectively with People

Chapter 7   Personal Communication Effectiveness   182

Chapter 8   Communication in the Workplace   216

Chapter 9   Getting Along with Your Manager, Coworkers, and Customers   244

Chapter 10   Managing Conflict   278

Chapter 11   Becoming an Effective Leader   310

Chapter 12   Motivating Others and Developing Teamwork   344

Chapter 13   Diversity and Cross-Cultural Competence   372

PART III   Developing Career Thrust

Chapter 14   Getting Ahead in Your Career   402

Chapter 15   Learning Strategies, Perception, and Life Span Changes   432

Chapter 16   Developing Good Work Habits   466

PART IV   Staying Emotionally Healthy

Chapter 17   Managing Stress and Personal Problems   494

Contents

Preface   *xiii*

PART I   **Understanding and Managing Yourself**

Chapter 1   **Human Relations and You**   **2**

What Is the Nature and Importance of Human Relations?   4

How Can Studying Human Relations Help You?   4

How Do Work and Personal Life Influence Each Other?   7

In What Way Does Human Relations Begin with
Self-Understanding?   10

How Did the Human Relations Movement Develop?   15

How Does Human Relations Knowledge and Skill Help You Deal
with Major Challenges in the Workplace?   19

What Major Factors Influence Job Performance
and Behavior?   23

Chapter 2   **Self-Esteem and Self-Confidence**   **34**

What Is the Nature of Self-Esteem, How Does It Develop,
and What Are Its Consequences?   36

How Do You Enhance Self-Esteem?   41

What Is the Importance of Self-Confidence, and What Are
Its Sources?   44

How Do You Develop and Strengthen Your Self-Confidence?   45

Chapter 3   **Self-Motivation and Goal Setting**   **62**

How Do Needs and Motives Influence Motivation?   64

How Do Goals Contribute to Motivation?   71

What Are Some Self-Motivation Techniques?   77

How Do You Develop the Self-Discipline to Achieve Goals
and Stay Motivated?   80

Chapter 4   **Emotional Intelligence, Attitudes, and Happiness**   **92**

What Is Emotional Intelligence?   94

What Are the Components of Attitudes, and How Are They
Acquired and Changed?   98

What Is Happiness, and How Can It Be Acquired
and Enhanced?   104

Chapter 5   **Values and Ethics**   **120**

In What Way Are Values a Part of Understanding Human
Relations?   122

Why Be Concerned About Business Ethics?   128

What Are Some Guidelines for Making Ethical Decisions
and Behaving Ethically?   135

> " The hallmark of this text is the
> use of many real-world
> examples of human relations
> issues and practices. "
>
> —Darlean McClure, College of the Sequoias

Chapter 6   Problem Solving and Creativity   150

What Are Some Personal Characteristics That Influence Your
Problem-Solving Ability?   152

What Are the Problem-Solving and Decision-Making Steps?   156

What Do I Need to Know About Creativity in Decision Making?   161

How Do I Improve My Creativity?   167

How Does Critical Thinking Relate to Problem Solving
and Creativity?   172

PART II   Dealing Effectively with People

Chapter 7   Personal Communication Effectiveness   182

How Does Communication Take Place?   184

How Does Interpersonal Communication Relate
to Relationship Building?   185

What Is Nonverbal Communication (Sending and Receiving
Silent Messages)?   187

What Are Some Frequent Roadblocks to Communication?   192

What Are Some Ways to Build Bridges to Communication?   197

How Do You Overcome Gender Barriers to Communication?   201

How Can You Enhance Your Listening Skills?   203

Chapter 8   Communication in the Workplace   216

What Are the Formal Channels of Communication Within
Organizations?   218

What Are the Informal Channels of Communication Within
Organizations?   223

What Are the Challenges to Interpersonal Communication
Created by Communication Technology?   226

How Does One Do an Effective Job of Conducting or Participating
in a Business Meeting?   234

**Chapter 9   Getting Along with Your Manager, Coworkers,
and Customers   244**

How Do You Develop a Good Relationship with Your Manager
or Team Leader?   246

How Do You Cope with a Problem Manager?   252

How Do You Build Good Coworker Relationships?   254

How Do You Build Good Relationships with Customers?   266

Chapter 10   Managing Conflict   278

Why Does So Much Conflict Exist?   280

The Good and Bad Sides of Conflict   287

What Are Some Techniques for Resolving Conflicts?   289

What Are Some Suggestions for Managing Anger?   299

"The self-assessment quizzes
are excellent.

—Jim Wilhelm, South Plains College

Chapter 11   **Becoming an Effective Leader   310**

What Are Some Traits and Characteristics of Effective
Leaders?   312

What Are Some Behaviors and Skills of Effective Leaders?   319

What Is Leadership Style, and What Is Style Flexibility?   325

How Does a Leader Get Along Well with Subordinates?   331

How Do You Develop Your Leadership Potential?   332

What Are Several Key Challenges of Being a First-Time
Leader?   334

Chapter 12   **Motivating Others and Developing Teamwork   344**

How Do You Diagnose What Motivates Others toward Good
Performance?   346

What Are Two Classic Approaches to Understanding Work
Motivation?   346

How Do You Motivate Through Empowerment, Job Design,
and Various Forms of Positive Reinforcement?   347

What Are Some Strategies and Tactics for Building
Teamwork?   354

How Does Understanding Group Dynamics Contribute to
Teamwork Development?   358

What Are the Characteristics of an Effective Work Group?   364

Chapter 13   **Diversity and Cross-Cultural Competence   372**

What Are the Major Dimensions of Differences in Cultural
Values?   374

What Are Some Barriers to Good Cross-Cultural Relations?   377

What Are Some Approaches to Improving Cross-Cultural
Relations?   380

How Do You Overcome Cross-Cultural Communication
Barriers?   390

Why Are Gender Differences in Leadership Style Regarded as
Cultural Differences?   392

What Are Some of the Legal Aspects of Working in a Culturally
Diverse Environment?   393

PART III   **Developing Career Thrust**

Chapter 14   **Getting Ahead in Your Career   402**

What Are the Basics of Conducting a Job Search?   404

What Are Some Effective Career Advancement Strategies
and Tactics?   412

Developing Your Networking Skills   423

Chapter 15   **Learning Strategies, Perception, and Life
Span Changes   432**

What Are the Major Learning Strategies and Processes?   434

What Are Several Different Learning Styles?   438

I really like . . . knowing
yourself before you can begin
to understand others and the
environment around you.

—Jewel Cherry, Forsyth Technical and
Community College

"One strength is the readability, the second strength is the practical approach, the third strength is the summary section, the fourth strength concerns the case studies. . . ."

—Reginald St. Clair, Mountain Empire Community College

How Does Perception Influence How People Interpret the World?   443

How Do We Respond to Life Span Changes and Challenges?   446

What Are Some Basic Concepts About Changing Careers?   453

What Are Some Tactics for Coping with Change?   456

Chapter 16   Developing Good Work Habits   466

How Does a Person Deal with Procrastination?   468

What Are Some Proper Attitudes and Values to Develop?   472

What Are Some Effective Time-Management Techniques?   475

How Does One Overcome Time Wasters?   482

PART IV   Staying Emotionally Healthy

Chapter 17   Managing Stress and Personal Problems   494

What Are the Physiology and Consequences of Stress?   496

What Are Some Sources of Stress in Personal Life?   499

What Are Some Key Sources of Work Stress?   503

What Are Several Effective Approaches to Managing Stress?   506

What Are Two Key Perspectives on Understanding and Dealing with Personal Problems?   513

Appendix   *527*
Glossary   *529*
Index   *537*

Welcome to the ninth edition of *Human Relations for Career and Personal Success: Concepts, Applications, and Skills.* This new edition continues the emphasis of the eighth edition on developing effective human relations skills for the workplace, including material on teamwork and motivating and influencing others. The purpose of this book is to show how you can become more effective in your work and personal life through knowledge of and skill in human relations. A major theme of this text is that career and personal success are related. Success on the job often enhances personal success, and success in personal life can enhance job success. Dealing effectively with people is an enormous asset in both work and personal life.

This text is written to help students deal with human relations problems in the workplace and in personal life. It is designed to be appropriate for human relations courses taught in colleges, career schools, vocational–technical schools, and other postsecondary schools. Managerial, professional, and technical workers who are forging ahead in their careers will also find this book immediately useful in improving workplace and personal relationships.

Organization of the Book

The text is divided into four parts, reflecting the major issues in human relations.

Part I covers four aspects of understanding and managing yourself. Chapter 1 focuses on the meaning of human relations, self-understanding, and the interrelationship of career and personal success. Chapter 2 explains how self-esteem and self-confidence are important parts of human functioning. Chapter 3 explains how to use self-motivation and goal setting to improve your chances for success. Chapter 4 deals with the importance of emotional intelligence and attitudes and factors associated with being happy. Chapter 5 explains the contribution of values and ethics to effective human relations. Chapter 6 explains the basics of solving problems and making decisions with an emphasis on creativity.

Part II examines the heart of human relations—dealing effectively with other people. The topics in Chapters 7 through 13 are, respectively, personal communication effectiveness; communication in the workplace; getting along with your manager, coworkers, and customers; managing conflict; becoming an effective leader; motivating others and developing teamwork; and developing cross-cultural competence.

Part III provides information to help career-minded people capitalize on their educations, experiences, talents, and ambitions. The topics of Chapters 14 through 16 are getting ahead in your career; learning strategies, perception, and life span changes; and developing good work habits.

Part IV deals with staying emotionally healthy, while Chapter 17 covers managing stress and personal problems.

Changes in the Ninth Edition

In addition to thoroughly updating material throughout the text, we have also made changes to the narrative to improve flow and readability and provide more examples and applications of concepts. Major changes in this regard include the following:

■ Many of the introductory cases, Human Relations in Action inserts, and case studies have been replaced with contemporary material. Sixteen chapter introduction cases are new. Fourteen Human Relations in Action inserts have been replaced with new inserts. Nineteen new end-of-chapter case studies are found in this edition, and six Internet skill-building exercises have been replaced with new exercises.

■ Narrative sections of the text are now "chunked" by headings into smaller segments with subheadings and bulleting, and explanations of research studies have substantially reduced. These changes improve flow and readability for students, yet still include the information supported by the research.

■ Many new self-assessments, role-plays, and class activities have been added to this edition, including five new skill-building exercises, four new self-assessment quizzes, seventeen new role-playing exercises, and fifteen new class activities.

Detailed chapter-by-chapter revisions and updates—in addition to the changes already mentioned—include the following:

Chapter 1, Human Relations and You

■ Case example of how understanding human relations might help the reader resolve a delicate situation.

■ Analysis of how work behavior is related to behavior at home.

■ The Johari Window as a method of self-disclosure.

■ Analysis of how human relations knowledge and skills can help the reader deal with major challenges in the workplace, as follows: dealing with workplace diversity and globalization; emphasis on employee creativity and innovativeness; being part of the virtual workplace and telecommuting; and increased emphasis on skill acquisition and upward mobility.

■ Role-playing exercise about kindness and recognition.

■ Class activity about the uniqueness of people.

Chapter 2, Self-Esteem and Self-Confidence

■ Long-term research about how self-esteem contributes to career success.

■ How self-esteem can regulate social relationships.

■ Leo Buscaglia's observations on how appreciating one's strengths enhances self-esteem.

■ How behaving as if you feel self-confident can enhance self-confidence.

■ The development of positive psychological capital.

■ The importance of avoiding overconfidence

Chapter 3, Self-Motivation and Goal Setting

■ Explanation of how using knowledge about self-discipline can help a person attain career goals.

■ Self-assessment quiz about one's position on the needs hierarchy.

■ Engagement as part of self-motivation.

■ Delaying gratification as part of self-discipline.

Chapter 4, Emotional Intelligence, Attitudes, and Happiness

■ Consequences of high and low emotional intelligence.

■ Giving personal support to others as part of organizational citizenship behavior.

■ Developing and maintaining friendships with happy people to enhance personal happiness.

■ The challenge of *hedonic adaptation*, or regarding exciting and new aspects of life as routine after a while.

Chapter 5, Values and Ethics

■ Stereotypes about Gen Y workers.

■ New findings on the extent of ethical problems.

■ Causing problems in order to take credit for fixing them as a form of unethical behavior.

■ The four-criteria ethics test.

■ The Mission and Values of Microsoft Corporation (updated).

Chapter 6, Problem Solving and Creativity

- Illustration about the cognitive intelligence, education, and experience of Captain "Sully" Sullenberger.
- Engaging in multicultural experiences to enhance creativity.
- Adequate physical exercise as a method of improving creativity.
- Relationship of critical thinking to problem solving and creativity.

Chapter 7, Personal Communication Effectiveness

- Allowing sender to finish his or her sentence to improve listening.
- Minimizing words that shut down discussion to keep the conversation flowing.

Chapter 8, Communication in the Workplace

- Social networking Web sites as part of organizational communication.
- Intranets and Wikis as part of organizational communication.
- Webinars as part of organizational communication.
- Social network analysis.
- Overconfidence in computer-generated data as a problem in organization communication.

Chapter 9, Getting Along with Your Manager, Coworkers, and Customers

- Self-Assessment Quiz 9-1 about interaction with managers (replaces previous quiz on same subject).
- Research study about how self-esteem and being at the center of a communication network are associated with popularity.

Chapter 10, Managing Conflict

- Differences of opinions on work-related issues and rights as a source of conflict.
- Cross-generational conflict.
- Reframing through cognitive restructuring and asking questions.
- Listening to investigate what the other side wants as a negotiation technique.
- Self-Assessment Quiz 10-2: How Much Am I Being Ostracized?

Chapter 11, Becoming an Effective Leader

- How a subordinate can adapt to various leadership styles.
- Adapting leadership style to cultural values.
- Challenges of being a first-time leader.

Chapter 12, Motivating Others and Developing Teamwork

- More strategies for building teamwork, including (a) making appropriate use of a team slogan, logo, and clothing and (b) stepping in to resolve conflict.
- How students might get into difficulty with a group assignment because of groupthink.

Chapter 13, Diversity and Cross-Cultural Competence

- How business practices are subject to cultural norms (example from India).
- Examples of legislation and court rulings to ensure equal rights in addition to federal legislation.

Chapter 14, Getting Ahead in Your Career

- Expansion of information about job résumé construction, including mention of the video résumé.
- Job hunting during difficult economic times.
- 10,000 Hour Rule about developing true expertise.
- Development of personal brand.
- The buddy system as a form of mentoring.
- Dealing constructively with the situation of having a subordinate older than you or a younger boss.

Chapter 15: Learning Strategies, Perception, and Life Span Changes

- Learning of habits in everyday life.
- Group learning (how groups learn).

- Successfully managing the teenage brain.
- The sandwich generation challenge.
- Acquiring cognitive fitness to adapt to life changes.
- Changing careers without changing employers.

Chapter 16: Developing Good Work Habits

- Planning for working with people from different time zones.
- ADHD as a cause of poor concentration on important tasks.

Chapter 17: Managing Stress and Personal Problems

- Challenge versus hindrance stressors.
- Job insecurity and job loss as stressors.
- Receiving organizational support to help manage stress.
- Soft addictions as a type of self-defeating behavior.
- Observing the discrepancy between your ideal life and what exists now to help overcome self-defeating behavior.

An accomplished author, Andrew J. DuBrin, PhD, brings to his work years of research experience in human relations and business psychology. His research has been reported in *Entrepreneur, Psychology Today, The Wall Street Journal, Fortune Small Biz*, and more than one hundred national magazines and local newspapers. He has published numerous articles, textbooks, and well-publicized professional books. Dr. DuBrin received his PhD from Michigan State University and is Professor Emeritus at the College of Business, Rochester Institute of Technology, where he has taught organizational behavior, leadership, and career management.

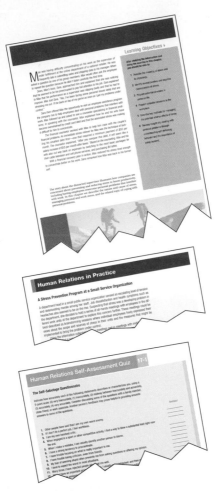

Human Relations for Career and Personal Success is not simply a textbook. The ninth edition contains a wealth of experiential exercises, including new cases and self-assessment quizzes that can be completed in class or as homework.

Chapter-Opening Cases Set the Stage

Chapter-opening cases introduce students to the topic and set the stage for the chapter narrative.

Pedagogical Features Relate Concepts to What's Happening Today, Personally and in the Workplace

- **Self-assessment quizzes** give students the opportunity to explore their own opinions, feelings, and behavior patterns as related to chapter topics. All chapters include one or more self-assessment quizzes.
- **Human Relations in Practice** boxes in all chapters illustrate real human relations business practices in today's business world.
- **Motivational "words of wisdom"** from a wide variety of business and world leaders and experts are included in all chapters.

Expanded Assignment Material

End-of-chapter assignment material is organized into two sections: **Concept Review and Reinforcement,** featuring exercises that focus on concept retention and developing critical-thinking skills, and **Developing Your Human Relations Skills,** focusing on developing skills that can be used immediately in life and on the job.

Concept Review and Reinforcement

Key Terms

Chapter Summary and Review provides an excellent detailed review of key chapter concepts.

Check Your Understanding provides questions, reviews key chapter topics, and stimulates thinking about the issues.

Web Corner provides informational Web sites and asks students to use the power of the Web in researching outside resources. Six of the Internet Skill Builder exercises have been replaced by new exercises.

Developing Your Human Relations Skills

Skills Exercises tie together chapter topics and allow students to apply what they have just learned.

New Role-Playing and Class Projects allow students to practice and model human relations situations in the classroom.

Two Human Relations Case Studies put students into a realistic scenario so they can practice making decisions in tough situations.

Resources for Students
Need Additional Practice and Support?

COMPANION WEB SITE

Go to www.pearsonhighered.com/dubrin to access links to online resources for each chapter and to prepare for tests. Here you will find a variety of new exercises, online assignments, and self-grading quizzes for each chapter, including multiple-choice questions, true/false questions, and essay questions to help students check mastery of the topics.

PRENTICE HALL SELF-ASSESSMENT LIBRARY (SAL)

SAL is a CD-ROM product developed by Steve Robbins that contains fifty-one research-based self-assessments that provide students with insights into their skills, abilities, and interests. It is easy to use, self scoring, and can be packaged with this text at a discounted price. Please contact your Pearson/Prentice Hall representative to obtain a review copy.

THE GOLDEN PERSONALITY TYPE PROFILER

This popular personality assessment provides students with information about five fundamental personality dimensions: Where you direct your energy (introverted or extraverted), the way you gather and interpret information, how you make decisions, how you approach life (e.g., organizing versus adapting), and how you respond to stress. The Golden assessment is similar to the Myers-Briggs full assessment program. It takes about 15 to 20 minutes to complete, and students receive an easy-to-use and practical feedback report based on their results. This tool helps students improve their self-knowledge and ability to work effectively with others by providing students with feedback on their leadership and organizational strengths, communication and teamwork preferences, motivation and learning style, and opportunities for personal growth. The Golden is typically used in a classroom setting to help prepare students for entry into the workforce or for career development. Instructional support materials are available so that instructors guide students through their feedback report and help them apply their results to build personal and interpersonal skills. An access code can be packaged with the text or can be purchased online at www.pearsonhighered.com.

Resources for Instructors

To access supplementary materials online, instructors need to request an instructor access code. Go to www.pearsonhighered.com/irc, where you can register for an instructor access code. Within forty-eight hours of registering, you will receive a confirming e-mail including an instructor access code. Once you have received your code, locate your text in the online catalog and click on the Instructor Resources button on the left side of the catalog product page. Select a supplement, and a log-in page will appear. Once you have logged in, you can access instructor material for all Prentice Hall textbooks.

INSTRUCTOR'S MANUAL WITH TEST ITEM FILE

The instructor's manual for this text contains a large number of multiple-choice and true/false test questions, chapter outlines and lecture notes, answers to discussion questions and case problems, and comments about the exercises.

PRENTICE HALL TEST GENERATOR

The computerized test-generation system gives you maximum flexibility in preparing tests. It can be used to create custom tests and print scrambled versions of a test at one time, as well as to build tests randomly by chapter, level of difficulty, or question type. The software also allows online testing and record keeping and the ability to add problems to the database.

POWERPOINT LECTURE PRESENTATION PACKAGE

Lecture presentation screens for each chapter are available online and on the IRC.

JWA HUMAN RELATIONS VIDEOS

JWA videos on human relations and interpersonal communication topics are available to qualified adopters. Contact your local representative for details.

Distance Learning Solutions: Convenience, Simplicity, Success

Readymade **WebCT** and **Blackboard** online courses are available. If you adopt a course, student access cards will be packaged with the text at no extra charge to the student. Courses include Research Navigator, a premium online research tool.

Pearson's **MySearchLab** is the easiest way for students to start a research assignment or research paper. Complete with extensive help on the research process and four exclusive databases of credible and reliable source material—including the EBSCO Academic Journal and Abstract Database, *New York Times* Search by Subject Archive, "Best of the Web" Link Library, and *Financial Times* Article Archive and Company Financials—Research Navigator helps students quickly and efficiently make the most of their research time.

Acknowledgments

A book of this nature cannot be written and published without the cooperation of many people. Many outside reviewers of this and the previous editions provided constructive suggestions for improving the book. The following reviewers provided detailed feedback that drove the refocusing of this edition:

Jessica Li, University of North Texas

Therese Nemec, Fox Valley Technical College

Marcia Polanis, Forsyth Technical Community College

Dr. Nora Jo Sherman, Houston Community College

Previous edition reviewers:

Daniel Bialis, Muskegon Community College

Jewel Cherry, Forsyth Technical Community College

Claudia Cochran, El Paso Community College

Darlean McClure, College of the Sequoias

Michelle Meyer, Joliet Junior College

Alvin Motley, Metropolitan Community College

Debra Rowe, Oakland Community College

Reginald St. Clair, Mountain Empire Community College

Rudy Soliz, Houston Community College

Carol Thole, Shasta College

James Van Arsdall, Metropolitan Community College

Susan Verhulst, Des Moines Area Community College

Jim Wilhelm, South Plains College

Mary D. Aun, DeVry Technical Institute

Donna Ana Branch and H. Ralph Todd Jr., American River College

Hollis Chaleau Brown, Oakton Community College

Sheri Bryant, DeKalb Technical Institute

Win Chesney, St. Louis Community College

Joy Colwell, Purdue University

Ruth Keller, Indiana Vo-Tech College

Robert F. Pearse, Rochester Institute of Technology

Steve Quinn, Olympic College

Bernice Rose, Computer Learning Center

Pamela Simon, Baker College

A special thanks goes to Terese Nemec and Kath Lich from Fox Valley Technical College and Sharon Chacon-Mineau from Northease Wisconsin Technical College for their assistance in revising and expanding the supplement materials that accompany this textbook.

Thanks also to my family members, whose emotional support and encouragement assist my writing: Melanie, Will, Carson, Douglas, Gizella, Camila, Sofia, Eliana, Drew, Rosie, and Clare. I also offer special thanks to Stefanie, the woman in my life.

Andrew J. DuBrin

Rochester, New York

Human Relations for Career and Personal Success

1

Human Relations and You

Outline

1 What Is the Nature and Importance of Human Relations?

2 How Can Studying Human Relations Help You?

3 How Do Work and Personal Life Influence Each Other?

4 In What Way Does Human Relations Begin with Self-Understanding?
General Information about Human Behavior
Informal Feedback from People
Feedback from Superiors
Feedback from Coworkers
Feedback from Self-Assessment Quizzes
Looking at the Self through the Johari Window
Two Self-Evaluation Traps

5 How Did the Human Relations Movement Develop?
Scientific Management
The Hawthorne Studies
The Threat of Unionization
The Philosophy of Industrial Humanism
Theory X and Theory Y of Douglas McGregor
Relevance of the History of Human Relations to Today's Workplace

6 How Does Human Relations Knowledge and Skill Help You Deal with Major Challenges in the Workplace?
Emphasis on Teamwork and Collaboration

High Expectations for Personal Productivity
Dealing with Workplace Diversity and Globalization
Emphasis on Employee Creativity and Innovativeness
Being Part of the Virtual Workplace and Telecommuting
Increased Emphasis on Skill Acquisition and Less on Upward Mobility

7 What Major Factors Influence Job Performance and Behavior?

andy Bellows was being honored as the local Woman of the Year by a public relations trade association. Bellows was the executive vice president of a private organization that promoted tourism and convention business in her geographic area. During the awards ceremony, several people who either report directly to Bellows or work closely with her were asked to comment on what makes Sandy Bellows so special.

Jack, the director of tourism publicity, spoke first. Among his comments were, "Sandy knows no limits to the kindness and respect she shows to others on her team. When a suggestion of mine might be way off base, Sandy will listen carefully and then compliment me for the good in my idea. But then she will ask me a few sharp questions that point me in the direction of coming up with a better solution to the problem I am facing."

Penny, the convention and banquet manager at a large hotel in the area, opened her comments about Bellows in these terms: "Sandy really knows what it means to partner with somebody in the community. She works with me and my staff in a fully cooperative way. She keeps emphasizing how the community can prosper only if we truly collaborate in finding ways to bring convention business to our city. Working with Sandy has helped we hotel managers realize that we are not competing against each other but against other areas of the country."

Megan, who has worked five years as the administrative assistant to Bellows, included this point in her comments: "Sandy makes me feel like the most important person in her workday. She asks my opinion about so many things. She frequently asks me what she can do to make my job run more smoothly. The impression I get is that Sandy makes a lot of other people feel important too."

Learning Objectives ▶

After studying the information and doing the exercises in this chapter, you should be able to:

1 Describe the nature and importance of human relations.

2 Understand how studying human relations will help you.

3 Pinpoint how work and personal life influence each other.

4 Understand how effective human relations begins with self-understanding.

5 Understand the timeline and development of the human relations movement.

6 Indicate how a knowledge of human relations will help you deal with major challenges in the workplace.

7 Understand the major factors influencing job performance and behavior.

The comments by this public-sector executive focus on the importance of effective human relations. Treating people with kindness helps Sandy Bellows deal effectively with the businesspeople her organization serves, as well as her employees. This book presents a wide variety of suggestions and guidelines for improving your personal relationships both on and off the job. Most of them are based on systematic knowledge about human behavior.

▶ Learning Objective 1 ▶

What Is the Nature and Importance of Human Relations?

Human relations
the art of using systematic knowledge about human behavior to improve personal, job, and career effectiveness

In the context used here, **human relations** is the art of using systematic knowledge about human behavior to improve personal, job, and career effectiveness. Human relations is far more than "being nice to people," because it applies systematic knowledge to treating people in such a way that they feel better and are more productive—such as providing a more relaxed work atmosphere to enhance worker creativity.

Similar to the field known as *organizational behavior*, human relations studies individuals and groups in organizations. Human relations, however, is essentially a less technical and more applied version of organizational behavior. In this text we make some references to research and theory, but the emphasis is on a more personal and applied approach to the subject matter.

Organizational effectiveness
the extent to which an organization is productive and satisfies the demands of interested parties, such as employees, customers, and investors

From the standpoint of management, human relations is quite important because it contributes to **organizational effectiveness**—the extent to which an organization is productive and satisfies the demands of interested parties, such as employees, customers, and investors. Steve Kent, an equities analyst (not a human relations specialist) at Goldman Sachs & Co., made extensive observations about the importance of treating employees well (using principles of human relations). He found that treating employees with respect and paying them fairly contributes to developing an efficient and creative organization. Business firms that go the extra mile to treat employees well often derive tangible benefits, such as a high quality of customer service.[1]

Why does paying more attention to the human element improve business performance? Organizational behavior professor Jeffery Pfeffer at Stanford University notes that people work harder when they have greater control over their work environment and when they are encouraged by peer pressure from teammates. Even more advantage comes from people working smarter. People-oriented management practices enable workers to use their wisdom and receive the training they need to perform better. Another contribution to improved performance stems from eliminating positions that focus primarily on watching and controlling people.[2] The accompanying Human Relations in Practice box insert provides additional information about the payoff from company management practicing good human relations.

▶ Learning Objective 2 ▶

How Can Studying Human Relations Help You?

Human relations knowledge and skills are also potentially beneficial for the individual as well as the organization. The following case history illustrates how a career-minded person made effective use of human relations principles to resolve a difficult situation that seemed to be blocking her career. You might be able to use the same approach if you face a similar problem.

Human Relations in Practice

Growing an Innovation Consulting Firm by Focusing on Positive Interpersonal Relationships

When the four founders of Jump Associates LLC were building the company, they wanted to avoid the ultracompetitive, sometimes backstabbing atmosphere found at other high-energy consulting agencies. So early on they began adopting a series of practices that promote considerate collaboration.

Every morning, all employees meet for a "scrum"—a short get-together where they're briefed on company news, do yoga-like exercises, and then play a quick brain-rousing game that forces them to think on their feet. Jump employees are also subject to a "no zinger" policy that bans them from saying anything demeaning or hurtful about another employee. What's more, employees are asked to occasionally do so-called affinity exercises where employees ask others to declare one thing they like about them and ask other icebreaker-type questions. The person who responded then poses those questions to the person who originally asked them. And a coach stops in the office a few days a month to help employees with any issue, such as improving their communications or resolving conflicts with a colleague.

"There are companies that try to systematize the nastier instincts in people," says cofounder and chief executive Dev Patnaik. At Jump, "we try to put in systems that make people better than they otherwise would be."

The layout and interior design of the office are also meant to spark team building. All employees, including all senior management, sit out in the open in "neighborhoods" of five or six workers.

Senior management also believes in relying on the latest team-building research and methods to improve effectiveness and camaraderie. New employees all take tests that measure learning knowledge and skills learning. Everyone's strengths are listed on a poster in the office in hopes that these skills will be used and discussed on a regular basis to improve team performance.

The test told Colleen Murray, a 35-year-old project leader, that among her top strengths are being disciplined, responsible, and deliberative. Her disciplined nature, she says, makes her a natural at spearheading projects and setting goals and deadlines. Managers say they took those qualities into account when moving her into leadership roles.

Question: Why would an emphasis on collaboration help a company that helps other companies be more innovative?

Source: Abridged from Kelly K. Spors, "Top Small Workplaces 2008: Jump Associates LLC," *The Wall Street Journal*, October 13, 2008, p. R5.

Ashley worked as a business analyst at a large hospital. Her responsibilities included searching for ways to improve work processes at the hospital, such as developing better forms for collecting information about patients and reducing the time outpatients spent in the waiting room. Ashley enjoyed her work and believed that she was gaining valuable experience toward her goal of becoming a hospital administrator.

Another contributor to Ashley's job satisfaction was her relationship with Paul, her boss. Ashley perceived her work relationship with him to be ideal. Paul kept feeding Ashley interesting assignments, gave her useful suggestions from time to time, and frequently praised her work. On her most recent performance evaluation, Ashley was described as "an ideal hospital business analyst with great potential."

Ashley's smooth working relationship with her manager quickly changed one January. Paul informed the group that the hospital had offered him a promotion to a much bigger role at the hospital and that although he enjoyed his present position, he felt obliged to accept the promotion. In Paul's place, the hospital appointed Jody, an experienced supervisor in another department within the hospital.

Within the first three weeks, Jody began criticizing Ashley's work. She told her that her approach to improving business processes was not up-to-date, and that it lacked the kind of depth the hospital needed. Ashley then worked diligently on her next project to make the kind of improvements Jody suggested. Jody then found something else to criticize, this time telling Ashley that her PowerPoint presentations supporting her report were too complex, making them difficult for hospital administrators to follow.

Soon Jody found ways to criticize Ashley personally, in addition to the work she was performing. She suggested that Ashley should be careful to never wear heels higher than one and one half inches to the office and that the tattoo on her neck was unprofessional. Jody also suggested to Ashley twice that she should make sure to use the Internet only for job-related purposes during working hours.

After five months of regular criticism from her boss, Ashley decided to talk over the strained relationship with David, a close friend. Ashley explained to David that the negative chemistry between her and her boss was giving her chest pains and interrupted sleep. Ashley also emphasized that she was worried about receiving such a poor evaluation that it would damage her career.

David advised Ashley to "do what she had to do," by confronting her boss about the unjustified criticisms. If that didn't work, Ashley should communicate directly with Jody's manager to get the problem resolved. David explained that "In the modern organization, you are expected to bring problems right out on the table."

Ashley thanked David for his advice and then did some careful reflection. On the surface, David's advice made sense, but with her career potentially at stake, Ashley did not want to operate on common sense alone. She remembered studying about attitude change somewhere in human relations or social psychology. A point that stuck in her mind was that favorable interactions lead to attitude change.

Ashley developed a game plan to look for ways to have positive interactions with Jody whenever possible. One day she thanked Jody for the suggestions she made about preparing less complicated PowerPoint slides. She also incorporated ideas from a recent article about business process reengineering into her next suggestion for improving the workflow in the hospital laundry. Another day Ashley complimented Jody about a business suit she was wearing. At a luncheon meeting with Jody and several other department members, Ashley wore a blouse that covered the tattoo on her neck.

Ashley's game plan of applying a little-known principle of human relations to improving her relationship with her boss soon started to pay off. Jody actually complimented Ashley's report and stated that she was a strong contributor to the hospital. The most concrete evidence of an improved relationship was that Jody rated Ashley as "exceeding expectations" the first time she formally evaluated her performance.

As the case history just presented indicated, another way of understanding the importance of human relations is to examine its personal benefits. A person who carefully studies human relations and incorporates its suggestions into his or her work and personal life should derive the five benefits discussed next. Knowledge itself, however, is no guarantee of success. Because people differ greatly in learning ability, personality, and life circumstances, some will get more out of studying human relations than will others. You may, for example, be getting along well with coworkers or customers, so studying this topic might seem unnecessary from your viewpoint. Or you may be so shy at this stage of your life that you are unable to capitalize on some of the suggestions for being assertive with people. You might have to work doubly hard to benefit from studying that topic. The major benefits from studying human relations are the following:

1. **Acquiring valid information about human behavior.** To feel comfortable with people and to make a favorable impression both on and off the job, you need to understand how people think and act. Studying human relations will provide you with some basic knowledge about interpersonal relationships, such as the meaning of self-esteem, why goals work, and win–win conflict resolution. You will even learn such things as effective methods of dealing with difficult people.

2. **Developing skills in dealing with people.** People who aspire to high-level positions or enriched social lives need to be able to communicate with others, work well on a team, manage stress, and behave confidently. Relating well to diverse cultural groups is also an asset. Studying information about such topics, coupled with practicing what you learn, should help you develop such interpersonal skills.

3. **Coping with job problems.** Almost everyone who holds a job inevitably runs into human relations problems. Reading about these problems and suggestions for coping with them could save you considerable inner turmoil. Among the job survival skills that you will learn about in the study of human relations are how to deal with difficult people and how to overcome what seems to be an overwhelming workload.

4. **Coping with personal problems.** We all have problems. An important difference between the effective and the ineffective person is that the effective person knows how to manage them. Among the problems studying human relations will help you cope with are self-defeating behavior, dealing with a difficult coworker, overcoming low self-confidence, and working your way out of heavy job stress.

5. **Capitalizing on opportunities.** Many readers of this book will someday spend part of their working time taking advantage of opportunities rather than solving daily problems. Every career-minded person needs a few breakthrough experiences to make life more rewarding. Toward this end, studying human relations gives you ideas for developing your career, becoming a leader, and becoming more creative.

You are invited to take the accompanying Human Relations Self-Assessment Quiz 1-1 to think through your current level of human relations effectiveness.

◀ Learning Objective 3 ◀

How Do Work and Personal Life Influence Each Other?

Most people reading this book will be doing so to improve their job effectiveness and careers. Therefore, the book centers on relationships with people in a job setting. Keep in mind that human relationships in work and personal life have much in common. Several studies have supported the close relationship between job satisfaction and life satisfaction. One such study conducted by Timothy A. Judge, psychology professor at the University of Florida, and Remus Ilies, psychology professor at Michigan State University, involved seventy-four university employees with administrative support positions, such as secretaries or office managers. The researchers collected reports of mood and job satisfaction at work, mood away from work, and job satisfaction. Data were collected using questionnaires posted on a Web site.

FIGURE 1-1

HOW WORK AND PERSONAL LIFE INFLUENCE EACH OTHER

> 1. Job satisfaction enhances life satisfaction.
> 2. An unsatisfying job can damage physical health.
> 3. Relationships with people on and off the job influence each other.
> 4. Certain skills contribute to success in both work and personal life.
> 5. How we behave at work is closely related to how we behave at home.

The major findings of the study were that mood influences job satisfaction, with a positive mood increasing satisfaction. The effect decreases rapidly because moods pass quickly. The researchers also found that employee's satisfaction with their jobs, measured at work, influences the mood at home. Workers who are more emotional by nature are more likely to experience these connections, such as joy or anger, on the job spilling over to home life. A related finding was that a mood developed on the job spilled over to the home later in the day.[3] In short, this study confirmed the old cartoons about a worker who is chewed out by the boss coming home and swearing at his or her dog or kicking the furniture!

Work and personal life influence each other in a number of specific ways, as outlined in Figure 1-1. First, the satisfaction you achieve on the job contributes to your general life satisfaction. Conversely, if you suffer from chronic job dissatisfaction, your life satisfaction will begin to decline. Career disappointments have been shown to cause marital relationships to suffer. Frustrated on the job, many people start feuding with their partners and other family members.

Second, an unsatisfying job can affect physical health, primarily by creating stress and burnout. Intense job dissatisfaction may even lead to heart disease, ulcers, intestinal disorders, and skin problems. People who have high job satisfaction even tend to live longer than those who suffer from prolonged job dissatisfaction. These benefits may be attributed to better physical health and passion for life. Finding the right type of job may thus add years to a person's life.

Third, the quality of your relationships with people at work and in personal life influence each other. If you experience intense conflict in your family, you might be so upset that you will be unable to form good relationships with coworkers. Conversely, if you have a healthy, rewarding personal life, it will be easier for you to form good relationships on the job. People you meet on the job will find it pleasant to relate to a seemingly positive and untroubled person.

Another way of explaining the third point is that how we behave at work is closely related to how we behave at home. Psychologist John M. Gottman, executive director of the Relationship Research Institute, has been studying married couples for over thirty-five years. He and his colleagues have used devices such as camcorders, heart monitors, and other biofeedback equipment to measure what takes place when couples experience moments of conflict or closeness. The research results indicate that successful couples look for ways to emphasize the positive and attempt to say yes as often as possible. Successful couples use conflict as a way of working through personality differences rather than to attack each other.

A useful inference from research at the Relationship Research Institute is that the way people manage their relationships in the workplace is closely linked to the way they manage their personal ones. People who frequently use the word *yes* in communications at home are likely to do the same on the job. Also, people who are abusive on the job are likely to be abusive at home.[4]

Personal relationships on the job also influence personal relationships off the job. Interacting harmoniously with coworkers can put one in a better mood for dealing with family and friends after hours. Crossing swords with employees and customers during working hours can make it difficult for you to feel comfortable and relaxed with people off the job.

Human Relations Self-Assessment Quiz   1-1

Human Relations Skills

For each of the following statements about human relations skills, indicate how strong you think you are right now. Attempt to be as objective as possible, even though most of us tend to exaggerate our skills in dealing with people. To help obtain a more objective evaluation of your capabilities, ask someone who knows you well (family member, friend, or work associate) to also rate you on these factors. Use the following scale: (1) very weak, (2) weak, (3) average, (4) strong, (5) very strong.

	Self-Rating	Rating by Other Person
1. Listen carefully when in conversation with another person	_____	_____
2. Smile frequently	_____	_____
3. Am tactful when criticizing others	_____	_____
4. Am comfortable in dealing with people from a different generation than myself	_____	_____
5. Am comfortable in dealing with a person from a different ethnic group than myself	_____	_____
6. Am comfortable in dealing with a person from a different race than myself	_____	_____
7. Let my feelings be known when I disagree with another person	_____	_____
8. Let my feelings be known when I am joyful about something	_____	_____
9. Have a neat, well-groomed appearance	_____	_____
10. Congratulate the winner when I lose an athletic or any other type of contest	_____	_____
11. Concentrate on another person when in conversation instead of accepting a call on my cell phone, making use of call waiting, or responding to e-mail	_____	_____
12. Compliment others when a compliment is merited	_____	_____
13. Have a good sense of humor	_____	_____
14. Am patient with people who do not understand what I am saying	_____	_____
15. Cooperate with others in a team effort	_____	_____
16. Have a controllable temper	_____	_____
17. Am respected for being honest and dependable	_____	_____
18. Hug people when the situation is appropriate	_____	_____
19. Am trusted by other people	_____	_____
20. Motivate others to do something they hadn't thought of doing	_____	_____
Total Score	_____	
Combined Score (self plus other)		_____

Interpretation

1. **Self-ratings:** If your self-rating is 85 or more, and your scoring is accurate, you have exceptional human relations skills. Scores between 60 and 84 suggest moderate, or average, human relations skills. Scores of 59 and below suggest below-average human relations skills in the areas covered in this quiz.
2. **Rating by other person:** Because people tend to judge us a little more critically than we judge ourselves in human relations skills, use the following scale: 80 or more suggests exceptional human relations skills; 55 to 79 suggests moderate, or average, human relations skills; 54 and below suggests below-average human relations skills.
3. **Combined ratings:** 165 or more suggests exceptional human relations skills; 115 to 163 suggests moderate, or average, human relations skills; 114 or below suggests below-average human relations skills.

Action plan: Whether you scored high, low, or medium on this quiz, there is always room for improvement, just as athletes, actors, and musicians are always looking to improve their art. Scores in the bottom category suggest a more urgent need for improvement in human relations skill.

Fourth, certain skills contribute to success in both work and personal life. For example, people who know how to deal effectively with others and get things accomplished on the job can use the same skills to enhance their personal lives. Similarly, people who are effective in dealing with friends and family members and who can organize things are likely to be effective supervisors.

Can you think of other ways in which success in work and success in personal life are related to each other?

▶ Learning Objective 4 ▶

In What Way Does Human Relations Begin with Self-Understanding?

Before you can understand other people very well, and therefore practice effective human relations, you must understand yourself. You already know something about yourself. An important starting point in learning more about yourself is self-examination. Suppose that instead of being about human relations, this book were about dancing. The reader would obviously need to know what other dancers do right and wrong. But the basic principles of dancing cannot be fully grasped unless they are seen in relation to your own style of dancing. Watching a video of your dancing, for example, would be helpful. You might also ask other people for comments and suggestions about your dance movements.

Self-understanding

gathering valid information about oneself; self-understanding refers to knowledge about oneself, particularly with respect to mental and emotional aspects

Self

a complex idea generally referring to a person's total being or individuality

Public self

what a person communicates about himself or herself and what others actually perceive about the person

Private self

the actual person an individual may be

Similarly, to achieve **self-understanding,** you must gather valid information about yourself. (Self-understanding refers to knowledge about you, particularly with respect to mental and emotional aspects.) Every time you read a self-help book, take a personality quiz, or receive an evaluation of your work from a manager or instructor, you are gaining some self-knowledge.

In achieving self-understanding, it is helpful to recognize that the **self** is a complex idea. It generally refers to a person's total being or individuality. To help clarify the meaning of the self, a distinction is sometimes made between the self a person projects to the outside world and the inner self. The **public self** is what the person is communicating about himself or herself and what others actually perceive about the person. The **private self** is the actual person you may be.[5] A similar distinction is made between the real self and the ideal self. Many people think of themselves in terms of an ideal version of what they are really like. To avoid making continuous distinctions between the various selves throughout this text, we will use the term *self* to refer to an accurate representation of the individual.

Some scientific evidence suggests that the self is based on structures within the brain. According to the research of Joseph LeDoux at New York University, the self is the sum of the brain's individual components, or subsystems. Each subsystem has its own form of memory, along with its interactions with other subsystems.[6] Two examples of subsystems in the brain are the center for speech and the center for hearing. The implication to recognize here is that the self could be an entity that is both psychological and biological.

While we discuss the self in depth in the first chapter, the chapters that follow also deal with the self. Most of this text is geared toward using human relations knowledge for self-development and self-improvement. Throughout the text you will find questionnaires designed to improve insight. The self-knowledge emphasized here deals with psychological (such as personality traits and thinking style) rather than physical characteristics (such as height and blood pressure). As outlined in Figure 1-2, here we discuss six types of information that contribute to self-understanding, along with potential problems in self-evaluation.

1. General information about human behavior
2. Informal feedback from people
3. Feedback from superiors
4. Feedback from coworkers
5. Feedback from self-assessment quizzes
6. The Johari Window

GENERAL INFORMATION ABOUT HUMAN BEHAVIOR

As you learn about people in general, you should also be gaining knowledge about yourself. Therefore, most of the information in this text is presented in a form that should be useful to you personally. Whenever general information is presented, it is your responsibility to relate such information to your particular situation, such as in studying sources of conflict. One such general cause is limited resources—that is, not everyone can have what he or she wants. See how this general principle applies to you. Here is an example involving others: "That's why I've been so angry with Melissa lately. She was the one given the promotion, whereas I'm stuck in the same old job."

In relating facts and observations about people in general to yourself, be careful not to misapply the information. Feedback from other people will help you avoid the pitfalls of introspection (looking into yourself).

INFORMAL FEEDBACK FROM PEOPLE

As just implied, **feedback** is information that tells you how well you have performed. You can sometimes obtain feedback from the spontaneous comments of others or by asking them for feedback. An order-fulfillment materials-handling specialist grew one notch in self-confidence when coworkers began to call him "Net Speed." He was given this name because of the rapidity with which he processed orders. His experience illustrates that a valuable source of information for self-understanding is what the significant people in your life think of you. Although feedback of this type might make you feel uncomfortable, when it is consistent, it accurately reflects how others perceive you.

With some ingenuity you can create informal feedback. (In this sense, the term *informal* refers to not being part of a company-sponsored program.) For example, you might send an e-mail to ten people in your social network asking them for a candid evaluation of your strengths and weaknesses. Make the promise that you will not retaliate if you don't like what you hear.

A few skeptics will argue that friends never give you a true picture of yourself but, rather, say flattering things about you because they value your friendship. Experience has shown, however, that if you emphasize the importance of their opinions, most people will give you a few constructive suggestions. You also have to appear sincere. Because not everyone's comments will be helpful, you may have to sample many people.

Feedback
information that tells one how well he or she has performed

FEEDBACK FROM SUPERIORS

Virtually all employers provide employees with formal or informal feedback on their performances. A formal method of feedback is called a *performance evaluation.* During a performance evaluation (or appraisal) your superior will convey to you what he or she thinks you are doing well and not so well. These observations become a permanent part of your human resources record. Informal feedback occurs when a superior discusses your job performance with you but does not record these observations.

The feedback obtained from superiors in this way can help you learn about yourself. For instance, if two different bosses say that you are a creative problem solver, you might conclude that you are creative. If several bosses tell you that you are too impatient with other people, you might conclude that you are impatient.

FEEDBACK FROM COWORKERS

Peer evaluations
system in which teammates contribute to an evaluation of a person's job performance

A sometimes-used practice in organizations is **peer evaluations,** a system in which teammates contribute to an evaluation of a person's job performance. Although coworkers under this system do not have total responsibility for evaluating each other, their input is taken seriously. The amount of a worker's salary increase could thus be affected by peer judgments about his or her performance. The results of peer evaluations can also be used as feedback for learning about yourself. Assume that coworkers agree on several of your strengths and needs for improvement. You can conclude that others who work closely with you generally perceive you that way.

Developmental opportunity
area for growth or weakness

Teammates might rate each other on performance dimensions such as cooperation with other members of the team, customer service attitude, productivity, and contributions to meetings. If several teammates rated you low in one of these dimensions, it could indicate a **developmental opportunity,** an area for growth, or weakness.

FEEDBACK FROM SELF-ASSESSMENT QUIZZES

Many self-help books, including this one, contain questionnaires that you fill out by yourself, for yourself. The information that you pick up from these questionnaires often provides valuable clues to your preferences, values, and personal traits. Such self-examination questionnaires should not be confused with the scientifically researched test you might take in a counseling center or guidance department or when applying for a job. Another source of useful self-assessment quizzes is www.queendom.com, which offers a variety of tests that contribute to self-understanding, including the classical intelligence quotient (IQ), mental toughness, risk-taking, and self-esteem tests, among many others.

The amount of useful information gained from self-examination questionnaires depends on your candor. Because no outside judge is involved in these self-help quizzes, candor usually is not a problem. An exception is that we all have certain blind spots. Most people, for example, believe that they have considerably above-average skills in dealing with people.

As a starting point in conducting self-examination exercises, you already completed Human Relations Self-Assessment Quiz 1-1. Quiz 1-2 gives you an opportunity to write some things down about yourself.

LOOKING AT THE SELF THROUGH THE JOHARI WINDOW

Johari Window
a grid showing how much information you know about yourself as well as how much other people know about you

A systematic approach to looking at yourself is through a model of communication called the Johari Window, which focuses on self-disclosure. The **Johari Window** is a grid showing how much information you know about yourself as well as how much other people know about you. (The term *Johari* came about because the method was created by Joseph Loft and Harry Ingram.)

Human Relations Self-Assessment Quiz   1-2

The Written Self-Portrait

A good starting point in acquiring serious self-knowledge is to prepare a written self-portrait in the major life spheres (or aspects). In each of the following spheres, describe yourself in about twenty-five to fifty words. For example, under the social and interpersonal sphere, a person might write, "I'm a little timid on the surface. But those people who get to know me well understand that I'm filled with enthusiasm and joy. My relationships with people last a long time. I'm on excellent terms with all members of my family. And my significant other and I have been together for five years. We are very close emotionally and should be together for a lifetime."

A. Occupational and school: _____

_____

_____

_____

B. Social and interpersonal: _____

_____

_____

_____

C. Beliefs, values, and attitudes: _____

_____

_____

_____

D. Physical description (body type, appearance, grooming): _____

_____

_____

_____

The basics of the model are outlined in Figure 1-3. One axis of the grid is the degree to which information about you is known to or understood by you. The other axis is the degree to which information about you is known to others. The horizontal dimension involves soliciting, or obtaining, feedback from others about you; the vertical dimension involves feedback about you to others, or self-disclosure.[7]

The basic premise of the model, as well as the lesson it teaches, is that we can improve our personal and professional relationships through understanding ourselves in depth. But you also have to take the next step of selecting those aspects of the self that are appropriate to share with others. A packaging specialist might want to reveal to coworkers that he does his best creative thinking when jogging alone. However, he might not want to reveal that he finds coworkers to be an annoying distraction while he is attempting to think creatively.

Another premise of the model is that the more we share of ourselves with others, the higher the probability of developing high-quality relationships. To develop

FIGURE 1-3 THE JOHARI WINDOW

Solicit Feedback →

	Known to Self	Unknown to Self
Known to Others	**Open Area:** known to self and others	**Blind Area:** blind to self, seen by others
Unknown to Others	**Hidden Area:** open to self, hidden from others	**Unknown Area:** unknown to self and others

Give Feedback ↓

these positive relationships, we need to be aware of the four areas (or four panes of the window) indicating what is known about us and what is hidden. Observe that the four areas, or panes, of the window are the basics of the communication model.

■ The **open area** consists of information that is known to us and others. Among these readily observable aspects would be hair color, skin color, physical appearance, and spoken communication skills. As a relationship builds we enlarge the open area by revealing more about ourselves. As the open area expands, relationships with others improve—unless you annoy others with too many details about your work and personal life.

Open area

pane of Johari Window consisting of information that is known to us and others

■ The **hidden area** contains information known to us about ourselves but is hidden from others. Frequent hidden areas are ambitions and dislikes of specific individuals. Over the long term, fewer hidden areas lead to more openness and closeness in relationships with others. Yet it is prudent to keep some areas hidden, such as describing a strong physical attraction toward your coworker's or manager's spouse.

Hidden area

pane of Johari Window that contains information known to us about ourselves but is hidden from others

■ The **blind area** contains information that others are aware of but we cannot see in ourselves in reference to both positive and negative qualities. Many people suffer from thinking that they are not physically attractive, yet others in general have an opposite perception. In the opposite direction, many people perceive themselves to be highly skilled in getting along with other people, yet most people might have an opposite point of view. Feedback from others, if not blocked by defensiveness, will help reduce the blind area. As your blind area decreases, you are likely to enlarge your open area because you will have more accurate data to work with.

Blind area

pane of Johari Window that contains information that others are aware of but we cannot see in ourselves in reference to both positive and negative qualities

■ The **unknown area** contains information that you and others do not know about you. It sometimes takes an unusual situation to bring out this unknown information, such as emerging as a leader when a crisis, such as a hurricane, hits your unit of the company.

Unknown area

pane of Johari Window that contains information that you and others do not know about you

The Johari Window is useful in reminding you of the importance of self-disclosure, such as in enlarging your open area. As you disclose more about yourself, others will reciprocate and disclose more about themselves. The mutual disclosures lead to enhanced positive feelings among people in both work and personal life.

TWO SELF-EVALUATION TRAPS

The theme of this section of the chapter is that self-awareness is a positive force in our lives. Yet self-awareness also has two negative extremes or traps. One of these extremes is that focusing on the self can highlight shortcomings the way staring into a mirror can dramatize every blemish and wrinkle on a face. Certain situations predictably force us to engage in self-reflection and become the object of our own attention. When we talk about ourselves, answer self-quizzes, stand before an audience or camera, or watch ourselves on a video, we become more self-aware and make comparisons to some arbitrary standard of behavior. The comparison often results in negative self-evaluation in comparison to the standard and a decrease in self-esteem as we discover that we fall short of standards.[8] Keeping the self-awareness trap in mind will help you minimize needless underevaluation, thereby benefiting from gathering feedback about yourself.

In contrast to underevaluation, it is also true that many people tend to overestimate their competence, such as thinking they deserve a bigger raise or an A in every course. A particular area in which people overestimate their competence is in the moral domain. Many people suffer from a "holier than thou" syndrome. A study with college students, for example, found that they consistently overrated the likelihood that they would act in generous or selfless ways. Eighty-four percent of the students initially predicted that they would cooperate with their partner, but in reality only 61 percent did.[9]

Cultural differences help explain at least some of the differences in underevaluation versus overevaluation. Several studies have shown, for example, that East Asians tend to underestimate their abilities, with an aim toward improving the self and getting along with others. North Americans are more likely to overestimate their abilities and not be so prone to look for areas of self-improvement.[10] Cultural differences reflect stereotypes that apply to the average individual from a culture.

The antidote to the twin self-evaluation traps is to search for honest and objective feedback from others to help you supplement your self-evaluation. Competing against peers, such as in school, sports, and contests on the job (for example, a sales contest or creative suggestion contest), can help you evaluate yourself more realistically. Next, we look more at human relations from the standpoint of the workplace rather than the individual.

How Did the Human Relations Movement Develop?

◀ Learning Objective 5 ◀

The **human relations movement** began as a concentrated effort by some managers and their advisers to become more sensitive to the needs of employees or to treat them in a more humanistic manner. In other words, employees were to be treated as human beings rather than as parts of the productive process. The human relations movement was supported directly by three different historic influences: the Hawthorne studies, the threat of unionization, and industrial humanism (see Figure 1-4).[11] Scientific management, which predated the growth of human relations in industry, contributed indirectly to the movement.

Human relations movement
movement that began as a concentrated effort by some managers and their advisers to become more sensitive to the needs of employees or to treat them in a more humanistic manner

SCIENTIFIC MANAGEMENT

The study of management became more systematized and formal as a byproduct of the Industrial Revolution, which took place from the 1700s through the 1900s. Approaches to managing work and people needed to be developed to manage all the new factories that were a central part of the Industrial Revolution. The focus of **scientific management** was on the application of scientific methods to increase individual workers' productivity. Frederick W. Taylor, considered the father of scientific management, was an engineer by background. He used scientific analysis

Scientific management
theory that focuses on the application of scientific methods to increase individual workers' productivity

FIGURE 1-4 INFLUENCES SUPPORTING THE HUMAN RELATIONS MOVEMENT

and experiments to increase worker output. Taylor's goal was to remove human variability so each worker could become essentially an interchangeable part. His model for human behavior was a machine, with inexpensive parts, each of which has a specific function. Using the principles of scientific management, a worker might assemble a washing machine with the least number of wasted motions and steps. United Parcel Service (UPS) relies heavily on the principles of scientific management to get the most productivity from carriers and shipping personnel, including tightly timing their deliveries.

With scientific management sounding so dehumanizing, how could the movement have contributed to good human relations? Taylor also studied problems such as fatigue and safety. He urged management to study the relationship between work breaks and the length of the workday and productivity. He convinced some managers that work breaks and shorter workdays could increase productivity. Furthermore, scientific management proposed that workers who produced more be paid more.

Scientific management also contributed to the human relations movement by creating a backlash against what many people thought was mistreatment of workers. The industrial engineer with his or her stopwatch and clipboard, hovering over a worker measuring each tiny part of the job and the worker's movements, became a hated figure.[12] The objection to this approach called for a better way to treat people, which came to be known as the human relations movement.

THE HAWTHORNE STUDIES

The human relations school of management is generally said to have begun in 1927 with a group of studies conducted at the Chicago-area Hawthorne plant of an AT&T subsidiary. These studies were prompted by an experiment carried out by the company's engineers between 1924 and 1927. Following the tradition of scientific management, these engineers were applying research methods to investigate problems of employee productivity.

Two groups were studied to determine the effects of different levels of light on worker performance. As prescribed by the scientific method, one group received increased illumination, whereas the other did not. A preliminary finding was that when illumination was increased, the level of performance also increased. Surprisingly to the engineers, productivity also increased when the level of light was decreased almost to moonlight levels. One interpretation of these findings was that the workers involved in the experiment enjoyed being the center of attention. In other words, they reacted positively because management cared about them. Such a phenomenon taking place in any work or research setting is now called the **Hawthorne effect.**[13]

Hawthorne effect

applying research methods to investigate problems of employee productivity using the scientific method; in the study, employees reacted positively because management cared about them

As a result of these preliminary investigations, a team of researchers headed by Harvard professors Elton Mayo and Fritz J. Roethlisberger conducted a series of experiments extending over a six-year period. The conclusions they reached served as the foundations for later developments in the human relations approach to management. It was found that economic incentives are less important than generally believed in influencing workers to achieve high levels of output. Also, leadership practices and work group pressures profoundly influence employee satisfaction and performance. An example of an effective leadership practice would be coaching and encouraging workers to higher performance. The researchers noted that any factor influencing employee behavior is embedded in a social system. For instance, to understand the impact of pay on performance, you have to understand the atmosphere that exists in the work group and how the leader approaches his or her job.

A major implication of the Hawthorne studies was that the old concept of an economic person motivated primarily by money had to be replaced by a more valid idea. The replacement concept was a social person, motivated by social needs, desiring rewarding on-the-job relationships and more responsive to pressures from coworkers than to control by the boss.[14] Do you believe that workers are more concerned with social relationships than with money?

THE THREAT OF UNIONIZATION

Labor union officials and their advocates contend that the benefits of unionization extend to many workers who themselves do not belong to unions. Management in nonunion firms will often pay employees union wages to offset the potential advantages of unionization. A similar set of circumstances contributed to the growth of the human relations movement. Labor unions began to grow rapidly in the United States during the late 1930s. Many employers feared that the presence of a labor union would have negative consequences for their companies. Consequently, management looked aggressively for ways to stem the tide of unionization, such as using human relations techniques to satisfy workers.[15] Their reasoning is still valid today: dissatisfied workers are much more likely to join a labor union, in hope of improving their working conditions.[16]

Today the threat of unionization is primarily in the public sector. Although unionization has declined considerably in manufacturing, about 36 percent of government workers, including those in education, are union members, compared with about 8 percent of workers in private-sector industries. In 1945, about 36 percent of the U.S. workforce was unionized, versus about 12 percent today.[17] The decline of manufacturing jobs has contributed to the decline of union membership.

THE PHILOSOPHY OF INDUSTRIAL HUMANISM

Partly as a byproduct of the Hawthorne studies, a new philosophy of human relations arose in the workplace. Elton Mayo was one of the two key figures in developing this philosophy of industrial humanism. He cautioned managers that emotional factors (such as a desire for recognition) were a more important contributor to productivity than physical and logical factors. Mayo argued vigorously that work should lead to personal satisfaction for employees.

Mary Parker Follett was another key figure in advancing the cause of industrial humanism. Her experience as a management consultant led her to believe that the key to increased productivity was to motivate employees, rather than simply ordering better job performance. The keys to both productivity and democracy, according to Follett, were cooperation, a spirit of unity, and a coordination of effort.[18]

THEORY X AND THEORY Y OF DOUGLAS McGREGOR

The importance of managing people through more effective methods of human relations was advanced by the writings of social psychologist Douglas McGregor. His famous position was that managers should challenge their assumptions about the nature of people. McGregor believed that too many managers assumed that people were lazy and indifferent toward work. He urged managers to be open to the possibility that under the right circumstances people are eager to perform well. If a supervisor accepts one of these extreme sets of beliefs about people, the supervisor will act differently toward them than if he or she believes the opposite. These famous assumptions that propelled the human relations movement are summarized as follows:

Theory X Assumptions

1. The average person dislikes work and therefore will avoid it if he or she can.

2. Because of this dislike of work, most people must be coerced, controlled, directed, or threatened with punishment to get them to put forth enough effort to achieve organizational goals.

3. The average employee prefers to be directed, wishes to shirk responsibility, has relatively little ambition, and highly values job security.

Theory Y Assumptions

1. The expenditure of physical and mental effort in work is as natural as play or rest.

2. External control and the threat of punishment are not the only means for bringing about effort toward reaching company objectives. Employees will exercise self-direction and self-control in the service of objectives to which they attach high valence.

3. Commitment to objectives is related to the rewards associated with their achievement.

4. The average person learns, under proper conditions, not only to accept but also to seek responsibility.

5. Many employees have the capacity to exercise a high degree of imagination, ingenuity, and creativity in the solution of organizational problems.

6. Under the present conditions of industrial life, the intellectual potentialities of the average person are only partially utilized.[19]

The distinction between Theory X and Theory Y has often been misinterpreted. McGregor was humanistic, but he did not mean to imply that being directive and demanding with workers is always the wrong tactic. Some people are undermotivated and dislike work. In these situations, the manager has to behave sternly toward group members to motivate them. If you are a Theory Y manager, you size up your group members to understand their attitudes toward work.

RELEVANCE OF THE HISTORY OF HUMAN RELATIONS TO TODAY'S WORKPLACE

Many of the pioneering ideas described in the history of human relations are still relevant, partly because human nature has not undergone major changes. Most of the core ideas in the history of the human relations movement are still part of the human relations and organizational behavior curriculum today, even though they have more research substantiation and new labels. A good example is the push toward creativity and innovation based on the involvement of many different workers, not only specialists from one department. The link to history is that Theory Y encourages empowering employees to use their ingenuity and creativity to solve organizational problems. Next is a bulleted summary of ideas from the human relations movement that still influence the practice of human relations today.

- Many principles of scientific management are useful in making workers more productive so business firms can compete better in a global economy.

- Ideas from the Hawthorne studies have helped managers focus on the importance of providing both congenial work surroundings and adequate compensation to motivate and retain workers.

- Industrial humanism is widely practiced today in the form of looking for ways to keep workers satisfied through such methods as flexible work arrangements, family leave, and dependent care benefits.

- Theory Y has prompted managers to think through which style of leadership works best with which employees. Specifically, a modern manager is likely to grant more freedom to employees who are well motivated and talented. Spurred partially by Theory X, few managers today believe that being the "bull of the woods" is the best way to supervise all workers.

How Does Human Relations Knowledge and Skill Help You Deal with Major Challenges in the Workplace?

◀ Learning Objective 6 ◀

Another major way in which human relations skills and knowledge can help you is in dealing effectively with major challenges in the modern workplace. Although it would be difficult to reach consensus on which are the major challenges in the workplace, our list at least touches the major themes. All of these themes, outlined in Figure 1-5, will be discussed in more depth at various places in the book.

EMPHASIS ON TEAMWORK AND COLLABORATION

The modern workplace emphasizes teamwork and collaboration. Similarly, many of the courses you have taken emphasize collaborative projects inside and outside of the classroom. The story about the consulting firm presented earlier in the chapter indicates that company management invests time and money to enhance collaboration among coworkers. A current thrust in office design is to move people away from private offices and cubicles to encourage collaboration.[20] The reasoning being that you are more likely to confer with coworkers who are in open view than with those hidden in their own work area. Another approach to enhancing teamwork and collaboration is to send employees to offsite or outdoor training to participate in exercises that require collaboration, such as refurbishing an old house.

A subtle aspect of collaboration is that the modern employee is supposed to think of the demands of people working in different functions of the organization, not just in terms of his or her own function (or department). The buzzword for people who think only in terms of their own function or discipline (such as marketing or

FIGURE 1-5

**MAJOR WORKPLACE
CHALLENGES OF TODAY**
Human relations skills are helpful in dealing
with the major challenges in the modern
workplace.

accounting) is having a *silo mentality*.[21] A silo, as you probably already know, is high and narrow, thereby blocking out other points of view.

The human relations lesson for you with respect to teamwork and collaboration is that you need to acquire skills that facilitate working smoothly in joint effort with others. Among these dozens of skills would be learning to accept criticism from coworkers and also being willing to offer them constructive criticism.

HIGH EXPECTATIONS FOR PERSONAL PRODUCTIVITY

For many years business organizations as well as governmental and educational institutions have been focusing on getting more work accomplished with fewer people. Many large firms have shrunk their workforce almost in half without experiencing a substantial decrease in sales volume. Much of this increased productivity stems from advances in technology, yet some of the productivity gains stem from employees working harder, smarter, and longer. This translates into you having to produce more than your counterparts of yesteryear. Higher productivity is expected of workers at all levels, including managers, corporate professionals, and entry-level workers. Here is an example of productivity measurement applied to a store cashier:

> A clock starts ticking the moment a cashier at Meijer Inc. scans a customer's first item, and it doesn't shut off until his register spits out a receipt. To assess his efficiency, the store's computer takes into account everything from the kinds of merchandise he is bagging to how his customers are paying. Each week, he gets scored. If he falls below 95% of the baseline score too many times, the 185-store megastore chain is likely to bounce him to a lower-paying job or fire him.[22]

With so many retail stores under the gun to cut costs and improve profit margins, "labor-waste elimination" systems such as the one mentioned above have come into widespread use. Employees working in manufacturing, whatever their job title, are typically expected to be highly efficient. An extreme example is that several automobile manufacturers worldwide, including Tata Motors of India, are attempting to produce automobiles that can be sold profitably for around $5,000. Initially, the hope was to sell a Tata auto for $3,500 which proved to be unrealistic.[23] In addition to using the latest labor-saving technology, these companies expect managers and professionals to work at a fast pace, relying on less staff assistance.

To deal successfully with the push for increased productivity, you have to acquire excellent work habits and time-management skills. Such skills are related to human relations because being in control of your work makes it easier to relate effectively to others, partially because you will be less stressed. Human relations skills at a high level are also called for in helping management determine which approaches to enhanced productivity are sensible, and therefore not counterproductive. A cashier who is working like a robot might lower customer service by failing to establish rapport with customers. The cashier might also neglect to smile, violating an important part of relationship building with customers.

DEALING WITH WORKPLACE DIVERSITY AND GLOBALIZATION

The domestic workforce has become more culturally diverse, and more people in high-level positions are from culturally diverse groups. You deal well with diversity when you relate comfortably to people from a range of cultural and demographic groups. (A cultural group refers mostly to values and customs, whereas a demographic group refers to a statistical category, such as being a Filipino or under age twenty-five.) *Diversity* includes all categories of people. A strong example of this inclusion is the global constituency teams formed by Merck & Co., the pharmaceutical giant. The teams represent the following diverse groups: Asians, blacks, Latinos, indigenous peoples, generational differences, interfaith, differently abled, and lesbian, gay, bisexual, and transgendered. (Age groups are not considered separately.) The leader of all these teams is chief diversity officer Deborah Dagit, who is four feet tall and who made the following comment:

> As a person with a visible disability, I have a special gift and a unique challenge. Because of my packaging, and because there are not many people with disabilities who do the work that I do, I have been given opportunities I might otherwise not have had. Having a disability is a tool in my toolbox.[24]

The globalization of the workforce requires many workers to work comfortably with people from different countries and time zones. Visiting another country might require a quick adaptation to another culture, such as being offered food during a business dinner that you consider to be a household pet or repulsive in some other way.

A specific career challenge created by globalization is that you have to develop skills so valuable that your job is not in danger of being sent offshore. We all know that countless thousands of manufacturing and call-center jobs have been sent overseas. Less well publicized is that many higher-level positions such as those related to research and development, product design, and medical diagnostics have also been sent to other countries. Many American patients now have surgery performed in India and China to lower costs, assuming the health of the patient allows for such rigorous travel. Your job is less likely to be outsourced if you have established valuable personal relationships, such as an industrial sales representative who knows his or her customers well.

The general challenge created by the diverse domestic and international workforce is that you need to develop cross-cultural skills, including being able to work comfortably with generational differences. So many workers today have been relating to diverse groups for so much of their lives that cross-cultural skills are more widespread than they were years ago. Participating in sports during youth, for example, has helped many people develop cross-cultural skills.

EMPHASIS ON EMPLOYEE CREATIVITY AND INNOVATIVENESS

Workplaces today frequently demand creativity and innovativeness from all types of workers, not just those involved in such functions as research and development, advertising, engineering, and product development. Creativity in the present context refers to having imaginative, useful suggestions. Many people have imaginative ideas that are not useful, such as suggesting that the company become more environmentally friendly by having employees commute to work via jet packs rather than private vehicles. (Maybe jetpacks will be useful by the next edition of this book.)

The creativity demanded by organizations from employees outside of traditionally creative roles, such as those in advertising, often focuses on searching for new ways to solve basic problems, including how to decrease costs and improve profits. A representative example is Costco, a discount warehouse chain that relies heavily on membership fees. The company fears that raising prices on merchandise might drive away dues-paying customers. As a result, employees search continuously for ways to reduce the cost of merchandise so the store price is lower. A few years ago, Procter & Gamble announced a 6 percent price increase on Bounty paper towels. Costco management responded imaginatively by purchasing hundreds of truckloads of Bounty paper at the old price and storing the towels. As a result, customers saved psychologically important pennies. At the time the company was also exploring the possibilities of growing its own pumpkins to help maintain a low price tag on its store-baked pies. Costco CEO James Sinegal says, "If that stuff doesn't turn you on then you're in the wrong business."[25]

Although being a creative problem solver is not directly an interpersonal skill, being creative will help you develop a better reputation within your company and perhaps help you hold on to an important job. The current emphasis on creative problem solving in the workplace suggests that you will have to emphasize the creativity that you probably already have—even if you don't yet use it extensively.

BEING PART OF THE VIRTUAL WORKPLACE AND TELECOMMUTING

Workplace trends such as more emphasis on diversity and creativity are intangible, or difficult to measure. A tangible, or measurable, workplace trend is the movement toward many workers being given the opportunity, or forced to, work outside of the traditional office. Forcing refers to demand that employees work from home to reduce real estate costs for the company.

Virtual office

one in which employees work together as if they were part of a single office despite being physically separated

A **virtual office** is one in which employees work together as if they were part of a single office despite being physically separated. Highly coordinated virtual office members form a virtual team. For example, you might be on the same team with five other workers who are physically located in different parts of country or even another country. Or a few of your team members might be at different places of a large office building or factory. Communication among team members is mostly online, with telephone calls supplementing the online messages. Members of the virtual team might hold a physical meeting on occasion. Companies who make extensive use of virtual offices rely heavily on Web-based technology. Among the specific tools are an Intranet (company Internet), a method of scheduling meetings, document management, and news updates.[26]

Being a successful member of a virtual office and a virtual team requires that you have particularly good skills in relating to people you do not see frequently. Among these skills are knowing how to give sincere compliments with instant messaging, keeping your manager updated on your contribution, and making the most out of the occasional face-to-face meeting.

Telecommuting, or working from a remote location, makes a virtual office possible. Yet many workers telecommute as independent workers rather than as part of a team. About 26 million corporate workers in the United States now telecommute at least one day a week. The special human relations demands that telecommuting places on the worker include being sufficiently self-disciplined to work without a supervisor present and making a good face-to-face impression during the time one spends in the physical office. You also have to be able to size up the company atmosphere to understand whether telecommuting places you in a favorable or an unfavorable light with management.[27]

INCREASED EMPHASIS ON SKILL ACQUISITION AND LESS ON UPWARD MOBILITY

A subtle trend in the workplace is for employers to encourage employees to continuously acquire new skills and knowledge, while at the same time offering fewer opportunities for promotion than in the past. A positive force behind this development is that technology and workplace procedures change so rapidly that continuous learning by workers is necessary for organizations of all types to stay competitive. A not-so-positive reason for the emphasis on growth by acquiring new skills is that organizations offer fewer opportunities for vertical mobility (essentially promotions). Most organizations today have substantially decreased their number of layers as well as the number of managers. Some of the best-known business firms, such as General Motors and Hewlett Packard, have eliminated over 30,000 positions.

An example of today's emphasis on continuous learning is the lifelong learning account (LiLA) offered by some employers. LiLA offers an investment program for adult education to which employees and employers contribute, with the employee owning the plan and keeping it even if he or she leaves the organization. An employee could use the money in the plan to invest in learning at the present employer or use the same funds to invest in education at a future employer. One of the goals of the plan is to assist working adults to remain competitive in the workforce.[28]

The new emphasis on learning in organizations requires that to succeed, you need to actively participate in learning through such means as self-study, taking courses, and participating in training and seminars. If you are concerned about the challenge of fewer opportunities for promotion, you need to place extra effort into tactics for career advancement, such as building your personal brand (your unique basket of strengths).

What Major Factors Influence Job Performance and Behavior?

◀ Learning Objective 7 ◀

Part of understanding human relations is recognizing the factors or forces that influence job performance and behavior. In overview, the performance and behavior of workers is influenced by factors related to the employee, manager, job, and organization as discussed next and outlined in Figure 1-6. Here we present a sampling of these many factors, because a comprehensive understanding of them would encompass the study of human relations, organizational behavior, and management.

1. **Factors related to the employee.** The major influence on how a worker performs and behaves, or acts, on the job stems from his or her personal attributes. The worker's mental ability influences how quickly and accurately he or she can solve problems. Physical ability would influence some types of performance, such as the ability to stand up for long periods of time as a store manager or lift

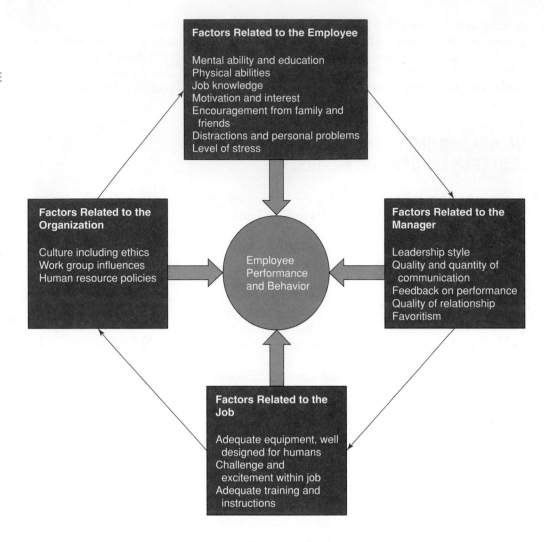

boxes as a warehouse attendant. Job knowledge is obviously important, such as a financial consultant being knowledgeable about a variety of investments. Employees who are well motivated and interested in the work are likely to perform better and behave in a more professional manner. Workers who receive encouragement from friends and family are likely to perform better. Being distracted, such as Internet surfing during the workday or experiencing heavy personal problems, can influence performance negatively. Having the right amount of stress can boost performance, whereas being overstressed can lower performance and lead to distracting behavior, such as being confused.

2. **Factors related to the manager.** The manager, or supervisor, is another major influence on work behavior. A manager whose style, or approach, is warm and supportive is likely to bring out the best in many employees. But some workers require a more directive and demanding supervisor to perform at their best. Ample communication among the manager and group members is likely to enhance performance and guide employees toward doing what is expected of them. Most workers need considerable feedback from their supervisor to stay on track and be highly motivated. A high-quality relationship between the manager and group members leads to high performance, more loyalty, and lower absenteeism. Favoritism is another key factor related to the manager. A manager who plays favorites is less likely to gain the cooperation of the entire group.

3. **Factors related to the job.** The job itself influences how well the worker might perform and behave. Given the right equipment, designed well for human use, a

worker is likely to perform better, such as being less likely to have aches, pains, and wrist injuries as a result of many hours of keyboarding. A proven strategy for improving worker motivation is to give the employee an exciting, challenging job, such as the opportunity to make presentations to management about a project. Adequate training and instructions can also be a big boost to job performance.

4. **Factors related to the organization.** The organization as a whole can have a profound influence on the individual worker's performance and behavior. The *culture*, or atmosphere and values of a company, establishes an unwritten standard for how employees perform and behave. At Google, for example, employees are placed in an atmosphere where being creative and making suggestions is expected. And all Southwest Airlines employees know that having fun is supposed to be part of the job. The culture of the organization also influences the ethical behavior of employees, with some companies expecting honest treatment of workers and employees. Other companies are much less ethical and encourage tactics such as deceiving customers. The work group, as part of the organization, can influence the employee by encouraging teamwork and high productivity, among other methods. Human resource policies are another notable influence on the individual. If your company offers you generous medical and dental benefits and allows time off for family emergencies, it becomes easier to concentrate on the job.

The four factors just listed often have a combined influence on the worker. Let us take an extreme example: Jack, a well-motivated and talented assistant hotel manager, reports to a manager with whom he has a great relationship, which includes giving Jack ample feedback on his performance. Jack finds his job challenging, and his hotel has the advanced equipment necessary for success. The hotel has a friendly climate, along with generous benefits. As a result of this combination of factors, Jack is an outstanding performer who approaches his job with a high degree of professionalism.

Concept Review
and Reinforcement

Human relations, 4

Organizational effectiveness, 4

Self-understanding, 10

Self, 10

Public self, 10

Private self, 10

Feedback, 11

Peer evaluations, 12

Developmental opportunity, 12

Johari Window, 12

Open area, 14

Hidden area, 14

Blind area, 14

Unknown area, 14

Human relations movement, 15

Scientific management, 15

Hawthorne effect, 16

Virtual office, 22

Summary and Review

Human relations is the art and practice of using systematic knowledge about human behavior to improve personal, job, and career effectiveness. From the standpoint of management, human relations is important because it contributes to organizational effectiveness. Treating employees with respect and paying them fairly contributes to developing an efficient and creative organization.

Major benefits of studying human relations include the following:

■ Acquiring information about human behavior
■ Developing skills in dealing with people
■ Coping with job problems
■ Coping with personal problems
■ Capitalizing on opportunities

Work and personal life often influence each other in several ways, as follows:

■ Mood influences job satisfaction, but the effect passes quickly.
■ Job satisfaction influences the mood at home, with more emotional employees more likely to experience this relationship.
■ A high level of job satisfaction tends to spill over to your personal life. Conversely, an unsatisfactory personal life could lead to negative job attitudes.
■ Your job can affect physical and mental health. Severely negative job conditions may lead to a serious stress disorder, such as heart disease.
■ The quality of relationships with people at work and in one's personal life influence each other.
■ Certain skills (such as the ability to listen) contribute to success at work and in one's personal life.

■ How we behave at work is closely related to how we behave at home.

To be effective in human relationships, you must first understand yourself. Six sources of information that contribute to self-understanding are as follows:

1. General information about human behavior
2. Informal feedback from people
3. Feedback from superiors
4. Feedback from coworkers
5. Feedback from self-examination exercises
6. Looking at the self through the Johari Window

Be aware of the self-evaluation traps of highlighting your shortcomings and unrealistically overevaluating your competence. Cultural differences help explain some of the differences in underevaluation versus overevaluation.

The human relations movement was a concentrated effort to become more sensitive to the needs of employees and to treat them in a more humanistic manner. Along with the indirect influence of scientific management, the movement was supported directly by four historic influences:

1. Scientific management applied scientific methods to increase worker productivity.
2. The Hawthorne studies showed that concern for workers can increase their performance as much as or more than improving physical working conditions.
3. Employers used the threat of unionization, in which management employed human relations techniques to deter workers from joining a labor union.

4. The philosophy of industrial humanism, in which motivation and emotional factors are important.

Many of the pioneering ideas described in the history of human relations are still relevant, partly because human nature has not undergone major changes. An example of a pioneering idea in use is that Theory Y has prompted managers to think through which leadership style works best with which employees.

Human relations knowledge and skill will help you deal with major challenges in the workplace, as follows:

- Emphasis on teamwork and collaboration
- High expectations for personal productivity
- Dealing with workplace diversity and globalization
- Emphasis on employee creativity and innovativeness
- Being part of the virtual workplace and telecommuting
- Increased emphasis on skill acquisition and less on upward mobility

The major factors influencing job performance and behavior are related to the employee, manager, job, and organization.

Check Your Understanding

1. Why do you think good human relations skills are so important for supervisors who direct the work activities of entry-level workers?
2. Give an example of a business executive, politician, athletic coach, or professor who you think has exceptional human relations skills. On what basis did you reach your conclusion?
3. Give an example from your own experience of how work life influences personal life and vice versa.
4. How might a person improve personal life to the extent that the improvement would also enhance job performance?
5. How might a person improve his or her job or career to the extent that the improvement would actually enhance personal life?

6. Of the five sources of information about the self described in this chapter, which one do you think is likely to be the most accurate? Why?
7. Imagine yourself as a manager or small-business owner. How might you apply the Hawthorne effect to increase the productivity of workers reporting to you?
8. In what way might the chief diversity officer mentioned in this chapter being four feet tall enhance the credibility of her position?
9. How do you think having good human relations skills and knowledge might add to your job security in a competitive workplace?
10. In your current job, or any previous one, which set of factors had the biggest impact on your performance and behavior—those related to the employee, manager, job, or organization? How do you know?

Web Corner

The Dale Carnegie organization has long been associated with teaching human relations effectiveness. The company stemmed from the work of Dale Carnegie, who many years ago popularized the idea of "winning friends and influencing people." Visit www.dalecarnegie.com to understand what type of skills Dale Carnegie teaches. Compare the course listing to subjects listed in the table of contents in this text. What similarities do you see?

INTERNET SKILL BUILDER

The Importance of Human Relations Skills in Business

One of the themes of this chapter and the entire book is that human relations skills are important for success in

business. But what do employers really think? To find out, visit the Web sites of five of your favorite companies, such as www.apple.com or www.ge.com. Go to the employment section and search for a job that you might qualify for now or in the future. Investigate which human relations or interpersonal skills the employer mentions as a requirement, such as "Must have superior spoken communication skills." Make up a list of the human relations, or interpersonal, skills you find mentioned. What conclusions do you reach from this exercise?

Developing Your Human Relations Skills

Human Relations Application Exercises

Applying Human Relations Exercise 1-1

Learning about Each Other's Human Relations Skills

A constructive way of broadening your insights about human relations skills is to find out what other people perceive as their strengths in dealing with others. Toward this end, each class member comes to the front of the class, one by one, to make a two-minute presentation on his or her best ability in dealing with people. To help standardize the presentations, each student answers the following question: "What I do best with people is _____."

In this exercise, and all other class presentation exercises contained in the text, students are asked to share only those ideas they would be comfortable in sharing with the class. Here, for example, you might be very good at doing something with people about which you would be embarrassed to let others know.

As the other students are presenting, attempt to concentrate on them and not be so preoccupied with your presentation that you cannot listen. Make note when somebody says something out of the ordinary. When the presentation is over, the class will discuss answers to the following questions:

1. What was the most frequent human relations capability mentioned?
2. To what extent do classmates appear to be exaggerating their human relations skills?
3. What omissions did you find? For example, were there any important human relations skills you thought a few students should have mentioned but did not?

Applying Human Relations Exercise 1-2

My Human Relations Journal

A potentially important aid in your development as a person with effective human relations skills is to maintain a journal or diary of your experiences. Make a journal entry within 24 hours of carrying out a significant human relations action or failing to do so when the opportunity arose. You therefore will have entries dealing with human relations opportunities both capitalized on and missed. Here is an example: "A few of my neighbors were complaining about all the vandalism in the neighborhood. Cars were getting dented and scratched, and lamplights were being smashed. A few bricks were thrown into home windows. I volunteered to organize a neighborhood patrol. The patrol actually helped cut back on the vandalism." Or, in contrast, given the same scenario: "I thought that someone else should take care of the problem. My time is too valuable." (In the first example, the key human relations skill the person exercised was leadership.)

Also include in your journal such entries as feedback you receive on your human relations ability, good interpersonal traits you appear to be developing, and key human relations ideas about which you read.

Review your journal monthly, and make note of any progress you think you have made in developing your human relations skills. Also consider preparing a graph of your human relations skill development. The vertical axis can represent skill level on a 1 to 100 scale, and the horizontal axis might be divided into time internals, such as calendar quarters.

Human Relations Case Study 1-1

We Can't Afford Good Human Relations around Here

Tammy Horton was happy to be hired by Bradbury Foods as a supervisor in the main food processing plant. It was apparent to her that being a supervisor so soon after graduation from career school would be a real boost to her career. After about a month on the job, Tammy began to make some critical observations about the company and its style of management.

To clarify issues in her own mind, Tammy requested a meeting with Marcus Green, plant superintendent. The meeting between Horton and Green included a conversation of this nature:

Marcus: Have a seat, Tammy. It's nice to visit with one of our new supervisors. Particularly so when you didn't say you were facing an emergency that you and your boss couldn't handle.

Tammy: (*nervously*) Marcus, I want to express my appreciation for your willingness to meet with me. You're right, I'm not facing an emergency, and I am not here to complain about my boss. But I do wonder about something. That's what I came here to talk to you about.

Marcus: That's what I like to see—a young woman who takes the initiative to ask questions about things that are bothering her.

Tammy: To be truthful, I am happy here and I'm glad I joined Bradbury Foods. But I'm curious about one thing. As you may know, I majored in business at my career college. A few of the courses I took emphasized using human relations knowledge and skills to manage people—you know, kind of psychology on the job. It seems like the way to go if you want to keep employees productive and happy. Here at Bradbury it seems that nobody uses human relations knowledge and skills. I know that we're a successful company. But some of the management practices seem out of keeping with the times. The managers make all the decisions. Everybody else listens and carries out orders. Even professionals on the payroll have to use time recording devices for checking in and checking out. I've been here for almost two months and I haven't even heard the term "human relations" used once.

Marcus: Oh, I get your point. You're talking about using human relations around here. I know all about that. The point you are missing, Tammy, is that human relations is for big, profitable companies. That stuff works great when business is good and profit margins are high. But around here business is so-so, and profit margins in the food business are thinner than a potato chip. Maybe someday when we get fat and profitable we can start using human relations. In the meantime, we've all got a job to do.

Tammy: I appreciate your candid answer, Marcus. But when I was in career school, I certainly heard a different version of why companies use human relations.

Questions

1. What is your evaluation of Marcus's contention that human relations knowledge is useful primarily when a firm is profitable?

2. To what extent should Tammy be discouraged?

3. What should Tammy do next about her concerns about the application of human relations knowledge at Bradbury?

4. Based on your experiences, how representative of most managers is Marcus's thinking?

Human Relations Case Study 1-2

Is This Any Way to Run a Trucking Company?

J. A. Frate Inc. tries to make sure its most dedicated drivers feel valued and want to stay for the long haul. The company was founded by CEO R. Douglas Jennings, who says he has always run J. A. Frate with the goal of treating employees as fairly and kindly as possible.

Managers hire only experienced truck drivers—those with at least two years on the job—and those who dress and act professionally, Mr. Jennings says. The company then motivates its fifty-some drivers to do their best by giving recognition and prizes to those who show special effort. Each month the company's Driver Recognition Committee selects "Drivers of the Month" and usually divvies $200 in Wal-Mart gift certificates among them. The recognition is based on a point system where drivers can be docked points for issues such as damaged freight, tardiness, or sloppy log books.

Each year, one driver is designated "Driver of the Year" and wins a larger prize. Joe Rhamey, a driver who's worked with J. A. Frate since 1991, won in 2006 and 2007. Last year, the company bought a new truck tractor for him to drive but added about $4,000 of embellishments that drivers usually don't get, such as satellite radio, power windows, and chrome wheels. "They just come up with these things, and you think, 'Wow, that's nice,'" says Rhamey, who is fifty-four.

Employees are also encouraged to suggest changes, with the top three suggestions each quarter winning

$100, $50, and $25 respectively. All of these efforts pay off in employee retention. The average tenure of current employees is 7.3 years.

Here is how management at J. A. Frate handled a particularly challenging predicament: Soon after the September 11, 2001, terrorist attacks, the company lost two big clients and laid off six drivers—the only layoffs in its thirty-seven-year history. The board of directors then asked remaining employees to vote on taking a 10 percent pay cut, promising to reinstate their normal wages after three months. The majority of employees voted for the cut.

Within six months, the company rehired all the drivers it had laid off and reinstated their pre–September 11 wages. In 2006, it reimbursed the missed income to all employees who had taken the 10 percent pay cut, as well as those who had been laid off.

Questions

1. What does this case tell you about the importance of good human relations in a basic industry like trucking?

2. Why bother spending company money giving frills like chrome wheels, power windows, and satellite radio to a trucker? Isn't the trucker already getting paid to do a job?

3. Why might giving recognition to truck drivers, such as the "Drivers of the Month" award, be especially effective with members of this occupational group?

4. Think of all the money executives at J. A. Frate have given to employees in gift certificates and back pay. Is this any way to run a trucking company?

Source: Abridged from Kelly K. Spors, "Top Small Workplaces 2008: J. A. Frate Inc.," *Wall Street Journal*, October 13, 2008, p. R5.

Human Relations Role-Playing Exercise

Kindness and Recognition

Here, as in all chapters, a role-playing (or role-assuming) exercise will be presented to provide practice in implementing a specific human relations skill or technique. The role-plays will typically be presented in front of others for about five to ten minutes. A natural and easy way of carrying out most of these role-plays is for you to get a general idea of the role and then spontaneously say and do what you think a person in that role might do and say. For many of the role-plays, it will be helpful for you to read the relevant text material to assist you in refining your skill. For these two introductory role-plays, just rely on whatever knowledge and skills you already have.

Scenario 1: Kindness at the Not-for-Profit Agency Getting back to the chapter-opening story, one person plays the role of Sandy Bellows who is presented with what appears to be a way-off-base suggestion from a staff member. The staff member suggests that their organization should raise more funds by requiring each person who works at the agency to be assigned a monthly collection quota. The money would be collected from anybody in their network, including family members, friends, neighbors, and work associates. The staff members who failed to meet quota for three consecutive months

would be eligible to be fired. One person plays the role of the staff member who makes the suggestion. Another person plays the role of Bellows, who will reject the suggestion with kindness. Run the conversation for about six minutes.

Scenario 2: Giving Recognition to a Trucker Getting back to Case Study 1-2, one person plays the role of a supervisor at J. A. Frate, the trucking company. While at headquarters he runs into Billy Joe, who has stopped by to fill out some forms for the human resources department. The supervisor is aware that Billy Joe achieved better than average performance last month and would like to give him appropriate recognition. But Billy Joe was certainly not the *top* performer among the truck drivers. Another student plays the role of Billy Joe, who feels somewhat underappreciated and would like some recognition. The two role-players carry out an on-the-spot recognition session rather than meeting in a cubicle or conference room.

For both scenarios, observers rate the role-players on two dimensions, using a 1 to 5 scale from very poor to very good. One dimension is "effective use of human relations techniques." The second dimension is "acting ability." A few observers might voluntarily provide feedback to the role-players in terms of sharing their ratings and observations. The course instructor might also provide feedback.

Class Activity: The Unique People

Most of the self-assessment quizzes and human relations exercises presented throughout this book are performed by students working individually or in small groups. At the end of each chapter we present an additional activity geared toward enhanced human relations knowledge or skill that is to be performed by the entire class, often interacting with each other. The unit of contribution might be you working alone, but at some point the contributions become collective.

Our first class activity is geared toward reinforcing the idea that part of effective human relations is to recognize that people are different in many ways, stemming from their group characteristics, culture, personality, problem-solving ability, experiences, and interests, among many other factors. Each student in the class, or only those who volunteer, come up to the front of the class one at a time to make a one-minute presentation about any way in which he or she is unique. Here are three statements of uniqueness among an infinite number of possibilities: "I graduated number one in my high school class of fifty-seven students." "I was born and raised in China, but I don't like to eat in Chinese restaurants. I prefer Applebee's and Outback Steakhouse." "I rigged up my house to be smart. I can use my BlackBerry to start the air-conditioning or the oven in my house from miles away."

After the unique aspects of each class member are presented, volunteers might offer feedback to participants by completing the following statements:

1. "What really surprised me was _____."
2. "What made me really think positively about _____ was the fact that he (or she) _____."
3. "I really learned something about human relations today. Now I know that _____."

REFERENCES

1. Steven Kent, "Happy Workers Are the Best Workers," *Wall Street Journal*, September 6, 2005, p. A20.

2. Jeffery Pfeffer, *The Human Equation* (Boston: Harvard Business School Press, 1998), p. 59; Pfeffer, "Producing Sustainable Competitive Advantage through the Effective Management of People," *Academy of Management Executive*, November 2005, pp. 95–108.

3. Timothy A. Judge and Remus Ilies, "Affect and Job Satisfaction: A Study of Their Relationship at Work and Home," *Journal of Applied Psychology*, August 2004, pp. 661–673.

4. "Making Relationships Work: A Conversation with Psychologist John M. Gottman," *Harvard Business Review*, December 2007, pp. 45–50.

5. C. R. Snyder, "So Many Selves," *Contemporary Psychology*, January 1988, p. 77.

6. Cited in Etienne Benson, "The Synaptic Self," *Monitor on Psychology*, November 2002, p. 40.

7. Joseph Luft, *Group Process: An Introduction to Group Dynamics* (New York: Mayfield Publishing Company/ McGraw-Hill, 1984); Luft, *Of Human Interaction* (Palo Alto, CA: National Press, 1969); Suzanne C. De Janasz, Karen O. Dowd, and Beth Z. Schneider, *Interpersonal Skills in Organizations* (New York: McGraw-Hill, 2002), pp. 31–32.

8. Saul Kassin, *Psychology*, 3rd ed. (Upper Saddle River, NJ: Prentice Hall, 2001), p. 74.

9. Research summarized in Tori DeAngelis, "Why We Overestimate Our Competence," *Monitor on Psychology*, February 2003, p. 61.

10. Ibid.

11. Robert Kreitner, *Management*, 5th ed. (Boston: Houghton Mifflin, 1992), pp. 51–52.

12. Edward G. Wertheim, "Historical Background of Organizational Behavior." Retrieved March 15, 2006, from: http:// web.cba.neu.edu/~Wertheim/introd/history.htm

13. Elton Mayo, *The Human Problems of Industrial Civilization* (New York: Viking Press, 1960).

14. James A. F. Stoner and R. Edward Freeman, *Management*, 4th ed. (Upper Saddle River, NJ: Prentice Hall, 1989), p. 49.

15. Kreitner, *Management*, p. 50.

16. Alan B. Krueger, "Job Satisfaction Is Not Just a Matter of Dollars," *New York Times*. Retrieved December 8, 2005, from: www.nytimes.com

17. "Union Members Summary," *Bureau of Labor Statistics News* Retrieved January 25, 2008, from: www.bls.gov/ news

18. Kreitner, *Management*, p. 62.

19. Douglas McGregor, *The Human Side of Enterprise* (New York: McGraw-Hill, 1960), pp. 33–48.

20. Susan Berfield, "After the Layoff, the Redesign," *Business Week*, April 14, 2008, p. 56.

21. Cliff Edwards, Kenji Hall, and Ronald Grover, "Sony Chases Apple's Magic," *Business Week*, November 10, 2008, p. 51.

22. Vanessa O'Connell, "Stores Count Seconds to Cut Labor Costs," *Wall Street Journal*, November 17, 2008, pp. A1, A15.

23. David Welch and Nandini Lakshman, "My Other Car Is a Tata," *Business Week*, January 14, 2008, p. 33.

24. Ann Pomeroy, "A Passion for Diversity," *HR Magazine*, March 2008, p. 49. The other information about Merck & Co. is from page 48 of the same source.

25. Jane McGregor, "Artful Discounts," *Business Week*, October 20, 2008, p. 59.

26. Simona Covel, "Making a Virtual Company a Reality," *Wall Street Journal*, January 10, 2008, p. B4.

27. Cindy Krischer Goodman, "Telecommuting: Driving Down the Cost of Working," *Miami Herald*, June 25, 2008. Available at: www.miamiherald.com

28. Susan Ladika, "When Learning Lasts a Lifetime," *HR Magazine*, May 2008, pp. 56–60.

2

Self-Esteem and Self-Confidence

Outline

1 What Is the Nature of Self-Esteem, How Does It Develop, and What Are Its Consequences?
The Development of Self-Esteem
The Consequences of Self-Esteem

2 How Do You Enhance Self-Esteem?
Attain Legitimate Accomplishments
Be Aware of Personal Strengths
Minimize Settings and Interactions That Detract from Your Feelings of Competence
Talk and Socialize Frequently with People Who Boost Your Self-Esteem
Model the Behavior of People with High Self-Esteem

3 What Is the Importance of Self-Confidence, and What Are Its Sources?

4 How Do You Develop and Strengthen Your Self-Confidence?
Take an Inventory of Personal Assets and Accomplishments
Develop a Solid Knowledge Base
Use Positive Self-Talk
Avoid Negative Self-Talk
Use Positive Visual Imagery
Set High Expectations for Yourself (the Galatea Effect)
Strive for Peak Performance
Behave as if You Feel Confident
Bounce Back from Setbacks and Embarrassments
Strive to Develop Psychological Capital
Avoid Overconfidence

Family members who are entrepreneurs helped Eran Dekel start his own fashion company. But it was a chance connection with an uncle who owns a clothing store that started him in the fashion business. "My uncle asked me to help him liquidate some designer suits on the Internet. Right away, I thought of eBay," Dekel says. "When the first suit sold for a 300 percent profit, a light went on in my head." The same uncle helped him find wholesale suppliers—one of the biggest hurdles for any beginning eBay seller.

eBay challenges individuals to do their own market research to select, price, and present merchandise. Dekel, who graduated from Cooper Union in New York City with a degree in engineering, saw such activities as an extension of his studies. "The problem-solving and analytical capabilities I learned in college really prepared me for this type of business," he says. "You have to perform both quantitative and qualitative reasoning in determining what products to sell, and you need to know how to think outside the box when it comes to completing transactions."

After finding success on eBay, Dekel was able to launch his own DeCalo Fashion Web site (www.decalofashion.com), and he shows boundless enthusiasm. "The potential for success is within each individual," he says. "You can't be afraid to take risks or try something new."

Dekel's success with his high-end retail business helped him develop the confidence to expand his professional activities. In 2006 he founded Innovative Language Learning (innovativelanguage.com), a training company that offers skill development in seven languages: Japanese, Korean, Spanish, Italian, German, French, and Arabic. Experts in each of these languages offer the online courses.[1] By operating his online language laboratory, Dekel placed himself in competition with well-established companies Pimsleur Approach (www.pimslcurapproach.com) and Rosetta Stone (rosettastone.com).

Learning Objectives ▶

After studying the information and doing the exercises in this chapter, you should be able to:

1 Describe the nature, development, and consequences of self-esteem.

2 Explain how to enhance self-esteem.

3 Describe the importance of self-confidence and self-efficacy.

4 Pinpoint methods of strengthening and developing your self-confidence.

The story just presented illustrates how self-confidence, such as being willing to take risks and try something new, helps a person succeed in a competitive field. Dekel also has to have high self-esteem to think that his analytical skills are so good that he can compete in the worlds of fashion and language training. Many other people you will meet in this book score high in self-esteem and self-confidence—otherwise they would never have been so successful. In this chapter the focus is on two of the biggest building blocks for more effective human relations: the nature and development of self-esteem and self-confidence.

▶ Learning Objective 1 ▶

What Is the Nature of Self-Esteem, How Does It Develop, and What Are Its Consequences?

Self-esteem

the experience of feeling competent to cope with the basic challenges in life and of being worthy of happiness

Understanding the self from various perspectives is important because who you are and what you think of yourself influences many facets of your life, both on and off the job. A particularly important role is played by **self-esteem,** the experience of feeling competent to cope with the basic challenges in life and of being worthy of happiness.[2] In more general terms, self-esteem refers to a positive overall evaluation of oneself.

A useful distinction is that our self-concept refers to what we *think* about ourselves, whereas self-esteem is what we *feel* about ourselves.[3] People with positive self-esteem have a deep-down, inside-the-self feeling of their own worth. Consequently, they develop positive self-concepts. Before reading further, you are invited to measure your current level of self-esteem by taking the Human Relations Self-Assessment Quiz 2-1. Next the nature of self-esteem and many of its consequences are examined.

THE DEVELOPMENT OF SELF-ESTEEM

Part of understanding the nature of self-esteem is to know how it develops. Self-esteem comes about from a variety of early life experiences. People who were encouraged to feel good about themselves and their accomplishments by family members, friends, and teachers are more likely to enjoy high self-esteem. Early life experiences play a key role in the development of both healthy self-esteem and low self-esteem, according to research synthesized at the Counseling and Mental Health Center of the University of Texas.[4] Childhood experiences that lead to healthy self-esteem include the following:

■ Being praised

■ Being listened to

■ Being spoken to respectfully

■ Getting attention and hugs

■ Experiencing success in sports or school

In contrast, childhood experiences that lead to low self-esteem include the following:

■ Being harshly criticized

■ Being yelled at or beaten

■ Being ignored, ridiculed, or teased

■ Being expected to be "perfect" all the time

■ Experiencing failures in sports or school

■ Often being given messages that failed experiences (losing a game, getting a poor grade, and so forth) were failures of one's whole self

A widespread explanation of self-esteem development is that compliments, praise, and hugs alone build self-esteem. Yet many developmental psychologists

Human Relations Self-Assessment Quiz | 2-1

The Self-Esteem Checklist

Indicate whether each of the following statements is mostly true or mostly false as it applies to you.

	Mostly True	Mostly False
1. I am excited about starting each day.		
2. Most of any progress I have made in my work or school can be attributed to luck.		
3. I often ask myself, "Why can't I be more successful?"		
4. When my manager or team leader gives me a challenging assignment, I usually dive in with confidence.		
5. I believe that I am working up to my potential.		
6. I am able to set limits to what I will do for others without feeling anxious.		
7. I regularly make excuses for my mistakes.		
8. Negative feedback crushes me.		
9. I care very much how much money other people make, especially when they are working in my field.		
10. I feel like a failure when I do not achieve my goals.		
11. Hard work gives me an emotional lift.		
12. When others compliment me, I doubt their sincerity.		
13. Complimenting others makes me feel uncomfortable.		
14. I find it comfortable to say, "I'm sorry."		
15. It is difficult for me to face up to my mistakes.		
16. My coworkers think I am not worthy of promotion.		
17. People who want to become my friends usually do not have much to offer.		
18. If my manager praised me, I would have a difficult time believing it was deserved.		
19. I'm just an ordinary person.		
20. Having to face change really disturbs me.		

Scoring and Interpretation:

The answers in the high self-esteem direction are as follows:

1. Mostly True	**8.** Mostly False	**15.** Mostly False
2. Mostly False	**9.** Mostly False	**16.** Mostly False
3. Mostly False	**10.** Mostly False	**17.** Mostly False
4. Mostly True	**11.** Mostly True	**18.** Mostly False
5. Mostly True	**12.** Mostly False	**19.** Mostly False
6. Mostly True	**13.** Mostly False	**20.** Mostly False
7. Mostly False	**14.** Mostly True	

17–20 You have very high self-esteem. Yet if your score is 20, it could be that you are denying any self-doubts.

11–16 Your self-esteem is in the average range. It would probably be worthwhile for you to implement strategies to boost your self-esteem (described in this chapter) so that you can develop a greater feeling of well-being.

0–10 Your self-esteem needs bolstering. Discuss your feelings about yourself with a trusted friend or with a mental health professional. At the same time, attempt to implement several of the tactics for boosting self-esteem described in this chapter.

Questions:
1. How does your score on this quiz match your evaluation of your self-esteem?
2. What would it be like being married to somebody who scored 0 on this quiz?

"Parents need to fill a child's bucket of self-esteem so high that the rest of the world can't poke enough holes in it to drain it dry."

—Alvin Price, child development specialist, quoted in Ken Dooley, ed., *Good Stuff* (Malvern, PA: Progressive Business Publications, 2005), p. 6.

(Adapted to the world of work, this quote reads: "Supervisors need to fill a worker's bucket of self-esteem so high that the rest of the world can't poke enough holes in it to drain it dry.")

seriously question this perspective. Instead, they believe that self-esteem results from accomplishing worthwhile activities and then feeling proud of these accomplishments.[5] Receiving encouragement, however, can help the person accomplish activities that build self-esteem.

Leading psychologist Martin Seligman argues that self-esteem is caused by a variety of successes and failures. To develop self-esteem, people need to improve their skills for dealing with the world.[6] Self-esteem, therefore, comes about by genuine accomplishments, followed by praise and recognition. Heaping undeserved praise and recognition on people may lead to a temporary high, but it does not produce genuine self-esteem. The child develops self-esteem not from being told he or she can score a goal in soccer but from scoring that goal.

Although early-life experiences have the major impact on the development of self-esteem, experiences in adult life also affect self-esteem. David De Cremer, of the Tilburg University (Netherlands), and his associates conducted two studies with Dutch college students about how the behavior of leaders and fair procedures influence self-esteem. The study found that self-esteem was related to procedural fairness and leadership that encourages self-rewards. The interpretation given of the findings is that a leader/supervisor can facilitate self-esteem when he or she encourages self-rewards and uses fair procedures.[7] A takeaway from this study would be that rewarding yourself for a job well done, even in adult life, can boost your self-esteem a little.

THE CONSEQUENCES OF SELF-ESTEEM

No single factor is as important to career success as self-esteem, as observed by psychologist Eugene Raudsepp. People with positive self-esteem understand their own competence and worth and have positive perceptions of their abilities to cope with problems and adversity.[8] Kendrick Melrose, former CEO of Toro, illustrates this fundamental point. Toro employees were bedraggled because of some rough business years, and they were reluctant to make decisions. Melrose helped them learn how to make decisions as a team. He said, "The transformation in management philosophy built self-esteem. It built innovation, creativity, risk, ownership."[9] Here we look at the major consequences of self-esteem, as outlined in Figure 2-1.

Good Mental Health

One of the major consequences of high self-esteem is good mental health. People with high self-esteem feel good about themselves and have positive outlooks on life. One of the links between good mental health and self-esteem is that high self-esteem helps prevent many situations from being stressful. Few negative comments from others are likely to bother you when your self-esteem is high. A person with low self-esteem might crumble if somebody insulted his or her appearance. If you have high self-esteem you might shrug off the insult as simply being the other person's point of view. If faced with an everyday setback, such as losing keys, if you

FIGURE 2-1

CONSEQUENCES OF SELF-ESTEEM

1. Good mental health
2. Profiting from negative feedback
3. Career success
4. Organizational prosperity
5. Envying too many people (negative consequence)
6. Serves as a guide for regulating social relationships
7. Poor romantic relationships when self-esteem is low

have high-self-esteem you might think, "I have so much going for me, why fall apart over this incident?"

Profiting from Negative Feedback

Although people with high self-esteem can readily shrug off undeserved insults, they still profit well from negative feedback. Because they are secure, they can profit from the developmental opportunities suggested by negative feedback. Workers with high self-esteem develop and maintain favorable work attitudes and perform at high levels. These positive consequences take place because such attitudes and behaviors are consistent with the personal belief that they are competent individuals. Mary Kay Ash, the legendary founder of a beauty products company, put it this way: "It never occurred to me I couldn't do it. I always knew that if I worked hard enough, I could." Furthermore, research has shown that high-self-esteem individuals value reaching work goals more than do low-self-esteem individuals.[10]

Career Success

A major consequence of having high self-esteem is that you have a better chance of attaining career success, as mentioned at the beginning of this section and supported by long-term research. The study in question was known as the National Longitudinal Survey of Youth, involving over 12,000 young men and women. The group was studied over a twenty-five-year period beginning in 1979. Self-Assessment Quiz 2-2 gives you the opportunity to take the same survey used in the study to measure *core self-evaluation* (quite similar to self-esteem). Individuals with high core self-evaluations are better motivated, perform better on the job, tend to hold more challenging jobs, and have higher job satisfaction.

Among the many results of the study were that people with higher core evaluations performed better in their first jobs. Furthermore, over time those people with high core evaluations increase their career success at a faster pace than those with below-average core evaluations. Over a twenty-five-year span, the career success they have over others doubles. Success was measured in terms of job satisfaction, pay, and holding a higher-status position.[11] A practical conclusion to take away from this study is that if you have a high core self-evaluation, it will pay impressive career dividends.

Organizational Prosperity

The combined effect of workers having high self-esteem helps a company prosper. Self-esteem is a critical source of competitive advantage in an information society. Companies gain the edge when, in addition to having an educated workforce, employees have high self-esteem, as shown by such behaviors as the following:

- Being creative and innovative
- Taking personal responsibility for problems
- Feeling of independence (yet still wanting to work cooperatively with others)
- Trusting one's own capabilities
- Taking the initiative to solve problems[12]

Behaviors such as these help you cope with the challenge of a rapidly changing workplace where products and ideas become obsolete quickly. Workers with high self-esteem are more likely to be able to cope with new challenges regularly because they are confident that they can master their environments.

Human Relations Self-Assessment Quiz   2-2

National Longitudinal Survey of Youth Measure of Core Self-Evaluation

	True	False
1. I have little control over the things that happen to me.	_____	_____
2. There is little I can do to change many of the important things in my life.	_____	_____
3. I feel that I am a person of worth, on an equal basis with others.	_____	_____
4. I feel that I have a number of good qualities.	_____	_____
5. All in all, I am inclined to feel that I am a failure.	_____	_____
6. I feel I do not have much to be proud of.	_____	_____
7. I wish I could have more respect for myself.	_____	_____
8. I've been depressed.	_____	_____
9. I've felt hopeful about the future.	_____	_____
10. What happens to me in the future depends on me.	_____	_____
11. What happens to me is of my own doing.	_____	_____
12. When I make plans, I am almost certain to make them work.	_____	_____

Scoring and Interpretation:

The answers in the high core self-evaluation direction are as follows:

1. False	5. False	9. True
2. False	6. False	10. True
3. True	7. False	11. True
4. True	8. False	12. True

Although there are no specific categories for scores, the more statements you answered in the direction of high core self-evaluation, the more likely it is that you have the type of core self-evaluation that will facilitate career success.

Questions: 1. How does your score on this quiz match your evaluation of your core self-evaluation?
2. How does your score on this quiz compare to your score on Self-Assessment Quiz 2-1?
3. How can you explain the fact that responses to the above statements were found to be related to long-term career success?

Source: The statements are from the National Longitudinal Survey of Youth (NLSY79), a study commissioned and operated by the Bureau of Labor Statistics, U.S. Department of Labor. The statements are also reported in Timothy A. Judge and Charlice Hurst, "How the Rich (and Happy) Get Richer (and Happier): Relationship of Core Self-Evaluations to Trajectories in Attaining Work Success," *Journal of Applied Psychology*, July 2008, p. 863.

Envying Too Many People

A potential negative consequence of low self-esteem is envying too many people. If you perceive that many individuals have much more of what you want and are more worthwhile than you, you will suffer from enormous envy. To decrease pangs of envy, it is best to develop realistic standards of comparison between you and other people in the world.

If high school basketball player Joshua measures his self-esteem in terms of how well he stacks up with basketball superstar and super-millionaire LeBron James, young Joshua will take a lot of blows to his self-esteem. However, if Joshua compares himself to other players on his team and in his league, his self-esteem will be higher because he has chosen a more realistic reference group. For example,

Joshua might think that Kent, the starting point guard on his team has a good chance of winning a basketball scholarship to college, speaks intelligently, and is well groomed. Joshua works hard to develop the same potential and behaviors. When he believes he has succeeded, Joshua will experience a boost in self-esteem.

According to economist Robert H. Frank of Cornell University, our own reference group has the biggest impact on self-esteem. He wrote, "When you see Bill Gates's mansion, you don't actually aspire to have one like it. It's who is local, who is near you physically and who is most like you—your family members, coworkers and old high school classmates—with whom you compare yourself. If someone in your reference group has a little more, you get a little anxious."[13]

Serves as a Guide for Regulating Social Relationships

Another consequence of self-esteem is that you can use it as a guide in regulating social relationships. According to Mark Leary, director of social psychology at Duke University, self-esteem provides a gauge of performance during social interactions: "Self-esteem rises and falls, acting as an internal barometer of how well you're faring, telling you to fix this problem here, and helping you understand that you don't have to worry about it there."[14]

Following this reasoning, fluctuations in self-esteem provide information that is useful in working your way through social relationships. For example, if you are talking and the person you are talking to yawns, your self-esteem drops, signaling you to change the topic. When you tell a joke, and people laugh, your self-esteem climbs rapidly. If we did not feel bad when we bored or offended others, or satisfied when we delighted them, we would not be inclined to change course.[15]

Poor Romantic Relationships when Self-Esteem Is Low

Low self-esteem can have negative consequences for romantic relationships because people with self-doubts consistently underestimate their partners' feelings for them. People with low **self-respect** distance themselves from the relationship—often devaluing their partner—to prepare themselves for what they think will be an inevitable breakup. John G. Holmes, a psychologist at the University of Waterloo in Ontario, Canada, says, "If people think negatively about themselves, they think their partner must think negatively about them—and they're wrong."[16]

Self-respect
how you think and feel about yourself

How Do You Enhance Self-Esteem?

◀ Learning Objective 2 ◀

Improving self-esteem is a lifelong process because self-esteem is related to the success of your activities and interactions with people. Following are approaches to enhancing self-esteem that are related to how self-esteem develops.

ATTAIN LEGITIMATE ACCOMPLISHMENTS

To emphasize again, accomplishing worthwhile activities is a major contributor to self-esteem in both children and adults. Self-esteem therefore stems from accomplishment.[17] Giving people large trophies for mundane accomplishments is unlikely to raise self-esteem. More likely, the person will see through the transparent attempt to build his or her self-esteem and develop negative feelings about the self. The general-information point of view is the opposite: accomplishment stems from a boost in self-esteem. The two different viewpoints are diagrammed in Figure 2-2.

FIGURE 2-2

GOAL ACCOMPLISHMENT AND SELF-ESTEEM

The Social Science Perspective

Person establishes goal. → Person pursues goal. → Person achieves goal. → Person develops esteem-like feelings.

The General Information Perspective

Person develops esteem-like feelings. → Person establishes a goal. → Person pursues the goal. → Person achieves the goal.

What about you? Would your self-esteem receive a bigger boost by (a) receiving an A in a course in which 10 percent of the class received an A or by (b) receiving an A in a class in which everybody received the same grade?

Another way of framing the attainment of legitimate accomplishments is that to boost your self-esteem, you must engage in behaviors and make choices that are worthy of esteem. To implement this strategy, you must first size up what your reference group regards as esteemed. For most reference groups, or the people whose opinion matters to you, esteem-worthy behavior would include the following:

- Successfully completing a program of studies

- Occupying a high-status job and staying long enough to accomplish something worthwhile

- Investing time and money in charitable activities

- Taking pride in your physical appearance and condition

- Having a social networking Web profile (such as on Facebook) that is filled with honorable and sensible content

As you have probably observed, all these esteem-worthy accomplishments reflect values about what is important. For example, a person might have criminals and swindlers in his or her reference group. Self-esteem for this person based on the acclamation of others would therefore stem from such activities as defrauding others of money and not paying taxes.

BE AWARE OF PERSONAL STRENGTHS

Introspection
the act of looking within oneself

Another method of improving your self-esteem is to develop an appreciation of your strengths and accomplishments. Appreciating your strengths and accomplishments requires that you engage in **introspection,** the act of looking within oneself. Although introspection may sound easy, it requires considerable discipline and concentration to actually observe what you are doing. A simple example is that we are often not even aware of some of our basic habits, such as biting the lip when nervous or blinking when attempting to answer a difficult question.

Research conducted with more than sixty executives showed that their self-concepts became more positive after one month of stopping to appreciate their strengths and accomplishments for a few minutes every day.[18] A good starting point is to list your strengths and accomplishments on paper. This list is likely to be more impressive than you expected.

You can sometimes develop an appreciation of your strengths by participating in a group exercise designed for such purposes. A group of about seven people meet to form a support group. All group members first spend about ten minutes answering the question, "What are my three strongest points, attributes, or skills?" After each group member records his or her three strengths, he or she discusses them with the other group members.

Each group member then comments on the list. Other group members sometimes add to your list of strengths or reinforce what you have to say. Sometimes you may find disagreement. One member told the group, "I'm handsome, intelligent, reliable, athletic, self-confident, and very moral. I also have a good sense of humor." Another group member retorted, "And I might add that you're unbearably conceited."

The late Leo Buscaglia (aka Dr. Hug) was a major contributor to emphasizing the importance of people appreciating their strengths to boost their self-esteem. Part of his program for enhancing human relationships was for people to love others as well as themselves. A representative example of Buscaglia's advice for being aware of your personal strengths is as follows:

> A wonderful realization will be the day you realize that you are unique in all the world. There is nothing that is an accident. You are a special combination for a purpose—and don't let them tell you otherwise, even if they tell you that purpose is an illusion. (Live an illusion if you have to.) You are that combination so that you can do what is essential for you to do. Don't ever believe that you have nothing to contribute. The world is an incredible unfilled tapestry. And only you can fulfill that space that is yours.[19]

MINIMIZE SETTINGS AND INTERACTIONS THAT DETRACT FROM YOUR FEELINGS OF COMPETENCE

Most of us have situations in work and personal life that make us feel less than our best. If you can minimize exposure to those situations, you will have fewer feelings of incompetence. The problem with feeling incompetent is that it lowers your self-esteem. An office supervisor said she detests company picnics, most of all because she is forced to play softball. At her own admission, she had less aptitude for athletics than any able-bodied person she knew. In addition, she felt uncomfortable with the small-talk characteristic of picnics. To minimize discomfort, the woman attended only those picnics she thought were absolutely necessary. Instead of playing on the softball team, she volunteered to be the equipment manager.

A problem with avoiding all situations in which you feel incompetent is that it might prevent you from acquiring needed skills. Also, it boosts your self-confidence and self-esteem to become comfortable in a previously uncomfortable situation.

TALK AND SOCIALIZE FREQUENTLY WITH PEOPLE WHO BOOST YOUR SELF-ESTEEM

Psychologist Barbara Ilardie says that the people who can raise your self-esteem are usually those with high self-esteem themselves. They are the people who give honest feedback because they respect others and themselves. Such high-self-esteem individuals should not be confused with yes-people who agree with others simply to be liked. The point is that you typically receive more from strong people than weak ones. Weak people will flatter you but will not give you the honest feedback you need to build self-esteem.[20]

A related approach to boosting self-esteem is to create a blog in which you enter positive comments, still photos, and videos about you. You invite others to respond with positive comments about you, thereby boosting your good feelings about yourself. A downside here, however, is that some people respond to warm invitations with negative and hurtful commentary. An underlying problem here is that many people are quite uninhibited when responding to a blog.[21] Have you ever noticed how nasty and uninhibited people can be on the Web?

MODEL THE BEHAVIOR OF PEOPLE WITH HIGH SELF-ESTEEM

Observe the way people who are believed to have high self-esteem stand, walk, speak, and act. Even if you are not feeling so secure inside, you will project a high-self-esteem image if you act assured. Raudsepp recommends, "Stand tall, speak clearly and with confidence, shake hands firmly, look people in the eye and smile frequently. Your self-esteem will increase as you notice encouraging reactions from others."[22] (Notice here that self-esteem is considered to be about the same idea as self-confidence.)

Choose your models of high self-esteem from people you know personally as well as celebrities you might watch on television news and interview shows. Observing actors on the large or small screen is a little less useful because they are guaranteed to be playing a role. Identifying a teacher or professor as a self-esteem model is widely practiced, as is observing successful family members and friends.

▶ Learning Objective 3 ▶

What Is the Importance of Self-Confidence, and What Are Its Sources?

Self-efficacy

confidence in your ability to carry out a specific task in contrast to generalized self-confidence

Although self-confidence can be considered part of self-esteem, it is important enough to study separately. **Self-efficacy** is confidence in your ability to carry out a specific task in contrast to generalized self-confidence. When self-efficacy is high, you believe you have the ability to do what is necessary to complete a task successfully.

The Importance of Self-Confidence and Self-Efficacy

Self-confidence has also long been recognized as a trait of effective leaders. A straightforward implication of self-efficacy is that people who think they can perform well on a task do better than those who think they will do poorly. Various studies have shown that people with a high sense of self-efficacy tend to have good job performance, so being self-confident is important for your career. They also set relatively high goals for themselves.[23]

The importance of self-confidence for your career can be illustrated by the tactics of Jack Welch, the former CEO of General Electric (GE), who is regarded by many business writers as one of the most influential leaders of all time. Welch has become a well-known business author and columnist, in addition to remaining active in directing several companies. Welch once said that his most important responsibility at GE was building the self-confidence of managers throughout the company. Although an intimidating and demanding boss, Welch would help managers develop their self-confidence by giving them lots of opportunities to succeed on major assignments.

The Sources of Self-Confidence

Research by college professors and psychological consultants George P. Hollenbeck and Douglas T. Hall suggests that our feelings of self-confidence stem from five sources of information.[24] The first source is the *actual experience,* or *things we have done.* Having done something before and having succeeded is the most powerful way to for you to build self-confidence. If you successfully inserted a replacement battery in your watch without destroying the watch, you will be confident in making another replacement.

The second source of self-confidence is the *experiences of others,* or *modeling.* You can gain some self-confidence if you have carefully observed others perform a task, such as resolving conflict with a customer. You might say to yourself, "I've seen Tracy calm down the customer by listening and showing sympathy, and I'm confident I can do the same thing."

The third source of self-confidence is *social comparison,* or *comparing yourself to others.* If you see other people with capabilities similar to your own perform a task well, your will gain in confidence. A person might say, "If that person can learn how to work with enterprise software, I can do it also. I'm just as smart."

The fourth source of self-confidence is *social persuasion,* or *the process of convincing another person.* If a credible person convinces you that you can accomplish a particular task, you will often receive a boost in self-confidence large enough to give the task a try. If the encouragement is coupled with guidance on how to perform the task, your self-confidence gain will be higher. So the boss or teacher who says, "I know you can do it, and I'm here to help you," knows how to build self-confidence.

The fifth source of self-confidence is *emotional arousal,* or *how you feel about events around you and manage your emotions.* People rely somewhat on inner feelings to know if they are self-confident enough to perform the task. Imagine a person standing on top of a high mountain ready to ski down. However, he or she is trembling and nauseous with fear. Contrast this beginner to another person who simply feels mildly excited and challenged. Skier number one has a self-confidence problem, whereas skier number two has enough confidence to start the descent. (Have your emotional sensations ever influenced your self-confidence?)

The more of these five sources of self-confidence are positive for you, the more likely your self-confidence will be positive. Human Relations Self-Assessment Quiz 2-3 provides some insight into your level of self-confidence.

How Do You Develop and Strengthen Your Self-Confidence?

◀ Learning Objective 4 ◀

Strengthening your confidence often facilitates success. As explained by motivational speaker and author Valorie Burton, a lack of authentic confidence holds most people from attaining their goals. People who are more successful are not necessarily better equipped than others, but they are bolder in their belief in themselves.[25] Self-confidence is generally achieved by succeeding in a variety of situations. A confident civil engineer may not be generally self-confident unless he or she also achieves success in activities such as forming good personal relationships, navigating complex software, writing a letter, learning a second language, and displaying athletic skills.

Although this general approach to building self-confidence makes sense, it does not work for everyone. Some people who seem to succeed at everything still have lingering self-doubt. Low self-confidence is so deeply ingrained in this type of personality that success in later life is not sufficient to change things. Following are ten specific strategies and tactics for building and elevating self-confidence. They will generally work unless the person has deep-rooted feelings of inferiority.

Human Relations Self-Assessment Quiz 2-3

How Self-Confident Are You?

Indicate the extent to which you agree with each of the following statements. Use a 1 to 5 scale: (1) disagree strongly, (2) disagree, (3) neutral, (4) agree, and (5) agree strongly.

	DS	D	N	A	AS
1. I frequently say to people, "I'm not sure."	5	4	3	2	1
2. I perform well in most situations in life.	1	2	3	4	5
3. I willingly offer advice to others.	1	2	3	4	5
4. Before making even a minor decision, I usually consult with several people.	5	4	3	2	1
5. I am generally willing to attempt new activities for which I have very little related skill or experience.	1	2	3	4	5
6. Speaking in front of the class or other group is a frightening experience for me.	5	4	3	2	1
7. I experience stress when people challenge me or put me on the spot.	5	4	3	2	1
8. I feel comfortable attending a social event by myself.	1	2	3	4	5
9. I'm much more of a winner than a loser.	1	2	3	4	5
10. I am cautious about making any substantial change in my life.	5	4	3	2	1

Total score: _____

Scoring and Interpretation:

Calculate your total score by adding the numbers circled. A tentative interpretation of the scoring is as follows:

45–50 Very high self-confidence with perhaps a tendency toward arrogance

38–44 A high, desirable level of self-confidence

30–37 Moderate, or average, self-confidence

10–29 Self-confidence needs strengthening

Questions: 1. How does your score on this test fit with your evaluation of your self-confidence?

2. What would it be like working for a manager who scored 10 on this quiz?

The tactics and strategies described here and outlined in Figure 2-3 are arranged approximately in the order in which they should be tried to achieve best results.

TAKE AN INVENTORY OF PERSONAL ASSETS AND ACCOMPLISHMENTS

Many people suffer from low self-confidence because they do not appreciate their own good points. Therefore, a starting point in increasing your self-confidence is to take an inventory of personal assets and accomplishments. A slight variation of this activity was offered previously as a method of developing self-esteem. Personal assets should be related to characteristics and behaviors rather than tangible assets, such as an inheritance or an antique car.

Accomplishments can be anything significant in which you played a key role in achieving the results. Try not to be modest in preparing your list of assets and accomplishments. You are looking for any confidence booster you can find. Two lists

FIGURE 2-3

TECHNIQUES FOR STRENGTHENING YOUR SELF-CONFIDENCE

prepared by different people will suffice to give you an idea of the kinds of assets and accomplishments that might be included.

Amy

Good listener; most people like me; good messaging skills; good posture; inquisitive mind; good at solving problems; above-average Internet search skills; good sense of humor; patient with people who make mistakes; better-than-average appearance. Organized successful fund drive that raised $40,000 for church; graduated tenth in high school class of 500; achieved first place in industrial bowling league; daughter has an excellent career.

Todd

Good mechanical skills, including automotive repair and computer repair; work well under pressure; good dancer; friendly with strangers; great physical health (drug and disease free); good cook; can laugh at my own mistakes; favorable personal appearance; respectful of authority. Made award-winning suggestion that saved company $45,000; scored winning goal in college basketball tournament; dragged child out of burning building; dynamite blogger.

The value of these asset lists is that they add to your self-appreciation. Most people who lay out their good points on paper come away from the activity with at least a temporary boost in self-confidence, and perhaps self-esteem. The temporary boost, combined with a few successful experiences, may lead to a long-term gain in self-confidence.

An important supplement to listing your own assets is hearing the opinion of others on your good points. This tactic has to be used sparingly, however, and mainly with people who are personal-growth minded. A good icebreaker is to tell your source of feedback that you have to prepare a list of your assets for a human relations exercise. Because that person knows of your work on your capabilities, you hope that he or she can spare a few minutes for this important exercise. For many people, positive feedback from others does more for building self-confidence than does feedback from you. The reason is that self-esteem depends to a large extent on what people think others think about them. Consequently, if other people—whose judgment you trust—think highly of you, your self-image will be positive.

DEVELOP A SOLID KNOWLEDGE BASE

A bedrock strategy for projecting self-confidence is to develop a base of knowledge that enables you to provide sensible alternative solutions to problems. Intuition is very important, but working from a base of facts helps you project a confident image. Formal education is an obvious and important source of information for your knowledge base. Day-by-day absorption of information directly and indirectly related to your career is equally important. A major purpose of formal education is to get you in the right frame of mind to continue your quest for knowledge.

In your quest for developing a solid knowledge base to project self-confidence, be sensitive to abusing this technique. If you bombard people with quotes, facts, and figures, you are likely to be perceived as an annoying know-it-all.

USE POSITIVE SELF-TALK

Positive self-talk

saying positive things about yourself to yourself

A basic method of building self-confidence is to engage in **positive self-talk,** saying positive things about you to yourself. The first step in using positive self-talk is to objectively state the incident that is casting doubt about self-worth.[26] The key word here is *objectively.* Terry, who is fearful of poorly executing a report-writing assignment, might say, "I've been asked to write a report for the company, and I'm not a good writer."

The next step is to objectively interpret what the incident *does not* mean. Terry might say, "Not being a skilled writer doesn't mean that I can't figure out a way to write a good report or that I'm an ineffective employee."

Next, the person should objectively state what the incident *does* mean. In doing this, the person should avoid put-down labels such as *incompetent, stupid, dumb, jerk,* or *airhead.* These terms are forms of negative self-talk. Terry should state what the incident does mean: "I have a problem with one small aspect of this job."

The fourth step is to objectively account for the cause of the incident. Terry would say, "I'm really worried about writing a good report because I have very little experience in writing along these lines."

The fifth step is to identify some positive ways to prevent the incident from happening again. Terry might say, "I'll get out my textbook on business communications and review the chapter on report writing" or "I'll enroll in a course or seminar on business report writing."

The final step is to use positive self-talk. Terry imagines his boss saying, "This report is really good. I'm proud of my decision to select you to prepare this important report."

Positive self-talk builds self-confidence and self-esteem because it programs the mind with positive messages. Making frequent positive statements or affirmations about the self creates a more confident person. An example would be, "I know I can learn this new equipment rapidly enough to increase my productivity within five days."

Business coach Gary Lockwood emphasizes that positive self-talk is also useful for giving you the confidence to get people past difficult times. "It's all in your head," he said. "Remember you are in charge of your feelings. You are in control of your attitude." Instead of berating yourself after making a mistake, learn from the experience and move on. Say to yourself, "Everyone makes mistakes," "Tomorrow is another day," or "What can I learn from this?"[27]

AVOID NEGATIVE SELF-TALK

In addition to making positive statements, you should minimize negative statements about yourself to bolster self-confidence. A lack of self-confidence is reflected in statements such as, "I may be stupid, but . . .," "Nobody asked my opinion," "I know I'm usually wrong, but . . .," "I know I don't have as much education as some people, but. . . ." Self-effacing statements such as these serve to reinforce low self-confidence.

It is also important not to attribute to yourself negative, irreversible traits, such as "idiotic," "ugly," "dull," "loser-type," "hopeless," "nerdy," and "dorky." Instead, look on your weak points as areas for possible self-improvement. Negative self-labeling can do long-term damage to your confidence. If a person stops that practice today, his or her self-confidence may begin to increase.

USE POSITIVE VISUAL IMAGERY

Assume you have a situation in mind in which you would like to appear confident and in control. An example would be a meeting with a major customer who has told you by e-mail that he is considering switching suppliers. Your intuitive reaction is that if you cannot handle his concerns without fumbling or appearing desperate, you will lose the account. An important technique in this situation is **positive visual imagery,** or picturing a positive outcome in your mind. To apply this technique in this situation, imagine yourself engaging in a convincing argument about why your customer should retain your company as the primary supplier. Imagine yourself talking in positive terms about the good service your company offers and how you can rectify any problems.

> **Positive visual imagery**
> picturing a positive outcome in your mind

Visualize yourself listening patiently to your customer's concerns and then talking confidently about how your company can handle these concerns. As you rehearse this moment of truth, create a mental picture of you and the customer shaking hands over the fact that the account is still yours.

Positive visual imagery helps you appear confident because your mental rehearsal of the situation has helped you prepare for battle. If imagery works for you once, you will be even more effective in subsequent uses of the technique.

SET HIGH EXPECTATIONS FOR YOURSELF (THE GALATEA EFFECT)

If you set high expectations for yourself, and you succeed, you are likely to experience a temporary or permanent boost in self-confidence. The **Galatea effect** is a type of self-fulfilling prophecy in which high expectations lead to high performance. The term Galatea effect stems from Greek mythology. Galatea was a maiden who was originally a statue carved by Pygmalion. She was later brought to life by Aphrodite in response to the sculptor's pleas. Similar to positive self-talk, if you believe in yourself, you are more likely to succeed. You expect to win, so you do. The Galatea effect does not work all the time, but it does work some of the time for many people.

> **Galatea effect**
> a type of self-fulfilling prophecy in which high expectations lead to high performance

Workplace behavior researchers D. Brian McNatt and Timothy A. Judge studied the Galatea effect with seventy-two auditors within three offices of a major accounting firm for a three-month period. The auditors were given letters of encouragement to strengthen their feelings of self-efficacy. Information in the letters was based on facts about the auditors, such as information derived from their résumés and company records. The results of the experiment showed that creating a Galatea effect bolstered self-efficacy, motivation, and performance. However, the performance improvement was temporary, suggesting that self-expectations need to be boosted regularly.[28]

STRIVE FOR PEAK PERFORMANCE

Peak performance
exceptional accomplishment in a given task

A key strategy for projecting confidence is to display **peak performance,** or exceptional accomplishment in a given task. The experience is transient but exceptionally meaningful. Peak performance refers to much more than attempting to do your best. Experiencing peak performance in various tasks over a long time period would move a person toward self-actualization (full use of potential).[29] To achieve peak performance, you must be totally focused on what you are doing. When you are in the state of peak performance, you are mentally calm and physically at ease. Intense concentration is required to achieve this state. You are so focused on the task at hand that you are not distracted by extraneous events or thoughts. To use an athletic analogy, you are *in the zone* while you are performing the task. In fact, many sports psychologists and other sports trainers work with athletes to help them attain peak performance.

The mental state achieved during peak performance is akin to a person's sense of deep concentration when immersed in a sport or hobby. On days when tennis players perform way above their usual game, they typically comment, "The ball looked so large today. I could read the label as I hit it." On the job, focus and concentration allow the person to sense and respond to relevant information coming both from within the mind and from outside stimuli. When you are at your peak, you impress others by responding intelligently to their input. While turning in peak performance, you are experiencing a mental state referred to as *flow*.

Although you are concentrating on an object or sometimes on another person during peak performance, you still have an awareness of the self. You develop a strong sense of the self, similar to self-confidence and self-efficacy, while you are concentrating on the task. Peak performance is related to self-confidence in another important way. Achieving peak performance in many situations helps you develop confidence. Here are two representative examples of peak performance:

- A real estate agent sells $17 million of homes in her region in one year, 40 percent higher than any other agent in her area.

- A customer-service specialist becomes certified as a Black Belt in the quality-improvement process called Six Sigma and then leads a team that moves a call center from a customer satisfaction rating of 75 to 98 percent.

BEHAVE AS IF YOU FEEL CONFIDENT

A principle of psychology developed about 100 years ago states that your behavior leads to attitudes. As you change your behavior, your attitudes will begin to change. This same idea can be used to project confidence. A useful example is the often-feared situation of making a presentation. Executive coach Gail Golden says that you should enter the room purposefully, holding your back straight. Look up and out at the audience instead of looking down at your notes or at the screen of your computer graphic presentation. Speak in a loud, clear voice, and look the audience in the eye or on their foreheads.[30] Behaving in this manner will often make you feel more confident within several minutes.

BOUNCE BACK FROM SETBACKS AND EMBARRASSMENTS

Resilience is a major contributor to personal effectiveness. Overcoming setbacks also builds self-confidence. An effective self-confidence builder is convincing yourself that you can conquer adversity, such as setbacks and embarrassments, thus being resilient. The vast majority of successful leaders have dealt successfully with at least one significant setback in their careers, such as being fired or demoted. In contrast, crumbling after a setback or series of setbacks will usually lower self-confidence. Two major suggestions for bouncing back from setbacks and embarrassments are presented next.

Get Past the Emotional Turmoil

Adversity has enormous emotional consequences. The emotional impact of severe job adversity can rival the loss of a personal relationship. The stress from adversity leads to a cycle of adversity followed by stress, followed by more adversity. A starting point in dealing with the emotional aspects of adversity is to *accept the reality of your problem.* Admit that your problems are real and that you are hurting inside. The next step is *not to take the setback personally.* Remember that setbacks are inevitable as long as you are taking some risks in your career. Not personalizing setbacks helps reduce some of the emotional sting. If possible, *do not panic.* Recognize that you are in difficult circumstances under which many others panic. Convince yourself to remain calm enough to deal with the severe problem or crisis. Also, *get help from your support network.* Getting emotional support from family members and friends helps overcome the emotional turmoil associated with adversity.

Human Relations in Practice

Eddie Lampert Uses Self-Confidence to Make Billions and Escape Kidnappers

By the time financier Eddie Lampert was forty-two years old, he had amassed a fortune estimated at nearly $2 billion. He is the owner of the private investment fund ESL Investments. After his fund acquired the bankrupt discounter Kmart, Lampert then acquired Sears Roebuck & Co. to form Sears Holding Company, with Lampert as chair. In his dealings with business associates, Big Eddie brims with self-confidence in his decision making. During a meeting with Sears executives, he asked again and again, "What's the benefit of that?" or "Why invest in that?" He shot down a modest $2 million proposal to improve lighting in the stores.

In 2003, he was kidnapped at gunpoint in a parking garage by four hoodlums who had been searching for wealthy people on the Internet. He was held bound in a bathtub at a motel. The men told Lampert they had been hired to kill him for $5 million but would let him go for $1 million. As the kidnappers became increasingly nervous, Lampert convinced them that if they would release him, he would pay them $40,000 a couple of days later. The hoodlums let him off on the side of a road in Greenwich, Connecticut. "It was very much like going to your own funeral," he says. Two days later Lampert was back in Kmart negotiations, with all the more confidence in his negotiating skills.

Source: Patricia Sellers, "Eddie Lampert: The Best Investor of His Generation," *Fortune, Investor's Guide*, February 6, 2006; Robert Berner, "The Next Warren Buffet," *Business Week*, November 22, 2004, pp. 144–154.

A type of emotional turmoil that faces many people at some point in their careers is to be fired for what the company thinks is poor performance. Being fired hurts most people deeply, but by following the steps previously described, the impact can be softened and can ultimately lead to heightened self-confidence. A surprisingly large number of successful entrepreneurs were at one time fired from a corporate job, often because they were seen as mavericks who would not follow rules well.

Find a Creative Solution to Your Problem

An inescapable part of planning a comeback is to solve your problem. You often need to search for creative solutions. Jason, a business student in Chicago, ran a sub shop to earn a living and support himself through college. Layoffs at nearby companies had driven his sales way down below the point at which it paid to keep the sub shop open. In the process of exploring all the possibilities of what he could do in a hurry to earn a living, Jason observed that loads of old buildings in downtown Chicago were being rebuilt and turned into apartments and retail space. Jason then thought of starting an "interior demolition" company, combining efforts with two relatives in the home repair business. Jason's creative solution accomplished what needed to be done to regain his financial equilibrium. His self-confidence continues to surge as his interior demolition business has prospered. If the preceding steps work for you and you bring your level of self-confidence to where you want it to be, you will have achieved a major milestone in applying human relations to yourself.

STRIVE TO DEVELOP POSITIVE PSYCHOLOGICAL CAPITAL

Positive psychological capital
a positive psychological state of development in which you have a storehouse of hope, self-efficacy, optimism, and resilience

A comprehensive way of becoming more self-confident is to develop **positive psychological capital,** a positive psychological state of development in which you have hope, self-efficacy, optimism, and resilience. Note that self-efficacy and resilience have already been included in our study of self-confidence. In more detail, the components of positive psychological capital are as follows:

- *Hope* refers to persevering toward goals and, when necessary, redirecting paths to a goal in order to succeed. In everyday language, don't give up when pursuing your goals.

- *Self-efficacy* refers to having the confidence to take on and invest the necessary effort to succeed at challenging tasks. Experience is a big help here, because if you have successfully completed the same task, or a similar one, previously you will be more confident that you can succeed.

- *Optimism* refers to making a positive attribution about succeeding now and in the future. If you are a natural pessimist you will have to work harder at looking for the positive aspects of a given situation.

- *Resiliency* refers to dealing with problems and adversity by sustaining effort and bouncing back to attain success. Conquering a major setback would be an enormous contributor to your self-confidence.

An encouraging note about positive psychological capital is that people can develop it. An experiment conducted with 187 working adults found that a Web-based, highly-focused two-hour training program raised the average level of psychological capital. The increase in psychological capital was measured by more positive responses after training to such statements as, "If I should find myself in a jam at work, I could think of many ways to get out of it" (hope).[31] Should the participants in the study really do a better job of getting out of jams in the future, you could be even more confident about how well training improves psychological capital.

AVOID OVERCONFIDENCE

As with most human qualities, self-confidence can be a negative factor if carried to the extreme. The overly self-confident individual might become intimidating and unwilling to listen to the advice of others. During a group meeting, the highly self-confident person might typically make a comment before giving others their fair turn to speak. Overconfident individuals are so self-centered that they do not even notice eyes rolling when they hog the meeting.

The potential disadvantages of extremely high self-confidence also apply to too much concern about the self in general, including self-esteem. Too much attention to the self can lead a person to be self-centered, self-conscious, and uninterested in other people and the outside world. You have probably met people who include in almost every conversation a statement about their health or an activity of theirs, indicating their self-centeredness. An illustration of this problem is as follows:

> Psychoanalyst Kerry J. Sulkowicz, who specializes in workplace problems, was asked about dealing with an employee who turns every interaction into a conversation about her. Sulkowicz responded that the employee's need for attention may arise from early-life experiences of emotional deprivation and neglect. She compensates by her greediness in grabbing attention. The advice offered to deal with the situation included politely but firmly telling the employee that her work is valued but she does not seem to realize how much she redirects the subject to herself.[32]

The right balance is to be concerned about yourself, your self-esteem and self-confidence, and your personal growth yet still focus on the outside world. Focusing on the outside world can ultimately strengthen you because you develop skills and interests that will enhance your self-esteem and self-confidence.

Concept Review
and Reinforcement

Key Terms

Self-esteem, 36   Self-efficacy, 44   Galatea effect, 49
Self-respect, 41   Positive self-talk, 48   Peak performance, 50
Introspection, 42   Positive visual imagery, 49   Positive psychological capital, 52

Summary and Review

- Self-esteem refers to feeling competent and being worthy of happiness. People with high self-esteem develop positive self-concepts.
- Self-esteem develops from a variety of early-life experiences. People who were encouraged to feel good about themselves and their accomplishments by key people in their lives are more likely to enjoy high self-esteem.
- Of major significance, self-esteem also results from accomplishing worthwhile activities and then feeling proud of these accomplishments. Praise and recognition for accomplishments also help develop self-esteem.
- Self-esteem is important for career success. Good mental health is another major consequence of high self-esteem. One of the links between good mental health and self-esteem is that high self-esteem helps prevent many situations from being stressful. High self-esteem helps us profit from negative feedback.
- Workers with high self-esteem develop and maintain favorable work attitudes and perform at a high level. A company with high self-esteem workers has a competitive advantage.
- High self-esteem is associated with long-term career success, including job satisfaction, higher pay, and occupying high-status positions. Companies also prosper when workers have high self-esteem.
- A potential negative consequence of low self-esteem is envying too many people. Our own reference group has the biggest impact on self-esteem.
- Low self-esteem can have negative consequences for romantic relationships because people with self-doubts consistently underestimate their partners' feelings for them.
- Self-esteem can be useful in guiding social relationships because you can adjust your behavior as your esteem feelings fluctuate.

Self-esteem can be enhanced in many ways:

- Attain legitimate accomplishments, including engaging in behaviors and making choices that are esteem worthy.
- Be aware of your personal strengths.
- Minimize settings and interactions that detract from your feelings of competence.
- Talk and socialize frequently with people who boost your self-esteem.
- Model the behavior of people with high self-esteem.

Various studies have shown that people with a high sense of self-efficacy tend to have good job performance, so self-confidence is important for your career. Our feelings of self-confidence stem from five sources of information:

1. Actual experiences, or things that we have done
2. Experiences of others, or modeling
3. Social comparison, or comparing yourself to others
4. Social persuasion, the process of convincing another person
5. Emotional arousal, or how people feel about events around them and managing emotions

A general principle of boosting your self-confidence is to experience success (goal accomplishment) in a variety of situations. The specific strategies for building self-confidence described here are as follows:

- Take an inventory of personal assets and accomplishments.

- Develop a solid knowledge base.
- Use positive self-talk.
- Avoid negative self-talk.
- Use positive visual imagery.
- Set high expectations for yourself (the Galatea effect).
- Strive for peak performance.
- Behave as if you feel self-confident.

- Bounce back from setbacks and embarrassments.
- Strive to develop psychological capital (hope, self-efficacy, optimism, and resiliency).

Avoiding overconfidence will help you make more effective use of your self-confidence. To achieve the right level of self-confidence and self-esteem, maintain focus on others also.

Check Your Understanding

1. Do you see any relationship between a person having loads of tattoos all over the body, including the neck and arms, and his or her self-esteem? Explain your reasoning.
2. A study by economists indicated that workers with higher levels of self-esteem tended to be more productive. What would be an explanation for this finding?
3. In what way has a teacher, instructor, or professor ever raised your self-esteem? How long-lasting was the effect?
4. How might you improve your self-efficacy for a specific job that you are performing?
5. When you meet another person, on what basis do you conclude that he or she is self-confident?
6. What steps could you take in the next thirty days to increase your positive psychological capital?
7. In what way does your program of studies contribute to building your self-esteem and self-confidence?
8. Many pharmaceutical firms actively recruit cheerleaders as sales representatives to call on doctors to recommend their brand of prescription drugs. The firms in question say that cheerleaders make good sales reps because they are so self-confident. What is your opinion on this controversial issue?
9. Visualize yourself applying for your dream job, and because you want the job so badly you do not feel highly self-confident. What steps can you take to appear self-confident?
10. Interview a person whom you perceive to have a successful career. Ask that person to describe how he or she developed high self-esteem. Be prepared to discuss your findings in class.

Web Corner

Integrating self-esteem into the fabric of society
www.self-esteem-nase.org

Building your self-confidence
www.mindtools.com/selfconf.html (includes video)

INTERNET SKILL BUILDER 2-1

Learning More about Your Self-Esteem

The National Mental Health Information Center has a Web site (listed below) that provides a self-help guide to building self-esteem. Many of the suggestions in the booklet the Web site provides reinforce what you have studied in this chapter. The help offered is mostly from the perspective of people who have low esteem and are working to improve their situation. As you read the booklet and do the self-esteem-building exercises, you are asked to keep the following statement in mind: "I am a very special, unique, and valuable person. I deserve to feel good about myself." http://mentalhealth.samhsa. gov/publications/allpubs/SMA-3715/introduction.asp

INTERNET SKILL BUILDER 2-2

Developing Your Self-Confidence Online

As described in this chapter, self-confidence is a major contributor to leadership effectiveness in a variety of situations. www.self-confidence.co.uk offers a free self-confidence course online. After you sign up for the course, you will receive your first installment immediately. After that you will receive one tutorial a week for six weeks. The lessons include self-confidence-boosting stories, information and quotes, and skill-development exercises. Sponsors of the site will invite you to take related courses for a fee.

Developing Your Human Relations Skills

Applying Human Relations Exercise 2-1

The Self-Esteem-Building Club

You and your classmates are invited to participate in one of the most humane and productive possible human relations skill-building exercises: membership in the "self-esteem-building club." Your assignment is for three consecutive weeks to help build the self-esteem of one person. Before embarking on the exercise, review the information about self-esteem development in the chapter. One of the most effective tactics would be to find somebody who has a legitimate accomplishment and give that person a reward or thank-you. Record carefully what the person did, what you did, and any behavioral reactions of the person whose self-esteem you attempted to build. The incident could become part of your human relations journal. An example follows, written by a 46-year-old student of human relations:

Thursday night two weeks ago I went to the athletic club to play racquetball. Different from usual, I had a date after the club. I wanted to look good, so I decided to wear my high school class ring. The ring doesn't have much resale value, but I was emotionally attached to it, having worn it for special occasions for twenty-eight years. I stuffed the ring along with my watch and wallet in my athletic bag.

When I was through with racquetball, I showered and got dressed. My ring was missing from my bag even though my wallet and watch were there. I kind of freaked out because I hate to lose a prized possession. I shook the bag out three times, but no luck. Very discouraged, I left my name, telephone number, and e-mail address at the front desk just in case somebody turned in the ring. I kept thinking that I must have lost the ring when I stopped at the desk to check in.

The next morning before going to class, I got a phone call from a front-desk clerk at the club. The clerk told me that Karl, from the housekeeping staff, heard a strange noise while he was vacuuming near the front desk. He shut off the vacuum cleaner immediately and pulled out my ring. To me, Karl was a hero. I made a special trip to the club that night to meet with Karl. I shook his hand, and gave him a $10

bill as a reward. I also explained to Karl what a difference he had made in my mood. I told him that honest, hardworking people like him who take pride in their work make this world a better place. It made my day when Karl smiled and told me it was a pleasure to be helpful.

Your instructor might organize a sharing of self-esteem-building episodes in the class. If the sharing does take place, look for patterns in terms of what seemed to work in terms of self-esteem building. Also, listen for any patterns in failed attempts at self-esteem building.

Applying Human Relations Exercise 2-2

Building Your Self-Confidence and Self-Efficacy

Most people can use a boost to their self-confidence. Even if you are a highly confident individual, perhaps there is room for building your feelings of self-efficacy in a particular area—for example, as a proud and successful business owner learning a new skill such as editing digital photos or speaking a foreign language. For this skill-building exercise, enhance your self-confidence or self-efficacy in the next two weeks by trying out one of the many suggestions for self-confidence building described in the text.

As part of planning the implementation of this exercise, think about any area in which your self-confidence could use a boost. A candid human relations student, who was also a confident cheerleader, said, "Face it, I suck at PowerPoint presentations. I put up so many details on my slides that the audience is trying to read my slides instead of looking at me. I have to admit that my PowerPoint presentation consists mostly of my reading my slides to the audience. I'm much better at cheerleading." So this student studied information in her human relations text about making better graphic presentations. She revamped her approach to using her slides as headlines and talking points. She tried out one presentation in class and one at her church. She received so many compliments on her presentations that she now has much higher self-efficacy with respect to PowerPoint presentations.

Human Relations Class Activity

The Self-Esteem and Self-Confidence Survey

Here is an opportunity to engage in data collection about a vital human relations topic. Each class member is required to obtain survey data from five people, asking each person four questions, as follows: (Survey anybody convenient, including yourself.)

1. What is your sex (gender)?
2. What is your age?
3. How would you rate your self-esteem from 1 (low) to 10 (high)?
4. How would you rate your self-confidence from 1 (low) to 10 (high)?

Use any method of data collection you would like, including face-to-face interviews, e-mail, chat, instant messaging, social networking site, or phone. The results of the survey are entered into a class database run by one or two volunteers. After all data have been collected, one of the volunteers analyzes the data in terms of the following results:

1. Percent of respondents who are male and percent female
2. Average age
3. Average self-esteem rating
4. Average self-confidence rating
5. Average self-esteem and self-confidence ratings of men and women
6. Average self-esteem and self-confidence ratings of respondents of (a) those twenty-five and younger and (b) those twenty-six and older

Class discussion might include any conclusions drawn from the results and how the results fit expectations. For example, a few students might comment about what they predicted would be the average score on self-esteem and self-confidence or any sex or age differences they might have predicted. What about you? How do your self-esteem and self-confidence ratings compare to the survey average?

Human Relations Case Study 2-1

Cindy Struggles in Customer Service

Cindy, age twenty-four, had never looked forward to frequent conflict at home or on the job. She is good natured and gets along with most people as long as they are not abrasive and rude. Despite knowing that she does not feel at her best in dealing with angry people, Cindy accepted a position as a customer service representative in big-box discount department store. The position requires her to work 37½ hours per week, split among days and evenings, including weekends. Customer service at this store involves mostly exchanges of merchandises, granting refunds for returned merchandise, and occasionally listening to complaints about service at the store or about advertised merchandise not being available.

Cindy's supervisor, Derek, explained that the most demanding part of the job would be refusing refunds to customers who had obviously abused merchandise or had bought the merchandise with the intent of using it for a while and then expecting a full refund. Cindy cringed at the thought of standing up to angry customers, but she told Derek that she was up to the challenge.

After a three-day training and orientation program at the store, Derek said that Cindy was ready to work at the customer service desk on her own. Cindy accepted Derek's decision that she was ready to deal with customer demands, but she was trembling underneath. She thought, "How will I handle it if one of those abusive customers tries to rip us off?"

For the first few days, the customer requests were relatively easy for Cindy to manage. Many of the customers brought back merchandise neatly packed in the original boxes, with no visible damage to the merchandise. Several other customers wanted to exchange merchandise for a different size or color. One Friday evening, the relative tranquility of Cindy's job changed suddenly.

A woman around thirty-five years old brought back a long overcoat, saying, "I want my money back. I don't like this coat." Cindy noticed that the coat had a mud stain, so she politely asked, "Ma'am, is it possible that you have worn this coat, and maybe gotten it a little bit dirty?"

"I just wore the coat once. What's wrong with that? I want my money back right now, or I am going to complain to your supervisor." Cindy began to tremble and thought that she just didn't want to get in a fight with a cheat and a thief. She thought that the customer really never intended to keep the coat but just wanted to pretend to buy the coat, all the time expecting a refund after wearing the coat once or twice. So Cindy replied to the customer, "I might be stretching store policy a little, but I think I can give you a full refund."

Later that night Cindy wondered if she had the courage to go back to the job tomorrow. She kept thinking about whether she had enough nerve to deal with demanding customers, even when she knew they were being unreasonable.

Questions

1. In what way does this case deal with self-confidence?

2. What steps do you recommend that Cindy take to enhance her self-confidence?

3. What steps do you recommend that Derek take to boost Cindy's self-confidence?

4. What should Cindy have told the customer who wanted to return the mud-stained coat?

Human Relations Role-Playing Exercise 2-1

Human Relations Case 2-1 provides the background information and story line for this role-play. One person plays the role of the customer attempting to obtain a full refund on the mud-stained overcoat. The other student plays the role of Cindy, who intends to quite confidently reject the customer's demand as being unreasonable.

Observers rate the role-players on two dimensions, using a 1 to 5 scale, from very poor to very good. One dimension is "effective use of human relations techniques." The second dimension is "acting ability." A few observers might voluntarily provide feedback to the role-players in terms of sharing their ratings and observations. The course instructor might also provide feedback.

Human Relations Case Study 2-2

Building Up Kristina

Kristina Wright entered the front door of the half of a house she was sharing with Wendy Lopez. Her housemate said, "I don't see a smile on your face. How did the job hunt go today?"

"Not too well," replied Kristina. "I had two interviews, but I doubt I will be called back. After all, there are dozens of applicants looking for administrative assistant positions with better qualifications than mine. In this economy you really have to know the right people to land a job."

"Will you please stop it, Kristina? You're as good as or better than the competition. You have your degree, and you have experience as an administrative intern. Besides that, you look great."

"That's easy for you to say, Wendy. You have a good job, and people like you. I'm simply average, average, average. Even Lucky [Kristina's cocker spaniel] has an average name. And thousands of girls are named Kristina."

"With an attitude like that," replied Wendy, "you won't get hired. Be proud of who you are. You are somebody special."

"Thanks for the ego boost, my ever-faithful friend. But I almost don't have the courage to go back out there tomorrow and face any more interviews."

Questions

1. What seems to be Kristina's problem, based on the brief information you have been given?

2. What recommendations can you make to Kristina to boost her self-confidence enough to get through any upcoming job interviews she might have?

3. How helpful have the words of encouragement and advice been that Wendy has given Kristina so far?

Human Relations Role-Playing Exercise 2-2

Boosting Kristina's Self-Esteem

Human Relations Case Study 2-2 provides the background information and story line for this role-play. One person plays the role of Kristina Wright, who is feeling down on herself because her job hunt is going poorly. She wants to pour out her discouragement to her housemate, Wendy Lopez. Another student plays the role of Wendy Lopez, who wants to boost Kristina's self-esteem.

As with all role plays in this text, several different pairs might engage in the role-play. At least one student who plays the role of Wendy might be stern with Kristina in an attempt to get her to focus on her strengths. This approach is often referred to as *tough love*.

For both scenarios, observers rate the role-players on two dimensions, using a 1 to 5 scale, from very poor to very good. One dimension is "effective use of human relations techniques." The second dimension is "acting ability." A few observers might voluntarily provide feedback to the role-players in terms of sharing their ratings and observations. The course instructor might also provide feedback.

REFERENCES

1. Excerpted from Greg Holden, "Find Out How Entrepreneurs Tapped into the Power of eBay and Made Millions," *Entrepreneur*, May 2006, pp. 64–65. Additional facts from "Eran Kekel, Owner," at DecaloFashion.com, www.linkedin.com/in/businessman, p. 1; www.innovativelanguage.com

2. Nathaniel Branden, *Self-Esteem at Work: How Confident People Make Powerful Companies* (San Francisco: Jossey-Bass, 1998).

3. April O'Connell, Vincent O'Connell, and Lois-Ann Kuntz, *Choice and Change: The Psychology of Personal Growth and Interpersonal Relationships*, 7th ed. (Upper Saddle River, NJ: Pearson/Prentice Hall, 2005), p. 3.

4. "Better Self-Esteem." Retrieved February 1, 2006, from: www.utexas.edu/student/cmhc/booklets/selfesteem/selfest.html

5. A review of the scholarly research on this topic is contained in Mark R. Leary and Ray F. Baumeister, "The Nature and Function of Self-Esteem: Sociometer Theory," in *Advances in Experimental Social Psychology*, Vol. 32 (New York: Academic Press, 2000), pp. 1–49.

6. Randall Edwards, "Is Self-Esteem Really All That Important?" *APA Monitor*, May 1995, p. 43.

7. David De Cremer et al., "Rewarding Leadership and Fair Procedures as Determinants of Self-Esteem," *Journal of Applied Psychology*, January 2005, pp. 3–12.

8. Eugene Raudsepp, "Strong Self-Esteem Can Help You Advance," *Wall Street Journal*. Retrieved August 10, 2004, from: www.careerjournal.com

9. Larry Werner, "Coffee with Retired Toro CEO Kendrick Melrose," Minneapolis, MN *Star Tribune*, May 23, 2005, as reprinted by Center for Ethical Business Culture. Retrieved February 7, 2006, from: www.cebeglobal.org

10. Jon L. Pierce, Donald G. Gardner, Larry L. Cummings, and Randall B. Dunman, "Organization-Based Self-Esteem: Construct Definition, Measurement, and Validation," *Academy of Management Journal*, September 1989, p. 623.

11. Timothy A. Judge and Charlice Hurst, "How the Rich (and Happy) Get Richer (and Happier): Relationship of Core Self-Evaluations to Trajectories in Attaining Work Success," *Journal of Applied Psychology*, July 2008, pp. 849–863.

12. Nathaniel Branden, *Self-Esteem at Work: How Confident People Make Powerful Companies* (San Francisco: Jossey-Bass, 1998); Timothy A. Judge and Joyce E. Bono, "Relationship of Core Self-Evaluations Traits—Self-Esteem, Generalized Self-Efficacy, Locus of Control, and Emotional Stability—With Job Satisfaction and Job Performance: A Meta-Analysis," *Journal of Applied Psychology*, February 2001, pp. 80–92.

13. Quoted in Carlin Flora, "The Measuring Game: Why You Think You'll Never Stack Up," *Psychology Today*, September/October 2005, p. 44.

14. As quoted in Erika Casriel, "Stepping Out," *Psychology Today*, March/April 2007, p. 73.

15. Ibid.

16. Cited in Julia M. Klein, "The Illusion of Rejection," *Psychology Today*, January/February 2005, p. 30.

17. Research mentioned in book review by E. R. Snyder in *Contemporary Psychology*, July 1998, p. 482.

18. Daniel L. Aroz, "The Manager's Self-Concept," *Human Resources Forum*, July 1989, p. 4.

19. "Leo Buscaglia." Retrieved December 23, 2008, from: www.selfgrowth.com/experts/leo_buscaglia.html

20. Cited in "Self-Esteem: You'll Need It to Succeed," *Executive Strategies*, September 1993, p. 12.

21. Carlin Flora, "The Decline and Fall of the Private Self," *Psychology Today*, May/June 2007, pp. 82–87.

22. Raudsepp, "Strong Self-Esteem."

23. Marilyn E. Gist and Terence R. Mitchell, "Self-Efficacy: A Theoretical Analysis of Its Determinants and Malleability," *Academy of Management Review*, April 1992, pp. 183–211.

24. George P. Hollenbeck and Douglas T. Hall, "Self-Confidence and Leader Performance," *Organizational Dynamics*, Issue 3, 2004, pp. 261–264.

25. Ayana Dixon, "The Center of Success: Author Explains How Confidence Can Get You Further," *Black Enterprise*, March 2008, p. 123.

26. Jay T. Knippen and Thad B. Green, "Building Self-Confidence," *Supervisory Management*, August 1989, pp. 22–27.

27. "Entrepreneurs Need Attitude: Power of Being Positive Can Help You to Succeed in Spite of Setbacks," Knight Ridder, September 16, 2002.

28. D. Brian McNatt and Timothy A. Judge, "Boundary Conditions of the Galatea Effect: A Field Experiment and Constructive Replication," *Academy of Management Journal*, August 2004, pp. 550–565.

29. Frances Thornton, Gayle Privette, and Charles M. Bundrick, "Peak Performance of Business Leaders: An Experience Parallel to Self-Actualization Theory," *Journal of Business and Psychology*, Winter 1999, pp. 253–264.

30. "Present with Panache," *Manager's Edge*, June 2007, p. 8.

31. Fred Luthans, James R. Avey, and Jaime L. Patera, "Experimental Analysis of a Web-Based Training Intervention to Develop Positive Psychological Capital," *Academy of Management Learning and Education*, June 2008, pp. 209–221.

32. Kerry Sulkowicz, "Me, Me, Me, Me, Me," *Business Week*, April 23, 2007, p. 14.

3

Self-Motivation and Goal Setting

Outline

1 How Do Needs and Motives Influence Motivation?
The Need Theory of Motivation
Important Needs and Motives People Attempt to Satisfy
Maslow's Hierarchy of Needs
Engagement as Part of Self-Motivation

2 How Do Goals Contribute to Motivation?
Advantages of Goals
The Learning and Performing Orientations toward Goals
Goal Setting on the Job
Personal Goal Setting
Action Plans to Support Goals
Guidelines for Goal Setting
Problems Sometimes Created by Goals

3 What Are Some Self-Motivation Techniques?

4 How Do You Develop the Self-Discipline to Achieve Goals and Stay Motivated?

D etroit police chief James Barren began his position in fall 2008 not knowing whether he would have his position in six months, because special elections for a new mayor would be taking place at that time. Detroit police officers were bubbling with enthusiasm over the choice of Barren. They saw him as a tough street cop who is even-handed and apolitical.

"I'm just a police officer," Barren said. "My job is to fight crime, and that's what I stay focused on. I'm not political. The mayor gave me a mission; that mission is to make this city safe, care for the people in the city, and watch out for the officers. That's what I'm going to do."

Among Barren's immediate goals: boosting office morale, exploring the possibility of reopening a precinct or two, and finding new ways to fight crime with diminishing resources. Also, he planned to continue going on patrol with officers several nights a week.

Barren, who has a doctorate degree in counseling and ran his own counseling service before rejoining the department, said his background can only help. (Barren had previously worked for the Detroit Police Department for thirty-one years, including holding the position of deputy police chief. He was ousted in 2004 during a change in leadership at the Department.)

During his first nine months as police chief, Barren was highly regarded by the police force and city officials. However, the newly appointed mayor, Dave Bing, replaced him with Wayne County sheriff Wayne Evans. One speculation as to why Barren was fired was that he did not respond the way Bing wanted to the shooting of seven teenagers at a city bus stop. Another speculation was that Barren was fired for "political reasons," with Bing wanting to replace Barren with a close associate.[1]

After studying the information and doing the exercises in this chapter, you should be able to:

1 Explain how needs and motives influence motivation.

2 Identify several needs and motives that could propel you into action.

3 Pinpoint how the hierarchy of needs could explain your behavior.

4 Explain why and how goals contribute to self-motivation.

5 Describe how to set effective goals and the problems sometimes created by goals.

6 Describe several specific techniques of self-motivation.

7 Apply the self-discipline model to achieving your goals.

Whether or not you are interested in police work as a career, the story about Barren illustrates that setting goals, including being guided by a mission, contributes to job success. Another point illustrated is that an understanding of human relations, as evidenced by Barren's counseling background, is useful in a high-pressure position such as a police officer. Strong motivation is also important for personal life. Unless you direct your energies toward specific goals, such as improving your productivity or meeting a new friend, you will accomplish very little. Knowledge of motivation and goal setting as applied to yourself, therefore, can pay substantial dividends in improving the quality of your life. Knowledge about motivation and goal setting is also important when attempting to influence others to get things accomplished. Motivating others, for example, is a major requirement of the manager's job.

Being well motivated is also important simply to meet the demands of employers. Most organizations insist on high productivity from workers at all levels. Assuming that you have the necessary skills, training, and equipment, being well motivated will enable you to achieve high productivity.

The general purpose of this chapter is to present information that can help you sustain a high level of motivation, centering on the importance of needs and goals. Chapter 12 contains information that you will find useful for motivating other people. The story about the chief of police illustrates how knowledge about one aspect of motivation, goal setting, might lead to improved performance. Here is an example that might apply to you personally.

> Assume that similar to many readers of this book, you are ambitious. You have many interesting career goals. You want to finish your formal education, you want to obtain professional certification in your field, you want to attain a high level of responsibility in your career, and you want to be among the top 10 percent of incomer earners. Your plate is also filled with personal goals: You want to improve substantially in your favorite sport, become fluent in your second language, network all your electronic devices together, and double your network of friends.

> Despite all your exciting goals, you are not making much progress in attaining them. Could the problem be that your level of self-discipline is not quite high enough to propel you toward accomplishing these goals one by one? Not having sufficient self-discipline is the major reason most people fall short of reaching their goals. Later in the chapter, we describe a well-developed system for developing enough self-discipline for getting things done that are important to you.

▶ Learning Objective 1 ▶

How Do Needs and Motives Influence Motivation?

According to a widely accepted explanation of human behavior, people have needs and motives that propel them toward achieving certain goals. Needs and motives are closely related. A **need** is an internal striving or urge to do something, such as a need to drink when thirsty. It can be regarded as a biological or psychological requirement. Because the person is deprived in some way (such as not having enough fluid in the body), the person is motivated to take action toward a goal. In this case the goal might be simply getting something to drink.

Need
an internal striving or urge to do something, such as a need to drink when thirsty

A discussion of needs often triggers a discussion of the difference between *needs* and *wants*. A need is essentially a craving or urge that must be satisfied to maintain your equilibrium. In contrast, a want refers to more of a luxury—something you would like to have but is not necessary to keep your system balanced. A need is a more technical concept than is a want. Here are two examples of the difference between a need and a want.

> Visualize yourself jogging in 90-degree weather. Suddenly your need for water surfaces, so any old fountain water will satisfy your physiological craving. But at the same time, you want a prestige brand of flavored bottled water to drink. You don't need the bottled water, you want it.

> You have a need for recognition, so it is quite important for somebody to compliment you on having jogged during such extreme weather. This small amount of recognition will help you maintain your emotional equilibrium. On the other hand, you might have a want for the recognition that would stem from having won a marathon in your city.

FIGURE 3-1
THE NEED CYCLE

A **motive** is an inner drive that moves you to do something. The motive is usually based on a need or desire and results in the intention to attain an appropriate goal. Because needs and motives are so closely related, the two terms are often used interchangeably. For example, "recognition need" and "recognition motive" refer to the same thing.

Motive
an inner drive that moves a person to do something

THE NEED THEORY OF MOTIVATION

The central idea behind need theory is that unsatisfied needs motivate us until they become satisfied. When people are dissatisfied or anxious about their present status or performance, they will try to reduce this anxiety. This need cycle is shown in Figure 3-1. Assume that you have a strong need or motive to achieve recognition. As a result, you experience tension that drives you to find some way of being recognized on the job. The action you take is to apply for a position as the team leader of your group: being appointed as team leader would provide ample recognition, particularly if the team performs well. You are appointed to the position, and for now your need for recognition is at least partially satisfied as you receive compliments from your coworkers and friends. Once you receive this partial satisfaction, two things typically happen. Either you will soon require a stronger dose of recognition, or you will begin to concentrate on another need or motive, such as achievement. In either case, the need cycle will repeat itself. You might seek another form of recognition or satisfaction of your need for power. For example, you might apply for a position as department manager or open your own business. Ideally, in this former situation, your boss would give you more responsibility. This could lead to more satisfaction of your recognition need and to some satisfaction of your need for achievement. (The needs mentioned so far, and others, are defined next.)

The need theory suggests that self-interest plays a key role in motivation.[2] People ask, "What's in it for me?" (or "WIIFM," pronounced *wiff'em*), before engaging in any form of behavior. In one way or another, people act to serve their self-interest. Even when people act in a way that helps others, they are doing so because helping others helps them. For example, you may give money to poor people because this act of kindness makes you feel wanted and powerful.

IMPORTANT NEEDS AND MOTIVES PEOPLE ATTEMPT TO SATISFY

Work and personal life offer the opportunity to satisfy dozens of needs and motives. In this and the following section, important needs that propel people into action are described. As you read about these needs and motives, relate them to yourself. For example, ask yourself, "Am I a power-seeking person?"

FIGURE 3-2

PREFERENCES OF WORKERS
WITH STRONG ACHIEVEMENT
NEEDS

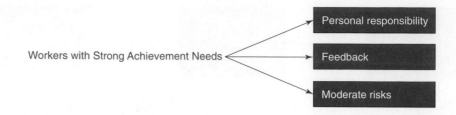

Workers with Strong Achievement Needs → Personal responsibility / Feedback / Moderate risks

Achievement

Need for achievement
the desire to accomplish something
difficult for its own sake

The **need for achievement** is the desire to accomplish something difficult for its own sake. People with a strong need for achievement frequently think of how to do a job better. Responsibility seeking is another characteristic of people with a high need for achievement. They are also concerned with how to progress in their careers. Workers with a high need for achievement are interested in monetary rewards primarily as feedback about how well they are achieving. They also set realistic yet moderately difficult goals, take calculated risks, and desire feedback on performance. (A moderately difficult goal challenges a person but is not so difficult as to most likely lead to failure and frustration.) In general, those who enjoy building businesses, activities, and programs from scratch have a strong need for achievement. Figure 3-2 outlines the preferences of workers with strong achievement needs.

Power

People with a high power need feel compelled to control resources, such as other people and money. Successful executives typically have a high power motive and exhibit three dominant characteristics: (1) They act with vigor and determination to exert their power, (2) they invest much time in thinking about ways to alter the behavior and thinking of others, and (3) they care about their personal standing with those around them.[3] The power need can be satisfied through occupying a high-level position or by becoming a highly influential person. Or you can name skyscrapers and hotels after yourself, following the lead of Donald Trump.

Affiliation

People with a strong affiliation need seek out close relationships with others and tend to be loyal as friends or employees. The affiliation motive is met directly through belonging to the "office gang," a term of endearment implying that your coworkers are an important part of your life. Many people prefer working in groups to individual effort because of the opportunity the former provides for socializing with others.

Recognition

People with a strong need for recognition want to be acknowledged for their contribution and efforts. The need for recognition is so pervasive that many companies have formal recognition programs in which outstanding or long-time employees receive gifts, plaques, and jewelry inscribed with the company logo. The recognition motive can be satisfied through means such as winning contests, receiving awards, and seeing your name online or in print. A major reason the need for recognition is such a useful motivator is that most people think they are underappreciated (and overworked).

Order

People with a strong need for order want to achieve arrangement, balance, neatness, and precision. The order motive can be quickly satisfied by cleaning and organizing your work or living space. Occupations offering the opportunity to satisfy the order motive almost every day include accountant, computer programmer, and paralegal.

Risk Taking and Thrill Seeking

Some people crave constant excitement on the job and are willing to risk their lives to achieve thrills. The need to take risks and pursue thrills has grown in importance in the high-technology era. Many people work for employers, start businesses, and purchase stocks with uncertain futures. Both the search of giant payoffs and daily thrills motivate these individuals.[4] A strong craving for thrills may have some positive

Human Relations Self-Assessment Quiz   3-1

The Risk-Taking Scale

Answer true or false to the following questions to obtain an approximate idea of your tendency to take risks or your desire to do so.

		True	False
1.	I eat sushi or other raw fish.	❑	❑
2.	I would rather be a stock broker than an accountant.	❑	❑
3.	I think that amusement park roller coasters should be abolished.	❑	❑
4.	I enjoy doing creative work.	❑	❑
5.	I enjoy (or did enjoy) the excitement of looking for new dates.	❑	❑
6.	I don't like trying foods from other cultures.	❑	❑
7.	I would choose bonds over growth stocks.	❑	❑
8.	Friends would say that I do not like to take risks.	❑	❑
9.	I like to challenge people in positions of power.	❑	❑
10.	I don't always wear seat belts while driving.	❑	❑
11.	I sometimes talk on my cell phone or send text messages while driving at highway speeds.	❑	❑
12.	I would love to be an entrepreneur (or I love being one).	❑	❑
13.	I purposely avoid traveling overseas to any country that is known to have civil unrest, including riots.	❑	❑
14.	Most days are boring for me.	❑	❑
15.	I would like helping out in a crisis such as a product recall.	❑	❑
16.	On the highway, I usually drive at least 10 miles per hour beyond the speed limit.	❑	❑
17.	I would like to go cave exploring (or already have done so).	❑	❑
18.	I like to have a daily dose of stimulation.	❑	❑
19.	I would be willing to have at least one-third of my compensation based on a bonus for good performance.	❑	❑
20.	I would be willing to visit a maximum security prison on a job assignment.	❑	❑

Scoring and Interpretation:

1. T	5. T	9. T	13. F	17. T
2. T	6. F	10. T	14. F	18. T
3. F	7. F	11. T	15. T	19. T
4. T	8. F	12. T	16. T	20. T

Give yourself one point each time your answer agrees with the key. If you score 16–20, you are probably a high risk taker. 10–15: You're a moderate risk taker. 5–9: You are cautious. 0–4: You're a very low risk taker.

Questions: 1. How does your self-evaluation of your risk-taking tendencies compare with your score on this quiz?

2. Do you see any needs for improvement in terms of becoming more (or less) of a risk taker?

Source: The idea of a test about risk-taking comfort, as well as several of the statements on the quiz, come from psychologist Frank Farley.

consequences for the organization, including willingness to perform such dangerous feats as setting explosives, capping an oil well, controlling a radiation leak, and introducing a product in a highly competitive environment. However, extreme risk takers and thrill seekers can create such problems as being involved in a disproportionate number of vehicular accidents and making imprudent investments. Take Human Relations Self-Assessment Quiz 3-1 to measure your tendency toward risk taking.

MASLOW'S HIERARCHY OF NEEDS

Maslow's hierarchy of needs
the best-known categorization of needs; according to psychologist Abraham H. Maslow, people strive to satisfy the following groups of needs in step-by-step order: physiological needs, safety needs, social needs, esteem needs, and self-actualizing needs

The best-known categorization of needs is **Maslow's hierarchy of needs.** At the same time, it is the most widely used explanation of human motivation. According to psychologist Abraham H. Maslow, people strive to satisfy the following groups of needs in step-by-step order:

1. *Physiological needs* refer to bodily needs, such as the requirements for food, water, shelter, and sleep.

2. *Safety needs* refer to actual physical safety and to a feeling of being safe from both physical and emotional injury.

3. *Social needs* are essentially love, affection, or belonging needs. Unlike the two previous levels of needs, they center on a person's interaction with other people.

4. *Esteem needs* represent an individual's demand to be seen as a person of worth by others—and to him- or herself.

5. *Self-actualizing needs* are the highest level of needs, including the needs for self-fulfillment and personal development.[5]

A diagram of the needs hierarchy is presented in Figure 3-3. Notice the distinction between higher-level and lower-level needs. With few exceptions, higher-level needs are more difficult to satisfy. A person's needs for affiliation might be satisfied by being a member of a friendly work group. Yet to satisfy self-actualization need, such as self-fulfillment, a person might have to develop an outstanding reputation in his or her company.

The needs hierarchy implies that most people think of finding a job as a way of obtaining the necessities of life. Once these are obtained, a person may think of

FIGURE 3-3

MASLOW'S HIERARCHY OF NEEDS

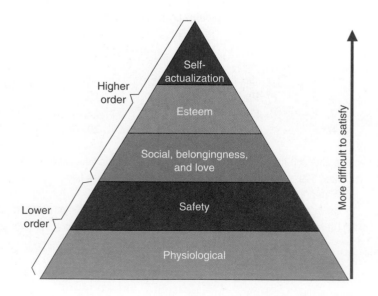

achieving friendship, self-esteem, and self-fulfillment on the job. When a person is generally satisfied at one level, he or she looks for satisfaction at a higher level. As Maslow described it, a person is a "perpetually wanting animal." Very few people are totally satisfied with their lot in life, even the rich and famous.

The extent of need satisfaction is influenced by a person's job. Some construction jobs, for example, involve dangerous work in severe climates, thus frustrating both physiological and safety needs. Ordinarily there is much more opportunity for approaching self-actualization when a person occupies a prominent position, such as a top executive or famous performer. However, a person with low potential could approach self-actualization by occupying a lesser position. In the current era, workers at all levels are threatened with the frustration of security needs because so many companies reduce the number of employees to save money.

How do Maslow's needs and the other needs described in this chapter relate to self-motivation? First you have to ask yourself, "Which needs do I really want to satisfy?" After answering the question honestly, concentrate your efforts on an activity that will most likely satisfy that need. For instance, if you are hungry for power, strive to become a high-level manager or a business owner. If you crave self-esteem, focus your efforts on work and social activities that are well regarded by others. The point is that you will put forth substantial effort if you think the goal you attain will satisfy an important need.

To learn more about how the needs hierarchy fits your need makeup, take Human Relations Self-Assessment Quiz 3-2. The class activity presented toward the end of the chapter will also enlarge your understanding of the need hierarchy.

ENGAGEMENT AS PART OF SELF-MOTIVATION

Another way of looking at self-motivation is that if you are strongly motivated you are engaged in your work, or committed to the job and company. Employees engaged in their work are more willing to help supervisors and coworkers and to voluntarily promote the company outside of work. Several studies have found that most American workers are not fully engaged in their work. They do what is expected of them but do not contribute the extra mental and physical effort to be outstanding. According to a Gallup Organization survey of a few years back, about 70 percent of employees are "disengaged," meaning that they are no longer committed to the company. Furthermore, the longer employees stay, the more disengaged they become.[6] Tim Galbraith is vice president for people development at Yum Brands Inc., the company whose brands include KFC, Taco Bell, Pizza Hut, and Long John Silver's. He explains that an employee who's truly engaged says, "I'm willing to give a little bit more. I'm willing to help my team members when I see they're in need. Or, I'm willing to clean without being told by my manager."

To measure attitudes related to engagement, some KFC and Long John Silver's ask employees to respond to statements such as the following:

- My restaurant is a great place to work.

- People on my team help out, even if it is not their job.

- I understand the employee benefits that are available to me.[7]

You might wonder how the third question ties in with employee engagement. The reasoning is that engaged employees are quite aware of what opportunities and advantages the company makes available to them.

Human Relations Self-Assessment Quiz   3-2

My Standing on the Need Hierarchy

Respond to each of the following statements in terms of its importance to you, as follows: (1) not important, (2) a little bit important, (3) average importance, (4) important, and (5) very important.

Statement Number	Statement	Importance (1 to 5)
1.	Having a good reputation	
2.	Loving another person	
3.	Having a high evaluation of myself	
4.	Being somebody special and important	
5.	Having coworkers who are not physically abusive	
6.	Being respected by others	
7.	Feeling emotionally close to another person	
8.	Becoming much more than I am now	
9.	Avoiding big surprises in my work routine	
10.	Feeling useful and necessary in the world	
11.	Being a member of a group I care about	
12.	Feeling well rested	
13.	Feeling that I have the right balance of nutrients and chemicals in my body	
14.	Having a workplace that is relatively free of harmful germs	
15.	Being confident that I will achieve my full potential	
16.	Having an affectionate relationship with another person	
17.	Feeling completely self-fulfilled	
18.	Feeling comfortable rather than too hot or too cold	
19.	Not having to commute during hazardous road conditions	
20.	Eating food that has a pleasant taste	
21.	Being loved by another person	
22.	Becoming who I am capable of becoming	
23.	Having self-respect	
24.	Having enough food to eat	
25.	Avoiding loud, irritating noises	

Source: The ideas for the statements in the quiz stem from Abraham H. Maslow, "A Theory of Human Motivation," *Psychological Review*, July 1943, pp. 370–396.

Scoring and Interpretation:

The scoring key follows the five categories in the Maslow needs hierarchy. Enter your rating (1– 5) for each statement, and compute your total for each of the five categories of needs.

Ranking

Physiological

12_____   13_____   18_____   20_____   24_____   Physiological total_____   _____

Safety

5_____   9_____   14_____   19_____   25_____   Safety total_____   _____

Continued

Love

2_____   7_____   11_____   16_____   21_____   Love total_____   _____

Esteem

1_____   3_____   6_____   10_____   23_____   Esteem total_____   _____

Self-actualization

4_____   8_____   15_____   17_____   22_____   Self-actualization total_____   _____

The total for each of the five needs will be somewhere between 1 and 25. The highest score receives a rank of 1, and the lowest score receives a rank of 5. A tentative interpretation here is that your most important need category is the one with the highest rank, whereas the least important need category receives the lowest rank. A high-importance ranking might suggest that you are actively attempting to satisfy the need category in question. A low-importance ranking would suggest that you are not currently attempting to satisfy that need category because that category is already satisfied. It is also possible that you just don't care about the need category, such as not worrying about becoming self-actualized.

Questions: 1. What importance ranking to these needs categories might a person give who is unemployed and currently living in his or her SUV or minivan? Why?

2. Visualize one of your favorite celebrities. What importance rankings might one of your favorite celebrities give to these needs categories? Why?

How Do Goals Contribute to Motivation?

◀ Learning Objective 2 ◀

At some point in their lives, almost all successful people have established goals, attesting to the importance of goals. A **goal** is an event, circumstance, object, or condition a person strives to attain. A goal thus reflects your desire or intention to regulate your actions. Here we look at five topics to help you understand the nature of goals: (1) the advantages of goals, (2) different goal orientations, (3) goal setting on the job, (4) personal goal setting, and (5) guidelines for goal setting, as well as potential disadvantages of goals.

Goal
an event, circumstance, object, or condition a person strives to attain

ADVANTAGES OF GOALS

Goals and goal setting have become embedded into our society both on and off the job. Sales quotas and New Year's resolutions are examples of goal setting. Five of the potential advantages of goals are outlined in Figure 3-4.

Setting specific, reasonably difficult goals improves performance. One of many possible examples involves the American Pulpwood Association, which wanted to increase the productivity (employee cords per hour) of independent loggers in the

1. Reasonably difficult goals improve performance.
2. Goals can instill purpose, challenge, and meaning into ordinary tasks.
3. Goals focus our efforts in a specific direction.
4. Goals increase our chances for success because they serve as a standard for measuring success.
5. Goals serve as self-motivators and energizers.

FIGURE 3-4
ADVANTAGES OF GOALS

southern United States. Based on goal-setting theory, Pulpwood crew supervisors assigned a specific high goal for the loggers. They also handed out tally meters to enable the workers to keep count of the number of trees they cut down. Productivity soared in comparison to those crews who were simply urged to do their best. According to Gary Latham, professor of organizational effectiveness at the Rotman School of Management, goal setting instilled purpose, challenge, and meaning into what was previously seen as a boring, tiresome, task.[8]

Another advantage of goals is that when we guide our lives with goals, we tend to focus our efforts in a consistent direction. Your conscious goals affect what you achieve. Without goals, our efforts may become scattered in many directions. We may keep trying, but we will go nowhere unless we happen to receive more than our share of luck.

Goal setting increases our chances for success, particularly because success can be defined as the achievement of a goal. The goals you set for accomplishing a task can serve as a standard to indicate when you have done a satisfactory job. A sales representative might set a goal of selling $300,000 worth of merchandise for the year. By November, she might close a deal that places her total sales at $310,000. With a sigh of relief she can then say, "I've done well this year."

Goals serve as self-motivators and energizers. People who set goals tend to be motivated because they are confident that their energy is being invested in something worthwhile. Aside from helping you become more motivated and productive, setting goals can help you achieve personal satisfaction. Most people derive a sense of satisfaction from attaining a goal that is meaningful to them.

THE LEARNING AND PERFORMING ORIENTATIONS TOWARD GOALS

Another useful perspective on understanding how goals influence motivation is that goals can be aimed at either learning or hoping to perform well.[9] A learning-goal orientation means that an individual is focused on acquiring new skills and mastering new situations. For example, you might establish the goal of learning how to develop skill in making a computerized presentation package. You say to yourself, "My goal is to learn how to use PowerPoint [or similar software] so I know even more about how to apply information technology."

A performing-goal orientation is different. It is aimed at wanting to demonstrate and validate the adequacy of your competence by seeking favorable judgments about your competence. At the same time, the person wants to avoid seeking negative judgments. For example, your goal might be to make PowerPoint presentations that would highly impress whoever watched them. Your focus is on looking good and avoiding negative evaluations of your presentations.

Desire for Feedback

A person's goal orientation usually affects his or her desire for feedback. People with a learning-goal orientation are more likely to seek feedback on how well they are performing. In contrast, people with a performing-goal orientation are less likely to seek feedback. If you focus too much on setting performance goals, you might have a tendency to overlook the value of feedback. Yet the feedback could help you improve your performance in the long run.

Impact on Work Performance

Goal orientation is also important because it can affect work performance. Attempting to master skills often leads to better results than does attempting to impress others. A study of the effects of the two different goal orientations was conducted with 167 salespeople working for a medical supplies distributor. The salespeople were paid mostly on the commission of the gross profits they generated. The researchers found that a learning-goal orientation was associated with higher sales performance. In contrast, a performing-goal orientation was unrelated to sales performance. An important implication of the study is that even if you are an experienced worker, a focus on skill development is likely to lead to higher performance.[10]

Better Relationships with Supervisors

Another positive consequence of a mastery (or learning-goal) orientation is that it often prompts workers to develop better relationships with their supervisors. Workers with a mastery orientation are likely to have stronger job performance and job satisfaction than those workers with a performance orientation. The positive outcomes of stronger job performance and satisfaction appear to take place because the workers develop better relationships with their supervisors.[11]

A good reason exists as to why a learning-goal (or mastery) orientation is so important in today's business world. The purpose of a learning goal is to stimulate a person's imagination, to engage in discovery, and to think imaginatively. A performance goal focuses more on exerting effort to attain an objective using the knowledge one already possesses. When an effective strategy requires innovation that has yet to emerge—as is often the case—specific, high-learning goals should be set.[12] An example of a learning goal of high importance would be figuring out how to dispose of debris after a hurricane.

GOAL SETTING ON THE JOB

Virtually all organizations have come to accept the value of goal setting in producing the results they want to achieve. Goal-setting programs designed to boost performance or personal development are in frequent use.[13] The personal aspects of goal setting are described in the following section. In most goal-setting programs, executives at the top of the organization are supposed to plan for the future by setting goals such as "Improve profits 10 percent this year." Employees at the bottom of the organization are supposed to go along with such broad goals by setting more specific goals. An example is "I will decrease damaged merchandise by 10 percent this year. I will accomplish this by making sure that our shelving is adequate for our needs."

You participate in the goal-setting process by designing goals to fit into the overall mission of the firm. A bank teller might set a personal goal of this nature: "During rush periods, and when I feel fatigued, I will double count all the money that I handle." In some goal-setting programs, employees are requested to set goals that will lead to their personal improvement. An auditor for the state government set this goal for herself: "Within the next 12 months, I will enroll in and complete a supervisory training course in a local college." This woman aspired toward becoming a supervisor.

A sample set of work goals is shown in Figure 3-5. The service and repair shop supervisor who set these objectives took into account the requirements of his boss and the automobile dealership. Even if you set goals by yourself, they must still take into account the needs of your employer.

PERSONAL GOAL SETTING

If you want to lead a rewarding personal life, your chances of doing so increase if you plan it. Personal goals heavily influence the formulation of career goals as well. For this reason, it is worthwhile to set personal goals in conjunction with career goals. Ideally, they should be integrated to help achieve a balance between the

FIGURE 3-5

FORM USED IN AUTOMOBILE DEALERSHIP FOR STATEMENT OF GOALS

JOB TITLE AND BRIEF JOB DESCRIPTION

Manager, Service Department:
Responsible for supervision of service department of automobile dealership. Responsible for staffing service department with appropriate personnel and for quality of service to customers. Work closely with owner of dealership to discuss unusual customer problems. Handle customer complaints about mechanical problems of cars purchased at dealership.

Objectives for Scott Gilley

1. By December 31 of this year, decrease by 10 percent customer demands for rework.
2. Hire two general mechanics within 45 days.
3. Hire two body specialists within 45 days.
4. Decrease by 30 percent the number of repairs returned by customers for rework.
5. Reduce by 10 percent the discrepancy between estimates and actual bills to customers.
6. Schedule at least 20 percent of our service appointments through our Web site by January 15 of next year.

---

demands of work and personal life. For example, if your preferred lifestyle would be to live in a rural area, a career in manufacturing or food processing would be more sensible than a career in advertising. This is true because manufacturing and food processing within North America has moved mostly to rural areas, whereas advertising remains mostly in large cities.

Types of Personal Goals

Personal goals can be subdivided into those relating to social and family life, hobbies and interests, physical and mental health, career, and finances. An example of each type follows:

Social and family life. "By age 30 I would like to have a spouse and two children."

Hobbies and interests. "Become a black belt in karate by age 28."

Physical and mental health. "Be able to run four miles without stopping or panting for breath by April 15 of next year."

Career. "Become office manager by age 28."

Finances. "Within the next four years be earning $70,000 per year, adjusted for inflation."

Other categories of personal goals are possible, yet the list presented represents convenient categories for most people.

ACTION PLANS TO SUPPORT GOALS

Ideally, reading this chapter and doing the exercises in it will start you on a lifelong process of using goals to help you plan your life. But before you can capitalize on the benefits of goal setting, you need a method for translating goals into action. An **action plan** describes how you are going to reach your goal. The major reason you need an action plan for most goals is that without a method for achieving what you want, the goal is likely to slip by. If your goal were to build your own log cabin, part of your action plan would be to learn how to operate a buzz saw, to read a handbook on

Action plan
describes how you are going to reach your goal

FIGURE 3-6

GUIDELINES FOR GOAL SETTING

1. State each goal as a positive statement.
2. Formulate specific goals.
3. Formulate concise goals.
4. Set realistic as well as stretch goals.
5. Set goals for different time periods.

log cabin building, to learn how to operate a tractor, and so forth. Some goals are so difficult to reach that your action plan might encompass hundreds of separate activities. You would then have to develop separate action plans for each step of the way.

Some immediate goals do not really require an action plan. A mere statement of the goal may point to an obvious action plan. If your goal were to start painting your room, it would not be necessary to draw up a formal action plan such as, "Go to hardware store; purchase paint, brush, and rollers; borrow ladder and drop cloth from Ken; put furniture in center of room" and so on.

GUIDELINES FOR GOAL SETTING

Goal setting is an art in the sense that some people do a better job of goal setting than others. Following are suggestions on setting effective goals—those that lead to achieving what you hoped to achieve, as outlined in Figure 3-6.

Express Each Goal as a Positive Statement

Expressing your goals in positive statements is likely to be more energizing than focusing on the negative.[14] An example of a positive statement would be, "During the next year when I am attending networking events, I will create a positive, professional impression on everybody I meet." The negative counterpart would be, "During the next year, I will avoid making a fool of myself when I am attending networking events." Despite this suggestion, there are times when a negative goal is useful, such as in reducing errors.

Formulate Specific Goals

A goal such as "attain success" is too vague to serve as a guide to daily action. A more useful goal would be to state specifically what you mean by "success" and when you expect to achieve it. For example, "I want to be the manager of customer service at a telecommunications company by January 1, 2015, and receive above-average performance reviews."

Formulate Concise Goals

A useful goal can usually be expressed in a short, punchy statement—for example, "Decrease input errors in bank statements so that customer complaints are decreased by 25 percent by September 30 of this year." People new to goal setting typically commit the error of formulating lengthy, rambling goal statements. These lengthy goals involve so many different activities that they fail to serve as specific guides to action.

Set Realistic as Well as Stretch Goals

A realistic goal is one that represents the right amount of challenge for the person pursuing the goal. On the one hand, easy goals are not very motivational—they may not spring you into action. On the other hand, goals that are too far beyond your capabilities may lead to frustration and despair because there is a good chance you will fail to reach them. The extent to which a goal is realistic depends on a person's capabilities. An easy goal for an experienced person might be a realistic goal for a beginner. Self-efficacy is also a factor in deciding whether a goal is realistic. The higher your self-efficacy, the more likely you are to think that a particular goal is realistic. A person with high self-efficacy for learning Chinese might say, "I think learning two new Chinese words a day is realistic."

Several goals that stretch your capability might be included in your list of goals. An extreme stretch goal might be for a store manager trainee to become the vice president of merchandising for Target within four years. Another type of stretch goal is striving for a noble cause. A logging supervisor may not get excited about having the crew load a certain number of felled trees on a flatbed truck, but she might get excited about the trees being used to build homes, schools, and hospitals.

Set Goals for Different Time Periods

Goals are best set for different time periods, such as daily, short range, medium range, and long range. Daily goals are essentially a to-do list. Short-range goals cover the period from approximately one week to one year into the future. Finding a new job, for example, is typically a short-range goal. Medium-range goals relate to events that will take place within approximately two to five years. They concern such things as the type of education or training you plan to undertake and the next step in your career.

Long-range goals refer to events taking place five years into the future and beyond. As such, they relate to the overall lifestyle you wish to achieve, including the type of work and family situation you hope to have. Although every person should have a general idea of a desirable lifestyle, long-range goals should be flexible. You might, for example, plan to stay single until age 40. But while on vacation next summer, you might just happen to meet the right partner for you.

Short-range goals make an important contribution to attaining goals of longer duration. If a one-year work goal is to reduce mailing and shipping costs by 12 percent for the year, a good way to motivate workers is to look for a 1 percent saving per month. Progress toward a larger goal is self-rewarding.

PROBLEMS SOMETIMES CREATED BY GOALS

Despite the many advantages of goals, they can create problems. A major problem is that *goals can create inflexibility.* People can become so focused on reaching particular goals that they fail to react to emergencies, such as neglecting a much-needed machine repair to achieve quota. Goals can also make a person inflexible with respect to missing out on opportunities. Sales representatives sometimes neglect to invest time in cultivating a prospective customer because of the pressure to make quota. Instead, the sales rep goes for the quick sale with an established customer.

A problem related to inflexibility is that goals can sometimes become obsessions, leading you to neglect other phases of work or life. A worker might become so obsessed with accomplishing work by the end of a quarter that he or she refuses to take the time to help a coworker in need. Executive coach Marshall Goldsmith cautions, "I see too many older people wrecking their health in pursuit of their next achievement. I see too many younger people who are missing their youth, then postponing their love life, then not having children—all in the service of their career."[15]

A recommended approach to combating the potential inflexibility and obsessive nature of goals is to recognize and admit when you might be pursuing the wrong goal. Imagine that you decide to start a vineyard so you can create and market wine that retails for less than $15 per bottle. Among the hurdles you encounter are that (a) nobody wants to finance such a venture, and (b) the world already has far too many brands of wine. You finally surrender your wine-venture idea and look for a business activity with a greater chance of success. Life coach Pamela Mitchell explains the problem of pursuing wrong goals in the following terms:

> When we make the strategic decision to stop investing in actions that offer little return or negative outcomes, we are tapping into the power of positive quitting. It is important to discontinue activities that steal our time, drain our energy, waste our money, or diminish self-esteem and respect.[16]

Another problem is that *performance goals can sometimes detract from an interest in the task*. People with a performance-goal orientation (focusing on being judged as competent) will sometimes lose interest in the task. The loss of interest is most likely to occur when the task is difficult.[17] Assume that your primary reason for working as an information technology specialist is to perform well enough so that you can earn a high income. If carrying out your responsibilities encounters some hurdles, you may readily become discouraged with information technology as a field. But if your orientation is primarily to advance your knowledge about a dynamic field, you will not be readily frustrated when you encounter problems. You might even look on it as a learning opportunity.

A tight focus on goals can also encourage unethical behavior and a disregard for *how* the goals are attained. A sales representative might give kickbacks simply to gain a sale, and a CEO might lay off needed workers and neglect investing in new-product research simply to make certain profit figures. Too much emphasis on goals can also contribute to cheating in the form of people falsely reporting that they met a performance level.[18] An example would be a meat inspector claiming to have visited more meat packers than she actually did.

Despite the problems that can arise in goal setting, goals are valuable tools for managing your work and personal life. Used with common sense and according to the ideas presented in this chapter, they could have a major, positive impact on your life.

What Are Some Self-Motivation Techniques?

◀ Learning Objective 3 ◀

Many people never achieve satisfying careers and never realize their potential because of low motivation. They believe they could perform better but admit that "I'm simply not a high-initiative type" or "I'm simply not that motivated." Earlier we described how identifying your most important needs could enhance motivation. Here we describe six additional techniques for self-motivation.

1. Set goals for yourself. As shown throughout this chapter, goal setting is one of the most important techniques for self-motivation. If you set long-range goals and support them with a series of smaller goals set for shorter time spans, your motivation will increase.

2. Find intrinsically motivating work. A major factor in self-motivation is to find work that is fun or its own reward. **Intrinsic motivation** refers to the natural tendency to seek out novelty and challenges, to extend and use one's capacities, to explore, and to learn.[19] The intrinsically motivated person is involved in the task at hand, such as a technology enthusiast surfing the Web for hours at a time. Finding a job that offers you motivators in ample supply will help enhance your intrinsic motivation. For example, you might have good evidence from your past experience

Intrinsic motivation
the natural tendency to seek out novelty and challenges, to extend and use one's capacities, to explore, and to learn

that the opportunity for close contact with people is a personal motivator. Find a job that involves working in a small, friendly department or team.

Intrinsically motivating work often takes the form of *meaningful work*, or work that has personal meaning to you based on your values and interests. One person might think that working as a store manager for the Salvation Army is meaningful. Another person might think that working as an electronics technician at a missile defense systems company is meaningful. The accompanying Human Relations in Practice insert illustrates the motivational nature of meaningful work, including the opportunity to grow and learn.

Based on circumstances, you may have to take whatever job you can find, or you may not be in a position to change jobs. In such a situation, try to arrange your work so you have more opportunity to experience the reward(s) that you are seeking. Assume that solving difficult problems excites you but that your job is 85 percent routine. Develop better work habits so that you can take care of the routine aspects of your job more quickly. This will give you more time to enjoy the creative aspects of your job.

Human Relations in Practice

Employees Capitalize on Strengths at Consulting Engineering Firm

Leaders of consulting engineering firm McDonough Bolyard Peck Inc. (MBP) care as much about building employees as they do about construction projects for their private and public clients.

Established in 1989, the Fairfax, Va., firm provides construction management and engineering services for building, roads, bridges, and other projects. The company, with 160 employees in eight offices from Atlanta to Columbia, Maryland, ranked No. 20 one year on the "Best Small Companies to Work for in America" list.

Employees cite many examples of how leaders encourage their professional development—for example, by helping them obtain professional licenses and certifications, move into new jobs, or complete degrees. Several executives and managers started as interns in 1990.

At MBP, "Everyone is encouraged to strive toward getting better in an area of interest they can grow in," says Niyi Ladipo, a civil engineer and project manager. Executives encouraged her to develop her strength in cost estimating by providing textbooks and helping her prepare for the Certified Cost Engineer exam.

Chairman and CEO Charles Bolyard Jr. wants to help employees "capitalize on their strengths and work on the things that need some attention."

Informal mentoring supports individuals' development and involves about half the staff. HR personnel ask new employees after their first ninety days if they want a specific mentor or would like to be assigned one. But plenty of more formal training is available, too. Five percent of the budget is dedicated to employee training, including conferences and seminars.

"There is leadership in every person, and the company knows that. . . . Everyone is given latitude to develop as a leader," says Robert J. Carter, a project manager who was mentored by one of the principals and now mentors five people.

Project manager Ali Abdolahi says, "If I am helping subordinates to grow and achieve their goals, it helps me to grow, too."

Source: Leon Rubis, "Engineering People as Well as Projects," *HR Magazine*, July 2008, p. 35.

3. Get feedback on your performance. Few people can sustain a high level of motivation without receiving information about how well they are doing. Even if you find your work challenging and exciting, you will need feedback. One reason positive feedback is valuable is that it acts as a reward. If you learn that your efforts achieved a worthwhile purpose, you will feel encouraged. For example, if a graphics display you designed was well received by company officials, you would probably want to prepare another graphics display.

A study conducted with management students demonstrated that participants adjusted their goals upward after receiving positive feedback and downward after negative feedback. It was also found that when the students were more emotional about the feedback, the positive and negative results were more pronounced.[20] The link here to self-motivation is that when goals are higher, motivation will be higher.

4. Apply behavior modification to yourself. **Behavior modification** is a system of motivation that emphasizes rewarding people for doing the right things and punishing them for doing the wrong things. Many people have used behavior modification to change their own behavior. Specific purposes include overcoming eating disorders, tobacco addiction, Internet abuse, nail biting, and procrastination. To boost your own motivation through behavior modification, you would have to first decide what specific motivated actions you want to increase (such as working thirty minutes longer each day). Second, you would have to decide on a suitable set of rewards and punishments. You may choose to use rewards only because rewards are generally better motivators than punishments.

> **Behavior modification**
> system of motivation that emphasizes rewarding people for doing the right things and punishing them for doing the wrong things

5. Improve your skills relevant to your goals. The **expectancy theory of motivation** states that people will be motivated if they believe that their efforts will lead to desired outcomes. According to this theory, people hold back effort when they are not confident that their efforts will lead to accomplishments. You should, therefore, seek adequate training to ensure that you have the right abilities and skills to perform your work. The training might be provided by the employer or on your own through a course or self-study. Appropriate training gives you more confidence that you can perform the work. The training also increases your feelings of self-efficacy.[21] By recognizing your ability to mobilize your own resources to succeed, your self-confidence for the task will be elevated. Another motivational advantage of self-efficacy is that you are likely to commit more resources, such as time and money, to attaining a goal when you feel confident that you can perform the task.[22] For example, if you had confidence in your skills to develop an eBay business, you might be willing to spend a lot of time in designing the business and money in buying products to sell on the site.

> **Expectancy theory of motivation**
> people will be motivated if they believe that their efforts will lead to desired outcomes

6. Raise your level of self-expectation. Another strategy for increasing your level of motivation is to simply expect more of yourself. If you raise your level of self-expectation, you are likely to achieve more. Because you expect to succeed, you do succeed. The net effect is the same as if you had increased your level of motivation. The technical term for improving your performance through raising your own expectations is the Galatea effect. In one experiment, for example, the self-expectations of subjects were raised in brief interviews with an organizational psychologist. The psychologist told the subjects they had high potential to succeed in the undertaking they were about to begin (a problem-solving task). The subjects who received the positive information about their potential did better than those subjects who did not receive such encouragement.[23]

High self-expectations and a positive mental attitude take a long time to develop, but they are critically important for becoming a well-motivated person in a variety of situations.

> "Remind yourself that you have personal power, and that you can make things happen. Erase those negative mental tapes that say 'No, I can't.'"
>
> —E. Carol Webster, clinical psychologist, quoted in *Black Enterprise*, September 2005, p. 157.

7. Develop a strong work ethic. A highly effective strategy for self-motivation is to develop a strong work ethic. If you are committed to the idea that most work is valuable and that it is joyful to work hard, you will automatically become strongly motivated. A person with a weak work ethic cannot readily develop a strong one because the change requires a profound value shift. Yet if a person gives a lot of serious thought to the importance of work and follows the right role models, a work ethic can be strengthened. The shift to a strong work ethic is much like a person who has a casual attitude toward doing fine work becoming more prideful.

Psychological hardiness
mental state in which the individual experiences a high degree of commitment, control, and challenge

8. Develop psychological hardiness. A comprehensive approach to becoming better self-motivated would be to develop a higher degree of **psychological hardiness**—a mental state in which the individual experiences a high degree of commitment, control, and challenge. (The importance of commitment to company goals was described earlier in the chapter.) *Commitment* is a tendency to involve oneself in whatever one is doing or encounters, such as being committed to developing a successful computer game. Commitment also refers to a strong desire to follow through on the action plan in support of a goal. Many people set goals without following through. Commitment has also been defined as being willing to do whatever it takes.[24]

Control is a tendency to feel and act as if one is influential, rather than helpless, in facing twists and turns in life. *Challenge* is a belief that change rather than stability is normal in life and that changes lead to growth and are not threats to security. (Moving in these three directions would involve substantial personal development.) A study with more than six hundred college students demonstrated that those who scored higher on psychological hardiness tended to have stronger motivation to study and learn.[25] Psychological hardiness would also be helpful in work motivation.

▶ Learning Objective 4 ▶

How Do You Develop the Self-Discipline to Achieve Goals and Stay Motivated?

Self-discipline
the ability to work systematically and progressively toward a goal until it is achieved

Another perspective on achieving goals and staying motivated is that they require **self-discipline**—the ability to work systematically and progressively toward a goal until it is achieved. If you are self-disciplined, you work toward achieving your goals without being derailed by the many distractions faced each day. Self-discipline incorporates self-motivation because it enables you to motivate yourself to achieve your goals without being nagged or prodded with deadlines. Our discussion of how to develop self-discipline follows the model shown in Figure 3-7. You will observe

FIGURE 3-7

THE SELF-DISCIPLINE MODEL

that the model incorporates several of the ideas about goals already discussed in this chapter. Without realizing it, you have already invested mental energy into learning the self-discipline model. To think through your own tendencies toward being self-disciplined, you are invited to take Human Relations Self-Assessment Quiz 3-3. The components of self-discipline are described next.

Component 1: *Formulate a mission statement.* Who are you? What are you trying to accomplish in life? If you understand what you are trying to accomplish in life, you have the fuel to be self-disciplined. With a mission, activities that may appear mundane to others become vital stepping stones for you. An example would be learning Spanish grammar to help you become an international businessperson. To help formulate your mission statement, answer two questions: What are my five biggest wishes? What do I want to accomplish in my career during the next five years?

Component 2: *Develop role models.* An excellent method of learning how to be self-disciplined is to model your behavior after successful achievers who are obviously well disciplined. To model another person does not mean you will slavishly imitate every detail of that person's life. Instead, you will follow the general pattern of how the person operates in spheres related to your mission and goals. An ideal role model is the type of person whom you would like to become, not someone you feel you could never become.

Component 3: *Develop goals for each task.* Your mission must be supported by a series of specific goals that collectively will enable you to achieve your mission. Successfully completing goals eventually leads to fulfilling a mission. Each small goal achieved is a building block toward larger achievements.

Component 4: *Develop action plans to achieve goals.* Self-disciplined people carefully follow their action plans because they make goal attainment possible. It is helpful to chart your progress against the dates established for the sub-activities.

Component 5: *Use visual and sensory stimulation.* A self-disciplined person relentlessly focuses on a goal and persistently pursues that goal. To accomplish this consistent focus, self-disciplined people form images of reaching their goals—they actually develop a mental image of the act of accomplishing what they want. As mysterious as it sounds, visualization helps the brain convert images into reality. The more senses you can incorporate into your visual image, the stronger its power. Imagine yourself seeing, tasting, hearing, smelling, and touching your goal. Can you imagine yourself sitting in your condo overlooking the ocean, eating a great meal to celebrate the fact that the business you founded now has ten thousand employees?

Component 6: *Search for pleasure within the task.* A self-disciplined person finds joy, excitement, and intense involvement in the task at hand and therefore finds intrinsic motivation. Instead of focusing on the extrinsic (or external) reward, the love of the task helps the person in pursuit of the goal. An axiom of becoming wealthy is not to focus on getting rich. Instead, focus on work. If the task at hand does not thrill you, at least focus on the pleasure from the most enjoyable element within the task. A bill collector might not find the total task intrinsically motivating, but perhaps he or she enjoys developing skill in resolving conflict.

Component 7: *Compartmentalize spheres of life.* Self-disciplined people have a remarkable capacity to divide up (or compartmentalize) the various spheres of their lives to stay focused on what they are doing at the moment. While working, develop the knack of concentrating on work and putting aside thoughts about personal life. In the midst of social and family activities, concentrate on them rather than half thinking about work. This approach will contribute to both self-discipline and a better integration of work and family life.

"Nothing in the world can take the place of persistence. Persistence and determination alone are omnipotent. The slogan 'press on' has solved, and always will solve, the problems of the human race."

—Calvin Coolidge, thirtieth president of the United States

Human Relations Self-Assessment Quiz   **3-3**

The Self-Discipline Quiz

On the following scale, indicate the extent to which each of the following statements describes your behavior or attitude by circling one number for each: disagree strongly (DS), disagree (D), neutral (N), agree (A), agree strongly (AS). Consider asking someone who knows your behavior and attitudes well to help you respond accurately.

		DS	D	N	A	AS
1.	I have a strong sense of purpose.	1	2	3	4	5
2.	Life is a pain when you are always chasing goals.	5	4	3	2	1
3.	My long-range plans in life are well established.	1	2	3	4	5
4.	I feel energized when I have a new goal to pursue.	1	2	3	4	5
5.	It is difficult for me to picture an event in my mind before it occurs.	5	4	3	2	1
6.	When success is near, I can almost taste, feel, and see it.	1	2	3	4	5
7.	I consult my daily planner or a to-do list almost every day.	1	2	3	4	5
8.	My days rarely turn out the way I had planned.	5	4	3	2	1
9.	What I do for a living is not (or would not be) nearly as important as the money it pays.	5	4	3	2	1
10.	Some parts of my job are as exciting to me as any hobby or pastime.	1	2	3	4	5
11.	Working sixty hours per week for even a short period of time would be out of the question for me.	5	4	3	2	1
12.	I have personally known several people who would be good role models for me.	1	2	3	4	5
13.	So far I have never read about or known anybody whose lifestyle I would like to emulate.	5	4	3	2	1
14.	My work is so demanding that it's difficult for me to concentrate fully on my personal life when I'm not working.	5	4	3	2	1
15.	When I'm involved in an important work project, I can enjoy myself fully at a sport or cultural event after hours.	1	2	3	4	5
16.	If it weren't for a few bad breaks, I would be much more successful today.	5	4	3	2	1
17.	My best helping hand is at the end of my arm.	1	2	3	4	5
18.	I get bored easily.	5	4	3	2	1
19.	Planning is difficult because life is so unpredictable.	5	4	3	2	1
20.	I feel that I'm moving forward a little bit each day toward achieving my goals.	1	2	3	4	5

Scoring and Interpretation:

Calculate your score by adding the numbers circled.

90–100 points: You are a highly self-disciplined person who should be able to capitalize on your skills and talents. Studying about self-discipline might help you capitalize even further on your strong self-discipline.

60–89 points: You have an average degree of self-discipline, so studying the self-discipline model could point to areas for personal improvement.

40–59 points: You may be experiencing problems with self-discipline. Start putting into practice the ideas contained in the self-discipline model.

20–39 points: If your answers are accurate, you have enough problems with self-discipline to limit achieving many of the things in life important to you. In addition to studying the self-discipline model, study about work habits and time management.

Questions: 1. How does this score agree with your evaluation of your self-discipline?
2. Who might you use as a role model of a person with high self-discipline?

FIGURE 3-8 RELATIONSHIP BETWEEN SELF-DISCIPLINE SCORE AND KEY FACTORS

Key Factor	Average Score on Factor for 325 Adults	Relationship to Self-Discipline Score
1. Age	34.7 years	Almost zero
2. Years of formal education	15.9	Slightly positive
3. Salary in U.S. dollars	$45,899	Slightly positive
4. Self-rating of career on scale of 1 to 7	4.9	Quite positive
5. Self-rating of goal accomplishment on scale of 1 to 7	5.6	Quite positive
6. Self-discipline score on scale of 20 to 100	76.9	------

Source: Table derived from data presented in Andrew J. DuBrin, "Career-Related Correlates of Self-Discipline," *Psychological Reports*, 2001, Vol. 89, p. 109.

Component 8: *Minimize excuse making.* Self-disciplined people concentrate their energies on goal accomplishment rather than making excuses for why work is not accomplished. Instead of trying to justify why they have been diverted from a goal, high-achieving, self-disciplined people circumvent potential barriers. Undisciplined people, in contrast, seem to look for excuses. If you are an excuse maker, conduct a self-audit, writing down all the reasons blocking you from achieving any current goal. Be brutally honest in challenging each one of your excuses. Ask yourself, "Is this a valid excuse, or is it simply a rationalization for my getting sidetracked?"

The belief that self-discipline contributes to goal attainment and success is about as strong as the belief that a healthy diet and exercise contribute to physical health. Nonetheless, a study conducted with 325 working adults provides reassurance about the benefits of self-discipline. The study participants completed the self-discipline questionnaire previously presented, and they also answered questions about their age, education, salary, and how they felt about their career success and goal accomplishment. As shown in Figure 3-8, positive relationships were found between being self-disciplined and education, salary, career success, and goal attainment. Self-ratings of career success and goal accomplishment were the most strongly related.[26] In conclusion, self-discipline pays. Why do you think it was found that self-discipline was positively associated with years of formal education?

Another useful perspective on self-discipline is that a self-disciplined person is able to delay gratification. For many people this aspect of self-discipline could mean forgoing income now to complete a degree, and eventually earn more money. The ability to delay gratification begins early in life. An amusing study gave eighth-graders the opportunity to receive one dollar at the moment, or two dollars if they were willing to wait a week. The students who had the self-discipline to delay gratification consistently outperformed their more impulsive counterparts on grades and achievement test scores.[27] (Could it be that the children who delayed gratification to earn a bigger prize were simply smarter?)

Concept Review and Reinforcement

Key Terms

Need, 64
Motive, 65
Need for achievement, 66
Maslow's hierarchy of needs, 68

Goal, 71
Action plan, 74
Intrinsic motivation, 77
Behavior modification, 79

Expectancy theory of motivation, 79
Psychological hardiness, 80
Self-discipline, 80

Summary and Review

Self-motivation is important for achieving success in work and personal life. A well-accepted explanation of human behavior is that people have needs and motives propelling them toward achieving certain goals.

- The central idea behind need theory is that unsatisfied needs motivate us until they become satisfied.
- After satisfaction of one need, the person usually pursues satisfaction of another, higher need.

Work and personal life offer the opportunity to satisfy many different needs and motives. Among the more important needs and motives are achievement, power, affiliation, recognition, and order. The need for risk taking and thrill seeking is also important for some people.

According to Maslow's hierarchy of needs, people have an internal need pushing them on toward self-actualization.

- Needs are arranged into a five-step ladder. Before higher-level needs are activated, certain lower-level needs must be satisfied.
- In ascending order, the groups of needs are physiological, safety, social, esteem, and self-actualization (such as self-fulfillment).

Need theory helps in self-motivation. First identify the needs that you want to satisfy, and then focus your efforts on an activity that will satisfy those needs. Another way of looking at self-motivation is that if you are strongly motivated you are engaged in your work, or committed to the job and the company.

Substantial research indicates that setting specific, reasonably difficult goals improves performance. Goals are valuable because they

- Will improve performance if reasonably difficult
- Can instill purpose, challenge, and meaning into ordinary work
- Focus our efforts in a specific direction
- Increase our chances for success
- Serve as self-motivators and energizers

Goals can be aimed at either learning or performing. A learning-goal orientation means that an individual is focused on acquiring new skills and mastering new situations. A performing-goal orientation is aimed at wanting to demonstrate and validate the adequacy of your competence by seeking favorable judgments of competence. People with learning-goal orientations are more likely to

- Seek feedback on how well they are performing
- Focus on skill development that will lead to higher job performance
- Develop better relationships with their supervisors
- Be innovative in solutions to problems

Goal setting is widely used on the job. Goals set by employees at lower levels in an organization are supposed to contribute to goals set at the top.

Goal setting in personal life can contribute to life satisfaction. For maximum advantage, personal goals should be integrated with career goals. Areas of life in which personal goals may be set include

- Social and family
- Hobbies and interests

- Physical and mental health
- Career
- Financial

To increase their effectiveness, goals should be supported with action plans. Effective goals are

- Specific and concise
- Expressed as a positive statement
- Realistically challenging, yet also include stretch goals
- Set for different time periods

Goals have some problems associated with them. They can create inflexibility or become an obsession. Performing goals can detract from an interest in the task, and goals can encourage unethical behavior. To combat the potential inflexibility and obsessive nature of goals, recognize and admit when you are pursuing the wrong goal.

Key techniques of self-motivation include the following:

- Setting goals for yourself
- Finding intrinsically motivating work
- Getting feedback on your performance

- Applying behavior modification to yourself
- Improving your skills relevant to your job
- Raising your level of self-expectation
- Developing a strong work ethic
- Developing psychological hardiness (a high degree of commitment, control, and challenge)

Achieving goals and staying motivated require self-discipline. A model presented here for developing self-discipline consists of eight components:

1. Formulate a mission statement.
2. Develop role models.
3. Develop goals for each task.
4. Develop action plans.
5. Use visual and sensory stimulation.
6. Search for pleasure within the task.
7. Compartmentalize spheres of life.
8. Minimize excuse making.

A study found positive relationships between self-discipline scores and education, salary, satisfaction with career success, and satisfaction with goal attainment. Also, self-disciplined people are able to delay self-gratification.

Check Your Understanding

1. One of the biggest issues in labor-management relations today is that workers want employers to pay more of their health-care insurance. What does this issue tell us about the importance of satisfying the lower-level needs of workers?
2. Identify two business-related jobs for which a high need for risk taking and thrill seeking would be an advantage.
3. Identify any self-actualized person you know or have heard of and explain why you think that person is self-actualized.
4. Have you visited a KFC, Taco Bell, Pizza Hut, or Long John Silver's restaurant recently? (If you haven't, maybe you can answer this question in the future.) How engaged did these employees seem to you? Explain the basis for your evidence.
5. Why does a learning-goal orientation often contribute to more peace of mind than a performing-goal orientation?

6. Managers are supposed to be good motivators, and companies invest heavily in employee-motivation programs. So why do you have to worry about self-motivation?
7. Give examples of two jobs in your chosen field you think are likely to be intrinsically motivating. Explain your reasoning.
8. Explain how you might be able to use the Galatea effect to improve the success you achieve in your career and personal life.
9. What sacrifices might a highly self-disciplined person have to make in contrast to a lowly self-disciplined person?
10. Ask a person who has achieved career success how much self-discipline contributed to his or her success.

Web Corner

Self-motivation:
www.secretsofmotivation.com/self-motivation-tips.html

Self-discipline:
www.selfgrowth.com

INTERNET SKILL BUILDER:

Personal Goal Setting

At www.mindtools.com/page6.html you will find a pro-gram for personal goal setting useful for both career and personal success. The program includes a thoughtful, brief video. An important feature of the personal goal-setting plan is that it urges you to set goals in nine areas of life: artistic, attitude, career, education, family, finan-cial, physical, pleasure (really recreation), and public service. After reviewing the program, give your opinion of the usefulness of SMART goals. Also, how does the use of SMART goals compare to the suggestions for goal set-ting presented in this chapter?

Developing Your Human Relations Skills

Applying Human Relations Exercise 3-1

Goal-Setting and Action Plan Worksheet

Goal setting, along with developing action plans to support the goals, is a basic success strategy. Here you are being asked to refine a process you may have already begun. Consider entering more than one goal and accompanying action plan in each category. To clarify the meaning of the following entries, we provide examples in italics of a recent graduate entering the retail field. Before writing down your goals, consult the section "Guidelines for Goal Setting." If you are not currently employed, set up hypothetical goals and action plans for a future job.

Long-Range Goals (Beyond Five Years)

Work: *Ultimately become CEO of a major division of a retail company, perhaps the CEO of Bloomingdales.*

(Place your entry here.)

Action plan: *Work my way up, position by position, starting as assistant merchandising manager.*

(Place your entry here.)

Personal: *Married, with children, home ownership.*

(Place your entry here.)

Action plan: *Continue to develop relationship with my boyfriend as life partner. We will both save and invest at least 10 percent of our incomes each year.*

(Place your entry here.)

Medium-Range Goals (Two to Five Years)

Work: *Become merchandising manager for one store in a large retail chain.*

(Place your entry here.)

Action plan: *Will work hard as assistant merchandising manager, listen to and act on feedback from my supervisors, take courses in human relations and merchandising management.*

(Place your entry here.)

Personal: *Continue to develop relationship with my boyfriend and marry him within three years.*

(Place your entry here.)

Action plan: *Communicate in depth with each other regularly to build relationship. We will work on not criticizing each other so often. After he proposes marriage, we will use our business skills to plan the wedding.*

(Place your entry here.)

Short-Range Goals (within Two Years)

Work: *Do an outstanding job as assistant merchandising manager this month.*

(Place your entry here.)

Action plan: *Will take care of more e-mail and other routine work when not in the store. In this way I can put more time and energy into merchandising. I will ask my supervisor for feedback from time to time so I can make adjustments to my performance.*

(Place your entry here.)

Personal: *Get further into digital photography, particularly learning how to take action shots. Will go beyond the "point and click" approach to photography.*

(Place your entry here.)

Action plan: *I will study the camera manual more carefully and attend one of the digital photography workshops given at my former community college.*

(Place your entry here.)

Applying Human Relations Exercise 3-2

Need Identification among Members of Generations X and Y

Following is a list of work preferences characteristic among members of generations X and Y (collectively people born since 1965). Identify what psychological need or needs might be reflected in each work preference. Jot down the needs right after the work preference.

- They like variety, not doing the same thing every workday.
- Part of their career goals is to face new challenges and opportunities. It's not all based on money, but on growth and learning.

- They want jobs that are cool, fun, and fulfilling.
- They believe that if they keep growing and learning then that's all the security they need. Advancing their skill set and continuous learning is their top priority.
- They have a tremendous thirst for knowledge.
- Unlike many baby boomers, who tend to work independently, members of generations X and Y like to work in a team environment.
- They prefer learning by doing and making mistakes as they go along.
- They are apt to challenge established ways of doing things, reasoning that there is always a better way.

- They want regular, frequent feedback on job performance.
- Career improvement is a blend of life and job balance.

Questions

1. How well does the analysis presented apply to you? Do the statements fit your work preferences?

2. What needs are you (or will you be) attempting to satisfy on the job? How do you know?

Source: Reprinted with permission from the TemPositions Group of Companies, 420 Lexington Avenue, Suite 2100, New York, NY, 10170-0002.

Human Relations Class Activity

How Important Is Need Satisfaction to People?

Here is an opportunity to engage in data collection about a major human relations topic. Each class member agrees to obtain survey data about need satisfaction by having five people complete Self-Quiz 3-2. Perhaps a student will volunteer to make an electronic copy of the test. Obtain the sex and age of each participant. (Survey anybody convenient, including yourself.)

For each completed self-quiz, record the importance ratings for each of the five need categories: physiological, safety, love, esteem, and self-actualization. To quantify the fact that people may differ in the strength of certain needs, choose participants who appear to be in quite different life situations. For example, you might look for a full-time student, an unemployed person, a professional worker, an entry-level worker, and a retired person. (The research lesson here is that you obtain more interesting results when your sample is diverse.)

A couple of class volunteers will then compile the data for all the completed self-quizzes. Average importance ratings will be calculated for each of the five needs. An example result might be, "For the total group, the average importance rating for safety needs is 3.24." Also calculate average importance ratings by sex and age group, such as above and below age twenty-five.

Among the questions for class discussion are these:

1. Does our sample appear to show much variation in the importance ratings attached to needs?
2. Which need appears to be the most frustrated among the participants in our sample?
3. Which need appears to be the most satisfied among the participants in our sample?

You might also compare your pattern of importance ratings to the averages obtained for the sample. If your need-importance profile seems to be quite different, you might explain to yourself why this fact is most likely true.

Human Relations Case Study 3-1

Unengaged Monique at Shea, Cohen, Antonelli and Armstrong

Monique was happy to receive her associate's degree with a major in paralegal studies. At a minimum, she could now satisfy her parents' demands that she work in the legal field. Monique's father frequently told her

something to this effect: "Even if we have an occasional recession, people are going to keep suing each other. They might even sue more during hard times just to get some money." Monique's mother kept emphasizing that being a paralegal would give her status and make other people think that she is somebody important.

After a brief job hunt, Monique found a position at the legal firm of Shea, Cohen, Antonelli and Armstrong (often referred to as SCAA by insiders). Wanting to appear as professional as possible, Monique joined the South Carolina Paralegal Association, although she rarely attended meetings.

After an orientation period of several days, Monique was assigned to the residential and small business real estate department. Her work activities focused on the paperwork and electronic searches needed to support lawyers in closing on houses and small buildings. Monique thought to herself that it was curious that she and other paralegals did most of the work in preparing for closings, yet the lawyers were paid considerably more.

One evening while at the athletic club where she was a member, Monique met Kurt, one of her former classmates. When asked, "How's the job going at the law firm?" Monique replied, "To tell you the truth, Kurt, house closings are a lot like airplane rides. After a half dozen or so, they are all the same. I get no thrill out of all the prep work for the closing. Yet I do like to see the happy faces of the people when the deal is done."

One afternoon Monique was standing in line at Quizno's to order a toasted sub for lunch. Right in front of her was Louise, the database manager at SCAA. Louise invited Monique to sit together after they paid the cashier. During lunch, Louise said to Monique that she had some curious feedback she had been thinking of sharing with her.

"Please tell me, Louise. I hope I didn't make an error in providing background data for one of those dumb properties."

"No error in facts, but maybe an error in attitude. One of the attorneys was telling me that he and a couple of his colleagues refer to you as 'Monique Zombie.' Of course, I asked why. He said that it seems like you are just going through the motions with no passion about what you are doing."

"Honestly, Louise," responded Monique. "I would show a little more passion at SCAA if I were closing on skyscrapers or being paid what some of the partners in the firm are earning. Give me a break."

Questions

1. What can Monique do to become more engaged in her work?

2. What can Monique do to overcome the reputation of being a zombie on the job?

3. In what way might Monique's parents have contributed to her lack of commitment to paralegal work?

4. What might be the career consequences for Monique if she does not become more enthusiastic about her present work assignments?

Human Relations Case Study 3-2

How Self-Disciplined Is Gus?

Cora, an office temporary, noticed that Gus, one on the professionals in the office where she was assigned, was constantly seated in front of the computer. One day when Gus returned from lunch, Cora engaged him in general conversation about the weather and the recent Winter Olympics. Gus looked down at the time indicated on his cell phone and said, "Excuse me, but I have to get back to work."

Cora commented, "Excuse me for saying so, but don't you get bored just sitting in front of the computer all day? I mean, don't you just want to take a break and get some fresh air? How much can a human being stare at a monitor all day?" Gus smiled and replied, "It may look like I'm just sitting in front of a computer monitor all day just banging the keyboard, but the computer is a tool that helps me accomplish something very important. I'm analyzing data to help determine how our company can make products more environmentally friendly. Our company wants to be 'green.' In this way, I'm helping to improve the world."

Questions

1. Which elements of the self-discipline model is Gus applying?

2. To what extent might Cora have a self-discipline problem?

Human Relations Role-Playing Exercise

Getting Cora Focused

The scenario presented in Human Relations Case Study 3-2 depicts a problem often encountered in the workplace: You want to get your work accomplished, whereas a coworker wants to divert your attention. One student plays the role of Gus, who not only wants to pay attention to his work but also wants to help Cora become more self-disciplined and focused. If Cora interrupts him today, Gus will provide a little friendly coaching about her becoming more self-disciplined.

Another person plays the role of Cora, who is not a shirker, yet she thinks that Gus is somewhat of a nerd in his insistence on working all the time. She approaches Gus today to discuss how well her wedding plans are going and is even thinking of putting him on the list of invited guests.

For both scenarios, observers rate the role-players on two dimensions, using a 1 to 5 scale from very poor to very good. One dimension is "effective use of human relations techniques." The second dimension is "acting ability." A few observers might voluntarily provide feedback to the role-players in terms of sharing their ratings and observations. The course instructor might also provide feedback.

REFERENCES

1. Excerpted from "New Detroit Police Chief Setting Goals," *Detroit Free Press*, October 6, 2008. Updated facts from George Hunter and Christine Ferretti, "Bing Surprises Police Force, Replaces Chief with Evans," *Detroit Free Press*, July 4, 2009.

2. For a theoretical explanation of the principle of self-interest, see Dale T. Miller, "The Norm of Self-Interest," *American Psychologist,* December 1999, pp. 1053–1060.

3. David C. McClelland and Richard Boyatzis, "Leadership Motive Pattern and Long-Term Success in Management," *Journal of Applied Psychology,* December 1982, p. 737.

4. Marvin Zuckerman, "Are You a Risk Taker?" *Psychology Today,* November/December 2000, p. 53.

5. The original statement is Abraham H. Maslow, "A Theory of Human Motivation," *Psychological Review,* July 1943, pp. 370–396. See also Maslow, *Motivation and Personality* (New York: Harper & Row, 1954).

6. Cited in Steve Bates, "Getting Engaged," *HR Magazine,* February 2004, p. 46.

7. The information about Yum Brands, including the quotation, is from Erin White, "How Surveying Workers Can Pay Off," *Wall Street Journal,* June 18, 2007, p. B3.

8. Gary P. Latham, "The Motivational Benefits of Goal Setting," *Academy of Management Executive,* November 2004, pp. 126–129.

9. Don VandeWalle and Larry L. Cummings, "A Test of the Influence of Goal Orientation on the Feedback-Seeking Process," *Journal of Applied Psychology,* June 1997, pp. 390–400; VandeWalle, William L. Cron, and John W. Slocum, Jr., "The Role of Goal Orientation Following Performance Feedback," *Journal of Applied Psychology,* August 2001, pp. 629–640.

10. Don VandeWalle, Steven P. Brown, William L. Cron, and John W. Slocum, Jr., "The Influence of Goal Orientation and Self-Regulation Tactics on Sales Performance: A Longitudinal Field Test," *Journal of Applied Psychology,* April 1999, pp. 249–259.

11. Onne Janssen and Nico W. Van Yperen, "Employee Goal Orientations, The Quality of Leader-Member Exchange, and the Outcomes of Job Performance and Job Satisfaction," *Academy of Management Journal,* June 2004, pp. 368–384.

12. Gerard H. Seijts and Gary P. Latham, "Learning versus Performance Goals: When Should Each Be Used?" *Academy of Management Executive,* February 2005, p. 130.

13. VandeWalle and Cummings, "A Test of the Influence of Goal Orientation," p. 392.

14. Susan B. Wilson and Michael S. Dobson, *Goal Setting: How to Create an Action Plan and Achieve Your Goals,* 2nd ed. (New York: American Management Association, 2008).

15. "Personal Goal Setting: Find Direction. Live Life Your Way," www.mindtools.com/page6.html © Mind Tools Ltd, 1995–2008.

16. Quoted in "Too Obsessed with Personal Goals?" *Executive Leadership,* June 2008, p. 5. Adapted from "Are You Too Obsessed with Your Goals?" www.HarvardBusiness.org

17. Quoted in Marcia A. Reed-Woodard, "Throwing in the Towel: Sometimes Quitting Is Synonymous with Success," *Black Enterprise,* September 2007, p. 145.

18. Lisa D. Ordóñez, Maurice E. Schweitzer, Adam D. Galinsky, and Max H. Bazerman, "Goals Gone Wild: The Systematic Side Effects of Overprescribing Goal Setting," *Academy of Management Perspectives,* February 2009, p. 10.

19. Richard M. Ryan and Edward L. Deci, "Self-Determination Theory and the Facilitation of Intrinsic Motivation, Social Development, and Well-Being," *American Psychologist,* January 2000, p. 70.

20. Remus Ilies and Timothy A. Judge, "Goal Regulation across Time: The Effects of Feedback and Affect," *Journal of Applied Psychology,* May 2005, pp. 453–467.

21. P. Christopher Earley and Terri R. Lituchy, "Delineating Goals and Efficacy: A Test of Three Models," *Journal of Applied Psychology,* February 1992, p. 96.

22. Jeffrey B. Vancouver, Kristen M. More, and Ryan J. Yoder, "Self-Efficacy and Resource Allocation: Support for a Nonmonotonic, Discontinuous Model," *Journal of Applied Psychology,* January 2008, pp. 35–47.

23. Taly Dvir, Dov Eden, and Michal Lang Banjo, "Self-Fulfilling Prophecy and Gender: Can Women Be Pygmalion and Galatea?" *Journal of Applied Psychology,* April 1995, p. 268.

24. Tamara E. Holmes, "The Power of Commitment: Mere Motivation Is Often Not Enough to Achieve Your Goals," *Black Enterprise,* November 2007, p. 113.

25. Michael S. Cole, Hubert S. Field, and Stanley G. Harris, "Student Learning Motivation and Psychological Hardiness: Interactive Effects on Students' Reactions to a Management Class," *Academy of Management Learning and Education,* March 2004, pp. 64–85. The definition of *psychological hardiness* is from citations on page 66 of the same source.

26. Andrew J. DuBrin, "Career-Related Correlates of Self-Discipline," *Psychological Reports,* 2001, Vol. 89, pp. 107–110.

27. Ann Pleshette Murphy, "Teach Your Kids Patience, Now," *USA Weekend,* August 4–6, 2006, p. 6.

4

Emotional Intelligence, Attitudes, and Happiness

Outline

1 What Is Emotional Intelligence?
Key Components of Emotional Intelligence
Consequences of High and Low Emotional Intelligence
Acquiring and Developing Emotional Intelligence
Concerns and Cross-Cultural Considerations

2 What Are the Components of Attitudes, and How Are They Acquired and Changed?
Components of Attitudes
How Attitudes Are Formed
The Importance of Positive Attitudes
How Attitudes Are Changed
How Companies Encourage Positive Attitudes and Job Satisfaction
Organizational Citizenship Behavior

3 What Is Happiness, and How Can It Be Acquired and Enhanced?
The Spheres of Life and Happiness
The Keys to Happiness
The Five Principles of Psychological Functioning

At Star Automatic Merchandising, sales were down 45 percent for December in comparison to the previous December, and 26 percent for the year. Ben, the general manager, knew that business had to improve to keep his staff of twenty-five workers intact. He had recently received a visit from the corporate director of marketing and sales, who advised Ben to improve his region's sales or cut his division down enough to match its current sales volume.

Ben replied to the director that his sales staff was trying hard to get more business but that the business recession was a formidable force facing the group. The director said, "Just tell your sales force that they have to improve sales by 20 percent, or half of them will lose their jobs. And while you are at it, tell the service people to keep the vending machines we have in force closer to full capacity. Tell them their jobs are in jeopardy also."

Ben explained to the director that the entire staff was trying hard, and that motivation wasn't the problem. To which the director responded, "No excuses, Ben. We are facing an emergency need for revenue growth."

Ben called a meeting for Thursday at 4 p.m. with every member of Star who could possibly attend. With business down so much, rumors flew among the employee group that Ben would be making a layoff announcement.

At the meeting, Ben served pastries, bagels, fruit, and coffee. His gesture drew applause and good-natured kidding from the group. Karen, the administrative assistant, said to the group, "Please don't report Ben to the corporate group for having served non-vended food at our meeting."

As the meeting began, Ben could detect the fearful mood in the group. He said to the staff, "We're here today for a problem-solving meeting, not for a hatchet job. Let's begin by talking about how you feel about business prospects and your jobs."

With a collective sigh of relief, each Star worker expressed his or her attitude about business prospects. Phil, one of the junior sales representatives, volunteered to speak first, and said: "Of course, I'm frightened about poor sales right now. Yet, if we can just have a little more time, I know business will improve. I have been showing a few small companies how a Star Automatic Merchandising system can actually add a few hundred dollars to their bottom line each month. We offer the business owner a nice, fat little commission."

In turn, the other Star employees talked about how they felt about their jobs as well as the overall business.[1]

Learning Objectives ▶

After studying the information and doing the exercises in this chapter, you should be able to:

1 Explain how emotional intelligence contributes to effective human relations.

2 Understand the components of attitudes and how they are acquired and changed.

3 Appreciate the importance of positive attitudes.

4 Pinpoint why organizational citizenship behavior is so highly valued in the workplace.

5 Understand the nature of happiness and how it can be acquired and enhanced.

Ben's approach to working with his employees illustrates how important emotions are to workers and that they should be dealt with to achieve good business results. By dealing with employee feelings, Ben displayed good emotional intelligence, one of the major topics in this chapter. Other major sections of the chapter deal with related aspects of using emotion constructively: attitudes and happiness.

▶ Learning Objective 1 ▶

What Is Emotional Intelligence?

How effectively people use their emotions has a major impact on their success. The term *emotional intelligence* has gathered different meanings, all relating to how effectively a person makes constructive use of his or her emotions. John D. Mayer, a professor of psychology at the University of New Hampshire, along with Yale psychology professor Peter Saloey, originated the concept of emotional intelligence. Mayer explained that from a scientific (rather than a popular) viewpoint, **emotional intelligence** is the "ability to accurately perceive your own and others' emotions; to understand the signals that emotions send about relationships; and to manage our own and others' emotions."[2] A person with high emotional intelligence would be able to engage in such behaviors as sizing up people, pleasing others, and influencing them.

Emotional intelligence
the ability to accurately perceive emotions, to understand the signals that emotions send about relationships, and to manage emotions

KEY COMPONENTS OF EMOTIONAL INTELLIGENCE

Four key factors included in emotional intelligence are as follows:[3]

Self-awareness
the ability to understand moods, emotions, and needs as well as their impact on others; self-awareness also includes using intuition to make decisions you can live with happily

1. **Self-awareness.** The ability to understand your moods, emotions, and needs as well as their impact on others. Self-awareness also includes using intuition to make decisions you can live with happily. (A person with good self-awareness knows whether he or she is pushing other people too far.)

Self-management
the ability to control one's emotions and act with honesty and integrity in a consistent and acceptable manner

2. **Self-management.** The ability to control one's emotions and act with honesty and integrity in a consistent and acceptable manner. The right degree of self-management helps prevent a person from throwing temper tantrums when activities do not go as planned. Effective workers do not let their occasional bad moods ruin their day. If they cannot overcome the bad mood, they let coworkers know of their problem and how long it might last. (A person with low self-management would suddenly decide to drop a project because the work was frustrating.)

Social awareness
having empathy for others and having intuition about work problems

3. **Social awareness.** Includes having empathy for others and having intuition about work problems. A team leader with social awareness, or empathy, would be able to assess whether a team member has enough enthusiasm for a project to assign him or her to that project. Another facet of social skill is the ability to interpret nonverbal communication, such as frowns and types of smiles.[4] (A supervisor with social awareness, or empathy, would take into account the most likely reaction of group members before making a decision affecting them.)

Relationship management
the interpersonal skills of being able to communicate clearly and convincingly, disarm conflicts, and build strong personal bonds

4. **Relationship management.** Includes the interpersonal skills of being able to communicate clearly and convincingly, disarm conflicts, and build strong personal bonds. Effective workers use relationship management skills to spread their enthusiasm and solve disagreements, often with kindness and humor. (A worker with relationship management skill would use a method of persuasion that is likely to work well with a particular group or individual.)

Emotional intelligence thus incorporates many of the skills and attitudes necessary to achieve effective interpersonal relations in organizations. Many topics in human relations, such as resolving conflict and helping others develop, and positive political skills, would be included in emotional intelligence. Figure 4-1 outlines

FIGURE 4-1 THE LINK BETWEEN EMOTIONAL INTELLIGENCE AND OTHER TOPICS IN HUMAN RELATIONS

Chapter Number	Illustrative Links to the Emotional Intelligence (EI)
1. Human Relations and You	To understand yourself well, the self-awareness aspect of EI is essential.
2. Self-Esteem and Self-Confidence	Self-esteem focuses heavily on understanding your feelings, which makes EI quite important.
3. Self-Motivation and Goal Setting	Some aspects of self-motivation involve being able to read your own emotions. The self-management aspect of EI contributes to self-discipline.
4. Emotional Intelligence, Attitudes, and Happiness	EI is linked to attitudes because they have an emotional content. You need to understand your own emotions and feelings to be happy.
5. Values and Ethics	Values are colored with emotions, so understanding emotions helps develop your values. An important test of being ethical is to understand how you would feel if your behavior were made public. EI helps you understand these feelings.
6. Problem Solving and Creativity	Emotions and intuition contribute heavily to problem solving and creativity, so having good EI can be an asset.
7. Personal Communication Effectiveness	Personal communication includes relationship building, such as being supportive of others. A key part of EI is relationship building. Dealing with emotions and attitudes is also a contributor to overcoming barriers to communication.
8. Communication in the Workplace	Behaving effectively in meetings includes being able to understand the impact you are making on others and also reading the emotions of others. Both skills are part of EI.
9. Getting Along with Your Managers, Coworkers, and Customers	Managing relationships is one of the major components of EI. The social awareness aspect of EI includes having empathy for others, which is helpful in developing workplace relationships.
10. Managing Conflict	The relationship-management aspect of EI includes disarming conflict, so your emotional intelligence will help you deal with conflict. Also, being able to read the emotions of others will help you resolve conflict.
11. Becoming an Effective Leader	Several researchers believe that EI is the most important trait and characteristic of an effective leader. Your EI will also help you develop good relationships with subordinates.
12. Motivating Others and Developing Teamwork	When attempting to motivate others, it is helpful to understand their emotions and feelings and identify their major needs. Also, if your EI is good, you will be able to more readily praise others.
13. Diversity and Cross-Cultural Competence	A major contributor to effective cross-cultural relations is to have the cultural sensitivity to size up your environment and then act appropriately. Having cultural sensitivity and empathy is part of EI.
14. Getting Ahead in Your Career	Having good EI will help you build the relationships you need to succeed, such as during a job interview and with network members. Also, appropriate etiquette can contribute to career advancement, and EI helps you size up which standards of behavior are expected.
15. Learning Strategies, Perception, and Lifespan Changes	EI can help in such ways as having the self-awareness to understand your learning style and being able to recognize the subtle changes you need to make at various stages of life. Strong EI can also help you sharpen your perception because you will be able to recognize potential emotional biases.
16. Developing Good Work Habits	An important part of having good work habits is to understand your potential tendencies toward procrastination. The self-awareness aspect of EI is a major contributor to this type of self-reflection.
17. Managing Stress and Personal Problems	To understand how stress from work and personal life might be affecting you, you have to be able to read your emotions. Dealing well with personal problems also requires enough EI to read your emotions.

Human Relations Self-Assessment Quiz 4-1

What Is Your Emotional Intelligence?

Psychologists have developed various measures of emotional intelligence. The EQ (Emotional Quotient) test, found by visiting www.myskillsprofile.com, deals with sixteen emotional competencies. The feedback report provides a chart of your emotional competencies together with a detailed description of your profile. An advantage of this quiz is that it is based on the work of two of the original researchers in emotional intelligence, not the later popularizers of the concept.

and illustrates how emotional intelligence relates many other topics in human relations.

Tests of emotional intelligence typically ask you to respond to questions on a 1 to 5 scale (never, rarely, sometimes, often, consistently). For example, indicate how frequently you demonstrate the following behaviors:

I can laugh at myself.	1 2 3 4 5
I help others grow and develop.	1 2 3 4 5
I watch carefully the nonverbal communication of others.	1 2 3 4 5

Human Relations Self-Assessment Quiz 4-1 gives you an opportunity to measure your emotional intelligence.

CONSEQUENCES OF HIGH AND LOW EMOTIONAL INTELLIGENCE

Demonstrating good emotional intelligence is impressive because it contributes to performing well in the difficult arena of dealing with feelings. A worker with good emotional intelligence would engage in such behaviors as (a) recognizing when a coworker needs help but is too embarrassed to ask for help, (b) dealing with the anger of a dissatisfied customer, (c) recognizing that the boss is facing considerable pressure also, and (d) being able to tell whether a customer's "maybe" means "yes" or "no."

Another positive consequence of emotional intelligence is that if you know how to project positive emotion you will spread that positive feeling to others in your immediate workplace. **Emotional contagion** is the automatic and unconscious transfer of emotions between individuals based on cues the other person observes. The contagion takes place because people have a tendency to mimic and synchronize the facial expressions, sounds, postures, and movements of another person. As a result of the mimicking, the second person experiences the emotion of the first person.[5] Here is how you might use emotional contagion to solve a human relations problem: You are the team leader of a group of discouraged, disgruntled, and downtrodden people working in a distribution center of a large online retailer. You hear regular complaints such as, "We get treated like prison labor in a third-world country," "The computer systems keeps going down so we can't get our work done on time," "Even the Rollerblades management gives us to scoot around the center are in drastic need of repair." From time to time you tell the group to cheer up, but your words are not taken seriously.

Emotional contagion
the automatic and unconscious transfer of emotions between individuals based on cues the one person observes in another

Being skilled at emotional intelligence, you give emotional contagion a try. You enlist the help of the most cheerful member of the group, Willy, to duplicate your act so the effects of emotional contagion will be doubled. You and your confederate Willy come to work smiling, expressing positive thoughts, standing up straight, and making fist-to-fist contact with anybody who says something positive. Soon the positive mood and actions of you and Willy begin to rub off a little on other team-mates. The mood becomes positive enough to start working on problems instead of simply moaning and complaining.

A review of many studies concluded that employees with low emotional intelligence are more likely than their high-emotional-intelligence counterparts to experience negative emotional reactions to job insecurity, such as high tension. Furthermore, workers with low emotional intelligence are more likely to engage in negative coping behaviors, such as expressing anger and verbally abusing an immediate supervisor for the organization failing to provide job security.[6]

ACQUIRING AND DEVELOPING EMOTIONAL INTELLIGENCE

Many people believe that emotional intelligence can be acquired and developed, much like a person can learn to become more extraverted or learn to control his or her temper. Many consultants offer training programs for helping employees develop emotional intelligence, and school systems throughout North America provide students some training in emotional intelligence. Elkhonon Goldberg, a clinical professor of neurology at New York University School of Medicine, explains that emotional intelligence can be learned to a degree, much like musical talent or numerical ability can be developed. Having the right natural talent, however, is an important starting point. The combination of biological endowment (such as being aware of your emotions) and training will enable most people to enhance their emotional intelligence.[7]

Given that emotional intelligence is composed of different components, to acquire and develop such ability would usually require working on one component at a time. For example, if a person had difficulty in self-management, he or she would study and be coached in an aspect of self-management such as anger control. Training in anger management is widespread today because so many people have difficulty in managing their anger. Skill-Building Exercise 4-1 presented later in the chapter provides a step-by-step approach to the development of emotional intelligence.

CONCERNS AND CROSS-CULTURAL CONSIDERATIONS

A criticism of the idea of emotional intelligence is that it might simply be part of analytical (or traditional) intelligence. For example, if you can read the feelings of other people, aren't you just being smart? Another concern is that the popularized concept of emotional intelligence has become so broad it encompasses almost the entire study of personality. Emotional intelligence has become an all-inclusive term for many ideas about human behavior that were studied before and since the popularization of the term. Yet when emotional intelligence is regarded as a series of skills that can be developed, it has more scientific backing.[8]

As with all dimensions of human relations, in some situations it will be helpful to be aware of possible cross-cultural differences in what constitutes effective emotional intelligence. For example, an overt display of emotion might be more effective in a meeting conducted in Mexico City than London, because the typical Mexican businessperson is more open in expressing emotion than his or her typical British counterpart.

▶ Learning Objective 2 ▶

What Are the Components of Attitudes, and How Are They Acquired and Changed?

Attitude

a predisposition to respond that exerts an influence on a person's response to a person, a thing, an idea, or a situation

"You've got an attitude," said the supervisor to the store associate, thus emphasizing the importance of attitude to job performance. For mysterious reasons, the term *attitude* in colloquial language often connotes a *negative* attitude. More accurately, an **attitude** is a predisposition to respond that exerts an influence on a person's response to a person, a thing, an idea, or a situation. Attitudes are an important part of human relations because they are linked with perception and motivation. For example, your attitude toward a coworker influences your perception of how favorably you evaluate his or her work, and you will be better motivated if you have a positive attitude toward your work. Having and displaying positive attitudes will also help you build better relationships with coworkers, managers, and customers.

Our study of attitudes includes the components of attitudes, how attitudes are acquired, how they are changed, the importance of positive attitudes, how companies attempt to enhance positive attitudes and job satisfaction, and organizational citizenship behavior.

COMPONENTS OF ATTITUDES

Cognitive component

(of attitude) the knowledge or intellectual beliefs an individual might have about an object (an idea, a person, a thing, or a situation)

Affective component

(of attitude) the emotion connected with an object or a task

Attitudes are complex, having three components, as shown in Figure 4-2. The **cognitive component** refers to the knowledge or intellectual beliefs an individual might have about an object (an idea, a person, a thing, or a situation). A market researcher might have accumulated considerable factual information about statistics (such as sampling procedures) and software for running data. The researcher might, therefore, have a positive attitude toward statistics.

The feeling or **affective component** refers to the emotion connected with an object or a task. The market researcher mentioned might basically like statistical analysis because of some pleasant experiences in college associated with statistics.

FIGURE 4-2

THE THREE COMPONENTS OF ATTITUDES

Observe that the three components of attitudes influence each other and that the attitude toward a subject, person, object, or thing is the combined effect of the cognitive, affective, and behavioral components.

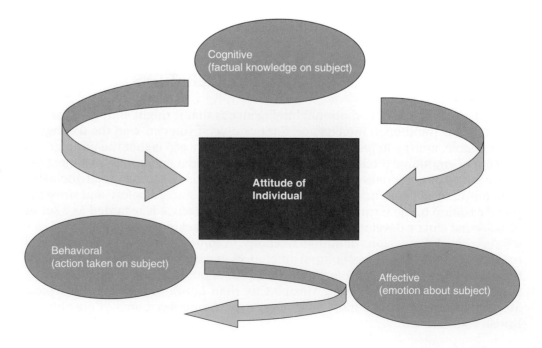

The **behavioral component** refers to how a person acts. The market researcher might make positive statements about statistical methods or emphasize them in his or her reports.

Behavioral component
(of attitude) how a person acts

The cognitive, affective, and behavioral aspects of attitudes are interrelated. A change in one of the components will set in motion a change in one or more of the others. If you have more facts about an object or process (cognitive), you form the basis for a more positive emotional response to the object (affective). In turn, your behavior toward that object would probably become more favorable. For example, if you have considerable information about the contribution of feedback to personal development, you might have a positive feeling toward feedback. When receiving feedback, therefore, you would act favorably.

At times, people do not experience the type of consistency previously described and feel compelled to search for consistency. **Cognitive dissonance** is the situation in which the pieces of knowledge, information, attitudes, or beliefs held by an individual are contradictory. When a person experiences cognitive dissonance, the relationship between attitudes and behaviors is altered. People search for ways to reduce internal conflicts when they experience a clash between the information they receive and their actions or attitudes. The same process is used when a person has to resolve two inconsistent sets of information.

Cognitive dissonance
situation in which the pieces of knowledge, information, attitudes, or beliefs held by an individual are contradictory

A typical example of cognitive dissonance on the job might occur when a worker believes that the report she submits to team members is of high quality; her teammates, however, tell her the report is flawed and requires substantial revisions. To reduce the dissonance, the worker might conveniently ignore the criticism. Or the worker might reason that she is the resident expert on the topic of the report, and her teammates, therefore, are not qualified to judge the merits of her report.

HOW ATTITUDES ARE FORMED

Attitudes usually are based on experience. Assume that you visited a convenience store, and you left your wallet on the counter without realizing it. Your wallet contained your credit cards, debit cards, driver's license, $150 in cash, and personal items. On returning home you receive a phone call from the clerk, informing you that he is holding your wallet for you. You most likely develop an immediate positive attitude toward the convenience store, the clerk, and perhaps toward other people of his ethnic group. Next we look more closely at the processes underlying attitude formation.[9]

A starting point in developing attitudes is to receive direct instruction from another individual. A friend whose opinion you respect tells you that e-filing of income tax is fast, efficient, and modern. You might quickly have a positive attitude toward e-filing. Similarly, you might develop a positive attitude through modeling the behavior of another person. You have seen that your trusted friend e-files her income tax, so you develop a positive attitude toward e-filing.

Conditioning, or making associations, also contributes to attitude formation, as in the example of the convenience store. The attitudes that we develop based on conditioning or associations usually develop after at least several exposures. You might develop a favorable attitude toward the human resources (HR) department if you asked for help several times, and each time you received useful advice. In contrast, you might have developed negative attitudes toward HR if a department representative was unhelpful at each visit.

The way we think about things, or our *cognitions*, can influence attitude formation. You might be quite content with your salary and benefits provided by your employer. You then visit www.salary.com and discover that you make much less than other workers in your city performing the same work. As a result, your attitude toward your salary and benefits plunges.

The deepest contributor to attitude formation could be a person's standing on the personality trait of optimism. People with a high degree of optimism are predisposed toward viewing events, persons, places, and things as positive, which in turn leads to a positive attitude. In contrast, people who have a high standing on pessimism will harbor many negative attitudes. Many workers who have chronically low job satisfaction are pessimistic at the core.[10]

THE IMPORTANCE OF POSITIVE ATTITUDES

Positive attitudes have always been the foundation of effective human relations, as reflected in the writings of Dale Carnegie, the pioneer of the popular (rather than scientific) approach to human relations. A sampling of Carnegie's wisdom is presented in Figure 4-3. In recent years positive attitudes have also become of interest to human relations specialists, as reflected in the fields called positive psychology and positive organizational studies. A major thrust of these fields is to enhance our experiences of enjoyment of work, as well as love and play. The assumption is that when employees are in a positive mood, they are typically more creative, better motivated to perform well, and more helpful toward coworkers.[11]

A worker who consistently maintains a *genuine* positive attitude will accrue many benefits. Being genuine is important because people with good emotional intelligence can readily detect a phony smile used as a cover-up for anger. Assuming the worker with a positive attitude backs it up with good performance, he or she is more likely to (a) be liked by customers, (b) close more sales, (c) receive good performance reviews, (d) receive favorable work assignments, and (e) be promoted.

A mild note of caution is that there is a negative side to workers being too positive. As analyzed by Judge and Ilies, putting on a happy face can lead to stress, burnout, and job dissatisfaction. Workers who have an unrealistically positive self-concept might become self-centered and manipulative and think they deserve more attention and rewards than other workers.[12] Also a little negativity and cynicism is helpful in jobs such as auditor, budget analyst, tax accountant, and store detective. Sometimes being suspicious and negative contributes to a job role.

FIGURE 4-3

THE WISDOM OF DALE CARNEGIE

The name Dale Carnegie is synonymous with a popularized approach to human relations. Carnegie (1888–1955) authored several best sellers, including *How to Win Friends and Influence People*, first published in 1937. More than 50 million copies of Carnegie's books have been printed, and they have been published in thirty-eight languages. Nine of Carnegie's suggestions for becoming a positive, friendlier person follow:

1. Don't criticize, condemn, or complain.
2. Give honest, sincere appreciation.
3. Arouse in the other person an eager want.
4. Become genuinely interested in other people.
5. Smile.
6. Remember that a person's name is to that person the sweetest and most important sound in any language.
7. Be a good listener. Encourage others to talk about themselves.
8. Talk in terms of the other person's interests.
9. Make the other person feel important—and do it sincerely.

Source: Dale Carnegie's Golden Book, Dale Carnegie Training, www.dalecarnegie.com, undated.

HOW ATTITUDES ARE CHANGED

In general, attitudes can be changed by reversing the processes by which they were formed. Yet, we can look at the process of attitude change more specifically. First, we might receive information from a source we trust. A manager might have negative attitudes toward the value of employee training but then reads in a reliable business magazine that IBM spends more than $4,000 per employee annually on training. As a consequence, the manager develops a more favorable attitude toward training. A person might also be reconditioned to bring about attitude change. A small-business owner might have a negative attitude toward e-filing income taxes because of the need to learn new skills combined with a fear of lack of security. After trying e-filing for two consecutive years because of being almost forced to by the law, the business owner receives refunds promptly and find the process not really so complicated. So her attitude toward e-filing becomes reconditioned in a positive direction.

Another way to change attitudes is to learn to look at the positive or negative aspect of situations, if you are a pessimist or optimist, respectively. A pessimistic person should concentrate on searching for the positive elements of a situation, such as a supervisor saying to himself or herself, "Okay, this employee is a pill, but maybe there is something good about him."

In contrast, a naturally optimistic person might learn to say, "I tend to fall in love with the credentials of most job candidates. So maybe I should scrutinize this candidate more carefully."

Looking at the positive aspects of a situation to change your attitude is often a question of where you choose to focus your attention. What we see tends to shape how we feel. Suppose you dislike your job. The way to change your attitude is to write down every single thing you like about your job, even something small, like the free espresso. It is also helpful to maintain a list of anything positive that happens to you during the workday. An example might be, "Today Laura showed me how to position my mouse over a false e-mail address to uncover the true address. I found that interesting." Keep in mind also that you are being paid, and without paid work a person cannot live independently.[13]

HOW COMPANIES ENCOURAGE POSITIVE ATTITUDES AND JOB SATISFACTION

From the standpoint of management it is beneficial for employees to have positive attitudes and job satisfaction. These two emotional states contribute to better customer service, less absenteeism and tardiness, less turnover, and often higher productivity. The logic is that satisfied employees will lead to satisfied customers, resulting in a more profitable business. Much of the effort of human resource professionals is aimed at making employees more content. Among the hundreds of possible company initiatives to foster positive attitudes and high job satisfaction among employees are flexible working hours, recognition awards, company picnics, financial bonuses, time off for birthdays, on-site haircuts, and on-premises child-care centers. Following are three specific examples of companies voted among the 100 Best Companies to Work For (as evaluated by *Fortune* magazine) to enhance employee attitudes and satisfaction:[14]

> ***Genentech, South San Francisco (biotechnology products).*** Employees receive free doggie day care, onsite farmer's market, and parties every Friday night. The company matches 401(k) payments 100 percent up to 5 percent of pay. (A 401(k) is a retirement fund contributed to by the employee and often the employer, with the balance being the property of the individual.)

W. L. Gore & Associates, Newark, Delaware (Gore-Tex fabrics, guitar strings, dental floss). To encourage job satisfaction as well as innovation, there are no bosses, job titles, or organization charts. Instead there are sponsors, team members, and leaders. The company attempts to hire candidates who are driven by opportunity rather than a job title or its associated status. Highly engaged employees are referred to as "passionate champions."

Principal Financial Group, Des Moines, Iowa (financial products). The company has a new, state-of-the-art child-care center. Employees can buy extra time off, and the majority receives retirement benefits of 100 percent of their income. During the financial upheaval in 2008, CEO Larry Zimpleman sent weekly e-mails to keep employees up-to-date and reassure them that the company was healthy.

The accompanying Human Relations in Practice provides an example of the steps a company will take to keep employees satisfied and why company leadership thinks keeping employees satisfied is important.

Human Relations in Practice

Job Satisfaction Counts at Advertising, Marketing, and Public Relations Agency

At Dixon Schwabl, an advertising, marketing, and public relations agency based in Victor, New York, creativity forms the cornerstone of the business. As a result, its seventy-seven employees are encouraged to share imaginative ideas in various forums. Six years ago when the company moved to its new office, employees were asked what they wanted in the space, and true to the company's extroverted culture, they didn't hold back.

Among employees' suggestions: windows that open, thermostat controls in each office, a giant slide, a fireplace in the conference room, and a padded "primal scream" room. The final design incorporates every idea, CEO Lauren Dixon says proudly.

"We never make a decision without putting it on the table for everyone's approval," Dixon says. "You might think our clients are number one, but really it's our employees. If we make our employees number one, they'll make our clients number one."

In its twenty-first year, Dixon Schwabl topped the *HR Magazine* annual list of the "Best Small Companies to Work For" in America. Leaders and employees of the privately held company, which has been on the list for four years, work hard to live its values of integrity, teamwork, fun, creativity, and community.

Company leaders have earned a reputation for listening to and valuing employees' opinions, offering the staff freedom and flexibility on the job, and providing benefits such as a generous health-care package and nutrition programs, profit sharing, and an array of training opportunities.

Questions

1. What factors in the job environment at Dixon Schwabl appear to be contributing to employee job satisfaction?
2. Why should company leaders care if its employees have "fun" on the job?
3. Put on your accounting hat. Explain whether a "padded primal scream room" is a good investment of company money.

Source: Abridged from Desda Moss, "Catering to a Creative Workforce," *HR Magazine*, July 2008, pp. 33–34.

Although companies invest considerable money in satisfying employees, a good deal of job satisfaction stems from positive interpersonal relationships in the work environment. A comprehensive study about job satisfaction was conducted with 540 people in a variety of positions, including teachers, physicians, and construction workers. The nature of the work, such as having a variety of interesting tasks to perform, contributed to job satisfaction. A bigger impact on job satisfaction, however, stemmed from frequent interaction with others, office friendship, and receiving emotional support from supervisors and coworkers.[15]

ORGANIZATIONAL CITIZENSHIP BEHAVIOR

An employee attitude highly valued by employers is **organizational citizenship behavior (OCB)**—the willingness to go beyond one's job description to help the company, even if such an act does not lead to an immediate reward. Being a good organizational citizen is also tied in with values, because the person who goes beyond the job description to help others most likely has a strong work ethic and values helping others. Several examples of good organizational citizenship follow:

Organizational citizenship behavior (OCB)
the willingness to go beyond one's job description to help the company, even if such an act does not lead to an immediate reward

- Melissa helps an employee in another department with a currency exchange problem because she has skill in this area, but Melissa's job does not involve working with currency exchange.

- Jeff is walking into the company from the company parking lot. He notices that a few beer bottles have been scattered on the lot. Worried about possible flat tires to employee vehicles, Jeff collects the bottles and disposes of them properly. He does not tell anybody about his good deed.

- Penelope, a gifted information technology person, is walking down the isle toward her cubicle. She notices a worker from another department with a panicked look on his face as he stares into his computer monitor. Penelope asks if there is anything she can do to help and proceeds to transfer valuable data from a corrupted file to a new file for the employee in panic.

Organizational citizenship behavior is so important to organizations that this set of attitudes has been the subject of many studies. A general finding has been that as a result of many workers being good organizational citizens, the organization functions more effectively in such ways as improved product quantity and quality.[16]

The personal support dimension of OCB will help you understand how citizenship behavior contributes directly to effective human relations in the workplace. **Personal support** refers to assisting others in the workplace through the use of interpersonal skills. As outlined in Figure 4-4, and presented next, the personal support dimension has four components, or subdimensions.[17] The three examples presented above involve a mixture of personal support and task-related assistance. Here is the difference: Penelope, just mentioned, is providing personal support when she helps the frustrated computer user calm down. She provides task-related assistance when she transfers the data to a new file.

Personal support
assisting others in the workplace through the use of interpersonal skills

1. **Helping.** Person-focused helping includes self-esteem maintenance and other more personal problem-solving behaviors. Penelope would be engaged in self-esteem maintenance if she said to the man she was helping, "Don't feel bad; even Bill Gates and Steve Jobs have trouble with corrupted files." Helping behavior contributes to organizational effectiveness when the help is of high technical quality. If Penelope calms down the man she is trying to help but does not help him with the corrupted file, not much has been accomplished for the organization.

2. **Courtesy.** In general, courtesy involves showing consideration and tact in interpersonal relationships. Although courtesy might be regarded as expected

FIGURE 4-4

THE FOUR COMPONENTS OF THE PERSONAL SUPPORT DIMENSION OF ORGANIZATIONAL CITIZENSHIP BEHAVIOR

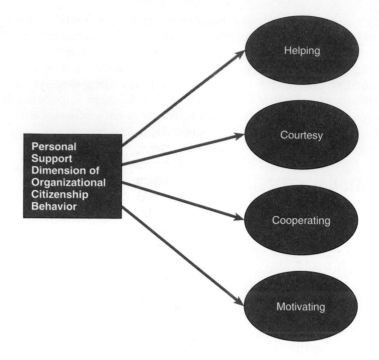

behavior on the job, many workers are rude and discourteous toward each other. Being courteous therefore stands out as part of organizational citizenship behavior. An example of courteous behavior during a department meeting would be to listen intently to the presenter without engaging in other activities, even if the person bored you.

3. **Cooperating.** A person who cooperates on the job willfully contributes time, effort, and resources to accomplish joint tasks. As a member of a team, you are expected to cooperate. In terms of citizenship behavior, cooperating includes accepting the suggestions of work associates, following their lead, and placing team objectives over personal interests. Included also in cooperation is informing others of events or requirements that may affect them. Cooperation is mostly clearly part of OCB when you go out of your way to cooperate with people outside of your immediate work unit. An example would be sending a job-relevant Web link to someone in another department.

4. **Motivating.** As related to organizational citizenship behavior, motivating behaviors include applauding the achievements and successes of coworkers, encouraging them when they face adversity, and helping them overcome setbacks. Expressing confidence in coworkers, and perhaps supervisors, is also part of the motivating component of personal support. In the example of Melissa presented above, she might have to encourage the person she is helping to study more about currency exchange. In sum, you are a good organizational citizen if you are helpful, courteous, cooperative, and motivational, even if these behaviors are not part of your job description.

▶ Learning Objective 3 ▶

What Is Happiness, and How Can It Be Acquired and Enhanced?

When asked "What is the most important thing in life?" most people respond, "Happiness." Research and opinion on the topic indicate that people can take concrete steps to achieve happiness. Planning for happiness is possible because it appears to be about 40 percent under people's control. Happier people have better physical health, achieve more career success, work harder, and are more caring and socially engaged. Misery can lead to self-obsession and inactivity.[18] Based partially on the importance of happiness for well-being, there has been a surge of writing and study about happiness in recent years. A course about positive psychology has become the most popular course at Harvard University, and at least one hundred other colleges and universities offer similar courses.[19]

Our approach to the unlimited topic of understanding how to achieve happiness involves a model of happiness, a listing of keys to happiness, and the five principles of psychological functioning.

THE SPHERES OF LIFE AND HAPPINESS

A practical way of understanding happiness is that it is a byproduct of having the various components of life working in harmony and synchrony. To understand this approach, visualize about six gears with teeth, spinning in unison. As long as all gears are moving properly (and no teeth are broken), a state of equilibrium and fluid motion is achieved. Similarly, imagine that life has six major components. The exact components will differ among people. For most people, the components would be approximately as follows:

1. Work and career

2. Interpersonal life, including loved ones and romantic life

3. Physical and mental health

4. Financial health

5. Interests and pastimes, including reading, surfing the Internet, and sports

6. A spiritual life or belief system, including religion, science, or astrology

When you have ample satisfactions in all six spheres, you achieve happiness. However, when a deficiency occurs in any of these six factors, your spheres are no longer in harmony, and dissatisfaction or unhappiness occurs. Yet sometimes if you are having problems in one sphere, satisfaction in the other spheres can compensate temporarily for a deficiency in one. For the long range, a state of happiness depends on all six spheres working in harmony. In short, the theme of this book surfaces again: Work and personal life are mutually supportive. Figure 4-5 presents the spheres-of-life model of happiness.

People vary as to how much importance they attach to each sphere of life. A person with intense career ambitions, for example, might place less weight on the interests sphere than would a more leisure-oriented person. However, if any of these spheres are grossly deficient, total happiness will not be forthcoming. Another source of variation is that the importance people attach to each sphere may vary according to the stage of life. If you are a full-time student, for example, you might need just enough money to avoid worrying about finances. However, after about ten years of full-time career experience, your expenses might peak. You would then attach more importance to the financial sphere.

"Don't worry, be happy."
—Bobby McFerrin, jazz
vocalist and classical conductor.

THE KEYS TO HAPPINESS

If you are aware of known contributors to happiness, you might be able to enhance your happiness. Fortunately there is some consistency in information about what makes people happy. Here we summarize and synthesize a wide range of research and opinion on the keys to happiness.[20]

FIGURE 4-5

THE SPHERES-OF-LIFE MODEL OF HAPPINESS

Give High Priority to the Pursuit of Happiness

Having the intention or goal of being happy will enhance your chances of being happy. A key principle is to discover what makes you happy and make the time to pursue those activities, as spending time doing what you enjoy contributes directly to happiness. University of California–Riverside psychology professor Sonja Lyubormirsky has researched routines to help people become happy by focusing on happiness, thereby systematically pursuing happiness. Her research shows that you need to put intentional effort into becoming happier. If people think about happy life events every day for three days, within four weeks they are happier than they were before they started this routine.[21] If you are going through a particularly unhappy period, you may have to stretch to think of a few happy life events. For example, did anybody pay you a compliment about anything you did or said recently? Did you help anybody recently who thanked you for your kindness?

Develop and Maintain Friendships with Happy People

New evidence indicates that getting connected to happy people improves a person's own happiness. Nicholas Christakis, a professor of medical sociology at Harvard Medical School, and James Fowler, a political scientist at the University of California–San Diego, surveyed the emotional state of about 5,000 people and the 50,000 social ties they shared. Happiness level, or emotional state, was measured at various points. Happiness was measured by asking people how often during the past week they could say, (a) I enjoyed life, (b) I was happy, (c) I felt hopeful about the future, and (d) I felt that I was just as good as other people.

The study found that happiness is contagious. If a participant's friend was happy, that participant was 15 percent more likely to be happy. If the friend of a participant's friend was happy, the original participant was 10 percent more likely to be happy. The happiness chain even extended further out, with a happy friend of a friend, of a friend giving a 5.6 percent boost to the original participant's happiness.

Another key finding was that people with the most social connections, including friends, spouses, neighbors, and relatives, were also the happiest. Each additional person in your network makes you happier. Spouses and other live-in partners who are happy increase the likelihood of their partners being happy by 8 percent. Happy siblings living nearby boosted life satisfaction 14 percent, and happy neighbors increased happiness levels by 34 percent.

The "friends" in this study were mostly traditional friends, not the type of "friends" you contact on social networks like MySpace and Facebook. Yet the study also found that people who are smiling on their Facebook photos tend to cluster together, forming an online social circle.[22]

Develop a Sense of Self-Esteem

Self-love must precede love for others. High self-esteem enables one to love and be loved. Developing a good self-image leads to the self-esteem required for loving relationships. An early contributor to the importance of thinking positively about oneself was Emile Coué, a French psychologist. He made a name for himself in the twentieth century by teaching that mental health could be achieved by repeating the sentence, "Every day and in every way I'm becoming better and better."[23]

A feeling of self-worth is important because it helps prevent being overwhelmed by criticism. An important part of developing self-esteem is to not want financial success more than other things. Insecure people seek society's approval in the form of purchasing consumer goods and accumulating investments. (In this way the person might be admired by others.) The accompanying Core Self-Evaluation Scale is a scientifically developed instrument that gives you an opportunity to assess how positively you think about yourself. You will recall another core self-evaluation scale was presented in Chapter 2.

Work Hard at What You Enjoy and Achieve the Flow Experience

To achieve happiness, it is necessary to find a career that fits your most intense interests. In addition, it helps to achieve regularly the flow experience of total involvement in what you are doing at the moment. Happiness stemming from flow is powerful because it is not dependent on favorable external circumstances, such as recognition or love. The individual creates the happiness that follows from flow. Hard work contributes to happiness in another important way. A fundamental secret of happiness is accomplishing things and savoring what you have accomplished. Happiness researcher David T. Lyken argues that happiness is available to anyone who develops skills, interests, and goals that he or she finds meaningful and enjoyable.[24] A log cabin dweller who lived off the land and whose goal was to be close to nature would therefore be happier than a wealthy person in a luxurious house who was not leading the lifestyle he or she wanted.

Appreciate the Joys of Day-to-Day Living

A major obstacle to happiness is **hedonic adaptation**—the tendency to adapt to regard exciting new aspects of life as routine after a while.[25] Imagine a person who wants a luxurious lifestyle finally purchases a fiftieth-story condominium penthouse overlooking a harbor. At first the view is breathtaking, yet after a while looking at the harbor becomes routine. To overcome the hedonic adaptation you therefore have to learn to appreciate the joys of day-to-day living. The essence of being a happy person is to savor what you have right now. As Benjamin Franklin said, "Happiness is produced not so much by great pieces of good fortune that seldom happen as by the little advantages that occur every day."

Part of the same key to happiness is the ability to live in the present without undue worry about the future or dwelling on past mistakes. Be on guard against becoming so preoccupied with planning your life that you neglect to enjoy the happiness of the moment.

Hedonic adaptation
the tendency to adapt to regard exciting new aspects of life as routine after a while

Human Relations Self-Assessment Quiz   4-2

The Core Self-Evaluation Scale

Below are several statements about you with which you may agree or disagree. Using the response scale below, indicate your agreement or disagreement with each item by placing the appropriate number on the line preceding that item.

1	2	3	4	5
Strongly Disagree	Disagree	Neutral	Agree	Strongly Agree

1. _____ I am confident I get the success I deserve.
2. _____ Sometimes I feel depressed.
3. _____ When I try, I generally succeed.
4. _____ Sometimes when I fail, I feel worthless.
5. _____ I complete tasks successfully.
6. _____ Sometimes, I do not feel in control of my work.
7. _____ Overall, I am satisfied with myself.
8. _____ I am filled with doubts about my competence.
9. _____ I determine what will happen in my life.
10. _____ I do not feel in control of my success in my career.
11. _____ I am capable of coping with most of my problems.
12. _____ There are times when things look pretty bleak and hopeless to me.

_____ Total Score

Scoring and Interpretation:

The scoring for items 1, 3, 5, 7, 9, and 11 proceeds as follows: 5, 4, 3, 2, 1 to indicate a positive attitude toward yourself. The scoring for questions 2, 4, 6, 8, 10, and 12 proceeds as follows: 1, 2, 3, 4, 5 to indicate a positive attitude toward yourself. Add all your scores to attain your total score. The higher the score, the more positive your attitude toward yourself. Scores of 48 and higher suggest a very positive attitude, scores between 37 and 47 suggest a neutral attitude, and scores between 12 and 35 indicate a negative attitude toward yourself. The mean score for several different groups of people, including working adults and students, is 45.

Source: Timothy A. Judge, Amir Erez, Joyce E. Bono, and Carl J. Thoresen, "The Core Self-Evaluation Scale: Development of a Measure," *Personnel Psychology,* Summer 2003, p. 315. This measure is nonproprietary (free) and may be used without permission.

Be Fair, Kind, and Helpful, and Trust Others

The Golden Rule is a true contributor to happiness. It is also important to practice charity and forgiveness. Helping others brings personal happiness. Knowing that you are able to make a contribution to the welfare of others gives you a continuing sense of satisfaction and happiness. Related to fairness and kindness is trust of others. Happy people have open, warm, and friendly attitudes.

Have Recreational Fun in Your Life

A happy life is characterized by fun, zest, joy, and delight. When you create time for fun (in addition to the fun in many kinds of work), you add an important element to your personal happiness. But if you devote too much time to play, you will lose out on the fun of work accomplishments. In choosing fun activities, avoid overplanning.

Because novelty contributes to happiness, be ready to pursue an unexpected opportunity or to try something different.

Learn to Cope with Grief, Disappointment, Setbacks, and Stress

To be happy, you must learn how to face problems that occur in life without being overwhelmed or running away. It is also important to persevere in attempting to overcome problems rather than to whine or engage in self-pity. Once you have had to cope with problems, you will be more able to appreciate the day-to-day joys of life. An example of an everyday problem that ranks high on the misery list is lengthy commutes to work, by private or public transportation.[26] If you cannot change the length of the commute for now, find ways to make commuting more enjoyable, such as finding a radio station that provides information useful for your professional growth or is simply enjoyable.

Live with What You Cannot Change

Happiness guru Martin Seligman says that attempting to change conditions unlikely to change sets us up for feeling depressed about failing. Weight loss is a prime example. Nineteen out of twenty people regain weight they lost. It is, therefore, better to worry less about weight loss and concentrate on staying in good physical condition by engaging in moderate exercise. Good condition contributes much more to health than does achieving a weight standard set primarily to achieve an aesthetic standard. You can then concentrate on being happy about your good physical condition instead of being unhappy about your weight.[27]

Energize Yourself through Physical Fitness

Engage in regular physical activity, such as dancing or sports that make you aerobically fit. Whether it is the endorphins released by exercise, dopamine released by the excitement, or simply the relaxed muscles, physical fitness fosters happiness. Another important part of energizing yourself is to attain adequate rest. Happy people invest time in revitalizing sleep and solitude.

Satisfy Your Most Important Values

Based on a survey of more than six thousand individuals, social psychologist Steven Reiss concluded that people cannot find lasting happiness by aiming to have more fun or seeking pleasure. Instead, you have to satisfy your basic values or desires and take happiness in passing. To increase your value-based happiness, you have to first identify your most important desires and then gear your life toward satisfying these values. Among these key values are curiosity, physical activity, honor, power, family, status, and romance.[28] For example, if power and romance are two of your basic values, you can achieve happiness only if your life is amply provided with power and romance. Religion also fits into the realm of values, and religious people tend to be happier than nonreligious people.[29]

To attain happiness by living your values, you first have to know what your values are. Physician and happiness counselor Russ Harris suggests that you answer the following question to identify your key values: "Imagine you could wave a magic wand to ensure that you would have the approval and admiration of everyone on the planet, forever. What, in this case, would you choose to do with your life?"[30] (The topic of values will be explored in Chapter 5.)

Earn Enough Money to Avoid Feeling Miserable

The role of money as a contributor to happiness is the subject of endless debate. Money cannot buy happiness, but having enough money to purchase the things that make you happy is important. Whether an iPod or a penthouse condominium with a view of the water would make you happy, they both require money—even though the amounts differ. However, the pursuit of money for its own sake is less likely to contribute to happiness.

According to Arthur C. Brooks, a professor at the Syracuse University Maxwell School of Public Affairs, some research by economists suggests that people with a lot of money tend to express a higher degree of subjective happiness than people with very little. Data from the National Opinion Research Center indicate that people in the top 20 percent income bracket are about 50 percent more likely to say they are "very happy" than people in the bottom 20 percent. Those in the higher bracket are also about half as likely to say they are "not too happy."[31, 32]

Another consideration is that not being able to pay for what you consider a necessity may lead to low self-esteem and unhappiness. Even if a person does not equate money with happiness, having a car repossessed or a house foreclosed contributes to at least a temporary state of unhappiness. Yet despite this obvious truth, many people in poor countries are happy. For example, surveys taken over a twenty-year period indicate that the Inuit people of northern Greenland score an average of 5.8 on a scale of 1 to 7 in response to a question about life satisfaction. Survey respondents on the list of the *Forbes* magazine wealthiest 400 also averaged 5.8 on the same scale.[33] People in rich countries are not consistently happier than people in poor countries. Yet the underlying principle could be the same. As long as you have enough money to pay for what you consider to be necessities, money is not a factor in your happiness.

Lead a Meaningful Life

Most of the principles previously stated, as well as the spheres-of-life happiness model, all point toward the conclusion that having a meaningful life is a major contributor to happiness. A meaning or an important purpose helps a person get through periodic annoyances that temporarily lower happiness. Seligman says that the ultimate level of happiness is the meaningful life. It consists of identifying your core strengths and then using them in the services of something you perceive to be bigger than you are.[34] For example, if you are a greeting card designer and you perceive that you are contributing to improved personal relationships, you are likely to be happy.

THE FIVE PRINCIPLES OF PSYCHOLOGICAL FUNCTIONING

According to clinical psychologist Richard Carlson, the best way to achieve inner serenity (or happiness) is to follow the five principles of psychological functioning.[35] These principles act as guides toward achieving a feeling of inner happiness. The first is *thinking*, which creates the psychological experience of life. Feelings come about only after you thought about something or somebody. If you think of another person as attractive, it will lead to a warm feeling toward that person. People who learn to direct their thinking in positive directions will contribute to their own happiness. Remember that you produce your own thoughts.

The second principle is *moods*, meaning that the positive or negative content of your thinking fluctuates from moment to moment and day to day. Practice ignoring your low (bad) moods rather than analyzing them, and you will see how quickly they vanish. Developing this skill will contribute substantially to healthy psychological functioning. The third principle is *separate psychological realities*. Because each person thinks in a unique way, everyone lives in a separate psychological reality. Accept the idea that others think differently from you, and you will have much more compassion and fewer quarrels. As a result, you will be happier. Also, if you accept the principle of separate realities, you will waste less time attempting to change people. At the same time, others will like you more, thus contributing to your happiness.

The fourth principle of psychological functioning is *feelings.* Combined with emotions, feelings are a built-in feedback mechanism that tells us how we are doing psychologically. If your feelings turn negative suddenly, you know that your thinking is dysfunctional. It is then time to make a mental readjustment. If you feel discontented, for example, it is necessary to clear the head and start thinking positively. As a consequence, you will experience contentment and happiness. A key point is that the person will maintain a sense of well-being as long as he or she does not focus on personal concerns.

The fifth principle is *the present moment.* Learning to pay attention to the present moment and to your feelings enables people to live at peak efficiency without the distraction of negative thinking. Much like the flow experience, the present moment is where people find happiness and inner peace. Carlson advises, "The only way to experience genuine and lasting contentment, satisfaction, and happiness is to learn to live your life in the present moment."[36]

Concept Review
and Reinforcement

Emotional intelligence, 94
Self-awareness, 94
Self-management, 94
Social awareness, 94
Relationship management, 94
Emotional contagion, 96
Attitude, 98

Cognitive component
(of attitude), 98
Affective component
(of attitude), 98
Behavioral component
(of attitude), 99
Cognitive dissonance, 99

Organizational citizenship behavior
(OCB), 103
Personal support, 103
Hedonic adaptation, 107

Summary and Review

Emotional intelligence generally refers to how effectively a person makes constructive use of his or her emotions. The four key components of emotional intelligence are

1. Self-awareness (understanding the self)
2. Self-management (emotional control)
3. Social awareness (includes empathy and intuition)
4. Relationship management (includes interpersonal skills)

Demonstrating good emotional intelligence is impressive because it contributes to performing well in the difficult area of dealing with feelings. Another positive consequence of emotional intelligence is that if you know how to project positive emotion you will spread those positive feelings to others in the workplace. In some situations it will be helpful to be aware of possible cross-cultural differences in what constitutes effective emotional intelligence.

The combination of biological endowment and training will enable most people to enhance their emotional intelligence.

Attitudes are complex, having three components

1. Cognitive (knowledge or beliefs)
2. Affective (emotional)
3. Behavioral (how a person acts)

Cognitive dissonance occurs when the three components are not consistent with each other. Attitudes are formed based on experience, including receiving instruction from another person, conditioning, and cognitions (the way we think about something). The trait of optimism versus pessimism influences attitudes

strongly. A worker who maintains a genuine positive attitude will accrue many benefits, yet being too positive can have disadvantages.

Attitudes can be changed by reversing the process by which they were formed. Looking at the positive or negative aspect of a situation can also lead to attitude change. From the standpoint of management it is beneficial for employees to have positive attitudes and job satisfaction. Much of job satisfaction stems from good interpersonal relationships in the workplace. Organizational citizenship behavior is highly valued by employers because such attitudes can lead to improved product quality and quantity. Personal support is one aspect of organizational citizenship behavior and includes helping, courtesy, cooperating, and motivating.

Planning for happiness appears to be about 40 percent under a person's control. A practical way of understanding happiness is that it is a byproduct of having the spheres of life working in harmony and synchrony. For most people these spheres would be the following:

- Work and career
- Interpersonal life, including romance
- Physical and mental health
- Financial health
- Interests and pastimes
- Spiritual life or belief system

Contributors or keys to happiness include the following:

- Giving priority to happiness
- Developing and maintaining friendships with happy people

- Self-esteem
- Working hard at things enjoyed, and achieving the flow experience
- Appreciation of the joys of day-to-day living
- Fairness, kindness, helpfulness, and trust
- Recreational fun
- Coping with grief, disappointment, setbacks, and stress
- Living with what you cannot change
- Energizing yourself through physical fitness
- Satisfying your most important values
- Earning enough money to avoid feeling miserable

According to Richard Carlson, the best way to achieve inner serenity (or happiness) is to follow the five principles of psychological functioning.

- First is thinking which brings about feelings.
- Second is moods, including the idea that you can ignore bad moods.
- Third is separate psychological realities, meaning that each person thinks in a unique way.
- Fourth is feelings, which can be turned from negative to positive.
- Fifth is the present moment, which is where people find happiness and inner peace.

Check Your Understanding

1. What has one of your professors or instructors done recently to demonstrate good emotional intelligence in dealing with students?
2. Describe what a business executive, entertainer, or well-known athlete has done recently to demonstrate low emotional intelligence. Explain your reasoning.
3. Suppose the vast majority of company managers had high emotional intelligence. How might this fact give the company a competitive advantage?
4. Imagine yourself as a manager or team leader. What could you do to make positive use of emotional contagion with the people in your group?
5. How is a person supposed to maintain a positive attitude when major things in life are going wrong, such as a job loss, a personal bankruptcy, a broken relationship, or the premature death of a loved one?
6. What are some of the skills a person needs to acquire to become happy?
7. How do your "spheres of life" compare with those in Figure 4-5?
8. When you are happiest, are you more productive professionally/academically?
9. Why might being very happy prompt some people to become less competitive in their careers?
10. Happiness researchers agree that having a high income is not necessarily associated with happiness. Yet at the same time activities that bring happiness, such as dining in restaurants, or taking vacations with friends and family, require considerable money. How does a person resolve this conflict?

Web Corner

Emotional intelligence:
www.emotionalintelligence.com; www.eiconsortium.org

The Happiness Test:
www.pathwaytohappiness.com/happiness_test.htm

Positive attitudes:
www.attitudeiseverything.com.

Positive Psychology Center:
www.ppc.sas.upenn.edu

INTERNET SKILL BUILDER

Daily Doses of Happiness on the Web

Visit www.thehappyguy.com to receive your "daily dose of happiness." This site offers you happiness quotes and suggestions for self-actualization. The "Happy Guy" promises to help you achieve such ends as becoming inspired about life, discovering the meaning of happiness, and achieving personal growth. After trying out this program of happiness and personal growth, you be the judge. Have you made strides toward becoming happier? Do you feel any better emotionally? What impact do the Daily Happiness mugs have on your personal well-being? Be happy!

Developing Your Human Relations Skills

Applying Human Relations Exercise 4-1

Enhancing Your Emotional Intelligence

A realistic starting point in improving your emotional intelligence is to work with one of its four components at a time, such as the empathy aspect of social awareness. A complex behavior pattern or trait such as emotional intelligence takes considerable time to improve, but the time will most likely be a good investment. Follow these steps:

1. Begin by obtaining as much feedback as you can from people who know you. Ask them if they think you understand their emotional reactions and how well they think you understand them. It is helpful to ask someone from another culture or someone who has a severe disability how well you communicate with him or her. (A higher level of empathy is required to communicate well with somebody much different from you.) If you work with customers, ask them how well you appear to understand their position.
2. If you find any area of deficiency, work on that deficiency steadily. For example, perhaps you are not perceived as taking the time to understand a point of view quite different from your own. Attempt to understand other points of view. Suppose you believe strongly that only people with lots of money can be happy. Speak to a person with a different opinion and listen carefully until you understand that person's perspective.
3. At a minimum of a few weeks later, obtain more feedback about your ability to empathize. If you are making progress, continue to practice.
4. Prepare a document about your skill development. Describe the steps you took to enhance your empathy, the progress you made, and how people react differently to you now. For example, you might find that people talk more openly and freely with you now that you are more empathetic.
5. Then repeat these steps for another facet of emotional intelligence. As a result you will have developed another valuable interpersonal skill.

Applying Human Relations Exercise 4-2

Achieving Happiness

The following exercises will help you develop attitudes that contribute mightily to happiness.

1. **Start the day off right.** Begin each day with five minutes of positive thought and visualization. Commit to this for one week. When and how do you plan to fit this into your schedule?

_____

_____

_____

2. **Make a list of five virtues in which you believe.** Examples would include patience, compassion, and helping the less fortunate.

_____

_____

_____

3. **Each week, for the next five weeks, incorporate a different virtue into your life.** On a simple index card, write this week's virtue in bold letters, such as "helping the less fortunate." Post the card in a prominent place. After you have completed one incident of helping the less fortunate, describe in about ten to twenty-five words what you did. Also record the date and time.

_____

_____

_____

4. **Look for good things about new acquaintances.** List three students, customers, or coworkers you have just met. List three *positive* qualities about each.

_____

_____

_____

5. **List the positive qualities of fellow students or coworkers you dislike or have trouble working with.** Remember, keep looking for the good.

_____

_____

_____

6. **Think of school assignments or job tasks you dislike, and write down the merits of these tasks.** Identify the benefits they bring you.

_____

_____

_____

7. **Look at problems as opportunities.** What challenges are you now facing? In what way might you view them that would inspire and motivate you?

_____

_____

_____

Source: Adapted from Stu Kamen, "Turn Negatives into Positives," *Pryor Report Success Workshop*, May 1995, pp. 1–2.

Human Relations Class Activity

The World's Happiest Person

Hundreds of thousands of articles and Web sites have been devoted to the subject of the world's happiest, man, woman, or person. Class time and resources most likely prohibit you from searching the globe for that person, but you and your classmates can search for that person in your classroom. If you are taking this course online, the work can be accomplished by e-mail or course Web site.

After about five minutes of reflection, each class member should decide whether he or she is totally happy, or almost totally happy. Several class members who feel that they might qualify for the title of World's Happiest Person (at least who comes closest within this classroom) volunteer to explain why to the rest of the class. Candidates for the Happiest Person category will make about a three-minute presentation of precisely why they feel so happy. As you listen to these presentations, attempt to identify any of the principles of happiness covered in this chapter.

After the presentations are completed, spend a few minutes looking for trends to arrive at a few conclusions. For discussion points, you might complete these sentences:

1. All the happy people seem to think that _____.
2. I notice that each candidate for the World's Happiest Person seemed to _____.
3. A difference I noticed between me and the volunteers (or between me and the rest of the volunteers) is that _____.
4. In terms of the candidates smiling, I noticed that _____.

The conclusions you reach can become information for class discussion. Look to see if many class members arrived at similar conclusions—perhaps in response to the four questions.

Human Relations Case Study 4-1

The Very Positive Kelly Malibu

Kelly Malibu, twenty-seven, is the manager of Deco, a woman's store that features clothing with an art deco design. Deco is one of several specialty retail stores owned by Max and Mary Lowenstein. When the store opened

three years ago, Malibu was hired as the manager. Max Lowenstein said, "Kelly was a wonderful fit. She had retailing in her blood, having worked at women's stores since age seventeen. She also had supervisory experience and is so upbeat. Our one concern was that she might be too nice to be a tough boss when needed."

Malibu is responsible for merchandising. Twice a year she makes trips to New York to buy designs imported from Asia in bulk, and she also purchases some clothing online. Malibu contends that the most difficult part of her responsibilities is dealing with employees and customers. "When I deal with vendors, things usually go pretty smoothly," she says. "The vendors are usually trying to please me. We sometimes haggle a little bit about price, but we can usually work out a deal. We have the occasional dispute about returning merchandise that we cannot sell. I know that some big retailers insist on a generous return policy."

"My attitude is that our vendors are themselves small outfits operating on slim margins. So I hate to cut too deeply into their profits. If we can't sell a few dresses at Deco unless we practically give them away, it's as much my fault as that of the manufacturer or distributor. I guessed wrong on what our clientele wants. Max and Mary don't agree with my philosophy 100 percent, but they do respect my right to manage the store as I see fit."

Malibu notes that keeping her store associates productive and happy can be a challenge. Deco has two full-time associates and three part-time associates. One challenge is that her part-time associates make frequent requests for a change of schedule to fit their personal life or school demands. A recent Columbus Day was a good example of this problem.

She says, "Columbus Day is usually one of our best days outside of the holiday season. So I wanted to make sure we had two part-time sales associates on board to supplement the two full-time associates." Three days before Columbus Day, Tracy, one of the part-timers, told her she had to complete a mammoth project for her computer science class, so she wouldn't be able to work that day. "My instinct was to tell Tracy that if she couldn't be here on Columbus Day, she could set sail for another job. Then I thought of my own experiences in college. A computer science project can suck up all your mental energy and make it difficult to concentrate on anything else. So I let Tracy off the hook.

"Kim, another one of our associates, said she would be out of town for her brother's wedding. She had given me two month's notice about the wedding, so I couldn't insist that she be here. Bruce, another one of our associates, said he couldn't work on Columbus Day because he would be running a marathon. My first thoughts were to tell Bruce that running a marathon was no excuse for missing work. However, as I thought it through I realized that completing a marathon would add considerably to Bruce's self-esteem. As a result, I simply wished Bruce the best of luck in the marathon. I know that Bruce appreciated my understanding.

"That left me with one sales associate, Nicki, who could work on Columbus Day. I made up for one of the missing sales associates with my mom, who isn't a bad last-minute substitute.

"My biggest hassle with customers is when they want to see the manager because of a dispute with the associate about a return. You know that quite often they bought the dress, blouse, or suit with the intention of using it for a special occasion and then returning it for a full refund. I usually go along with the return as a way of building customer goodwill. But I have my limits. No returns when clothing has food or perspiration stains."

Questions

1. In what way does Malibu demonstrate empathy?

2. In what way does Malibu demonstrate a positive attitude?

3. To what extent do you think Malibu would be a more effective manager if she were less empathic and positive?

Human Relations Role-Playing Exercise

Empathizing with Tracy

Human Relations Case Study 4-1 serves as the background information and storyline for this role-playing exercise. One person plays the role of Kelly Malibu, the store manager of Deco. She has made her staffing plans for Columbus Day, in anticipation of heavy store traffic over the holiday. Kelly wants to have two part-timers on board to supplement the two full-time associates. Three days before Columbus Day, Tracy, one of the part-timers, told her that she has to complete a mammoth project for her computer science class, so she wouldn't be able to work that day. Another student plays the role of Tracy, who wants her job at Deco, but she also wants to receive a good grade in her computer science class.

Kelly wants to demonstrate good emotional intelligence, including empathy and emotional control, yet she also wants the store to be properly staffed. Tracy expects Kelly to understand her predicament.

For both scenarios, observers rate the role-players on two dimensions, using a 1 to 5 scale from very poor to very good. One dimension is "effective use of human relations techniques." The second dimension is "acting ability." A few observers might voluntarily provide feedback to the role-players in terms of sharing their ratings and observations. The course instructor might also provide feedback.

Human Relations Case Study 4-2

Alex Explodes in Anger

Alex worked as an accountant in the fraud investigation unit of the welfare department of a state government. He said that one of the things he liked about his job was that he was indirectly helping people in need. Although he was not dealing directly with welfare clients, he helped the state uncover fraud in providing financial assistance to hordes of people. Alex reasoned that when fraudulent applications for public assistance are uncovered, more money is available for families that really need the money. One such case Alex helped uncover involved a woman making $30,000 per year selling stolen electronics goods on her Web site, yet she claimed to be unemployed.

Although Alex did not have major problems with his coworkers and management, he incurred some difficulties. He would become quite irritated when his work was interrupted by an e-mail message or a phone call from a work associate. He would often respond in writing: "I can't answer you now. I'm busy with something important." By phone he would respond in an abrupt tone: "Call me later. I'm busy now."

One day Alex came to work in a particularly bad mood. He smashed the bumper on his car by backing into a two-foot-high guard rail in a parking lot, he had a fight with his girlfriend, and his favorite NFL team was eliminated from the playoffs. The same day, Alex was due for a performance and salary review. Marilyn, his supervisor, told him that he would not be receiving merit pay because he was a poor team player. (Merit pay is a bonus for good performance beyond a cost-of-living adjustment.) Alex became red in the face and explained that he was one of the most valuable people in the agency because his detection of fraud saved the agency over $500,000 during the past year. Alex left the evaluation interview without even saying thank you or goodbye to Marilyn.

Before leaving the office, Alex sent an e-mail to Marilyn with distribution to every e-mail account in the agency, with the subject line, "Getting Ripped Off." The rest of the e-mail explained in a couple of hundred words how much he had contributed to the agency and how because of office politics he was not receiving merit pay.

Still feeling mistreated when he returned home, Alex made in the following entry in his blog:

Our investigation unit should be investigated itself. I have personally found five instances in which state funds are being diverted to personal use. Did you know that our director uses a state limousine for trips to race tracks and gambling casinos? Did you know that three of the officials in our department ran up a $650 tab at a fancy restaurant and charged it to the state as a business expense?

Two hours after Alex arrived at the office the next morning, Marilyn and the agency head came to his cubicle to tell Alex he was immediately suspended from his job because of insubordination. Also, a strong recommendation was being made to the state review board that he be fired and never allowed to work for the state again. As he left the office, Alex said angrily, "Don't you guys believe in free speech?"

Questions

1. Which aspects of low emotional intelligence did Alex display?

2. How justified is Alex's suspension along with the recommendation for termination?

3. You be the career coach: What can Alex do to patch the problems he has created with his career?

REFERENCES

1. Case researched by Jacqueline Jakus, January 2009.
2. Quoted in "Leading by Feel: Be Realistic," *Harvard Business Review*, January 2004, p. 28.
3. Daniel Goleman, Richard Boyatzis, and Annie McKee, "Primal Leadership: The Hidden Driver of Great Performance," *Harvard Business Review*, December 2001, pp. 42–51.
4. David A. Morand, "The Emotional Intelligence of Managers: Assessing the Construct Validity of a Nonverbal Measure of 'People Skills,'" *Journal of Business and Psychology*, Fall 2001, pp. 21–23.
5. Stefanie K. Johnson, "I Second That Emotion: Effects of Emotional Contagion and Affect at Work on Leader and Follower Outcomes," *Leadership Quarterly*, February 2008, p. 2.
6. Peter J. Jordan, Neal M. Ashkanasy, and Charmine E. J. Hartel, "Emotional Intelligence as a Moderator of Emotional and Behavioral Reactions to Job Insecurity," *Academy of Management Review*, July 2002, pp. 361–372.
7. "Leading by Feel: Train the Gifted," *Harvard Business Review*, January 2004, p. 31.
8. This is one of the major themes from Kevin R. Murphy, ed., *A Critique of Emotional Intelligence: What Are the Problems and How Can They Be Fixed?* (Mahwah, NJ: Lawrence Erlbaum, 2006).
9. Based to some extent on information synthesized in Dodge Fernald, *Psychology* (Upper Saddle River, NJ: Prentice Hall, 1997), pp. 562–563.
10. L. A. Burke and L. A. Witt, "Personality and High-Maintenance Employee Behavior," *Journal of Business and Psychology*, Spring 2004, pp. 349–363.
11. Timothy A. Judge and Remus Ilies, "Is Positiveness in Organizations Always Desirable?" *Academy of Management Executive*, November 2004, 152.
12. Ibid., pp. 153–155.
13. Judith Sills, "Take This Job and Love It," *Psychology Today*, November/December 2008, pp. 58–59.
14. "The 100 Best Companies to Work for 2008," pp. 61–94; Robert Levering and Milton Moskowitz, "The 100 Best Companies to Work for 2009: And the Winners Are . . ." *Fortune*, February 2, 2009, pp. 67–78.
15. Frederick P. Morgeson and Stephen E. Humphrey, "The Work Design Questionnaire (WDQ): Developing and Validating a Comprehensive Measure for Assessing Job Design and the Nature of Work," *Journal of Applied Psychology*, November 2006, pp. 1321–1339.
16. Mark C. Ehrant and Stefanie E. Nauman, "Organizational Citizenship Behavior in Work Groups: A Group Norms Approach," *Journal of Applied Psychology*, December 2004, pp. 960–974.
17. Nicole M. Dudley and Jose M. Cortina, "Knowledge and Skills That Facilitate the Personal Support Dimension of Citizenship," *Journal of Applied Psychology*, November 2008, pp. 1249–1270.
18. Research reported in "So What Do You Have to Do to Find Happiness?" *Sunday Times Magazine*, available at www.timesonline.co.uk, October 2, 2005; Amy Novotney, "The Happiness Diet: Sonjya Lyubomirsky Argues that Limiting Overthinking Can Improve Our Emotional Well-Being," *Monitor on Psychology*, April 2008, pp. 24–25.
19. Carlin Flora, "The Pursuit of Happiness," *Psychology Today*, January/February 2009, pp. 60–69.
20. The major sources of information for this list are Mihaly Csikzentmihalyi, "Finding Flow," *Psychology Today*, July/August 1997, pp. 46–48, 70–71; Flora, "The Pursuit of Happiness," pp. 60–69; Richard Corliss, "Is There a Formula for Joy?" *Time*, January 20, 2003, pp. 72–74; David G. Meyers, "Pursuing Happiness," *Psychology Today*, available at www.psychologytoday.com/articles; retrieved March 1, 2006; Martin Seligman, *What You Can Change and What You Can't* (New York: Knopf, 1994).
21. Cited in Novotney, "The Happiness Diet," p. 24.
22. Study cited in Alice Park, "The Happiness Effect. How Emotions and Even Behaviors Can Spread Like an Epidemic," *Time*, December 22, 2008; Maggie Fox, "Happiness Is Contagious, Study Finds," *Scientific American*, www.sciam.com. Accessed December 5, 2008.
23. Quoted in George Melloan, "The Rich Are Getting Richer, but So Are Others," *Wall Street Journal*, December 23, 2003, p. A15.
24. David T. Lykken, *Happiness: What Studies on Twins Show Us about Nature, Nurture, and Happiness Set Point* (New York: Golden Books, 1999), p. 67.
25. Jonathan Clements, "The Pursuit of Happiness: Six Experts Tell What They've Done to Achieve It," *Wall Street Journal*, December 6, 2006, p. D1.
26. Clements, "The Pursuit of Happiness," p. D1.
27. Martin Seligman, "Don't Diet, Be Happy," *USA Weekend*, February 4–6, 1994, p. 12.
28. Steven Reiss, "Secrets of Happiness," *Psychology Today*, January/February 2001, pp. 50–52, 55–56.
29. Corliss, "Is There a Formula for Joy?" p. 74.
30. Quoted in Flora, "The Pursuit of Happiness," p. 69.
31. Arthur C. Brooks, "Money Buys Happiness," *Wall Street Journal*, December 8, 2005, p. A16.
32. Jonathan Clements, "Money and Happiness: Here's Why You Won't Laugh All the Way to the Bank," *Wall Street Journal*, August 16, 2006, p. D1.
33. Sharon Begley, "Wealth and Happiness Don't Necessarily Go Hand in Hand," *Wall Street Journal* (Science Journal), August 13, 2004, p. B1.
34. Quoted in Corliss, "Is There a Formula for Joy?" p. 74.
35. Richard Carlson, *You Can Be Happy No Matter What: Five Principles Your Therapist Never Told You*, revised edition (Novato, CA: New World Library, 1997).
36. Ibid., p. 71.

5
Values and Ethics

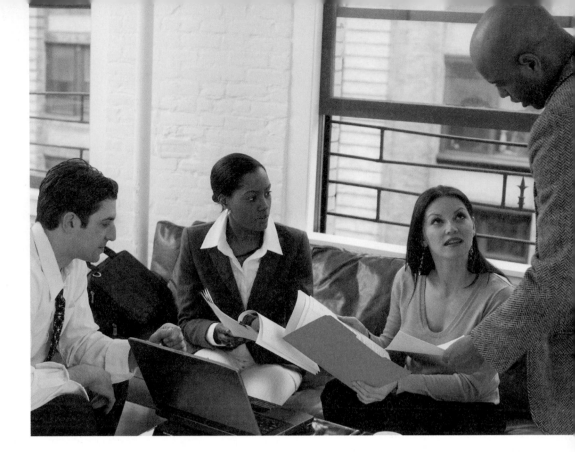

Outline

1 In What Way Are Values a Part of Understanding Human Relations?
How Values Are Learned
The Classification and Clarification of Values
The Mesh between Individual and Job Values

2 Why Be Concerned About Business Ethics?
Why Being Ethical Isn't Easy
The Extent of Ethical Problems
Frequent Ethical Dilemmas

3 What Are Some Guidelines for Making Ethical Decisions and Behaving Ethically?
Developing the Right Character Traits
Using a Guide to Ethical Decision Making
Developing Strong Relationships with Work Associates
Using Corporate Ethics Programs
Follow an Ethical Role Model in the Company
Follow an Applicable Code of Professional Conduct

A ndrew Ajello, a regional sales executive in the eastern United States for Danish diabetes-drug maker Novo Nordisk AS, embraces an increasingly popular management theory: To improve productivity, treat workers of different ages differently.

Ajello persuaded his employer to let young sales reps drive Jeeps, while keeping traditional sedans for others. He highlights team results over individual members so that team-oriented twenty-somethings feel part of a group effort. He hires consultants to train managers on generational issues and asks managers to discuss their own experiences at meetings.

Ajello now heads a group of about 650 people, including substantial portions of boomers, Generation Xers, and those from Generation Y, and he sees plenty of potential for generational conflict. Many of his reps, for example, report to younger bosses.

At one point in his career, half of Ajello's sales reps were Generation Xers, who according to a book he read, tend to dislike bureaucracy and formality. His first target was voice mail. At the time, most managers communicated with staffers through mass voice mails. Ajello found that it was alienating his Gen X reps.

Instead of voice mails, he started holding casual weekly meetings at 5 p.m. Over sodas and chicken wings, he gathered the reps, asked how they were doing, and shared tips and news. Younger reps relished the informal environment. But Ajello appealed to the competitive streak in older reps by singling out top performers. He reassured one worried thirty-year veteran, telling him, "You're the expert in what you do." Both groups responded well: Sales improved.

Ajello also changed the format of sales performance emails he sent to the team. The messages typically started by ranking each salesperson's performance. But he feared the competition would offend team-oriented twenty-somethings. So Ajello started each email with a message about group success, and he thanked everyone for their contribution. Then he listed the sales results to please the competitive boomers.[1]

Learning Objectives ▶

After studying the information and doing the exercises in this chapter, you should be able to:

1 Understand the nature of values and how they are learned.

2 Be able to classify values and explain generational differences in values.

3 Pinpoint the nature of value clarification and how the meshing of individual and organizational values is important.

4 Understand the importance of business ethics, the difficulty of being ethical, and the extent of ethical problems in business.

5 Identify workplace situations that often present ethical dilemmas.

6 Follow the guidelines for making ethical decisions and behaving ethically.

The story about the pharmaceutical company sales executive illustrates how it is possible to make the workplace more productive and satisfying when differences in generational values are taken into account. In this chapter we study values, an important force contributing to a person's level of ethical behavior, as well as ethics. Values and ethics are foundation topics in human relations because our values and ethics influence how we treat others and how we are treated in return.

▶ Learning Objective 1 ▶

In What Way Are Values a Part of Understanding Human Relations?

Value
the importance a person attaches to something; values are also tied to the enduring belief that one's mode of conduct is better than another mode of conduct

Ethics
the moral choices a person makes

Morals
an individual's or a society's determination of what is right and wrong

One group of factors influencing how a person behaves on the job is that person's values and beliefs. A **value** refers to the importance a person attaches to something. Values are also tied to the enduring belief that one's mode of conduct is better than another mode of conduct. If you believe that good interpersonal relations are the most important part of your life, your humanistic values are strong. Similarly, you may think that people who are not highly concerned about interpersonal relations have poor values.

Values are closely tied in with **ethics**—the moral choices a person makes. A person's values influence which kinds of behaviors he or she believes are ethical. Ethics converts values into action. A business owner who highly values money and profits might not find it unethical to raise prices higher than needed to cover additional costs. A corporate executive who strongly values family life might suggest that the company invest company funds in an on-premises dependent-care center. Another concept that ties in closely with values and ethics is **morals,** which are an individual's or a society's determination of what is right or wrong. Your morals are influenced by your values. If you value truth telling, for example, you would consider it immoral to lie to a coworker.

HOW VALUES ARE LEARNED

People are not born with a particular set of values. Instead, people acquire values in the process of growing up, and many values are learned by the age of four. One important way we acquire values is through observing others, or modeling. Models can be teachers, friends, brothers, sisters, and even public figures. If we identify with a particular person, the probability is high that we will develop some of his or her major values, such as those of a parent, instructor, or coach.

Given that values are acquired in the process of growing up, your culture influences your values, as will be explained more in detail in Chapter 13. For now, consider this illustration. People growing up in a Malaysian culture, as well as other Far East cultures, learn to value age, hierarchy, and wisdom. When meeting the seventy-year-old CEO of his company, the young Malaysian customer service rep might say, "Sir, I am honored to have the opportunity to speak with you and benefit from your wisdom." In contrast, a young American worker might say, "Hi, Joe. How's it going?" (Of course, we are exaggerating a stereotype.)

Another major way values are learned is through the communication of attitudes. The attitudes that we hear expressed directly or indirectly help shape our values. Assume that using credit to purchase goods and services was considered an evil practice among your family and friends. You might, therefore, hold negative values about installment purchases.

Unstated but implied attitudes may also shape your values. If key people in your life showed a lack of enthusiasm when you talked about work accomplishments, you might not place such a high value on achieving outstanding results. If, however, your family and friends centered their lives on their careers, you might develop similar values. (Or, you might rebel against such a value because it interfered with a more relaxed lifestyle.) Many key values are also learned through religion and thus become the basis for society's morals. For example, most religions emphasize treating other people fairly and kindly. To "knife somebody in the back" is considered immoral both on and off the job.

Later Life Influences on Values

Although many core values are learned early in life, our values continue to be shaped by events late in life. The media, including dissemination of information about popular culture, influence the values of many people throughout their lives. The aftermath of Hurricane Katrina intensified a belief in the value of helping less fortunate people. Volunteers from throughout the United States invested time, money, and energy into helping rebuild New Orleans and several other Gulf Coast cities. Influential people, such as NBA players, were seen on television building houses for Katrina victims. Such publicity sent a message that helping people in need is a value worth considering.

The current publicity given to building a sustainable environment, or "being green," has shaped the values of countless thousands of people throughout the world. Many people regard being green as an important value and are attracted to business firms, such as Ford Motor Company, that have a green agenda. William C. Ford Jr., the executive chairman at Ford, said this about Barack Obama shortly before the latter's inauguration: "One of the things I feel very encouraged about is the president-elect and where he'd like to take this country in terms of energy, and I completely buy into his vision."[2]

The media, particularly advertisements, can also encourage the development of values that are harmful to a person intent on developing a professional career. People featured in advertisements for consumer products, including snack food, beer, and vehicles, often flaunt rudeness and sloppy grammar. The message comes across to many people that such behavior is associated with success.

Changes in technology can also change our values. As the world has become increasingly digitized, more and more people come to value a *digital lifestyle* as the normal way of life. The changes in values lead to curious changes in the behavior of people. Eastman Kodak Co. chair and chief executive Antonio Perez commented on how people have shifted away from storing prints of photos in shoeboxes, thereby being in danger of losing many important memories. Perez said, "As much as we complain about the old shoebox, it was brilliant. Because it was just a matter of going through the attic. This is going to be a lot more difficult in digital, as you all know. Formats are going to change. Hard drives will crash."[3] Of course, people who truly value stored memories can make prints.

The Influence of Company Values

Values can sometimes be learned later in life when we are introduced to values that did not capture our attention earlier. It is possible that the teaching and demands of an employer will help us acquire new values. A relevant example is the effort and time IBM invests in teaching company values to employees. Several years ago chairman, president, and CEO Sam Palmisano wanted to update company values at IBM. He spearheaded an effort called ValuesJam in which more than one thousand employees contributed information about the company's values into a Web site. After analyzing more than 1 million words of input, three new values emerged for IBM:

- Dedication to every client's success

- Innovation that matters—for our company and the world (such as using software to help develop new disease-fighting drugs)

- Trust and personal responsibility in all relationships[4]

IBM employees at every level are expected to incorporate these values into interaction with coworkers and customers. A sales representative when meeting a

FIGURE 5-1

THE MISSION AND VALUES
OF MICROSOFT CORPORATION

Our Mission

At Microsoft, our mission and values are to help people and businesses throughout the world realize their full potential.

Our Values

As a company, and as individuals, we value integrity, honesty, openness, personal excellence, constructive self-criticism, continual self-improvement, and mutual respect. We are committed to our customers and partners and have a passion for technology. We take on big challenges and pride ourselves on seeing them through. We hold ourselves accountable to our customers, shareholders, partners, and employees by honoring our commitments, providing results, and striving for the highest quality.

Questions

1. Based on your knowledge of Microsoft, how well do company practices match up to their values?
2. If you were (or are) a Microsoft employee, how would (or do) these values inspire you toward ethical behavior and high performance?

Source: www.microsoft.com/mscorp/mission.

customer might say to himself or herself, "What IBM product or service might help this company be more successful," rather than, "What IBM product or service can I sell this company so I can meet my sales quota?" Figure 5-1 presents another example of company values that are supposed to guide employee behavior.

Another value that individuals may acquire as a result of being part of an organization is *corporate spiritualism*. This type of spiritualism takes place when management is just as concerned about nurturing employee well-being as they are about profits. A practice such as a work/life program contributes to this style of corporate spiritualism.[5] The purpose of a work/life program is to make it easier for workers to effectively manage both work and personal life responsibilities. Flexible working hours and dependent-care assistance are prime examples, but even the presence of a dry cleaner on company premises can help workers balance the demands of work and personal life.

THE CLASSIFICATION AND CLARIFICATION OF VALUES

Because values can be related to anything we believe in, a large number of values exist. Several attempts have been made to classify values, and each one is closely tied to psychological needs. If you value something strongly, such as accomplishing worthwhile activities, it leads to a need such as achievement. If you value independence, it will most likely lead to a need for autonomy. The following classification of values involves needs and is linked to both career and personal life. The basis of the value classification is to categorize people into four types emphasizing different values and needs.[6]

- *Humanists* are driven primarily by a need for self-awareness, personal growth, and a sense of being individual and unique. Humanism is their most important value.

- *Strategists* highly value a sense of mastery and personal achievement. They are likely to say, "I am what I do." Strategists might believe that insight and understanding are important, but they place the highest value on tangible accomplishments.

- *Pragmatists* strive for a corner in the world anchored by power, influence, stability, and control. They search for roles and settings that provide them with formal power, respect, and prestige. A pragmatist, therefore, highly values career success in the traditional meaning of the term—high compensation and rank.

- *Adventurers* place low value on status and conformity. Instead, they have a powerful drive for excitement and adventure. The adventurer might say, "I don't want to play it safe. I want to play often and big. Play is good. Just do it." The adventurer has high standing on the traits of risk taking and thrill seeking.

Another key value that influences both work and personal life is *conscientiousness*. As a personality trait, conscientiousness is regarded as one of the basic components of personality. But the same trait also functions as a value, with the conscientious person striving to be industrious, well organized, self-controlling, responsible, traditional, and virtuous.[7] Dozens of studies have demonstrated that workers with a high standing on conscientiousness tend to perform well in a wide variety of positions.[8] As a result, employers look for conscientious workers when choosing among job candidates for both initial hiring and later promotion.

Generational Differences in Values

Differences in values among people often stem from age, or generational, differences. Workers older than fifty, in general, may have different values than people who are much younger. A subtle point, however, is that quite often generational values and attitudes we pick up at a certain age may persist for many years.[9] Assume that as a teenager and young adult, Jen develops a passion for using communication technology devices, as well as for living a balanced lifestyle (a fair balance between work and personal life). Although Jen has acquired these values early in life, the same values are likely to persist for many years. However, as Jen gets older she may become more risk averse, such as not changing jobs unless forced to and obeying speed limits—with the increased conservatism being linked to age rather than her generation.

Generational differences in values have often been seen as a clash between baby boomers and members of Generation X and Generation Y. According to the stereotype, boomers see Generation X and Generation Y as disrespectful of rules, not willing to pay their dues, and being disloyal to employers. Generation X and Generation Y see boomers as worshipping hierarchy (layers of authority), being overcautious, and wanting to preserve the status quo.

Figure 5-2 summarizes these stereotypes with the understanding that massive group stereotypes like this are only partially accurate because there are literally millions of exceptions. For example, many baby boomers are fascinated with communication technology, and many members of Generation Y like hierarchy. Also, you may have observed that many people in their fifties and sixties are so wedded to communication technology that they incessantly use their BlackBerry (or other brand of personal digital assistant) on and off the job. Now the vast majority of workers are tethered to communication technology, not just members of Generation X and Generation Y.

Expanding and clarifying the list of values the members of Generation Y emphasize are a fun work environment, opportunities for growth, and a wide range of projects on which to work. The same group, similar to career-oriented workers of all ages, wants opportunities to learn and develop new skills paid for by the company. In addition, the majority of Generation Y employees value friendly relationships among employees, including effective teamwork.[10]

Heather Huhman, a person who has mentored people seeking entry-level positions, offers a useful perspective for understanding value-based generational difference. She contends that earlier generations have developed negative stereotypes

"Above all, Gen Y is tech savvy. Their lifestyle is all about technology. They are consumed by entertainment and accomplished at multitasking."
—Elizabeth Gillespie, vice president of marketing for Jones Lang LaSalle Americas Inc., a real estate firm.

FIGURE 5-2 VALUE STEREOTYPES FOR SEVERAL GENERATIONS OF WORKERS

Baby Boomers (1946–1964)	Generation X (1965–1980)	Generation Y (1981–2002) Millennials
Uses technology as a necessary tool, but not obsessed with technology for its own sake	Techno-savvy	Techno-savvy, and even questions the value of standard IT techniques such as e-mail, with a preference for communications on a Web site
Appreciates hierarchy	Dislikes hierarchy	Dislikes hierarchy, prefers participation
Tolerates teams but values independent work	Teamwork very important	Teamwork very important
Strong career orientation	Strives for work–life balance but will work long hours for now; prefers flexible work schedule	Strives for work–life balance and may object to work interfering with personal life; expects flexible work schedule
More loyalty to organization	Loyalty to own career and profession	Loyalty to own career and profession and feels entitled to career goals
Favors diplomacy and tact	Candid in conversation	Quite direct in conversation
Seeks long-term employment	Will accept long-term employment if situation is right	Looks toward each company as a stepping stone to better job in another company
Believes that issues should be formally discussed	Believes that feedback can be administered informally and welcomes feedback	Believes that feedback can be given informally, even on the fly, and craves feedback
Somewhat willing to accept orders and suggestions	Often questions why things should be done in a certain way	Frequently asks why things should be done in a certain way, and asks a lot of questions
Willing to take initiative to establish starting and completion dates for projects	Slight preference for a manager to provide structure about project dates	Prefers structure on dates and other activities based on childhood of structured activities
Regards rewards as a positive consequence of good performance and seniority	Expects frequent rewards	Feels strong sense of entitlement to rewards, including promotions
Will multitask in front of work associates when it seems necessary	Feels comfortable in multitasking while interacting with work associates	Assumes that multitasking, including listening to music on earphones while dealing with work associates, is acceptable behavior

Note: Disagreement exists about which age brackets fit baby boomers, Generation X, and Generation Y, with both professional publications and dictionaries showing slight differences.

Sources: The majority of ideas in this table are from Robert McGarvey, "The Coming of Gen X Bosses," *Entrepreneur*, November 1999, pp. 60–64; Gregg Hammill, "Mixing and Managing Four Generations of Employees," *FDUMagazine Online*, Winter/Spring 2005, p. 5; Sommer Kehrli and Trudy Sopp, "Managing Generation Y: Stop Resisting and Start Embracing the Challenges Generation Y Brings to the Workplace," *HR Magazine*, May 2006, pp. 113–119; Ron Alsop, *The Trophy Kids Grow Up: How the Millennial Generation Is Shaking Up the Workforce* (San Francisco: Jossey-Bass/Wiley, 2008); Alsop, "Schools, Recruiters Try to Define Traits for Future Students," *Wall Street Journal*, February 14, 2006, p. B6; Kathryn Tyler, "Generation Gaps: Millennials May Be Out of Touch with the Basics of Workplace Behavior," *HR Magazine*, January 2008, pp. 69–72.

about Gen Y people and offers the following advice for members of Gen Y to overcome such stereotypes.[11]

Stereotype 1: *They are entitled.* Memorize the phrase, "What can I do to help?" Offering help to others helps overcome the stereotype of being self-centered. Another approach is to suggest something of benefit to the organization, and volunteer to develop it.

Stereotype 2: *They are needy for feedback.* Ask your manager how he or she likes to communicate, and follow that preference, such as by instant messaging rather than traditional e-mail, or vice versa. Make appointments to get the feedback you want instead of popping in unexpectedly.

Stereotype 3: *They have no work ethic.* Ask your supervisor to be specific about what he or she expects. The supervisor is likely to perceive the questioning as a sign of interest and commitment. At the same time you are likely to get the information you need to perform your job well.

Stereotype 4: *They are self-centered.* Show that you are a team player by being a good organizational citizen. (A team player is the opposite of being self-centered.) At the same time, displaying initiative and leadership will show that you want to help the company as well as coworkers.

Stereotype 5: *They are not loyal.* Be willing to commit to work, the job, and the team. Talk about projects and activities you have been committed to for a long time. Also, talk about responsibilities and positions in the company that you would like to pursue in the future.

Stereotype 6: *They are oblivious to time. (They dislike rigid time schedules even though they are willing to work extra-long hours on emergency projects.)* To overcome this stereotype, it is best to select a job that fits your own personal time clock, such as flexibility in doing some work offsite. Also, show some acceptance toward the attitude that all work should be conducted during traditional office hours.

Stereotype 7: *They lack manners.* Study the company culture to understand what level of politeness and manners are expected in dealing with superiors, coworkers, and customers. For example, is it appropriate to send e-mail attachments to coworkers without writing anything on the e-mail message itself? Are you expected to greet customers with a smile and establish eye contact?

Stereotype 8: *They resist policies they disagree with.* If you have a grievance about a particular policy, approach your supervisor to discuss the problem. For example, a Gen Y person might feel outraged about a policy that prohibits using company computers to shop online during working hours. Discussing this issue with the supervisor might help him or her understand the justification for the policy.

Stereotype 9: *Their helicopter parents are flying low overhead.* To combat this stereotype, avoid all references to parents when negotiating conditions of work, such as salary and benefits. Never make a statement like, "My father said this starting salary is too low."

Stereotype 10: *They lack presence when speaking (such as vocalized pauses and overuse of "like" and "you know").* Using a camcorder and or a speech coach, most people can learn to speak in a more refined and polished manner.

Although stereotypes do give us some general ideas, they can be insulting and patronizing. For example, many Gen Y people have highly polished speaking skills. At the same time, being a baby boomer does not automatically grant a person refined speaking skills.

Value Clarification

The values that you develop early in life are directly related to the kind of person you are and to the quality of the relationships you form.[12] Recognition of this fact has led to exercises designed to help people clarify and understand some of their own values. At times the values you clarify will match with the value categories previously listed, including company values and generational differences in values. At other times, your personal value list will be different. Human Relations Skill-Building Exercise 5-1 at the end of the chapter gives you an opportunity to clarify your values.

THE MESH BETWEEN INDIVIDUAL AND JOB VALUES

Under the best of circumstances, the values of employees mesh with those required by the job. When this state of congruence exists, job performance is likely to be high. Suppose that Jacquelyn strongly values giving people with limited formal education an opportunity to work and avoid being placed on welfare. So she takes a job as a manager of a dollar store that employs many people in their stores who would ordinarily have limited opportunity for employment. Jacquelyn is satisfied because she and her employer share a similar value.

Person–role conflict

the demands made by the organization or a superior clash with the basic values of the individual

When the demands made by the organization or a superior clash with the basic values of the individual, he or she suffers from **person–role conflict.** The individual wants to obey orders but does not want to perform an act that seems inconsistent with his or her values. A situation such as this might occur when an employee is asked to produce a product that he or she feels is unsafe or is of no value to society.

> *A manager of a commercial weight-reduction center resigned after two years of service. The owners pleaded with her to stay based on her excellent performance. The manager replied, "Sorry, I think my job is immoral. We sign up all these people with great expectations of losing weight permanently. Most of them do achieve short-term weight reduction. My conflict is that more than 90 percent of our clientele regain the weight they lost once they go back to eating standard food. I think we are deceiving them by not telling them up front that they will most likely gain back the weight they lose."*

What constitutes a good fit between personal values and organizational values may change at different stages of a person's career because of a change in values. At one point in a person's career, he or she may think that founding a business is important because the new firm might create employment. At another stage of the same person's career, he or she might believe that working for the nonprofit sector is more meritorious.

A starting point in finding a good fit between individual and organizational values is to identify what type of work would be the most meaningful to you. Po Bronson, a writer specializing in social documentaries, observes that people "thrive by focusing on the question of who they really are—and connecting to work that they truly love (and, in so doing, unleashing a productive and creative power that they never imagined)."[13] After identifying your passion in terms of work, you would then seek an employment opportunity that provides such work. For example, a manager might discover that helping young people learn useful job skills brings her the most professional excitement. She might then seek an opportunity to manage a manufacturing apprenticeship program in her company.

▶ Learning Objective 2 ▶

Why Be Concerned About Business Ethics?

When asked why ethics (the moral choices a person makes) is important, most people would respond something to the effect that, "Ethics is important because it's the right thing to do. You behave decently in the workplace because your family and religious values have taught you what is right and wrong." All this is true, but the justification for behaving ethically is more complex, as described next.[14]

A major justification for behaving ethically on the job is to recognize that people are motivated by both self-interest and moral commitments. Most people want to maximize gain for themselves. At the same time, most people are motivated to do something morally right. As one of many examples, vast numbers of people donate money to charity, although keeping that amount of money for themselves would provide more personal gain.

Many business executives want employees to behave ethically because a good reputation can enhance business. A favorable corporate reputation may enable firms to charge premium prices and attract better job applicants. A favorable reputation also helps attract investors, including mutual fund managers whose primary responsibility is to purchase stock in companies. Certain mutual funds, for example, invest only in companies that are environmentally friendly. Managers want employees to behave ethically because unethical behavior—for example, employee theft, lost production time, and lawsuits—is costly.

Behaving ethically is also important because many unethical acts are also illegal, which can lead to financial loss and imprisonment. A company that knowingly allows workers to engage in unsafe practices might be fined and the executives may be held personally liable. Furthermore, unsafe practices can kill people. Low ethics have also resulted in financial hardship for employees as company executives raid pension funds of other companies they purchase, sharply reducing or eliminating the retirement funds of many workers.

Extreme acts of unethical behavior can lead a company into bankruptcy, such as the famous scandals at Enron Corporation. Among the worst ethical violations were hiding financial losses by passing the losses on to phony subsidiaries, encouraging employees to invest their life savings in company stock that was doomed to failure, and creating power shortages in California to artificially inflate energy prices. Furthermore, company executives sometimes held business meetings at strip clubs—at company expense.[15]

A subtle reason for behaving ethically is that high ethics increases the quality of work life. Ethics provides a set of guidelines that specify what makes for acceptable behavior. Being ethical will point you toward actions that make life more satisfying for work associates. A company code of ethics specifies what constitutes ethical versus unethical behavior. When employees follow this code, the quality of work life improves. Several sample clauses from ethical codes are as follows:

- Demonstrate courtesy, respect, honesty, and fairness.

- Do not use abusive language.

- Do not bring firearms or knives to work.

- Do not offer bribes.

- Maintain confidentiality of records.

- Do not harass (sexually, racially, ethnically, or physically) subordinates, superiors, coworkers, customers, or suppliers.

To the extent that all members of the organization abide by this ethical code, the quality of work life will improve. At the same time, interpersonal relations in organizations will be strengthened. To help raise your awareness of your own ethical thoughts and behaviors, take Human Relations Self-Assessment Quiz 5-1.

WHY BEING ETHICAL ISN'T EASY

As analyzed by Linda Klebe Treviño, an organizational behavior professor at Pennsylvania State University, and Michael E. Brown, a management professor at Penn State–Erie, behaving ethically in business is more complex than it seems on the surface, for a variety of reasons.[16] To begin with, ethical decisions are complex. For example, someone might argue that hiring children for factory jobs in overseas countries is unethical. Yet if these children lose their jobs, many would starve or

Human Relations Self-Assessment Quiz   5-1

The Ethical Reasoning Inventory

Describe how well you agree with each of the following statements. Use the following scale: disagree strongly (DS), disagree (D), neutral (N), agree (A), agree strongly (AS). Circle the number in the appropriate column.

	DS	D	N	A	AS
1. When applying for a job, I would cover up the fact that I had been fired from my most recent job.	5	4	3	2	1
2. Cheating only a few dollars in one's favor on an expense account is okay if a person needs the money.	5	4	3	2	1
3. Employees should report on each other for wrongdoing.	1	2	3	4	5
4. It is acceptable to give approximate figures for expense account items when one does not have all the receipts.	5	4	3	2	1
5. I see no problem with conducting a little personal business on company time.	5	4	3	2	1
6. Simply to make a sale, I would stretch the truth about a delivery date.	5	4	3	2	1
7. I would fix up a purchasing agent with a date simply to close a sale.	5	4	3	2	1
8. I would flirt with my boss simply to get a bigger salary increase.	5	4	3	2	1
9. If I received $500 for doing some odd jobs, I would report it on my income tax return.	1	2	3	4	5
10. I see no harm in taking home a few office supplies.	5	4	3	2	1
11. It is acceptable to read the e-mail messages and faxes of coworkers, even when not invited to do so.	5	4	3	2	1
12. It is unacceptable to call in sick to take a day off, even if only done once or twice a year.	1	2	3	4	5
13. I would accept a permanent, full-time job even if I knew I wanted the job for only six months.	5	4	3	2	1
14. I would first check company policy before accepting an expensive gift from a supplier.	1	2	3	4	5
15. To be successful in business, a person usually has to ignore ethics.	5	4	3	2	1
16. If I felt physically attracted toward a job candidate, I would hire that person over a more qualified candidate.	5	4	3	2	1
17. On the job, I tell the truth all the time.	1	2	3	4	5
18. If a student were very pressed for time writing a paper, it would be acceptable to either have a friend write the paper or to purchase one.	5	4	3	2	1
19. I would authorize accepting an office machine on a thirty-day trial period, even if I knew we had no intention of buying it.	5	4	3	2	1
20. I would never accept credit for a coworker's ideas.	1	2	3	4	5

Scoring and Interpretation:

Add the numbers you have circled to obtain your total score.

90–100 You are a strongly ethical person who may take a little ribbing from coworkers for being too straitlaced.

60–89 You show an average degree of ethical awareness and therefore should become more sensitive to ethical issues.

41–59 Your ethics are underdeveloped, but you at least have some awareness of ethical issues. You need to raise your level of awareness of ethical issues.

20–40 Your ethical values are far below contemporary standards in business. Begin a serious study of business ethics.

turn to crime to survive. Second, people do not always recognize the moral issues involved in a decision. A handyman on a work assignment who finds a butcher knife under the bed might not think that he has a role to play in perhaps preventing murder. Sometimes language hides the moral issue involved, such as when the term *file sharing* replaces *stealing* in terms of online music.

Another complexity in making ethical decisions is that people have different levels of moral development. At one end of the scale, some people behave morally simply to escape punishment. At the other end of the scale, some people are morally developed to the point that they are guided daily by principles of justice and right, such as wanting to help as many people as possible. The environment in which we work also influences our behaving ethically. Suppose a restaurant owner encourages such practices as serving customers food that was accidentally dropped on the kitchen floor. An individual server is more likely to engage in such behavior to obey the demand of the owner.

Despite the difficulties in being ethical, many people in the workplace are ethically strong. The accompanying Human Relations in Practice presents examples of people in business who have been recognized for their outstanding ethical behavior.

Human Relations in Practice

Three of the Most Influential People in Business Ethics 2008

Each year *Ethisphere* magazine prepares a list of 100 people who stood out for their positive achievements in the business world. The list stems from the recommendations of a group of distinguished business professors as well as the editors of *Ethisphere*. Three of the choices, along with their rank, are as follows:

1. Liu Qi—Chairman of the Organizing Committee of the 2008 Olympics, who was selected because he was stern on corruption. The Olympic Committee for the Beijing Olympics was recognized as being one of the most stringent ever in fighting corruption in bids, even to the point of exceeding Western standards. This action stands in contrast to the typical stereotype of China, which is often thought of as having a secretive government. Qi relies on China's definition of "tough enforcement" on ethical issues.

11. David Steiner—CEO of Waste Management was selected because of his environmentally friendly approach to discarding waste. Steiner assigned top priority to sustainability and healthy-environment initiatives. One example is that he built over fifty "landfill conversion facilities" that will use the gas emitted from landfills to generate renewable energy.

83. Brenda C. Barnes—CEO of Sara Lee welcomed back employees who took time off to take care of family responsibilities. Barnes launched a new initiative called the "returnship program" at Sara Lee in 2008. The program was modeled after her experience taking time off work to spend more time at home with her family. She took a lot of criticism for that move back in 1997 and began the returnship program to help other professionals ease back into full-time professional work.

Source: Based on facts from "100 Most Influential People in Business Ethics 2008," www.ethisphere.com/100-most-influential-people-in-business-ethics-2008, December 31, 2008.

THE EXTENT OF ETHICAL PROBLEMS

The ethical misdeeds of executives have received substantial publicity in recent years. But ethical violations by rank-and-file employees are widespread, particularly with respect to lying. According to two separate surveys, more than one-third of workers admit to having fabricated their need for sick days. More employees are stretching the reasons for taking time off. Job applicants reporting false or embellished academic credentials have increased.[17] Here are the major findings of a survey conducted by the Ethics Resource Center:[18]

■ Ethical misconduct is quite high and is back at the pre-Enron levels. More than 50 percent of employees have witnessed ethical misconduct of some kind.

■ Many employees do not report the unethical conduct they observe because they are fearful about retaliation and skeptical that their reporting will make a difference. One in eight employees claims to have experienced some form of retaliation for reporting misconduct.

■ The number of companies that are successful in attaining a strong organizational ethical culture has declined in recent years. Only 9 percent of companies appear to have strong ethical cultures.

Although these findings might suggest that unethical behavior is on the increase, another explanation is possible. Workers today might be more observant of ethical problems and more willing to note them on a survey.

Going beyond surveys of what individuals believe, some company practices of today might be considered unethical in terms of people getting harmed. Today, there is much less disgrace in a company declaring bankruptcy, thereby leaving many debts unpaid and abandoning employees' pensions. (The federal government is then forced to take over the pension plan and pays the workers a small percentage of the pension for which they were hoping.) *Fortune* magazine writer Justin Fox represents the ethical thinking of the executives who feel no guilt about bankruptcy in these words: "Chapter 11 [a type of bankruptcy] encourages risk taking, helps the economy adapt to changing times, and helps companies rebound from past mistakes. American business wouldn't be where it is today without it."[19]

A widespread concern about business ethics relates to top-level business executives being paid so highly in relation to other workers. According to the Congressional Research Service, the average pay for CEOs is 180 times that paid to the average worker in the company. In 1994, the multiple was 90.[20] In addition, CEOs of major corporations receive many additional benefits, including chauffeurs and company-paid luncheons in a private dining room.

Figure 5-3 presents seven examples of unethical and/or criminal behavior in business and government. As you scrutinize the examples, you will notice the variety of organizations and types of unethical behavior.

FREQUENT ETHICAL DILEMMAS

Certain ethical mistakes, including illegal actions, recur in the workplace. Familiarizing yourself with these mistakes can be helpful in monitoring your own behavior. Here we describe a number of common ethical problems faced by business executives as well as workers at lower job levels.[21]

The Temptation to Illegally Copy Software

A rampant ethical problem is whether to illegally copy computer software. According to the Business Software Alliance, approximately 38 percent of

FIGURE 5-3 EXAMPLES OF UNETHICAL BEHAVIOR IN THE WORKPLACE BY EXECUTIVES AND CORPORATE PROFESSIONALS

Person and Organization	Ethical and or Criminal Offense
J. Terrence Lanni, chairman and chief executive of MGM Mirage	A corporate biography of Lanni on MGM's Web site said he held an MBA in finance from USC. A newspaper investigation revealed that the university had no record that Lanni had earned an MBA from the school. The 66-year-old executive then resigned, stating that he wanted to spend more time with his wife.
Bernard L. Madoff, former NASDAQ chairman and then chairman of own investment company	Charged with having perpetrated a mammoth Ponzi scheme in which investors may have lost as much as $50 billion. The victims included prominent families, charities, and high-risk investment funds (hedge funds). (A Ponzi scheme involves taking people's money without really investing it and paying them returns with money collected from new investors.) The Madoff firm was liquidated. Madoff was later sentenced to 150 years in prison.
Dole Food executives	Company management concealed from poor Central American farm workers the potential danger of male sterilization posed by a pesticide, Fumazone, used in the Nicaragua banana fields. Jurors awarded $2.8 million to six workers and held Dole responsible for 80 percent of the damages.
Department head and workers in the Royalty in Kind division of Mineral Management Services of the U.S. Interior Department, Denver, Colorado	Thirteen workers were charged by government investigators with having engaged in secret sex and drug abuse with oil company employees and accepted thousands of dollars in gifts while managing billions of dollars worth of energy contracts. Employees were also accused of rigging contracts, helping workers fix problems in their contracts, and working part-time as private oil consultants.
Executives at Goldman Sachs & Co.	Company executives and brokers encouraged some of their major clients to place investment bets against California bonds, even though Goldman Sachs had collected millions of dollars in fees to help the state sell some of the same bonds. The company did not inform the California treasurer that it was proposing a way for investment clients to profit from California's deepening financial problems. (The bets involved selling clients *credit default swaps* that are essentially an insurance policy against a bond default.)
Seven town board members in Franklin County, New York	Undue influence was placed on board members to approve multimillion-dollar wind farms, with turbines two hundred feet or taller. Some of the public officials who approved the contract were leasing their own land to the developers.
Matthew DePante and father Joseph DePante, Action Research Group, Inc.	Working for HP, among other clients, the company obtained consumer private phone records without their knowledge and sold them to third parties. ARG used "pretexting," or false pretenses, to obtain confidential information. ARG and several of its subcontractors were later fined.

Sources: In order of use, as follows: Keith J. Winstein and Tamara Audi, "MGM Mirage CEO Resigns amid Questions about MBA," *Wall Street Journal,* November 14, 2008, p. B1; Roger Parloff, "As if a Credit Tsunami Weren't Enough: The Case of Accused Ponzi Schemer Bernard L. Madoff," *Fortune,* January 19, 2009, p. 6; John Spano, "Dole Food Workers Win Court Battle," *Miami Herald* (miamiherald.com), November 6, 2007; "Interior Dept. Scandal: Sex, Drugs, Energy Deals Probed at Denver Office," *Denver Post* (denverpost.com), September 20, 2008; Sharona Coutts, Marc Lifsher, and Michael A. Hiltzik, "Goldman Sachs Urged Bets against California Bonds It Helped Sell," *Los Angeles Times,* November 11, 2008; Joseph Spector, "Whistle Blown on Wind Power," *Democrat and Chronicle* (Rochester, NY), July 28, 2008, pp. 1A, 10A; Dibya Sarkar, "Court Penalizes Investigators in HP Spying Case," Associated Press, May 29, 2008.

applications used in business are illegal.[22] The illegal copying of software deprives software developers of profits they deserve for having produced the software. Such pirating also leads to the loss of potential jobs for many software developers because the companies that produce the software have less revenue.

Treating People Unfairly

Being fair to people means equity, reciprocity, and impartiality. Fairness involves the issue of giving people equal rewards for accomplishing equal amounts of work. The goal of human resource legislation is to make decisions about people based on their qualifications and performance—not on the basis of demographic factors such as sex, race, or age. A fair working environment is where performance is the only factor that counts (equity). Employer–employee expectations must be understood and met (reciprocity). Prejudice and bias must be eliminated (impartiality).

"Follow the Platinum Rule: Treat people the way *they* wish to be treated."

—Eric Harvey and Scott Airitam, authors of *Ethics 4 Everyone.*

Treating people fairly—and therefore ethically—requires an underemphasis on political factors. Yet this ethical doctrine is not always easy to implement. It is human nature to want to give bigger rewards (such as fatter raises or bigger orders) to people we like.

Sexual Harassment

Sexual harassment is a source of conflict and an illegal act. Sexual harassment is also an ethical issue because it is morally wrong and unfair. All acts of sexual harassment flunk an ethics test. Before sexually harassing another person, the potential harasser should ask, "Would I want a loved one to be treated this way?"

Conflict of Interest

Conflict of interest

judgment or objectivity is compromised because of two competing ends that must be satisfied

Part of being ethical is making business judgments only on the basis of the merits or facts in a situation. Imagine that you are a supervisor who is romantically involved with a worker within the group. When it comes time to assign raises, it will be difficult for you to be objective. A **conflict of interest** occurs when your judgment or objectivity is compromised. Conflicts of interest often take place in the sales end of business. If a company representative accepts a large gift from a sales representative, it may be difficult to make objective judgments about buying from the representative. Yet being taken to dinner by a vendor would not ordinarily cloud one's judgment. Another common example of a conflict of interest is making a hiring decision about a friend who badly needs a job but is not well qualified for the position.

Dealing with Confidential Information

An ethical person can be trusted by others not to divulge confidential information unless the welfare of others is at stake. Suppose a coworker tells you in confidence that she is upset with the company and therefore is looking for another job. Behaving ethically, you do not pass this information along to your supervisor, even though it would help your supervisor plan for a replacement. Now suppose the scenario changes slightly. Your coworker tells you she is looking for another job because she is upset. She tells you she is so upset that she plans to destroy company computer files on her last day. If your friend does find another job, you might warn the company about her contemplated activities.

The challenge of dealing with confidential information arises in many areas of business that affect interpersonal relations. If you learned that a coworker was indicted for a crime, charged with sexual harassment, or facing bankruptcy, there would be a temptation to gossip about the person. A highly ethical person would not pass along information about the personal difficulties of another person.

Misrepresentation of Employment History

Many people are tempted to distort in a positive direction information about their employment history on their job résumé, job application form, and during the interview. Distortion, or lying, of this type is considered unethical and can lead to immediate dismissal if discovered. The hotel and casino executive mentioned in Figure 5-3 falsely claimed to have attained an advanced business degree and evidently stepped down because of it.

Possible Ethical Violations with Computers and Information Technology

As computers dominate the workplace, many ethical issues have arisen in addition to pirating software. One ethical dilemma that surfaces frequently is the fairness of tracking the Web sites a person visits and those from which he or she buys. Should this information be sold, like a mailing list? Another issue is the fairness of having an employee work at a keyboard for sixty hours in one week when such behavior frequently leads to repetitive-motion disorder. And is it ethical for workers to spend so much time doing online shopping and placing bets online during the working day?

Causing Problems in Order to Take Credit for Fixing Them

A longstanding workplace problem gaining recent attention involves employees who quietly cause problems so they can later take the credit for their resolution. The advantage derived from fixing problems is that such behavior is considered quite valuable by most employers. The problem repaired might be fictitious, or simply exaggerated, as in the following example:

> The night manager of a suburban restaurant in Atlanta telephoned owner J. D. Clockdale to brag about how well she had dealt with an irate female customer. The customer went ballistic about a botched order but calmed down after the manager gave her a free meal, as told by the night manager. Clockdale later found out what really took place by reviewing a surveillance video and telephoning the customer, who was an acquaintance. The order mistake was minor, and remedied without much drama. Clockdale confronted the night manager, who confessed that she made up the altercation to look good because she wanted more responsibility.[23]

You may have observed that these common ethical problems are not always clear-cut. Aside from obvious matters, such as prohibitions against stealing, lying, cheating, and intimidating, subjectivity enters into ethical decision making.

What Are Some Guidelines for Making Ethical Decisions and Behaving Ethically?

◀ Learning Objective 3 ◀

Following guidelines for ethical behavior is the heart of being ethical. Although many people behave ethically without studying ethical guidelines, they are usually following guidelines programmed into their minds early in life. The Golden Rule exemplifies a guideline taught by parents, grandparents, and kindergarten teachers. In this section we approach ethical guidelines from six perspectives: (1) developing the right character traits, (2) following a guide for ethical decision making, (3) developing close relationships with work associates, (4) using corporate programs for ethics, (5) following an ethical role model, and (6) following an applicable professional code of conduct.

DEVELOPING THE RIGHT CHARACTER TRAITS

Character trait
an enduring characteristic of a person
that is related to moral and ethical
behavior that shows up consistently

Character traits develop early in life, yet with determination and self-discipline many people can modify old traits or develop new ones. A **character trait** is an enduring characteristic of a person that is related to moral and ethical behavior that shows up consistently. For example, if a person has the character trait of untruthfulness, he or she will lie in many situations. Conversely, the character trait of honesty leads to behaving honestly in most situations.

The Character Counts Coalition is an organization formed to encourage young people to develop fairness, respect, trustworthiness, responsibility, caring, and good citizenship. The coalition has developed a list of ten key guidelines as a foundation for character development.[24] If you develop, or already have, these traits, it will be easy for you to behave ethically in business. As you read the following list, evaluate your own standing on each character trait. Remember, however, that extra effort is required to evaluate one's character traits, because most people have an inflated view of their own honesty and integrity.

1. **Be honest.** Tell the truth; be sincere; do not mislead or withhold information in relationships of trust; do not steal.

2. **Demonstrate integrity.** Stand up for your beliefs about right and wrong; be your best self; resist social pressure to do wrong.

3. **Keep promises.** Keep your word and honor your commitments; pay your debts and return what you borrow.

4. **Be loyal.** Stand by family, friends, employers, community, and country; do not talk about people behind their backs.

5. **Be responsible.** Think before you act; consider consequences; be accountable and "take your medicine."

6. **Pursue excellence.** Do your best with what you have; do not give up easily.

7. **Be kind and caring.** Show you care through generosity and compassion; do not be selfish or mean.

8. **Treat all people with respect.** Be courteous and polite; judge all people on their merits; be tolerant, appreciative, and accepting of individual differences.

9. **Be fair.** Treat all people fairly; be open-minded; listen to others, and try to understand what they are saying and feeling.

10. **Be a good citizen.** Obey the law and respect authority; vote; volunteer your efforts; protect the environment.

If you score high on all of the preceding character traits and behaviors, you are an outstanding member of your company, community, and school. Your ethical behavior is superior.

USING A GUIDE TO ETHICAL DECISION MAKING

Ethical screening
running a contemplated decision
or action through an ethics test,
particularly when a contemplated
action or decision is not clearly ethical
or unethical

A powerful strategy for behaving ethically is to follow a guide for ethical decision making. Such a guide for making contemplated decisions includes testing their ethics. **Ethical screening** refers to running a contemplated decision or action through an ethics test. Such screening makes the most sense when the contemplated action or decision is not clearly ethical or unethical. If a sales representative were to take a favorite customer to Pizza Hut for lunch, an ethical screen would not be necessary. Nobody would interpret a "veggie super" to be a serious bribe. Assume, instead, that the sales rep offered to give the customer an under-the-table gift of $1,000 for placing a large offer with the rep's firm. The sales representative's behavior would be so blatantly unethical that conducting an ethical screen would be unnecessary.

Several guidelines, or ethical screens, have been developed to help the leader or other influence agent decide whether a given act is ethical or unethical. We present two such typical guides here.

Center for Business Ethics Guide

The Center for Business Ethics at Bentley College has developed six questions to evaluate the ethics of a specific decision:[25]

- **Is it right?** This question is based on the deontological (the study or morality) theory of ethics that there are certain universally accepted guiding principles of rightness and wrongness, such as "thou shall not steal." A person dining at a restaurant who is trying to cut back in expenses might contemplate giving tips of 5 percent. Before doing so, he or she wonders, "Is this right?"

- **Is it fair?** This question is based on the deontological theory of justice that certain actions are inherently just or unjust. For example, it is unjust to fire a high-performing employee to make room for a less competent person who is a relative by marriage.

- **Who gets hurt?** This question is based on the utilitarian notion of attempting to do the greatest good for the greatest number of people. The owner of an automotive service center might say to himself or herself, "I would save us substantial money by purchasing bottom-grade brake linings and tires. But I can do more good for the safety of our customers if I invest in higher quality on those two items."

- **Would you be comfortable if the details of your decision or actions were made public in the media or through e-mail?** This question is based on the principle of disclosure. For example, would you be willing to post on a blog the outcome of a decision you made with respect to an ethical temptation, such as potential job discrimination?

- **What would you tell your child, sibling, or young relative to do?** This question is based on the deontological principle of reversibility, which evaluates the ethics of a decision by reversing the decision maker. Would you say to a younger family member, "The way to write a good term paper is to pluck one from the Internet"?

- **How does it smell?** This question is based on a person's intuition and common sense. For example, not paying overtime to employees who work through their lunch hour would "smell" bad to a sensible person.

Four-Criteria Ethics Test

Another useful ethics test, or screen, asks employees to consider four criteria when contemplating the ethics of a potential action. The approach is similar in nature to the Center for Business Ethics Guide:[26]

- The test of *common sense*: "Does this action I am about to take make sense?" The hiring manager might say, "Does it really make sense for me to tell this candidate that she has to go out to dinner and dancing with me to see if she is qualified for the position?"

- The test of *one's best self*: "Is this action or decision I am getting ready to take compatible with my concept of myself at my best?" A competitive person might reflect, "Would I be at my best criticizing my rival in a meeting just to make him look bad?"

- The *light of day* approach, or making the action public. (This question is used in most ethics tests and could apply to e-mail, the Web, and YouTube, among other ways of making decisions and actions public.) A person might reflect, "Would I want to send a message to my followers on Twitter that I backstabbed my coworker this morning?"

- The test of the *purified idea*: (An idea is purified when an influential person makes it pure.) "Am I thinking this action or decision is right just because someone with appropriate authority or knowledge thinks it is right?" Assume that you are a sale representative and your boss tells you it acceptable to list as completed sales a promise of a big order that will be arriving early next year. You know that your boss wants to close the year with more sales, yet you know such an accounting trick is unethical. You pass the test of the purified idea if you resist the suggestion of going along with the plan made pure by your boss.

Ethical issues that require a run through the guide are usually subtle rather than blatant, a decision that falls into the gray zone. You can use an ethical decision-making guide to help solve important human relations problems. Visualize yourself in the same or similar predicament faced by Sara.

Sara and an acquaintance of hers, Ashley, were rivals for a promotion to supervisor of the pension department at a financial services firm. Ashley was often rude toward Sara, making the rivalry more intense. Both were attending the same barbeque. It soon became apparent that Ashley was drinking way too much beer. Finally, Ashley jumped into pool dressed in a tank top and cutoff jeans, while holding a bottle of beer in her left hand. Sara was taking videos anyway, so she filmed Ashley's leap into the pool and obvious drunken behavior.

That night Sara thought she could place her rival Ashley in an unfavorable light by posting the video on YouTube and then having a friend alert an executive at the financial services firm to the availability of the video. Sara hesitated long enough to think through the ethics of what she was doing, including how she would feel if her decision were made public. As a result, Sara did not transmit the video to YouTube, and she also deleted the pool scene from her camcorder.

DEVELOPING STRONG RELATIONSHIPS WITH WORK ASSOCIATES

A provocative explanation of the causes of unethical behavior emphasizes the strength of relationships among people.[27] Assume that two people have close professional ties to each other, such as having worked together for a long time or knowing each other both on and off the job. As a consequence, they are likely to behave ethically toward one another on the job. In contrast, if a weak professional relationship exists between two individuals, either party is more likely to engage in an unethical relationship. The owner of an auto service center is more likely to behave unethically toward a stranger passing through town than toward a long-time customer. The opportunity for unethical behavior between strangers is often minimized because individuals typically do not trust strangers with sensitive information or valuables.

The ethical-skill-building consequence of information about personal relationships is that building stronger relationships with people is likely to enhance ethical behavior. If you build strong relationships with work associates, you are likely to behave more ethically toward them. Similarly, your work associates are likely to behave more ethically toward you. The work associates we refer to are all your contacts.

USING CORPORATE ETHICS PROGRAMS

Many organizations have various programs and procedures for promoting ethical behavior. Among them are committees that monitor ethical behavior, training programs in ethics, and vehicles for reporting ethical violations. The presence of these programs is designed to create an atmosphere in which unethical behavior is discouraged and reporting on unethical behavior is encouraged.

Ethics Hotlines

Ethics hotlines are one of the best-established programs to help individuals avoid unethical behavior. Should a person be faced with an ethical dilemma, the person calls a toll-free line to speak to a counselor about the dilemma. Sometimes employees ask questions to help interpret a policy, such as, "Is it okay to ask my boss for a date?" or "Are we supposed to give senior citizen discounts to customers who qualify but do not ask for one?" At other times, a more pressing ethical issue might be addressed, such as, "Is it ethical to lay off a worker only five months short of his qualifying for a full pension?"

At times an ethical problem of such high moral intensity is presented that employee confidentiality cannot be maintained. But the ethics office handles the inquiries in as confidential a manner as practical and assigns them case identification numbers for follow-up.[28]

Ethics Training Program

Wells Fargo & Co., a mammoth bank, emphasizes both a code of conduct and ethics training. Its Code of Ethics and Business Conduct specifies policies and standards for employees, covering a variety of topics from maintaining accurate records to participating in civic activities. Each year, employees also participate in ethics training. Any Wells Fargo employee may ask questions or report ethical breaches anonymously using an ethics hotline or dedicated e-mail address. The company will fire violators, dismissing about one hundred people a year for misconduct ranging from conflicts of interest to cheating on incentive plans.

Patricia Callahan, executive vice president and director of human resources at the bank, says, "I'm the biggest soft touch in the world. But when someone lies or cheats, you can't have people like that representing us to our customers, whose trust is all we have."[29]

A group of human resource professionals said that no amount of training will ensure that employees will choose the ethical path in every situation. Also, which behavior is the most ethical is not always clear-cut. Nevertheless, the human resource specialists noted that training can start a useful dialogue about right and wrong behavior that employees could recall when faced with an ethical temptation.[30]

The Right Corporate Culture

A corporate ethics program works best when placed in a corporate culture that promotes ethical behavior. When top management holds meetings at strip clubs, such as Enron executives did on occasion, it is difficult to seriously preach the importance of ethics. Executives have to communicate regularly about the importance of high ethics and corporate values. For example, when sales representatives are asked about their total sales, they should also be asked how ethically they behaved in attaining the sales.[31] A positive example of an ethical corporate culture is the Vanguard Group mutual fund company. The scandals in the mutual fund industry in recent years never touched Vanguard. Company leaders consistently talk about the client-oriented practices that are as important as legal controls. Vanguard's orientation for new employees includes a history lesson, examples of commitment to client service, and a clear warning: "Cross the line, and there's no second chance. It's clear from day one," says managing director Mike Miller.[32]

FOLLOW AN ETHICAL ROLE MODEL IN THE COMPANY

An important influence on your ethical behavior can be the behavior of other people whom you regard as ethical role models. The role model is not necessarily a top-level manager. He or she could be the purchasing agent who refuses to accept tickets to sporting events from vendors, the coworker who goes on a business trip and returns the part of the travel advance not spent, or the supervisor who tells workers the truth about company problems that might affect them. According to a series of interviews, general categories of attitudes and behaviors characterize ethical role models in organizations as follows:

- Everyday interpersonal behaviors, such as taking responsibility for others

- High ethical expectations for oneself, such as working extra hours simply to make sure performance evaluations of group members were completed on time

- High ethical expectations for others, such as expecting others to avoid favoritism, including not recommending unqualified friends and relatives for jobs at the company

- Fairness in dealing with others, such as getting their input on a problem situation involving them

Quite often these role models were managers the participants in the study knew well rather than distant executives. As one of the interviewees in the study responded, "I had an opportunity to interact with him on a daily basis in close confines. I had the chance to see that the actions matched the verbal message."[33]

FOLLOW AN APPLICABLE CODE OF PROFESSIONAL CONDUCT

Professional codes of conduct are prescribed for many occupational groups, including physicians, nurses, lawyers, paralegals, purchasing managers and agents, and real estate salespeople.

A useful ethical guide for members of these groups is to follow the code of conduct for their profession. If the profession or trade is licensed by the state or province, a worker can be punished for deviating from the code of conduct specified by the state. The code of conduct developed by the profession or trade is separate from the legal code but usually supports the same principles and practices. Some of these codes of conduct developed by the professional associations are fifty and sixty pages long, yet all are guided by the kind of ethical principles implied in the ethical decision-making guide described earlier. Figure 5-4 presents a sampling of provisions from these codes of conduct.

FIGURE 5-4 EXCERPTS FROM CODES OF PROFESSIONAL CONDUCT

Professional Organization	Sample of Ethical Guidelines and Regulations
Institute of Management Accountants	1. Maintain an appropriate level of professional competence by ongoing development of their knowledge and skills. 2. Refrain from disclosing confidential information acquired in the course of their work, and monitor their activities to assure the maintenance of that confidentiality. 3. Avoid actual or apparent conflicts of interest, and advise all appropriate parties of any potential conflict.
National Association of Legal Assistants	1. A legal assistant (paralegal) must not perform any of the duties that attorneys only may perform nor take any actions that attorneys may not take. 2. A legal assistant may perform any task which is properly delegated and supervised by an attorney, as long as the attorney is ultimately responsible to the client, maintains a direct relationship with the client, and assumes professional responsibility for the work product. 3. A legal assistant must protect the confidences of a client and must not violate any rule or statute now in effect or hereafter enacted controlling the doctrine of privileged communications between a client and an attorney.
National Association of Purchasing Management	1. Avoid the intent and appearance of unethical or compromising practice in relationships, actions, and communications. 2. Refrain from any private business or professional activity that would create a conflict between personal interests and the interest of the employer. 3. Refrain from soliciting or accepting money, loans, credits, or prejudicial discounts, and the acceptance of gifts, entertainment, favors, or services from present or potential suppliers which might influence, or appear to influence purchasing decisions.
Project Management Institute	1. We fulfill the commitments that we undertake—we do what we say we will do. 2. We protect proprietary or confidential information that has been entrusted to us. 3. We do not hire or fire, reward or punish, or award or deny contracts based on personal considerations, including but not limited to, favoritism, nepotism, or bribery.

Source: Institute of Management Accountants Code of Ethics; National Association of Legal Assistants Professional Standards; National Association of Purchasing Management Principles and *Standards of Purchasing Practice*; *PMI Code of Ethics and Professional Conduct*, Project Management Institute.

Concept Review and Reinforcement

Key Terms

Value, 122
Ethics, 122
Morals, 122

Person–role conflict, 128
Conflict of interest, 134
Character trait, 136

Ethical screening, 136

Summary and Review

Values, morals, and beliefs influence how a person behaves on the job, and values are closely tied in with ethics, the moral choices a person makes. Values are learned in several ways, as follows:

■ Observing others or modeling
■ Communication of attitudes by others
■ Unstated but implied attitudes of others
■ Later life influences, such as stories reported by the media
■ Demands of employers that may help us acquire new values, including corporate spiritualism

Values are closely tied to psychological needs. One way of categorizing values is as follows:

■ Humanists (includes personal growth)
■ Strategists (mastery and personal achievement)
■ Pragmatists (power and control)
■ Adventurers (excitement and adventure)

Conscientiousness is another value that influences both work and personal life.

Differences in values often stem from generational differences, such as members of Generation X and Generation Y being less concerned about hierarchy than are baby boomers. Earlier generations have developed negative stereotypes about Gen Y people, yet Gen Y people can often overcome these stereotypes.

Value clarification can lead to a better understanding of your values. When individual and job values mesh, performance may be higher. A person may suffer from person–role conflict when personal and job values clash. To find a good value fit, it helps to identify the type of work that would be most meaningful to you.

Business ethics are important to study for many reasons, including the following:

■ People are motivated by both self-interest and moral commitments.
■ A good ethical reputation can enhance business.
■ Many unethical acts are illegal.
■ High ethics increases the quality of work life because they provide guidelines for acceptable behavior.

Being ethical isn't easy, because ethical decisions are complex, people have different levels of moral development, and our work environment influences our ethical behavior. Surveys reveal that unethical behavior is widespread. Also, much questionable unethical behavior exists, including companies declaring bankruptcy while at the same time granting top-level executives extraordinary compensation.

Common ethical problems faced by business executives as well as workers at lower job levels include the following:

■ The temptation to illegally copy software
■ Sexual harassment
■ Conflict of interest
■ Dealing with confidential information
■ Accurate presentation of employment history
■ Possible ethical violations with computers and information technology
■ Causing problems in order to take credit for fixing them

Guidelines for making ethical decisions and behaving ethically include the following:

- Develop the right character traits (such as honesty, integrity, and loyalty).

- Use a guide to ethical decision making (the process of ethical screening).
- Develop strong relationships with work associates.
- Use corporate ethics programs.
- Follow an ethical role model in the company.
- Follow an applicable code of professional conduct.

Check Your Understanding

1. Identify several of your values that you think will help you succeed. Why do you think these values will help you?
2. What evidence would you need to conclude that there was a good fit between your values and those of your employer?
3. Get together in a brainstorming group to identify what you think might be a few values important to (a) Wal-Mart and (b) Toyota. Support your reasoning.
4. Assume that company management brags about its values of being altruistic and humanitarian. Should such a company then shelter the homeless at night on company premises? Why or why not?
5. Give an example of an action in business that might be unethical but not illegal.
6. Some companies send advertisements to cell phone users by voice and text message, thereby consuming minutes paid for by the phone owner. What is your evaluation of the ethics of transmitting these advertisements?

7. A 25-year-old is applying for a position as an assistant loan officer at a bank, and the bank is ready to make an offer. The hiring manager then decides against the offer when she discovers by Internet that the candidate spent one night in jail seven years ago after being arrested as an antiwar demonstrator. How ethical is the hiring manager's decision?
8. If so many successful business executives and people in public office have been charged with ethical violations, why should you worry about being ethical?
9. The number of deaths and serious injuries caused by automobile and small-truck drivers sending and receiving text messages continues to increase. What ethical responsibility should cell phone manufacturers and phone service providers have for preventing or reducing these accidents?
10. Some hospitals prohibit doctors from accepting any gift but a free lunch from pharmaceutical companies. Are these hospitals going overboard on ethics? Explain your reasoning.

Web Corner

Choosing a Career Based on Values
www.careersonline.com.au/disc/vwp.html

Learning More About Business Ethics
www.ethicsandbusiness.org/links/

Making Ethical Business Decisions
www.entre-ed.org/_teach/ethics.htm

INTERNET SKILL BUILDER

Assume that you have accepted in position in your field with Levi Strauss & Co., the manufacturer of work and casual clothing. You want to fit in well with the company. One of your strategies is to demonstrate regularly that you conform to the company values of empathy, originality, integrity, courage, and vision. Details about these values are found by visiting http://www.levistrauss.com/company/valuesandvision.aspx, or simply visit the company Web site and look for the values statement.

The skill aspect of this exercise is for you to explain in about twenty-five words how you will demonstrate that you have incorporated each one of these values into your thinking and actions. For example, to demonstrate *integrity*, you might say something to the effect of, "Whenever I tell a supervisor or coworker that I will do something, I will follow through promptly. If the activity will take a long time, I will furnish a couple of progress reports."

Developing Your
Human Relations Skills

Applying Human Relations Exercise 5-1

Value Clarification

Learning how to clarify your values can be uplifting and, at the same time, can help you make career choices based on these values. Ideally, you might pursue career opportunities that give you an opportunity to satisfy your most important career values, such as a person who highly values "making an above-average income" pursing a career in industrial sales. And a person who values "helping people less fortunate than me" might pursue a career in youth work.

Rank from 1 to 20 the importance of the following values to you as a person. The most important value on the list receives a rank of 1; the least important a rank of 20. Use the space next to "Other" if the list has left out an important value in your life.

_____ Having my own place to live

_____ Having one or more children

_____ Having an interesting job and career

_____ Owning a car

_____ Having a good relationship with coworkers

_____ Having good health

_____ Sending and receiving e-mail messages and instant messages and using the Web

_____ Being able to stay in frequent contact with friends by cell phone and text messaging

_____ Watching my favorite television shows

_____ Participating in sports or other pastimes

_____ Following a sports team, athlete, music group, or other entertainer

_____ Being a religious person

_____ Helping people less fortunate than me

_____ Loving and being loved by another person

_____ Having physical intimacy with another person

_____ Making an above-average income

_____ Being in good physical condition

_____ Being a knowledgeable, informed person

_____ Completing my formal education

_____ Other

1. Discuss and compare your ranking of these values with the person next to you.
2. Perhaps your class, assisted by your instructor, can arrive at a class average on each of these values. How does your ranking compare to the class ranking?
3. Look back at your own ranking. Does it surprise you?
4. Are there any surprises in the class ranking? Which values did you think would be highest and lowest?

Applying Human Relations Exercise 5-2

Ethical Decision Making

Working in small groups, take one or more of the following ethical dilemmas through the six steps for screening contemplated decisions. (See page 137.) You might supplement the preceding analysis with the briefer ethical decision-making guides. If more than one group chooses the same scenario, compare your answers for the various steps.

Scenario 1: To Recycle or Not. Your group is the top management team at a large insurance company. Despite the movement toward digitizing all records, your firm still generates tons of paper each month. Customer payments alone account for truckloads of envelopes each year. The paper recyclers in your area claim they can hardly find a market any longer for used paper, so they will be charging you just to accept your paper for recycling. Your group is wondering whether to recycle.

Scenario 2: The Hole in the Résumé. Emily has been working for the family business as an office manager for five years. Because the family business is being sold, Emily has started a job hunt. She also welcomes the opportunity to work in a larger company so she could learn more about how a big company operates. As she begins preparing her job résumé, she ponders how to classify the year of unemployment prior to working at the family business. During that year she worked a total of ten weeks in entry-level jobs at three fast-food restaurants. Otherwise she filled her time with such activities as walking in the park, watching daytime television shows, surfing the Internet, engaging in MySpace activities, playing video games, and pursuing her hobby of visiting graveyards.

Emily finally decides to tack that year onto the five years in the family business. She indicates on her résumé that she has been working *six* years at the family business. As Emily says, "It's a tight job market for office managers, and I don't want to raise any red flags." Evaluate the ethics of Emily's decision to fill in the year off from work, and perhaps offer her some advice.

Scenario 3: The Deep Discounted Flat-Screen HDTV. You are in the market for a large, flat-screen HDTV. The model you want retails for about $3,500 even in big-box discount stores like Wal-Mart and Kmart. A friend of yours says to you, "Why be a jerk and pay $3,500 for basically the same product you can get for $2,000 from an online electronics dealer I know about." You are interested because a $1,500 discount on essentially the same TV set seems quite good to you. Yet with your knowledge of business, you wonder how an online retailer can beat the rock-bottom prices at Wal-Mart and Kmart.

With a smile, your friend says, "The HDTV sets the online retailer sells are stolen by sea pirates from Africa. Somehow they get their way up through the marketing channels into an online retailer. The retailer didn't steal them; the pirates did. So you are clean. Besides, the pirates are desperate, hungry people forced into crime."

Your decision is whether to purchase your HDTV online, knowing that the merchandise was hijacked by modern-day sea pirates.

Human Relations Class Activity

My Biggest Ethical Challenge and Its Resolution

The first step in this class activity is for each student to think of an ethical challenge, or temptation, he or she has faced in recent years and how he or she resolved the challenge. You may need about five minutes to think through your ethical challenge and its resolution. Students should keep in mind that they will be asked to share the scenario with classmates, so a scenario should be chosen that they would be comfortable sharing with others. Each student in the class, or perhaps volunteers, then makes about a two-minute presentation of his or her challenge and resolution. Here is an example contributed by a student named Danielle:

About five years ago, I was facing financial pressures because of bills and things like that. I was due a $357 tax refund form the IRS, and I really needed the money. Then something bizarre happened. I received a refund for $357 one Monday, which pleased me no end. Then it blew my mind when I received refund checks for $357 on Tuesday and Wednesday also. The money would have been so helpful. But then I thought of the ethical problems. The federal government is in worse shape than me and needs every penny. Also, what if I got audited?

My resolution of the ethical dilemma was to contact the IRS on its Web site and explain my dilemma. Five weeks later I received a letter from the IRS instructing me to return the money. I hated sending those two extra refunds back, but I can sleep better knowing that I did the right thing.

The class will vote by secret ballot as to which three students presented ethical challenges and resolutions that were the most instructive for the rest of the class. The votes can be made on small slips of paper, or by computer if the classroom is so equipped. After the votes are tallied, the class might discuss why the scenarios receiving the most votes were so instructive.

PS, What would you have done if you had been in Danielle's position?

Human Relations Case Study 5-1

The Undercover Recruiter

It was a humid June morning on David Perry's fourth day of masquerading as a snack-food vendor inside an industrial park. He had one day left on the canteen truck he'd rented for $500. The executive recruiter, wearing a hairnet and an apron, finally got a customer to tell him what he needed to know: the identity of a technology guru a client had hired Perry to poach from a competitor.

Perry's client didn't know this person's name. So for days, the recruiter had been asking every coffee, cigarette, and sandwich buyer who the "genius" was behind the large, publicly traded company's top-selling piece of software. Finally, an unsuspecting patron spilled the beans, and Perry got his man. "It was real hard detective work, but it was fun," he says.

For Perry, chasing down a potential recruit is a sport that leads him to use unconventional methods. "How else can you get at those people?" says Perry, whose search firm, Perry-Martel International Inc., employs three researchers, plus his wife, Anita, who handles miscellaneous tasks. "They're behind steel gates." The firm is located in Ottawa, the capital city of Canada.

Once, after dozens of failed attempts to reach through normal channels the CEO of a technology firm, Perry says, he hopped a plane and sneaked into the basement of his quarry's [target's] New York workplace and gave a janitor $100 and a self-addressed envelope. The recruiter says he was counting on his target's having a private washroom with a phone—and asked the janitor to send him his number. Perry says those digits arrived in the mail a few days later. Soon after, he scored a meeting with the executive, who agreed to take the position Perry was hawking: CEO of a large, publicly traded software company in New York.

A few years ago Blake Carruthers, a sales executive was skiing on an expert-level hill at a Québec, Canada, ski area when he spotted Perry, an amateur skier, with his arms flailing for the executive's attention and seemingly stuck halfway down the slope. "Within 30 seconds he goes, "I got this opportunity I want to talk to you about,'" recalls Carruthers, who had been dodging the recruiter's phone calls.

In 22 years, Perry says he has completed 991 searches for positions. He says, "I don't care if you're available or not. I don't care if you want to move. I have to get in front of you and tell you why you should listen to me."

Source: Sarah E. Needleman, "Snack Vendor—or Undercover Recruiter?" *Wall Street Journal*, September 9, 2008, pp. D1, D6.

Questions

1. How ethical are the methods Perry uses to conduct his executive searches?

2. If you think that Perry might be unethical, on which specific criteria of ethical behavior does he fall short?

3. Imagine yourself as a manager visiting a ski slope for recreational purposes. What would your reaction be to an executive recruiter who flagged you down on the slope?

4. To what extent do you think Perry has a values problem?

Human Relations Role-Playing Exercise

Business Ethics on the Ski Slope

The case about the undercover recruiter serves as the scenario and the story line for this role-play. One person plays the role of Blake Carruthers, the sales executive who is taking a weekend ski vacation in Quebec with his family. (No prior skiing experience necessary for this role-play.) As the sales exec is skiing down the hill, he encounters search consultant David Perry motioning to him. Another person plays the role of Perry, who intends to make the pitch about the job opening he is trying to fill. Blake is concerned about the ethics David is displaying by trapping him into a conversation. David feels he is just doing whatever it takes to get the job done. Blake openly challenges David's ethics.

The role-play will be more authentic if the role-players act as if they are skiing, rather than seated at a desk. If the role-players happen to be wearing a cap and gloves today, the role-play will be more authentic, but simulating ski conditions is not a requirement for the success of this role-play.

For both scenarios, observers rate the role-players on two dimensions, using a 1 to 5 scale from very poor to very good. One dimension is "effective use of human relations techniques." The second dimension is "acting ability." A few observers might voluntarily provide feedback to the role-players in terms of sharing their ratings and observations. The course instructor might also provide feedback.

Human Relations Case Study 5-2

The Highly Rated but Expendable Marsha

Department manager Nicholas had thought for a long time that Marsha, one of his financial analysts, created too many problems. Although Marsha performed her job in a satisfactory manner, she required a lot of supervisory time and attention. She frequently asked for time off when her presence was needed the most because of a heavy workload in the department. Marsha sent Nicholas many long and complicated e-mail messages that required substantial time to read and respond to. When Nicholas responded to Marsha's e-mail messages, she would typically send another e-mail back asking for clarification.

Marsha's behavior during department meetings irritated Nicholas. She would demand more time than any other participant to explain her point of view on a variety of issues. At a recent meeting, she took ten minutes explaining how the company should be doing more to help the homeless and invest in the development of inner cities.

Nicholas coached Marsha frequently about the problems she was creating, but Marsha strongly disagreed with his criticism and concerns. At one time, Nicholas told Marsha that she was a high-maintenance employee. Yet Marsha perceived herself as a major contributor to the department. She commented once, "Could it be, Nick, that you have a problem with an assertive woman working in your department?"

Nicholas developed a tactic to get Marsha out of the department. He would give her outstanding performance evaluations, emphasizing her creativity and persistence. Marsha would then be entered into the company database as an outstanding employee, thereby making her a strong candidate for transfer or promotion. Within six months, a manager in a new division of the company took the bait. She requested that Marsha be recruited into her department as a senior financial analyst. Nicholas said to the recruiting manager, "I hate to lose a valuable contributor like Marsha, but I do not want to block her career progress."

Two months later, Marsha's new manager telephoned Nicholas and asked, "What's the problem with Marsha? She's kind of a pill to have working with us. I thought she was an outstanding employee."

Nicholas responded, "Give Marsha some time. She may be having a few problems adjusting to a new environment. Just give her a little constructive feedback. You'll find out what a dynamo she can be."

Questions

1. How ethical was Nicholas in giving Marsha a high-performance evaluation for the purposes of attracting her to other departments?

2. What should the manager do who was hooked by Nicholas's bait of the high-performance evaluation?

3. What might the company do to prevent more incidents of inflated performance evaluations for the purpose of transferring an unwanted employee?

Human Relations Role-Playing Exercise

Confronting the Ethical Deviant

One student plays the role of the manager who transferred Marsha into his or her department. The new manager has become suspicious that Nicholas might have manipulated Marsha's performance evaluations to make her appear like a strong candidate for transfer or promotion. In fact, the new manager thinks he may have caught an ethical deviant. Another student plays the role of Nicholas, who wants to defend his reputation as an ethical manager. During the role-play, pay some attention to ethical issues. As usual, other students will provide feedback on the effectiveness of the interaction they observed.

REFERENCES

1. Excerpted from Erin White, "Age Is as Age Does: Making the Generation Gap Work for You," *Wall Street Journal*, June 30, 2008, p. B6.
2. Bill Vllasic, "Ford Scion Looks Beyond Bailout to Green Agenda," *New York Times* (nytimes.com), November 24, 2008, p. 1.
3. Ben Rand, "'On Track' at Kodak," *Democrat and Chronicle* (Rochester, NY), May 21, 2006, p. 4E.
4. Paul Hemp and Thomas A. Stewart (interview with Samuel J. Palmisano), "Leading Change When Business Is Good," *Harvard Business Review*, December 2004, p. 63.
5. Joanne Cole, "Building Heart and Soul," *HRfocus*, October 1998, pp. 9–10.
6. Douglas B. Richardson, "Know Thyself: An Easy Approach," www.CareerJournal.com as reproduced in www.shrm.org/jobs/043/May.
7. Brent W. Roberts, Oleksandr S. Chernyshenko, Stephen Stark, and Lewis R. Goldberg, "The Structure of Conscientiousness: An Empirical Investigation Based on Seven Major Personality Questionnaires," *Personnel Psychology*, Spring 2005, pp. 103–139.
8. A recent review of the evidence is Nicole N. Dudley et al., "A Meta-Analytic Investigation of Conscientiousness in the Prediction of Job Performance: Examining the Intercorrelations and the Incremental Validity of Narrow Traits," *Journal of Applied Psychology*, January 2006, pp. 40–57.
9. Opinion of Peter Cappelli cited in White, "Age Is as Age Does," p. B6.
10. Kathryn Tyler, "The Tethered Generation," *HR Magazine*, May 2007, p. 42; "Get Ready for 'Millennials' at Work," *Manager's Edge*, January 2006, p. 1.
11. Heather Human, "Avoiding Gen Y Stereotypes on the Job," *San Francisco Examiner* (www.examiner.com), December 3, 2008.
12. David C. McClelland, "How Motives, Skills, and Values Determine What People Do," *American Psychologist*, July 1985, p. 815.
13. Po Bronson, "What Should I Do with My Life?" *Fast Company*, December 2002, p. 68.
14. Linda K. Treviño and Katherine A. Nelson, *Managing Business Ethics: Straight Talk about How to Do It Right* (New York: Wiley, 1995), pp. 24–35; O. C. Ferrell, John Fraedrich, and Linda Ferrell, *Business Ethics: Ethical Decision Making and Cases,* 4th ed. (Boston: Houghton Mifflin, 2000), pp. 13–16; Anita Bruzzese, "Tools Take Ethics to the Real World," Gannett News Service, May 16, 2005.
15. Erin Kelly, "Unethical Behavior Is on Rise, Experts Fear," Gannett News Service, March 5, 2006.
16. Linda Klebe Treviño, "Managing to Be Ethical: Debunking Five Business Ethics Myths," *Academy of Management Executive*, May 2004, pp. 69–72.
17. Data from Ethics Resource Center and Kronos Inc., reported in Sue Shellenbarger, "How and Why We Lie at the Office: From Pilfered Pens to Padded Accounts," *Wall Street Journal*, March 24, 2005, p. D1.
18. "National Business Ethics Survey: An Inside View of Private Sector Ethics," *Kiplinger Business Resource Center* (www.kiplinger.com), February 2008, pp. 1–2.
19. Justin Fox, "Three Cheers for Bankruptcy," *Fortune*, October 17, 2005, p. 34.
20. Carol Hymowitz, "Pay Gap Fuels Worker Woes," *Wall Street Journal*, April 28, 2008, p. B8.
21. Treviño and Nelson, *Managing Business Ethics*, pp. 47–64.
22. Reported in Anne Broache, "Study: Pirates Cost Software Industry $48 Billion," http://news.cnet.com, May 14, 2008, p. 1.
23. Phred Dvorak, "'Munchausen at Work': Employees Advance by Fixing Problems They Had Created," *Wall Street Journal*, August 25, 2008, p. B4.
24. Michael S. Josephson, "Does Character Still Count?" *USA Weekend*, September 23–25, 1994, p. 20; www.character-counts.org. Accessed January 20, 2009.
25. James L. Bowditch and Anthony E. Buono, *A Primer of Organizational Behavior* (New York: Wiley, 2001), p. 4.
26. Curtis C. Verschoor, "What's Ethical? Here's a Simple Test," *Strategic Finance*, March 2000, p. 24, as reported in Suzanne C. de Janasz, Karen O. Dows, and Beth Z. Schneider, *Interpersonal Skills in Organizations* (New York: McGraw-Hill, 2002), p. 385.
27. Daniel J. Brass, Kenneth D. Butterfield, and Bruce C. Skaggs, "Relationships and Unethical Behavior: A Social Network Perspective," *Academy of Management Review*, January 1998, pp. 14–31.
28. Daryl Koehn, "An Interview with William Griffin." Retrieved March 8, 2006. from: www.stthom.edu/cbes/griffin.html
29. Quoted in "The Optima Awards: They've Got Game," *Workforce Management*, March 2005, p. 44.
30. Jean Thilmany, "Supporting Ethical Employees," *HR Magazine*, September 2007, p. 106.
31. Kathryn Tyler, "Do the Right Thing: Ethics Training Programs Help Employees Deal with Ethical Dilemmas," *HR Magazine*, February 2005, pp. 99–102.
32. Quoted in Jonathan Pont, "Doing the Right Thing to Instill Business Ethics," *Workforce Management*, April 2005, p. 27.
33. Gary R. Weaver, Linda Klebe Treviño, and Bradley Agle, "'Somebody I Look Up To': Ethical Role Models in Organizations," *Organizational Dynamics*, Issue 4, 2005, pp. 313–330.

6

Problem Solving and Creativity

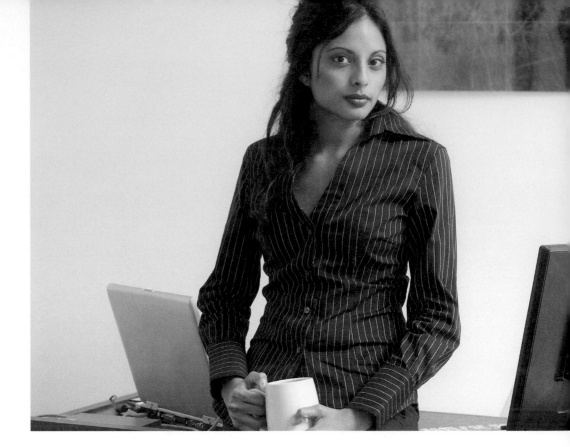

Outline

1 What Are Some Personal Characteristics That Influence Your Problem-Solving Ability?
Cognitive Intelligence, Education, and Experience
Emotional Intelligence
Flexibility versus Rigidity
Intuition
Concentration
Decisiveness and Perfectionism
Risk Taking and Thrill Seeking
Values of the Decision Maker

2 What Are the Problem-Solving and Decision-Making Steps?
Awareness of the Problem
Identify Causes of the Problem
Find Creative Alternatives
Weigh Alternatives and Make the Choice
Implement the Choice
Evaluate the Choice
Brain Teasers for Improving Your Problem-Solving Ability

3 What Do I Need to Know About Creativity in Decision Making?
Measuring Your Creative Potential
Characteristics of Creative Workers
The Conditions Necessary for Creativity

4 How Do I Improve My Creativity?
Concentrate Intensely on the Task at Hand
Overcome Traditional Mental Sets
Discipline Yourself to Think Laterally
Conduct Brainstorming Sessions
Establish Idea Quotas for Yourself
Engage in Multicultural Experiences
Obtain Adequate Physical Exercise
Play the Roles of Explorer, Artist, Judge, and Lawyer

5 How Does Critical Thinking Relate to Problem Solving and Creativity?

Learning Objectives ▶

After studying the information and doing the exercises in this chapter, you should be able to:

1 Understand how personal characteristics influence the ability to solve problems and make decisions.

2 Apply the problem-solving and decision-making steps to complex problems.

3 Summarize the characteristics of creative people.

4 Describe various ways of improving your creativity.

5 Know the basic steps in critical thinking.

I n its early days, Chris Wallace's company didn't always have enough work to keep its staff fully occupied designing Web sites for its clients. But it didn't want to lose any talent. So he and his co-founders decided to tell employees they could pursue their own interests in their downtime, doing just about whatever they wanted, on the clock.

An unexpected side benefit emerged. Employees spend some of their spare time writing music and building photography and video skills. When the company needed ideas to pitch to potential clients, it tapped into employees' personal growth projects. Wallace says he has had meetings with potential clients where 40 percent of the work he showed them was done by employees in their downtime.

His company, SuperGroup Creative Omnimedia Inc. has grown to fifteen employees and close to $3 million in annual revenue. Downtime is less frequent these days, but management's philosophy is the same: As long as employees get their work done, they're free to pursue outside projects from their cubicles. The company continues to lean on employees' personal projects to help win new clients and expand the work it does with existing clients.

The model works, Wallace says, because of the company's small size and collegial atmosphere. Most people in SuperGroup's Atlanta headquarters know what their colleagues are working on in their personal lives. Twice a week, the whole staff gathers to discuss both company business and personal projects. "A larger organization wouldn't have that intimate knowledge," says Wallace, who is the company's director of technology.

For employees, the cross-pollination between their work and personal lives can be an opportunity to turn a hobby into a line on their résumés—and an ego boost. "I jumped at the chance to put my music out in front of anybody," says Elliott Rothman, a SuperGroup Web developer. Music he wrote and his guitar playing were used in a successful project to the Weather Channel, a client.

On average, employees spend about a half day each week working on outside pursuits. Wallace says occasionally employees have to be reminded that clients come first and they need to drop whatever they're doing if a client has an urgent request.[1]

The story about SuperGroup illustrates that putting aside time for exploring ideas can result in creative solutions to business problems. At the same time, the story illustrates a major theme of this book—work life and personal life often support each other. The general purpose of this chapter is to help you become a more effective and creative problem solver when working individually or within groups.

Two key definitions will help you understand the nature of the material in this chapter. A **problem** is a gap between what exists and what you want to exist. If you are a Web site developer, and far fewer people are visiting your site than your company is hoping for, you have a problem. **Decision making** refers to choosing one alternative from the various alternative solutions that can be pursued. After exploring a number of possibilities for your Web site, you must choose one.

The general purpose of this chapter is to help you become a more effective and creative problem solver when working individually or in groups. Whether you are solving problems by yourself or as part of a group, the principles apply equally well.

Problem
gap between what exists and what you want to exist

Decision making
choosing one alternative from the various alternative solutions that can be pursued

▶ Learning Objective 1 ▶

What Are Some Personal Characteristics That Influence Your Problem-Solving Ability?

Many personal characteristics influence the type of problem solver and decision maker you are or are capable of becoming. Fortunately, some personal characteristics that influence your decision-making ability can be improved through conscious effort. For instance, if you make bad decisions because you do not concentrate on the details of the problem, you can gradually learn to concentrate better. Most of the personal characteristics described next can be strengthened through the appropriate education, training, and self-discipline. Figure 6-1 outlines these characteristics.

COGNITIVE INTELLIGENCE, EDUCATION, AND EXPERIENCE

In general, if you are intelligent, well educated, and well experienced, you will make better decisions than people without these attributes. (The term *cognitive intelligence* refers to the intellectual, or traditional, type of intelligence that is necessary for such tasks as solving math problems and conjugating verbs.) Cognitive intelligence helps because, by definition, intelligence denotes the ability to solve problems. Education improves the problem-solving and decision-making process because it gives you a background of principles and facts on which to rely.

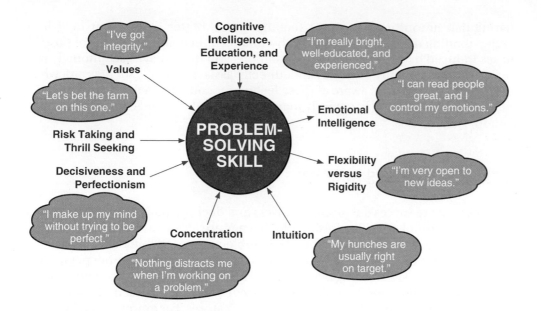

FIGURE 6-1

INFLUENCES ON PROBLEM-SOLVING SKILL

Experience facilitates decision making because good decisions tend to be made by people who have already faced similar situations in the past. All things being equal, would you prefer to take your computer problem to an experienced or an inexperienced specialist? Or what about flying with an experienced airline pilot?

On January 16, 2009, airline pilot Chesley "Sully" Sullenberger, age fifty-seven, became an international hero after landing an engine-damaged jet airplane safely into the Hudson River in New York City. Captain Sullenberger had forty years of flying experience, including twenty-eight years with US Airways. He was also well educated, including degrees from the U.S. Air Force Academy and two other universities, and a specialist in airline safety. In short, Sullenberger's intelligence, education, and experience contributed to his heroic feat.

EMOTIONAL INTELLIGENCE

Being able to deal effectively with your feelings and emotions and those of others can help you make better decisions. This type of intelligence has to do with the ability to connect with people and understand their emotions. A worker with high emotional intelligence would be able to engage in such behaviors as sizing up people, pleasing others, and influencing them.[2]

Emotional intelligence is important for decision making because how effective you are in managing your feelings and reading those of other people can affect the quality of your decisions. For example, if you cannot control your anger, you are likely to make decisions that are motivated by retaliation, hostility, and revenge. An example would be shouting and swearing at your team leader because of a work assignment you received. Your emotional intelligence could also influence your career decision making. If you understand your own feelings, you are more likely to enter an occupation or accept a position that matches your true attitude.

Another part of emotional intelligence related to problem solving is that contrary to common knowledge, experiencing intense emotions can facilitate decision making. Instead of attempting to block your emotions, you allow them to surface to facilitate making sharper decisions. A study with 101 members of stock investment clubs found that the investors who experienced more intense feelings achieved higher decision-making performance. Among the dozens of emotions and feelings recorded were "happy," "enthusiastic," "nervous," and "depressed." An equally important finding was that investors who were better able to identify and distinguish among their current feelings made better investment decisions. Understanding their feelings apparently enhanced their ability to control possible biases induced by these feelings.[3] For example, you might have exceptionally positive feelings about any company that directly assists animals, such as a pet-food manufacturer. If you are aware of these feelings, it could prevent you from making the mistake of investing in a poorly managed dog and cat food company based on your love of animals.

FLEXIBILITY VERSUS RIGIDITY

Some people are successful problem solvers and decision makers because they approach every problem with a fresh outlook. They are able to avoid developing rigid viewpoints. Flexible thinking enables the problem solver to think of original—and therefore creative—alternative solutions to solving a problem. Another perspective on the same issue is that being open-minded helps a person solve problems well. In recent years several major retailers have become more flexible in their thinking about inner cities as profitable locations for their stores. For example, the Kmart division of Sears Holdings Inc. has been successful with many of its new inner-city stores. The link between flexibility and creativity will be described in more detail in the discussion of the characteristics of creative people.

INTUITION

Intuition

an experience-based way of knowing or reasoning in which weighing and balancing of evidence are done automatically

Effective decision makers do not rely on careful analysis alone. Instead, they also use their **intuition,** an experience-based way of knowing or reasoning in which weighing and balancing of evidence are done automatically. Judgments and decisions reached through intuition are rapid, and they are largely unconscious—we are not completely aware of how we reached the decision.[4] Intuition appears to be composed of the interplay between knowing (intuition-as-expertise) and sensing (intuition-as-feeling). The best use of intuition, therefore, involves both bringing past facts in mind to deal with the situation and a sudden emotional hunch at the same time.[5] An experienced real estate developer might look at an old building and within ten minutes decide it would be a good investment to rehabilitate the structure. Based on hundreds of property evaluations, the developer knows that rehabilitating an old building can be profitable. At the same time, the developer visualizes what the old building would look like when rehabilitated.

Relying on intuition is like relying on your instincts when faced with a decision. Intuition takes place when the brain gathers information stored in memory and packages it as a new insight or solution. Intuitions, therefore, can be regarded as stored information that is reorganized or repackaged. Developing good intuition may take a long time because so much information has to be stored. Cognitive psychologist Gary Klein, the founder of Klein Associates, explains it this way:

> We sometimes think that experts are weighted down by information, by facts, by memories—that they make decisions slowly because they must search through so much data. But in fact, we've got it backward. The accumulation of experience does not weight people down—it lightens them up. It makes them fast.[6]

Despite its merits, intuition has its drawbacks. Our hunches based on the combination of experience and emotion can sometimes lead us astray when a more analytical approach would have led to a better decision. For example, a charming and articulate job candidate might be chosen mostly on the basis of intuition. A background check based on rational analysis might have revealed that the candidate is a procrastinator and a criminal. One way to improve intuition is to get feedback on the decisions we make, so we can sharpen future decisions.[7] For example, a credit analyst in a bank profits from feedback about the future payment records of the loans he or she approved.

CONCENTRATION

Mental concentration is an important contributor to making good decisions. Many people who solve problems poorly do so because they are too distracted to immerse themselves in the problem at hand. In contrast, effective problem solvers often achieve the **flow experience**—total absorption in their work. When flow occurs, things seem to go just right. The person feels alive and fully attentive to what he or she is doing. As a byproduct of the flow experience, a good solution to a problem may surface. If you fail to concentrate hard enough, you may overlook an important detail that could affect the outcome of the decision. For example, a person about to purchase an automobile might be excited about the high gas mileage but forget to check the vehicle's ability to withstand a crash.

A major factor affecting your ability to concentrate is how well rested you are. Being well rested helps you concentrate more, and being sleep deprived lowers concentration.[8] Negative stress can also adversely affect concentration, resulting in poorer decisions. Many serous automobile accidents are caused by fatigued drivers who could not concentrate well at the moment.

Flow experience
total absorption in work; when flow occurs, things seem to go just right

DECISIVENESS AND PERFECTIONISM

Some people are ill suited to solving problems and making decisions because they are fearful of committing themselves to any given course of action. "Gee, I'm not sure, what do you think?" is their typical response to a decision forced on them. If you are indecisive, this characteristic will have to be modified if you are to become successful in your field. A manager has to decide which person to hire. And a photographer has to decide which setting is best for the subject. As the old saying goes, at some point "you have to fish or cut bait." The combination of being indecisive and a perfectionist can lead to procrastination. Also, being a procrastinator can make one indecisive. Perfectionism contributes to delayed decision making because the person keeps working on a project before deciding to submit it to somebody else.

RISK TAKING AND THRILL SEEKING

The need for taking risks and seeking thrills is yet another personality characteristic that influences problem-solving skill. For some types of problems, the high risk taker and thrill seeker is at an advantage. Firefighters have to take risks to save people from burning buildings and remove people trapped in collapsed buildings. An information technology specialist might have to engage in a risky maneuver to salvage data from a crashed hard drive. Risk taking and thrill seeking can also lead to poor problem solving and decision making, such as a merchandiser buying a huge inventory of a highly original fashion. The experienced decision maker needs to know when to take high risks and seek thrills and when to be more conservative.

Another influence on decision making related to risk is the common tendency to focus on avoiding loss—or being averse to taking a risk. According to the Nobel Prize–winning research of Daniel Kahneman and Amos Tverseky, an individual's response to loss is much more intense than his or her response to gains. This is one reason why so many people are tempted to hold on to a losing stock or refuse to leave a casino despite a long losing streak.[9] The same phenomenon of loss aversion helps explain why flat-rate telephone plans are so popular, even when they cost more than variable-rate plans.[10]

VALUES OF THE DECISION MAKER

Values influence decision making at every step. The right values for the situation will improve problem solving and decision making, whereas the wrong values will lead to poor decisions. Ultimately, all decisions are based on values. A manager who places a high value on the well-being of employees tries to avoid alternatives that create hardships for workers. Another value that significantly influences problem solving and decision making is the pursuit of excellence. A worker who embraces the pursuit of excellence (and is, therefore, conscientious) will search for the high-quality alternative solution.

▶ Learning Objective 2 ▶

What Are the Problem-Solving and Decision-Making Steps?

Whatever complex problem you face, it is best to use the standard problem-solving and decision-making steps as a guide. These steps are similar to the systematic approach used in the scientific method and also contribute to critical thinking as explained later in the chapter. Figure 6-2 summarizes the steps involved in problem solving and decision making. It assumes that problem solving should take place in an orderly flow of steps. Paying attention to this model is important because deviating too far will often result in decision failure. Paul C. Nutt studied 356 decisions in medium to large organizations in the United States and Canada. He found that one-half of these decisions failed, meaning that the decision was not fully used

FIGURE 6-2

PROBLEM-SOLVING AND DECISION-MAKING STEPS

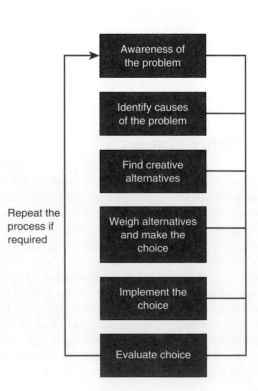

after two years. The typical reason for failure is that the decision makers did not take a systematic approach, such as searching for many alternative solutions. The managers involved also committed the human relations error of not involving enough people in the decisions.[11]

Although the problem-solving and decision-making steps appear logical, we emphasize again that people are frequently not entirely rational when making decisions. Emotions and personality traits can cloud decision making.

AWARENESS OF THE PROBLEM

Problem solving and decision making begin when somebody is aware that a problem exists. In most decision-making situations, problems are given to another person. At other times, people create their own problems to solve, or they find problems. Scotch tape had its origins in 1930, when somebody noticed a problem. The story goes like this:

> Richard Drew, a young engineer, was working for the Minnesota Mining and Manufacturing Co. (3M today), whose only product at the time was sandpaper. Drew was product testing one brand of sandpaper at a local body shop when he noticed that car painters were having trouble making clean dividing lines on two-color paint jobs. In 1925, as a solution to the problem, Drew invented a masking tape using crepe paper with lines of pressure-sensitive glue running along the edges. A problem encountered was that the tape kept falling off.
>
> An automotive painter told a 3M representative to "Take this tape back to those Scotch [negative stereotype that Scotch people are cheap] bosses of yours and tell them to put more adhesive on it." The bosses did, the tape worked, and the name was soon applied to the entire line of 3M tapes. Five years later, Drew overcame numerous production hurdles and developed the Scotch Brand Cellulose Tape that has become a worldwide staple.[12]

After you are aware that a problem exists or have identified it, recognize that it may represent an important opportunity. For example, if you are bothered enough by a problem facing your company, you might volunteer to be the person in charge of overcoming the problem.

IDENTIFY CAUSES OF THE PROBLEM

The causes of problems should be diagnosed and clarified before any action is taken because they are not always what they seem to be on the surface. Some may be more complicated than suspected or may even be the wrong problem you need to solve in a particular situation. Five key elements to ask questions about (along with some sample questions) are as follows:

1. **People.** What do the people involved contribute to the problem? Are they competent? Do they have an attitude problem?

2. **Materials.** Do we have the right materials available? Is the quality of the materials adequate?

3. **Machines and facilities.** Do we have the right machines and facilities to do the job? Have the machines and facilities changed?

4. **Physical environment.** Is anything wrong with the environment (such as toxic fumes making people sick)? Has the environment changed?

5. **Methods.** Are the processes and procedures adequate? Have new methods been introduced that workers do not understand?

FIGURE 6-3

BASIC CAUSE-AND-EFFECT DIAGRAM

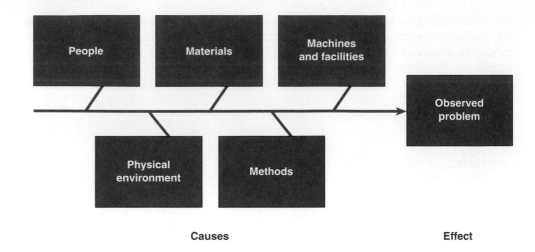

The approach to analyzing causes is often placed in a cause-and-effect diagram, as shown in Figure 6-3. The approach is sometimes referred to as a *fishbone diagram* because of the angles of the lines leading to the various causes. Notice that all the causes contribute to the problem at the right. Even when you have identified the general source of a problem, you may still need to dig further as to what, when, and where a problem *did not* occur. Suppose a friend talks about a fear of public speaking. By asking a few "but not" questions, you might be able to identify a major cause of the problem. Let's try out the method:

Your friend:	I'm horribly afraid of public speaking. I hate going up in front of class.
You:	But have you ever not been afraid of speaking to a group of people?
Your friend:	Yes, I can remember once feeling okay speaking at a victory dinner for my high school soccer team. We came in first place in the region.
You:	What did you talk about?
Your friend:	I told a cute story about how my mother and father put a soccer ball in my crib. I hugged it every day like it was a teddy bear.
You:	So why weren't you afraid of giving that talk?
Your friend:	I knew what I was talking about. I didn't have to rehearse.
You:	What else was different about the talk?
Your friend:	It wasn't like talking to strangers. I was just there with my buddies and our coaches.
You:	What you are really telling me is that public speaking is okay when you are well prepared and you are in a comfortable surrounding?
Your friend:	Thanks for helping me understand my problem.

FIND CREATIVE ALTERNATIVES

Creativity and imagination enter into problem solving and decision making. Successful decision makers have the ability to think of different alternatives. The person who pushes to find one more alternative to a problem is often the person who finds a breakthrough solution. The more alternatives you generate, the more likely you will find a useful solution to your problem. In the words of business strategy expert and consultant Gary Hamel, "Innovation is a numbers game. It takes 1,000 wacky ideas to find 100 things worth putting any money at all on, to find 10 ideas worth really investing in, to wind up with one really great idea."[13]

WEIGH ALTERNATIVES AND MAKE THE CHOICE

This stage refers simply to examining the pros and cons of the various alternatives in the previous stages and then making a choice. In a major decision, each alternative would have to be given serious consideration. In practice, weighing alternatives often means jotting down the key good and bad points of each possible choice. The essence of decision making is selecting the right course of action to follow. You have to choose an alternative, even if it is not to go ahead with a new plan of action. For instance, after conducting a job campaign, you could decide *not* to change jobs. Instead of coming to a decision, some people overanalyze a problem. Do you suffer from "analysis paralysis," or do you make up your mind after a reasonable amount of thought?

In choosing an alternative, it is helpful to remember that most problems really have multiple solutions. You therefore do not have to be overly concerned with finding the only correct answer to your problem. For instance, there might be several effective ways of reducing the costs of running a department.

Another useful consideration about choices is that it is best to reduce the number of possible choices you have to make. With too many choices, you might freeze in terms of decision making, such as trying to choose one among fifteen different television sets. Psychology professor Barry Schwartz of Swarthmore College notes that as we face more and more options we become overloaded. "Choice no longer liberates, but debilitates. It might even be said to tyrannize."[14]

IMPLEMENT THE CHOICE

After you decide which course of action to take, you have to put the choice into effect. Some decisions are more difficult to implement than others. Decisions made by top management, for example, are sometimes so difficult to implement that they have to be reversed. An executive at a major online retailer announced a new policy that all customer problems would have to be resolved by e-mail and that the toll-free number for customer assistance would be disbanded. Hundreds of customers complained about the new policy by e-mail, and many customer accounts became inactive. The executive reconsidered the decision in terms of its effect on customer service and goodwill and reinstated the toll-free line. The general point is that to implement many decisions, the human element must be taken into consideration.

EVALUATE THE CHOICE

The decision-making sequence is not complete until the decision has been evaluated. Evaluation may take a considerable period of time because the results of your decision are not always immediately apparent. Suppose you receive two job offers. It might take several months to a year to determine whether you are satisfied with the job you accepted. It would be necessary to look at the factors you think are most important in a job. Among them might be "Is there opportunity for advancement?" "Are the people here friendly?" "Is the work interesting?"

Evaluating your choice would be further complicated by the difficulty of determining how you might have fared in the job you didn't accept. Now and then, you might obtain some information to suggest what that alternative held in store for you, as did a woman who turned down a job offer with a new and promising company. She questioned that decision until she read one morning a year later that the company had gone into bankruptcy.

What happens when your evaluation of a decision is negative? You go back to the drawing board, as the line and arrow on the left-hand side of Figure 6-2 indicates. Because your first decision was not a good one, you are faced with another problem situation. A helpful decision-making aid is to visualize what you would do if the alternative you chose proved to be dreadful—the **worst-case scenario.** Suppose, for example, you choose a job that proves to be unsuited to your talents. Would you resign as soon as your mistake became apparent, or would you sweat it out for a year to show some employment stability? Or would you retain the job while starting to look for a more suitable job? Developing a worst-case-scenario plan helps prevent you from becoming overwhelmed by a bad decision. Closely related to the worst-case scenario is establishing an **exit strategy** that determines in advance how you will get out of a bad decision, such as having joined a failing family business.

Worst-case scenario
helpful decision-making aid that involves visualizing what you would do if the alternative chosen proved to be dreadful

Exit strategy
determining in advance how to get out of a bad decision, such as having joined a failing family business

BRAIN TEASERS FOR IMPROVING YOUR PROBLEM-SOLVING ABILITY

A widely accepted belief is that solving difficult problems and puzzles enhances your problem-solving ability. Among these brain teasers could be crossword puzzles, some types of video games, and various types of word puzzles. Just to give you a brief mental workout, here we present an example of frame games (Figure 6-4) and Sudoku (Figure 6-5). You may be less familiar with the frame game, so here is an example: The words in the box below symbolize a popular saying ("dog days"):

Sunday Poodle
Monday German Shepherd
Tuesday Springer Spaniel

FIGURE 6-4

FRAME GAMES

Source: The frame games are from Terry Stickels, "Frame Games," *USA Weekend*, March 10–12, 2006, p. 26; Stickels, *USA Weekend*, December 19–21, 2008, p. 11; Stickels, USAWeekend.com, July 26, 2008, p. 11.

Can you solve these puzzles? Each communicates a well-known saying, person, place, or thing.

SPINAL
SPINAL
SPINAL
SPINAL

SHOP   SHOP
U

	6		1		4		5	
		8	3		5	6		
2								1
8			4		7			6
		6				3		
7			9		1			4
5								2
		7	2		6	9		
	4		5		8		7	

FIGURE 6-5

SUDOKU

Fill in the Sudoku grid so that every row, every column, and every 3 x 3 box contains the digits 1 through 9.

Performing activities such as these regularly might sharpen your mental acuity for problem solving on the job and in school. The answers to the Sudoku and the frame games are presented following the references in this chapter.

What Do I Need to Know About Creativity in Decision Making?

◀ Learning Objective 3 ◀

Creativity is helpful at any stage of problem solving but is essential for being aware of problems, analyzing their causes, and searching for alternative solutions. Simply put, **creativity** is the ability to develop good ideas that can be put into action. Finding a creative idea usually involves a flash of insight as to how to solve a problem, such as that experienced by the person who thought of Scotch tape. The flash of insight might take place at the workplace or while engaged in other activity, such as jogging, walking, showering, or watching a movie. If you are aware that you have a problem to solve, the sudden insight is more likely to flash into your mind. For example, you might want to solve the problem of adding a couple of more influential people into your network. So while you are taking out the garbage, the names of a couple of potential contacts might surface into your brain. Your mind has been working on your problem below your level of awareness.

Creativity
the ability to develop good ideas that can be put into action

When many people see or hear the word *creativity*, they think of a rarefied talent. A more helpful perspective is to recognize that not all creativity requires wild imagination. The emphasis here is on creativity applied to business and personal life rather than on creativity in science, technology, and the arts.

A major theme of this chapter is that for the vast majority of people, it is possible to improve their creativity. As explained in the *Encyclopedia of Creativity*, creativity can be taught, learned, enhanced, and mastered. Enough is known about creativity that it can be integrated into every level in the educational system.[15]

"Imagination is a very special thing, and we always try to find students with that ability."
—David Greenberg, senior vice president, human resources, for L'Oréal USA. Quoted in the *Wall Street Journal*, September 12, 2006, p. B8.

MEASURING YOUR CREATIVE POTENTIAL

One way to understand creativity is to try out exercises used to measure creative potential. Begin with Human Relations Self-Assessment Quiz 6-1, which measures creativity based on verbal ability.

CHARACTERISTICS OF CREATIVE WORKERS

Creative workers tend to have different intellectual and personality characteristics from their less creative counterparts. In general, creative people are more mentally

Human Relations Self-Assessment Quiz 6-1

Creative Personality Test

Answer each of the following statements as mostly true or mostly false. We are looking for general trends, so do not be concerned that under certain circumstances your answer might be different in response to a particular statement.

	Mostly True	Mostly False
1. I think novels are a waste of time, so I am more likely to read a nonfiction book.		
2. You have to admit, some crooks are ingenious.		
3. I pretty much wear the same style and colors of clothing regularly.		
4. To me most issues have a clear-cut right side or wrong side.		
5. I enjoy it when my boss hands me vague instructions.		
6. When I'm surfing the Internet, I sometimes investigate topics about which I know very little.		
7. Business before leisure activities is a hard-and-fast rule in my life.		
8. Taking a different route to work is fun, even if it takes longer.		
9. From time to time I have made friends with people of a different sex, race, religion, or ethnic background from myself.		
10. Rules and regulations should be respected, but deviating from them once in a while is acceptable.		
11. People who know me say that I have an excellent sense of humor.		
12. I have been known to play practical jokes or pranks on people.		
13. Writers should avoid using unusual words and word combinations.		
14. Detective work would have some appeal to me.		
15. I am much more likely to tell a rehearsed joke than make a witty comment.		
16. Almost all advertising on television bores me.		
17. Why write letters or send e-mail greetings to friends when there are so many clever greeting cards already available in the stores or online?		
18. For most important problems in life, there is one best solution available.		
19. Pleasing me means more to me than pleasing others.		
20. I'm enjoying taking this test.		

Scoring and Interpretation:

Give yourself a plus 1 for each answer scored in the creative direction as follows:

1. Mostly False	8. Mostly True	15. Mostly False
2. Mostly True	9. Mostly True	16. Mostly False
3. Mostly False	10. Mostly True	17. Mostly False
4. Mostly False	11. Mostly True	18. Mostly False
5. Mostly True	12. Mostly True	19. Mostly True
6. Mostly True	13. Mostly False	20. Mostly True
7. Mostly False	14. Mostly True	

A score of 15 or more suggests that your personality and attitudes are similar to those of a creative person. A score of between 9 and 14 suggests an average similarity with the personality and attitudes of a creative person. A score of 8 or less suggests that your personality is dissimilar to that of a creative person. You are probably more of a conformist and not highly open-minded in your thinking at this point in your life. To become more creative, you may need to develop more flexibility in your thinking and a higher degree of open-mindedness.

flexible than others, which allows them to overcome the traditional ways of looking at problems. This flexibility often shows up in practical jokes and other forms of playfulness, such as making up a rap song about the company's product line. The characteristics of creative workers can be grouped into three broad areas: knowledge, intellectual abilities, and personality.[16]

Knowledge

Creative thinking requires a broad background of information, including facts and observations. Knowledge supplies the building blocks for generating and combining ideas. This is particularly true because, according to some experts, creativity always comes down to combining things in a new and different way. A few of the new smaller market energy drinks, for example, are a combination of caffeinated and alcoholic beverages. (These drinks are controversial, however, and might be subject to legal challenges.) Taking Human Relations Self-Assessment Quiz 6-2 will help you appreciate how possessing knowledge contributes to thinking creatively.

Intellectual Abilities

In general, creative workers tend to be bright rather than brilliant. Extraordinarily high intelligence is not required to be creative, but creative people are good at generating alternative solutions to problems in a short period of time. According to Tufts University dean of the School of Arts and Sciences and professor of psychology Robert Sternberg, the key to creative intelligence is **insight,** an ability to know what information is relevant, to find connections between the old and the new, to combine facts that are unrelated, and to see the "big picture."[17] Creative people also maintain a youthful curiosity throughout their lives, and the curiosity is not centered on only their own field of expertise. Instead, their range of interests encompasses many areas of knowledge, and they generate enthusiasm toward almost any puzzling problem.

Creative people are able to think divergently. They can expand the number of alternatives to a problem, thus moving away from a single solution. Yet the creative thinker also knows when it is time to think convergently, narrowing the number of useful solutions. For example, the divergent thinker might think of twenty-seven different names for a Web site to sell high-fashion buttons. Yet at some point, he or she will have to converge toward choosing the best name, such as www.chicbutton.com.

Creativity can stem from both *fluid intelligence* and *crystallized intelligence.* Fluid intelligence depends on raw processing ability, or how quickly you learn information and solve problems. Like raw athletic ability, fluid intelligence begins to decline by age thirty, particularly because our nerve conduction slows. Crystallized intelligence is accumulated knowledge that increases with age and experience.

Personality

The emotional and other nonintellectual aspects of a person heavily influence creative problem solving. Creative people tend to have a positive self-image without being blindly self-confident. Because they are self-confident, creative people are able to cope with criticism of their ideas. Creative people have the ability to tolerate the isolation necessary for developing ideas. Talking to others is a good source of ideas. Yet at some point, the creative problem solver has to work alone and concentrate.

Creative people are frequently nonconformists and do not need strong approval from the group. Many creative problem solvers are thrill seekers who find developing imaginative solutions to problems to be a source of thrills. Creative people are also persistent, which is especially important for seeing that a new idea is implemented.

Insight
an ability to know what information is relevant, to find connections between the old and the new, to combine facts that are unrelated, and to see the "big picture"

Human Relations Self-Assessment Quiz   6-2

Rhyme and Reason

A noted creativity expert says that exercises in rhyming release creative energy—they stir imagination into action. While doing the following exercises, remember that rhyme is frequently a matter of sound and does not have to involve similar or identical spelling. This exercise deals with light and frivolous emotions. After each "definition," write two rhyming words to which it refers.

Examples

1. Large hog   Big _____   pig _____
2. Television   Boob _____   tube _____
3. A computer command tool for the home   House _____   mouse _____

Now try these:

1. Happy father
2. False pain
3. Formed like a simian
4. Highest-ranking police worker
5. Voyage by a large boat
6. Corpulent feline
7. Melancholy fellow
8. Clever beginning
9. Heavy and unbroken slumber
10. Crazy custom
11. Lengthy melody
12. Weak man
13. Instruction at the seashore
14. Criticism lacking in effectiveness
15. A person who murders for pleasurable excitement
16. Musical stringed instrument with full, rich sounds
17. Courageous person who is owned as property by another
18. Mature complaint
19. Strange hair growing on the lower part of a man's face
20. Drooping marine crustacean
21. A computer whiz with a ridiculous sense of humor
22. You make one up now for the most important question of all

Answers and Interpretation:

The more of these rhymes you were able to come up with, the higher your creative potential. You would also need an advanced vocabulary to score very high (for instance, you have to know what a simian and a crustacean are). Ten or more correct rhymes would tend to show outstanding creative potential, at least in the verbal area. Here are the answers:

1. Glad dad	7. Sad lad	13. Beach teach	19. Weird beard
2. Fake ache	8. Smart start	14. Weak critique	20. Limp shrimp
3. Ape shape	9. Deep sleep	15. Thriller killer	21. Absurd nerd
4. Top cop	10. Mad fad	16. Mellow cello	22. 2 bonus points
5. Ship trip	11. Long song	17. Brave slave	
6. Fat cat	12. Frail male	18. Ripe gripe	

Continued

If you can think of a sensible substitute for any of these answers, give yourself a bonus point. For example, for number 21, how about a freak geek?

Source: The current test is an updated version of Eugene Raudsepp with George P. Hough, Jr., *Creative Growth Games* (New York: Harcourt Brace Jovanovich, 1977). Reprinted with permission.

Selling a creative idea to the right people requires considerable follow-up. Creative people enjoy dealing with uncertainty and chaos. A creative person, for example, would enjoy the challenge of taking over a customer service department that was way behind schedule and ineffective. Less creative people become frustrated quickly when their jobs are unclear and disorder exists.

Self-reflection and a concentration on feelings are characteristic of many creative people. The quiet thinking is helpful in finding useful ideas, as in thinking of how to solve a difficult problem while walking alone or taking a shower. Creative people are also open and responsive to feelings and emotions in the world around them.

THE CONDITIONS NECESSARY FOR CREATIVITY

Creativity is not simply a random occurrence. Well-known creativity researcher and professor of business administration at Harvard Business School, Teresa M. Amabile, has summarized twenty-two years of her research about creativity in the workplace. Her findings are also supported by others.[18] Creativity takes place when three components come together: expertise, creative thinking skills, and the right type of motivation. *Expertise* refers to the necessary knowledge to put facts together. The more ideas floating around in your head, the more likely you are to combine them in some useful way, as already described.

Creative thinking refers to how flexibly and imaginatively individuals approach problems. If you know how to keep digging for alternatives and to avoid getting stuck in the status quo, your chances of being creative multiply. Along these same lines, you are much more likely to be creative if you are intentionally seeking ideas, such as always being on the lookout for ways to save money. Persevering, or sticking with a problem to a conclusion, is essential for finding creative solutions. A few rest breaks to gain a fresh perspective may be helpful, but the creative person keeps coming back until a solution emerges. Or the creative idea might surface outside of the work setting, as described earlier.

The right type of *motivation* is the third essential ingredient for creative thought. A fascination with or passion for the task is much more important then searching for external rewards. People will be the most creative when they are motivated primarily by the satisfaction and challenge of the work itself. Passion for the task and high intrinsic motivation contribute to a total absorption in the work and intense concentration, resulting in the flow experience. A creative businessperson, such as an entrepreneur developing a plan for worldwide distribution of a product, will often achieve the experience of flow. One analysis of creativity suggests that hard work and the love of the task can be at least as important as raw talent in ensuring creative success.[19] In addition to the internal conditions that foster creativity, five factors outside the person are key:

1. An environmental need must stimulate the setting of a goal. This is another way of saying, "Necessity is the mother of invention." For example, several years ago independent hardware stores were faced with the challenge of large chains, such as Home Depot and Lowe's, driving them out of business. Many of these independent

Human Relations in Practice

With barely a second thought, Mark Grandusky bent over and snatched a seventy-five-pound weight off the floor with one hand and placed it on a two-foot table. No, he's not a circus strongman. Grandusky is sales manager for one of the fastest-selling products at Gorbel Inc., of Fishers, New York, a maker of jib cranes and overhead lifting devices. He was demonstrating the company's G-Force line of "intelligent lifting devices," designed to lift loads of up to 660 pounds. "We give workers a way to safely lift and move things more efficiently with less product damage," he said.

Gorbel was founded in 1977 as a maker of overhead cranes to help manufacturers move multi-ton loads from place to place. In the later 1980s, though, company leaders noticed that manufacturers were cutting costs by taking advantage of new technology to make lighter products.

Gorbel, which has about two hundred workers, responded by creating a line of lifting devices for lighter loads and stumbled into the growing ergonomics market in which employers seek to reduce workplace injuries by taking the strain off their workers' backs, shoulders, and arms, said David Butwid, the company's vice president of global sales and marketing.

"We were just following a trend," said Butwid. "We didn't know workers' compensation was having such a profound effect on the pocketbook of corporations. The accountants figured if they can make things safe, they can reduce workers' compensation."

The G-Force, which rides on an overhead track, uses servomechanisms to read motion feedback and provide constant corrections to the movement of the object, creating a seemingly limitless range of direction.

A typical chain-driven lift, by contrast, requires workers to push up-down, side-to-side buttons to get an object into proper position. "Workers hate equipment that can't do a job as fast as they can," said Butwid. "They won't use something that slows them down."

Clients include manufacturers of heavy machinery, automobiles, and automobiles parts. Butwid said Gorbel is exploring other potential uses for the technology, such as lifting patients in medical centers. "We're looking for ways to expand outside the manufacturing sector, and we know the market is there. The market for lifting and moving devices in the medical industry is large enough for us to do more research," he said.

Questions

1. What environmental need, or needs, led to the development of the G-Force line of intelligent lifting devices?
2. Working alone or in a group, identify another potential market for the G-Force lifting devices.

Source: Patrick Flanigan, "An Uplifting Business: Crane Company's Products Take Strain off Workers' Backs," *Democrat and Chronicle* (Rochester, NY), December 2, 2007, p. 1E; retrieved February 2, 2009, from: www.gorbel.com/gforce/g-force.asp

stores survived by forming buying alliances with each other so that they could purchase inventory in larger quantities—and therefore at lower prices. The independents also emphasize doing home repairs, such as fixing ripped screens and broken windows. The accompanying Human Relations in Practice insert illustrates creativity surfacing because of an environmental need.

2. Another condition that fosters creativity is enough conflict and tension to put people on edge. Robert Sutton, professor of engineering at Stanford University, advises managers to prod happy people into fighting among themselves to stimulate creativity. The fights should be about ideas, not personality conflicts and name calling. For example, a group member should be given time to defend his or her work, and then the ideas should be sharply criticized by the other group members.[20] Cirque du Soleil, the world-famous circus, capitalizes on the importance of conflict for creativity. Cirque officials generally ensure there is a mix of nationalities and viewpoints when they assemble a creative team. Daniel Lamarre, the troupe's president, says that easy consensus is the enemy of groundbreaking ideas. The ideas, in this context, usually refer to fascinating acts.[21]

3. Another external factor for creativity is encouragement, including a permissive atmosphere that welcomes new ideas. A manager or team leader who encourages imagination and original thinking and does not punish people for making honest mistakes is likely to receive creative ideas from people. W. L Gore is often cited among the world's most innovative companies. You may be familiar with their waterproof fabrics and guitar strings. The cornerstone of Gore's innovative culture has been a permissive atmosphere. In the words of human resources associate Jackie Brinton, "We believe in the power of the individual who is given the freedom to do great things and in the beauty of small teams, even though we're now operating on a global, coordinated scale."[22]

4. Humor is a key environmental condition for enhancing creativity. Humor has always been linked to creativity. Humor gets the creative juices flowing, and effective humor requires creativity. Thomas Edison started every workday with a joke-telling session. Mike Vance, chair of the Creative Thinking Association of America, says, "Humor is unmasking the hypocritical. What makes us laugh often is seeing how things are screwed up—then sometimes seeing how we can fix them. Whenever I go into a company and don't hear much laughter, I know it's not a creative place.[23]

5. A final key environmental condition to be considered here is how much time pressure the problem solver should face to trigger creativity. Conventional wisdom says that people produce the best when pressure is highest—for example, thinking of ways to keep a business running after a disaster, such as a fire, flood, or terrorist attack. Yet studies show that the more workers feel pressed for time, the less likely they are to produce creative output, such as solving a tricky problem or envisioning a new product, or to have other such "ah ha!" experiences that result in innovation. Time pressures may diminish creativity because they limit a worker's freedom to think through different options and directions. A subtle finding, however, is that time pressures may help creativity if the worker is focused on a single task that he or she considers important.[24] So if you are under heavy time pressure to arrive at a creative solution, focus on one task.

Despite the theme of permissiveness in several of the conditions for enhancing creativity, constraints also have their place. Individuals or teams with budget constraints and time constraints sometimes find that these constraints help them rise to the occasion. Marissa Ann Mayer, the vice president for search products and user experience at Google, contends that constraints can actually speed product development. Google often gets a sense of just how good a new concept is if they simply prototype it (try it out) for a single day or week. Another constraint would be limiting team size to two or three people.[25]

How Do I Improve My Creativity?

◀ Learning Objective 4 ◀

Because of the importance of creative problem solving, many techniques have been developed to improve creativity. Here we look at both specific techniques and general strategies for becoming more creative. The goal of these experiences is to think like a creative problem solver. Such a person lets his or her imagination wander. He or she ventures beyond the constraints that limit most people. The result of thinking more creatively is to bring something new into existence. *Something new* can be a totally new creation or a combination of existing things and ideas. To focus again on the subject, when we refer to creativity in business we are not necessarily thinking of revolutionary ideas that create a new industry. The new design of containers for prescription medicine is a representative example. Old prescription bottles were difficult to open and read, whereas the new prescription bottles are color coded to specific medicines and easy to read and open.[26] Nevertheless, many of the older-style prescription bottles are still in use.

CONCENTRATE INTENSELY ON THE TASK AT HAND

The ability to concentrate was mentioned earlier as a characteristic that contributes to effective problem solving in general. The ability to eliminate distractions also contributes mightily to generating new ideas. At times we think we are thinking intently about our problem, yet in reality we may be thinking about something that interferes with creativity. Among the office distractions that interfere with concentration are phone calls, a computer beep informing you of an incoming message, a person in the next cubicle talking loudly on the phone, and a friendly hello from a work associate walking past your cubicle. All the methods that follow for creativity enhancement require concentration.

OVERCOME TRADITIONAL MENTAL SETS

Traditional mental set
fixed way of thinking about objects and activities

An important consequence of becoming more intellectually flexible is that you can overcome a **traditional mental set,** a fixed way of thinking about objects and activities. Overcoming traditional mental sets is important because the major block to creativity is perceiving things in a traditional way. All creative examples presented so far in this chapter have involved this process, and here is another one. You may be familiar with the Nalgene sports bottle for carrying water and other fluids. Aside from its decorative colors, a key feature is its durability. The bottle had its origins in chemical laboratories—the traditional use for a durable plastic bottle. However, by the 1970s, managers at Nalgene noticed that scientists were using the durable bottles to hold water for camping and hiking. The company soon started a division to market its "laboratory" bottles to Boy Scouts and other hikers.[27] Today, the company is challenged to keep up with the demand for the Nalgene bottle. In 2008, however, their bottles made with bisphenol A (BPA) were recalled from stores because of consumer worries about risks associated with the chemical. Nalgene management quickly solved the problem by using BPA-free alternatives.[28]

An effective way of overcoming a traditional mental set (or thinking outside the box) is to challenge the status quo. If you want to develop an idea that will impress your boss or turn around an industry, you must use your imagination. Question the old standby that things have always been done in a particular way.

Vertical thinking
analytical, logical process that results in few answers; the vertical thinker looks for the one best solution to a problem, much like solving an equation in algebra

DISCIPLINE YOURSELF TO THINK LATERALLY

A major challenge in developing creative thinking skills is to learn how to think laterally in addition to vertically. **Vertical thinking** is an analytical, logical process that results in few answers. The vertical thinker is looking for the one best solution to a problem, much like solving an equation in algebra. In contrast, **lateral thinking** spreads out to find many different alternative solutions to a problem. In short,

Lateral thinking
process of spreading out to find many different alternative solutions to a problem

critical thinking is vertical, and creative thinking is lateral. A vertical thinker might say, "I must find a part-time job to supplement my income. My income is not matching my expenses." The lateral thinker might say, "I need more money. Let me think of the various ways of earning more money. I can find a second job, get promoted where I am working, cut my expenses, run a small business out of my home . . ."

To learn to think laterally, you have to develop the mental set that every problem has multiple alternative solutions. Do not leave the problem until you have sketched out multiple alternatives. Use a pencil or pen and paper or a computer screen, but do not walk away from your problem until you have thought of multiple alternatives.

CONDUCT BRAINSTORMING SESSIONS

The best-known method of improving creativity is **brainstorming,** a technique by which group members think of multiple solutions to a problem. Using brainstorming, a group of six people might sit around a table generating new ideas for a product. During the idea-generating part of brainstorming, potential solutions are not criticized or evaluated in any way. In this way, spontaneity is encouraged. Brainstorming continues as a standard procedure for producing creative ideas in all types of organizations. If you engage in brainstorming on the job or in personal life, you will be both solving a real problem and enhancing your creative thinking skills at the same time. Rules for brainstorming are presented in Figure 6-6. Brainstorming has many variations, including an electronic approach and brainwriting.

> **Brainstorming**
> technique by which group members think of multiple solutions to a problem

An important strategy for enhancing the outcome of brainstorming is to have intellectually and culturally diverse group members. Some group leaders purposely choose people of different problem-solving styles (such as sensation and intuitive types) to encourage more diverse thinking. The sensation type might have more "brainstorms" based on facts, whereas the intuitive type might have more brainstorms based on hunches. Cultural diversity is likely to improve brainstorming because people with different cultural experiences often bring different viewpoints to bear on the problem. A basic example is that when developing new food products, members with different ethnic backgrounds are chosen for a brainstorming group. You will recall that Cirque du Soleil relies on heterogeneous groups to produce new ideas.

Collecting creative ideas is so important to the lifeblood of business firms that the brainstorming process continues to be refined. A recent approach is to hypnotize employees to enhance their ability to think creatively. Corporate hypnotist Hal Goldberg says hypnosis works by making people ultra-relaxed through breathing, meditation, and visualization. Relaxation lowers inhibitions, and when people are less inhibited, they offer "their craziest ideas, which are sometimes the best," says Goldberg.[29]

FIGURE 6-6

RULES AND GUIDELINES FOR BRAINSTORMING

1. Use groups of about five to seven people.
2. Encourage the spontaneous expression of ideas. All suggestions are welcome, even if they are outlandish or outrageous. The least workable ideas can be edited out when the idea-generation phase is completed.
3. Quantity and variety are very important. The greater the number of ideas, the greater the likelihood of a breakthrough idea.
4. Encourage combination and improvement of ideas. This process is referred to as *piggybacking* or *hitchhiking*.
5. One person serves as the secretary and records the ideas, perhaps posting them on a whiteboard or a computer with a projection device.
6. Do not overstructure by following any of the preceding rules too rigidly. Brainstorming is a spontaneous process.

Brainwriting

Brainwriting
arriving at creative ideas by jotting
them down

In many situations, brainstorming by yourself produces as many or more useful ideas than does brainstorming in groups. **Brainwriting** is arriving at creative ideas by jotting them down yourself. The creativity-improvement techniques discussed so far will help you develop the mental flexibility necessary for brainstorming. After you have loosened up your mental processes, you will be ready to tackle your most vexing problems. Self-discipline is very important for brainwriting because some people have a tendency to postpone something as challenging as thinking alone. A variation of brainwriting is for group members to pass along their ideas from working alone to another member who reads them and adds his or her own ideas.

Brainwriting supports group brainstorming in two important ways. One approach is for team leaders to alert participants of the upcoming brainstorming session and encourage them to bring creative ideas into the meeting. David Perkins, a professor at the Harvard Graduate School of Education, says, "The best way to get good ideas is to get people to write them down privately and then bring them in."[30] A second approach is to permit participants to submit additional ideas up to twelve hours after the meeting. In this way participants who were shy about submitting a particular idea in a group will have a voice.[31] Also, we often think of the right thing to say after an event— the phenomenon of "I wish I would have thought of that then instead of now."

In the various types of brainstorming just discussed, collecting wild ideas is only the start of the process. After ideas are collected, the group or each member carefully evaluates and analyzes the various alternatives. (You also need to refine your ideas from brainwriting.) It is usually important to also specify the implementation details. For example, how do you actually convert an industrial robot into an amusement park ride?

ESTABLISH IDEA QUOTAS FOR YOURSELF

To enhance creativity, many companies assign idea quotas to workers. For example, workers might be instructed to bring one good idea for earning or saving money to every meeting. Establishing idea quotas is similar to brainwriting with a goal in mind. An easy way of getting started is to establish a monthly minimum quota of one creative idea to improve your personal life and one to improve your job or school performance. Although this exercise might only take about five minutes of thinking each month, it could have a tremendous impact on your life. After you have gained the skill of developing one good idea per month, you might up your quota to two or three ideas. As with any creative idea, you will need an action plan to make the idea a reality. For example, one creative idea might be "I will sell buried treasure on eBay." Next, you have to find the buried treasure or find a supplier, photograph the treasure, and so forth.

ENGAGE IN MULTICULTURAL EXPERIENCES

A recent analysis of many studies supports the assumption that multicultural experience fosters creativity.[32] *Multicultural experience* in this context refers to all direct and indirect experiences of encountering or interacting with people from foreign cultures. This definition is helpful because it suggests that travel to other countries is not the only way to obtain multicultural experience. For example, eating in a foreign-themed restaurant or interacting with people from another culture via the Internet would give you at least some multicultural experience.

Multicultural experience fosters creativity in several ways. First, you might obtain direct access to novel ideas and concepts from other cultures. For example, an American visitor to Japan might observe that many Japanese people read novels on their cell phones and then convince his or her company to start a similar service in the United States.

Second, multicultural living experience may allow people to recognize that the same surface behavior has different functions and implications. For example, in some cultures leaving food on your plate is a compliment to the host, implying that you had enough food. In another culture, leaving food on the plate would suggest the food wasn't good. A stretch application of this concept is that the act of using a fountain pen might be perceived as (a) a means of signing an important document or (b) as a gesture of status. The latter is why expensive fountain pens still sell even if their practical use is limited.

Third, exposure to foreign cultures might shake up a person's thinking enough to access unconventional knowledge when back in their own cultures. For example, you might observe that people in parts of Canada and Iceland actually pay to stay in a hotel made of ice and sleep in sleeping bags in their ice beds. As a hotel manager, you might say to yourself, "Maybe we can charge people to stay overnight in a swamp here in Florida."

Fourth, exposure to other cultures may lead to a psychological readiness to recruit ideas from unfamiliar sources and places. The well-traveled manager might now be more willing to ask entry-level workers for their suggestions on improving products, services, and work procedures. Or during "Bring Your Child to Work Day," the manager might ask the visiting children for useful suggestions.

Fifth, cultural exploration might foster a willingness to synthesize seemingly incompatible ideas from diverse cultures. For example, the rickshaws used in Asia sparked the idea for a similar service to provide transportation to businesspeople and tourists in crowded cities such as New York City and London. The modern rickshaw is usually bicycle driven and referred to as a pedicab.

OBTAIN ADEQUATE PHYSICAL EXERCISE

Physical exercise plays an important role in preparing you for creative thinking. Physical movement stimulates the brain by bringing it more blood and oxygen.[33] At the same time, the exercise may reduce stress that makes it difficult to concentrate enough to think creatively. Exercise also enhances activity in the frontal lobe, the region of the brain involved in abstract reasoning and attention. Participating in physical activity may also foster creativity because many flashes of insight occur while engaged in leisure pursuits.

Phillip A. Newbold, the CEO of Memorial Hospital in South Bend, Indiana, runs the Innovation Café, a laboratory for collecting creative ideas. He holds regular brainstorming sessions in which participants are often required to stand up for the entire twenty-one-minute exercise so they practice thinking on their feet. Newbold, sixty-one years old, runs, bikes, swims, and competes in ironman triathlons. He says, "I couldn't do my innovation marathon if I weren't in marvelous physical shape."[34] The fact that physical activity can boost creative thinking should not be interpreted in isolation. Without other factors going for you, such as a storehouse of knowledge and passion for the task, physical exercise will not lead to mental breakthroughs.

PLAY THE ROLES OF EXPLORER, ARTIST, JUDGE, AND LAWYER

A method for improving creativity has been proposed that incorporates many of the suggestions already made. The method calls for you to adopt four roles in your thinking.[35]

1. Be an explorer. Speak to people in different fields and get ideas that you can use. For example, if you are a telecommunications specialist, speak to salespeople and manufacturing specialists.

2. **Be an artist by stretching your imagination.** Strive to spend about 5 percent of your day asking "what if" questions. For example, a sales manager at a fresh-fish distributor might ask, "What if some new research suggests that eating fish causes intestinal cancer in humans?" Also remember to challenge the commonly perceived rules in your field. A bank manager challenged why customers needed their canceled checks returned each month. This questioning led to some banks not returning canceled checks unless the customer paid an additional fee for the service. (As a compromise, most banks send customers photocopies of about ten checks on one page.)

3. **Know when to be a judge.** After developing some wild ideas, at some point you have to evaluate them. Do not be so critical that you discourage your own imaginative thinking, but be critical enough to prevent attempting to implement weak ideas.

4. **Achieve results by playing the role of a lawyer.** Negotiate and find ways to implement your ideas within your field or place of work. The explorer, artist, and judge stages of creative thought might last only a short time toward developing a creative idea. Yet you may spend months or even years getting your brainstorm implemented. For example, it took a long time for the developer of the electronic pager to finally get the product manufactured and distributed on a large scale.

▶ **Learning Objective 5** ▶

How Does Critical Thinking Relate to Problem Solving and Creativity?

Critical thinking

solving problems and making decisions through a systematic evaluation of evidence

Another way of understanding and improving problem solving and creativity is to regard both processes as being part of critical thinking. Probably any course you have ever taken, including mathematics, chemistry, history, political science, and English literature, was aimed partially at improving your critical thinking. This is true because critical thinking is a broad concept that includes many different cognitive, or intellectual, behaviors that focus on problem solving. **Critical thinking** refers to solving problems and making decisions through a systematic evaluation of evidence.[36] A person who thinks clearly and rationally is engaged in critical thinking, and the problem-solving steps described in this chapter help you think critically. Also, the suggestions for improving creativity will help you attain high-quality solutions to problems. Critical thinking proceeds in steps, as shown in Figure 6-7.

Step 1   is to have a healthy degree of skepticism about the argument or proposition being presented. Probe for logical flaws in the argument the other

FIGURE 6-7

STEPS IN CRITICAL THINKING

person might have made. The other person's emotional state might have made him or her a little irrational. Visualize yourself as a store manager in a chain of furniture stores. The CEO introduces a plan for saving money by firing two-thirds of the experienced full-time store associates and replacing them with part-time workers at modest wages. You are quite skeptical that this plan will help the company in the long run.

Step 2   is to evaluate the stated or unstated assumptions underlying the argument. You say to yourself, "The CEO is assuming that part-time, inexperienced associates will sell as much furniture and accessories as our experienced associates did. He is also assuming that knowledge of the business does not account for much. Another assumption is that the part-timers who replace the full-timers will be as loyal, even if not given benefits. I doubt these assumptions are correct." Evaluating assumptions is important because a persuasive speaker will often influence us not to carefully evaluate the logic of his or her position.

Step 3   is to imagine and attempt to evaluate alternative arguments. Here are a couple of other assumptions you might make: "Experienced and knowledgeable store associates are the lifeblood of our business. They are worth the compensation they receive because they generate more business and create a greater base of satisfied customers. Many part-time workers might sell furniture as a supplement to their regular job. Instead of feeling committed to our company, they might have high turnover."

Step 4   is to make a decision. You have given careful thought to top-management's plan, including having conducted some research. Your decision is to write an e-mail to the CEO that includes these thoughts: "I know we want to trim costs and increase profits. Our best profit generators are experienced, dedicated store associates. They give great decorating ideas to customers. Home Depot once tried to save money by dumping full-time associates. Customer service became so bad that the plan was reversed. Circuit City tried the same stunt of saving money by firing experienced store associates, and they went bankrupt."

Critical thinking is often difficult to accomplish for a variety of personal and situational factors that might prevent or limit us from critically evaluating a problem. The factors that influence problem-solving skill listed in Figure 6-1 might be considered as potential constraints on critical problem solving. Here we highlight a few possible constraints.

One personal factor is a person's emotional state. When we are too emotional in a negative or positive direction, our ability to critically evaluate a situation is diminished. Another personal factor is cognitive skills, including knowledge and wisdom. A person who is mentally sharp and has more knowledge is better able to think critically than a person with less cognitive skills and less knowledge. (In the above example, being familiar with the Home Depot and Circuit City experiences in reducing the number of full-time associates was quite useful.)

Situational factors, including the atmosphere of the company, also influence critical thinking. For example, in some companies critical thinking by employees about major issues is welcomed. In some other company atmospheres, critical thinking of issues outside your immediate area is discouraged. Another situational factor would be a crisis situation, such as a worker not taking time to reflect carefully on alternatives when he or she is charged with using company resources to establish a child pornography Web site. (The worker also did not engage in critical thinking when establishing the Web site.)

Concept Review
and Reinforcement

Key Terms

Problem, 152
Decision making, 152
Intuition, 154
Flow experience, 155
Worst-case scenario, 160

Exit strategy, 160
Creativity, 161
Insight, 163
Traditional mental set, 168
Vertical thinking, 168

Lateral thinking, 168
Brainstorming, 169
Brainwriting, 170
Critical thinking, 172

Summary and Review

Problem solving occurs when you try to remove an obstacle that is blocking a path you want to take or when you try to close the gap between what exists and what you want to exist. Decision making takes place after you encounter a problem and you select one alternative from the various courses of action that can be pursued. Many traits and characteristics influence the type of problem solver you are now or are capable of becoming. Among them are the following:

- Cognitive intelligence, education, and experience
- Emotional intelligence
- Flexibility versus rigidity
- Intuition
- Concentration
- Decisiveness and perfectionism
- Risk taking and thrill seeking
- Values of the decision maker

The decision-making process outlined in this chapter uses both the scientific method and intuition for making decisions in response to problems. Decision making follows an orderly flow of events:

1. You are aware of a problem or create one of your own.
2. You identify causes of the problem.
3. You find creative alternatives.
4. You weigh the alternatives and make a choice.
5. You implement the choice.
6. You evaluate whether you have made a sound choice. If your choice was unsound, you are faced with a new problem, and the cycle repeats itself.

Creativity is the ability to look for good ideas that can be put into action. Creative workers tend to have different intellectual and personality characteristics than their less creative counterparts. In general, creative people are more mentally flexible than others, which allows them to overcome the traditional way of looking at problems. These characteristics are as follows:

- **Knowledge.** Creative thinking requires a broad background of information, including facts and observations.
- **Intellectual abilities.** Creative workers tend to be bright rather than brilliant. The key to creative intelligence is insight. Creativity can stem from both fluid (raw) intelligence and crystallized (accumulated) intelligence.
- **Personality.** The emotional and other nonintellectual aspects of a person heavily influence creative problem solving. For example, creative people are frequently nonconformists and thrill seekers.

Creativity takes place when three components come together:

1. Expertise
2. Creative thinking skills (being flexible and imaginative)
3. The right type of motivation (passion for the task and intrinsic motivation)

Four factors outside the person play a key role in fostering creativity: an environmental need, enough conflict and tension to put people on edge, encouragement from management, and the presence of humor. Unless a person is working on a highly focused task, time pressures are likely to diminish creativity. Constraints, such as time and budgets, can often enhance creativity.

Methods of improving your creativity include the following:

- Concentrate intensely on the task at hand.
- Overcome traditional mental sets.
- Discipline yourself to think laterally.
- Conduct brainstorming sessions, including brainwriting.
- Borrow creative ideas.

- Establish idea quotas for yourself.
- Engage in multicultural experiences.
- Obtain adequate physical exercise.
- Play the roles of explorer, artist, judge, and lawyer.

Another way of understanding and improving problem solving and creativity is to regard both processes as part of critical thinking. The process has four steps:

1. Be skeptical of the argument or proposition offered.
2. Evaluate the stated or unstated assumptions underlying the argument.
3. Imagine and attempt to evaluate alternative arguments.
4. Make a decision.

Check Your Understanding

1. What would be some of the symptoms or signs of a "rigid thinker"?
2. Provide an example of how you or somebody you know is risk averse or loss averse.
3. Provide an example of how you have used intuition to your advantage in work or personal life.
4. Furnish an example from your own life in which you became aware of a problem. What led to this awareness?
5. Why does knowledge lead to creativity?
6. Provide an example of how a supervisor or teacher of yours encouraged you to be creative. How effective was this encouragement?

7. Why is being passionate about the task at hand almost essential for being creative?
8. If it is really true that being hypnotized helps workers become more creative, explain whether managers should order workers to be hypnotized.
9. How might having just a couple of creative ideas during your work life have a major impact on the success of your career?
10. Ask an experienced manager or professional how important creative thinking has been in his or her career. Be prepared to report back to class with your findings.

Web Corner

Problem-solving techniques:
www.mindtools.com

Development of Creative Thinking:
www.cre8ng.com

INTERNET SKILL BUILDER

Many Web sites offer creativity training and an opportunity for self-assessment with respect to creativity. One such site is www.creax.com, which offers creativity services as well as a comprehensive forty-question test

of creativity tendencies. The CREAX creativity test measures your creativity in eight different areas and visually depicts how your score compared to others who took the test. After you take the test, compare your results to the creativity test you took in this chapter. Also decide if the CREAX test is measuring personal characteristics that contribute to creative thinking, or if actual creative thinking is being tested. If CREAX is no longer in operation, insert "creativity training" in your search engine to find a comparable site.

Developing Your
Human Relations Skills

Human Relations Application Exercises

Applying Human Relations Exercise 6-1

Using the Problem-Solving Process

Imagine that you have received $2 million in cash with the income taxes already paid. The only stipulation is that you will have to use the money to establish some sort of enterprise, either a business or a charitable foundation. Solve this problem using the following worksheet. Describe what thoughts you have or what actions you will take for each step of problem solving and decision making.

I. *Identify causes of the problem.* Have you found your own problem, or was it given to you?

II. *Diagnose the problem.* What is the true decision that you are facing? What is your underlying problem?

III. *Find creative alternatives.* Think of the many alternatives facing you. Let your imagination flow and be creative.

IV. *Weigh alternatives and make the choice.* Weigh the pros and cons of each of your sensible alternatives.

Alternatives	Advantages	Disadvantages
1.		
2.		
3.		
4.		
5.		

V. Based on your analysis in step IV, choose the best alternative.

VI. *Implement the choice.* Outline your action plan for converting your chosen alternative into action.

VII. *Evaluate the choice.* Do the best you can here by speculating how you will know if the decision you reached was a good one.

Applying Human Relations Exercise 6-2

Stretch Your Imagination

A global contest was organized by Stanford University through its Technology Ventures program. Anyone in the world was permitted to enter. The assignment was to take ordinary rubber bands and "add value" to them. Entries were submitted by video, posting them on YouTube. Entrants included people from many different occupations, including computer scientists. The winner received the Genius Award.

Here is where you fit in. By brainwriting or brainstorming, come up with at least six ways of adding value (making more useful) to a rubber band, or a bunch of rubber bands. You must stretch your imagination to be successful. After the brainstorming sessions have been completed, perhaps taking ten minutes of class time, a representative of each group might share results with the class. Students might then assign a Genius Award to the entry that seems the most useful. Or the instructor might be the judge.

Source: The facts about the contest stem from Lee Gomes, "Our Columnist Judges a Brainstorming Bee, and Meets a Genius," *Wall Street Journal*, March 5, 2008, p. B1.

Human Relations Class Activity

Hunting for Unusual Advertising Placements

In recent years, shopping mall owners and managers have searched for more outlets for advertising to help cope with the lost revenue from vacant stores. In-mall advertising includes vacant storefronts, adhesive ads that cover tabletops in food courts, and security vehicles with advertising painted on the exterior. The nature of this class activity is for students to look around for out-of-the-ordinary ad placements inside shopping malls or anyplace else. Instead of going on a field trip, just stay alert to these ads during your regular activities. Each student will submit up to five unusually placed ads by the completion date of the activity. One or two class members might volunteer to compile the database. It will be helpful to make a frequency chart with entries such as "Advertising on park bench: Five were cited."

After the results are shown to class members, either in class or by email, answer the following questions:

1. Which were the most creative places to put an ad?
2. Which ads were the most likely to be effective in terms of attracting customers?

3. What problems are these ads solving?
4. Where else might an ad be placed that wasn't spotted by class members?

Source: Several of the facts for this skill-building exercise (but not the exercise itself) stem from Kris Hudson, "This Space for Rent—To Advertisers, if Not Retail Tenants," *Wall Street Journal*, October 22, 2008, p. C12.

Human Relations Case Study 6-1

Crystal Icing Catches on Big Time

Several years ago, Gina Smith had a hobby—a simple diversion for an artsy mom who spent her nights adorning everyday objects with shiny Swarovski crystals. But these days, Smith's work has gone far beyond a simple pastime. Her company, Crystal Icing, has blinged out everything from cell phones to electric guitars for everyone from average people to celebrities like Mariah Carey, Jennifer Lopez, and Paris Hilton.

A recent project for Smith, thirty, and co-owner Wasim Khaled, twenty-nine, is Ed Hardy Icing, a partnership established in August with the popular Ed Hardy Clothing Company. A licensing agreement allows Crystal Icing to put Ed Hardy designs in crystal form on cell phones, faceplates, and laptops. Business has quadrupled recently, with the Ed Harding line being distributed in twenty-one countries.

The Ed Hardy deal came on top of partnerships already established with companies like Nintendo, Yahoo!, Sony, and T-Mobile. Khaled and Smith have put licensing offers on hold from Snoop Dogg's Rich & Famous clothing line and Baby Phat because of not having enough employees. Crystal Icing has just ten employees (including Smith and Khaled) handling custom orders in their Rochester, New York, office. The company also has order-fulfillment centers in Los Angeles and New York City. Smith and Khaled handle public relations and distribution relations and manage the entire Ed Hardy Icing line themselves.

Smith started the company in her living room by selling Crystal Icing kits on eBay. The business was a side project to her full-time job in telecommunication sales, which is how she met Khaled. They began talking, and Khaled—an IT specialist who was running a Web design company on the side—agreed to produce a Web site for Crystal Icing and become a full partner.

Crystal Icing's big break came thanks to Carrie Bradshaw, Sarah Jessica Parker's character on HBO's *Sex and the City*. In one of the shows, Bradshaw was seen sporting a crystallized cell phone. The show's trendsetting impact on pop culture led fans to hit the Web in search of the phone. And what they found was Crystal Icing, thanks to Khaled's search-engine optimization of the company's Web site. The irony is that Crystal Icing didn't make the phone seen on *Sex and the City*. It came from a similar company called NYC Peach. But that didn't matter; Crystal Icing was off and running.

The company's first major event came when Smith and Khaled were asked by New York City planner David Tutera to crystallize compact mirrors for the 2006 Academy Awards pre-show gift baskets, which eventually led to Fusion Beauty contracting Crystal Icing for an entire line of products. Work with companies like T-Mobile and L'Oréal soon followed.

In July 2008, Khaled was at a trade show in Las Vegas when he decided to drive to Christian Audigier's headquarters in Los Angeles with a story that he had traveled all the way from the East Coast for a scheduled meeting.

Khaled lucked out. While he was there, Audigier walked in. Khaled showed the designer a crystallized cell phone he had brought with him. "He was like, 'This is beautiful, beautiful,'" recalls Khaled, mimicking Audigier's French accent. The licensing agreement was signed a week later, and Crystal was faced with the daunting tasks of creating the Ed Hardy Icing brand for a trade show the following month.

"If we had known what getting this license would entail, and how much work it would have been, it might have scared us off," says Khaled with a laugh. "But our lack of knowledge actually helped us out."

Questions

1. In what way has Gina Smith demonstrated that she is creative?

2. In what way has Wasim Khaled demonstrated that he is creative?

3. What is your evaluation of the ethics of the co-owners of Crystal Icing? What is the basis for your conclusion?

4. What other products do you think Crystal Icing might profitably crystallize?

5. What problem does Crystal Icing appear to be solving?

Source: Adapted and abridged from Troy L. Smith, "Crystal Icing Puts Bling on Just About Everything," *Democrat and Chronicle* (Rochester, NY) January 7, 2009, pp. 5B, 6B.

Human Relations Case Study 6-2

Stefanie Ponders a Career Decision

Four years ago when Stefanie was twenty-one years old, she secured a position as a data-entry specialist in the customer support center for business software at a telecommunications company. For Stefanie, this position was an important starting point for moving up the career ladder. Within one year, Stefanie's advancement began. She was promoted to the position of customer support representative, in which she helped customers resolve software problems related to large-size commercial printers. Stefanie worked on problems both online and by telephone.

Two years ago, Stefanie received some disappointing news from her manager. As company revenues declined, Stefanie's position was eliminated. Her boss reassured Stefanie that she was an above-average performer and that she could possibly be called back should business conditions improve.

Stefanie was quite discouraged, yet she took action to move to what she thought be a more stable career. Stefanie enrolled in a three-month course at a beauty school, which would certify her as a cosmetologist. One week after graduating, Stefanie found a position as a hair stylist and nail specialist with a cosmetology studio in a home for seniors. She worked an average of thirty hours per week as a contract employee. Most of her work consisted of styling and shampooing the hair of women in their seventies and eighties.

Four months into her new position, Stefanie's manager at the telecommunications company telephoned her with positive news. Stefanie would be invited back to the company just four months from the date of the call. Stefanie expressed her appreciation for the exciting news and said she would get back to her manager with a decision soon.

Stefanie explained to her best friend, "I don't know what to do. I loved my job at the company. My work as a cosmetologist is going okay, and I'm kind of still learning. If I go back to the company, maybe I would be laid off again. Also, I don't know if it's such a good idea to quit a job so soon after beginning."

Questions

1. How should Stefanie systematically go about deciding whether to return to the company that laid her off?

2. What might be an imaginative solution to Stefanie's dilemma?

3. To what extent might Stefanie be facing an ethical issue if she leaves her position as a cosmetologist in a few months?

Source: Case researched by Stefanie Donaldson, February 2, 2009.

Human Relations Role-Playing Exercise

Helping Stefanie Make a Career Decision

The case about Stefanie's dilemma serves as background material and the story line for this role-play. One person plays the role of Stefanie, who meets with her best friend to discuss what kind of decision she should reach about being called back to the company. Another student plays the role of the best friend, who will do more than simply listen. The best friend will attempt to facilitate Stefanie using the problem-solving and decision-making steps to help her arrive at a sound decision.

For both scenarios, observers rate the role-players on two dimensions, using a 1 to 5 scale from very poor to very good. One dimension is "effective use of human relations techniques." The second dimension is "acting ability." A few observers might voluntarily provide feedback to the role-players in terms of sharing their ratings and observations. The course instructor might also provide feedback.

REFERENCES

1. Simona Covel, "Tapping the Creativity of Downtime," *Wall Street Journal*, July 24, 2008, p. B5.

2. Daniel Goleman, *Working with Emotional Intelligence* (New York: Bantam, 1998).

3. Myeong-Gu Seo and Lisa Feldman Barrett, "Being Emotional During Decision Making—Good or Bad? An Empirical Investigation," *Academy of Management Journal*, August 2007, pp. 923–940.

4. Erik Dane and Michael G. Pratt, "Exploring Intuition and Its Role in Managerial Decision Making," *Academy of Management Review*, January 2007, pp. 33–54.

5. Eugene Sadler-Smith and Erella Shefy, "The Intuitive Executive: Understanding and Applying 'Gut Feel' in Decision-Making," *Academy of Management Executive*, November 2004, p. 76.

6. Quoted in Bill Breen, "What's Your Intuition?" *Fast Company*, September 2000, p. 300.

7. Lea Winerman, "What We Know without Knowing," *Monitor on Psychology*, March 2005, p. 52.

8. Christopher M. Barnes and John R. Hollenbeck, "Sleep Deprivation and Decision-Making Teams: Burning the Midnight Oil or Playing with Fire?" *Academy of Management Review*, January 2009, p. 64.

9. Research reported in Amy Cynkar, "A Towering Figure," *Monitor on Psychology*, April 2007, pp. 38–39.

10. David A. Shaywitz, "Free to Choose but Often Wrong," *Wall Street Journal*, June 24, 2008, p. A17.

11. Paul C. Nutt, "Surprising but True: Half the Decisions in Organizations Fail," *Academy of Management Executive*, November 1999, pp. 75–90; Nutt, *Why Decisions Fail* (San Francisco: Berrett-Koehler, 2002).

12. Carol Polsky, "This Invention Is So Useful, It Has Stuck around for 75 Years," *Newsday* syndicated story, May 13, 2000.

13. Quoted in Ann Pomeroy, "Cooking Up Innovation," *HR Magazine*, November 2004, pp. 49–50.

14. Cited in Dan Heath and Chip Heath, "Analysis of Paralysis," *Fast Company*, November 2007, p. 68.

15. Mark A. Runco and Steven R. Pritzker, eds., *Encyclopedia of Creativity*, vol. 1 (San Diego: Academic Press, 1999), p. xv.

16. Richard W. Woodman, John E. Sawyer, and Ricky W. Griffin, "Toward a Theory of Organizational Creativity," *Academy of Management Review*, April 1993, pp. 293–321; Greg R. Oldham and Anne Cummings, "Employee Creativity: Personal and Contextual Factors at Work," *Academy of Management Journal*, June 1996, pp. 607–634; Robert J. Sternberg, "Creativity as a Decision," *American Psychologist*, May 2002, p. 376; Zak Stambor, "Self-Reflection May Lead Independently to Creativity, Depression," *Monitor on Psychology*, June 2005, p. 13.

17. Robert J. Sternberg, ed., *Handbook of Creativity* (New York: Cambridge University Press, 1999).

18. Teresa M. Amabile, "How to Kill Creativity," *Harvard Business Review*, September–October 1998, pp. 78–79.

19. Teresa M. Amabile, "Beyond Talent: John Irving and the Passionate Craft of Creativity," *American Psychologist*, April 2001, p. 335.

20. Robert I. Sutton, "The Weird Rules of Creativity," *Harvard Business Review*, September 2001, p. 101.

21. Linda Tischler, "Join the Circus," *Fast Company*, July 2005, p. 56.

22. Patrick J. Kiger, "Small Groups: Big Ideas," *Workforce Management*, February 27, 2006, p. 2.

23. Cited in Robert McGarvey, "Turn It On," *Entrepreneur*, November 1996, pp. 156–157.

24. Research cited in Bridget Murray, "A Ticking Clock Means a Creativity Drop," *Monitor on Psychology*, November 2002, p. 24; Interview with Teresa M. Amabile in Bill Breen, "The 6 Myths of Creativity," *Fast Company*, December 2004, pp. 77–78.

25. Marissa Ann Mayer, "Creativity Loves Constraints," *Business Week*, February 13, 2006, p. 102.

26. Bruce Nussbaum, "Get Creative! How to Build Innovative Companies," *Business Week*, August 1, 2005, pp. 66–67.

27. "Sports Bottles Oh So Cool," *Democrat and Chronicle* (Rochester, NY), August 23, 2003, p. 14D.

28. "Nalgene Nixes Plastic Bottles with BPA." *YourLawyer.com*, April 21, 2008, pp. 1–2.

29. Quoted in "You are Getting Creative . . . Very Creative," *Business Week*, May 12, 2008, p. 018.

30. Quoted in Jared Sandberg, "Brainstorming Works Best if People Scramble for Ideas on Their Own," *Wall Street Journal*, June 13, 2006, p. B1.

31. "Expand Brainstorming," *Manager's Edge*, November 2008, p. 6.

32. Angela Ka-yee Leung, William W. Maddux, Adam D. Galinksy, and Chi-yue Chiu, "Multicultural Experience Enhances Creativity: The When and How," *American Psychologist*, April 2008, pp. 169–181.

33. Joann S. Lublin, "A CEO's Recipe for Fresh Ideas," *Wall Street Journal*, September 2, 2008, p. D4.

34. "Creativity Step by Step: A Conversation with Twyla Tarp," *Harvard Business Review*, April 2008, p. 51.

35. "Be a Creative Problem Solver," *Executive Strategies*, June 6, 1989, pp. 1–2.

36. Saul Kassin, *Psychology*, 2nd ed. (Upper Saddle River, NJ: Prentice Hall, 2001), p. 278. The critical-thinking steps described in this section are from the same source.

Answers to brain teasers are as follows:

The answers to the frame games are (1) "spinal column" and (2) "shop till you drop." The Sudoku solution is presented in the grid.

9	6	3	1	7	4	2	5	8
1	7	8	3	2	5	6	4	9
2	5	4	6	8	9	7	3	1
8	2	1	4	3	7	5	9	6
4	9	6	8	5	2	3	1	7
7	3	5	9	6	1	8	2	4
5	8	9	7	1	3	4	6	2
3	1	7	2	4	6	9	8	5
6	4	2	5	9	8	1	7	3

7

Personal Communication Effectiveness

Outline

1 How Does Communication Take Place?

2 How Does Interpersonal Communication Relate to Relationship Building?

3 What Is Nonverbal Communication (Sending and Receiving Silent Messages)?
Environment or Setting
Distance from the Other Person
Posture
Hand Gestures
Facial Expressions and Eye Contact
Voice Quality
Personal Appearance
Nonverbal Communication and Airport Security

4 What Are Some Frequent Roadblocks to Communication?
Limited Understanding of People
One-Way Communication
Different Interpretation of Words (Semantics)
Credibility of the Sender and Mixed Signals
Distortion of Information
Different Perspectives and Experiences
Emotions and Attitudes
Communication Overload
Improper Timing

Poor Communication Skills
Cultural and Language Barriers

5   What Are Some Ways to Build Bridges to Communication?
Appeal to Human Needs, and Time Your Messages
Repeat Your Message, Using More than One Channel
Have an Empowered Attitude, and Be Persuasive
Discuss Differences in Frames of Reference
Check for Comprehension and Feelings through Feedback
Minimize Defensive Communication
Combat Communication Overload
Use Mirroring to Establish Rapport
Engage in Small Talk and Constructive Gossip

6   How Do You Overcome Gender Barriers to Communication?

7   How Can You Enhance Your Listening Skills?
Active Listening

After studying the information and doing the exercises in this chapter, you should be able to:

1   Explain the basic communication process.

2   Explain the relationship-building aspect of interpersonal communication.

3   Describe the nature and importance of nonverbal communication in the workplace.

4   Identify roadblocks to communication.

5   Know how to build bridges to communication.

6   Overcome many gender communication barriers.

7   Enhance your listening skills.

ock star Bono was visiting then-Senator Jesse Helms's Capitol Hill office to enlist his help in the global war against AIDS. Bono had all the facts and figures at his fingertips, and he launched into a detailed appeal based on these data. He was, in essence, speaking to Helms the same way he had recently spoken to executives and technical experts at the many foundations and corporations he had approached about the issue. But within a few minutes, Bono sensed that he was losing Helms's attention, and he instinctively changed his pitch.

Knowing that Helms was a deeply religious man (and drawing on his own born-again Christian values), Bono began speaking of Jesus Christ's concern for the sick and the poor. He argued that AIDS should be considered the twenty-first-century equivalent of leprosy, an affliction cited in many Bible stories of the New Testament. Helms immediately sat up and began listening, and before the meeting was over he had promised to become the Senate champion for Bono's cause.[1]

Whether or not you believe that combating AIDS is a worthy cause, or believe in Christian values, the story about Bono's conversation with Helms sends a key message about personal communication effectiveness. You have to understand your listener's viewpoint and interests to get through to him or her—or even to get the person to listen.

Effective communication skills are also important for many other reasons. Communication is so vital that it has been described as the glue that holds organizations and families together. Most job foul-ups and personal relationship disputes are considered to be a result of communication problems. Furthermore, to be successful in work or personal life, you usually have to be an effective communicator. You can't make friends or stand up against enemies unless you can communicate with them. And you can't accomplish work through others unless you can send and receive messages effectively.

In this chapter we explain several important aspects of interpersonal communication, such as the communication process and overcoming various communication barriers. Many factors contribute to enhanced communication, leading in turn to more effective human relations. Explanation should also lead to skill improvement. For example, if you understand the steps involved in getting a message across to another person, you may be able to prevent many communication problems.

▶ Learning Objective 1 ▶

How Does Communication Take Place?

A convenient starting point in understanding how people communicate is to look at the steps involved in communicating a message. **Communication** is the sending and receiving of messages. A diagram of how the process takes place is shown in Figure 7-1. The theme of the model is that two-way communication involves three

Communication
the sending and receiving of messages

FIGURE 7-1

THE COMMUNICATION PROCESS

When sending a message to another person, one has to take into account potential barriers to communication. Feedback from the receiver helps clarify if the message has been sent as intended.

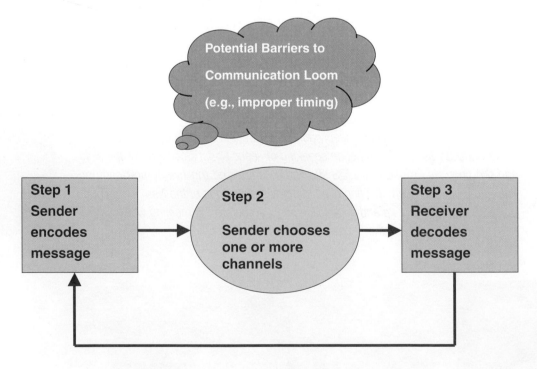

major steps and that each step is subject to interference or noise. Assume that Crystal, a customer, wishes to inform Tony, a used-car sales representative, that she is willing to make an offer of $8,000 on a used car. The price tag on the car is $8,750.

Step 1. **Sender encodes the message.** **Encoding** is the process of organizing ideas into a series of symbols, such as words and gestures, designed to communicate with the receiver. Word choice has a strong influence on communication effectiveness. The better a person's grasp of language, the easier it is for him or her to encode. Crystal says, "Tony, this car obviously is not in excellent condition, but I am willing to give you $8,000 for it."

> **Encoding**
> the process of organizing ideas into a series of symbols, such as words and gestures, designed to communicate with a receiver

Step 2. **Sender chooses one or more channels.** The message is sent via a communication channel or medium, such as voice, telephone, paper, e-mail, or messaging. It is important to select a medium that fits the message. It would be appropriate to use the spoken word to inform a coworker that he swore under his breath at a customer. It would be less appropriate to send the same message through e-mail. Many messages on and off the job are sent nonverbally through the use of gestures and facial expressions. For example, a smile from a superior during a meeting is an effective way of communicating the message "I agree with you." Crystal has chosen the oral medium to send her message.

Step 3. **Receiver decodes the message.** In **decoding,** the receiver interprets the message and translates it into meaningful information. Decoding is the process of understanding a message. Barriers to communication are most likely to surface at the decoding step. People often interpret messages according to their psychological needs and motives. Tony wants to interpret Crystal's message that she is very eager to purchase this car. Therefore, he may listen attentively for more information demonstrating that she is interested in purchasing the car. Effective decoding is also dependent on the receiver understanding the words chosen by the sender. Breadth of vocabulary as well as cultural factors can influence the interpretation of a word or phrase. For example, if Crystal says the car is "bad," she could mean that the car is in poor condition *or* that it is wonderful, depending on her vernacular.

> **Decoding**
> the process of understanding a message; the receiver interprets the message and translates it into meaningful information

Decoding the message leads naturally to action—the receiver does something about the message. If the receiver acts in the manner the sender wants, the communication has been successful. If Tony says, "It's a deal," Crystal had a successful communication event. Many missteps can occur between encoding and decoding a message. **Barriers to communication** or unwanted interference or **noise** can distort or block a message. If Crystal has an indecisive tone and raises her voice at the end of her statement, it could indicate that she is not really serious about offering a maximum of $8,000 for the car.

> **Barriers to communication (or noise)**
> missteps that can occur between encoding and decoding a message; unwanted interference that can distort or block a message

How Does Interpersonal Communication Relate to Relationship Building?

◀ Learning Objective 2 ◀

Another way of understanding the process of interpersonal communication is to examine how communication is a vehicle for building relationships. According to Texas Tech business communication professors Rich Sorenson, Grace De Bord, and Ida Ramirez, we establish relationships along two primary dimensions: dominate–

subordinate and cold–warm. In the process of communicating, we attempt to *dominate or subordinate*. When we dominate, we attempt to control communication. When we subordinate, we attempt to yield control, or think first of the wishes and needs of the other person. Dominators expect the receiver of messages to submit to them; subordinate people send a signal that they expect the other person to dominate.[2]

We indicate whether we want to dominate or subordinate by the way we speak or write, or by the nonverbal signals we send. The dominator might speak loudly or enthusiastically, write forceful messages filled with exclamation points, or gesture with exaggerated, rapid hand movements. He or she might write a harsh e-mail message, such as, "It's about time you started taking your job seriously and put in some real effort."

In the subordinate mode, we might speak quietly and hesitantly, in a meek tone, being apologetic. A subordinate person might ask, "I know you have better things on your mind than to worry about me, but I was wondering when I can expect my reimbursement for travel expenses?" In a work setting we ordinarily expect people with more formal authority to have the dominant role in conversations. However, in more democratic, informal companies, workers with more authority are less likely to feel the need to dominate conversations.

The *cold–warm dimension* also shapes communication because we invite the same behavior that we send. Cold, impersonal, negative messages evoke similar messages from others. In contrast, warm verbal and nonverbal messages evoke similar behavior from others. Getting back to the inquiry about the travel-expense check, here is a colder-versus-warmer response by the manager:

Colder: Travel vouchers really aren't my responsibility. You'll just have to wait like everybody else.

Warmer: I understand your problem. Not getting reimbursed on time is a bummer. I'll follow up on the status of your expense check sometime today or tomorrow.

The combination of dominant and cold communication sends the signal that the sender of the message wants to control and to limit, or even withdraw from, a personal relationship. A team leader might say that she cannot attend a Saturday morning meeting because she has to go out of town for her brother's wedding. A dominant and cold manager might say, "I don't want to hear about your personal life. Everyone in this department has to attend our Saturday meeting."

Subordinate actions combined with warm communication signal a desire to maintain or build the relationship while yielding to the other person. A manager communicating in a warm and subordinate manner in relation to the wedding request might say, "We'll miss you on Saturday morning because you are a key player in our department, but I recognize that major events in personal life sometimes take priority over a business meeting."

Figure 7-2 summarizes how the dual dimensions of dominate–subordinate and cold–warm influence the relationship-building aspects of communication. Rather than regarding these four quadrants of relationships as good or bad, think of your purposes. In some situations you might want to dominate and be cold, yet in most situations you might want to submit a little and be warm in order to build a relationship. For example, being dominant and cold might be necessary for a security officer who is trying to control an unruly crowd at a sporting event.

Observe that the person in the quadrant *dominate–cold* has an impersonal relationship with the receiver, and the person in the *warm–subordinate* quadrant has a supportive relationship with the receiver. Being *dominant and warm* leads to a personal relationship, whereas as being *subordinate and cold* leads to an accepting relationship. The combinations of *dominate–cold* and *warm–subordinate* are more likely to produce the results indicated.

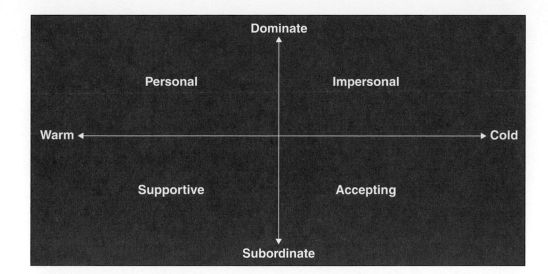

FIGURE 7-2

COMMUNICATION DIMENSIONS OF ESTABLISHING A RELATIONSHIP

Source: Adapted with permission from Rich Sorenson, Grace De Bord, and Ida Ramirez, *Business and Management Communication: A Guide Book*, 4th ed. (Upper Saddle River, NJ: Prentice Hall, 2001), p. 7.

What Is Nonverbal Communication (Sending and Receiving Silent Messages)?

◀ Learning Objective 3 ◀

So far we have been considering mostly spoken communication. But much of the communication among people includes nonspoken and nonwritten messages. These nonverbal signals are a critical part of everyday communication. As a case in point, *how* you say "thank you" makes a big difference in the extent to which your sense of appreciation registers. In **nonverbal communication,** we use our body, voice, or environment in numerous ways to help put a message across. Sometimes we are not aware how much our true feelings color our spoken message.

Nonverbal communication
using the body, voice, or environment in numerous ways to help get a message across

One problem of paying attention to nonverbal signals is that they can be taken too seriously. Just because some nonverbal signals (such as yawning or looking away from a person) might reflect a person's real feelings, not every signal can be reliably connected with a particular attitude. Jason may put his hand over his mouth because he is shocked. Lucille may put her hand over her mouth because she is trying to control her laughter about the message, and Ken may put his hand over his mouth as a signal that he is pondering the consequences of the message. Here we look at eight categories of nonverbal communication that are generally reliable indicators of a person's attitude and feelings.

ENVIRONMENT OR SETTING

Where you choose to deliver your message indicates what you think of its importance. Assume that your supervisor invites you over for dinner to discuss something with you. You will think it is a more important topic under these circumstances than if it were brought up when the two of you met in the supermarket. Other important environmental cues include room color, temperature, lighting, and furniture arrangement. A person who sits behind an uncluttered large desk, for example, appears more powerful than a person who sits behind a small, cluttered desk.

Few people in an organization have the authority to control the physical factors of room color, temperature, and lighting, but there are exceptions. An office or building painted gray in the interior might suggest an impersonal, strictly business atmosphere. A business owner who keeps the temperature at 62°F during cold months or 75°F during warm months communicates a message of frugality.

DISTANCE FROM THE OTHER PERSON

How close you place your body relative to another person's also conveys meaning when you send a message. If, for instance, you want to convey a positive attitude toward another person, get physically close to him or her. Putting your arm around someone to express interest and warmth is another obvious nonverbal signal. However, many people in a work setting abstain from all forms of touching (except for handshakes) because of concern that touching might be interpreted as sexual harassment. Cultural differences must be kept in mind in interpreting nonverbal cues. A French male is likely to stand closer to you than a British male, even if they had equally positive attitudes toward you. A set of useful guidelines has been developed for estimating how close to stand to another person (at least in many cultures).[3] They are described here and diagrammed in Figure 7-3.

Intimate distance covers actual physical contact to about eighteen inches. Usually, it is reserved for close friends and loved ones or other people you feel affectionate toward. Physical intimacy is usually not called for on the job, but there are exceptions. For one, confidential information might be whispered within the intimate distance zone.

Personal distance covers from about one and a half to four feet. In this zone it is natural to carry on friendly conversations and discussions. When people engage in a heated argument, they sometimes enter the personal distance zone. One example is a baseball coach getting up close to an umpire and shouting in his face.

Social distance covers from four to twelve feet and in general is reserved for interaction that is businesslike and impersonal. We usually maintain this amount of distance between ourselves and strangers, such as retail sales associates.

Public distance covers from twelve feet to the outer limit of being heard. This zone is typically used in speaking to an audience at a large meeting or in a

FIGURE 7-3
FOUR CIRCLES OF INTIMACY

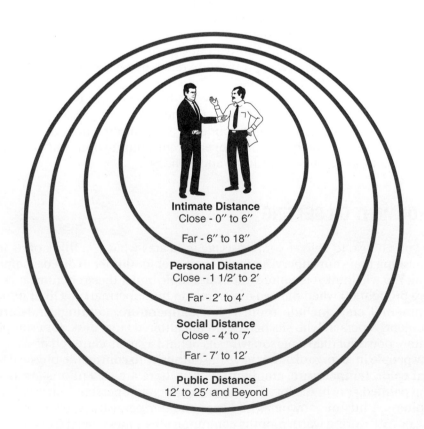

Intimate Distance
Close - 0″ to 6″

Far - 6″ to 18″

Personal Distance
Close - 1 1/2′ to 2′

Far - 2′ to 4′

Social Distance
Close - 4′ to 7′

Far - 7′ to 12′

Public Distance
12′ to 25′ and Beyond

classroom, but a few insensitive individuals might send ordinary messages by shouting across a room. The unstated message suggested by such an action is that the receiver of the message does not merit the effort of walking across the room.

People sometimes manipulate personal space in order to dominate a situation. A sales representative might move into the personal or intimate circle of a customer simply to intimidate him or her. Many people become upset when you move into a closer circle than that for which a situation calls. They consider it an invasion of their personal space, or their "territorial rights."

POSTURE

Certain aspects of your posture communicate a message. Leaning toward another individual suggests that you are favorably disposed toward his or her message. Leaning backward communicates the opposite. Openness of the arms or legs serves as an indicator of liking or caring. In general, people establish closed postures (arms folded and legs crossed) when speaking to people they dislike. Standing up straight generally indicates high self-confidence. Stooping and slouching could mean a poor self-image. In any event, there is almost no disadvantage to standing up straight.

Related to posture are the nonverbal signals sent by standing versus sitting. Sitting down during a conversation is generally considered to be more intimate and informal than standing. If you do sit down while conversing, be sure to stand up when you wish the conversation to end. Standing up sends a message to the other person that it is time to leave. It also gives you the chance to be more attentive and polite in saying good-bye.

HAND GESTURES

An obvious form of body language is hand gestures. Hand gestures are universally recognized as conveying specific information to others within the same culture. If you make frequent hand movements, you will generally communicate a positive attitude. If you use few gestures, you will convey dislike or disinterest. An important exception here is that some people wave their hands vigorously while arguing. Some of their hand movements reflect anger. Another example is that open-palm gestures toward the other person typically convey positive attitudes. As will be described in Chapter 13, many hand gestures have culture-specific meanings. An off-color example follows:

> In many cultures holding your hand in front of you as if pushing something away tells the other person to stop—you have had enough. In West Africa, the same gesture means "There are different men who could be your father," thereby insulting the receiver's mother.[4]

It is often said that gestures speak louder than words, because if there is a discrepancy between words and gestures, the receiver will usually take your gestures more seriously. In general more weight is given to nonverbal cues than verbal cues when a discrepancy exists between the two.[5]

> *Imagine that you have been interviewed for a job you really want. At the close of the interview, the interviewer looks at you with a solemn face, and his arms are crossed with his hands tucked under his armpits. He says in a monotone, "We will get back to you soon." Most likely, you will continue your job search.*

FACIAL EXPRESSIONS AND EYE CONTACT

When used in combination, the head, face, and eyes provide the clearest indications of attitudes toward other people. Lowering your head and peering over your glasses, for instance, is the nonverbal equivalent of the expression "You're putting me on." As is well known, maintaining eye contact with another person improves communication with that person. To maintain eye contact, it is usually necessary to correspondingly move your head and face. Moving your head, face, and eyes away from another person is often interpreted as a defensive gesture or one suggesting a lack of self-confidence. Would you hire a job candidate who didn't look at you directly? Yet again, cultural differences can influence the meaning of eye contact. In some Asian cultures, looking down rather than maintaining eye contact is a sign of respect.

The face is often used as a primary source of information about how we feel. We look for facial clues when we want to determine another person's attitude. You can often judge someone's current state of happiness by looking at his or her face. The expression "sourpuss" attests to this observation. Happiness, apprehension, anger, resentment, sadness, contempt, enthusiasm, and embarrassment are but a few of the emotions that can be expressed through the face.

VOICE QUALITY

More significance is often attached to the *way* something is said than to *what* is said. A forceful voice, which includes a consistent tone without vocalized pauses, connotes power and control. Closely related to voice tone are volume, pitch, and rate of speaking. Anger, boredom, and joy can often be interpreted from voice quality. Anger is noted when the person speaks loudly with a high pitch and at a fast rate, with irregular inflection. Boredom is indicated by a monotone. Joy is often indicated by loud volume, high pitch, fast rate, upward inflection, and regular rhythm.

Avoiding an annoying voice quality can make a positive impact on others. The research of Jeffrey Jacobi, voice coach and founder of Jacobi Voice, provides some useful suggestions. A while back he surveyed a nationwide sample of one thousand men and women and asked, "Which irritating or unpleasant voice annoys you the most?" His results are still valid today. The most irritating quality was a whining, complaining, or nagging tone.

Jacobi notes that we are judged by the way we sound. He also contends that careers can be damaged by voice problems, such as those indicated in the survey. "We think about how we look and dress. And that gets most of the attention. But people judge our intelligence much more by how we sound than how we dress."[6] Human Relations Self-Assessment Quiz 7-1 provides more details about his findings.

PERSONAL APPEARANCE

Your external image plays an important role in communicating messages to others. Job seekers show recognition of this aspect of nonverbal communication when they carefully groom for a job interview. People pay more respect and grant more privileges to people they perceive as being well dressed and attractive. The meaning of being well dressed depends heavily on the situation and the culture of the organization. In an information technology firm, neatly pressed jeans, a stylish T-shirt, and clean sport shoes might qualify as being well dressed. The same attire worn in a financial service firm would qualify as being poorly dressed. In recent years, more formal business attire has made a comeback, as reflected in more space in department stores being devoted to suits for men and women.

Human Relations Self-Assessment Quiz   7-1

Voice Quality Checkup

The study of voice quality (cited in the text) ranked voice quality, in decreasing order of annoyance, as follows:

- Whining, complaining, or nagging tone—44.0 percent
- High-pitched, squeaky voice—15.9 percent
- Mumblers—11.1 percent
- Very fast talkers—4.9 percent
- Weak and wimpy voice—3.6 percent
- Flat, monotonous tone—3.5 percent
- Thick accent—2.4 percent

Ask yourself and two other people familiar with your voice if you have one or more of the preceding voice-quality problems. If your self-analysis and feedback from others does indicate a serious problem, get started on self-improvement. Record your voice and attempt to modify the biggest problems. Another avenue of improvement is to consult with a speech coach or therapist.

Tattoos and body piercing represent another aspect of personal appearance that sends a strong nonverbal message. The message that tattoos and body piercing send, however, depends to a large extent on the values and preferences of the receiver. A positive message sent by visible tattoos and piercing is that the individual is cool, modern, fashionable, and youthful in outlook. A negative message is the person with visible tattoos and piercing is immature, daring, and nonconscientious. As the percentage of people wearing visible tattoos and body piercing continues to increase, less significance will probably be attached to them. For example, about thirty years ago when a man appeared in the office wearing a pierced earring, it was considered shocking. Today, the same behavior is unremarkable—at least to many people.

Common sense and research indicate that a favorable personal appearance leads to higher starting salaries and, later, salary increases. One study showed that people perceived to be physically attractive tend to receive salaries 8 to 10 percent higher. A possible explanation offered for the results is that employers might attribute other positive attributes to employees they perceive as physically attractive.[7]

NONVERBAL COMMUNICATION AND AIRPORT SECURITY

An advanced workplace application of nonverbal communication is to help combat drug trafficking and terrorism. The art of spotting nervous or threatening behavior has gained respect among airport security officials. Since the terrorist attacks on September 11, 2001, the Federal Bureau of Investigation (FBI) started teaching nonverbal behavior analysis to all new FBI recruits. In the past, passengers were selected to be interrogated mostly on the basis of what they looked like, such as a negative ethnic stereotype. Customs agents are now trained to observe what people do and to ask pointed questions when suspicious nonverbal behavior surfaces. Among the indicators of suspicious behavior are darting eyes, hand tremors, a fleeting style, and an enlarged carotid artery (indicating the rapid blood flow associated with anxiety). Failure to make eye contact with the customs official is a strong red flag.[8]

Behavior detection officer is the term given to airport security officers who specialize in detecting nonverbal signs of stress, fear, and deception. Part of the officer's responsibility is to roam a major airport and watch for anyone who seems nervous or out of place, or is acting suspiciously. Particularly suspicious are passengers traveling without bags, sweating, and constantly checking people passing by, especially those with badges and guns. Facial movements detecting a lie, such as rapid eye movements, are also regarded as suspicious.

Other suspicious nonverbal communication cues are passengers avoiding eye contact or veering away when police approach. Suspicious-appearing people are routinely brought in for questioning, but nonverbal behavior alone is not sufficient evidence to be charged with attempting a crime.[9]

The American Civil Liberties Unions objects to nonverbal behavior detection because it is easy to find these negative nonverbal behaviors if you look for them. The many flight cancellations and delays, for example, trigger many passengers into looking stressed and suspicious.

▶ **Learning Objective 4** ▶

What Are Some Frequent Roadblocks to Communication?

Communication rarely proceeds as effectively as we would like. Many different factors filter out a message on its way to the intended receiver, shown as potential barriers in Figure 7-1. In this section we look at some of the human roadblocks to communication. If you are aware of their presence, you will be better able to overcome them.

Routine or neutral messages are the easiest to communicate. Communication roadblocks are most likely to occur when a message is complex, is emotionally arousing, or clashes with the receiver's mental set. An emotionally arousing message would deal with such topics as job security or money. A message that clashes with a receiver's mental set requires that person to change his or her familiar pattern of receiving messages. The next time you order a meal in a restaurant, order dessert first and an entrée second. The server will probably not "hear" your dessert order because it deviates from the normal ordering sequence. The roadblocks or barriers described here are as follows:

1. Limited understanding of people

2. One-way communication

3. Different interpretation of words (semantics)

4. Credibility of the sender and mixed signals

5. Distortion of information

6. Different perspectives and experiences

7. Emotions and attitudes

8. Communication overload

9. Improper timing

10. Poor communication skills

11. Cultural and language barriers

LIMITED UNDERSTANDING OF PEOPLE

If you do not understand people very well, your communication effectiveness will be limited. To take a basic example, if you frame your message in terms of what can be done for you, you may be in trouble. It's much more effective to frame your message in terms of what you can do for the other person. Suppose a person in need of money wants to sell food supplements to a friend. Mentioning financial need is a very self-centered message. It could be made less self-centered:

> ***Very self-centered.*** "You've got to buy a few food supplements from me. I can't meet my credit card payments."

> ***Less self-centered.*** "Would you be interested in purchasing a few food supplements that would bring you more energy and help you live longer? If your answer is yes, I can help you."

Limited understanding of people can also take the form of making false assumptions about the receiver. The false assumption serves as a communication roadblock. A supervisor might say to a telemarketer (a person who sells over the phone), "If you increase sales by 15 percent, we will promote you to lead telemarketer." When the telemarketer does not work any harder, the supervisor thinks the message did not get across. The false assumption the supervisor made was that the telemarketer wanted a position with supervisory responsibility. What false assumptions have you made lately when trying to communicate with another person?

Limited understanding of another person can sometimes be attributed to cultural differences. For example, a supervisor might send a message to Kim, a South Korean American in her group, that she can win an Employee of the Month award if she increases her productivity by 5 percent. Kim does not receive the message well because according to her cultural beliefs, it is negative behavior to stand out from the group. (After Kim assimilates more into the American culture, she will most likely receive the message more clearly.)

ONE-WAY COMMUNICATION

Effective communication proceeds back and forth. An exchange of information or a transaction takes place between two or more people. Person A may send messages to person B to initiate communication, but B must react to A to complete the communication loop. One reason written messages sometimes fail to achieve their purpose is that the person who writes the message cannot be sure how it will be interpreted. One written message that is subject to many interpretations is, "Your idea is of some interest to me." (How much is *some*?) Face-to-face communication helps clarify meanings.

Instant messaging helps overcome the one-way barrier because the receiver reacts immediately to your message. An example: "You said ship the first batch only to good customers. Who do you consider to be a *good* customer?" Ten seconds later comes the reply: "A good customer bought at least $4,000 worth of goods last year and is up-to-date on payments." Three seconds later, the first person writes, "Got it." E-mail is also widely used to clarify messages and engage in two-way communication.

A quick way to bring about the exchange of information necessary for two-way communication is to ask a question. An example here would be, "Are you clear on what I mean by a *good customer*?"

DIFFERENT INTERPRETATION OF WORDS (SEMANTICS)

Semantics is the study of the meaning and changes in the meaning of words or symbols. These different meanings can create roadblocks to communication.

Semantics
the study of the meaning and changes in the meaning of words or symbols

Often the problem is trivial and humorous; at other times, semantic problems can create substantial communication barriers. Consider first an example of trivial consequence.

Two first-time visitors to Montreal, Quebec, entered a restaurant for dinner. After looking over the menu, the husband suggested they order the shrimp cocktail entrées. He said to his wife, "A whole shrimp dinner for $11.95 Canadian is quite a deal. I guess it's because Montreal is a seaport." When the entrées arrived, the visitors were sadly disappointed because they were the size of an *appetizer*.

The husband asked the server why the entrées were so small in Montreal. With a smile, the server replied, "You folks must be Americans. In French-speaking countries, the entrée is the beginning of the meal, like the word *enter*. In the United States, it's just the reverse—the entrée is the main meal. Are you now ready to order your main meal?"

Of greater consequence is the use of a word or term without thorough explanation that could cause people to act in an unintended direction. An example is for a manager to use the term *restructure* when speaking to employees or outsiders. Four common interpretations of the word are the following: (1) refinance the company debt, (2) declare bankruptcy, (3) change the organization structure, or (4) lay off many workers. A negative consequence of not knowing the true meaning of the term would be for a competent employee to seek employment elsewhere because he or she feared being laid off.

CREDIBILITY OF THE SENDER AND MIXED SIGNALS

Mixed signals
type of message in which the sender might recommend one thing to others yet behave in another way

The more trustworthy the source or sender of the message, the greater the probability that the message will get through clearly. In contrast, when the sender of the message has low credibility, many times it will be ignored. Communications can also break down for a subtle variation of low credibility. The disconnect occurs from **mixed signals,** a type of message in which the sender might recommend one thing to others yet behave in another way himself or herself. A team leader might tell others that a tidy worker is a productive worker. However, his or her own cubicle contains a four-month supply of empty soft-drink cans, and old papers consume virtually every square inch of his or her desk.

Mixed signals also refers to sending different messages about the same topic to different audiences. For example, company representatives might brag about the high quality of the company's products in public statements. Yet on the shop floor and in the office, the company tells its employees to cut costs whenever possible to lower costs.

DISTORTION OF INFORMATION

A great problem in sending messages is that people receiving them often hear what they want to hear. Without malicious intent, people modify your message to bolster their self-esteem or improve their situation. An incident that occurred between Danielle and her supervisor is fairly typical of this type of communication roadblock. Danielle asked her supervisor when she would be receiving a salary increase. Regarding the request as far-fetched and beyond the budget at the time, Danielle's supervisor replied, "Why should the company give you a raise when you are often late for work?"

Danielle *heard* her supervisor say, "If you come to work on time regularly, you will receive a salary increase." One month later, Danielle said to her supervisor that she had not been late for work in a month and should now be eligible for a raise. Her supervisor replied, "I never said that. Where did you get that idea?"

DIFFERENT PERSPECTIVES AND EXPERIENCES

People perceive words and concepts differently because their experiences and vantage points differ. On the basis of their perception of what they have heard, many Latino children believe that the opening line of the "Star-Spangled Banner" is "José, can you see . . ." (note that few children have *seen* the national anthem in writing). Cultural differences create different perspectives and experiences, such as workers from Eastern cultures tending to have high respect for authority. A worker from India might more readily accept a message from the boss than would his or her counterpart from California or Sweden. In the last two places, workers have a more casual attitude toward authority.

EMOTIONS AND ATTITUDES

Have you ever tried to communicate a message to another person while that person is emotionally aroused? Your message was probably distorted considerably. Another problem is that people tend to say things when emotionally aroused that they would not say when calm. Similarly, a person who has strong attitudes about a particular topic may become emotional when that topic is introduced. The underlying message here is try to avoid letting strong emotions and attitudes interfere with the sending or receiving of messages. If you are angry with someone, for example, you might miss the merit in what that person has to say. Calm down before proceeding with your discussion or attempting to resolve the conflict. Emotional intelligence makes a key contribution in this situation.

COMMUNICATION OVERLOAD

A major communication barrier facing literate people is being bombarded with information. **Communication overload** occurs when people are so overloaded with information that they cannot respond effectively to messages. As a result, they experience work stress. Workers at many levels are exposed to so much printed, electronic, and spoken information that their capacity to absorb it is taxed. The problem is worsened when low-quality information is competing for your attention. An example is a flashing pop-up ad informing you that you have just won a free laptop computer, and all you have to do is follow a link to claim your prize. The human mind is capable of processing only a limited quantity of information at a time. Workers who intentionally multitask, such as reading instant messages and filling in a spreadsheet at the same time, aggravate the problem of communication overload. More information about this problem is in Chapter 16 about developing good work habits.

> **Communication overload**
> phenomenon that occurs when people are so overloaded with information that they cannot respond effectively to messages

IMPROPER TIMING

Many messages do not get through to people because they are poorly timed. You have to know how to deliver a message, but you must also know *when* to deliver it. Sending a message when the receiver is distracted with other concerns or is rushing to get somewhere is a waste of time. Furthermore, the receiver may become discouraged and therefore will not repeat the message later.

The art of timing messages suggests not to ask for a raise when your boss is in a bad mood or to ask a new acquaintance for a date when he or she is preoccupied. However, do ask your boss for a raise when business has been good, and do ask someone for a date when you have just done something nice for that person and have been thanked.

POOR COMMUNICATION SKILLS

A message may fail to register because the sender lacks effective communication skills. The sender might garble a written or spoken message so severely that the receiver finds it impossible to understand. Also, the sender may deliver the message so poorly that the receiver does not take it seriously. A common deficiency in sending messages is to communicate with low conviction by using *wimpy* words, backpedaling, and qualifying. Part of the same idea is to use affirmative language, such as saying "when" instead of "if." Also, do not use phrases that call your integrity into question, such as "to be perfectly honest" (implying that you usually do not tell the truth).[10] To illustrate, here are three statements that send a message of low conviction to the receiver: "I think I might be able to finish this project by the end of the week." "It's possible that I could handle the assignment you have in mind." "I'll do what I can."

Another communication skill deficiency that can serve as a communication barrier is to have a regional accent so strong that it detracts from your message. Your regional accent is part of who you are, so you may not want to modify how you speak. Nevertheless, many public personalities, business executives, and salespeople seek out speech training or speech therapy to avoid having an accent that detracts from their message.[11] Also, at high-level positions people typically want to be universal in their appeal. You may notice that commentators on national television usually speak in a universal, rather than regional, manner.

Communication barriers can result from deficiencies within the receiver. A common barrier is a receiver who is a poor listener. Improving listening skills is such a major strategy for improving communication skills that it receives separate mention later in this chapter.

> "You can have brilliant ideas; but if you can't get them across, your ideas won't get you anywhere."
>
> —Lee Iacocca, former Chrysler chairman and Ford CEO

CULTURAL AND LANGUAGE BARRIERS

Communication barriers in work and personal life can be created when the sender and receiver come from different cultures and are not fluent in each other's language. Quite often cultural differences and language differences exist at the same time. A cultural difference creating a barrier to communication often takes this form: A supervisor from a culture that emphasizes empowering (giving power to) employees is giving instructions to an employee from a culture that believes the boss should make all the decisions. In response to a question from the subordinate, the supervisor says, "Do what you think is best." The subordinate has a difficult time understanding the message because he or she is waiting for a firm directive from the boss.

A language communication barrier is sometimes amusing, such as an American worker complimenting another by saying, "You have been working like a dog" on this project. The second person might interpret the comment as suggesting he or she must be punished to work hard. At other times language barriers cause accidents. Many foreign-language-speaking construction workers in the United States encounter accidents because they do not clearly understand the instructions about danger.

A notable problem with language barriers has stemmed from the practice of *offshoring* (sending overseas) customer service and call center positions to India, as well as Mexico and the Philippines. For Mexicans and Filipinos, English is usually their second language so they have an accent unfamiliar to many Americans. Although English might be the primary or strong second language of Indian workers, it is not a type of English familiar to many Americans. As a result, many Americans who are not familiar with the accents of English-speaking Indians will say, "I can't understand the person who is trying to help me." Many of these people hang up in frustration. Several U.S.-based telecommunication companies have therefore reestablished customer service centers in the United States.

To help overcome cultural and language barriers, many companies invest considerable time and money in cross-cultural training, as will be explained in Chapter 14.

What Are Some Ways to Build Bridges to Communication?

◀ Learning Objective 5 ◀

With determination and awareness that communication roadblocks and barriers do exist, you can become a more effective communicator. It would be impossible to remove all barriers, but they can be minimized. The following nine techniques are helpful in building better bridges to communication.

1. Appeal to human needs, and time your messages.

2. Repeat your message, using more than one channel.

3. Have an empowered attitude, and be persuasive.

4. Discuss differences in frames of reference.

5. Check for comprehension and feelings through feedback.

6. Minimize defensive communication.

7. Combat communication overload.

8. Use mirroring to establish rapport.

9. Engage in small talk and constructive gossip.

APPEAL TO HUMAN NEEDS, AND TIME YOUR MESSAGES

People are more receptive to messages that promise to do something for them. In other words, if a message promises to satisfy a need that is less than fully satisfied, you are likely to listen. The person in search of additional money who ordinarily does not hear low tones readily hears the whispered message, "How would you like to earn $500 in one weekend?"

Timing a message properly is related to appealing to human needs. If you deliver a message at the right time, you are taking into account the person's mental condition at the moment. A general principle is to deliver your message when the person might be in the right frame of mind to listen. The right frame of mind includes such factors as not being preoccupied with other thoughts, not being frustrated, being in a good mood, and not being stressed out. (Of course, all this severely limits your opportunity to send a message!)

REPEAT YOUR MESSAGE, USING MORE THAN ONE CHANNEL

You can overcome many roadblocks to communication by repeating your message several times. It is usually advisable not to say the same thing so as to avoid annoying the listener with straight repetition. Repeating the message in a different form is effective in another way: The receiver may not have understood the message the way in which it was first delivered. Repetition, like any other means of overcoming communication roadblocks, does not work for all people. Many people who repeatedly hear the message "text messaging while driving is dangerous" are not moved by it. It is helpful to use several methods of overcoming roadblocks or barriers to communication.

A generally effective way of repeating a message is to use more than one communication channel. For example, follow up a face-to-face discussion with an e-mail message or phone call or both. Your body can be another channel or medium to help impart your message. If you agree with someone about a spoken message, state your agreement and also shake hands over the agreement. Can you think of another channel by which to transmit a message?

HAVE AN EMPOWERED ATTITUDE, AND BE PERSUASIVE

A positive attitude helps a person communicate better in speaking, writing, and nonverbally. Being positive is a major factor in being persuasive, as mentioned previously in avoiding wimpy words. *Empowerment* here refers to the idea that the person takes charge of his or her own attitude.[12] Developing a positive attitude is not always easy. A starting point is to see things from a positive perspective, including looking for the good in people and their work. If your work is intrinsically motivating, you are likely to have a positive attitude. You would then be able to communicate about your work with the enthusiasm necessary. Figure 7-4 summarizes key ideas about persuasive communication, a topic most readers have most likely studied in the past.[13] If you can learn to implement most of the nine suggestions, you are on your way toward becoming a persuasive communicator. In addition, you will need solid facts behind you, and you will need to make skillful use of nonverbal communication.

DISCUSS DIFFERENCES IN FRAMES OF REFERENCE

Frame of reference
model, viewpoint, or perspective

Another way of understanding differences in perspectives and experiences is to recognize that people often have different frames of reference that influence how they interpret events. A **frame of reference** is a model, viewpoint, or perspective. When two people with different frameworks look at a situation, a communication problem may occur. For instance, one person may say, "I have just found the *ideal* potential mate." To this person, an *ideal* mate would be a person who was kind, caring, considerate, in good health, gainfully employed, and highly ethical. The listener may have a perception of an *ideal* potential mate as someone who has a superior physical appearance and is wealthy (a traditional stereotype). Until the two people understand each other's frame of reference, meaningful communication about the prospective mate is unlikely. The solution to this communication clash is to discuss the frame of reference by each side defining the perception of an *ideal* mate.

CHECK FOR COMPREHENSION AND FEELINGS THROUGH FEEDBACK

Don't be a hit-and-run communicator. Such a person drops a message and leaves the scene before he or she is sure the message has been received as intended. It is preferable to ask for feedback. Ask receivers for their understanding or interpretation of what you said. For example, you might say after delivering a message, "What is your understanding of our agreement?" Also use nonverbal indicators to gauge how well you delivered your message. A blank expression on the receiver's face might indicate no comprehension. A disturbed, agitated expression might mean that the receiver's emotions are blocking the message.

A comprehension check increases in importance when possible cultural and language barriers exist. A simple direct inquiry about comprehension is often effective, such as, "Is what I said okay with you" or "Tell me what I said." A friendly facial expression should accompany such feedback checks, otherwise your inquiry will come across like a challenge.

FIGURE 7-4 KEY PRINCIPLES OF PERSUASIVE COMMUNICATION

1. *Know exactly what you want.* First clarify ideas in your mind.
2. *Never suggest an action without describing its end benefit.* Explain how your message will benefit the receiver.
3. *Get a yes response early on.* It is helpful to give the persuading session a positive tone by establishing a "yes pattern" at the outset.
4. *Use powerful words.* Sprinkle your speech with phrases like "bonding with customers," and "vaporizing the competition."
5. *When you speak, begin with your headline—the most important point.* After the headline, provide more information as needed. To come up with the right headline, imagine what you would say if you had only ten minutes to deliver your message. An environmental specialist might begin a message to management with, "My new program will help us save the planet."
6. *Minimize raising your pitch at the end of sentences.* Part of being persuasive is not to sound unsure and apologetic.
7. *Back up conclusions with data.* You will be more persuasive if you support your spoken and written presentations with solid data, but do not become an annoyance by overdoing it.
8. *Minimize "wimp" phrases.* (As discussed earlier in this chapter.)
9. *Avoid or minimize common language errors.* Do not say "could care less," when you mean "couldn't care less," or "orientated" when you mean "oriented."
10. *Avoid overuse of jargon and clichés.* To feel "in" and cool, many workers rely heavily on jargon and clichés, such as referring to their "fave" (for *favorite*) product or that "At the end of the day," something counts. It is also helpful to minimize the use of catchphrases like *bottom line, quantum leap,* and *cutting edge.* The problem is that if you make frequent use of overused expressions, you may give the impression of not thinking critically.
11. *Frame your position in the direction you want.* Describe in a positive way the option you want the receiver to choose, or describe in a negative way the option you don't want the receiver to choose. For example, if you want to convince others of the advantages of global outsourcing, you might refer to it as *seeking wage rates that will make us competitive.* If you want to convince others of the disadvantages of global outsourcing, you might refer to it as *shipping jobs from our country overseas.*

In addition to looking for verbal comprehension and emotions when you have delivered a message, check for feelings after you have received a message. When a person speaks, we too often listen to the facts and ignore the feelings. If feelings are ignored, the true meaning and intent of the message are likely to be missed, thus creating a communication barrier. Your boss might say to you, "You never seem to take work home." To clarify what your boss means by this statement, you might ask, "Is that good or bad?" Your boss's response will give you feedback on his or her feelings about getting all your work done during regular working hours.

When you send a message, it is also helpful to express your feelings in addition to conveying the facts. For example, "Our customer returns are up by 12 percent [fact], and I'm quite disappointed about those results [feelings]." Because feelings contribute strongly to comprehension, you will help overcome a potential communication barrier.

MINIMIZE DEFENSIVE COMMUNICATION

Defensive communication
tendency to receive messages in such a way that one's self-esteem is protected

Distortion of information was described previously as a communication barrier. Such distortion can also be regarded as **defensive communication,** the tendency to receive messages in such a way that our self-esteem is protected. Defensive communication is also responsible for people sending messages to look good. For example, when criticized for achieving below-average sales, a store manager might shift the blame to the sales associates in her store. Overcoming the barrier of defensive communication requires two steps. First, people have to acknowledge the existence of defensive communication. Second, they have to try not to be defensive when questioned or criticized. Such behavior is not easy because of **denial,** the suppression of information we find uncomfortable. For example, the store manager previously cited would find it uncomfortable to think of herself as being responsible for below-average performance.

Denial
the suppression of information one finds uncomfortable

COMBAT COMMUNICATION OVERLOAD

You can decrease the chances of suffering from communication overload by such measures as carefully organizing and sorting information before plunging ahead with reading. Speed-reading may help, provided that you stop to read carefully the most relevant information. Or you can scan through hard-copy reports, magazines, and Web sites looking for key titles and words that are important to you. Recognize, however, that many subjects have to be studied carefully to derive benefit. It is often better to read thoroughly a few topics than to skim through lots of information.

Being selective about your e-mail and Internet reading goes a long way toward preventing information overload. Suppose you see an e-mail message titled "Car Lights Left on in Parking Lot." Do not retrieve the message if you distinctly remember having turned off your lights or you did not drive to work. E-mail programs and Internet search software are available to help users sort messages according to their needs. You can help prevent others from suffering from communication overload by being merciful in the frequency and length of your messages. Also, do not join the ranks of pranksters who send loads of jokes via e-mail and who widely distribute their personal blogs.

A useful way of combating information (or communication) overload when making a decision is to aim for the *flat maximum.* This point takes place where you have gotten rid of dead weight and can choose any of the remaining options because they are pretty much equal.[14] An example would be in purchasing a new laptop computer. After having eliminated five models that do not fit your requirements, perhaps you would regard the other models as equally useful. When you have stopped processing information and have made your decision, your mind will be clearer to receive other messages.

USE MIRRORING TO ESTABLISH RAPPORT

Mirroring
form of nonverbal communication to overcome communication barriers by subtly imitating another; used to improve rapport with another person

Another approach to overcoming communication barriers is to improve rapport with another person. A form of nonverbal communication, called **mirroring,** can be used to establish such rapport. To mirror someone is to subtly imitate that individual. The most successful mirroring technique for establishing rapport is to imitate the breathing pattern of another person. If you adjust your own breathing rate to someone else's, you will soon establish rapport with that person. Mirroring sometimes takes the form of imitating the boss in order to communicate better and win favor. Many job seekers now use mirroring to get in sync with the interviewer. Is this a technique you would be willing to try?

Mirroring takes practice to contribute to overcoming communication barriers. It is a subtle technique that requires a moderate skill level. If you mirror (or match) another person in a rigid, mechanical way, you will appear to be mocking that person. And mocking, of course, erects rather than tears down a communication barrier.

ENGAGE IN SMALL TALK AND CONSTRUCTIVE GOSSIP

The terms *small talk* and *gossip* have negative connotations for the career-minded person with a professional attitude. Nevertheless, the effective use of small talk and gossip can help a person melt communication barriers. Small talk is important because it contributes to conversational skills, and having good conversational skills enhances interpersonal communication. Trainer Randi Fredeig says, "Small talk helps build rapport and eventually trust. It helps people find common ground on which to build conversation."[15] A helpful technique is to collect tidbits of information to use as small talk to facilitate work-related or heavy-topic conversation in personal life. Keeping informed about current events, including sports, television, and films, provides useful content for small talk.

Being a source of positive gossip brings a person power and credibility. Workmates are eager to communicate with a person who is a source of not-yet-verified developments. Having such inside knowledge enhances your status and makes you a more interesting communicator. Positive gossip would include such tidbits as mentioning that the company will be looking for workers who would want a one-year assignment in Europe or that more employees will soon be eligible for profit-sharing bonuses. In contrast, spreading negative gossip will often erode your attractiveness to other people.[16]

How Do You Overcome Gender Barriers to Communication?

◀ Learning Objective 6 ◀

Another strategy for overcoming communication barriers is to deal effectively with potential cultural differences. Two types of cultural differences are those related to gender (male versus female role) and those related to geographic differences. Of course, not everybody agrees that men and women are from different cultures. Here we describe gender differences, whereas cultural differences are a separate topic.

Despite the movement toward equality of sexes in the workplace, substantial interest exists in identifying differences in communication style between men and women. The basic difference between women and men, according to the research of Deborah Tannen, professor of sociolinguistics at Georgetown University, is that men emphasize and reinforce their status when they talk, whereas women downplay their status. As part of this difference, women are more concerned about building social connections.[17] People who are aware of these differences face fewer communication problems between themselves and members of the opposite sex.

As we describe these differences, recognize that they are group stereotypes. Individual differences in communication style are usually more important than group styles (men versus women). Here we will describe the major findings of gender differences in communication patterns.[18]

1. **Women prefer to use conversation for rapport building.** For most women, the intent of conversation is to build rapport and connections with people. It has been said that men are driven by transactions, whereas women are driven by relations. Women are therefore more likely to emphasize similarities, to listen intently, and to be supportive.

2. Men prefer to use talk primarily as a means to preserve independence and status by displaying knowledge and skill. When most men talk, they want to receive positive evaluations from others and maintain their hierarchical status within the group. Men are, therefore, more oriented to giving a *report*, whereas women are more interested in establishing *rapport*.

3. Women want empathy, not solutions. When women share feelings of being stressed out, they seek empathy and understanding. If they feel they have been listened to carefully, they begin to relax. When listening to the woman, the man may feel blamed for her problems or that he has failed the woman in some way. To feel useful, the man might offer solutions to the woman's problem.

4. Men prefer to work out their problems by themselves, whereas women prefer to talk out solutions with another person. Women look on having and sharing problems as an opportunity to build and deepen relationships. Men are more likely to look on problems as challenges they must meet on their own. Similarly men are more hesitant to ask questions when faced with a problem, and women gather information by asking questions. The communication consequence of these differences is that men may become uncommunicative when they have a problem.

5. Men tend to be more directive and less apologetic in their conversation, whereas women are more polite and apologetic. Women are therefore more likely to frequently use the phrases "I'm sorry" and "thank you," even when there is no need to express apology or gratitude. Men less frequently say they are sorry, because they perceive communications as competition, and they do not want to appear vulnerable.

6. Women tend to be more conciliatory when facing differences, whereas men become more intimidating. Again, women are more interested in building relationships, whereas men are more concerned about coming out ahead.

7. Men are more interested than women in calling attention to their accomplishments or hogging recognition. One consequence of this difference is that men are more likely to dominate discussions during meetings. Another consequence is that women are more likely to help a coworker perform well. In one instance, a sales representative who had already made her sales quota for the month turned over an excellent prospect to a coworker. She reasoned, "It's somebody else's turn. I've received more than my fair share of bonuses for the month."

8. Women are more likely to use a gentle expletive, whereas men tend to be harsher. For example, if a woman locks herself out of the car, she is likely to say, "Oh dear." In the same situation, a man is likely to say, "Oh _____." (Do you think this difference really exists?)

(Here we could be dealing with both a sex and generational difference, with recent generations of women being more likely to swear than previous generations.)

The use of expletives is more consequential than simply a difference in communication style. Many people feel uncomfortable, and even harassed, when hearing expletives in the workplace. A constructive counterapproach to the expletive user is to express your discomfort and politely ask for the person to refrain from swearing in your presence. An example of this approach is as follows:

> You make me feel uncomfortable when you use expletives in my presence. I'm not challenging your right to swear, but I just wish you could avoid swearing in front of me.

Another counterapproach is to repeat what the expletive user just said, so the person will understand the inappropriateness of the swearing. Precede the statement just made with, "You just referred to one of our coworkers as a "_____ son of a _____."

How can this information just presented help overcome communication problems on the job? As a starting point, remember that gender differences often exist. Understanding these differences will help you interpret the communication behavior of people. For example, if a male coworker is not as polite as you would like, remember that he is simply engaging in gender-typical behavior. Do not take it personally.

A woman can remind herself to speak up more in meetings because her natural tendency might be toward holding back. She might say to herself, "I must watch out to avoid gender-typical behavior in this situation." A man might remind himself to be more polite and supportive toward coworkers. The problem is that, although such behavior is important, his natural tendency might be to skip saying thank you.

Men and women should recognize that when women talk over problems, they might not be seeking hard-hitting advice. Instead, they may simply be searching for a sympathetic ear so they can deal with the emotional aspects of the problem.

A general suggestion for overcoming gender-related communication barriers is for men to improve communication by listening with more empathy. Women can improve communication by becoming more direct.

How Can You Enhance Your Listening Skills?

◀ Learning Objective 7 ◀

Improving your receiving of messages is another part of developing better face-to-face and telephone communication skills. Unless you receive messages as they are intended, you cannot perform your job properly or be a good companion. Listening is a particularly important skill for anybody whose job involves solving problems for others because you need to gather information to understand the nature of the problem. Improving employee listening skills is important because insufficient listening is extraordinarily costly. Listening mistakes lead to reprocessing letters and e-mail messages, rescheduling appointments, reshipping orders, and recalling defective products. Effective listening also improves interpersonal relationships because people listen to feel understood and respected. Human Relations Self-Assessment Quiz 7-2 gives you the opportunity to think through possible listening traps you may have developed. The accompanying Human Relations in Practice illustrates how being a good listener can enrich the lives of others.

A fundamental reason so many people do not listen well is because of the difference between the average speed of talking and the average speed of processing information. Humans speak at an average pace of 110 to 200 words per minute. In contrast, they can understand or process information in the range of 400 to 3,000 words per minute.[19] As a result, the mind tends to wander while listening to the slow pace of the sender talking.

ACTIVE LISTENING

A major component of effective listening is to be an **active listener.** The active listener listens intensely, with the goal of empathizing with the speaker. **Empathy** means understanding another person's point of view. If you understand the other person's paradigm, you will be a better receiver and sender of messages. Empathy does not necessarily mean that you sympathize with the other person. For example, you may understand why some people are forced to beg in the streets, but you may have very little sympathy for their plight.

Active listener
person who listens intensely, with the goal of empathizing with the speaker

Empathy
understanding another person's point of view

Human Relations Self-Assessment Quiz 7-2

Listening Traps

Communication specialists have identified certain behavior patterns that interfere with effective hearing and listening. After thinking carefully about each trap, check how well the trap applies to you: not a problem, or need improvement. To respond to the statements accurately, visualize how you acted when you recently were in a situation calling for listening.

	Not a Problem	Need Improvement
1. **Mind reader.** You will receive limited information if you constantly think, "What is this person really thinking or feeling?"	❑	❑
2. **Rehearser.** Your mental rehearsals for "Here's what I'll say next" tune out the sender.	❑	❑
3. **Filterer.** You engage in selective listening by hearing only what you want to hear. (Could be difficult to judge because the process is often unconscious.)	❑	❑
4. **Dreamer.** You drift off during a face-to-face conversation, which often leads you to an embarrassing, "What did you say?" or "Could you repeat that?"	❑	❑
5. **Identifier.** If you refer everything you hear to your experience, you probably did not really listen to what was said.	❑	❑
6. **Comparer.** When you get sidetracked sizing up the sender, you are sure to miss the message.	❑	❑
7. **Derailer.** You change the subject too quickly, giving the impression that you are not interested in anything the sender has to say.	❑	❑
8. **Sparrer.** You hear what is said but quickly belittle or discount it, putting you in the same class as the derailer.	❑	❑
9. **Placater.** You agree with everything you hear just to be nice or to avoid conflict By behaving this way, you miss out on the opportunity for authentic dialogue.	❑	❑

Interpretation:

If you checked "Need Improvement" for five or more of the above statements, you are correct—your listening needs improvement! If you checked only two or fewer of the above traps, you are probably an effective listener and a supportive person.

Source: Reprinted with permission from *Messages: The Communication Skills Book* (Oakland, CA: New Harbinger Publications, 1983).

Accepting the Sender's Figure of Speech

A useful way of showing empathy is to accept the sender's figure of speech. By so doing, the sender feels understood and accepted. Also, if you reject the person's figure of speech by rewording it, the sender may become defensive. Many people use the figure of speech "I'm stuck" when they cannot accomplish a task. You can facilitate smooth communication by a response such as, "What can I do to help you get unstuck?" If you respond with something like, "What can I do to help you think more clearly?" the person is forced to change mental channels and may become defensive.[20]

Feedback and Paraphrasing

As a result of listening actively, the listener can feed back to the speaker what he or she thinks the speaker meant. Feedback of this type relies on both verbal and nonverbal communication. Feedback is also important because it facilitates two-way

Human Relations in Practice

Big Success Tony Wainwright Listened Well

Barry Farber, top-rated sales, management, and motivation speaker, reflects fondly about a person he admired, in these terms: "I met Tony Wainwright, chairman of a $2.5 billion corporation, author, playwright, incredible philanthropist, and one of the world's foremost salespeople. He became my greatest mentor and one of my best friends.

"Tony passed away not long ago. I miss him every day. Shortly after he died, I began to wonder: What set him apart from the other people who tried to do what he did but failed? As I thought about Tony's life—not just his sales life, but about everything he did—I realized that what made him great was his uncanny ability to listen. He listened—truly listened to everyone he met.

"When you had a conversation with Tony, he made you feel as if your ideas were worth their weight in gold. (Not that everything you said was right—if you were on the wrong track, he would let you know.) He would make you feel special, as if you were the most important appointment he had in his life, and his only purpose was to find out what was on your mind. Then he'd tell you how you could make your idea 20 times larger than anything you'd conceived. His belief in you was so strong that you had to believe it, too. That's what made him such a great salesperson: He sold you on yourself."

Source: Abridged from Barry Farber, "All Ears? Sales Success: In Business and in Life, Learning to Listen Is One of the Most Important Skills You Can Develop," *Entrepreneur*, April 2004, pp. 83–84.

communication. To be an active listener, it is also important to **paraphrase,** or repeat in your own words what the sender says, feels, and means. In your paraphrasing, avoid rewording a person's figure of speech so long as that phrase is acceptable to you. You might feel awkward the first several times you paraphrase. Therefore, try it with a person with whom you feel comfortable. With some practice, it will become a natural part of your communication skill kit. Here is an example of how you might use paraphrasing:

> *Other Person:* I'm getting ticked off at working so hard around here. I wish somebody else would pitch in and do a fair day's work.
>
> *You:* You're saying that you do more than your fair share of the tough work in our department, and it's ticking you off.
>
> *Other Person:* You bet. Here's what I think we should be doing about it. . . .

Life coach Sophronia Scott advises that, after you have paraphrased, it is sometimes helpful to ask the person you listened to whether your impression of what he or she said is correct. Your goal is not to make others repeat themselves but to extend the conversation so you can obtain more useful details.[21]

Paraphrase
repeating in one's own words what a sender says, feels, and means

Minimize Distractions

If feasible, keep papers and your computer screen out of sight when listening to somebody else. Having distractions in sight creates the temptation to glance away from the message sender. Avoid answering a cell telephone call unless you are anticipating an emergency call. At the start of your conversation, notice the other person's eye color to help you establish eye contact. (But don't keep staring at his or her eyes!) A major technique of active listening is to ask questions rather than making conclusive statements. Asking questions provides more useful information. Suppose a teammate is late with data you need to complete your analysis. Instead of saying, "I must have your input by Thursday afternoon," try, "When will I get your input?"

Allow Sender to Finish His or Her Sentence

Be sure to let others speak until they have finished. Do not interrupt by talking about you, jumping in with advice, or offering solutions unless requested. Equally bad for careful listening is finishing the sentence of a receiver. Almost all people prefer to complete their own thoughts, even though there are two curious traditions that run counter to this idea. One is that business partners who have been working together for many years, and understand each other well, have a tendency to finish the other partner's sentence. Couples in personal life behave similarly. Also, have you noticed how when you start to enter a phrase into a major search engine, suddenly you are given about ten choices that are not necessarily what you are planning to write? (Of course, this is responding to writing and not really listening, but the overtaking of your thinking is the same.)

Minimize Words That Shut Down Discussion

A key part of listening is to keep the conversation flowing. According to executive coach Marshall Goldsmith, an especially useful approach to keep conversation going in most work situations is for the listener to minimize certain negatively toned words that frequently shut down conversation. When you say, "no," "but," or "however," you effectively shut down or limit the conversation. No matter what words follow, the sender receives a message to the effect, "You are wrong and I am right." Even if you say, "I agree, but…" the shut-down message still comes through. The other person is likely to get into the defensive mode.[22]

After the person has finished talking, there are times it will be appropriate to say, "no," "but," or "however." Assume, for example, that a worker says to the business owner that the company should donate one-third of its profits to charity each year. The owner might then reply, "I hear you, but if we give away all that money, our profits will be too slim to grow the business."

Avoid the Need to Lie or Fake When You Have Not Been Paying Attention

A consequence of active listening is that you will avoid the need to pretend that you have been paying attention. Performance management coach Joe Takash suggests that you,

> Remind yourself that other people can sense if you're not listening. Force yourself to be honest and admit that you didn't catch everything that was said. That means asking the other person to repeat or requesting clarification. In this way you're being honest rather than deceitful—and deceit kills results-producing relationships fast.[23]

PERSONAL COMMUNICATION STYLE

Personal communication style
verbal and nonverbal communication style for a unique approach to sending and receiving information

In this chapter we have described many aspects of how people communicate, including gender-specific tendencies. How you combine verbal and nonverbal communication becomes part of your **personal communication style,** or your unique approach to sending and receiving information. Your personal communication style is a major component of your personality because it differentiates you from others. Hundreds of styles are possible, including the following:

- Katherine speaks loudly, smiles frequently, and moves close to people when speaking. Her communication style might be described as aggressive.

- Oscar speaks softly, partially covers his mouth with his hand while talking, and looks away from others. His communication style might be defined as passive or wimpy.

- Tim speaks rapidly, uses a colorful vocabulary, smiles frequently, and makes sweeping gestures. His communication style might be defined as flamboyant.

Concept Review and Reinforcement

Communication, 184
Encoding, 185
Decoding, 185
Barriers to communication
(or noise), 185
Nonverbal communication, 187

Semantics, 193
Mixed signals, 194
Communication overload, 195
Frame of reference, 198
Defensive communication, 200
Denial, 200

Mirroring, 200
Active listener, 203
Empathy, 203
Paraphrase, 205
Personal communication
style, 206

Summary and Review

Communication is the sending and receiving of messages. Therefore, almost anything that takes place in work and personal life involves communication. The steps involved in communication are sending, transmission over a channel, and decoding.

Communication is a vehicle for building relationships. We establish relationships along two primary dimensions: dominate–subordinate and cold–warm.

- In the process of communicating, we attempt to dominate or subordinate.
- We indicate whether we want to dominate or subordinate by the way we speak or write or by nonverbal signals we send.
- The four combinations of dominate–subordinate and cold–warm lead to different types of relationships— impersonal, accepting, supportive, or personal.

Nonverbal communication, or silent messages, are important parts of everyday communication. Nonverbal communication includes the following:

- Environment or setting in which the message is sent
- Distance from the other person
- Posture
- Hand gestures
- Facial expressions and eye contact
- Voice quality
- Personal appearance

An advanced application of nonverbal communication is to help combat drug trafficking and terrorism by spotting nervous or threatening behavior.

Roadblocks to communication are most likely to occur when messages are complex or emotional or clash with the receiver's mental set. Communication roadblocks include the following:

- Limited understanding of people
- One-way communication
- Semantics
- Credibility of the sender and mixed signals
- Distortion of information
- Different perspectives and experiences
- Emotions and attitudes
- Communication overload
- Improper timing
- Poor communication skills
- Cultural and language barriers

Strategies to overcome communication roadblocks include these:

- Appealing to human need and timing your messages
- Repeating your message using more than one channel
- Having an empowered attitude and being persuasive
- Discussing differences in paradigms
- Checking for comprehension and feelings
- Minimizing defensive communication
- Combating communication overload
- Using mirroring to establish rapport
- Engaging in small talk and constructive gossip

Some opinion and evidence exists about gender differences in communication style. For example, women prefer to use conversation for rapport building, and men prefer to use talk primarily as a means to preserve independence and status by displaying knowledge and skill. Understanding gender differences will help you interpret the communication behavior of people.

Improving your receiving of messages is another part of developing better communication skills. Unless you receive messages as intended, you cannot perform your job properly or be a good companion. A major component of effective listening is to be an active listener. The active listener uses empathy and can feed back to the speaker what he or she thinks the speaker meant.

Active listening also involves:

- Accepting the sender's figure of speech
- Feedback and paraphrasing
- Minimizing distractions
- Allowing the sender to finish his or her sentences
- Minimizing words that shut down discussion

How you combine verbal and nonverbal communication becomes your personal communication style.

Check Your Understanding

1. Based on Figure 7-1, describe one way in which you could use interpersonal communication to build a better relationship.
2. How can knowing the three major steps in communication help a person communicate more effectively?
3. Many people contend they communicate much more formally when on the job and much more informally (including using a more limited vocabulary) when among family members and friends. What do you see as the potential advantages and disadvantages of using two communication styles?
4. Why is nonverbal communication so important for the effectiveness of a manager or sales representative?
5. What can a person do to send more positive nonverbal communication signals with his or her handshake?
6. Assume that a person who is intent on a career in business chooses to have several tattoos. Which type of tattoo is likely to send the most positive message about his or her maturity and seriousness?
7. Shortly after experienced IT executive Carol Bartz, age sixty, was appointed as the new CEO of Yahoo! Inc., she made the following comments: "Let's give Yahoo! some frickin' breathing room," and "I promise to get outward looking and kick some butt."[23] What is your evaluation of this type of communication style for an Internet company executive?
8. Based on your own observations, identify a term or phrase in the workplace that creates semantic problems.
9. So what if differences in communication patterns between men and women have been identified? What impact will this information have on your communication with men and women?
10. How would you rate the persuasive communication skills of the current president of the United States? Have you any suggestions as to how the president could improve?

Web Corner

Effective listening:
www.womensmedia.com/seminar-listening.html

Exploring nonverbal communication:
http://nonverbal.ucsc.edu/

INTERNET SKILL BUILDER

Infoplease offers some practical suggestions for improving your listening skills that both support and supplement the ideas offered in this chapter. Infoplease divides listening into three basic steps: hearing, understanding, and judging. Visit the site at www.infoplease.com/homework/listeningskills1.html. The Web site includes a video of a person offering a service that will enable you to earn money as a public speaker. What is your opinion of this man's persuasiveness and credibility? What is you opinion of the effectiveness of his nonverbal communication?

Developing Your Human Relations Skills

Applying Human Relations Exercise 7-1

I Want a Raise

The purpose of this exercise is to practice your persuasive skills using a topic of interest to many people—obtaining a salary increase. One by one, students make a presentation in front of the class, presenting a persuasive argument as to why they merit a salary increase. The instructor will decide whether to use a handful of volunteers or the entire class. The audience represents the boss. The student will first explain his or her job title and key responsibilities. (Use your imagination here.) Next, make a three-minute convincing argument as to why you merit a salary increase and perhaps indicate how much you want. You will probably have about 15 minutes to prepare, inside or outside of class.

After the presentations, volunteers will offer feedback on the effectiveness of selected presentations. During the presentations of the other students, make a few notes about the presenter's effectiveness. You may need a couple of minutes between presenters to make your notes. Consider these factors:

- Overall, how convincing was the presenter? If you were the boss, would you give him or her the requested salary increase?
- Which techniques of persuasion did he or she use?
- What aspect of the presentation was unconvincing or negative?

What lessons did you take away from this exercise about persuasive communication?

Applying Human Relations Exercise 7-2

Active Listening

Before conducting the following role-plays, review the suggestions for active listening in this chapter. The suggestion about paraphrasing the message is particularly relevant because the role-plays involve emotional topics.

The Cost-Cutting Coworker

One student plays the role of a coworker who has just been appointed as the cost-cutting coordinator for the department. The cost cutter has decided to explain his or her new responsibilities to coworkers one at a time before calling a group meeting. He or she wants to emphasize how everybody has an important role in saving the company money, even in such minor initiatives as copying on two sides of a sheet of paper and not throwing out pencils until they are less than three inches long. The second worker decides to listen intently to the first worker. Other class members will rate the second student on his or her listening ability.

The Failed Nurse

One student plays the role of a coworker who has just been notified that she has failed her licensing exam to become a registered nurse (RN). She now faces being dismissed from the hospital because she has failed to obtain her license for the second time. She worries about what she will be able to do to earn a living. Another student plays the role of a coworker she corners to discuss his problems. The second worker decided to listen intently to her problems but is pressed for time. Other class members will rate the second student on his or her listening ability.

When evaluating the active listening skills of the role-players, consider using the following evaluating factors, on a scale of 1 (low) to 5 (high):

Evaluation Factor	Rating 1 2 3 4 5
1. Maintained eye contact	
2. Showed empathy	
3. Paraphrased what the other person said	
4. Focused on other person instead of being distracted	
5. Asked questions	
6. Let other person speak until he or she was finished	

Total Points: _____

Human Relations Class Activity

How Good Should Our Communication Skills Be?

"How good do my communication skills have to be to succeed in the workplace?" is a question on the minds of many career-oriented people. The purpose of this exercise is to observe the verbal and nonverbal communication skills of people who appear to have succeeded in their careers. The class in its entirety will observe a business leader or sports leader, such as a coach or an athletic director, being interviewed on television. Business channels and sports channels might be a good source of material, as might YouTube. Larry King is another potential source of useful interviews. The transmission can be real time or previously recorded, and it should last approximately five to ten minutes.

As you observe the leader (or perhaps two leaders) on television or on the Internet, grade the person or persons on two dimensions: verbal communication skills and nonverbal communication skills. Use a standard A though F system. Back up your grading with a few written comments, such as "Great eye contact with the interviewer," or "Dull, unanimated person. Put me to sleep." Also, attempt to answer the following questions:

1. What kind of impact is the presenter having on your classmates? To answer this question, take a few quick peeks around the room during the presentation, and observe the nonverbal communication of your classmates.
2. To what extent would this person be a good communications role model for me?
3. What, if any, communication tips did I learn from the person or persons in the interview(s)?

A couple of minutes after the grading and written observations are completed, the class will discuss some of the student observations. Be alert to whether consensus exists about the quality of the communications skills observed.

Human Relations Case Study 7-1

The Scrutinized Team Member Candidate

HRmanager.com is a human resources management firm that provides human resource services such as payroll, benefits administration, affirmative action programs, and technical training to other firms. By signing up with HRmanager, other firms can outsource part or all of their human resources functions. During its seven years of operation, HRmanager has grown from three to fifty employees and last year had total revenues of $21 million.

Teams perform most of the work, led by a rotating team leader. Each team member takes an eighteen-month turn at being a team leader. CEO and founder Jerry Clune regards the four-person new ventures team as vital for the future of the company. In addition to developing ideas for new services, the team members are responsible for obtaining clients for any new service they propose that Clune approves. The new ventures team thus develops and sells new services. After the service is launched and working well, the sales group is responsible for developing more clients.

As with other teams at HRmanager, the team members have a voice as to who is hired to join their team. In conjunction with Clune, the new ventures team decided it should expand to five members. The team posted the job opening for a new member on an Internet recruiting service, ran classified ads in the local newspaper, and also asked present employees for referrals. One of the finalists for the position was Gina Cleveland, a 27-year-old business graduate. In addition to interviewing with Clune and the two company vice presidents, Cleveland spent a half day with the new ventures team, breakfast and lunch included. More than two hours of that time was spent in a team interview in which Gina sat in a conference room with the four team members.

The team members agreed that Cleveland appeared to be a strong candidate on paper. Her education and experience were satisfactory, her résumé was impressive, and she presented herself well during a telephone-screening interview. After Cleveland completed her time with the new ventures team, Lauren Nielsen, the team leader, suggested that the group hold a debriefing session. The purpose of the session would be to share ideas about Cleveland's suitability for joining the team.

Nielsen commented, "It seems like we think that Gina is a strong candidate based on her credentials and what she said. But I'm a big believer in nonverbal communication. Studying Gina's body language can give us a lot of valuable information. Let's each share our observations about what Gina's body language tells us she is *really* like. I'll go first."

Lauren: I liked the way Gina looked so cool and polished when she joined us for breakfast. She's got all the superficial movements right to project self-confidence. But did anybody else notice how she looked concerned when she had to make a choice from the menu? She finally did choose a ham-and-cheese omelet, but she raised her voice at the end of the sentence when she ordered it. I got the hint that Gina is not very confident.

I also noticed Gina biting her lips a little when we asked her how creative she thought she was. I know that Gina said she was creative and gave us an example of a creative project she completed. Yet nibbling at her lips like that suggests she's not filled with firepower.

Michael: I didn't make any direct observations about Gina's being self-confident or not, but I did notice something that could be related. I think Gina is on a power trip, and this could indicate high or low self-confidence. Did anybody notice how Gina put her hands on her hips when she was standing up? That's a pure and clear signal of somebody who wants to be in control. Her haircut is almost the same length and style as most women who've made it to the top in *Fortune* 500 companies.

Another hint I get of Gina's power trip is the way she eyed the check in the restaurant at lunch. I could see it in her eyes that she really wanted to pay for the entire team. That could mean a desire to control and show us that she is very important. Do we want someone on the team with such a strong desire to control?

Brenda: I observed a different picture of Gina based on her nonverbal communication. She dressed just right for the occasion—not too conservatively, not too far business casual. This tells me she can fit into our environment. Did you notice how well groomed her shoes were? This tells you she is well organized and good at details. Her attaché case was a soft, inviting leather. If she were really into power and control, she would carry a hard vinyl or aluminum attaché case. I see Gina as a confident and assertive person who could blend right into our team.

Larry: I hope that because I'm last, I'm not too influenced by the observations that you three have shared so far. My take is that Gina looks great on paper but that she may have a problem in being a good team player. She's too laid-back and distant. Did you notice her handshake? She gave me the impression of wanting to have the least possible physical contact with me. Her handshake was so insincere. I could feel her hand and arm withdrawing from me as she shook my hand.

I also couldn't help noticing that Gina did not lean much toward us during the roundtable discussion. Do you remember how she would pull her chair back ever so slightly when we got into a heavy discussion? I interpreted that as a sign that Gina does not want to be part of a close-knit group.

Lauren: As you have probably noticed, I've been typing as fast as I can at my laptop, taking notes on what you have said. We have some mixed observations here, and I want to summarize and integrate them before we make a decision. I'll send you an e-mail with an attached file of my summary observations by tomorrow morning. Make any changes you see fit and get back to me. After we have finished evaluating Gina carefully, we will be able to make our recommendations to Jerry.

Questions

1. To what extent are new ventures team members making an appropriate use of nonverbal communication to size up Gina Cleveland?

2. Which team member do you think made the most realistic interpretation of nonverbal behavior? Why?

3. Should Lauren, the team leader, have told Gina in advance that the team would be scrutinizing her nonverbal behavior? Justify your answer.

Human Relations Case Study 7-2

The Financial Services Coach

Kristine Florentine is an account representative (stockbroker) at a branch office of a financial services firm. Her manager, Chad Olsen, is concerned that Kristine is 25 percent below quota in sales of a new hedge mutual fund offered by the company. (In the past, hedge funds were only for the wealthiest investors.) Chad sets up an appointment with Kristine to spur her to achieve quota. The conversation proceeds, in part, in this manner:

Chad: My most important responsibility is to help team members work up to their potential. I wanted to get together with you today to see if there is any way I can help you. During the past quarter you were 25 percent below quota in your sales of the new hedge fund.

Kristine: I know that I am under quota, but I can't help it. It's tough pushing a hedge fund these days. Our clients are becoming conservative, and they don't want to jump into an investment they don't understand well and is associated with taking a high risk.

Chad: Why don't your clients understand the hedge fund?

Kristine: It's a fund that the average investor does not understand. The information I send them is pretty complicated for a layperson.

Chad: What steps could you take to make this hedge fund easier for our clients and prospects to understand?

Kristine: Maybe I could work up a thirty-second presentation that would give a nice overview of the hedge fund. This would enable me to make a quick pitch over the telephone. I could get back with more details by email.

Chad: Now you're making good sense. But I'm disappointed that an intelligent person like you didn't think of that before. Do you have a self-confidence problem when it comes to making quota on a new product?

Kristine: Most people would have a self-confidence problem if they were going through what I am these days. It's not that easy concentrating on my work.

Chad: I don't like to hear excuses, but I'll make an exception this time. What are you going through that makes it difficult for you to concentrate on your work, Kristine?

Kristine: My sister and I are pretty close, and she's in big trouble. I mean *big* trouble. She was down on her luck, so she started dealing drugs. I warned her. My folks warned her, but she wouldn't listen. She got busted recently and faces a ten-year prison term.

Chad: Sorry to hear about your sister. But can't you keep things in perspective? You weren't involved in her drug dealing, were you?

Kristine: What's really dragging me down is that my sister used to tell me that I was her role model. Some role model. Her life is ruined.

Chad: Now I understand why you are so down. However, let's meet again real soon to talk about your sales on the hedge fund.

Questions

1. Identify the strengths in Chad's listening technique.

2. Identify the areas for improvement in Chad's listening technique.

3. How effective is Chad as a coaching style of manager?

Human Relations Role-Playing Exercise

Listening to Kristine's Tale of Woe

The case about the financial services coach serves as the scenario and the story line for this role-play. One student plays the role of Kristine, who believes that her distress about her sister's personal problem is a valid reason for her below-average performance. Her hope is that her boss, Chad, will listen carefully to her tale of woe and be empathetic. She will try to get Chad to listen more attentively to her. Another person plays the role of Chad, who is quite work oriented. He is willing to listen to an employee's personal problems, but he believes that his most important role is to focus on business results.

For both scenarios, observers rate the role-players on two dimensions, using a 1 to 5 scale from very poor to very good. One dimension is "effective use of human relations techniques." The second dimension is "acting ability." A few observers might voluntarily provide feedback to the role-players in terms of sharing their ratings and observations. The course instructor might also provide feedback.

REFERENCES

1. "'The Art of Woo': Selling Your Ideas to the Entire Organization, One Person at a Time," Knowledge@Wharton (www.knowledgeatwharton.com), October 17, 2007, p. 1.

2. Rich Sorenson, Grace De Bord, and Ida Ramirez, *Business and Management Communication: A Guide Book*, 4th ed. (Upper Saddle River, NJ: Prentice Hall, 2001), pp. 6–10.

3. Edward T. Hall, "Proxemics—A Study of Man's Spatial Relationships," in *Man's Image in Medicine and Anthropology* (New York: International Universities Press, 1963); Pauline E. Henderson, "Communication without Words," *Personnel Journal*, January 1989, pp. 28–29.

4. Brochure for Executive Advantage program, Washington, DC, offered by Letitia Baldrige, 1997, p. 6.

5. Nick Morgan, "How to Become an Authentic Speaker," *Harvard Business Review*, November 2008, p. 116.

6. Jeffrey Jacobi, *The Vocal Advantage* (Upper Saddle River, NJ: Prentice Hall, 1996).

7. Genviève Coutu-Bouchard, "L'effet Pygmalion," *Montréal Campus*, April 24, 2002, p. 11.

8. Ann Davis, Joseph Pereira, and William M. Bulkeley, "Silent Signals: Security Concerns Bring New Focus on Body Language," *Wall Street Journal*, August 15, 2002, pp. A1, A6;

9. Del Quentin Wilber and Ellen Nakashima, "They Don't Like Your Looks," *Washington Post*, September 19, 2007, p. DO1.

10. "Weed Out Wimpy Words," *WorkingSMART*, March 2000, p. 2; George Walther cited in "Power Up Your Persuasiveness," *Executive Leadership*, July 2003, p. 1.

11. Joe Neumaier, "Sweet Sounds of Success: Dialect Coach Sam Chwat Accents Hollywood's Best," *USA Weekend*, July 12–14, 2002, p. 12.

12. Sharon Lund O'Neill, "An Empowered Attitude Can Enhance Communication Skills," *Business Education Forum*, April 1998, pp. 28–30.

13. Several of the ideas are from "Six Ways to Be More Persuasive," *Manager's Edge*, November 2008, p. 3; Charles Harrington Elster, "Cubicle Conversation," *Wall Street Journal*, July 23, 2008, p. A15; "Talk in Headlines," *Manager's Edge*, April 2008, p. 8. For more details about point 9 in Figure 7-4, see Brian Fugere, Chelsea Hardaway, and Jon Warshawsky, *Why Business People Speak like Idiots* (New York: Free Press, 2005); Jessica E. Vascellaro, "Yahoo Chief to Deliver More Straight Talk," *Wall Street Journal*, January 26, 2009, p. A2.

14. Chris Pentila, "I Know Too Much!" *Entrepreneur*, February 2007, p. 83.

15. Quoted in Jacquelyn Lynn, "Small Talk, Big Results," *Entrepreneur*, August 1999, p. 30.

16. Nancy B. Kurland and Lisa Hope Pelled, "Passing the Word: Toward a Model of Gossip and Power in the Workplace," *Academy of Management Review*, April 2000, pp. 428–438.

17. Deborah Tannen, *Talking from Nine to Five* (New York: William Morrow, 1994).

18. Deborah Tannen, *You Just Don't Understand* (New York: Ballantine, 1990); John Gray, *Men Are from Mars, Women Are from Venus* (New York: HarperCollins, 1992); Deborah Tannen, "The Power of Talk: Who Gets Heard and Why," *Harvard Business Review*, September–October 1995, pp. 138–148; Laurie Arliss, *Gender Communication* (Englewood Cliffs, NJ: Prentice Hall, 2005).

19. One source of this widely quoted statistic is Jared Sandberg, "Bad at Complying? You Might Just Be a Very Bad Listener," *Wall Street Journal*, September 25, 2007, p. D1.

20. Daniel Araoz, "Right-Brain Management (RBM): Part 2," *Human Resources Forum*, September 1989, p. 4.

21. Cited in "Five Keys to Effective Listening," *Black Enterprise*, March 2005, p. 113.

22. Ideas from Marshall Goldsmith cited in "Eliminate Bad Words," *Manager's Edge*, special issue, 2008, p. 5.

23. Quoted in Mimi Whitefield, "Listen Up—Your Job Could Depend on It," *Miami Herald* (www.miamiherald.com), April 20, 2009.

8

Communication in the Workplace

Outline

1 What Are the Formal Channels of Communication Within Organizations?
Company Blogs as Formal Channels
Social Networking Web Sites, Intranets, and Webinars
Communication Channels for Managing Crises
Communication Directions

2 What Are the Informal Channels of Communication Within Organizations?
Networks of Contacts
The Grapevine
Chance Encounters and Management by Walking Around

**3 What Are the Challenges to Interpersonal Communication Created
by Communication Technology?**
E-mail and Communication among People
Use Presentation Technology to Your Advantage
Improve Your Telephone, Voice Mail, and Speakerphone Communication Skills
Telecommuting and the Remote Workforce
The Multitasking Movement
Overconfidence in Computer-Generated Data

**4 How Does One Do an Effective Job of Conducting or Participating
in a Business Meeting?**

One year Monsanto Co. wanted to raise the visibility of some projects and go beyond statistics to make a case for bioengineered crops. So the St. Louis agricultural products company took a page from YouTube's playbook. Tom McDermott, a Monsanto public-relations manager, sent camera crews to the Philippines, Australia, and other countries to film testimonials from farmers using Monsanto products to grow genetically modified corn, soybeans, and other crops, which are sometimes targeted for protests by environmentalists.

He then posted the clips on a Monsanto Web site, hoping to attract attention from customers, employees, and policy makers. Today the site attracts more than 15,000 visitors a month, and Monsanto is aiming to boost viewership to 200,000 within one year.

The company, which hadn't used online video before, joined a growing crowd of large businesses taking advantage of the fast-evolving medium to tackle communication chores. While video has been commonplace on the Internet since the 1990s, companies such as YouTube have developed consumer services that make it much easier to post and view movie and video clips.[1]

Learning Objectives ▸

After studying the information and doing the exercises in this chapter, you should be able to:

1 Describe the formal channels of communication within organizations.

2 Describe the informal channels of communication within organizations.

3 Identify the challenges to interpersonal communication created by communication technology.

4 Be ready to do an effective job of conducting or participating in a business meeting.

The story about Monsanto using a modern form of communication to disseminate an unpopular message illustrates the effort business enterprises put into getting their message across to interested parties. Effective communication contributes to organization success in many ways, such as keeping employees informed as to what needs to be accomplished and identifying problems before they cripple a company. For example, a lab technician might quickly warn her manager that a new food supplement being sold by the company had an unacceptably high level of mercury, thereby avoiding a recall and lawsuits. Another example of the benefit of effective communication is that workers kept up-to-date about key issues that affect them are much more likely to stay on the job. In this chapter we study communication in organizations from several perspectives: formal and informal communication channels, the communication challenges created by information technology, and dealing effectively with meetings.

▶ Learning Objective 1 ▶

What Are the Formal Channels of Communication Within Organizations?

Formal communication channels
the official pathways for sending information inside and outside an organization

Messages in organizations are sent over both formal (official) and informal (unofficial) channels. **Formal communication channels** are the official pathways for sending information inside and outside an organization. The primary source of information about formal channels is the organization chart. It indicates the channels the messages are supposed to follow. By carefully following an organization chart, an entry-level worker would know how to transmit a message to someone in the executive suite. Formal communication channels are often bypassed through information technology. Using e-mail, instant messaging, and company blogs, anybody can send a message to anybody else in the organization. During an emergency, workers are also likely to bypass formal channels, such as a technician telephoning the plant manager directly about a chemical spill.

Relatively recent formal channels of communication include company blogs, social networks, intranets, and webinars, as well as procedures for crisis management. We also look at communication directions.

Web sites have now become the premier formal crisis communication channel. Formal channels during a crisis are necessary for informing employees about a disaster, work assignments, health services and grief counseling, and assistance in returning to work. Other formal communication channels during a crisis include television or radio.

COMPANY BLOGS AS FORMAL CHANNELS

The company blog (or, more precisely, a Web log or journal) is a widely used formal mode of communication, paralleling the use of blogs in private life. Blogs originated by consumers are often used to complain about products or services and less often to compliment a company. Blogs were first used by business to communicate with customers in a personal, direct manner and perhaps form a bond with them. The blog can provide customers with a behind-the-scenes look at the company.[2] A company can also use a blog to defend its side of the story in the face of criticism, similar to the use of YouTube described in the chapter opener. Today, about 10 percent of major business corporations have entered the *blogosphere*.

The blog communicates business information but with a soft, human touch. For example, a product manager for bicycle helmets might write,

> *Just the other day, I heard from a mother of a six-year-old in our housing development. Little Jason complained about having to wear a helmet simply to ride his tricycle around the neighborhood. But then he was hit lightly by a car and thrown five feet. He escaped with a few scratches and bruises but no head injury. I'm so happy for Jason and so thankful to our fine staff who built that bike helmet to get the job done.*

The company blog can also be used to communicate with employees in a relaxed, casual tone. Employees, as well as customers, can interact with the Web log by providing comments that can be a source of valuable feedback to management and communicated directly to other visitors to the site. Blogs are also useful for communicating about shared projects, as a substitute for cutting back on large numbers of shared e-mail messages. Publishing company Ziff Davis found that by encouraging employees to use internal blogs, group e-mails were reduced from about one hundred per day to one per week. A company spokesperson said, "We've saved a month in a four-month software project, and everyone is on the same page."[3]

An individual who establishes a blog on his or her own to chat about the employer creates an *informal* rather than a formal channel—when the blog is not authorized by the company. Several years ago, Whole Foods Market Inc. amended its company code of conduct to restrict Internet postings by company officials. Based on problems created by the CEO with his anonymous blogs, the revised code bars executives and directors from posting messages about Whole Foods, its competitors, or vendors that are not sponsored by the company.[4]

Bloggers who publish negative information about their employer, or publish unprofessional photos of themselves, are liable to being fired. The rationale behind these firings is that the employee is making unwarranted use of his or her association with the company. To prevent problems of negativity appearing on personal blogs by employees, many companies now establish guidelines, such as "no disclosure of negative information about the company," "no nude photos," or "no profanity."

A general guideline for the use of offensive blogs is that a person's First Amendment right to free speech is not protected if it defames a company or divulges trade secrets on a Web posting. As explained by Nancy Flynn, executive director of the ePolicy Institute, "You could find yourself on the wrong side of a civil lawsuit."[5]

SOCIAL NETWORKING WEB SITES, INTRANETS, AND WEBINARS

Formal communication channels in the workplace have kept pace with Internet-based communication technology. An important implication of this development is that workers at all levels are expected to use these channels to send and receive messages and to work collaboratively with each other. Here we describe three key Internet-based workplace communication channels: social networking Web sites, intranets, and webinars.

Social Networking Web Sites

As a majority of workers have become members of social networking Web sites such as MySpace, Facebook, LinkedIn, and Twitter, these sites have become natural channels for members of the same company to communicate. Twitter is used for brief messages of up to 140 characters, such as "Jogged today. Feel great." Because of their more widespread membership, MySpace and Facebook are more likely to be used as official workplace communication channels. Also, Facebook and MySpace have networks dedicated to companies or coworkers. Nevertheless, Twitter is becoming quite competitive in the workplace.

Social networking technologies on the job are quite similar to their use in personal life. Members are allowed to create profiles of themselves and link up with others in a virtual community.[6] The focus on the workplace site, however, is to communicate work-related messages. The sites are also useful for workers offering support to each other, such as encouraging another Facebook member when he or she is facing a challenging problem. Another official use of social networking by corporations is for recruiting workers, with many companies posting positions on these sites. Also, site members can pass along recruiting information to their network friends.

Yet another business application of social networks is to connect workers looking for mentors with more experienced workers who are available for mentoring. Members create profiles, ask questions of potential mentors, and arrange for in-person meetings. The same software has a "praise" tab, enabling site members to write quick notes of appreciation to each other.

Social networking sites also have an application that rests at the border between a formal and informal communication channel. For example, all employees might be encouraged to join Facebook so they can network with each and build their working relationships. Facebook becomes a virtual watercooler. In the words of Jeremy Burton, CEO of Serena Software Inc., "Social networking tools like Facebook can bring us back together, help us to get to know each other as people, help us understand our business and our products, and help us better serve our customers."[7]

A concern about social networking sites in the workplace is that they facilitate spending time on nonwork matters, such as pausing to watch a coworker's surfing video instead of reviewing his or her input. Nestlé USA has created a social network with its own firewall. Employees can post content related to nutrition and health but are prohibited from using the site for dating or selling products or services.[8] Another problem is that the same social networking site that displays a professional presence might present unprofessional images and content.

Assume that your vice president of finance sends you a finance message from her Facebook page. Will you take her seriously when her page also includes photos of her mud wrestling in a bikini? (This is the reason that many companies implement a company-specific social networking site rather than a public site.)

The accompanying Human Relations in Practice presents an example of the successful application of a social networking site in the workplace.

Human Relations in Practice

Alpine Access Uses Social Networking to Get Work Accomplished

When Denver-based Alpine Access wanted to provide a place for its home-based customer service representatives to trade ideas, it turned to a method usually reserved for college students and other young people.

"To meet the needs of our employees, we wanted to provide a watercooler in a virtual way," said David Parkhurst, director of client operations for Alpine Access. "It's a trend where people use technology to get what they need from one another rather than the traditional, institutional organization."

Alpine has about 7,500 home-based operators in the U.S. who take calls for a number of corporations, such as Office Depot and J. Crew. Parkhurst said the company wanted to unify all its workers, offering them a common online space to trade ideas and socialize.

Community builds morale, so Alpine enlisted the help of HiveLive Inc., a Boulder-based company that develops social networking platforms for businesses. Within 45 days of launching the Web-based HiveLive application at Alpine, 1,500 people were using it. Now employees are trading photos and recipes, and have even set up a classified marketplace to buy and sell items.

"Web 2.0 and social networks, blogs, wikis, tags, all shifted the way we connect and share with each other," said John Kembel, co-founder and chief executive of HiveLive. "Either from a competitive point of view or the effectiveness of doing business with each other, people realize they need to bring different communication tools to the business."

Source: Excerpted from Kimberly S. Johnson, "Work, Connected by Social Networking, *Denver Post* (denverpost.com), February 11, 2008.

Intranets

An **intranet** is essentially a company version of the Internet with the basic purpose of giving employees a central place to find what they need amidst a sea of digital information.[9] The intranet serves as a useful communication channel because updated information is readily available to workers, and the information is centralized, current, and correct. For example, an employee might want to know the company's per diem allowance for meals while traveling. Instead of having to send an e-mail to the boss or human resources department, the employee can search the intranet.

Intranet
a company version of the Internet with the basic purpose of giving employees a central place to find what they need amidst a sea of digital information

The intranet is also used for much more than a file for routine information. More advanced uses include posting a video displaying a new product or service, describing the company's stand on a particular environmental issue, or posting a motivational message from the CEO. The company might also post a vision statement focusing on its exciting plans for the future. Another useful purpose is to use the intranet as a storage place for the minutes of meetings.

An intranet can also have a wiki feature in which workers are encouraged to add information of their own to certain content, similar to Wikipedia. Employee interaction of this type is helpful when those adding input are well informed and serious. The wiki approach facilitates worker collaboration, including the modification of documents as needed. The on-the-spot modification replaces sending hundreds of e-mails with attachments back and forth. To guard against misinformation being circulated, the company restricts which content allows for employee interaction. For example, the company cannot allow employees to modify per diem meal allowances.

For intranets to work well as a formal communication channel, they must have the same features of a useful commercial Web site, such as being able to find the information you need readily.

Some company intranets have added a human touch by adding such features as a phone book, menus from the company cafeteria, a classified ad section, and a dating site. Again, we see how a formal communication channel can also serve an informal, social purpose.

Webinars

Another formal communication channel is a web-based method of holding a seminar, referred to as a **webinar.** The speaker sends information to participants, who can interact with the conference presenter by computer. Collaboration is possible through such means as asking and answering questions. A telephone hookup is also typically used, including a speakerphone so many people at the same time can tune in on the information flow. Slides are displayed throughout the presentation.

Webinar
a web-based method of holding a seminar

The participants in the webinar often are working alone, yet they can be gathered in groups at one or more locations. The meetings can include PowerPoint presentations and streaming videos. Chat is another possible feature, so participants can react to the points raised by other participants.

Webinars as a formal communication channel are efficient and save travel costs and time, but, as with some other forms of communication technology, they have a limited human touch. For example, it is more difficult to inspire a worker with a message to his or her computer screen than an in-person message complete with many nonverbal cues.

COMMUNICATION CHANNELS FOR MANAGING CRISES

Many companies have developed formal communication channels for managing crises, such as fires and explosions, massive product recalls, financial scandals, and terrorist attacks. One of the most crucial parts of a disaster plan is how to communicate with the company's workforce during a crisis. A key part of the challenge is to locate and reestablish contact with employees who may be scattered in the streets or stranded in airports around the world. Aon Corporation, an international insurance, risk-management, and consulting company, improvised to use its Web site as an official communication channel during the crisis of September 11, 2001. A company official said, "With everything else down, we decided to use the company Web site. That seemed like the only option we had."[10]

A more subtle type of crisis is widespread employee fear that the company might lay off large numbers of workers or go out of business. An effective communication strategy is for top management to quickly allay fear if the company is not truly in danger. A few years ago the bankruptcy of Lehman Brothers Holdings created fear for employees at the Navy Federal Credit Union in Vienna, Virginia. The credit union responded with a letter from the president that presented a realistic but positive assessment of the company. He emphasized that the credit union is conservative and never entered into subprime (high-risk) lending.[11]

COMMUNICATION DIRECTIONS

Another aspect of formal communications is the directions messages follow in the organization. Messages in organizations travel in four primary directions: downward, upward, horizontally, and diagonally.

Downward Communication

Downward communication
the transmission of messages from higher to lower levels in an organization

Downward communication is the flow of messages from one level to a lower level. It is typified by a middle manager giving orders to a lower-level supervisor or by top management sending announcements to employees. Information is sometimes transmitted from a higher level to a lower one without the sender inviting a response. When this occurs, the feedback built into two-way communication is lost.

Upward Communication

Upward communication
the transmission of messages from lower to higher levels in an organization

Open-door policy
communication channel that is structured upward that allows employees to bring a gripe to top management's attention without first checking with the employee's manager

Upward communication is the transmission of messages from lower to higher levels in an organization. It is the most important channel for keeping management informed about problems within the organization. Simply talking regularly to employees improves upward communication. An **open-door policy** is a more structured upward communication channel that allows employees to bring a gripe to top management's attention without first checking with their manager. Managers who are willing to listen to bad news without becoming upset at the messenger are more likely to receive upward communication. Alan Lafley, the former chief executive at Procter & Gamble, was recognized for his ability to listen to problems without becoming vindictive. As a result, he often received early warning of impending problems. Upward communication is more widely used in less bureaucratic firms than in highly bureaucratic firms. Almost all executives contend that they value upward communication, regardless of whether the majority of employees agree.

Horizontal Communication

Horizontal communication is sending messages among people at the same organization level. It often takes the form of coworkers from the same department talking to one another. Horizontal communication is the basis for cooperation and collaboration. When coworkers are not sharing information with and responding to one another, they are likely to fall behind schedule. Also, efforts are duplicated and quality suffers. Another type of horizontal communication takes place when managers communicate with other managers at the same level.

Diagonal Communication

Diagonal communication is the transmission of messages to higher or lower organizational levels in different departments. Because these pathways are infrequently spelled out on the organization chart, diagonal communication is usually an *informal* channel. A typical diagonal communication event occurs when a manager from one department contacts a lower-ranking person from a department outside of his or her chain of command. Diagonal communication becomes an *informal* pathway.

What Are the Informal Channels of Communication Within Organizations?

◀ Learning Objective 2 ◀

Informal communication channels are the unofficial network of channels that supplements the formal channels. Most of these informal channels arise out of necessity. For example, people will sometimes depart from the official communication channels to consult with a person with specialized knowledge. Suppose an administrative professional in the hospital admissions department spoke and wrote fluent German. Employees from other departments would regularly consult her when they were dealing with a customer from Germany. Here we study several aspects of informal communication channels: networks of contacts, the grapevine, rumors, chance encounters, and management by walking around.

Informal communication channels
unofficial networks of channels that supplement the formal channels

NETWORKS OF CONTACTS

Perhaps the most useful aspect of informal communication channels is that they enable workers to accomplish many tasks they would not be able to if they relied exclusively on formal channels. The network of contacts often means in practice that an individual worker might be in touch with people in his or her formal and informal channels to get work accomplished. However, the emphasis is on the informal communication channels.

The Shadow Organization and Social Network Analysis

Some observers believe that the network of contacts explains how work really gets accomplished. According to this viewpoint, all companies have hidden **shadow organizations** where much of the real work gets accomplished.[12] For example, in most firms there are "tech fixers" who supplement—but do not replace—the technical support center. Suppose a worker is stuck with an information technology problem, such as a document being filled with mysterious codes that he or she cannot eliminate. The worker might get in immediate contact with a tech fixer (whose formal job responsibilities do not include solving technical problems outside his or her department) for help with the problem.

Shadow organizations
where much of the real work gets accomplished, the shadow organization is revealed by network analysis, which traces who talks to whom

The shadow organization is revealed by **social network analysis,** the mapping and measuring of relationships and links between and among people, groups, and organizations.[13]

Social network analysis
the mapping and measuring of relationships and links between and among people groups, and organizations that reveals the shadow organization

The nodes in the network are the people, and the links show relationships or flow between and among the nodes as shown in Figure 8-1. Social network analysis helps explain how work gets accomplished in a given unit, such as shown in the interactions among Susan, Tim, and Tara on the right side of Figure 8-1. Perhaps the

FIGURE 8-1

A BASIC UNIT OF A SOCIAL NETWORK ANALYSIS

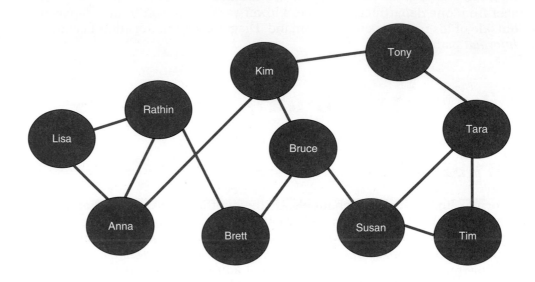

three of them mutually discuss credit risks. The interrelations can become quite complicated, because of the many number of people and interactions among them.

Social network analysis helps management survey the informal interactions among employees that can lead to innovative ideas. At the same time, the maps can point to areas where workers should be collaborating but are not. In this way, the maps help facilitate knowledge sharing. The maps can also be used to pinpoint the interactions one manager has so he or she can give the information to a successor.

Another insight gleaned for social network analysis is that the line indicates who trusts whom because they exchange ideas and go to each other for advice. According to corporate anthropologist Karen Stephenson, knowing who trusts whom is as important as knowing who reports to whom. Finding out who trusts whom is part of the social network analysis and is revealed by asking employees questions such as the following:[14]

- Whom do you go to for a quick decision?
- Whom do you hang out with socially?
- Whom do you turn to for advice?
- Whom do you go to with a good idea?
- Whom do you go to for career advice?

Your network of contacts can also extend outside the organization. A real estate developer, for example, might have contacts inside a bank who inform him of upcoming foreclosures. In this way the developer can make an early appraisal of the property to be ready with an effective bid on the foreclosed property. The mortgage specialist in the bank is part of the real estate developer's network of contacts.

A subtle perspective about social network analysis maps is that more connections aren't necessarily the best for the organization. If one person is too connected, he or she could be a bottleneck. Also, it is okay for some workers who spend a lot of time with customers or have expertise in highly specialized areas to show up on the outside of the web of interactions.

THE GRAPEVINE

The **grapevine** is the major informal communication channel in organizations. The grapevine refers to the tangled pathways that can distort information. The term referred originally to the snarled telegraph lines on the battlefield during the U.S. Civil War. The grapevine is often thought to be used primarily for passing along negative rumors and negative gossip. Gossips sometimes use the Internet and e-mail as channels for transmitting negative gossip. When left to fester, gossip can cause individuals chagrin and also lead to turnover, conflict, and lawsuits. Gossip often increases when workers are bored or lack ample information about company events.

Managers can often stop negative gossip by confronting the source of the gossip, demanding that he or she stop. Positive gossip, however, makes a contribution to the organization because trading information strengthens ties among workers and humanizes the workplace. Gossip can be viewed as the glue that binds social groups together.[15] An example of positive gossip would be, "I heard management is considering adding a paid holiday next year. Everyone with five or more service years gets his or her birthday off from work."

Another contribution of gossip is that it makes workers feel good, a situation that will sometimes enhance productivity. So long as gossip does not consume too much of the workday, the results may be positive. Marty Kotis, the CEO of a commercial real estate development firm, provides this analysis:

> I want people to enjoy coming to the office and working. I want them to get things done, and I don't think the two are mutually exclusive. I'm not a micromanager. I have a goal; they have to do it. If they want to relax along the way, that's great.[16]

The grapevine is sometimes used purposely to disseminate information along informal lines. For example, top management might want to hint to employees that certain work will be outsourced (sent to another company or outside the country) unless the employees become more productive. Although the plans are still tentative, feeding them into the grapevine may result in improved motivation and productivity.

Rumors

Rumors are an important informal communication force within organizations, and they tend to thrive in organizations with poor corporate communication, such as a penitentiary. Respondents to a worldwide survey agreed that rumors are an important early source of information. To ensure that rumors are more helpful than harmful, management might promote healthy, accurate communication. Consultant and author Tom E. Jones reinforces the importance of open communication to combat rumors. He recommends that unless the company is bound by some legal restriction, top-level management should tell everyone what they know about the facts. "Don't wait until you have all the details. Just get the truth out there fast."[17]

A problem with inaccurate rumors is that they can distract workers, create anxiety, and decrease productivity. A frequent byproduct of false rumors about company relocation or a pending merger is that some of the more talented workers leave in the hopes of more stable employment.

CHANCE ENCOUNTERS AND MANAGEMENT BY WALKING AROUND

Another informal channel of significance is the *chance encounter*. Unscheduled informal contact between managers and employees can be an efficient and effective communication channel. John P. Kotter, professor of leadership at Harvard Business School, found that effective managers do not confine their communication to formal

Grapevine
major informal communication channel in organizations; the grapevine refers to the tangled pathways that can distort information

meetings.[18] Instead, they collect valuable information during chance encounters. Spontaneous communication events may occur in the cafeteria, near the water fountain, in the halls, and on the elevator. In only two minutes, the manager might obtain the information that would typically be solicited in a thirty-minute meeting or through a series of e-mail or text-messaging exchanges. A representative question might be, "What seems to be the buzz on our newest product?"

One important communication channel can be classified as either formal or informal. **Management by walking around** involves managers intermingling freely with workers on the shop floor or in the office, as well as with customers. By spending time in personal contact with employees, the manager enhances open communication. During contacts with employees the manager will often ask questions such as, "How are you enjoying your work?" or "What bottlenecks have you encountered today?" Because management by walking around is systematic, it could be considered formal. However, a manager who circulates throughout the company is not following the formal paths prescribed by the organization chart. Management by walking around differs from chance encounters in that the latter are unplanned events; the former occur intentionally.

Another perspective on management by walking around is that it is similar to a physician making rounds to visit his or her hospital patients. Instead of visiting patients, the manager drops by to see employees and engages in brief, informal conversations. Sample questions to ask on rounds include, "What is working well today?" "Do you have the tools and equipment you need to do your job?" "Is there anything I could do better?"[19] Recognizing the nature of the rounds, the employees are likely to respond with brief, spontaneous, and useful feedback—assuming the manager making the rounds is trusted!

Management by walking around

managers intermingle freely with workers on the shop floor or in the office, as well as with customers; enhances open communication

▶ Learning Objective 3 ▶

What Are the Challenges to Interpersonal Communication Created by Communication Technology?

Rapid advances in information (or communication) technology may enable workers to communicate more easily and quickly than they could even a few years ago. Quite often the influence has been positive, but at other times the effectiveness of interpersonal communication has decreased. Six developments that illustrate the impact of information technology on interpersonal communication are e-mail, presentation technology, telephones and voice mail, telecommuting, multitasking, and overconfidence in computer-generated data. (The author realizes that telephones are not usually considered part of communication or information technology, but they, too, are electronic devices that create communication challenges.)

E-MAIL AND COMMUNICATION AMONG PEOPLE

E-mail, including instant messaging and text messaging, is the information technology system with the most dramatic impact on interpersonal communication in the current era. For both work and personal life, e-mail is typically less formal than a letter but more formal than a phone conversation. The major impact of e-mail on interpersonal communication is that written messages replace many telephone and in-person exchanges. Team members often keep in regular contact with each other without having lengthy meetings or phone conversations.

E-mail including attachments of graphics and videos has become the dominant form of communication on the job. Several potential communication problems that e-mail and instant messaging create should be kept in mind to minimize these problems.[20]

Indiscriminate Message Sending

A major problem with e-mail is that it encourages indiscriminate sending of messages Some professional workers receive an average of three hundred e-mail messages per day, and some workers check their e-mail over thirty times an hour. Some of these workers make cynical comments such as, "My job is answering e-mail" or "I answer e-mail during the day and do my work at night and on weekends." Some workers conduct virtual joke-telling contests over e-mail, with some of the jokes being perceived as offensive by many other workers. The proliferation of electronic junk mail (spam) has prompted most company officials to take corrective action, such as the installation of spam filters.

To discourage excessive use of e-mails, several companies have experimented with prohibiting the use of e-mail on Fridays or on weekends. The purpose is to both ease the e-mail overload and encourage workers to interact with each other in person or by phone. Many workers hide behind e-mail instead of dealing directly with coworkers. Although the bans typically allow sending e-mails to customers and clients or responding to urgent matters, the usual flow of e-mail is halted. Many workers have complained about such limits to e-mail because it disrupts their work routine too severely. Another problem is that banning e-mail messages on Friday results in many workers stockpiling their e-mails and sending them on Monday morning or over the weekend.[21] Another company banned "reply to all" e-mails, and cut down on e-mail dramatically.

To minimize feeling overwhelmed by e-mail, it is best to schedule blocks of time for sending and answering e-mail—assuming you have the type of work that allows you to limit e-mail. Many successful people control e-mail, rather than letting it control them. Jeff Bezos, founder and CEO of Amazon.com, is besieged by people sending him e-mails. To protect his creativity and time for interacting with his staff, Bezos reserves part of every Tuesday for reading and responding to e-mail messages.[22] (Of course, the customer service rep does not have this luxury of time blocking.)

Excessive use of e-mail drains company productivity because workers who receive an e-mail typically spend about four minutes reading it and recovering from the interruption before they can return to other work. But for workers such as an online customer service representative, dealing with e-mail is their entire job.[23]

Too Much Informality

The informal style of many e-mail exchanges can lead a person to believe that incorrect spelling, poor grammar, and disconnected thoughts are acceptable in all forms of business communication. The opposite is true. To appear professional and intelligent, writers of business e-mail messages should use correct spelling, grammar, capitalization, and punctuation. A conflict here, however, is that some professional people have begun to incorporate the informal writing style into their e-mails, including the lowercase *i* instead of *I*. Furthermore, some book titles from prestigious publishing companies use all lowercase.

E-mail has become a tool for office politicians who search for ways to look good themselves and make others look bad. Many office politicians use e-mail to give credit to themselves for their contributions to a project, perhaps using a companywide distribution list. When something goes wrong, such as a failed project, the office politician will inform hundreds of people that it was not his or her fault.

Avoidance of In-Person Reprimands

Many supervisors and other workers use e-mail to reprimand others because, by sending a message over the computer, they can avoid face-to-face confrontation. E-mail is well suited for managers who would prefer to avoid face-to-face contact with group members. Harsh messages sent over e-mail create several problems. First, it is shocking to be reprimanded or insulted in writing. Second, the person cannot offer a defense except by writing back an e-mail message explaining his or her position. Third, the recipient, not knowing what to do about the harsh message, may brood and become anxious.

Negotiations and E-mail

The use of e-mail and instant messaging during negotiations points to the strengths and limitations of this form of communication. E-mail should be used to supplement, not substitute for, face-to-face negotiations. Professor Janet Nadler of Northwestern University School of Law conducted a study in which students paired up to negotiate a commercial transaction. Half of the students used e-mail exclusively, and half conducted a brief phone conversation before beginning the negotiation via e-mail. The students who first interacted by phone were four times more likely to reach an agreement than those who relied only on e-mail. The problem highlighted by the experiment is that there are no audio or visual cues (such as facial expressions or voice tone) to establish rapport when using e-mail.[24]

Alternatives to E-mail

Some business firms have counterattacked the problems associated with e-mail by shifting to related technologies. The major problem counterattacked is the time drain of sending and responding to e-mail messages. Workers at such well-known organizations as Disney, Eastman Kodak, and the U.S. military are replacing e-mail with other software tools that function in real time. Among them are private workplace wikis, blogs, instant messaging, RSS, and more elaborate forms of groupware that allow workers to create Web sites for the team's use on a specific project. A *wiki* is a site allows a group of people to comment on and edit each other's work. *RSS* is the abbreviation for really simple syndication, which enables people to subscribe to the information they need. E-mail will probably remain strong for one-to-one communication, but the tools just mentioned will be relied on more heavily for collaboration.[25]

Figure 8-2 presents suggestions for good etiquette when using e-mail, including messaging. The good etiquette leads to more productive use of e-mail.

USE PRESENTATION TECHNOLOGY TO YOUR ADVANTAGE

Speakers in all types of organizations supplement their talk with computer slides, such as those created with PowerPoint, and often organize their presentation around them. Many people want presentations reduced to bulleted items and eye-catching graphics. (Have you noticed this tendency among students?) The communication challenge here is that during an oral presentation the predominant means of connection between sender and receiver is eye contact. When an audience is constantly distracted from the presenter by movement on the screen, sounds from the computer, or lavish colors, eye contact suffers, as does the message.

One of the biggest challenges is to learn how to handle equipment and maintain frequent eye and voice contact at all times. Several professionals in the field of

FIGURE 8-2 E-MAIL AND MESSAGING ETIQUETTE

Observing the following tips will enhance your e-mail etiquette and electronic communication effectiveness.

Keep it simple. Each message should have only one piece of information or request for action, so that it's easier for the receiver to respond. But avoid sending an e-mail with an attachment without some type of greeting or explanation. Do not allow e-mail threads longer than a couple of pages. E-mail messages longer than one screen often are filed instead of read.

Include an action step. Clearly outline what type of reply you're looking for as well as any applicable deadlines.

Use the subject line to your advantage. Generic terms such as *details* or *reminder* do not describe the contents of your message or whether it's time sensitive. So the receiver may delay opening it. "Came in Under Budget" illustrates a specific (and joyful) title. Do not forward a long chain of e-mails without changing the subject; otherwise, you might have a confusing subject line, such as "RE: FW: RE: FW: RE: FW."

Take care in writing e-mails. Clearly organize your thoughts to avoid sending e-mails with confusing, incomplete, or missing information. Use business writing style, and check carefully for grammatical and typographical errors. (Also, generally avoid the trend to set I lowercase.) When in doubt, use traditional formatting rather than bright colors and unusual fonts, because many people prefer standard formatting.

Inform receivers when sending emails from a wireless device. If you use a BlackBerry or comparable device, include a tagline informing people that you are using such a device, which will help explain your terseness. Without explanation, you might project an image of rudeness or limited writing skill.

Be considerate. Use "please" and "thank you" even in brief messages. Part of being considerate, or at least polite, is to begin your e-mail with a warm salutation, such "Hello, Gina," rather than jumping into the subject with no greeting. Avoid profane or harsh language. Another way of being considerate is to send emails only when necessary, to help combat information overload. Sending copies to only recipients who need or want the information is part of being considerate.

Don't include confidential information. The problem is that e-mail is occasionally forwarded to unintended recipients. If your message is in any way sensitive or confidential, set up a meeting or leave a voice mail in which you request confidentially.

Do not use e-mail to blast a coworker and send copies to others. Criticizing another person with e-mail and copying others is equivalent to blasting him or her during a large meeting.

Ask before sending huge attachments. Do not clog e-mail systems without permission.

Encourage questions and demands for clarification. E-mail functions best when it is interactive, so ask receivers to send along questions the might have about your message, including any requests for clarification.

Consider the timing of e-mail messages. An e-mail that makes a major request should be sent earlier in the day so the person has time to process the request. Good news can be sent almost anytime. For some recipients, bad news is best sent early in the day so they can ask for your support in dealing with the problem. But very bad news (such as being laid off) is best delivered in person. Some people prefer to receive bad news later in the day so it will not interrupt their entire workday.

Instant messaging requires a few additional considerations for practicing good electronic etiquette:

Don't be Big Brother. Some bosses use instant messaging to check up on others, to make sure they are seated at their computer. Never intrude on workers unless it is urgent.

Lay down the instant-messaging law. Make sure your message has some real value to the recipient before jumping right in front of someone's face. Instant messaging is much like walking into someone's office or cubicle without an appointment or without knocking.

Take it offline. When someone on your buddy list becomes too chatty, don't vent your frustration. By phone, in-person, or through regular e-mail, explain tactfully that you do not have time for processing so many instant messages. Suggest that the two of you get together for lunch or coffee soon.

Set limits to avoid frustration. To avoid constant interruptions, use a polite custom status message, such as "I will be dealing with customers today until 4:40."

Source: "Communicating Electronically: What Every Manager Needs to Know," *Communication Solutions*, Sample Issue, 2008, p. 2; Monte Enbysk, "Bosses: 10 Tips for Better E-mails," *Microsoft Small Business Center*, www.microsoft.com/smallbusiness/resources/technology/communications/bosses-10-tips-for-better-emails.aspx; Heinz Tschabitscher, "The Ten Most Important Rules of Email Etiquette." Accessed September 9, 2003, at: http://email.about.com/cs/netiquettetips/tp/core_netiquette.htm

business communication offer these sensible suggestions for overcoming the potential communication barrier of using presentation technology inappropriately:[26]

- **Reveal points only as needed.** Project the overhead transparencies or computer slides only when needed, and use a cursor, laser pointer, or metal pointer for emphasis.

- **Talk to the audience and not the screen.** A major problem with computer slides is that the presenter as well as the audience is likely to focus continually on the slide. If the presenter minimizes looking at the slide and spends considerable time looking at the audience, it will be easier to maintain contact with the audience. A related problem is when the speaker simply reads the slides to the audience without adding other content.

- **Keep the slide in view until the audience gets the point.** A presenter will often flash a slide or transparency without giving the audience enough time to comprehend the meaning of the slide. It is also important for presenters to synchronize the slides with their comments.

- **Reduce the text on each page of your PowerPoint presentation to a bare minimum.** Few people can really listen to you and read your slides at the same time, even if they think they are effective at multitasking. For many audiences, using the text as an outline of your talk, or talking points, is the most effective use of the slides.

- **Make sure to triple-check your presentation for spelling errors.** A spelling error projected on a screen can quickly become a joke passed around the room.

The point again is not to avoid the new technologies for communication but to use them to your advantage skillfully.

IMPROVE YOUR TELEPHONE, VOICE MAIL, AND SPEAKERPHONE COMMUNICATION SKILLS

A direct way of overcoming communication barriers is to use effective telephone and voice mail communication skills, because these two communication media often create communication problems. Also, many businesses attract and hold on to customers because their representatives interact positively with people through the telephone and voice mail. Many other firms lose money, and nonprofit organizations irritate the public because their employees have poor communication and voice mail skills. Furthermore, despite the widespread use of computer networks, a substantial amount of work among employees is still conducted via telephone and voice mail. For example, investment firms, such as Merrill Lynch, do not send sensitive financial information by e-mail but instead rely on telephone conversations.

Speakerphones present some of their own communication challenges. Small noises, such as crumpling paper, eating crunchy food, and placing a handset on a hard desk, magnify when broadcast over a speakerphone. If other people are present in the office, advise the person you are telephoning at the beginning of the conversation.[27] Doing so may save a lot of embarrassment, such as the caller making negative comments about your boss or coworker. Most of the previous comments about overcoming communication barriers apply to telephone communications, including speakerphones. Keep in mind these four representative suggestions for improving telephone effectiveness:

"Say your phone number slowly. I can't tell you how many people have zipped through it."

—Michael Shepley, the owner of a public relations firm in New York City

- Vary your voice tone and inflection to avoid sounding bored or uninterested in your job and the company.

- Smile while speaking on the phone—somehow a smile gets transmitted over the telephone wires or optic fibers!

- Although multitasking has become the mode, when speaking on a telephone do not conduct a conversation with another person simultaneously, do not read e-mails, and do not have a television or radio playing in the background. (The last point is a challenge for people who work from home.) Business callers expect your undivided attention.

- Do not eat while talking on the phone, even though it is widely practiced. Many people are repelled by the sound of a person eating while talking—much like talking with food in your mouth in a restaurant. Loudly slurping a beverage is also objectionable to most people.

TELECOMMUTING AND THE REMOTE WORKFORCE

A **telecommuter** is an employee who works at home or other offsite location full-time or part-time and sends output electronically to a central office. An estimated 45 million people in the United States work at home, out of their cars, or as corporate employees working on the premises of the corporation's customer. Collectively, they are referred to as the remote (or distributed) workforce.[28] Technology companies rely the most heavily on the distributed workforce. The majority of people who work at home do so only a day or two per week at their residence. Also, millions of people work from their homes in self-employment. Concerns about lengthy commutes, contagious diseases, and the high cost of gasoline have made working at home even more attractive for many workers in recent years. Some people believe that the pollutants from driving a gasoline-powered vehicle contribute to global warming. Furthermore, some people find workplaces to have too many interruptions and distractions, such as conversations with coworkers, superiors, and meetings.

> **Telecommuter**
> employee who works at home or other offsite location full-time or part-time and sends output electronically to a central office

Advantages of Telecommuting

An analysis of forty-six studies involving close to thirteen thousand employees found many important advantages of telecommuting. Remote workers tend to be more productive, are less likely to quit, and have higher job satisfaction than those who spend the entire workweek in the office. Employees gained the most benefits from telecommuting when managers granted them flexibility on when and how they worked from home or another remote location. (Some telecommuters work mostly from cafés like Starbucks.) An example of flexibility would be letting teleworkers be on the job outside the confines of a rigid schedule, such as from 9 until 5.[29]

For the advantages of remote work to materialize, workers have to be judged on measured output rather than the time invested. An example of measured output for a teleworker would be the number of medical claims applications produced in a week.

Interpersonal Communication Problems

Telecommuters can communicate abundantly via electronic devices, but they miss out on the face-to-face interactions so vital for dealing with complex problems. Another communication problem telecommuters face is feeling isolated from activities at the main office and missing out on the encouragement and recognition that take place in face-to-face encounters. (Of course, many telecommuters prefer to avoid such contact.) Many telecommuters have another communications problem: Because they have very little face-to-face communication with key people in the organization, they believe they are passed over for promotion. Most telecommuters spend some time in the traditional office, yet they miss the day-by-day contact.

Another communication problem with telecommuting is that it lacks a solid human connection. As one telecommuting marketing consultant put it, face time is critical for building empathy. "It's a human connection. It takes time, and human beings need visual cues, the symbols of being together and caring for one another."[30] To combat the problem of isolation, most companies schedule some face time with remote workers, perhaps every few months. At a minimum, a supervisor might phone the teleworkers at least once a week or hold a monthly videoconference.[31]

Characteristics of Successful Telecommuters

A worker needs the right personality characteristics and work habits to be successful as a remote worker. Successful telecommuters should be able to work well without supervision and be highly self-disciplined to avoid falling to the many distractions at home or another remote location.[32] You also need to be able to work well in isolation and not be dependent on frequent interaction with coworkers or a supervisor. High-maintenance employees who need frequent praise and attention are much better suited for working in a traditional office than telework.[33]

THE MULTITASKING MOVEMENT

A major consequence of electronic communication devices is that they encourage multitasking, for good or for bad. It has become standard communication practice for many workers to read e-mail while speaking on the phone, to surf the Internet while in a business meeting, and to check text messages while listening to a presentation. Some customer-contact workers even conduct cell phone conversations with friends while serving customers. Many workers are now using two or three computer monitors so they can write reports while attending to e-mail. Multitasking has become a way of life for many members of Generation Y, who grew up studying while watching television and chatting with their friends on a cell phone.

The Benefits of Multitasking

Advocates of multitasking contend that it increases productivity, such as accomplishing two or more tasks at once. A prime example is Marissa Mayer, vice president of search products and user experience at Google (and a former computer science major). Among the comments she makes in describing the "secrets of her greatness" are as follows:

> I don't feel overwhelmed with information. I really like it. I use Gmail for my personal e-mail—15 to 20 e-mails a day—but on my work e-mail I get as many as 700 to 800 a day, so I need something really fast. I use an e-mail application called Pine, a Linux-based utility I started using in college. . . . I do marathon e-mail catch-up sessions, sometimes on a Saturday or Sunday. I'll just sit down and do e-mail for 10 to 14 hours straight. I almost always have the radio or my TV on. Sometimes it's the news. Sometimes it's a sitcom. I actually like the two streams of information. I guess I'm a typical 25 to 35 year old who's now really embracing the two-screen experience.[34]

Cognitive Problems Associated with Multitasking

Although many workers can multitask successfully, the bulk of scientific evidence suggests that performing more than one demanding cognitive activity at once lowers accuracy and productivity, because you can devote 100 percent of your attention to only one task at a time. Would you want a brain surgeon to operate on a loved one while he or she chatted on the cell phone with an investment consultant? Or, to take a less than life-and-death situation, would you want your tax accountant to e-file your return while making calculations on someone else's return? Two dramatic examples from transportation accidents in recent years illustrate the potential disadvantages of multitasking and the advantages of concentrating on one task at a time.

> A Los Angeles, California, train wreck in September 2008 killed 25 people and injured 135, with 40 of them injured critically. Two teenage train buffs told a TV station that the engineer, who died in the accident, sent them a text message one minute before the wreck.[35]
>
> On January 15, 2009, Captain Chesley "Sully" Sullenberger and his crew on the US Airways flight 1549 made a spectacular landing in the Hudson River, New York City, saving the lives of 150 people on board. Sullenberger and his crew, consisting of a co-pilot and three flight attendants, concentrated on the task at hand.[36] No evidence was found that Sullenberger was engaged in any activity not directly related to avoiding the major potential catastrophe of an airline crash in New York. The captain and the crew obviously had loads of information to process, but all relating to the same survival task.

Decades of research indicate that the quality of mental output and depth of thought deteriorate as a person attends to more than one task simultaneously. One of the problems is that the brain does not handle multitasking well. The brain rapidly toggles (an on-an-off switch effect) among tasks rather than performing true simultaneous processing. The problem is more acute for complex and demanding tasks that require action planning, such as deciding how to respond to a customer complaint or solving an accounting problem. Highly practiced and routine tasks, such as sealing an envelope, suffer less from multitasking.

David E. Meyer, the director of the Brain, Cognition and Action Laboratory at the University of Michigan, notes that when people attempt to perform two or more related tasks at the same time or alternating rapidly—instead of doing them sequentially—two negative consequences occur. Errors increase substantially, and the amount of time required to perform the task may double.[37]

Interpersonal Consequences of Multitasking

Another byproduct of the multitasking movement with implications for interpersonal relationships is that electronic devices have facilitated breaking down the distinction between work and personal life. While out of the office, including vacations, is easy to be in frequent contact with the office digitally. A study conducted at Brigham Young University found that 60 percent of U.S. executives do not take a vacation without staying in touch with the office.[38] On the positive side, the wired worker can be more productive, such as providing input on an important work issue at any time. Also, if you take care of a few work problems while away from the office, you will be less overwhelmed with work when you return. On the negative side, interpersonal relationships may become impoverished because the wired worker concentrates less on friends and family even during leisure time.

Digital connectivity in the form of multitasking can weaken human connections in another way. When talking to people face-to-face it is more polite to focus on them rather than paying attention to your BlackBerry, iPhone, or computer screen.[39] We caution, however, that some people in the workplace regard multitasking while talking to them as acceptable and typical behavior.

Whether communication in the workplace is formal or informal, electronic or printed, the human touch should be included for the highest level of effectiveness. Many of the points already made about informal communication illustrate this point. Consider also that an adhesive note (Post-it style) is useful in obtaining a quick response from a colleague. A study by psychology professor Randy Garner at Sam Houston University in Texas examined response rates to a questionnaire. Volunteers who were asked to fill out a survey were more likely to comply, and give more complete answers, if it included a handwritten sticky note. Writing on the survey cover page was not as effective. Garner believes that the sticky note is perceived as a request for a personal favor, even between strangers.[40]

OVERCONFIDENCE IN COMPUTER-GENERATED DATA

A subtle communication problem from heavy reliance on computers is that many people regard computerized data as infallible. Neglected in this assumption is the reality that humans, with all their possible shortcomings, entered the data into the computer. Communication problems occur because somebody acts on the computer-generated data and neglects to challenge or double-check the data. The same person might be unwilling to listen to a plea that the information is incorrect. As a result, the computer-generated data create a barrier to listening. Three examples follow of the phenomenon in question, and you can probably provide a personal example.

- A woman named Beatrice applied for a position as a front-desk clerk at a hotel. It appeared to the woman that she would be hired, but she was turned down at the last moment. She was told that a Google check revealed that she had been involved in an armed robbery of a convenience store several years ago. Beatrice explained that the Beatrice from the robbery had the same name, but they were not the same person. The hiring manager said, "Sorry, we rely heavily on Google results." (The error here was not validating the Google entry about the criminal Beatrice.)

- The brand manager for a new machine to repair potholes discovered that the distributor's new catalog had no mention of the machine, although the information about the machine had been available for six months. Furious, the brand manager phoned the distributor, who contended, "We had some problems with our database. We'll put your machine in the next catalog coming out early next year." (The error here was not comparing the list of new products with the final entries in the catalog.)

- Your bank statement indicates that you are overdrawn by $251. You review your statement three times and are convinced that you have a positive balance of $85. The bank officer shuts you off by saying, "All our calculations are done by computer, so they are correct." (The error here is a classic case of assuming that the computer must be right and you must be wrong.)

The message from these examples is not that communication technology was in error but that somebody neglected to prevent a communication problem by verifying that the information was correct.

▶ Learning Objective 4 ▶

How Does One Do an Effective Job of Conducting or Participating in a Business Meeting?

Much of workplace communication, including group decision making, takes place in meetings. Among the many purposes of meetings are disseminating information, training, building team spirit, and problem solving, including brainstorming. When conducted properly, meetings accomplish the purpose. Yet, when conducted poorly, meetings represent a substantial productivity drain. The following suggestions apply to those who conduct physical and electronic meetings, and some are also relevant for participants. Videoconferencing is sometimes used to conduct meetings with people in dispersed locations, as is teleconferencing. The globalization of business, as well as interest in reducing travel costs, has increased the demand for videoconferencing. By following these nine suggestions, you increase the meeting's effectiveness as a communication vehicle.

1. **Start with a key meeting outcome.** Before the meeting is called, the meeting leader defines the one thing that must be accomplished to consider the meeting a success. The outcome in mind is best framed even before establishing the agenda, because knowing what should be accomplished will help establish the agenda.[41] To illustrate, a hospital administrator establishes the key meeting outcome of "find new ways to shorten waiting time in the emergency room." The agenda might then include discussing what other hospitals have done to shorten waiting times in the emergency room.

2. **Meet only for valid reasons.** Many meetings lead to no decisions because they lacked a valid purpose in the first place. Having an agenda for the meeting is a valid reason because the agenda is an important purpose for getting together. Meetings are necessary only in situations that require coordinated effort and group decision making. E-mails and intranet exchanges can be substituted for meetings when factual information needs to be disseminated and discussion is unimportant. When looking to meet for valid reasons, be aware of possible cultural differences in the motives for having a meeting. In many cultures, meetings are conducted to build relationships. For example, a key to doing business in Asia is to get to know work associates on a personal level before getting down to problem solving, buying, or selling.[42] So for an Asian manager, conducting a meeting to build personal relationships *is* a valid reason. For many Americans, also, an important purpose of face-to-face meetings is to build relationships. In the words of business columnist Jared Sandberg, "We are, by nature, needy huddlers and cuddlers."[43]

3. **Start and stop on time, and offer refreshments.** Meetings appear more professional and action oriented when the leader starts and stops on time. If the leader waits for the last member to show up, much time is lost and late behavior is rewarded. Stopping the meeting on time shows respect for the members' time. Offering refreshments is another tactic for emphasizing the importance of the meeting and also enhances satisfaction with the meeting. Agree in advance on when and if there will be a break to reduce anxiety about when the break will occur.

4. **Keep comments brief and to the point.** A major challenge facing the meeting leader is to keep conversation on track. Verbal rambling by participants creates communication barriers because other people lose interest. An effective way for the leader to keep comments on target is to ask the contributor of a non sequitur, "In what way does your comment relate to the agenda?"

5. **Encourage critical feedback and commentary.** Meetings are more likely to be fully productive when participants are encouraged to be candid with criticism and negative feedback. Openness helps prevent groupthink and also brings important problems to the attention of management.

6. **Strive for wide participation.** One justification for conducting a meeting is to obtain a variety of input. Although not everybody is equally qualified to voice a sound opinion, everyone should be heard. A skillful leader may have to limit the contribution of domineering members and coax reticent members to voice their ideas. Asking participants to bring several questions to the meeting will often spur participation. The meeting leader should not play favorites by encouraging the participation of some members and ignoring others. If the meeting leader spends the entire time making a PowerPoint presentation, participation will be discouraged. The slides should supplement the meeting and be starting points for discussion.

7. **Solve small issues ahead of time with e-mail or other forms of electronic communication.** Meetings can be briefer and less mundane when small issues are resolved ahead of time. E-mail is particularly effective for resolving minor administrative issues and also for collecting agenda items in advance. Intranets and blogs can serve the same purpose.

8. **Consider "huddling" when quick action is needed.** A huddle is a fast-paced, action-oriented way to bring workers together into brief meetings to discuss critical performance issues. A department store manager might bring together five floor managers ten minutes before opening to say, "We have a line-up of about five hundred customers waiting to get in because of our specials today. Is everybody ready for the rush of excitement? What problems do you anticipate?" The huddle is particularly important when it would be difficult for the workers to attend a long meeting. Huddles are often accomplished standing up, which helps keep the meetings brief.

9. **Ensure that all follow-up action is assigned and recorded.** All too often, even after a decision has been reached, a meeting lacks tangible output. Distribute a memo summarizing who is responsible for taking what action and by what date.

10. **Minimize distractions during the meeting.** The group should agree on whether meeting participants will be allowed to use laptop computers for purposes other than recording information in the meeting. Agree also on whether using cell phones and text messaging is acceptable during the meeting. For example, Tim Brown, CEO of design firm IDEO, believes that it is unacceptable to use a PDA during a meeting because engaging with the people present is important.[44] If handouts are used, allow participants enough time to read them so one person is not presenting while the others are reading. Ensure beforehand that computer-related equipment, such as the projector, is working and that it is compatible with the presenter's software.

Concept Review and Reinforcement

Key Terms

Formal communication
    channels, 218
Intranet, 221
Webinar, 221
Downward communication, 222

Upward communication, 222
Open-door policy, 222
Informal communication
    channels, 223
Shadow organizations, 223

Social network analysis, 223
Grapevine, 225
Management by walking
    around, 226
Telecommuter, 231

Summary and Review

Messages in organizations are sent over both formal (official) and informal (unofficial) channels. Three key aspects of the formal channels are as follows:

- The company blog is a rapidly growing type of formal communication. It communicates business information with a soft, human touch.
- Formal communication channels in the workplace have kept up with Internet-based communication technology. Four such channels are social networking sites (such as Facebook), intranets, wikis, and webinars.
- Many companies have developed formal communication channels for managing crises, such as fires and terrorist attacks.
- Messages in organizations travel in four primary directions: downward, upward, horizontally, and diagonally. An open-door policy facilitates upward communication.
- An informal communication channel supplements the formal channel.
- A major informal communication channel is the network of contacts that employees use to accomplish work, sometimes referred to as the shadow organization. Social networking analysis is used to map the shadow organization.
- The grapevine is the major informal communication channel, and it carries rumors and gossip.
- Chance encounters between managers and employees foster informal communication, as does management by walking around.

Communication technology creates challenges for interpersonal communication, despite all its advantages, as follows.

- E-mail, including instant messaging and text messaging, has the most dramatic impact on interpersonal communication in organizations. Some workers are overwhelmed by e-mail, whereas others have the system under control.
- E-mail encourages informal, unprofessional communication, and the system is too often used to play office politics.
- E-mail should be used to supplement, not as a substitute for, face-to-face negotiations.
- Some business firms have counterattacked the problems associated with e-mail by shifting to related technologies.
- Presentation technology creates challenges of its own, including the need to learn how to handle equipment and maintain eye contact at the same time. It is important to talk to the audience and not the screen and reduce the text on each page to a bare minimum.
- Effective telephone and voice mail communication skills are helpful in overcoming communication problems. Remember to vary your voice tone and avoid multitasking while speaking.
- Telecommuters are now referred to as the remote or distributed workforce.
- Telecommuters may miss out on the face-to-face interactions necessary for dealing with complex problems.
- Telecommuting is also a challenge because it lacks a solid human connection.
- Electronic communication facilitates the multitasking that is so popular with Generation Y.
- Advocates of multitasking claim it enhances productivity.

- The bulk of scientific evidence suggests that performing more than one demanding cognitive activity at once lowers accuracy and productivity. Mental output and depth of thought deteriorate while multitasking.
- Multitasking has facilitated breaking down the distinction between work and personal life.
- A subtle communication problem from heavy reliance on computers is that many people regard computerized data as infallible. As a result, the user of the data might not listen to pleas that the information is incorrect.

Much of workplace communication takes place in meetings. Among the many suggestions for productive meetings are the following:

- Start with a key meeting outcome.
- Meet only for valid reasons.
- Start and stop on time, and offer refreshments.
- Solve small issues ahead of time with e-mail.
- Minimize distractions during the meeting.

Check Your Understanding

1. Suppose you thought that the CEO of your company was moving the company in the wrong direction, and you want to tell him or her. Explain which communication channel you would choose to deliver your message.
2. In what ways have communication technologies made the workplace more democratic?
3. In what way might management by walking around undermine the authority of the supervisor?
4. How might an e-mail message contain nonverbal communication?
5. To what extent do you think that clip art can enhance the communication effectiveness of a PowerPoint presentation?

6. What do you think would the advantages and disadvantages of having a "no e-mail on Friday" policy at a busy office?
7. Give three examples of business situations in which telephone conversations still play a key role.
8. Give an example from your own life in which multitasking has enhanced your performance.
9. Give an example from your own life in which multitasking has lowered your performance.
10. Why are face-to-face meetings still so popular even in high-technology companies?

Web Corner

Suggestions for writing better e-mails:
http://www.mindtools.com/CommSkll/EmailCommunication.htm

How to run an effective business meeting:
http://www.meetingwizard.org/meetings/effective-meetings.cfm

INTERNET SKILL BUILDER

Use your preferred search engine or engines to identify ten different positions for either telecommuting part of the workweek or completely working at home. It is also possible that you might receive an unsolicited e-mail message with a work-at-home opportunity. Which of the positions that you find would you regard as a legitimate career opportunity? Which of these positions would your regard as a scam? Explain the basis for your conclusions about both the legitimate and scam job opportunities.

Developing Your
Human Relations Skills

Applying Human Relations Exercise 8-1

Designing an Office for a Virtual-Customer Agent

Work in a team to design a home office for a virtual-customer agent, a worker whose responsibilities are to fill orders for merchandise for three different companies. The agent receives calls through a toll-free number and then uses the computer to enter the order. He or she also processes orders online. The office in question will be placed somewhere in a three-bedroom house that also has a family room, kitchen, basement, and enclosed porch.

While designing the office, include such factors as the layout of the furniture and equipment, the equipment needed, and any decorations. Keep in mind ergonomic factors that focus on making the equipment easy to use and with low risk for physical problems such as carpal tunnel syndrome and backaches. Because the virtual agent will have to pay for the office setup, derive a tentative budget.

Draw your design on any convenient format, including a flip chart, whiteboard, blackboard, or computer screen. Your team leader might be asked to present the design to the rest of the class so class members can compare the effectiveness of each design. Class members evaluating the home office design might use the following evaluation factors in addition to whatever their intuition suggests:

- To what extent does the office design help reduce possible conflict with other people living in the same household?
- How might this design offer productivity advantages over a conventional office?
- When and if customers or company representatives call into this office, how professional will the setup sound?
- How will this office design contribute to job satisfaction?

Applying Human Relations Exercise 8-2

Evaluating a Business Meeting

The class organizes into teams of about six students to conduct a meeting to formulate plans for building temporary housing for homeless people downtown in your city or a nearby city. Three other students, or the entire class, will observe the meeting. This exercise should take about thirty-five minutes, and it can be done inside or outside of class. Each team takes on the assignment of formulating plans for building temporary shelters for the homeless. The dwellings you plan to build, for example, might be two-room cottages with electricity and indoor plumbing. During the time allotted to the task, formulate plans for going ahead with shelters for the homeless. Consider dividing up work by assigning certain tasks to each team member. Sketch out tentative answers to the following questions: (a) How will you obtain funding for your venture? (b) Which homeless people will you help? (c) Where will your shelters be? (d) Who will do the actual construction?

After the meeting is completed, the three observers will provide feedback to the team members about the effectiveness of the meeting, using the following criteria:

1. How effective was the teamwork? Support your conclusion with an example of specific behavior.
2. How well did group members stay on track in terms of focusing on their goal?
3. Did the team members make any introductory warm-up comments to help build rapport?
4. To what extent was the participation among team members balanced?
5. Did the team move toward any conclusions or action plans?
6. Choose another criterion you think might be relevant.

Company Messages on Company Web Sites or YouTube

The introductory case in this chapter mentions that many companies are using their Web site or YouTube to disseminate important messages to stakeholders. The class assignment here is for each class member to search company Web sites or YouTube for a serious message to employees or other stakeholders, such as customers and stockholders. If you choose YouTube, the video you choose should appear to have been authentically prepared by a company representative, not the work of a prankster. Finding a serious message might take some digging because so many corporate messages posted on YouTube are strictly for entertainment purposes. But it is also possible to find video messages on an occasional company Web site.

At some point the class meets in a setting where it is possible to project videos on a large screen. Even if the screen is a large monitor for a PC, the activity will work. Depending on how much class time is available for the project, about six volunteers project their

chosen video on the screen. As class members watch the selection of videos, form an impression of the communication effectiveness of each video. Answer such questions as:

- What message is the business organization really getting across to its intended audience?
- How convincing is the video in sending its message?
- How sincere does the message appear to be?

After students have reflected on the videos, have a brief class discussion of the answers to the above questions.

Human Relations Case Study 8-1

Karl Walks Around

Karl Bennett, a supervisor in a call center located in Iowa, was urged by his manager to walk around the center from time to time to chat informally with the call center workers. His boss said to Karl, "It's always good to know what the call center specialists are feeling and thinking. You might pick up some good ideas." Bennett had studied the technique of *management by walking around* in a human relations course, so he was enthusiastic about the idea.

Karl chose a Tuesday evening to conduct his walk around and decided to stop by the cubicles of four call center operators to test the technique. If it worked well, he would walk around again in another week.

Karl first stopped by the cubicle of Mandi, making sure first that she was not on the telephone with a customer. "I just dropped by to say hello and see how things are going," said Karl. "I take it everything is going fine, and that you have no problems," he continued. "Am I right?"

Mandi answered, "Yes, no real problems. Thanks for stopping by."

Next, Karl stopped by the cubicle of Pete, a relatively new operator. "How's it going Pete?" asked Karl. "What kind of problems might you be facing?"

Pete answered, "I'm having trouble understanding the accent of some of my customers. And some of the customers say I talk too fast. Other than that, the job is going well."

"That's interesting," said Karl. "But I see I have a couple of e-mails waiting for me on my BlackBerry. Maybe you do talk too fast. I'll get back to you later."

Karl thought to himself that the walk around was going fine so far. He then dropped by Brittany's cubicle. "What's happening, Brittany?" asked Karl as Brittany was completing a customer inquiry about a defective piece of equipment. Brittany raised the palm of her right hand to signal that she was not quite finished with the call.

Karl then asked, "Are your wedding plans going along okay?"

Brittany replied, "Yes, Karl. Everything is fine. Thanks for stopping by."

A few minutes later, Karl completed his walk around by stopping to visit Derek, a rabid Chicago Bears fan. "Hey, Derek, how goes it?" said Karl. "I think the Bears are headed to the league championship this year. What do you think?"

Derek answered, "Oh, yes, the Bears are strong this season, and I'm optimistic. But as long as you have dropped by, I wanted to mention that our instruction manuals seem to be too complicated. People are calling in again and again with the most basic questions, like how to find the serial number."

"Don't worry too much about that. A lot of our customers can hardly read these days. I think the term is *functionally illiterate*," said Karl with a smile.

Questions

1. How successful is Karl in using his walk around to uncover useful information?

2. What can Karl do to increase his questioning effectiveness?

Derek Wants More from Karl

The case about Karl walking around serves as the scenario and story line for this role-play. One student plays the role of Karl, who is making the rounds. His last stop of the day is a visit with Derek, who is encountering some problems with customers who find the instruction manuals to be too complicated. Karl seems to want to dismiss the problem by blaming the lack of comprehension on the poor reading ability of some customers.

Another student plays the role of Derek, who is quite serious about serving the needs of customers and wants to discuss the situation further. He believes that a supervisor should give careful thought to any customer problem. Derek therefore wants to engage Karl in more of a problem-solving discussion.

Is Telecommuting Good for Us?

Susan Lepsch and Russell Stratton, co-owners of Lepsch and Stratton Travel Agency, met for breakfast on the first Monday in July. "Either we take decisive action or we stop complaining about too little office space and too much turnover," said Russ. "We've expanded despite people making their own travel arrangements over the Internet. Our focus on giving advice that you don't get with the online travel agencies has helped us grow. We should expand our office from four thousand to five thousand square feet. Our volume of business is good, but not good enough to cover that much increase in expenses."

Sue responded, "I've read that one of the best ways to keep good office staff is to give them a work schedule that makes life easy. If we allowed our staff to telecommute, we could get by without the additional space. This would save us a lot of money."

"I'm willing to try the program on a voluntary basis," said Russ. "Who should we start with?"

"The likely candidates are the support specialists and one direct-mail specialist. Those people could do a substantial portion of their work at home if they had the right equipment. Our staff members all have PCs or laptops at home, but they might not have powerful enough equipment to run our software. They would need upgrades." Sue and Russ later identified five volunteers for the telecommuting program.

The telecommuting program was launched September 1. During mid-November, Sue and Russ decided to evaluate the new system. Neither partner had heard of any substantial complaint about the program from the employees or from travel clients because of poor service. If the program were working well, the present space could be retained, thus avoiding the expense and effort of relocation.

Sue began her evaluation of telecommuting by describing her experiences in supervising the work of Kim and Betty. "I was worried about the possibility of Kim not doing her job because she wasted time on the telephone and with e-mail. That proved to be not a problem. Kim did all the work that was required."

Russ spoke to Kristin, the direct-mail specialist, about her experiences as a teleworker. Kristin replied, "My reaction has been mixed. I enjoy being treated like a true professional. Nobody has to watch over me to see that I get my work done. Besides, our work is driven by clients anyway. I like saving commuting time, so I have a little more time for reading the newspaper and taking care of errands.

"What I don't like is being so alienated from the office. I want to move up to supervisor as our agency expands substantially. If you two hardly ever see me, I could easily be passed over for promotion. Another problem I didn't anticipate is the distraction at home. My daughter asks me for rides, and my friends drop by. People simply don't take working at home as seriously as working in an office building."

Sue asked Cindy, one of the support specialists, for her reaction to working at home. With a gleam in her eye and a smile, Cindy replied, "Telecommuting has helped make my life work. My biggest problem before working at home was that I had a latchkey child. Trevor, my son, is too old for child care yet too young to go home unsupervised. He gets home at around 3:15 in the afternoon.

When he arrives, he knows that I'm working, but it's better than my not being on the premises. By not worrying so much about Trevor on my working days, I feel much less stressed and better able to concentrate on my work."

Russ interviewed Tony, another support specialist, about his telecommuting experiences. "On a scale of 1 to 10," said Tony, "I would rate teleworking a 5. I like being able to avoid commuting on a day when road conditions are bad. And I like getting home from work at 4:31 after having stopped work at 4:30. The pay is the same, so I have no complaints there."

"What reservations do you have?" Russ asked.

"I miss the interaction with the office buddies," said Tony. "I never wanted to be a loner. I like people. I like taking coffee breaks with coworkers. At home, I drink my coffee at my desk. For a break, I take out the garbage. If I'm lucky, I say hello to the mail carrier."

After this round of interviews, Sue and Russ had not made up their minds about the effectiveness of the telecommuting program. Sue mentioned, however, "I don't know how far we will go with telecommuting. But I do know that we will always need somebody around the office to talk to our clients both in person and on the phone."

Questions

1. What is your opinion of the effectiveness of the telecommuting program at the travel agency so far?

2. What evidence should Sue and Russ be seeking to know if the telecommuting program is beneficial to the travel agency?

3. What recommendations do you have for Tony so his teleworking will become a more positive experience for him?

REFERENCES

1. Bobby White, "Firms Take a Cue from YouTube: Companies Use Online Video to Reduce Costs, Communicate with Staff," *Wall Street Journal*, January 2, 2007, p. B3.

2. Michelle Conlin and Andrew Park, "Blogging with the Boss's Blessing," *Business Week*, June 28, 2004, p. 102; Marci Alboher, "Blogging's a Low-Cost, High-Return Marketing Tool," *New York Times* (nytimes.com), December 27, 2007, p. 2.

3. Cited in "Try Internal Blogs to Boost Productivity," *Executive Leadership*, September 2007, p. 3.

4. David Kesmodel, "Whole Foods Bars Executives from Web Forums," *Wall Street Journal*, November 7, 2007, p. A14.

5. Cited in Erika D. Smith, "Web Opens Another Defensive Front for Companies," *Indianapolis Star* syndicated story, July 1, 2007.

6. Ed Frauenhelm, "Social Revolution," *Workforce*, October 22, 2007, pp. 1, 28–37.

7. Bill Roberts, "Social Networking at the Office," *HR Magazine*, March 2008, pp. 81–83.

8. Roberts, "Social Networking at the Office," p. 82.

9. Vauhini Vaura, "The Winning Formula," *Wall Street Journal*, May 14, 2007, p. R1.

10. Patrick Kiger, "Lessons from a Crisis: How Communication Kept a Company Together," *Workforce*, November 2001, p. 28.

11. Jeremy Smerd and Jessica Marquez, "Calming Worried Workers," *Workforce Management*, October 6, 2008, pp. 1–3.

12. Mark Hendricks, "The Shadow Knows," *Entrepreneur*, January 2000, p. 110; Jennifer Reingold and Jia Lynn Yang, "What's Your OQ?" *Fortune*, July 23, 2007, pp. 98–106.

13. Valdis Krebs, "Social Network Analysis: A Brief Introduction." Retrieved August 10, 2007 from www.orgnet.com.

14. Cited in Ethan Watters, "The Organization Woman," *Business Week*, April 10, 2006, pp. 106–110.

15. Samuel Greengard, "Gossip Poisons Business: HR Can Stop It," *Workforce*, July 2001, pp. 26–27; Lea Winerman, "Have Your Heard the Latest?" *Monitor on Psychology*, April 2006, pp. 56–57.

16. Quoted in Joyce Rosenberg, "Business Owners Should Welcome Small Talk," Associated Press, January 14, 2008.

17. Quoted in Anne Fisher, "Psst! Rumors Can Help at Work," *Fortune*, December 12, 2005, p. 202.

18. John P. Kotter, *The General Managers* (New York: Free Press, 1991).

19. "'Making Rounds like a Physician," *Manager's Edge*, February 8, 2006. As adapted from Quint Studer, *Hardwiring Excellence* (Gulf Breeze, FL: Fire Starter Publishing, 2005).

20. "Communicating Electronically: What Every Manager Needs to Know," *Communication Solutions*, Sample Issue, 2008; "Using E-Mail and Voice Mail Effectively," *Business Education Forum*, October 1998, pp. 6–9, 51; Andrew Blackman, "Spam's 'Easy Target,'" *Wall Street Journal*, August 19, 2003, pp. B1, B4.

21. Sue Shellenbarger, "A Day without Email Is Like . . ." *Wall Street Journal*, October 11, 2007, p. D1.

22. Letitia Baldrige, *How to Cope with E-mails*, Richmond, VA: Briefings Publishing Group. Retrieved February 15, 2003, from: www.briefings.com.

23. Jon Hurdle, "Program Tackles E-mail Addiction," Reuters News Agency, February 20, 2007.

24. Janice Nadler, "Rapport in Legal Negotiation: How Small Talk Can Facilitate Email Dealmaking," *Harvard Negotiation Law Review*, Vol. 9, 2004, pp. 225–253.

25. Michelle Conlin, "E-Mail Is So Five Minutes Ago: It's Being Replaced by Software That Promotes Real-Time Collaboration," *Business Week*, November 28, 2005, pp. 111–112; Luis Suarez, "I Freed Myself from E-mail's Grip," *New York Times* (nytimes.com), June 29, 2008.

26. Jean Mausehund and R. Neil Dortch, "Presentation Skills in the Digital Age," *Business Education Forum*, April 1999, pp. 30–32; Michael Patterson, "The Pitch Coach," *Business Week SmallBiz*, Fall 2005, p. 61.

27. John T. Adams, III, "When You're on a Speakerphone, Don't Make Noise," *HR Magazine*, March 2001, p. 12.

28. Ravi S. Gajendran and David A. Harrison, "The Good, the Bad and the Unknown about Telecommuting: Meta-Analysis of Psychological Mediators and Individual Consequences," *Journal of Applied Psychology*, November 2007, p. 1524.

29. Gajendran and Harrison, "The Good, the Bad and the Unknown," pp. 1524–1541.

30. "Work à la Modem," *Business Week*, October 4, 1999, p. 176.

31. "Bridge Gaps with Remote Workers," *Manager's Edge*, July 2008, p. 1.

32. Michelle Conlin, "Telecommuting: Out of Sight, Yes. Out of Mind, No." *Business Week*, February 18, 2008, p. 60.

33. "Telecommuting Tips," *Manager's Edge*, December 2007, p. 1.

34. "Secrets of Greatness: How I Work," *Fortune*, March 20, 2006, p. 68.

35. Steve Gorman, "Text Messaging Figures in L.A. Train Wreck Probe," www.reuters.com, September 15, 2008.

36. Laura Browne, "Captain 'Sully' Sullenberger Leadership Lessons for Business," *Women's Business Examiner*, February 9, 2009.

37. The scientific information about multitasking is reviewed in Claudia Wallis, "The Multitasking Generation," *Time*, March 27, 2006, pp. 48–55. See also Joshua Rubinstein, David Meyer, and Jeffrey Evans, "Human Perception and Performance," *Journal of Experimental Psychology*, no. 4, 2001.

38. Mike DeGiorgi, "How to Know When You're Way Too Plugged In," *Executive Leadership*, April 2007, p. 7.

39. "The Perils of Multitasking," *Management People at Work*, Sample Issue, 2008, p. 2.

40. Research reported in "Post-It Persuasion: Read Me Now!" *Psychology Today*, December 2005, p. 32.

41. "Never Hold Another Bad Meeting," *Manager's Edge*, October 2008, p. 6.

42. Ed Frauenheim, "Custom-Fit Communication," *Workforce Management*, November 21, 2005, p. 30.

43. Jared Sandberg, "Another Meeting? Good. Another Chance to Hear Myself Talk," *Wall Street Journal*, March 11, 2008, p. B1.

44. "Bringing Design to Blue Chips: Tim Brown, CEO, IDEO," *Fortune*, November 12, 2007, p. 32.

9

Getting Along with Your Manager, Coworkers, and Customers

Outline

1 How Do You Develop a Good Relationship with Your Manager or Team Leader?
Achieve Good Job Performance
Display a Strong Work Ethic
Demonstrate Good Emotional Intelligence
Be Dependable and Honest
Be a Good Organizational Citizen
Create a Strong Presence
Find Out What Your Manager Expects of You
Minimize Complaints
Avoid Bypassing Your Manager
Engage in Favorable Interactions with Your Manager

2 How Do You Cope with a Problem Manager?
Reevaluate Your Manager
Confront Your Manager about the Problem
Overrespond to Your Manager's Pet Peeves
Learn from Your Manager's Mistakes

3 How Do You Build Good Coworker Relationships?
Have High Self-Esteem and Be the Center of a Communication Network
Develop Allies through Being Civil
Make Other People Feel Important
Maintain Honest and Open Relationships
Be a Team Player

Follow Group Standards of Conduct
Express an Interest in the Work and Personal Lives of Coworkers
Use Appropriate Compliments
Deal Effectively with Difficult People
Face Maturely the Challenge of the Office Romance

4 How Do You Build Good Relationships with Customers?

Learning Objectives ▶

After reading the information and doing the exercises in this chapter, you should be able to:

1 Select several tactics for developing a good relationship with your manager or team leader.

2 Deal effectively with a problem manager.

3 Describe methods of getting along with coworkers.

4 Identify tactics that help a person become a good team player.

5 Pinpoint tactics for dealing effectively with difficult people.

6 Specify approaches to building good relationships with customers.

R ay Isaac, 42, is the president of Isaac Heating & Air Conditioning, a company with 160 employees that provides heating and air conditioning, and installation service. He said that the company recently revised its rank order of priorities, as follows: safety, employee, customer, then company.

"Very rarely," says Isaac, "are you going to have a miserable employee who goes out and makes a happy customer. And we kind of stole that from Wegmans [an upscale national supermarket chain]. They put their employee first, and you know what, it seems to be working for them, so we'll do the same thing.

"But we have a customer satisfaction goal. There's one question on our customer satisfaction surveys: 'How likely are you to recommend Isaac to a friend or relative?' It goes from 0, not likely at all, to 10, extremely likely. There are two scores that are promoters, 10s and nines. Eight and seven are neutral.

All those surveys end up on my desk, and if I get an eight or below, I'm sending it back to the department managers and asking them to call the customer and find out why, because an eight is just as bad as a 0 for us. If they're not a promoter, if they're not dead set on using anybody else but Isaac, we need to make sure we're doing everything correct."[1]

The story about the heating and air-conditioning company illustrates a basic truth about success in business: You need to have good relationships with employees to facilitate their having good relationships with customers. At the same time, the customer-contact workers must develop good relationships with customers for the company to obtain referrals.

Political skills
an interpersonal style that combines awareness of others with the ability to communicate well; developing effective relationships with work associates, including customers

Developing effective relationships with work associates, including customers, has been seen as having good **political skills,** an interpersonal style that combines awareness of others with the ability to communicate well. People with political skill are charming and engaging, which inspires confidence, trust, and sincerity.[2] Based on these attributes, the person with political skill effectively influences others. This chapter presents information about developing productive relationships with three major groups of work associates: managers, coworkers, and customers. Along the way, we include information about coping with difficult bosses and coworkers.

▶ Learning Objective 1 ▶

How Do You Develop a Good Relationship with Your Manager or Team Leader?

Getting along well with your manager is the most basic strategy of getting ahead in your career. If you cannot gain favor with the boss, it will be difficult to advance to higher positions or earn much more money. Obtaining good performance reviews and receiving favorable work assignments also depends on a good relationship with the person to whom you report. The boss might be more of a traditional boss, such as a person with the title of manager or supervisor. Or the boss might be a team leader who typically has less formal authority than a manager or supervisor. Your manager or team leader is always the person who is contacted first when someone wants to determine what kind of employee you are. Usually this information is sought when you are being considered for transfer, promotion, or a position with another firm.

Getting along with the boss is particularly important when the economy is sluggish or when the threat of outsourcing exists. Workers who have good relationships with their manager have more job security than those with poor relationships. In this section we present a variety of approaches that lead to constructive relationships with an immediate superior. The goal is to be legitimately perceived as a strong contributor to your work unit.

ACHIEVE GOOD JOB PERFORMANCE

Maintaining good job performance remains the most effective strategy for impressing your manager. When any rational manager evaluates a group member's performance, the first question asked is, "Is this employee getting the job done?" And you cannot get the job done if you are not competent. Many factors contribute to whether you can become a competent performer. Among them are your education, training, personality characteristics, job experience, and special skills, such as being able to organize your work.

An advanced way of displaying good job performance is to assist your manager with a difficult problem he or she faces. Your manager, for example, might need to operate equipment outside his or her area of expertise. If you show the manager how to operate the equipment, he or she will think highly of your job performance. Another example would be helping your manager get ready for an important meeting with higher management by preparing attention-getting PowerPoint slides.

An effective way of enhancing your job performance is to offer alternative solutions to complex problems. In this way you are more likely to follow a path favored by your boss, leading to good performance. The director of a senior living residence asked an administrator to find a way to reduce the number of falls by residents—a problem that plagues people of advanced age. Instead of suggesting one idea, the administrator offered several suggestions, as follows:

- Let's check to see if all our residents use footwear with appropriate treads.

- Instruct our health-care aides to coach all our residents about the proper use of canes.

- The entire staff should check periodically to see if our residents are making good use of handrails at the facility.

The director liked the idea of alternatives so much that she said, "Great ideas. Let's implement all three instead of just using one idea, as I had suggested."

A subtle issue about performing well to please your manager is that your manager has to be aware of your good performance and give you proper credit. One useful approach is to assist your boss by keeping him or her informed about exactly what work you are doing, the problems you are solving, and the successes you have attained.[3]

DISPLAY A STRONG WORK ETHIC

A strong **work ethic** is a firm belief in the dignity and value of work and therefore is important for favorably impressing a manager. An employee with a strong work ethic will sometimes be excused if his or her performance is not yet exceptional. This is true because the manager assumes that a strong work ethic will elevate performance eventually. Six suggestions follow for demonstrating a strong work ethic.

Work ethic
a firm belief in the dignity and value of work and, therefore, important for favorably impressing a manager

1. Work hard and enjoy the task. By definition, a person with a strong work ethic works diligently and has strong internal motivation. The person may appreciate external rewards yet appreciates the importance of any work that adds value to society.

2. Demonstrate competence even on minor tasks. Attack each assignment with the recognition that each task performed well, however minor, is one more career credit. A minor task performed well paves the way for your being given more consequential tasks.

3. Assume personal responsibility for problems. An employee with a problem will often approach the manager and say, "We have a tough problem to deal with." The connotation is that the manager should be helping the employee with the problem. A better impression is created when the employee says, "I have a tough problem to deal with, and I would like your advice." This statement implies that you are willing to assume responsibility for the problem and for any mistake you may have made that led to the problem.

4. Assume responsibility for free-floating problems. A natural way to display a strong work ethic is to assume responsibility for free-floating (nonassigned) problems. Taking on even a minor task, such as ordering lunch for a meeting that is running late, can enhance the impression one makes on a manager.

5. Get your projects completed promptly. A byproduct of a strong work ethic is an eagerness to get projects completed promptly. People with a strong work ethic respect deadlines imposed by others. Furthermore, they typically set deadlines of their own more tightly than those imposed by their bosses.

6. Accept undesirable assignments willingly. Look for ways to express the attitude, "Whether this assignment is glamorous and fun is a secondary issue. What counts is that it is something that needs doing for the good of the company."

DEMONSTRATE GOOD EMOTIONAL INTELLIGENCE

Dealing effectively with feelings and emotions is a big challenge in the workplace. Demonstrating good emotional intelligence is impressive because it contributes to performing well in the difficult arena of dealing with feelings. A worker with good emotional intelligence would engage in such behaviors as (a) recognizing when a coworker needs help but is too embarrassed to ask for help, (b) dealing with the anger of a dissatisfied customer, (c) recognizing that the boss is facing considerable pressure also, and (d) being able to tell whether a customer's "maybe" means "yes" or "no."

Many of the competencies described throughout this chapter are facilitated by emotional intelligence. Nevertheless, being aware of strategies and tactics for dealing effectively with others helps you capitalize on your emotional intelligence.

BE DEPENDABLE AND HONEST

Dependability is a critical employee virtue. If an employee can be counted on to deliver as promised and to be at work regularly, that employee has gone a long way toward impressing the boss. A boss is uncomfortable not knowing whether an important assignment will be accomplished on time. If you are not dependable, you will probably not get your share of important assignments. Honesty is tied to dependability because a dependable employee is honest about when he or she will have an assignment completed. Dependability and honesty are important at all job levels. One of the highest compliments a manager can pay an employee is to describe the employee as dependable. Conversely, it is considered derogatory to call any employee undependable.

BE A GOOD ORGANIZATIONAL CITIZEN

An especially meritorious approach to impressing key people is to demonstrate organizational citizenship behavior. An effective way of being a good organizational citizen is to step outside your job description. Job descriptions are characteristic of a well-organized firm. If everybody knows what he or she is supposed to be doing, there will be much less confusion, and goals will be achieved. This logic sounds impressive, but job descriptions have a major downside. If people engage only in work included in their job description, an "it's not my job" mentality pervades. An effective way to impress your manager, therefore, is to demonstrate that you are not constrained by a job description. If something needs doing, you will get it done regardless of whether it is your formal responsibility.

An impressive way of stepping outside your job description is to anticipate problems, even when the manager had not planned to work on them. Anticipating problems is characteristic of a resourceful person who exercises initiative. Instead of working exclusively on problems that have been assigned, the worker is perceptive enough to look for future problems. Anticipating problems impresses most managers because it reflects an entrepreneurial, take-charge attitude.

CREATE A STRONG PRESENCE

A comprehensive approach to impressing your manager or team leader and other key people in the workplace is to create a strong presence, keeping yourself in the forefront. Such actions impress key people and simultaneously help advance your career. Stephanie Sherman, a career consultant, offers this advice for creating a strong presence:

- Get involved in high-visibility projects, such as launching a new product or redesigning work methods. Even an entry-level position on such a project can help a worker get noticed.

- Get involved in teams because they give you an opportunity to broaden your skills and knowledge.

- Get involved in social and community activities of interest to top management, such as those sponsored by the company. Behave professionally, and use your best manners.

- Create opportunities for yourself by making constructive suggestions about earning or saving money. Even if an idea is rejected, you will still be remembered for your initiative.

- Show a willingness to take on some of the tasks that your manager doesn't like to do but would be forced to do if you did not step in.[4]

A powerful way of creating a strong presence with a newly appointed manager is to take the initiative to state that you want to be part of his or her team. Instead of acting envious toward the new manager, approach the person with a statement of this effect: "I am experienced in my job, and I want to help. I may not be perfect, but I accept your goals for our unit."[5]

FIND OUT WHAT YOUR MANAGER EXPECTS OF YOU

You have little chance of doing a good job and impressing your manager unless you know what you are trying to accomplish. Work goals and performance standards represent the most direct ways of learning your manager's expectations. A **performance standard** is a statement of what constitutes acceptable performance. These standards can sometimes be inferred from a job description. Review your work goals and ask clarifying questions. An example would be, "You told me to visit our major customers who are sixty days or more delinquent on their accounts. Should I also visit the three of these customers who have declared bankruptcy?" In addition to having a clear statement of your goals, it is helpful to know the priorities attached to them. In this way you will know which task to execute first.

> **Performance standard**
> a statement of what constitutes acceptable performance

A subtle aspect of understanding the expectations of your boss is adapting to his or her preferred style of work. Managers vary in terms of wanting written versus oral briefings. Some managers prefer to receive e-mail messages from you regularly, others once a week. In one situation, a manager asked his new CEO how he preferred to communicate. The CEO said he prefers a direct, collaborative style. As a result, the two agreed to get together in person frequently when both in town, from about 5:30 to 6 p.m.[6]

Some managers want to be treated informally, much like being a coworker. A minority of managers wanted to be treated as if they were royalty. Matching your work style to the work style of your boss can help build a strong relationship between the two of you.

MINIMIZE COMPLAINTS

Being open and honest in expressing your feelings and opinions is part of having good human relations skills. Nevertheless, this type of behavior, when carried to excess, could earn you a reputation as a whiner. Few managers want to have a group member around who constantly complains about working conditions, coworkers, working hours, pay, and so forth. An employee who complains too loudly and frequently quickly becomes labeled a pill or a pest.

Another important reason a boss usually dislikes having a direct report (subordinate) who complains too much is that listening to these complaints takes up considerable time. Most managers spend a disproportionate amount of time listening to the problems of a small number of ineffective or complaining employees. Consciously or unconsciously, a manager who has to listen to many of your complaints may find a way to seek revenge.

How, then, does an employee make valid complaints to the manager? The answer is to complain only when justified. And when you do offer a complaint, back it up with a recommended solution. Anyone can take potshots at something. The valuable employee is the person who supports these complaints with a constructive action plan. An example follows of a complaint, supported by action plans for its remedy:

> When a customer wants a refund of more than $50 we have to receive authorization from you. The problem is that you may be out of contact with us temporarily, even by your BlackBerry. The $50 rule was probably established twenty years ago and has not been adjusted for inflation. If authorization were only required for refunds of $100 or more, we could reduce a lot of bottlenecks.

One possibility for minimizing the need for complaints is to attempt to look at decisions from the boss's point of view. The company might decide to prohibit workers from using instant messaging for personal reasons during working hours. Instead of complaining that the prohibition on instant messages is unjust, the worker might attempt to understand why company management thinks instant messages lower productivity.

AVOID BYPASSING YOUR MANAGER

A way to embarrass and sometimes infuriate your manager is to repeatedly go to his or her superior with your problems, conflicts, and complaints. Such bypasses have at least three strongly negative connotations. One is that you don't believe your boss has the power to take care of your problem. Another is that you distrust his or her judgment in the matter at hand. A third is that you are secretly launching a complaint against your manager.

The boss bypass is looked on so negatively that most experienced managers will not listen to your problem unless you have already discussed it with your immediate superior. There *are* times, however, when running around your manager is necessary, such as when you have been unable to resolve a conflict directly with him or her (see the following section). Should your manager be involved in highly immoral or illegal actions, such as sexual harassments or taking kickbacks from vendors, a boss bypass might be warranted. But even under these circumstances, you should politely inform your manager that you are going to take up your problem with the next level of management.

In short, if you want to keep on the good side of your manager, bring all problems directly to him or her. If your boss is unable or unwilling to take care of the problem, you might consider contacting your boss's superior. Nonetheless, considerable tact and diplomacy are needed. Do not imply that your manager is incompetent but merely that you would like another opinion about the issues at stake. If an organization has a formal system for filing complaints, such as an open-door policy, it can be used to substitute for a boss bypass but should be used only when you are unable to resolve a problem with your boss.

ENGAGE IN FAVORABLE INTERACTIONS WITH YOUR MANAGER

The many techniques described previously support the goal of engaging in favorable interactions with your manager. Human Relations Self-Assessment Quiz 9-1 contains a list of behaviors used by employees to create positive interactions with their supervisors. Use these behaviors as a guide for skill building.

According to a synthesis of findings by organizational behavior professor Cecily D. Cooper at the University of Miami, an effective way of ingratiating yourself to your boss, as well as to others in the workplace, is to make effective use of humor. **Ingratiating** is an attempt to increase one's attractiveness to others, so as to influence their behavior. The most effective type of humor for building a relationship with the boss should be work related and hint at a strength of the boss, department, or company. If the humor is well received, it helps build a relationship with the manager (or other targets of the humor as well).[7] Here's an attempt at ego-building humor that worked well with one vice president. The department administrative assistant said, "Herb, we all know what a reputation you've developed in the company. When you are promoted to CEO, will you take the old gang for a ride in your corporate jet?"

> **Ingratiating**
> an attempt to increase one's attractiveness to others to influence their behavior

Delivering Bad News

Although favorable interactions with a manager are valuable for relationship building, there are times when a group member has to deliver bad news. For example, you might have to inform the manager about a burst water pipe in the mainframe computer room or a bunch of customer complaints about a new product. You want to avoid being the messenger who is punished because he or she delivered bad

Human Relations Self-Assessment Quiz 9-1

Manager Interaction Checklist

Use the following behaviors as a checklist for achieving favorable interactions with your present manager or a future one. The more of these actions you engage in, the higher the probability that you are building a favorable relationship with your manager.

1. Express agreement with manager's opinion whenever I truly agree.
2. Ask for assistance in areas in which I know that my manager enjoys giving assistance or providing an opinion.
3. Am polite toward my manager, including smiling frequently and expressing appreciation.
4. Avoid profanity in front of my boss, even if he or she uses profanity on the job.
5. Bring forth solutions to important problems facing the group or organization.
6. Contribute willingly to payroll deductions for charity such as United Way.
7. Put considerable effort into working on problems that I know are important to my manager.
8. Almost never miss or be late for a meeting called by my manager.
9. Almost always get a work assignment done on time.
10. Often volunteer to help my manager accomplish a significant task.
11. Compliment my manager when he or she has accomplished something substantial.
12. Occasionally take on work that is outside my job description and then explain to my manager what I did and why I did it.
13. Almost never complain about work or personal life to my manager.
14. In a meeting, I explain to the group why I think the manager's new idea will work.
15. Inform my boss should I hear that a customer or client enjoys our product or service.

news. Attempt to be calm and businesslike. Do not needlessly blame yourself for the problem. Mention that *we are* or *the company is* facing a serious challenge. If possible, suggest a possible solution, such as, "I have already investigated a backup computer service we can use until the damage is repaired."

Cross-Cultural Factors

When working to establish a good relationship with your manager, keep in mind that cultural factors could influence how a given tactic should be modified for best effectiveness. An example would be that displaying strong work ethic to a supervisor from Japan would be different from displaying the same ethic to a manager from France. The Japanese manager might think that working fifty-five hours a week indicates a strong work ethic, whereas the French manager might think that forty hours a week of hard work is exceptional. Another cultural factor in establishing a good relationship could be the amount of respect shown to the manager. A typical American manager might expect an informal, friendly relationship, with the two of you acting like equals. However, a manager from China might expect much more respect. In one situation a manager from China in charge of a chemistry lab in the United States became angry when workers addressed him by his first name. He expected to be addressed as "Dr." plus his last name.

▶ Learning Objective 2 ▶

How Do You Cope with a Problem Manager?

Up to this point we have prescribed tactics for dealing with a reasonably rational boss. At some point in their careers, many people face the situation of dealing with a problem manager—one who makes it difficult for the subordinate to get the job done. At times, differences in values and goals could be creating the problem. The problem is sometimes attributed to the boss's personality or incompetence. A frequent personality problem is being a **bully**—a cruel and aggressive boss who intimidates and verbally abuses subordinates. People who report to a bully often feel belittled and sapped of energy.[8] Some bullies swear at group members, others insult them with statements such as, "Have you been stupid all your life, or is your stupidity something new?" A territory manager for a midsize technology company describes his toxic, bullying boss in these terms:

Bully
a cruel and aggressive boss who intimidates and verbally abuses subordinates

> *The guy has temper tantrums, screams, uses obscenities to me on the phone, plays my colleagues off against each other, and goes into long, nonproductive tirades about customers, the industry, and members of his staff. I really love this job except for my manager. And I'm good at it. So I didn't quit. Instead I developed a formula for dealing with him (such as spending an hour and one-half each day catering to the boss's needs).[9]*

Our concern here is with constructive approaches to dealing with the delicate situation of working for a problem manager.

REEVALUATE YOUR MANAGER

Some employees think they have problem managers when those bosses simply have major role, goal, or value differences. (A role in this context is the expectations of the job.) The problem might also lie in conflicting personalities, such as being outgoing or shy. Another problem is conflicting perspectives, such as being detail oriented as opposed to taking an overall perspective. The differences just noted can be good or bad, depending on how they are viewed and used. For example, a combination of a detail-oriented group member with an "overall perspective" boss can be a winning combination.[10]

Another approach to being more cautious in evaluating your manager is to judge slowly and fairly. Many decisions your manager makes may prove to be worthwhile if you give the decisions time.[11] Top management at your company might issue an order that employees cannot surf the Web for personal reasons on the job. You might think this rule is unfair and treats workers like adolescents. If you wait for the result of the decisions, you might find that productivity improves. Another benefit might be that many workers no longer have to work late because they save time by not surfing.

CONFRONT YOUR MANAGER ABOUT THE PROBLEM

A general-purpose way of dealing with a problem manager is to confront the problem and then look for a solution. Because your manager has more formal authority than you, the confrontation must be executed with the highest level of tact and sensitivity. A beginning point in confronting a manager is to gently ask for an explanation of the problem. Suppose, for example, you believed strongly that your team leader snubs you because he or she dislikes you. You might inquire gently, "What might I be doing wrong that is creating a problem between us?"

Another situation calling for confrontation would be outrageous behavior by the manager, such as swearing at and belittling group members. For example, a worker reported that in meetings his manager openly belittles his peers and the people higher in the organization. The worker was concerned that this behavior fosters poor morale and unprofessional attitudes among team members and hurts productivity.[12] Because several or all group members are involved in the example cited, a group discussion of the problem might be warranted. You and your coworkers might meet as a group to discuss the impact of the manager's style on group morale and productivity. This tactic runs the risk of backfiring if the manager becomes defensive and angry. Yet confrontation is worth the risk because the problem of abuse will not go away without discussion.

Confrontation can also be helpful in dealing with the problem of **micromanagement,** the close monitoring of most aspects of group member activities by the manager. "Looking over your shoulder constantly" is an everyday phrase for micromanagement. If you feel that you are being supervised so closely that it is difficult to perform well, confront the situation. Say something of this nature: "I notice that you check almost everything I do lately. Am I making so many errors that you are losing confidence in my work?"[13] As a consequence, the manager might explain why he or she is micromanaging or begin to check on your work less frequently.

Micromanagement
the close monitoring of most aspects of group member activities by the manager

OVERRESPOND TO THE MANAGER'S PET PEEVES

The territory manager mentioned above developed a tactic for dealing with his problem manager that is likely to work for you. If your boss has a pet peeve, cater to that demand. The manager in question knew that his boss likes orders to get processed immediately. (The boss's pet peeve is a delay in the processing of an order.) So the manager tried to process an order upon arrival. If he couldn't get to it immediately, he would send an e-mail stating that he is tied up on another project. Eight out of ten times, the boss would then do the order processing for the manager.[14] To be less manipulative, you might do an honest job of staying on top of any task that you boss deems to be extra important.

LEARN FROM YOUR MANAGER'S MISTAKES

Just as you can learn from watching your manager do things right, you can also learn from watching him or her do things wrong. In the first instance, we are talking about using your manager as a positive model. Modeling of this type is an important source of learning on the job. Using a superior as a negative model can also be of some benefit. As an elementary example, if your manager criticized you in public and you felt humiliated, you would have learned a good lesson in effective supervision: Never criticize a subordinate publicly. By serving as a negative example, your manager has taught you a valuable lesson.

Learning from a problem manager's mistakes can also occur when a manager is fired. Should your manager be fired, analyze the situation to avoid the mistakes he or she made. Enlist the help of others in understanding what went wrong. Did the manager get along poorly with higher-level managers? Was the manager lacking in technical expertise? Did the manager work hard enough? Did the manager commit ethical or legal violations, such as sexual harassment or stealing company property? Whatever the reason, you will learn quickly what behavior the company will not tolerate. If your manager was fired simply as a way to cut costs, there is still a lesson to be learned. Attempt to prove to the company that your compensation is a good investment for the company because your work is outstanding.

> "If you're not looking at your work relationships as a resource, you should be. Relationships need to be nurtured and developed, like any other skill or asset. Assess the quality of your relationships, and make a concerted effort to improve the ones lower on the scale."
>
> —Steve Ameson

Statement from this leadership coach appeared in his column, "Evaluate Your Work Relationships," *San Francisco Examiner* (www.examiner.com), January 8, 2009, p. 1.

▶ Learning Objective 3 ▶

How Do You Build Good Coworker Relationships?

If you are unable to work cooperatively with others you are unlikely to be recommended for promotion to a supervisory position. It will also be difficult to hold onto your job. Poor relationships with coworkers can lead to frustration, stress, and decreased productivity, whereas getting along with them makes the workplace more satisfying. You need their cooperation and support, and they need yours. When workers need help in getting a job done, they will choose a coworker who is congenial over one who might have the edge in expertise.[15] Furthermore, the leading reason employees are terminated is not poor technical skills but rather inability or unwillingness to form satisfactory relationships with others on the job. In this section we describe basic tactics for developing and maintaining good coworker relationships, as outlined in Figure 9-1.

If your goal is to become part of the *in-crowd* in your work group, building coworker relationships is all the more important. According to clinical psychologist and author Judith Sills, the in-crowd is the group of cool kids at your office, those with access to the boss, power, and information.[16] A relevant point here is that to become part of the select, informal group you must work extra hard at cultivating members of that group.

HAVE HIGH SELF-ESTEEM AND BE AT THE CENTER OF A COMMUNICATION NETWORK

A starting point in building effective coworker relationships is to have the right personality structure and to be at the center of a communications network. Brent A. Scott, a professor of management at Michigan State University, and Timothy A. Judge, a professor of industrial/organizational psychology at the University of

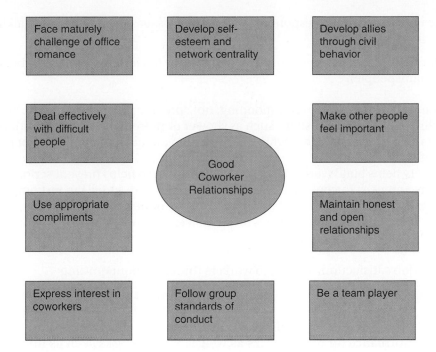

FIGURE 9-1

APPROACHES TO BUILDING COWORKER RELATIONSHIPS

Florida, conducted two studies to investigate what made workers popular, or generally accepted by one's peers.

> The study with the most informative results involved 139 healthcare employees from 22 groups of a large hospital, with most of the work being conducted in teams. Popularity was measured in terms of how well the employee was liked by coworkers on a 1-to-5 scale. Self-esteem was measured by significant others of the study participants completing a core self-evaluation quiz about the participant. [You will recall having completed two different core self-evaluation quizzes in Chapters 2 and 4, both of which focus on self-esteem.] Work communication centrality was measured by asking each coworker to "check the names of people with whom you communicate as part of the job during a typical workweek."

The results showed that having a high core self-evaluation (self-esteem) and being at the center of communications was related to popularity. The more popular employees also received more citizenship behavior from coworkers and less incidences of counterproductive, or disruptive, behavior—both of which reflect better coworker relationships.[17]

DEVELOP ALLIES THROUGH BEING CIVIL

People who are courteous, kind, cooperative, and cheerful develop allies and friends in the workplace. Practicing basic good manners, such as being pleasant and friendly, is also part of being civil. Being civil helps make you stand out, because many people believe that crude, rude, and obnoxious behavior has become both the norm and a national problem. Uncivil behaviors characteristically involve rudeness and discourteousness. A poll of nearly eight hundred U.S. workers found that 10 percent witnessed incivility every day on the job, and 20 percent said they were direct targets of incivility at least once a week.[18] Examples of incivility include the following:

- A salesperson makes sarcastic comments about another employee in front of a customer.
- A coworker initiates cell phone calls while listening to a presentation at a meeting.

- One worker continues responding to e-mail messages while another is talking to him in person.

- A person whistles or sings constantly in the office (an intensely annoying behavior for many people).[19]

Being civil also involves not snooping, not spreading malicious gossip, and not weaseling out of group presents, such as shower or retirement gifts. In addition, it is important to be available to coworkers who want your advice as well as your help in times of crisis.

Civility helps build workplace relationships and also helps prevent serious negative consequences to coworkers. Studies conducted with judicial court employees and municipal workers studied incivility in terms of being a personal target, or as part of the group atmosphere. It was found that experience with incivility had these harmful effects:

- Lower job satisfaction, leading to workers thinking about quitting

- A negative impact on mental health, which in turn damaged physical health[20]

A laboratory study with college students found similar results. Rudeness reduced performance on routine tasks as well as creative tasks such as finding new uses for a brick. In addition, students who were treated rudely were less likely to be helpful, as measured by a willingness to assist the experimenter pick up a jar of ten pencils the experimenter had "accidentally dropped."[21]

Closely related to being civil is maintaining a positive outlook. Everyone knows that you gain more allies by being optimistic and positive than by being pessimistic and negative. Nevertheless, many people ignore this simple strategy for getting along well with others. Coworkers are more likely to solicit your opinion or offer you help when you are perceived as a cheerful person.

MAKE OTHER PEOPLE FEEL IMPORTANT

A fundamental principle of fostering good relationships with coworkers and others is to make them feel important. Making others feel important is honest because everybody in an organization has a contribution to make, including the CEO, payroll coordinator, and window washer.

Although the leader has primary responsibility for satisfying this recognition need, coworkers also play a key role. One approach to making a coworker feel important would be to bring a notable accomplishment of his or hers to the attention of the group. Human Relations Self-Assessment Quiz 9-2 gives you an opportunity to think through your tendencies to make others feel important.

MAINTAIN HONEST AND OPEN RELATIONSHIPS

Self-disclosure
the process of revealing one's inner self to others

In human relations we attach considerable importance to maintaining honest and open relationships with other people. The mechanism underlying openness is **self-disclosure,** the process of revealing your inner self to others. (You will recall that self-disclosure was mentioned in Chapter 1 in relation to the Johari Window.) A person with a high degree of self-disclosure is open, whereas a person with a low degree of self-disclosure is closed. Nevertheless, you must be careful of excessive self-disclosure. Many people feel uneasy if another person is too self-revealing. The overly candid person risks being rejected. For instance, if you communicate all your negative feelings and doubts to another person, that person may become annoyed and pull away from you. It would be too open to tell an office mate, "I am ticked off

Human Relations Self-Assessment Quiz 9-2

How Important Do I Make People Feel?

Indicate on a 1 to 5 scale how frequently you act (or would act if the situation presented itself) in the ways indicated: very infrequently (VI), infrequently (I), sometimes (S), frequently (F), very frequently (VF). Circle the number underneath the column that best fits your answer.

	VI	I	S	F	VF
1. I do my best to correctly pronounce a coworker's name.	1	2	3	4	5
2. I avoid letting other people's egos get too big.	5	4	3	2	1
3. I brag to others about the accomplishments of my coworkers.	1	2	3	4	5
4. I recognize the birthdays of friends in a tangible way.	1	2	3	4	5
5. It makes me anxious to listen to others brag about their accomplishments.	5	4	3	2	1
6. After hearing that a friend has done something outstanding, I shake his or her hand.	1	2	3	4	5
7. If a friend or coworker recently received a degree or certificate, I would offer my congratulations.	1	2	3	4	5
8. If a friend or coworker finished second in a contest, I would inquire why he or she did not finish first.	5	4	3	2	1
9. If a coworker showed me how to do something, I would compliment that person's skill.	1	2	3	4	5
10. When a coworker starts bragging about a family member's accomplishments, I do not respond.	5	4	3	2	1

Total Score _____

Scoring and Interpretation:

Total the numbers corresponding to your answers. Scoring 40 to 50 points suggests that you typically make people feel important; 16 to 39 points suggests that you have a moderate tendency toward making others feel important; 10 to 15 points suggests that you need to develop skill in making others feel important. Study this chapter carefully.

that the manager has us sharing the same cubicle, but I'll put up with it until you quit or are fired."

Giving coworkers frank but tactful answers to their requests for your opinion is one useful way of developing open relationships. Assume that a coworker asks your opinion about a document he intends to send to his boss. As you read it, you find it somewhat incoherent and filled with spelling and grammatical errors. An honest response to this document might be, "I think your idea is a good one, but I think your memo needs more work before that idea comes across clearly."

Accurately expressing your feelings also leads to constructive relationships. If you arrive at work upset over a personal problem and appearing obviously fatigued, you can expect some reaction. A peer might say, "What seems to be the problem? Is everything all right?" A dishonest reply would be, "Everything is fine. What makes you think something is wrong?" In addition to making an obviously untrue statement, you would also be perceived as rejecting the person who asked the question.

If you prefer not to discuss your problem, an honest response on your part would be, "Thanks for your interest. I am facing some problems today. But I think things will work out." Such an answer would not involve you in a discussion of your personal problems. Also, you would not be perceived as rejecting your coworker. The same principle applies equally well to personal relationships.

BE A TEAM PLAYER

Team player
one who emphasizes group accomplishment and cooperation rather than individual achievement and not helping others

An essential strategy for developing good relationships with coworkers is to be a team player. A **team player** is one who emphasizes group accomplishment and cooperation rather than individual achievement and not helping others. Team play is important because of the emphasis on having teams of workers decide how to improve productivity and reduce costs. You will also have to be a team player if you reach the pinnacle of power in your organization. Executives are expected to be good team players as well as individual decision makers. But team play is even more important on the way to becoming an executive, because impatience and making unilateral decisions is more tolerated in the executive suite. Being an effective team player is important because without such capability collaborative effort is not possible.

Here we describe a representative group of behaviors that contribute to team play. In addition, engaging in such behavior helps you be perceived as a team player.

1. **Share credit with coworkers.** A direct method of promoting team play is to share credit for good deeds with other team members. Instead of focusing on yourself as the person responsible for a work achievement, point out that the achievement was a team effort. You will make a poor team player if you try to grab all the glory for ideas that work and distance yourself from ideas that do not work. An effective team member wants all other members to succeed. You will stand out by praising the people you work with rather than hogging any praise for the team.

2. **Display a helpful, cooperative attitude.** Working cooperatively with others is virtually synonymous with team play. Cooperation translates into such activities as helping another worker with a computer problem, covering for a teammate when he or she is absent, and making sure a coworker has the input required from you on time. A helpful cooperative attitude is the main component of organizational citizenship behavior.

3. **To establish trust, keep confidential information private and give honest opinions.** Trust is important for teamwork because trust is a major contributor to cooperation.[22] Confidential information shared with you by a teammate should not be shared with others. Trust is exceedingly difficult to regain after a person has been betrayed. Giving honest opinions helps develop trust because the recipient of your honesty will regard you as a person of integrity. However, tact and diplomacy are still important. A dishonest opinion can often be detected through your nonverbal cues, such as discomfort in your voice tone.

Assume that a friend of yours is starting a business selling antique toys over the Internet. She asks you if you like her proposed domain name, www.OldjunkRus.com. You think the name is both ridiculous and an infringement on the Toys "R" Us name; yet you say, "Hey, terrific" with a sickened look on your face. You might lose some of your friend's trust.

4. **Share information and opinions with coworkers.** Teamwork is facilitated when group members share information and opinions. This is true because one of the benefits of group effort is that members can share ideas. The result is often a better solution to problems than would have been possible if people worked alone. The group thus achieves **synergy,** a product of group effort whereby the output of the group exceeds the output possible if the members worked alone.

Synergy
a product of group effort whereby the output of the group exceeds the output possible if the members worked alone

Another important aspect of sharing information and opinion with teammates is to provide technical expertise, or knowledge of the task. Most people are selected for a work team primarily because their specialized knowledge. To use your expertise to advantage, you must be willing to share it with teammates. Some experts perceive their specialized knowledge as a source of power. As a consequence, they are hesitant to let others share their knowledge for fear of losing power.

5. Provide emotional support to coworkers. Good team players offer each other emotional support. Such support can take the form of verbal encouragement for ideas expressed, listening to a group member's concerns, or complimenting achievement. An emotionally supportive comment to a coworker who appears to be experiencing stress might be, "This doesn't look like one of your better days. What can I do to help?" According to one study, emotionally supporting coworkers facilitates their being able to service customers better.[23] Perhaps when workers feel emotionally supported, it is easier for them to have a positive attitude toward customers.

6. Follow the Golden Rule. The ancient adage "Treat others the way you would like them to treat you" provides a firm foundation for effective teamwork. Although some may dismiss the Golden Rule as a syrupy platitude, it still works. For example, you would probably want someone to help you with a perplexing problem, so you take the initiative to help others when you have the expertise needed.

7. Avoid actions that could sabotage or undermine the group in any way. Frequently criticizing group members directly or complaining about them to outsiders works against the best interest of the group. Members within the group, as well as the team leader, will most likely hear that you criticized them to an outsider, thus doing severe damage to your ability to work cooperatively with them.

8. Attend company-sponsored social events. A worker's reputation as a team player is often judged both on the job and in company-sponsored social events, such as parties, picnics, and athletic events. If you attend these and participate fully, your reputation as a team player will be enhanced. Company-sponsored social events are also important because they provide an opportunity to build rapport with coworkers. Rapport, in turn, facilitates teamwork.

9. Avoid backstabbing. A special category of disliked behavior is **backstabbing,** an attempt to discredit by underhanded means, such as innuendo, accusation, and the like. A backstabber might drop hints to the boss, for example, that a coworker performs poorly under pressure or is looking for a new job. Sometimes the backstabber assertively gathers information to backstab a coworker. He or she might engage another worker in a derogatory discussion about the boss and then report the coworker's negative comments back to the boss. A person who develops a reputation as a backstabber will receive poor cooperation from coworkers. The person might also be considered untrustworthy by management, thus retarding his or her own career.

> **Backstabbing**
> an attempt to discredit by underhanded means such as innuendo, accusation, or the like

These nine points contribute specifically to effective team play. Recognize also that all other actions directed toward good coworker relationships will enhance team play.

FOLLOW GROUP STANDARDS OF CONDUCT

The basic principle to follow in getting along with coworkers is to follow **group norms.** These refer to the unwritten set of expectations for group members—what people ought to do. Norms become a standard of what each person should do or not do within the group. Norms also provide general guidelines for reacting constructively to the behavior of coworkers. Norms are a major component of the **organizational culture,** or values and beliefs of the firm that guide people's actions. In one firm, the norms and culture may favor hard work and high quality. In another firm, the norms and culture may favor a weaker work ethic.

Group norms also influence the social aspects of behavior on the job. These aspects of behavior relate to such things as the people with whom to have lunch, getting together after work, joining a company team, and the type of clothing to

> **Group norms**
> unwritten set of expectations for group members—what people ought to do; basic principle to follow in getting along with coworkers
>
> **Organizational culture**
> values and beliefs of the firm that guide people's actions

wear to work. Sharing laughter, such as poking positive fun at coworkers, is another example of an important social behavior linked to a group norm.

Workers learn about norms through both observation and direct instruction from other group members. If you do not deviate too far from these norms, the group will accept much of your behavior. If you deviate too far, you will be subject to much rejection and feelings of isolation. In some instances, you might even be subjected to verbal abuse if you make the other employees look bad.

Getting along too well with coworkers has its price as well. The risk of conforming too closely to group norms is that you lose your individuality. You become viewed by your superiors as "one of the office gang" rather than a person who aspires to move up in the organization. It is important to be a good team player, but to advance in your career you must also find a way to distinguish yourself, such as through creative thinking and outstanding performance.

EXPRESS AN INTEREST IN THE WORK AND PERSONAL LIVES OF COWORKERS

Almost everyone is self-centered to some extent. Thus, people favor topics closely related to themselves, such as their children, friends, hobbies, work, or possessions. Sales representatives rely heavily on this fact in cultivating relationships with established customers. They routinely ask the customer about his or her hobbies, family members, and work activities. You can capitalize on this simple strategy by asking coworkers and friends questions such as these:

How is your work going? (*highly recommended*)

How did you gain the knowledge necessary for your job?

How does the company use the output from your department?

How did your son enjoy computer camp?

Closely related to expressing interest in others is to investigate what you have in common, both professionally and personally, with peers. You might identify common interests, such as a focus on the company's market share, or a personal interest, such as hiking.[24]

A danger in asking questions about other people's work and personal life is that some questions may not be perceived as well intentioned. There is a fine line between honest curiosity and snooping. You must stay alert to this subtle distinction.

USE APPROPRIATE COMPLIMENTS

An effective way of developing good relationships with coworkers and friends is to compliment something with which they closely identify, such as their children, spouses, hobbies, or pets. Compliments are also effective because they are a form of flattery. Paying a compliment is a form of positive reinforcement—rewarding somebody for doing something right. The right response is therefore strengthened or reinforced. A compliment is a useful multipurpose reward.

Another way of complimenting people is through recognition. The suggestions made earlier about making people feel important are ways of recognizing people and therefore compliments. Investing a small amount of time in recognizing a coworker can pay large dividends in terms of cultivating an ally. Recognition and compliments are more likely to create a favorable relationship when they are appropriate. *Appropriate* in this context means that the compliment fits the accomplishment. Praise that is too lavish may be interpreted as belittling and patronizing. Let's look at the difference between an appropriate and an exaggerated compliment over the same issue.

An executive secretary gets a printer operating that was temporarily not printing documents.

> ***Appropriate compliment.*** Nice job, Stephanie. Fixing the printer took considerable skill. We can now resume making hard copies of documents.

> ***Exaggerated compliment.*** Stephanie, I'm overwhelmed. You're a world-class printer specialist. Are there no limits to your talents?

Observe that the appropriate compliment is thoughtful and is proportionate to what Stephanie accomplished. The exaggerated compliment is probably wasted because it is way out of proportion to the magnitude of the accomplishment.

Cultural factors can mediate (influence) the most effective approach for getting along with coworkers. Although there is a strong tendency for people from another country to quickly adapt to the culture of your country, you still have to be sensitive to cultural differences for rapport building. An example would be for an American not to be disappointed when a British coworker offers modest, instead of effusive, compliments for a job well done. The American might have just won a sales contest and informs her British coworker of the feat. He responds, "Certainly, in the right direction." (Your disappointment might come across as a frown or some other subtle rejection.)

DEAL EFFECTIVELY WITH DIFFICULT PEOPLE

A major challenge in getting along well with coworkers is dealing constructively with **difficult people.** A coworker is classified as difficult if he or she is uncooperative, disrespectful, touchy, defensive, hostile, or even very unfriendly. The difficult person often meets or exceeds performance standards yet annoys coworkers and superiors.[25] Other symptoms of being a difficult person include bullying and incivility. Three examples of difficult people follow:

Difficult people
a coworker is classified as difficult if he or she is uncooperative, touchy, defensive, hostile, or even very unfriendly

- **The lone wolf.** Can't stand being part of anything: a team, a project, or group functions. Independent to a fault—makes no attempt to hide solitary preferences.

- **Chicken Little.** No matter how sunny things seem to be, he or she will always find a cloud to cast a shadow. ("What a great Web site we have. Twenty thousand visitors in the first week." "Yeah, but are more than 1 percent buying anything?")[26]

- **The high-maintenance person.** Requires so much assistance, special attention, and extra help that it wears you down. No matter what type of help you offer, they want a little more. If you bring a high-maintenance worker a soft drink, he or she is likely to say, "Didn't they have any decaffeinated soft drinks?"

- **The office magpie.** Always eager to chat and assumes that other workers want to do likewise. Whenever he or she is not faced with a pressing deadline barges into your workspace to shoot the breeze. Also known to send dozens of e-mails, along with chatty personal comments, over the same issue.[27]

In dealing with difficult coworkers, as well as difficult bosses, it is important to recognize that their problems could go much deeper than those of the types of individuals mentioned. Such individuals could be suffering from one or more of the personality disorders summarized in Figure 9-2. A **personality disorder** is a pervasive, persistent, inflexible, maladaptive pattern of behavior that deviates from expected cultural norms. The disorder is learned early in life and causes distress to

Personality disorder
pervasive, persistent, inflexible, maladaptive pattern of behavior that deviates from expected cultural norms

FIGURE 9-2

TEN MAJOR PERSONALITY DISORDERS

Source: "Personality Disorders," in *Diagnostic and Statistical Manual* (IV-TR) (Washington, DC: American Psychiatric Association, 2000).

The ten personality disorders recognized by the American Psychiatric Association are grouped into three clusters. Many difficult people may in reality suffer from a personality disorder, such as the "control freak," who is experiencing an obsessive-compulsive disorder.

Cluster A: The Odd or Eccentric Group
1. *Paranoid Personality.* Pattern of distrust and suspiciousness with a tendency to attribute evil motives to others.
2. *Schizoid Personality.* Pervasive pattern of detachment from social relationships and restriction of emotion in interpersonal settings.
3. *Schizotypal Behavior.* Appearance or thinking that is consistently strange or odd.

Cluster B: The Dramatic, Emotional, and Erratic Group
4. *Antisocial.* Chronic maladaptive behavior that disregards the rights of others.
5. *Borderline.* Instability of interpersonal relationships, self-image, and mood.
6. *Histrionic.* Excessive emotionality and attention-seeking behavior.
7. *Narcissistic.* Behavior includes grandiosity, need for admiration, and lack of empathy.

Cluster C: The Anxious and Fearful Group
8. *Avoidant.* Pattern of social inhibition, feelings of inadequacy, and hypersensitivity to negative evaluation.
9. *Dependent.* Predominantly dependent and submissive behavior.
10. *Obsessive-compulsive.* Preoccupation with orderliness, perfectionism, and control at the expense of flexibility and efficiency.

the person and/or conflicts with others. Individuals with personality disorders range from harmless eccentrics to dangerous, aggressive individuals.[28] If your difficult coworker has a severe personality disorder, the techniques described in the following paragraphs will not work as well as they would with a difficult person who has a mild disorder. About 5 to 10 percent of the population suffer from a personality disorder, and the negative behavior is the most likely to be triggered by heavy stress.

Rather than attempt to list different tactics for dealing with specific types of difficult people, here we present five widely applicable approaches for dealing with such individuals. Keep in mind that dealing with a difficult coworker requires grace and a firm grip on your own patience and temperament.[29]

Take Problems Professionally, Not Personally

A key principle in dealing with difficult people is to take what they do professionally, not personally. Difficult people are not necessarily out to get you. You may simply represent a stepping stone for them to get what they want.[30] For example, if a coworker insults you because you need his help Friday afternoon, he probably has nothing against you personally. He just prefers to become mentally disengaged from work that Friday afternoon. Your request distracts him from mentally phasing out of work as early as he would like.

Give Ample Feedback

The primary technique for dealing with counterproductive behavior is to feed back to the difficult person how his or her behavior affects you. Focus on the person's behavior rather than on characteristics or values. If a Chicken Little type is annoying you by constantly pointing out potential disasters, say something to this effect: "I have difficulty maintaining my enthusiasm when you so often point out the possible negatives." Such a statement will engender less resentment than saying, "I find you to be a total pessimist, and it annoys me."

When the difficult person says something particularly hurtful, be explicit about its effect on you, as follows: "That remark sounded nasty, not funny," and ask "Were you intending to hurt my feelings?" or "Why did you make that sour expression?"[31]

Listen and Respond

Closely related to giving feedback is listening and responding. Give the difficult person ample opportunity to express his or her concerns, doubts, anger, or other feelings. Face the person directly and maintain eye contact. Then acknowledge your awareness of the person's position.[32] An example: "Okay, you tell me that management is really against us and therefore we shouldn't work so hard." After listening, present your perspective in a way such as this: "Your viewpoint may be valid based on your experiences. Yet so far, I've found management here to be on my side." This exchange of viewpoints is less likely to lead to failed communication than if you are judgmental with a statement such as, "You really shouldn't think that way."

Use Tact and Diplomacy in Dealing with Annoying Behavior

Coworkers who irritate you rarely do annoying things on purpose. Tactful actions on your part can sometimes take care of these annoyances without your having to confront the problem. Close your door, for example, if noisy coworkers are gathered outside. Or try one woman's method of getting rid of office pests: She keeps a file open on her computer screen and gestures to it apologetically when someone overstays a visit.

Sometimes subtlety doesn't work, and it may be necessary to diplomatically confront the coworker who is annoying you. A useful approach is to precede a criticism with a compliment. Here is an example of this approach: "You're one of the best people I've ever worked with, but one habit of yours drives me bananas. Do you think you could let me know when you're going to be late getting back to the office after lunch?"[33]

Use Nonhostile Humor

Nonhostile humor can often be used to help a difficult person understand how his or her behavior is blocking others. Also, the humor will help defuse conflict between you and that person. The humor should point to the person's unacceptable behavior yet not belittle him or her. Assume that you and a coworker are working jointly on a report. For each idea that you submit, your coworker gets into know-it-all mode and informs you of important facts that you neglected. An example of nonhostile humor that might jolt the coworker into realizing that his or her approach is annoying is at follows:

> If there is ever a contest to choose the human with a brain that can compete against a Zip file, I will nominate you. But even though my brain is limited to human capacity, I still think I can supply a few facts for our report.

Your humor may help the other person recognize that he or she is attempting to overwhelm you with facts at his or her disposal. You are being self-effacing and thereby drawing criticism away from your coworker. Self-effacement (self-criticism) is a proven humor tactic.

Avoid Creating a Dependency on You

A trap to avoid with many difficult people, and especially the high-maintenance person, is to let him or her become too dependent on you for solutions to problems. In your desire to be helpful and supportive to coworkers, you run the risk of creating a dependency. A difficult person might be pestering you to regularly help solve some of his or her most challenging work problems. The high-maintenance worker might ask you to look up a number in the phone book, reboot a stalled computer, or help scrape ice from the windshield and windows of his or her car. You may want to be a good organizational citizen, yet you also need more time for your own work, and you do not want to make the person too dependent on you.[34] As an antidote to the problem, make frequent statements such as, "You have a telephone directory," "I know you can reboot your computer," and "Perhaps you can scrape the ice yourself, because I have to do the same thing with my SUV."

Reinforce Civil Behavior and Good Moods

In the spirit of positive reinforcement, when a generally difficult person is behaving acceptably, recognize the behavior in some way. Reinforcing statements would include, "It's fun working with you today" and "I appreciate your professional attitude."

Play the Reverse Gossip Game

Difficult people often gossip quite negatively about others to purposely create conflict within the unit. When you hear negative gossip about a coworker, you can quiet the difficult person by engaging in *reverse gossip* through mentioning the coworker's strengths.[35] Here is an example:

> Suppose the difficult person says, "Jim sure does take a lot of time away from the office to take care of personal issues." You reply, "I'm not sure about that, but I have observed that Jim has given us a bunch of useful ideas this year."

The tactics for dealing with difficult people described require practice to be effective. Also, you may have to use a combination of the seven tactics described in this section to deal effectively with a difficult person. The point of these tactics is not to out-manipulate or subdue a difficult person but to establish a cordial and productive working relationship. The accompanying Human Relations in Practice illustrates a successful approach to dealing with a difficult person.

FACE MATURELY THE CHALLENGE OF THE OFFICE ROMANCE

The office has become a frequent meeting place, with more romances beginning at work than over the Internet. Forty-six percent of respondents to a Vault.com Office Romance Survey said that they had dated someone from their own workplace.[36] People often work closely in teams and other joint projects, thus creating the conditions for romance to take place. Another basic reason why office romances are so frequent is that familiarity builds emotional and physical attraction. Based on research spanning twenty years, Cindy Hazan, an associate professor of human development at Cornell University, concludes that people need attachment. And proximity breeds attachment. "Proximity is really the core of attachment. Familiar people have a calming, soothing effect on us."[37]

Company Policies about Office Romances

Office romances can be disruptive to morale and productivity. Coworker romances are a more widespread potential problem because more romances take place between coworkers on the same level than between superiors and subordinates. To help deal with the potential negative aspects of office romance, some companies have established policies covering such relationships, including written agreements. The purpose of the consensual relationship contract (also referred to a *love contract*) is to avoid sexual harassment and retaliation lawsuits when the office

Human Relations in Practice

Telecommunications Manager Helps Jeff Overcome Obnoxious Behavior

Jessica, the CEO of a telecommunications company, was being distracted by the behavior of Jeff, the director of information technology (IT). The other key managers in the firm also suffered from Jeff's many moments of unpleasantness. Several times the director of finance suggested that Jessica just fire Jeff and be done with the problem of his rude disruptive behavior. Jessica's response was consistent: "Losing Jeff might mean it would be more peaceful around here. But at the same time we would be losing a talented guy who has spearheaded the services that generate most of our revenue. I would prefer to see if I might be able to help Jeff understand what he is doing wrong and perhaps change his approach."

At one meeting, Jessica said she wanted to spend about fifteen minutes talking about the tentative plans for a holiday party to celebrate a successful year. Jeff launched into a tirade about wasting company money on self-indulgence when so many people were being laid off at other companies. He also said that no company should hold a celebration when the city in which they were located had so many homeless people. The next day after the meeting Jeff sent an e-mail to every employee in the company explaining his position on the holiday party.

Following Jeff's latest outburst, Jessica took what she hoped would be constructive action to help him. First, she gathered feedback from the other key managers who attended the same meeting about how they negatively perceived Jeff's reaction to the planned holiday celebration. She shared the feedback with Jeff and explained, "I just want you to know how much you can upset people." The second part of Jessica's improvement plan for Jeff was to send him appreciative e-mails and text messages congratulating him on anything he did out of the ordinary in a positive direction. She would also make casual reminders of Jeff's past accomplishments.

When asked how her plan of helping Jeff was proceeding, Jessica replied, "I think I hit the right formula. Jeff really knows now bad his behavior was and how much he is loved and appreciated. The other managers and I have noted how much more relaxed and civil Jeff is now. But should he start being obnoxious again, he's going to get more feedback."

Source: The manager in question has chosen to remain anonymous.

---

romance terminates, especially when the two people are not at the same organizational level.[38] The contract is likely to emphasize that both parties must mutually and voluntarily consent to the social relationship. Furthermore, the policy states that the social relationship must not affect job performance or negatively impact the company's business.

Many companies are concerned about information leakage within their organization. If you date a person who has access to confidential information (such as trade secrets), management might be concerned that you are a security risk. You, therefore, might miss out on some opportunities for better assignments. Companies also worry about negative consequences stemming from office romances, such as sexual harassment claims, low morale of coworkers, lowered productivity from the couple involved in the romance, and an unprofessional atmosphere. Yet an important positive consequence to employers of an office romance is that while the relationship is working well, the couple may have a heightened interest in coming to work. Also, romance can trigger energy that leads to enhanced productivity.

A company practice, if not a true policy, about office romances, is that if there is a reporting relationship between the two of you, the person with the lower-ranking position will be asked to transfer to a new position or leave the company.[39]

Be Discreet with the Office Romance

Sensitivity is required to conduct an office romance that does not detract from your professionalism. It is important not to abuse company tolerance of the coworker romance. Do not invite the person you are dating to meals at company expense, take him or her on nonessential business trips, or create projects to work on jointly. Strive to keep the relationship confidential and restricted to after hours. Minimize talking to coworkers about the relationship. Engaging in personal conversations during work time or holding hands in the company cafeteria is unprofessional and taboo. Such behavior as holding hands or kissing in public view is regarded as poor office etiquette. Disappearing acts together during working hours are also taboo.

Should your coworker romance terminate, you face a special challenge. You must now work together cooperatively with a person toward whom you may have angry feelings. Few people have the emotional detachment necessary to work smoothly with a former romantic involvement. Extra effort, therefore, will be required on both your parts.

What should you do if you and your boss seem suited for a long-term commitment? Why walk away from Mr. or Ms. Right? My suggestion is that if you do become romantically involved, one of you should request a transfer to another department. Many office romances do lead to happy marriages and other long-term relationships. At the start of the relationship, however, use considerable discretion.

▶ Learning Objective 4 ▶

How Do You Build Good Relationships with Customers?

Success on the job also requires building good relationships with both external and internal customers. Business success is built on good relationships, as emphasized again and again by business advisors. *External customers* fit the traditional definition of customer that includes clients and guests. External customers can be classified as either retail or industrial. The latter represents one company buying from another, such as purchasing steel. *Internal customers* are the people you serve within the organization or those who use the output from your job. For example, if you design computer graphics, the other people in the company who receive your graphics are your internal customers.

Customer service orientation
approach of employee whose thoughts and actions are geared toward helping customers

The information already presented about getting along with your manager and coworkers dealt with internal customers. Here we emphasize providing good service (or delight) to external customers. An employee whose thoughts and actions are geared toward helping customers has a **customer service orientation.** Good service is the primary factor that keeps customers coming back. This is important because profits jump considerably as the customer is retained over time. Customer loyalty is therefore a major goal for almost all business firms. Occasionally, a place of business does not want the same person back, such as a bankruptcy counseling service. Nevertheless, the financial counselor still wants loyalty in the form of referrals for other services. Some techniques described here for serving external customers would also work well with internal customers and vice versa.

An overall approach to dealing effectively with customers is to be a good organizational citizen with respect to customer relationships. You gear a lot of your out-of-the-way effort into customer relationships. Specific behaviors of this type

1. Tells outsiders this is a good place to work.
2. Says good things about the organization to others.
3. Generates favorable goodwill for the company.
4. Encourages friends and family to use the firm's products and services.
5. Actively promotes the firm's products and services.
6. Follows customer service guidelines with extreme care.
7. Conscientiously follows guidelines for customer promotions.
8. Follows up in a timely manner to customer requests and problems.
9. Performs duties with unusually few mistakes.
10. Always has a positive attitude at work.
11. Regardless of circumstances, exceptionally courteous and respectful to customers.
12. Encourages coworkers to contribute ideas and suggestions for service improvement.
13. Contributes many ideas for customer promotions and communications.
14. Makes constructive suggestions for service improvement.
15. Frequently presents to others creative solutions to customer problems.
16. Takes home brochures to read up on products and services.

FIGURE 9-3

SERVICE-ORIENTED ORGANIZATIONAL CITIZENSHIP BEHAVIORS

Source: Portion of a table from Lance A. Bettencourt, Kevin P. Gwinner, and Matthew L. Meuter, "A Comparison of Attitude, Personality, and Knowledge Predictors of Service-Oriented Organizational Citizenship Behaviors," *Journal of Applied Psychology*, February 2001, p. 32.

are presented in Figure 9-3. Time-tested suggestions for high-level customer service are presented next.[40] Taken together, these suggestions will help you bond with a customer, forming a close and valued ongoing relationship. You will be able to implement principles of good service more readily if you are treated well by your employer. When workers feel valued, and are adequately compensated, they usually spread the sunshine to customers. Satisfied employees create satisfied customers.[41]

1. Establish customer satisfaction goals. Decide jointly with your manager how much you intend to help customers. Find answers to questions such as the following: "Is your company attempting to satisfy every customer within ten minutes of his or her request?" "Are you striving to provide the finest customer service in your field?" "Is your goal zero defections to competitors?" Your goals will dictate how much and the type of effort you put into pleasing customers.

2. Understand your customer's needs and place them first. The most basic principle of selling is to identify and satisfy customer needs. Many customers may not be able to express their needs clearly. Also, they may not be certain of their needs. To help identify customer needs, you may have to probe for more information. For example, an associate in a consumer electronics store may have to ask, "What uses do you have in mind for your television receiver aside from watching regular programs? Will you be using it to display digital photographs and videos?" Knowing such information will help the store associate identify which television receiver will satisfy the customer's needs.

After you have identified customer needs, focus on satisfying them rather than doing what is convenient for you or the firm. Assume, for example, that the customer says, "I would like to purchase nine reams of copier paper." The sales associate should not respond, "Sorry, the copying paper comes in boxes of ten, so it is not convenient to sell you nine reams." The associate might, however, offer a discount for the purchase of the full ten-ream box if such action fits company policy.

3. Show care and concern. During contacts with your customer, show concern for his or her welfare. Ask questions such as the following: "How have you enjoyed the television set you bought here awhile back?" "How are you feeling today?" After asking the question, project a genuine interest in the answer. A strictly business approach to showing care and concern is to follow up on requests. A phone call or e-mail message to the requester of your service is usually sufficient follow-up. A follow-up is effective because it completes the communication loop between two people.

Another way to show care and concern is to stay in touch with key customers. Interact with them on a personal level by making reference to their personal concerns.[42] For example, a heating and air-conditioning sales rep might send an e-mail to a customer asking how the new system is working and how the customer's child was doing in her youth soccer league.

4. **Communicate a positive attitude.** A positive attitude is conveyed by factors such as appearance, friendly gestures, a warm voice tone, and good telephone communication skills. If a customer seems apologetic about making a heavy demand, respond, "No need to apologize. My job is to please you. I'm here to serve." One reason a positive attitude is important is that hostility by the customer contact person leads to customer dissatisfaction. Lorna Doucet, a professor of organizational behavior at the University of Illinois, conducted a study in the telephone service center for a large retail bank. She found that hostility by the service provider had the strongest negative effect on customers when it was combined with low technical performance (poor answers) by the call center representative. (Perceived hostility was measured by questionnaires.) Hostility was more tolerated if the customers received the answers they needed.[43]

5. **Make the buyer feel good.** A fundamental way of building a customer relationship is to make the buyer feel good. Also, make the buyer feel good because he or she has bought from you. Offer compliments about the customer's healthy glow or a report that specified vendor requirements (for an industrial customer). Explain how much you value the customer's business. An effective feel-good line is, "I enjoy doing business with you." Smiling is a useful technique for making the customer feel good. Also, smiling is a natural relationship builder and can help you bond with your customer. Smile several times during each customer contact, even if your customer is angry with your product or service. Yet guard against smiling constantly or inappropriately because your smile then becomes meaningless. False smiling if carried out regularly is stressful, so look for opportunities to smile genuinely.

6. **Strive for the "wow" experience.** One of the most effective ways to please a customer is to provide him or her with an unusually sensitive and warm surprise, often referred to as a "wow" experience. Alan J. Fuerstman, the chief executive of Montage Hotels and Resorts, defines *wow* as a "spontaneous, personal gesture now." Employees at the chain attend training in how to deliver a wow experience to guests. Fuerstan provides this example:

> Lauren English, a server in our Mosaic Bar and Grill, was waiting on a couple staying with us, and we knew the woman was dying of cancer. Lauren asked if there was anything she could bring to make their stay more pleasant. The woman joked, "Well, lobster, crab, and caviar would be perfect." Later the couple heard a knock on their door. There was Lauren with a nicely turned out tray of crab cakes. "I didn't bring the lobster and caviar, but I hope crab will be all right." The woman cried, the husband cried, Lauren cried.[44]

7. **Display strong business ethics.** Ethical violations receive so much publicity that you can impress customers by being conspicuously ethical. Look for ways to show that you are so ethical that you would welcome making your sales tactics public knowledge. Also, treat the customer the same way you would treat a family member or a valued friend.

8. Be helpful rather than defensive when a customer complains. Take a complaint professionally rather than personally. Listen carefully and concentrate on being helpful. The upset customer cares primarily about having the problem resolved and does not care whether you are at fault. Use a statement such as, "I understand this mistake is a major inconvenience. I'll do what I can right now to solve the problem." Remember also that complaints that are taken care of quickly and satisfactorily will often create a more positive impression than mistake-free service. Another way of being helpful is to ask for enough details about what went wrong so that you can begin resolving the problem. Explain as soon as possible how you are going to fix the problem.

9. Invite the customer back. The southern U.S. expression "Y'all come back, now!" is well suited for good customer service. Specific invitations to return may help increase repeat business. The more focused and individualized the invitation, the more likely it will have an impact on customer behavior. ("Y'all come back, now!" is sometimes used too indiscriminately to be effective.) Pointing out why you enjoyed doing business with the customer and what future problems you could help with is an effective technique. Another way of encouraging the customer to return is to explain how much you value him or her.

10. Avoid rudeness. Although rudeness to customers is obviously a poor business practice, the problem is widespread. Rudeness by customer contact personnel is a major problem from the employer's standpoint. Be aware of subtle forms of rudeness, such as complaining about your job or working hours in front of customers. To elevate your awareness level about rudeness among customer contact personnel, do Human Relations Self-Assessment Quiz 9-3.

11. Keep electronic communications professional and polite. Many customer interactions take place by phone, e-mail, and Web site interactions. These electronic interactions are as important as those conducted face-to-face. The suggestions for proper e-mail etiquette and phone interactions described in Chapter 7 apply here. Above all, avoid the same informal breeziness that you might use in electronic interaction with friends. Be sure to check with company policy if it is acceptable to address customers by their first name only, as is widely practiced today.

The preceding eleven points emphasize the importance of practicing good human relations with customers and having a customer service orientation. Good customer service stems naturally from practicing good human relations.

As you deal with customers in our culturally diverse and enriched workplace, remember also to be aware of possible cross-cultural differences. Be alert to customs that could make a difference in terms of the customer feeling good about his or her experience with you. An illustrative cultural difference is that in the typical Asian family, older family members accompany younger members when a major purchase, such as a home, is being contemplated. Although the older family members may stay in the background, they might be a major financial and emotional influence on the purchase. So the eager real estate agent should not act as if the older family members are simply along for the ride. Instead, the agent should show respect by presenting vital details to all the family members, not only the couple making the purchase.

Human Relations Self-Assessment Quiz 9-3

Am I Being Rude?

Following is a list of behaviors of customer contact workers that would be interpreted as rude by many customers. Indicate whether you have engaged in such behavior in your dealings with customers or whether you are likely to do so if your job did involve customer contact.

	Yes	No
1. I talk to a coworker while serving a customer.	_____	_____
2. I conduct a telephone conversation with someone else while serving a customer.	_____	_____
3. I address customers by their first names without having their permission.	_____	_____
4. I address customers as "you guys."	_____	_____
5. I chew gum or eat candy while dealing with a customer.	_____	_____
6. I laugh when customers describe an agonizing problem they are having with one of our company's products or services.	_____	_____
7. I minimize eye contact with customers.	_____	_____
8. I say the same thing to every customer, such as "Have a nice day," in a monotone.	_____	_____
9. I accuse customers of attempting to cheat the company before carefully investigating the situation.	_____	_____
10. I hurry customers when my break time approaches.	_____	_____
11. I comment on a customer's appearance in a flirtatious, sexually oriented way.	_____	_____
12. I sometimes complain about or make fun of other customers when I am serving another customer.	_____	_____

Interpretation:

The more of these behaviors you have engaged in, the ruder you are and the more apt you are to lose potential business for your company. If you have not engaged in any of these behaviors, even when faced with a rude customer, you are an asset to your employer. You are also tolerant.

Concept Review
and Reinforcement

Key Terms

Political skills, 246
Work ethic, 247
Performance standard, 249
Ingratiating, 251
Bully, 252

Micromanagement, 253
Self-disclosure, 256
Team player, 258
Synergy, 258
Backstabbing, 259

Group norms, 259
Organizational culture, 259
Difficult people, 261
Personality disorder, 261
Customer service orientation, 266

Summary and Review

Adequate interpersonal skills are necessary for success in business. Developing a favorable relationship with your manager is the most basic strategy of getting ahead in your career. Specific tactics for developing a good relationship with your manager include the following:

- Achieve good job performance.
- Display a strong work ethic. (Use such means as demonstrating competence on even minor tasks, assuming personal responsibility for problems, and completing projects promptly.)
- Demonstrate good emotional intelligence. (Deal effectively with the emotional responses of coworkers and customers.)
- Be dependable and honest.
- Be a good organizational citizen. (Be willing to work for the good of the organization even without the promise of a specific reward.)
- Create a strong presence. (Keep yourself in the forefront.)
- Find out what your manager expects of you.
- Minimize complaints.
- Avoid bypassing your manager.
- Engage in favorable interactions with your manager. (At times you may have to deliver bad news.)

Coping with a manager you perceive to be a problem is part of getting along with him or her. The bully is a frequent type of problem manager. Consider the following approaches:

- Reevaluate your manager to make sure you have not misperceived him or her.
- It is important to confront your manager about your problem. Often this problem is a case of being micromanaged.

- Overrespond to the manager's pet peeves.
- Learning from your problem manager's mistakes (even if he or she gets fired) is recommended.

Methods and tactics for building coworker relationships include the following:

- Have high self-esteem and be at the center of a communication network.
- Develop allies through being civil, including maintaining a positive outlook.
- Make other people feel important.
- Maintain honest and open relationships (including self-disclosure).
- Be a team player. (Observe the nine approaches reported here.)
- Follow group standards of conduct.
- Express an interest in the work and personal life of coworkers.
- Use appropriate (nonexaggerated) compliments.

Deal effectively with difficult people, including the following:

- Take problems professionally.
- Give ample feedback.
- Listen and respond.
- Use tact and diplomacy in dealing with annoying behavior.
- Use nonhostile humor.
- Avoid creating a dependency on you.
- Reinforce civil behavior and good moods.
- Play the reverse gossip game.
- Face maturely the challenge of the office romance.

Team player approaches include sharing credit, maintaining a cooperative attitude, establishing trust, sharing information and opinions, providing emotional support, practicing the Golden Rule, avoiding sabotaging or undermining actions, sharing the glory, and avoiding backstabbing.

Job success also requires building good relationships with both internal and external customers. Techniques for providing high-level customer service include:

- Establishing customer satisfaction goals
- Understanding your customer's needs and placing them first

- Showing care and concern
- Communicating a positive attitude
- Making the buyer feel good
- Striving for the "wow" experience
- Displaying strong business ethics
- Being helpful rather than defensive when a customer complains
- Inviting the customer back
- Avoiding rudeness
- Keeping electronic communications professional and polite

Check Your Understanding

1. If team leaders don't have as much power as a regular manager, why is it still important to build a good relationship with your team leader?
2. How can a worker implement the tactic "engage in favorable interactions with your manager" without appearing to be "kissing up" to the boss?
3. Give an example of a technique you think would make a coworker feel important.
4. What explanation can you offer for the tendency for backstabbing to become more frequent during a recession?
5. Provide an example of a *group standard of conduct* in any place you have worked. What led you to conclude that the particular behavior was a group standard of conduct?
6. Many customer contact workers routinely say, "Have a nice day" when the customer's transaction has been completed. How effective is this expression in building customer relationships?

7. Suppose you thought the reason that a coworker of yours was a difficult person was because he or she had a true personality disorder. Would you recommend to that person directly that he or she seek mental health treatment? Explain your reasoning.
8. To what extent do you still have to worry about building good relationships with customers when you work for a company that sells only online?
9. If rudeness is so widespread today, why bother being polite and considerate on the job?
10. Ask a person who has achieved job success what he or she thinks are two important ways of getting along with coworkers and customers. Compare notes with classmates.

Web Corner

Getting along with your coworkers:
http://careerplanning.about.com/od/bosscoworkers/

Managing relationships with the boss:
www.howtoadvice.com/BossRelations

Customer relationships on the phone:
www.HeyCallCenters.com

INTERNET SKILL BUILDER

Visit http://careers.homedepot.com, and proceed to "Living Our Values." Identify which skills mentioned relate to workplace relationships, including communication skills and self-understanding. Reflect back on any time you have visited a Home Depot or a competitor's store. How realistic is Home Depot about the interpersonal and personal skills required for a sales associate? If you happen to know a Home Depot employee, obtain his or her input in formulating your answer to the preceding question.

Developing Your Human Relations Skills

Applying Human Relations Exercise 9-1

Giving Good Customer Service

Role-players in this exercise will demonstrate two related techniques for giving good customer service: show care and concern and make the buyer feel good. The role-players will carry out the scenarios in front of the class. For both role-plays, the provider of customer service should think through before starting the role-play what specifically he or she is attempting to accomplish. For example, the role-player might ask himself or herself, "How am I going to show care and concern?" or "What am I going to do to make the buyer feel good?"

Scenario 1: Show care and concern. A sales representative meets with two company representatives to talk about installing a new information system for employee benefits. One of the company representatives is from the human resources department and the other is from the information technology department. The sales representative will attempt to show care and concern for both company representatives during the same meeting.

Scenario 2: Make the buyer feel good. A couple, played by two role-players, enters a new-car showroom to examine a model they have seen advertised on television. Although they are not in urgent need of a new car, they are strongly interested. The sales representative is behind quota for the month and would like to close a sale today. The rep decides to use the tactic "make the buyer feel good" to help form a bond.

The rest of the class will provide some constructive feedback, and perhaps compliments, to the role-players. Use the evaluation dimensions in the table to help you evaluate the effectiveness of the customer service providers and customers. Use a scale of 1 to 5 in making your ratings: 1 = very poor, 2 = poor, 3 = average, 4 = good, and 5 = very good.

Other comments about the role players:

Customer Service Evaluation Factors	1 VP	2 P	3 A	4 G	5 VG
1. Maintained eye contact					
2. Was warm and supportive					
3. Smiled appropriately					
4. Displayed positive attitude					
5. Showed genuine concern					
6. Made buyer feel good					

Customer Evaluation Dimensions	1 VP	2 P	3 A	4 G	5 VG
1. Behaved realistically					
2. Showed respect for service provider					
3. Treated provider like a professional					
4. Showed appreciation for service provider's effort.					

Applying Human Relations Exercise 9-2

The Thirty-Second Elevator Speech

A longstanding tip in career development and impressing higher-ups is to make a thirty-second impromptu presentation when you have a chance encounter with a key person in your organization. If you work in an office tower, the chance encounter is likely to take place on an elevator—and it is generally frowned on to have long conversations in an elevator. So the term "elevator speech" developed, describing a brief opportunity to impress a key person. Imagine that you have a chance encounter with a high-ranking executive in your area on the elevator or escalator, in the parking lot, during a company picnic, or at some other location. You then give that person a thirty-second pitch geared to make a positive impression. Because you must boil your pitch down to thirty seconds, you will need to prepare for a long time. (Credit President Abraham Lincoln for that insight.)

About six different pairs (impresser and person to be impressed) will carry out this role-play in front of the class. The evaluators will put themselves in the role of the target key person of the thirty-second evaluation. Consider using the following scale and answering the two questions:

_____ Wow, I was impressed. (5 points)

_____ I was kind of impressed with the person I ran into. (4 points)

_____ He or she left me with at least an average impression. (3 points)

_____ I found the person to be somewhat annoying. (2 points)

_____ That person I met left with a terrible impression. (1 point)

1. What I liked about person's thirty-second pitch:
2. What I saw as possible areas for improvement:

Find a mechanism to feed back some of your observations to the role-players. Volunteer to present the findings in class, give the person your comments on note-paper, or send him or her an e-mail.

Human Relations Class Activity

How We Got in Good with the Boss

The purpose of this class activity is to further understand what workers have actually done to develop a positive relationship with a present or former boss. This activity would require about forty-five minutes of class time for a class of approximately thirty students. The first step is for each person to think through, and write down, an effective tactic he or she has used in developing a good relationship with a manager, past or present. Any type of work experience counts. If you have no formal work experience, perhaps the experience can be related to sports or a club. Include in your analysis how the boss reacted to the tactic.

After about four minutes of class time have been invested in thinking through the tactic-and-result scenarios, students will come up in front of the class one by one to present their findings. Presentations should be about sixty seconds. After all students have presented, have a brief class discussion centering on these points:

1. Which two tactics appear to be the most frequently mentioned?
2. Which two tactics appeared to be the most creative?
3. Which one or two tactics gave you a useful idea for the future?
4. How closely do some of the tactics conform to the suggestions for developing a relationship with the manager or team leader presented in the text?

Human Relations Case Study 9-1

Sara Struggles to Be Liked

Sara was excited about her opportunity to become a production coordinator at Tractor Co., one of the few American businesses still manufacturing and selling tractors for the commercial and residential markets. She also felt a sense of patriotism to work in manufacturing because only about 8 percent of the U.S. workforce was still making products. "I know that my grandparents are proud of me, because it was manufacturing that made this country great," said Sara.

Sara reported to Kelly, the production manager for domestic riding tractors, those used by homeowners and lawn care specialists. When Sara was first interviewed by Kelly, she thought she could work well enough with Kelly, but she didn't feel much spark between the two of them. Sara reasoned that a decent working rela-

tionship is all she would need with a boss. A close friendship would therefore not be so important.

As the weeks went by, Sara was eager to learn all she needed to be an outstanding production coordinator. She found that the production technicians were superhelpful in giving her hints about some of the real problems involved in getting the line of high-quality tractors ready for shipping to dealers.

Eager for feedback on how well she was performing her responsibilities, Sara would send the occasional progress report by e-mail to Kelly. Kelly typically did not respond to Sara's e-mails, but when she did her comment was something to the effect, "Message received. Thank you."

During a department meeting to discuss plans and problems, Sara thought she could do a better job of establishing rapport with Kelly. So she asked a question that she thought would delight Kelly: "Is it really true that we are one of the highest performing departments in Tractor Co. worldwide?" Kelly shrugged her shoulders and replied, "That would be news to me."

After the meeting, Sara thought that perhaps she was not being personal enough in building a better relationship with Kelly. So the following day when she saw Kelly for the first time in the morning, Sara said, "That's a sharp outfit you're wearing. You have given me a good idea for my own wardrobe." To which Kelly replied, "Thanks."

Questions

1. Is Sara trying too hard to get along better with Kelly?

2. Is Sara too worried about establishing better rapport with Kelly?

3. What recommendations can you offer Sara to improve her relationship with Kelly?

4. What suggestions might you offer Kelly to be a more effective manager from a human relations perspective?

Human Relations Role-Playing Exercise

Sara Attempts to Build Her Relationship with Kelly

The case study about Sara and Kelly serves as the background and the story line for this role-play. One person plays the role of Sara, who has been discouraged in her attempts to build a stronger relationship with her manager, Kelly. Sara decides that today she will use two specific tactics to improve her relationship with Kelly: "demonstrate a strong work ethic," and "find out what your manager expects of you." She plans to implement these tactics today when she will be discussing a new work assignment with Kelly. Another person plays the role of Kelly, who is expecting Sara to drop by her cubicle this morning to discuss the new work assignment. The person who plays the role of Kelly can act as she does in the case or can be more skilled at human relations.

For both scenarios, observers rate the role-players on two dimensions, using a 1 to 5 scale from very poor to very good. One dimension is "effective use of human relations techniques." The second dimension is "acting ability." A few observers might voluntarily provide feedback to the role-players in terms of sharing their ratings and observations. The course instructor might also provide feedback.

Human Relations Case Study 9-2

Alex Wants to Impress

Certified public accountant (CPA) Alex was looking for a way to document his contribution to a team whose work directly supported the mission of his firm. Alex's firm was experiencing a business plateau. As more large business firms gobbled up smaller companies, the demand for accounting services decreased. (Fewer companies were available to hire accountants.) In addition, more companies were doing their work internally and using software to replace some of the contributions of outside accountants.

Alex served on a client-development team that uncovered several productive ways of expanding the firm's practice. Among these initiatives was to advertise and hold tax seminars free to the public. The team received ample credit from the senior partners for helping the accounting practice grow, but Alex believed that he deserved more credit than several of the other team members. Nevertheless, he did not want to appear tacky by stating this observation to the senior partners. Instead, he wrote an e-mail message describing his contribution without asking for credit. His e-mail stated:

Hello Senior Partners,

Thanks for the opportunity to serve on the client development team. I'm pleased that the team accomplished its mission. My major assignment was to conduct tax seminars for the public. I am so pleased that the team accomplished its mission. I found that to be a professionally rewarding experience. Should the opportunity arise to help the firm again by conducting seminars, please consider me a candidate for the assignment.

Sincerely,

Alex Davenport

Alex thought, "This e-mail should work. I'll be seen as a fine team player and a great individual contributor at the same time."

Questions

1. What is your evaluation of Alex as a team player?

2. If Alex had asked your advice about sending the above e-mail, what would you have told him?

3. If you were a senior partner in Alex's firm, how would you reply to his memo?

REFERENCES

1. Excerpted from Sean Dobbin, "Emphasis on Staff, Customers Keeps Issac Heating Growing," *Democrat and Chronicle* (Rochester, NY), January 19, 2009, pp. 5B, 6B.
2. Gerald R. Ferris, Pamela L. Perrewé, William P. Anthony, and David C. Gilmore, "Political Skill at Work." *Organizational Dynamics,* Spring 2000, p. 25.
3. Judith Sills, "How to Improve Your Credit Rating," *Psychology Today*, March/April 2008, p. 67.
4. Quoted in Anita Bruzzese, "Get the Boss to Take Notice of You," Gannett News Service, April 21, 1997.
5. Kevin P. Coyne and Edward J. Coyne Sr., "Surviving Your New CEO," *Harvard Business Review*, May 2007, p. 66.
6. Erin White, "How to Keep Your Job, or Decide to Leave, if New CEO Arrives," *Wall Street Journal*, April 24, 2007, p. B5.
7. Cecily D. Cooper, "Just Joking Around? Employee Humor Expression as Ingratiatory Behavior," *Academy of Management Review*, October 2005, pp. 765–776.
8. Robert I. Sutton, cited in Ellen Simon, "Purge Jerks at Work, Says Author," Associated Press, March 18, 2007.
9. Anonymous, "How to Live with the S.O.B." *Business Week*, August 25/September 1, 2008, pp. 48–50.
10. J. Kenneth Matejka and Richard Dunsing, "Managing the Baffling Boss," *Personnel*, February 1989, p. 50.
11. "So You're Smarter than the Boss? Yeah, Right," *Executive Leadership*, June 2000, p. 5.
12. Cited in "Ask Annie," *Fortune*, April 1, 2002, p. 171.
13. "How's the View Back There?" *Working Smart*, December 1996, p. 1.
14. Anonymous, "How to Live with the S.O.B." pp. 40–49.
15. Janet Banks and Diane Coutu, "How to Protect Your Job in a Recession," *Harvard Business Review*, September 2008, p. 113.
16. Judith Sills, "Hanging with the In-Crowd," *Psychology Today*, November/December 2007, pp. 65–66.
17. Brent A. Scott and Timothy A. Judge, "The Popularity Contest at Work: Who Wins, Why, and What Do They Receive?" *Journal of Applied Psychology*, January 2009, pp. 20–33.
18. Christine M. Pearson and Christine L. Porath, "On the Nature, Consequences and Remedies of Workplace Incivility: No Time for 'Nice'? Think Again," *Academy of Management Executive*, February 2005, pp. 7–18.
19. Jared Sandberg, "Office Minstrels Drive the Rest of Us Nuts but Are Hard to Silence," *Wall Street Journal*, February 14, 2006, p. B1+.
20. Sandy Lim, Lilia M. Cortina, and Vicki J. Magley, "Personal and Workgroup Incivility: Impact of Work and Health Outcomes," *Journal of Applied Psychology*, January 2008, pp. 95–107.
21. Christine L. Porath and Amir Erez, "Does Rudeness Really Matter: The Effects of Rudeness on Task Performance and Helpfulness," *Academy of Management Journal*, October 2007, pp. 1181–1197.
22. Andrew C. Wicks, Shawn L. Berman, and Thomas M. Jones, "The Structure of Optimal Trust: Moral and Strategic Implications," *Academy of Management Review*, January 1999, p. 99.
23. Alex M. Susskind, K. Michele Kacmar, and Carl P. Borchgrevink, "Customer Service Providers' Attitudes Relating to Customer Service and Customer Satisfaction in the Customer-Server Exchange," *Journal of Applied Psychology*, February 2003, pp. 179–187.
24. "Build Allies for Personal Support," *Manager's Edge*, January 2003, p. 8.
25. Jathane Janove, "Jerks at Work," *HR Magazine*, May 2007, p. 111.
26. The first two types are from a brochure for ETC w/Career Track, Boulder, CO.
27. Matt Vilano, "How to Shush the Office Magpie," *New York Times.* Retrieved December 25, 2005, from: www.nytimes.com.
28. Charles G. Morris and Albert A. Maisto, *Psychology: An Introduction*, 11th ed. (Upper Saddle River, NJ: Prentice Hall, 2002), p. 537; Michael S. Beeson, "Personality Disorders." Retrieved March 25, 2006, from: www.emedicine.com/emerg/topic418.htm.
29. Naomi Cossack, "Skills Data, Retirement Benefits, Difficult Employees," *HR Magazine*, January 2007, p. 49.
30. Dru Scott, *Customer Satisfaction: The Other Half of Your Job* (Los Altos, CA: Crisp Publications, 1991), p. 16.
31. "Handle the Toughest Personalities," *Manager's Edge*, October 2008, p. 1.
32. "Master Dealing with Difficult People," *Manager's Edge*, March 2009, p. 8.
33. Jane Michaels, "You Gotta Get Along to Get Ahead," *Woman's Day*, April 3, 1984, p. 58.
34. Lin Grensing-Pophal, "High-Maintenance Employees," *HR Magazine*, February 2001, p. 89.
35. "Tame Team Tigers: How to Handle Difficult Personalities," *Manager's Edge*, Special Issue, 2008, p. 8.
36. Laura Tiffany, "How Useful Are Love Contracts?" *Entrepreneur*, October 2008, p. 84.
37. Carlin Flora, "Close Quarters: Why We Fall in Love with the One Nearby," *Psychology Today*, January/February 2004, p. 15.
38. Tiffany, "How Useful Are Love Contracts?" p. 84.
39. Kerry Sulkowicz, "In Cupid's Cubicle," *Business Week*, February 26, p. 18.
40. Linda Thornburg, "Companies Benefit from Emphasis on Superior Customer Service," *HR Magazine*, October 1993, pp. 46–49, 3–22; Hal Hardy, "Five Steps to Pleasing Difficult, Demanding Customers," *First Rate Customer Service* (sample issue distributed by Briefings Publishing Group, 2002).
41. Anne Fisher, "A Happy Staff Equals Happy Customers," *Fortune*, July 12, 2004, p. 52.
42. "The Art of the Schmooze," *Managing People at Work*, Sample Issue, 2006, p. 8.
43. Lorna Doucet, "Service Provider Hostility and Service Quality," *Academy of Management Journal*, October 2004, pp. 761–771.
44. Perry Garfinkel, "A Hotel's Secret: Treat Guests like Guests," *New York Times* (nytimes.com), August 23, 2008.

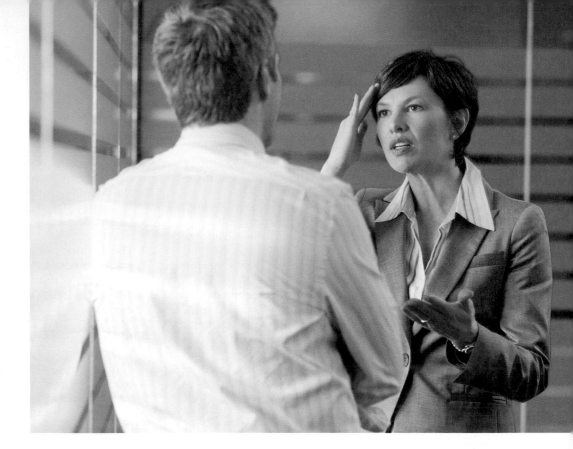

10

Managing Conflict

Outline

1 Why Does So Much Conflict Exist?
Competition for Limited Resources
Differences of Opinion on Work-Related Issues and Rights
Personality Clashes
Aggressive Personalities, Including Bullies
Culturally Diverse Teams and Factional Groups
Competing Work and Family Demands
Micro-Inequities as a Source of Conflict
Cross-Generational Conflict
Sexual Harassment: A Special Type of Conflict

2 The Good and Bad Sides of Conflict

3 What Are Some Techniques for Resolving Conflicts?
Being Assertive
Confrontation and Problem Solving Leading to Win–Win
Disarm the Opposition
Reframing (Including Cognitive Restructuring and Asking Questions)
Appeal to a Third Party
The Grievance Procedure
Negotiation and Bargaining Tactics

4 What Are Some Suggestions for Managing Anger?
Managing Your Own Anger
Managing Anger in Other People
Choosing a Tactic for Resolving a Conflict or Managing Anger

*J*ud, age thirty, is quite happy with his job as a construction supervisor at a construction engineering firm. The work is exciting and challenging, and in Jud's opinion offers him the opportunity to contribute some value to society. In Jud's words, "When you help construct something like an apartment building, you do some good for the world."

Suddenly, the tranquility in Jud's life changed. On the positive side he and his wife, Shannon, had their first baby, Quentin. After a three-month maternity leave, Shannon returned to work as a medical secretary. Jud and Shannon took turns dropping off Quentin at the day-care center and then picking him up at night. On days Quentin was ill, the couple each took a half-day off from work or had a relative care for Quentin.

On the negative side, one day Jud was told by his manager that he would be sent on a six-month assignment to a construction site three hundred miles away. The company would pay the travel expenses for one weekend trip home per month. Jud thought, "What do I do now? This assignment will throw my home life into turmoil. The father of an infant can't work out of town. Yet, if I turn down this assignment I might either be fired or regarded as being too inflexible for a career in management with the firm."

In anguish, Jud planned to discuss his conflict with Shannon that evening.

The situation just described illustrates a reality about the workplace. Conflict takes place frequently, and being able to manage it successfully enables the workers involved to function more peacefully, and the company to get more work done. **Conflict** is a condition that exists when two sets of demands, goals, or motives are incompatible. For example, if a person wants a career in retailing yet also wants to work a predictable eight-hour day with weekends off, that person faces a conflict. He or she cannot achieve both goals. A conflict can also be considered a dispute, feud, or controversy.

Our approach to studying conflict includes explaining why so much conflict exists, constructive approaches to resolving conflict, and the management of anger.

▶ Learning Objective 1 ▶

Conflict
condition that exists when two sets of demands, goals, or motives are incompatible

Why Does So Much Conflict Exist?

Many reasons exist for the widespread presence of conflict in all aspects of life. All these reasons are related to the basic nature of conflict—the fact that not every person can have what he or she wants at the same time. As with other topics in this book, understanding conflict helps you develop a better understanding of why people act as they do. Here we describe eight key sources of conflict.

COMPETITION FOR LIMITED RESOURCES

A fundamental reason you might experience conflict with another person is that not everybody can get all the money, material, supplies, or human help they want. Conflict also ensues when employees are asked to compete for prizes, such as bonuses based on individual effort or company-paid vacation trips. Because the number of awards is so limited, the competition becomes intense enough to be regarded as conflict. Conflict stemming from limited resources has become prevalent as so many companies attempt to reduce expenses. Many units of the organization have to compete for the limited money available to hire new people or purchase new technology.

Another type of limited resource that leads to conflict is trade names. Several companies or individuals might believe that they have the right to use a particular trade name. Instead of being able to resolve the conflict themselves, they often resort to litigation.

Imagine that a woman named Tiffany Horowitz wants to open a jewelry store called "Tiffany." Unfortunately, the lawyers for Tiffany & Co. will tell her to change the name on the storefront and Web site immediately or be sued for trademark infringement. Similarly, Anheuser Busch, the American brewery that makes Budweiser beer, and the Czechoslovakian brewery Budjovick Budvar have been in dispute for over a hundred years on who has the right to sell their Bud. The two brewers are also in conflict about who can use a particular slogan. The American Bud is the "King of Beers," and the Czech Bud is the "Beer of Kings." Who wins this conflict varies across different countries.[1] Somehow the executives of these two companies cannot settle their differences over a bottle of beer.

DIFFERENCES OF OPINION ON WORK-RELATED ISSUES AND RIGHTS

A natural source of conflict in the workplace centers on differences of opinion about work-related issues, including whose idea will work the best. One member of the design team for a luxury sports car might insist the paneling should be composed mostly of wood. Another might say that the car could get by with plastic paneling, saving the company considerable money. The two members might therefore enter into conflict.

Conflict from differences of opinion can last a long time and can lead to dismissal from the employer. Sallie Krawcheck, the former head of Citigroup's wealth management unit, stepped down after months of conflict with the chief executive. One difference of opinion was that Krawcheck pushed Citigroup to reimburse clients whose investments were severely depleted. She argued that the reimbursement would be preferable to alienating highly profitable clients. Other managers resisted her position, contending that the clients should have recognized the risks associated with their investments.[2]

Conflict over rights will often take the form of one group or individual feeling that it has the right to engage in certain behavior despite a rule or custom denying that right. Smoking is forbidden in most workplaces, with some employers forbidding workers to smoke anywhere on the property—especially at a medical facility. The smokers who have to walk or drive about a half mile become quite upset with the nonsmokers who have blocked what they consider their right to smoke immediately outside of a building. A frequent conflict over custom is when some office workers believe they have the right to wear low-cut jeans and shirts that display their midriff to work, but the company officials say that such clothing is unacceptable.

PERSONALITY CLASHES

Various value and personality differences among people contribute to workplace conflict. Many disagreements on the job stem from the fact that some people simply dislike each other. A **personality clash** is thus an antagonistic relationship between two people based on differences in personal attributes, preferences, interests, values, and styles. People involved in a personality clash often have difficulty specifying why they dislike each other. The end result, however, is that they cannot maintain an amiable work relationship. A strange fact about personality clashes is that people who get along well may begin to clash after working together for a number of years. Many business partnerships fold because the two partners eventually clash.

Personality clash
antagonistic relationship between two people based on differences in personal attributes, preferences, interests, values, and styles

AGGRESSIVE PERSONALITIES, INCLUDING BULLIES

Coworkers naturally disagree about topics, issues, and ideas. Yet some people convert disagreement into an attack that puts down other people and damages their self-esteem. As a result, conflict surfaces. **Aggressive personalities** are people who verbally and sometimes physically attack others frequently. Verbal aggression takes the form of insults, teasing, ridicule, and profanity. The aggression may also be expressed as attacks on the victim's character, competence, background, and physical appearance. When people are verbally abused, they are put on the defensive, making them feel uncomfortable.[3]

Aggressive personalities
people who verbally and sometimes physically attack others frequently

Aggressive personalities are also referred to as *bullies*. Among their typical behaviors are interrupting others, ranting in a loud voice, and making threats. A typical attitude of a bullying boss is "My way or the highway," sending the message that the employee's suggestions are unwelcome. Bullying managers were described in Chapter 9. Aggressiveness can also take the extreme form of the shooting or knifing of a former boss or colleague by a mentally unstable worker recently dismissed from the company. Violence has become so widespread that homicide is the second-highest cause of workplace deaths, with about six hundred workplace homicides each year in the United States since 2000.[4] Most of these deaths result from a robbery or commercial crime. Many of these killings, however, are perpetrated by a disgruntled worker or former employee harboring an unresolved conflict. As companies have continued to reduce their workforce despite being profitable, these incidents have increased in frequency. The accompanying Human Relations in Practice describes how one well-known company deals with the problem of potential employee violence.

CULTURALLY DIVERSE TEAMS AND FACTIONAL GROUPS

Conflict often surfaces as people work in teams whose members vary in many ways. Ethnicity, religion, and gender are three of the major factors that lead to clashes in viewpoints. Differing educational backgrounds and work specialties can

Human Relations in Practice

Pitney Bowes Attempts to Stamp Out Employee Violence

Pitney Bowes, the Stamford, Conn., mail and messaging management-equipment company, has a help line that employees can call anonymously if they're concerned that a colleague is exhibiting erratic or angry behavior, or has a problem such as substance abuse or depression. "We felt, on balance, it's better for employees to know they can call with concerns instead of sitting at their desks scared to death," says Michele Coleman Mayes, senior vice president and general counsel. Human-resource executives discretely investigate the complaints.

In January 2007, a guard at a Pitney Bowes facility in Phoenix quit his job and a few days later returned to the workplace and shot his replacement. The guard worked for a company from which Pitney Bowes subcontracts security personnel. The company now asks its subcontractors to do more-vigorous employee screenings.

The company also is offering managers training on how to identify signs of employee distress. "People bring all sorts of demons to work—from problems with spouses and kids to bipolar disease—that they shouldn't think they can solve on their own," says Ms. Mayes. Pitney Bowes has a staff physician that employees can consult and a program offering referrals to counselors.

If the employee is very distressed or potentially violent, a manager encourages counseling with a mental-health professional, and may suggest a transfer or a leave of absence or, as a last resort, may dismiss him or her. "We have to ask, 'What's in the best interests of all our employees?' because we're responsible for everyone's overall safety," says Ms. Mayes.

Source: Carol Hymowitz, "Bosses Have to Learn How to Confront Troubled Employees," *Wall Street Journal*, April 23, 2007, p. B1.

---

also lead to conflict. Workers often shut out information that doesn't fit comfortably with their own beliefs, particularly if they do not like the person providing the information. When these conflicts are properly resolved, diversity lends strength to the organization because the various viewpoints make an important contribution to solving a problem. Groups that are reminded of the importance of effective communication and taught methods of conflict resolution usually can overcome the conflict stemming from mixed groups.[5]

Another form of diversity occurs when groups contain different factions, such as those representing two different companies that merged. Often the factional group consists of two subgroups, each with several representatives, such as a cost-cutting task force consisting of three representatives each from marketing, operations, and finance. The potential for conflict within factional groups increases when the subgroups differ substantially in demographic characteristics such as age, gender, and educational levels.[6]

COMPETING WORK AND FAMILY DEMANDS

Balancing the demands of work and family life is a major challenge facing workers at all levels. Yet achieving this balance and resolving these conflicts is essential for being successful in career and personal life. The challenge of achieving balance is particularly intense for employees who are part of a two-wage-earner family. A heavy workload also intensifies the conflict because the person feel compelled to work long hours, including performing some work at home. Frequent business travel is another major contributor to work–family conflict.

Work–family conflict occurs when the individual has to perform multiple roles: worker, spouse or partner, and often parent. From the standpoint of the individual, this type of conflict can be regarded as work interfering with family life. From the standpoint of the employer, the same conflict might be regarded as family life interfering with work. Being a single parent can lead to even stronger work–family conflict when the other parent does not help manage unanticipated problems. An example would be managing the situation of a sick child not being able to attend school and refused from day care also because of the illness.

Attempting to meet work and family demands is a frequent source of conflict because the demands are often incompatible. Imagine having to attend your child's championship soccer game and then being ordered at the last minute to attend a late-afternoon meeting. As revealed in a study with working adults, another complication of work–family conflict is that when family life interferes with work, the person will often feel guilty. Guilt will be experienced also by some people who feel that work interferes with family life.[7] Feelings of guilt arise because the person might feel that when one is being paid for doing a job, the job should have higher priority than taking care of personal issues. Or the person might feel guilty because he or she believes that family remains a higher priority than work.

Some people attempt to resolve their work–family conflict by doing some work at family and personal events. Watch any Little League baseball game, high school tennis match, or youth soccer match, and you will see parents at the sidelines busily engaged with their BlackBerrys conducting work. Equally extreme is a recent trend for young people to do office work while on a date.

> A 36-year-old Los Angeles entrepreneur said her dates start like many other couple's. "We cook an amazing dinner, grab a little wine, and then we pull out our laptops and get some work done. Toiling side by side for hours, we laugh and have a great time." She says that working while on a date saves her from having no social life at all. "I probably wouldn't have left the house or office for a man if I couldn't bring my laptop along."[8]

The conflict over work versus family demands intensifies when the person is serious about both work and family responsibilities. The average American corporate professional works approximately fifty-five hours per week, including five hours on weekends. Adhering to such a schedule almost inevitably results in some incompatible demands from work versus those from family members and friends. Conflict arises because the person wants to work sufficient hours to succeed on the job yet still have enough time for personal life.

Cross-national differences based on culture can influence the extent to which workers experience work–family conflict. A study of 5,270 managers from twenty countries investigated how much work interfered with family life. Four clusters of countries were studied: the individualistic (Anglo) cluster versus three collectivistic (Asia, Eastern Europe, and Latin America). A collectivistic culture highly values the group. A finding was that work interfering with family life led to more dissatisfaction and intention to quit for people in individualistic than collectivistic societies. The researchers suggested that people in the collectivistic society might be more likely to remain loyal to the employer. Also, managers who value collectivism are more apt to respond to adverse conditions with greater affiliation toward coworkers.[9] A study with immigrant Latinos in the poultry-processing industry also suggested that workers with collectivistic beliefs experience less work–family conflict. For this group of Latinos, work is necessary and a vital method of ensuring family well-being.[10]

Work–family conflict
conflict that occurs when an individual has to perform multiple roles: worker, spouse or partner, and often parent

MICRO-INEQUITIES AS A SOURCE OF CONFLICT

Micro-inequity
small, semiconscious message sent
with a powerful impact on the receiver

Growing attention is being paid to snubbing, or ignoring, others as a source of conflict. A **micro-inequity** is a small, semiconscious message we send with a powerful impact on the receiver. A micro-inequity might also be considered a subtle slight. Conflict occurs because a person's feelings are hurt, and he or she feels trivialized. Two examples of workplace micro-inequities follow:

■ You check your messages on a cell phone, BlackBerry, or computer screen while a coworker is talking to you. (You are devaluing the other person's time and trivializing his or her importance.)

■ A manager dismisses the first idea offered in a meeting by responding, "Okay, so who would like to get the ball rolling?" (The person who offered the idea feels like his or her suggestion is not even worth consideration and therefore has hurt feelings.)

Many companies, including IBM and Wells Fargo, offer training seminars to help managers avoid micro-inequities, including those already mentioned as well as such things as mispronouncing the names of subordinates and looking at a watch while someone else is talking.[11]

CROSS-GENERATIONAL CONFLICT

As explained in Chapter 5, differences in values across generations lead to differences in behavior. The following list presents three examples of potential work-related conflict across generations. The illustrations presented are stereotypes that apply to a *typical* member of each generation.

■ **Preferred approach to communication.** Gen X members prefer to send text messages and use cell phones and IM. Gen Y members prefer e-mail, IM, and cell phones. Baby boomers prefer e-mail, cell phones, and face-to-face communication.

■ **Approach to problem solving.** Gen X members prefer to form a team to brainstorm a solution, as well as use the Web and social networking for research. Gen Y members prefer to think up a list of solutions on their own, then call a meeting to discuss the alternative solutions. Baby boomers like to think about what has worked in the past and how it can be replicated. Then they call a meeting to discuss possible alternatives.

■ **Requirement for being respected.** Gen X members want to have their ideas valued by coworkers. Gen Y members want to have their professionalism and growing knowledge valued. Baby boomers want to have their decades of work experience and input still valued.[12]

SEXUAL HARASSMENT: A SPECIAL TYPE OF CONFLICT

Sexual harassment
unwanted sexually oriented behavior
in the workplace that results in
discomfort or interference with the job

Many employees face conflict because they are sexually harassed by a supervisor, coworker, or customers. **Sexual harassment** is an unwanted sexually oriented behavior in the workplace that results in discomfort or interference with the job. It can include an action as violent as rape or as subdued as telling a sexually toned joke. The word *unwanted* is important for understanding sexual harassment. When workers enjoy or welcome sexual behavior, such as joking and flirting, that behavior is not considered harassment.[13] Customers and clients, as well as members of a person's own organization, can be the source of harassment. Sexual harassment creates conflict because the harassed person has to make a choice between two incompatible motives. One motive is to get ahead, keep the job, or have an unthreatening work environment. But to satisfy this motive, the person is forced to sacrifice the motive of holding on to his or her moral values or preferences. For example, a person might say, "I want a raise, but to do this, must I submit to being fondled by my boss?" Here we focus on the types and frequency of sexual harassment and guidelines for dealing with the problem.

Types, Frequency, and Effects of Harassment

Two types of sexual harassment are legally recognized. Both are violations of the Civil Rights Acts of 1964 and 1991 and are, therefore, a violation of your rights. Union contracts also prohibit sexual harassment. In quid pro quo sexual harassment, the individual suffers loss (or threatened loss) of a job benefit as a result of his or her response to a request for sexual favors. The demands of a harasser can be blatant or implied. An implied form of quid pro quo harassment might take this form: A manager casually comments to one of his or her employees, "I've noticed that workers who become very close to me outside of the office get recommended for bigger raises."

The other form of sexual harassment is hostile-environment harassment. Another person in the workplace creates an intimidating, hostile, or offensive working environment. No tangible loss or psychological injury has to be suffered under this form of sexual harassment.

A major problem in controlling sexual harassment in the workplace is that most workers understand the meaning and nature of quid pro quo harassment but are confused about what constitutes the hostile-environment type. For example, some people might interpret the following behaviors to be harassing, whereas others would regard them as friendly initiatives: (a) calling a coworker "sweetie" and (b) saying to a subordinate, "I love your suit. You look fabulous."

An employee who is continually subjected to sexually suggestive comments, lewd jokes, or requests for dates is a victim of hostile-environment harassment. When the offensive behavior stems from customers or vendors, it is still harassment. Although the company cannot readily control the actions of customers or vendors, the company may still be liable for such harassment. According to several legal decisions, it is a company's job to take action to remedy harassment problems involving employees.

Surveys as well as the opinions of human resource professionals suggest that somewhere between 50 and 60 percent of women are sexually harassed at least once in their careers. One study documented what has been observed in the past: Women in male-dominated organizations, such as a construction company, tend to be harassed more frequently than women in female-dominated organizations, such as a community service center. The same study found that women in male-dominated organizations who had relatively masculine personalities were sexually harassed the most. A "masculine" personality would include being highly aggressive and cold rather than warm.[14]

Aside from being an illegal and immoral act, sexual harassment has negative effects on the well-being of its victims. The harassed person may experience job stress, lowered morale, severe conflict, and lowered productivity.

The negative effects of sexual harassment toward women were documented by University of Calgary psychology professors Chelsea R. Willness and Kibeom Lee and business professor Piers Steel. The researchers analyzed data from forty-one studies involving nearly seventy thousand respondents. Sexual harassment experiences were associated with the negative outcomes of

- Decreased job satisfaction

- Lower commitment to the employer

- Withdrawing from work, such as being absent more frequently, escapist drinking, and a desire to quit

- Decreased productivity for both the individual and the work group

- Physical and mental health problems

- Symptoms of post-traumatic stress disorder

The negative effects in the list were more likely to occur when the climate (or culture) was more tolerant of sexual harassment.[15] To draw a stereotype not intended to offend male workers, it might be part of the climate in certain male-dominated industries for male workers to harass their female counterparts. For example, "flashing" women is considered to be part of the hazing ritual for recently hired women workers in certain male-dominated manufacturing settings.

Guidelines for Preventing and Dealing with Sexual Harassment

A starting point in dealing with sexual harassment is to develop an awareness of the types of behavior that are considered sexual harassment. Often the difference is subtle. Suppose, for example, you placed copies of two nudes painted by Renoir, the French painter, on a coworker's desk. Your coworker might call that harassment. Yet if you took that same coworker to a museum to see the originals of the same nude paintings, your behavior would usually not be classified as harassment. This example illustrates that the setting of the words or behavior influences whether they are harassing. College courses in understanding and dealing with pornography have grown in popularity, and these courses often show adult (sexually explicit) films as part of the curriculum.[16] If an accounting professor in a college of business showed the same films to accounting students, he or she would most likely be charged with sexual harassment.

Education about the meaning of sexual harassment is therefore a basic part of any company program to prevent sexual harassment. The situation and your tone of voice, as well as other nonverbal behavior, contribute to perceptions of harassment. For example, the statement "You look wonderful" might be perceived as good natured versus harassing, depending on the sender's voice tone and facial expression.

The easiest way to deal with sexual harassment is to speak up before it becomes serious. The first time it happens, respond with statements such as, "I won't tolerate that kind of talk," "I dislike sexually oriented jokes," or "Keep your hands off me." Write the harasser a stern letter shortly after the first incident. Confronting the harasser in writing dramatizes your seriousness of purpose in not wanting to be sexually harassed. If the problem persists, say something to the effect of, "You're practicing sexual harassment. If you don't stop, I'm going to exercise my right to report you to management." Don't leave any room for doubt that the behavior or words you heard were unwelcome. Recurring incidents should be reported to the immediate manager, a higher-level manager, or a human resources official. When the harasser is the manager, of course, reporting the incident to him or her is ineffective. In the typical situation, the employer will keep the information it gathers as confidential as possible, consistent with state, provincial, and federal laws. Both the accused and the complainant will have a chance to present the case.

Whether you are the accused employee, the complaining one, or a potential witness, confidentiality is crucial in dealing with accusations of harassment. Two people have their reputations on the line, and you may not have all the facts.

A recommended approach to dealing with continuing harassment from the same person or persons is to maintain a dated log of the incidents. If the incidents are severe, such as unwanted groping or hugs, a copy of the log might be sent to a high-level manager in the company and a human resources professional. The principle here is that any type of documentation is better than none when dealing with a workplace issue of legal consequences.[17]

Guidelines for Dealing with False Accusations of Sexual Harassment

Many workers, especially men, will be falsely charged with sexual harassment for such reasons as revenge related to another issue, a desire to get attention, or a misunderstanding of what constitutes sexual harassment. At the extreme, some women believe that if a man disagrees with them it is because he devalues the opinion of women. As such, he is engaging in sexism, which could be interpreted as sexual harassment. Next in frequency of false accusations of sexual harassment by women against men are false accusations by men against men. A remote third category is men falsely accusing women of harassment.

A strategy for a man defending against false accusations of sexual harassment is to establish the reputation of never engaging in sexual harassment. Among the possibilities here are (a) open no pornographic Web sites at work, (b) never touch women or men in the workplace except for a handshake or an occasional sideways hug in a group setting, (c) do not confer with a woman (or perhaps a man) face-to-face unless the door is open to an office or cubicle, and (d) don't make sexually toned comments or tell sexually oriented jokes.

When falsely charged of sexual harassment, the person should present a detailed account of his or her side of the story and point out that false accusations can be considered libel. The testimony of any witness to the alleged incident would also be helpful.

The Good and Bad Sides of Conflict

◀ Learning Objective 2 ◀

Conflict over significant issues is a source of stress. We usually do not suffer stress over minor conflicts such as having to choose between wearing one sweater or another. Like stress in general, we need an optimum amount of conflict to keep us mentally and physically energetic. Handled properly, moderate doses of conflict can be beneficial. Some of the benefits that might arise from conflict can be summarized around the following key points. Figure 10-1 outlines the positive as well as the negative consequences of conflict.

1. Talents and abilities may emerge in response to conflict. When faced with a conflict, people often become more creative than they are in a tranquil situation. Assume that your employer told you that it would no longer pay for your advanced education unless you used the courses to improve your job performance. You would probably find ways to accomplish such an end.

2. Conflict can help you feel better because it satisfies a number of psychological needs. By nature, many people like a good fight. As a socially acceptable substitute for attacking others, you might be content to argue over a dispute on the job or at home.

3. As an aftermath of conflict, the parties in conflict may become united. Two battling supervisors may become more cooperative toward each other in the aftermath of confrontation. A possible explanation is that the shared experience of being in conflict with each other *sometimes* brings the parties closer.

4. Conflict helps prevent people in the organization from agreeing too readily with each other, thus making some very poor decisions. Groupthink is the situation that occurs when group members strive so hard to get along that they fail to critically evaluate each other's ideas.

FIGURE 10-1

THE GOOD AND BAD SIDES OF CONFLICT

Conflict between people and groups can have both positive and negative consequences.

Interpersonal Conflict

Positive Consequences

- Talents and abilities emerge

- Need satisfaction leads to good feelings

- Unity after conflict

- Prevents premature agreement and poor decisions

Negative Consequences

- Poor well-being

- Wasted time and energy

- Financial and emotional costs

- Fatigue

- Self-interest dominates

- Workplace violence

Despite the positive picture of conflict just painted, it can also have detrimental consequences to the individual, the organization, and society. These harmful consequences of conflict make it important for people to learn how to resolve conflict:

1. Prolonged conflict can be detrimental to some people's emotional and physical well-being. As a type of stress, prolonged conflict can lead to such problems as heart disease and chronic intestinal disorders. President Lyndon B. Johnson suffered his first heart attack after an intense argument with a young newspaper reporter.

2. Relationships damaged by conflict can have consequences that impede individual, group, and organizational performance. When coworkers have a falling out, the repercussions for the people in conflict as well as coworkers can include emotional strain, poor listening, reduced information processing, distraction from work tasks, and a lowering of commitment and satisfaction. As a result, performance suffers for the individual, group, and organization.[18]

3. People in conflict with each other often waste time and energy that could be put to useful purposes. Instead of fighting all evening with your roommate, the two of you might fix up your place. Instead of writing angry e-mail messages back and forth, two department heads might better invest that time in thinking up ideas to save the company money.

4. The aftermath of extreme conflict may have high financial and emotional costs. Sabotage—such as ruining machinery or destroying a company database—might be the financial consequence. At the same time, management may develop a permanent distrust of many people in the workforce, although only a few of them are saboteurs.

5. Too much conflict is fatiguing, even if it does not cause symptoms of emotional illness. People who work in high-conflict jobs often feel spent when they return home from work. When the battle-worn individual has limited energy left over for family responsibilities, the result is more conflict. (For instance, "What do you mean you are too tired to visit friends?" or "If your job is killing your interest in having friends, find another job.")

6. People in conflict will often be much more concerned with their own interests than with the good of the family, organization, or society. An employee in the shipping department who is in conflict with his supervisor might neglect to ship an order. And a gang in conflict with another might leave a park or beach strewn with broken glass.

7. Workplace violence erupts, including the killing of managers, previous managers, coworkers, customers, as well as spouses and partners. Intense conflict can release anger, leading to aggressive behavior and violence. Disgruntled employees, such as those recently fired, may attempt revenge by assassinating work associates. For example, the shooter in an apparent murder–suicide at the Johnson Space Center unit of NASA in 2007 had received a poor performance evaluation and feared being fired.[19] The Human Relations in Practice insert presented earlier described one company's approach to warding off workplace violence. People involved in an unresolved domestic dispute sometimes storm into the partner's workplace to physically attack him or her. Unresolved conflict and frustration from financial, marital, or other domestic problems increase the odds of a person "going ballistic" at work.

What Are Some Techniques for Resolving Conflicts?

◀ Learning Objective 3 ◀

Because of the inevitability of conflict, a successful and happy person must learn effective ways of resolving conflict. An important general consideration is to face conflict rather than letting conflict slide or smoothing over it. Ignoring or smoothing over conflict does little to resolve the real causes of conflict and seldom leads to an effective long-term solution. Here we concentrate on methods of conflict resolution that you can use on your own. Most of them emphasize a collaborative or win–win philosophy. Several of the negotiating and bargaining tactics described may be close to the competitive orientation. Human Relations Self-Assessment Quiz 10-1 gives you the opportunity to think through your style of managing conflict.

BEING ASSERTIVE

Several of the techniques for resolving conflict described here require assertiveness. Learning to express your feelings to make your demands known is also an important aspect of becoming an effective individual in general. Expressing your feelings helps you establish good relationships with people. If you aren't sharing your feelings and attitudes with other people, you will never get close to them. Here we examine the nature of assertiveness and then describe several techniques for building assertiveness.

Assertive, Nonassertive, and Aggressive Behavior

As implied previously, **assertive** people state clearly what they want or how they feel in a given situation without being abusive, abrasive, or obnoxious. People who are assertive are open, honest, and "up front" because they believe that all people have an equal right to express themselves honestly. Assertive behavior can be understood

Assertive
characteristic of people who state clearly what they want or how they feel in a given situation without being abusive, abrasive, or obnoxious; open, honest, and up-front people who believe that all people have an equal right to express themselves honestly

Human Relations Self-Assessment Quiz   10-1

Collaborative versus Competitive Styles of Conflict Management

Answer on a 1 to 5 scale how well you agree with each of the following statements: disagree strongly, disagree, neutral, agree, and agree strongly.

	Disagree Strongly	Disagree	Neutral	Agree	Agree Strongly
1. I like to see the other side squirm when I resolve a dispute.	5	4	3	2	1
2. Winning is everything when it comes to settling conflict.	5	4	3	2	1
3. After I have successfully negotiated a price, I like to see the seller smile.	1	2	3	4	5
4. I have a "smash-mouth" attitude toward resolving conflict.	5	4	3	2	1
5. In most conflict situations, one side is clearly right, and the other side is clearly wrong.	5	4	3	2	1
6. I think there are effective alternatives to strikes for settling union versus management disputes.	1	2	3	4	5
7. The winner should take all.	5	4	3	2	1
8. Conflict on the job is like a prize fight: The idea is to knock out the opponent.	5	4	3	2	1
9. I like the idea of tournaments in which first-round losers receive another opportunity to play.	1	2	3	4	5
10. Nice guys and gals usually finish first.	1	2	3	4	5

Scoring and Interpretation:

Add the point value of your scores to obtain your total. Scores of 40 and higher suggest that you prefer a *collaborative*, or *win–win*, approach to resolving conflict. You tend to be concerned about finding long-term solutions to conflict that will provide benefits to both sides. Scores of 39 and lower suggest that you prefer a *competitive* approach to resolving conflict. You want to maximize gain for yourself, with little concern about the welfare of the other side.

Nonassertive
characteristic of people who let things happen to them without letting their feelings be known

Aggressive
characteristic of people who are obnoxious and overbearing; they push for what they want with almost no regard for the feelings of others

more fully by comparing it to that shown by two other types of people. **Nonassertive** people let things happen to them without letting their feelings be known. They also prefer to avoid conflict. **Aggressive** people are obnoxious and overbearing. They push for what they want with almost no regard for the feelings of others.

Another representative assertive behavior is to ask for clarification rather than contradicting a person with whom you disagree. The assertive person asks for clarification when another person says something irritating, rather than hurling insults or telling the other person he or she is wrong. For example, assume someone says to you, "Your proposal is useless." Aggressively telling the person, "You have no right to make that judgment," shuts out any possible useful dialogue. You will probably learn more if you ask for clarification, such as "What is wrong with my proposal?"

Gestures as well as words can communicate whether the person is being assertive, nonassertive, or aggressive. Figure 10-2 illustrates these differences.

Becoming More Assertive and Less Shy

Shyness, or not being assertive, is widespread, and about 50 percent of the U.S. population is shyer than they want to be. The personality trait of shyness has positive

FIGURE 10-2 ASSERTIVE, NONASSERTIVE, AND AGGRESSIVE GESTURES

Assertive	Nonassertive	Aggressive
Well balanced	Covering mouth with hand	Pounding fists
Straight posture	Excessive head nodding	Stiff and rigid posture
Hand gestures, emphasizing key words	Tinkering with clothing or jewelry	Finger waving or pointing
	Constant shifting of weight	Shaking head as if other person isn't to be believed
	Scratching or rubbing head or other parts of the body	
Moderately loud voice	Wooden body posture	Hands on hips
	Voice too soft with frequent pauses	Voice louder than needed, fast speech

aspects, such as leading a person to think more deeply and become involved in ideas and things. (Where would the world be today if Bill Gates weren't shy as a youth?) But shyness can also create discomfort and lower self-esteem.[20] There are a number of everyday actions a person can take to overcome being nonassertive or shy. Even if the actions described here do not elevate your assertiveness, they will not backfire and cause you discomfort. After reading the following five techniques, you might be able to think of others that will work for you.[21]

1. Set a goal. Clearly establish in your mind how you want to behave differently. Do you want to speak out more in meetings? Be able to express dissatisfaction to coworkers? You can overcome shyness only by behaving differently; feeling differently is not enough.

2. Appear warm and friendly. Shy people often communicate to others through their body language that they are not interested in reaching out to others. To overcome this impression, smile, lean forward, uncross your arms and legs, and unfold your hands.

3. Conduct anonymous conversations. Try starting a conversation with strangers in a safe setting, such as a sporting event, the waiting room of a medical office, at an airport, or a waiting line at the post office or supermarket. Begin the conversation with the common experience you are sharing at the time. Among them might be these:

"How many people do you estimate are in the audience?"

"How long does it usually take before you get to see the doctor?"

"What is your prediction about our plane arriving on time?"

"Where did you get that shopping bag? I've never seen one so sturdy before."

4. Greet strangers. For the next week or so, greet many of the people you pass. Smile and make a neutral comment such as "How ya doing?" or "Great day, isn't it?" Because most people are unaccustomed to being greeted by a stranger, you may get a few quizzical looks. Many other people may smile and return your greeting. A few of these greetings may turn into conversations. A few conversations may even turn into friendships. Even if the return on your investment in greetings is only a few pleasant responses, it will boost your confidence.

5. Practice being decisive. An assertive person is usually decisive, so it is important to practice being decisive. Some nonassertive people are even indecisive when asked to make a choice from a restaurant menu. They communicate their indecisiveness by asking their friend, "What are you going to have?" or asking the server, "Could you please suggest something for me?" or "What's good?" Practice quickly sizing up the alternatives in any situation and reaching a decision. This will help you be assertive and also project an image of assertiveness.

CONFRONTATION AND PROBLEM SOLVING LEADING TO WIN–WIN

Confrontation and problem solving

the most highly recommended way of resolving conflict; method of identifying the true source of conflict and resolving it systematically

The most highly recommended way of resolving conflict is **confrontation and problem solving.** It is a method of identifying the true source of conflict and resolving it systematically. The confrontation in this approach is gentle and tactful rather than combative and abusive. It is best to wait until your anger cools down before confronting the other person to avoid being unreasonable. Reasonableness is important because the person who takes the initiative in resolving the conflict wants to maintain a harmonious working relationship with the other party. Also, both parties should benefit from the resolution of the conflict.

Assume that Jason, the person working at the desk next to you, whistles loudly while he works. You find the whistling to be distracting and annoying; you think Jason is a noise polluter. If you don't bring the problem to Jason's attention, it will probably grow in proportion with time. Yet you are hesitant to enter into an argument about something a person might regard as a civil liberty (the right to whistle in a public place). An effective alternative is for you to approach Jason directly in this manner:

You: Jason, can I talk to you about a little problem that is bugging me?

Jason: Go ahead. I don't mind listening to a problem.

You: My problem is that when you whistle it distracts me and grates on my nerves. It may be my problem, but the whistling does bother me.

Jason: I guess I could stop whistling when you're working next to me. It's probably simply a nervous habit.

An important advantage of confrontation and problem solving is that you deal directly with a sensitive problem without jeopardizing the chances of forming a constructive working relationship in the future. One reason that the method works so effectively is that the focus is on the problem at hand and not on the individual's personality.

Win–win

belief that after conflict has been resolved both sides should gain something of value

The intent of confrontation and problem solving is to arrive at a collaborative solution to the conflict. The collaborative style reflects a desire to fully satisfy the desires of both parties. It is based on an underlying philosophy of **win–win,** the belief that after conflict has been resolved, both sides should gain something of value. The user of win–win approaches is genuinely concerned about arriving at a settlement that meets the needs of both parties or at least that does not badly damage the welfare of the other side. When collaborative approaches to resolving conflict are used, the relationships among the parties are built on and improved.

"Many people avoid confronting day-to-day issues because they're not certain how to open the door to conversation in a productive manner that will preserve the relationship."
—Deb Koen, vice president of Career Development Services, Rochester, New York

Here is an example of a win–win approach to resolving conflict. A manager granted an employee a few hours off on an occasional Friday afternoon because she was willing to be on call for emergency work on an occasional weekend. Both parties were satisfied with the outcome, and both accomplished their goals.

The opposite approach to win–win conflict resolution is *win–lose,* in which one side attempts to maximize gain at the expense of the other side. Win–lose is also referred to as a *zero-sum game*, in which one side wins nothing and the other side wins everything. Many people believe that win–lose is the best approach to resolving conflict—and that is one reason so much conflict goes unresolved in the form of physical attacks on people and bankruptcies. A person with a competitive orientation is likely to engage in power struggles in which one side wins and the other loses. "My way or the highway" is a win–lose strategy. An extreme example of a win–lose strategy would be to bad-mouth a rival so he or she gets fired.

If faced with an adversary who has a win–lose orientation, a plausible defense is to keep on pointing out the benefits of finding a solution that fits both sides. A sales representative for a company that makes steel buildings (often used for ware-housing) was about to be laid off because of poor business. He proposed to his boss, "Please give me one more chance. Give me just enough salary to pay my rent and feed our newborn child. All the rest of my income will come from commissions on the sales I make." The owner conceded, and the sales rep did earn his way, so a win–lose situation emerged into a win–win.

DISARM THE OPPOSITION

When in conflict, your criticizer may be armed with valid negative criticism of you. The criticizer is figuratively clobbering you with knowledge of what you did wrong. If you deny that you have made a mistake, the criticism intensifies. A simple technique has been developed to help you deal with this type of manipulative criticism. **Disarming the opposition** is a method of conflict resolution in which you disarm the criticizer by agreeing with his or her criticism of you. The technique assumes that you have done something wrong. Disarming the opposition generally works more effectively than counterattacking a person with whom you are in conflict.

Another reason disarming the opposition is effective is that it implies you are apologizing for a mistake or an error you have made. An apology often gets the other person on your side, or at least softens the animosity. By offering an apology and regretting your mistake, you are likely to gain sympathy from the person who disapproves of what you have done or who you have wronged.

Agreeing with criticism made of you by a manager or team leader is effective because, by so doing, you are in a position to ask that manager's help in improving your performance. Most managers and team leaders recognize that it is their responsibility to help employees overcome problems, not merely to criticize them. Imagine that you have been chronically late in submitting reports during the past six months. It is time for a performance review and you know you will be reprimanded for your tardiness. You also hope that your boss will not downgrade all other aspects of your performance because of your tardy reports. Here is how disarming the situation would work in this situation:

> **Disarming the opposition**
> method of conflict resolution in which
> you disarm the criticizer by agreeing
> with his or her criticism

Your boss:	Have a seat. It's time for your performance review, and we have a lot to talk about. I'm concerned about some things.
You:	So am I. It appears that I'm having a difficult time getting my reports in on time. I wonder if I'm being a perfectionist. Do you have any suggestions?
Your boss:	I like your attitude. I think you can improve on getting your reports in on time. Maybe you are trying to make your reports perfect before you turn them in. Try not to figure out everything to four decimal places. We need thoroughness around here, but we don't want to overdo it.

REFRAMING (INCLUDING COGNITIVE RESTRUCTURING AND ASKING QUESTIONS)

Another useful approach to resolving conflict is to reexamine or *reframe* the conflict situation by looking at in a different light. What follows are two practical approaches to reframing, one by searching for the positives in the situation and the other by asking questions.

Reframing through Cognitive Restructuring

Cognitive restructuring
technique of mentally converting negative aspects into positive ones by looking for the positive elements in a situation

An indirect way of resolving interpersonal conflict is to lessen the conflicting elements in a situation by viewing them more positively. According to the technique of **cognitive restructuring** you mentally convert negative aspects into positive ones by looking for the positive elements in a situation. How you frame or choose your thoughts can determine the outcome of a conflict situation. Your thoughts influence your actions. If you search for the beneficial elements in the situation, there will be less area for dispute. Although this technique might sound like a mind game to you, it can work effectively.

Imagine that a coworker of yours, Jeff, has been asking you repeated questions about how to carry out a work procedure. You are about ready to tell Jeff, "Go bother somebody else; I'm not paid to be a trainer." Instead, you look for the positive elements in the situation. You say to yourself, "Jeff has been asking me a lot of questions. This does take time, but answering these questions is valuable experience. If I want to become a manager, I'll have to help group members with problems."

After having completed this cognitive restructuring, you can then deal with the conflict situation more positively. You might say to Jeff, "I welcome the opportunity to help you, but we need to find a mutually convenient time. In that way, I can better concentrate on my own work." To get started with cognitive restructuring, do Applying Human Relations Exercise 10-2 at the end of the chapter.

Reframing by Asking Questions

Another way to use reframing is to step back, take a deep breath, and then ask the following questions about the conflict situation arising within the work group:

- Do I fully understand the situation?

- Am I sure what my coworker is really saying?

- Is the person really angry at me or just worried and anxious?

- Have I missed something important?

- Do I have all the facts?

- What is the real issue here?

- How do I want to react in this situation?

- How would I want to be treated if the situation were reversed?

By taking such an approach, you are more likely to communicate effectively and constructively with coworkers when conflict situations arise. You carefully talk through the issues rather than becoming explosive, defensive, and argumentative. A useful scenario for reframing through questioning would be when a coworker accuses you of not carrying your fair share of the workload.[22]

APPEAL TO A THIRD PARTY

Now and then you may be placed in a conflict situation in which the other party either holds most of the power or simply won't budge. Perhaps you have tried techniques such as confrontation and problem solving or disarming the opposition, yet you cannot resolve your conflict. In these situations you may have to enlist the help of a third party with power—more power than you or your adversary has. Among such third parties is your common boss, union stewards, or human resource managers. Filing a lawsuit against your adversary is another application of the third-party technique, such as filing an age-discrimination charge.

In some situations, simply implying that you will bring in a third party to help resolve the conflict situation is sufficient for you to gain advantage. One woman felt she was repeatedly passed over for promotion because of her sex. She hinted that if she were not given fairer consideration, she would speak to the Equal Employment Opportunity Commission (EEOC). She was given a small promotion shortly thereafter. Many conflicts about sexual harassment, as well as ethnic and racial harassment, are resolved through third-party appeal.

THE GRIEVANCE PROCEDURE

The formal process of filing a complaint and resolving a dispute within an organization is the **grievance procedure.** It can also be regarded as a formal method of resolving conflict, in which a series of third parties are brought into the picture. The third-party appeal described previously skips the step-by-step approach of a formal grievance procedure. In a unionized firm, the steps in the grievance procedure are specified in the written contract between management and labor. The grievance procedure is a key part of a labor agreement because one of the union's goals is to obtain fair treatment for union members. An example of a grievance about favoritism would be, "I get the worst assignments because I'm not one of the boss's fishing buddies." An example of a grievance about discrimination would be, "I didn't get the transfer to the receptionist job because I'm fifty-five years old."

> **Grievance procedure**
> formal process of filing a complaint and resolving a dispute within an organization

The steps in the grievance procedure may vary from one to six, depending on the labor agreement or company procedures. A summary of four typical steps in a grievance procedure is presented next and outlined in Figure 10-3. If the company does not have a labor union, a specialist from the human resources department might serve as a third party.

Step 1. **Initiation of the formal grievance.** Suppose that an employee feels that he or she has been treated unfairly or that his or her rights have been violated in some way. The employee then files a grievance with the supervisor (or team leader). Most grievances end at step 1 by conversation among the employee, union steward, and the supervisor. At this stage, it makes sense to use some of the techniques for resolving conflict already described. (If the workforce is not represented by a union, another type of grievance procedure might be used.)

Step 2. **Second level of management.** If the steward, supervisor or team leader, and employee cannot reach a satisfactory solution to the conflict, it goes to the next-highest level in the organization. At this point, the grievance must be documented in writing by both sides. Which people are involved at this level depends on the size of the firm. In a small firm, a high-ranking manager might be involved in step 2.

Step 3. **A higher-level manager and the local union president.** If the grievance is not resolved at step 2, higher-level officials from both the union and the

FIGURE 10-3 THE GRIEVANCE PROCEDURE

Step 1:   Initiation of formal grievance

Employee files grievance, and discussion is held with employee, supervisor or team leader, and union steward.

If not settled

Step 2:   Second-level manager

Grievance now goes to next-highest level of management and must be documented in writing by both sides.

If not settled

Step 3:   Higher-level manager and local union president

Higher-level officials from both union and employer step in to settle dispute.

If not settled

Step 4:   Arbitration

Independent arbitrator is called in to settle the issue.

employer become involved in settling the dispute. A general principle is that at each higher step in the grievance process, comparable levels of management from both company and union face each other, or a higher-level representative from the human resources department might be involved.

Step 4.   **Arbitration.** If the grievance cannot be settled at lower steps, an independent arbitrator may be called in to settle the issue. Only about 1 percent of grievances go all the way to arbitration. Arbitration is often used as an alternative to a strike. The arbitrator has the authority to settle the dispute and must be a person acceptable to both sides.

In a small organization, step 2 is sometimes omitted. After the grievance is discussed with the union steward, and it is not resolved, the grievance is taken to the chief executive or business owner, and then to arbitration if necessary.[23]

Mediation is often confused with arbitration. A mediator is a third party who enters a controversy but holds no power of decision. The mediator helps the two sides find a resolution to their conflict. Relatively few labor agreements allow for mediation, yet mediation might be used to settle a strike. A mediator works like a marriage counselor by helping both sides come to agreement by themselves.

A grievance procedure used in many firms without a union is the **jury of peers,** whereby unresolved grievances are submitted to a panel of coworkers. The

Jury of peers

grievance procedure used in many firms without a union whereby unresolved grievances are submitted to a panel of coworkers panel chosen is similar to a jury in a criminal case. Panel members weigh evidence and, after group discussion, vote for or against the grievant. The jury-of-peers method works well when the jury members are knowledgeable about organizational justice.

The grievance processes described are formal and legalistic. Nevertheless, to represent your interests well, it is helpful to use the informal conflict-resolution techniques described earlier, such as confrontation and problem solving. Grievances are less likely to lead to labor strikes in the current business environment, partly because labor unions in manufacturing (not in the public service sector) are less powerful than in the past. As more and more manufacturing jobs are being outsourced to lower-wage regions, including other countries, employees fear job loss. Worldwide competition has taken a lot of bargaining power away from workers and unions in the manufacturing sector. Also, an increasing number of manufacturing jobs are being automated, making workers feel more vulnerable.

NEGOTIATION AND BARGAINING TACTICS

Conflicts can be considered situations calling for **negotiating and bargaining,** conferring with another person to resolve a problem. When you are trying to negotiate a fair price for an automobile, you are also trying to resolve a conflict. At first the demands of both parties seem incompatible. After haggling for a while, you will probably reach a price that is satisfactory to both sides. Negotiation has many applications in the workplace, including buying, selling, arriving at a starting salary or raise, and deciding on a relocation allowance. Negotiation may also take place with coworkers when you need their assistance. For example, you might need to strike a bargain with a coworker to handle some of your responsibilities if you are faced with a temporary overload.

Negotiating and bargaining
situation of conferring with another person to resolve a problem

A sampling of negotiating tactics to help you resolve conflict is presented next. As with other techniques of resolving conflict already presented, choose those that best fit your style and the situation. Many people feel awkward at the prospects of negotiating with a stranger, yet by learning and practicing new skills most people can become better negotiators.[24]

Create a Positive Negotiating Climate

Negotiation proceeds much more swiftly if a positive tone surrounds the session, so it is helpful to initiate a positive outlook about the negotiation meeting. A good opening line in a negotiating session is, "Thanks for fitting this meeting into your hectic schedule." Nonverbal communication such as smiling and making friendly gestures helps create a positive climate. A calm voice helps build the trust necessary for creating a positive climate.

In negotiating with coworkers for assistance, a positive climate can often be achieved by phrasing demands as a request for help. Most people will be more accommodating if you say to them, "I have a problem, and I wonder if you could help me with it." The problem might be that you need the person's time and mental energy. By giving that person a choice of offering you help, you have established a much more positive climate than by demanding assistance.[25]

Another way of creating a positive negotiating climate is to validate the other side's position by describing his or her position in your own words (a form of paraphrasing). Make a positive comment to the other person that emphasizes the value in the relationship.[26] Assume that you are renting a condo and the owner wants to raise the rent 10 percent for next year. You might state, "I recognize that your costs are rising. You are also a great a landlord. But 10 percent more rent is a little beyond my budget."

Listen First to Investigate What the Other Side Wants

Listening skills are also part of effectiveness in negotiation. Negotiation professional Bobby Covie says, "There's a saying among negotiators that whoever talks the most during a negotiation loses." Being the first to listen helps establish trust. Listening also involves paying attention to what the other side is saying.[27] A person might begin a negotiating session claiming to want a bigger share of the division budget. Yet careful listening might indicate that he really is looking for his department to receive more respect and attention. So the issue is not financial.

As shown in the example just presented, listening helps you dig for information as to why the other side wants what it does.[28] If the other side wants a bigger budget just to have more respect, there are less expensive ways to grant respect than granting a bigger share of the budget. Perhaps the manager can give the person a classier job title, rename the department, or appoint the person to head a task force. For example, the head of marketing is renamed "chief of brands," and her department "brand development."

Allow Room for Compromise, but Be Reasonable

The basic strategy of negotiation is to begin with a demand that allows room for compromise and concession. Anyone who has ever negotiated the price of an automobile, house, or used furniture recognizes this vital strategy. If you are a buyer, begin with a low bid. (You say, "I'll give you $60 for that painting" when you are prepared to pay $90.) If you are the seller, begin with a high demand. (You say, "You can have this painting for $130" when you are ready to sell it for as low as $100.) As negotiations proceed, the two of you will probably arrive at a mutually satisfactory price. This negotiating strategy can also be used for such purposes as obtaining a higher starting salary or purchasing excess inventory.

Common sense, and perhaps greed, propels many negotiators to allow *too much* room for compromise. They begin negotiations by asking way beyond what they expect to receive or offering far less than they expect to give. As a result of these implausible demands, the other side may become hostile, antagonistic, or walk away from the negotiations. Beginning with a plausible demand or offer is also important because it contributes to a positive negotiating climate.

Focus on Interests, Not Positions

Rather than clinging to specific negotiating points, keep your overall interests in mind and try to satisfy them. A negotiating point might be a certain amount of money or a concession that you must have. Remember that the true object of negotiation is to satisfy the underlying interests of both sides. Among the interests you and the other side might be trying to protect are money, lifestyle, power, and the status quo. For example, instead of negotiating for a particular starting salary, your true interests might be to afford a certain lifestyle. If the company pays all your medical and dental coverage, you can get by with a lower salary. Or your cost of living might be much lower in one city than in another. Therefore, you can accept a lower starting salary in the city with a lower cost of living.

Make a Last and Final Offer

In many circumstances, presenting a final offer will break a deadlock. You might frame your message something like this: "All I can possibly pay for your guitar is $250. You have my number. Call me when it is available at that price." Sometimes the strategy will be countered by a last and final offer from the other side: "Thanks for your interest. My absolute minimum price for this guitar is $300. Call us if that should seem okay to you." One of you will probably give in and accept the other person's last and final offer.

Role-Play to Predict What the Other Side Will Do

An advanced negotiating technique is to prepare in advance by forecasting what the other side will demand or offer. Two marketing professors from New Zealand, J. Scott Armstrong and Kesten Green, have discovered that when people role-play conflicts, their ability to predict outcomes jumps remarkably. The researchers presented 290 participants with descriptions of six actual conflicts and asked them to choose the most likely eventual decisions. The conflicts involved labor–management, commercial, and civil disputes. Five of these conflicts were chosen for role-playing. Without the use of role-playing, the participants did not do much better than chance, with a 27 percent success ratio. Next, the researchers asked twenty-one international game theorists (specialists in predicting outcomes of events) to forecast the conflict outcomes. The game theorists were correct only 28 percent of the time. (Chance here would be one-fifth, or 20 percent.)

Next, 352 students were instructed to role-play the conflicts in the six situations. The average correct decision was 61 percent versus 27 percent for the comparable group. The authors note that in more than forty years of studying forecasting, they have never seen a technique that led to such improvement in predictive accuracy.[29]

The implication for making you a better negotiator is to role-play with a friend in advance of the negotiating session you will be facing. The role-play should help you predict what the other side and you will do so you will be better prepared. For example, if your role-play suggests that the company would be willing to give you a 15 percent bonus for incredible performance, ask for a 15 percent bonus.

Allow for Saving Face

We have saved one of the most important negotiating and conflict resolution strategies for last. Negotiating does not mean that you should try to squash the other side. You should try to create circumstances that will enable you to continue working with that person if it is necessary. People prefer to avoid looking weak, foolish, or incompetent during negotiation or when the process is completed. If you do not give your opponent an opportunity to save face, you will probably create a long-term enemy.

Saving face could work in this way. A small-business owner winds up purchasing a network system for about twice what he originally budgeted. After the sale is completed, the sales rep says, "I know you bought a more professional networking rig than you originally intended. Yet I know you made the right decision. You will be able to boost productivity enough with the networked PCs to pay back the cost of the networking system in two years."

What Are Some Suggestions for Managing Anger?

◀ Learning Objective 4 ◀

Limited ability to manage anger damages the careers and personal lives of many people. The ability to manage your anger, and the anger of others, is an important human relations skill now considered to be part of emotional intelligence. A person who cannot manage anger well cannot take good advantage of his or her intellectual intelligence. As an extreme example, a genius who swears at the manager regularly will probably lose his or her job despite being so talented. Concerns about employees becoming violent have prompted many companies to offer employees training in anger management. Also, employees who become verbally abusive on the job are often sent to such training.[30] Anger-management training is likely to encompass most of the suggestions presented next. Our concern here is with several tactics for managing your own anger and that of others effectively.

MANAGING YOUR OWN ANGER

A starting point in dealing with your anger is to recognize that at its best, anger can be an energizing force. Instead of letting it be destructive, channel your anger into exceptional performance. If you are angry because you did not get the raise you thought you deserved, get even by performing so well that there will be no question you deserve a raise next time. Develop the habit of expressing your anger before it reaches a high intensity. Tell your coworker that you do not appreciate his or her listening to an iPod while you are having dinner together the first time the act of rudeness occurs. If you wait too long, you may wind up grabbing the iPod and slamming it to the floor.

As you are about to express anger, *slow down.* (The old technique of counting to ten is still effective.) Slowing down gives you the opportunity to express your anger in a way that does not damage your relationship with the other person. Following your first impulse, you might say to the other person, "You're a stupid fool." If you slow down, this might translate into "You need training on this task."

Closely related to slowing down is a technique taught in anger-management programs: Think about the consequences of what you do when you are worked up. Say to yourself as soon as you feel angry, "Oops, I'm in anger mode now. I had better calm down before I say something or do something that I will regret later." To gauge how effectively you are expressing your anger, ask for feedback. Ask a friend, coworker, or manager, "Am I coming on too strong when I express my negative opinion?"[31]

MANAGING ANGER IN OTHER PEOPLE

A variation of confrontation and problem solving has developed specifically to resolve conflict with angry people: confront, contain, and connect. *Confront* in this context means that you jump right in and get agitated workers talking to prevent future blowups. The confrontation, however, is not aimed at arguing with the angry person. If the other person yells, you talk more softly. *Contain* refers to moving an angry worker out of sight and out of earshot. At the same time you remain impartial. The supervisor is advised not to choose sides or appear to be a friend.

You *connect* by asking open-ended questions such as "What would you like us to do about your concern?" to get at the real reasons behind an outburst. Using this approach, one worker revealed he was upset because a female coworker got to leave early to pick up her daughter at day care. The man also needed to leave early one day a week for personal reasons but felt awkward making the request. So instead of being assertive (explicit and direct) about his demands, he flared up.

An important feature of the confront–contain–connect technique is that it provides angry workers a place where they can vent their frustrations and report the outbursts of others. Mediator Nina Meierding says, "Workers need a safe outlet to talk through anger and not feel they will be minimized or put their job in jeopardy."[32]

CHOOSING A TACTIC FOR RESOLVING A CONFLICT OR MANAGING ANGER

How does a person know which of the tactics or strategies presented in this chapter will work best for a given problem? The best answer is to consider both your personality and the situation. With respect to your personality, or personal style, pick a tactic for resolving conflict that you would feel comfortable using. One person might say, "I would like the tactic of making a last and final offer because I like to control situations." Another person might say, "I prefer confrontation because I'm an open and up-front type of person." Still another person might say, "I'll avoid disarming the opposition for now. I don't yet have enough finesse to carry out this technique."

In fitting the strategy to the situation, it is important to assess the gravity of the topic for negotiation or the conflict between people. A woman might say to herself, "My boss has committed such a blatant act of sexual harassment that I had best take this up with a higher authority immediately." Sizing up your opponent can also help you choose the best strategy. If she or he appears reasonably flexible, you might try to compromise. Or if your adversary is especially upset, give that person a chance to simmer down before trying to solve the problem.

Another perspective on conflict resolution and anger management is to ponder whether you too frequently need to resolve conflict and manage anger with coworkers (or other students). One indirect measure of being perceived as too conflict-prone, or too angry, is the extent to which you are ostracized (excluded) by other group members. Ostracism might also take place because a person is unpopular for other reasons, such as having a bland personality. Self-Assessment Quiz 10-2 gives you an opportunity to think through whether you are being ostracized from a group of which you are a member.

Human Relations Self-Assessment Quiz   10-2

How Much Am I Being Ostracized?

Indicate how frequently each of the statements below relates to you based on a particular work group. If a recent work group does not come to mind, use a student group, athletic team, or club. 1 = Never, 2 = Once in a while, 3 = Sometimes, 4 = Fairly often, 5 = Often, 6 = Constantly, 7 = Always.

Statement	Frequency (1–7)
1. Others ignored you at work.	_____
2. Others left the area when you entered.	_____
3. Your greetings have gone unanswered at work.	_____
4. You involuntarily sat alone in a crowded lunchroom at work.	_____
5. Others avoided you at work.	_____
6. You noticed others would not look at you at work.	_____
7. Others at work shut you out of the conversation.	_____
8. Others refused to talk to you at work.	_____
9. Others at work treated you like you weren't there.	_____
10. Others at work did not invite you or ask you if you wanted anything when they went out for a coffee break.	_____

Total Score _____

Although the authors of this scientifically developed quiz do not offer a scoring key, the higher the score, the more evident it is that you have been ostracized from the group. A score of 20 or lower would indicate almost no ostracism. Scores between 21 and 50 would indicate some ostracism. A score of 51 or higher would indicate substantial ostracism.

Source: D. Lance Ferris, Douglas D. Brown, Joseph W. Berry, and Huiwen Lian, "The Development and Validation of the Workplace Ostracism Scale," *Journal of Applied Psychology*, November 2008, p. 1366.

Concept Review and Reinforcement

Conflict, 280
Personality clash, 281
Aggressive personalities, 281
Work–family conflict, 283
Micro-inequity, 284
Sexual harassment, 284

Assertive, 289
Nonassertive, 290
Aggressive, 290
Confrontation and problem solving, 292
Win–win, 292

Disarm the opposition, 293
Cognitive restructuring, 294
Grievance procedure, 295
Jury of peers, 296
Negotiating and bargaining, 297

Summary and Review

Conflict occurs when two sets of demands, goals, or motives are incompatible. Such differences often lead to a hostile or antagonistic relationship between people. A conflict can also be considered a dispute, feud, or controversy. Among the reasons for widespread conflict are the following:

- Competition for limited resources
- Differences of opinion on work-related issues and rights
- Personality clashes
- Aggressive personalities, including bullies
- Culturally diverse teams and factional groups
- Competing work and family demands
- Micro-inequities (semiconscious slights)
- Cross-generational conflict
- Sexual harassment

Sexual harassment is one of two types: quid pro quo (a demand for sexual favors in exchange for job benefits) and creating a hostile environment. It is important for workers to understand what actions and words constitute sexual harassment and how to deal with the problem.

The benefits of conflict include the emergence of talents and abilities, constructive innovation and change, and increased unity after the conflict is settled. Among the detrimental consequences of conflict are physical and mental health problems, wasted resources, the promotion of self-interest, and workplace violence.

Techniques for resolving conflicts with others include the following:

- Being assertive. To become more assertive, set a goal, appear warm and friendly, conduct anonymous conversations, greet strangers, and practice being decisive.
- Confrontation and problem solving leading to win–win. Get to the root of the problem and resolve it systematically. The intention of confrontation and problem solving is to arrive at a collaborative solution to the conflict. The opposite of win–win is win–lose, where each side attempts to maximize gain at the expense of the other.
- Disarm the opposition. Agree with the criticizer and enlist his or her help.
- Reframing. One approach is to use cognitive restructuring by mentally converting negative aspects into positive ones by looking for the positive elements in a situation. Also use reframing by asking questions such as, "Have I missed something important?"
- Appeal to a third party (such as a government agency).
- Use the grievance procedure (a formal organizational procedure for dispute resolution), used extensively in unionized companies.
- Use negotiation and bargaining tactics, including creating a positive negotiating climate; listening first to investigate what the other side wants; allowing room for compromise but being reasonable; focusing on interests, not positions; making a last and final offer; role-playing to predict what the other side will do; and allowing for face-saving.

Limited ability to manage anger damages the careers and personal lives of many people. The ability to manage anger is part of emotional intelligence.

In managing your own anger, remember that anger can be an energizing force.

■ Express your anger before it reaches a high intensity.
■ As you are about to express your anger, slow down.
■ Ask for feedback on how you deal with anger.
■ In dealing with the anger of others, use the confront, contain (move the angry worker out of sight), and connect (ask open-ended questions to get at the real reason behind the outburst) method.

In choosing a tactic for resolving conflict, consider both your personality or style and the nature of the situation facing you. The situation includes such factors as the gravity of the conflict and the type of person you are facing. Also, think through whether if you are so conflict-prone and angry that you are being ostracized from the group.

Check Your Understanding

1. Give an example from your life of how competition for limited resources can breed conflict.
2. Some conflicts go on for decades without being resolved, such as disputes between countries that last for up to a hundred years. Why is it so difficult to resolve such conflicts?
3. Imagine that after two weeks on a new job that you want, your boss begins to treat you in a bullying, intimidating manner. What would you say to that boss?
4. Many male managers who confer with a female worker in their offices leave the door open to avoid any charges of sexual harassment. Are these managers using good judgment, or are they being overly cautious?
5. Assume that a worker is being sexually harassed by the owner of the business where he or she works. How should the harassed person deal with the problem?
6. Identify several occupations in which conflict resolution skills are particularly important.
7. Visualize a person taking the road test part of obtaining a driver's license. The candidate has done a poor job of parallel parking, and the examiner looks at him or her with a frown and says, "Not very impressive." How can this candidate make best use of the tactic "disarming the opposition"?
8. How might a person use cognitive restructuring to help deal with the conflict of having received a below-average raise while expecting an above-average raise?
9. What is your explanation of the research showing that role-playing a negotiation scenario helps people make more accurate predictions about the outcome of conflicts?
10. What do you see as the potential advantages and disadvantages of having "working dates"?

Web Corner

Labor union approach to combating sexual harassment:
www.ueunion.org Look under "Search UE."

Cognitive restructuring:
http://www.mindtools.com/stress/rt/CognitiveRestructuring.htm

Shyness:
www.shyness.com (self-quizzes about shyness, plus the opportunity to participate in research about shyness)

INTERNET SKILL BUILDER

A good Web site dealing with improving your negotiating skills is www.negotiatingcoach.com. After scanning the site describe in your own words why improving negotiating skills is important and who needs to improve their negotiating skills. As the site opens, a presenter pops into view and provides an overview of the program. What is your evaluation of the presenter's communication skills? For example, how persuasive is she?

Developing Your Human Relations Skills

Applying Human Relations Exercise 10-1

Win–Win Conflict Management

The class is organized into groups of six, with each group being divided into conflict-resolution teams of three each. The members of the team would like to find a win–win solution to the issue separating each side. The team members are free to invent their own pressing issue or choose among the following:

- Management wants to control costs by not giving cost-of-living adjustments in the upcoming year. The employee group believes that a cost-of-living adjustment is absolutely necessary.
- City management has decided to take one giant step toward reducing carbon pollution by relying on giant wind turbines for some of its energy source. The people who live near the area where the windmills will be installed object strongly to the installation of these turbines, which they consider to be unsightly, noisy, and lethal for nearby birds.
- Starbucks Coffee would like to build in a new location, adjacent to a historic district in one of the oldest cities in North America. The members of the town planning board would like the tax revenue and the jobs that the Starbucks store would bring, but they still say they do not want a Starbucks store adjacent to the historic district.

After the teams have developed win–win solutions to the conflicts, the creative solutions can be shared with teammates. Explain why each of your solutions should be classified as win–win. Describe the benefits each side received from the resolution of conflict and why you classified the outcome as a benefit.

Applying Human Relations Exercise 10-2

Reframing Through Cognitive Restructuring

The following are examples of negative statements about others in the workplace. In the space provided, cognitively restructure (reframe) each comment in a positive way.

Negative: Nancy is getting on my nerves. It takes her two weeks longer than anyone else on the team to complete her input.

Positive:

Negative: Rob is so obsessed with sports he is hurting my productivity. Where does it say in the employee handbook that I have to spend thirty minutes on Monday listening to Rob's comments on his team's weekend performance? Doesn't he know that I have a job to do and that I just don't care about his team?

Positive:

Negative: My boss is driving me crazy. He's forever telling me what I did wrong and making suggestions for improvement. He makes me feel like I'm in elementary school.

Positive:

Negotiating for a Bigger Raise

During good times and bad times, most people would like to receive a bigger raise than the one the company or immediate manager has decided to grant. But it is not widely known which negotiating tactic or tactics is likely to be the most effective. The purpose of this class activity is to conduct a survey of written comments about the best way to negotiate for a bigger raise than management probably had in store for you (assuming that you worked for somebody else). In addition, the class will attempt to categorize the three most frequently occurring tactics. Following the text, the categories include "be the first to listen," "allow room for compromise, but be reasonable," "make a last and final offer," and so forth.

Method of data collection: Each class member sends an e-mail to two experienced working adults in your network, perhaps including yourself. Ask the person to complete the following sentence:

The best way to negotiate for a bigger raise for yourself is to _____.

After collecting the responses, send them to a master e-mail or Web page for your class.

Method of analysis: After every class member has taken the opportunity to review the master file, each student compiles (a) what he or she considers the three most frequently used approaches to asking for a bigger raise and (b) which negotiating and bargaining tactics

these approaches best fit. Here is an example for clarification: Suppose one of the most frequently used approaches is for the person wanting a bigger raise to state something to the effect of this: "Give me a bigger raise or I'll look elsewhere." This approach might be classified as "Make a last and final offer."

The analysis by individuals is then sent back to the master e-mail or Web site to prepare a final summary of the results. The class might then hold a discussion as to any takeaway lessons from this exercise.

Human Relations Case Study 10-1

The Apprehensive Sales Trainee

Maria was ecstatic about the position she just landed as a sales representative for a company that provides payroll and human resources services for small companies throughout the country. She was to be assigned a sales territory in Madison, Wisconsin, where she lived with her husband and three young children. Before working her territory, Maria had to attend ten days of training and orientation at company headquarters in Boston.

One of the key trainers in the program was the national sales manager, Todd, an energetic and successful man in his early forties. During a beverage break at the first morning of the training program, Todd approached Maria and complimented her on her "great tan," and "fabulous appearance." Maria was not particularly comfortable with the comments, but she let them pass.

Before the dinner meeting on the second night of the program, Todd came over to Maria and engaged her in a brief conversation about how she was enjoying the sales training. He then handed her a business card and said, "I imagine you might get lonely being away from home for so long, so here is my business card. Please get in touch if you would just like to hang out a little with me." Maria thought that Todd was stepping over the line of good business judgment, but she just smiled politely and said,

"Thanks anyway, but I am so overwhelmed with all this great information I am receiving, I have no spare time."

The following morning, Maria received a text message from Todd on her BlackBerry that said, "Your beauty is devastating. Get back."

Maria later phoned her best friend in Madison and said, "Todd carries a lot of weight being the national sales manager. But I think his behavior toward me borders on sexual harassment. Yet five days into my job, I guess I shouldn't attempt to rat on a company executive."

Maria's friend replied, "You have got to do something. That sales manager is a predator."

Questions

1. To what extent is Todd engaging in sexual harassment toward Maria?

2. If Todd is guilty, what type of sexual harassment is he committing?

3. What steps should Maria take so she can stop the harassment yet still maintain a good working relationship with Todd?

4. What would be the positives and negatives of Maria filing a complaint about Todd with the company?

Human Relations Role-Playing Exercise

Maria Tries to Fend Off Todd

The case about Maria, the sales trainee, provides the background information and story line for this role-play. One person plays the role of serious-minded

Maria, who wants to receive high ratings in her sales training. She does not want to create problems at the company, yet she recognizes she has the right to a harassment-free environment. Another student plays the role of Todd, who is infatuated with Maria and also believes that he is powerful and somewhat irresistible to women. Todd corners Maria during a cocktail hour prior to dinner on the third night of the sales training program. He once again starts to hit on her, and Maria wants to avoid being hit on. At a least a few sets of role-players should perform in front of the class for about seven minutes.

Observers rate the role-players on two dimensions, using a 1 to 5 scale from very poor to very good. One dimension is "effective use of human relations techniques." Focus on Maria's ability to effectively deal with sexual harassment. The second dimension is "acting ability." A few observers might voluntarily provide feedback to the role players in terms of sharing their ratings and observations. The course instructor might also provide feedback.

Human Relations Case Study 10-2

Caught in a Squeeze

Heather Lopez is a product development specialist at a telecommunications company. For the past seven months she has worked as a member of a product-development team composed of people from five different departments within the company. Heather previously worked full-time in the marketing department. Her primary responsibilities were to research the market potential of an idea for a new product. The product development team is now working on a product that will integrate a company's printers and copiers.

Heather's previous position in the marketing department was a satisfactory fit for her lifestyle. Heather thought that she was able to take care of her family responsibilities and her job without sacrificing one for the other. As Heather explains, "I worked about forty-five predictable hours in my other job. My hours were essentially 8:30 a.m. to 4:30 p.m. with a little work at night and on Saturdays. But I could do the work at night and on Saturdays at home.

"Brad, my husband, and I had a smooth-working arrangement for sharing the responsibility for getting our son, Christopher, off to school and picking him up from the after-school child-care center. Brad is a devoted accountant, so he understands the importance of giving high priority to a career yet still being a good family person."

In her new position as a member of the product-development team, Heather is encountering some unanticipated demands. Three weeks ago, at 3 p.m. on a Tuesday, Tyler Watson, Heather's team leader, announced an emergency meeting to discuss a budget problem with the new product. The meeting would start at four and probably end at about six-thirty. "Don't worry, folks," said the team leader, "if it looks like we are going past six-thirty, we will order in some Chinese food."

With a look of panic on her face, Heather responded to Tyler, "I can't make the meeting. Christopher will be expecting me at about five at the child-care center. My husband is out of town, and the center closes at six sharp. So count me out of today's meeting."

Tyler said, "I said that this is an emergency meeting and that we need input from all the members. You need to organize your personal life better to be a contributing member to this team. But do what you have to do, at least this once."

Heather chose to leave the office at four-thirty so she could pick up Christopher. The next day, Tyler did not comment on her absence, but he gave her a copy of the minutes and asked for her input. The budget problem surfaced again one week later. Top-level management asked the group to reduce the cost of the new product and its initial marketing costs by 15 percent.

Tyler said to the team on a Friday morning, "We have until Monday morning to arrive at a reduced cost structure on our product development. I am dividing up the project into segments. If we meet as a team Saturday morning at eight, we should get the job done by six at night. Get a good night's rest so we can start fresh tomorrow morning. Breakfast and lunch will be on the company."

Heather could feel stress overwhelming her body, as she thought, "Christopher is playing in the finals of his soccer league tomorrow morning at ten. Brad has made dinner reservations for six, so we can make it to the *The Lion King* at 8 p.m. Should I tell Tyler he is being unreasonable? Should I quit? Should I tell Christopher and Brad that our special occasions together are less important than a Saturday business meeting?"

Questions

1. What type of conflicts is Heather facing?

2. What should Heather do to resolve her conflicts with respect to family and work responsibilities?

3. What should the company do to help deal with the type of conflict Heather is facing? Or should the company not consider Heather's dilemma to be their problem?

Human Relations Role-Playing Exercise

Heather Attempts to Resolve Her Work–Family Conflict

Imagine that Heather in the case just presented decides that her job is taking too big a toll on her personal life, but she still values her job and does not want to quit. She decides to discuss her problem with her team leader, Tyler. From Tyler's standpoint, a professional person must stand ready to meet unusual job demands and cannot expect an entirely predictable work schedule.

One person plays the role of Heather and another the role of Tyler as they attempt to resolve this incident of work–family conflict.

Observers will look for (a) how well the conflict appears to have been resolved and (b) which techniques of conflict resolution Heather and Tyler used. Other feedback observations will also be welcome.

REFERENCES

1. Jacinthe Tremblay, "Lutte Sans Merci Entre Bud et Bud," *La Presse Affaires* (http://lapresseaffaires.cyberpresse.ca), August 18, 2007. ("Nonstop Struggle between Bud and Bud.")
2. David Enrich, "Krawcheck Is Leaving Citigroup," *Wall Street Journal*, September 23, 2008, p. C8.
3. Dominic A. Infante, *Arguing Constructively* (Prospect Heights, IL: Waveland Press, 1992); Siobhan Leftwich, "Hey, You Can't Say That! How to Cope with Verbally Abusive People," *Black Enterprise*, January 2006, p. 95.
4. "Workplace Homicides in 2007," *U.S. Bureau of Labor Statistics*, http://data.bls.gov, August 26, 2008.
5. Angela Pirisi, "Teamwork: The Downside of Diversity," *Psychology Today*, November/December 1999, p. 18.
6. Jiatao Li and Donald C. Hambrick, "Factional Groups: A New Vantage on Demographic Faultlines, Conflict, and Disintegration in Work Teams," *Academy of Management Journal*, October 2005, pp. 794–813.
7. Beth A. Livingston and Timothy A. Judge, "Emotional Responses to Work–Family Conflict: An Examination of Gender Role Orientation among Working Men and Women," *Journal of Applied Psychology*, January 2008, pp. 207–216.
8. Adapted from Sue Shellenberger, "Dinner and a PowerPoint," *Wall Street Journal*, June 28, 2007, p. D1.
9. Paul E. Spector et al. (consisting of 22 researchers), "Cross-National Differences in Relationships of Work Demands, Job Satisfaction, and Turnover Intentions with Work–Family Conflict," *Personnel Psychology*, Winter 2007, pp. 805-835.
10. Joseph G. Gryzwacz et al., "Work–Family Conflict: Experiences and Health Implications among Immigrant Latinos," *Journal of Applied Psychology*, July 2007, pp. 1119–1130.
11. The examples, but not the interpretations, are from Julie Fawe, "Why Your Boss May Start Sweating the Small Stuff," *Time*, March 20, 2006, p. 80. See also Joann S. Lublin, "How to Stop the Snubs That Demoralize You and Your Colleagues," *Wall Street Journal*, December 7, 2004, p. B1.
12. Chris Pentila, "Talking about My Generation," *Entrepreneur*, March 2009, p. 55.
13. Jennifer L. Berdhal and Karl Aquino, "Sexual Behavior at Work: Fun or Folly?" *Journal of Applied Psychology*, January 2009, p. 34.
14. Jennifer Berdahl, "The Sexual Harassment of Uppity Women," *Journal of Applied Psychology*, March 2007, pp. 425–437.
15. Chelsea R. Willness, Piers Steel, and Kibeom Lee, "A Meta-Analysis of the Antecedents and Consequences of Workplace Sexual Harassment," *Personnel Psychology*, Spring 2007, pp. 127–162.
16. Lisa Takeuchi Cullen, "Sex in the Syllabus," *Time*, April 3, 2006, pp. 80–81.
17. "Sexual Harassment Fact Sheet," www.doter.ost.dot.gov/Documents/complaint/Preventing_SexualHarassment.htm, p. 5.
18. Data synthesized in Hong Ren and Barbara Gray, "Repairing Relationship Conflict: How Violation Types and Culture Influence the Effectiveness of Restoration Rituals, *Academy of Management Review*, January 2009, p. 105.
19. Rasha Madkour, "NASA Gunman Thought He Was Going to Be Fired," The Associated Press, April 22, 2007, p. 19A.
20. Bernardo J. Carducci, *Shyness: A Bold Approach* (New York: HarperCollins, 1999).
21. Philip Zimbardo, *Shyness: What It Is, What to Do about It* (Reading, MA: Addison-Wesley, 1977), pp. 220–226; Mel Silberman with Freda Hansburg, *PeopleSmart* (San Francisco: Berrett-Koehler, 2000), pp. 75–76.
22. "Conquer Conflict with This Technique," *Manager's Edge*, September 7, 2005. As adapted from Maria Broomhower, "Dissolving Conflict through Reframing," http://www.conflict911.com.
23. Stephen P. Robbins and David A. DeCenzo, *Supervision Today!*, 4th ed. (Upper Saddle River, NJ: Pearson Prentice Hall, 2004), p. 438.
24. Marc Deiner, "Speak Up: Hate to Negotiate? That's Still No Excuse to Avoid Learning the Skill," *Entrepreneur*, September 2004, p. 79.
25. Joseph D'O'Brian, "Negotiating with Peers: Consensus, Not Power," *Supervisory Management*, January 1992, p. 4.
26. "To Agree or Disagree?" *Chicago Tribune Career Builder*, November 4, 2007, p. 1, Section 6.
27. Quoted in Brenda Goodman, "The Art of Negotiation," *Psychology Today*, January/February 2007, p. 65.
28. Deepak Malhotra and Max H. Bazerman, "Investigative Negotiation," *Harvard Business Review*, September 2007, pp. 72–78.
29. J. Scott Armstrong, "Forecasting in Conflicts: How to Predict What Your Opponents Will Do," *Knowledge@Wharton* (www.knowledge.wharton.upenn.edu), February 13, 2002, p. 1.
30. Linda Wasmer Andrews, "When It's Time for Anger Management," *HR Magazine*, June 2005, pp. 131–135.
31. Fred Pryor, "Is Anger Really Healthy?" *Pryor Management Newsletter*, February 1996, p. 3.
32. The quote and technique are both from Kathleen Doheny, "It's a Mad, Mad Corporate World," *Working Woman*, April 2000, pp. 71–72.

11

Becoming an Effective Leader

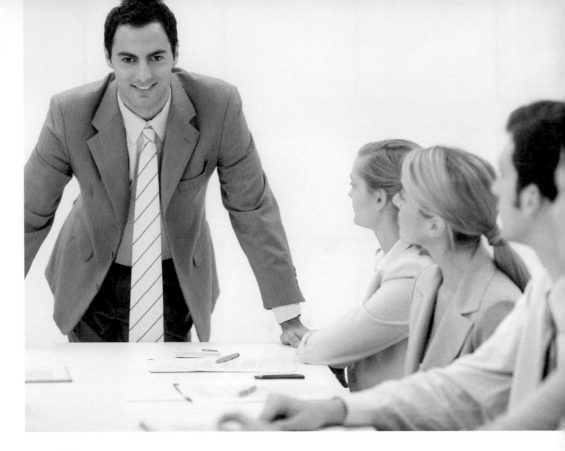

Outline

1 What Are Some Traits and Characteristics of Effective Leaders?
Self-Confidence and Courage
Emotional Intelligence
Trustworthiness and Character
Strong Work Motivation and High Energy
Cognitive Skills and Openness to Experience
Assertiveness
Charisma

2 What Are Some Behaviors and Skills of Effective Leaders?
Practice Strong Ethics
Direction Setting
Develop Partnerships with People
Help Group Members Reach Goals and Achieve Satisfaction
Set High Expectations
Give Frequent Feedback on Performance
Manage a Crisis Effectively
Ask the Right Questions
Be a Servant Leader

3 What Is Leadership Style, and What Is Style Flexibility?
The Classic Dimensions of Consideration and Initiating Structure
The Participative (Team) Leadership Style
Style Flexibility and Adaptability

4 How Does a Leader Get Along Well with Subordinates?
The Leader–Member Exchange Model
Suggestions for Attaining Good Relationships with Subordinates

5 How Do You Develop Your Leadership Potential?

6 What Are Several Key Challenges of Being a First-Time Leader?

O ne April day several years ago, Federal Deposit Insurance Corp. chairman Sheila Bair saw a stark reminder of the human side of the foreclosure crisis. Attending a foreclosure-prevention workshop in Los Angeles, she saw hundreds of homeowners of all backgrounds lined up for hours to be admitted to the event, where they desperately hoped to receive help or advice that would allow them to keep their homes.

For Bair, the outspoken and politically savvy head of the FDIC, the images of so many borrowers trying to salvage their lives left an impression.

"This myth of all these people making sophisticated calculations and trying to game the system, that wasn't it," Bair says of the event hosted by California governor Arnold Schwarzenegger. "These were just regular people, working families trying to hold onto their homes. They were scared, and I saw a lot of fear on their faces, and I think that struck me more than anything."

The event, like many others, solidified in Bair's mind that the federal government needed to take much more aggressive action to stem the record numbers of foreclosures at the center of the growing economic crisis. It also reinforced her belief that compassion should be a key part of the equation for policy makers.

"People say we should punish all these people because they got these mortgages they couldn't afford. Why? Who is that going to help?" Bair said in her office overlooking the Old Executive Office Building in Washington, DC. "It's going to put more empty houses on the market, and more houses where the lawn maybe isn't going to get mowed and the windows may be broken, or the owner isn't there so they aren't paying taxes."[1]

Leadership
the process of bringing about positive changes and influencing others to achieve worthwhile goals

To become chairman of the FDIC, Sheila Bair no doubt has many good leadership qualities, but on display here is one of the many leadership characteristics or behaviors described in this chapter—being compassionate to help work through a crisis. **Leadership** is the process of bringing about positive changes and influencing others to achieve group goals and coordinating the pursuit of these goals.[2] The key words in understanding leadership are *change* and *influence*. A leader often challenges the status quo and brings about improvements. A leader also influences people to do things, such as achieve higher performance that they would not do otherwise. We therefore measure the effectiveness of leaders in terms of the results they attain, such as running a profitable medical clinic or a winning athletic team.

Effective leadership at the top of organizations is necessary for their prosperity and even survival. Effective leadership is also important throughout the organization, particularly in working with entry-level workers. Good supervision is needed to help employees deal with customer problems, carry out their usual tasks, and maintain high quality.

The study of leadership warrants your attention because today people at all levels in the organization are expected to exert some leadership. Organizations seek people to exert leadership at all levels by giving many of them an opportunity to engage in such tasks as motivating others and setting goals.[3] Even if your job title does not include the mention of management responsibility, you will often be called on to be a temporary leader, such as being appointed the head of a committee or project. Our approach to the vast topic of leadership encompasses the attributes and behaviors of leaders, leadership style, getting along with subordinates, and developing your leadership potential.

▶ Learning Objective 1 ▶

What Are Some Traits and Characteristics of Effective Leaders?

Leadership effectiveness
inner quality of a leader who helps the group accomplish its objectives without neglecting satisfaction and morale

A major thrust to understanding leaders and leadership is to recognize that effective leaders have the "right stuff." In other words, certain inner qualities contribute to leadership effectiveness in a wide variety of situations. **Leadership effectiveness** in this situation means that the leader helps the group accomplish its objectives without neglecting satisfaction and morale. The characteristics that contribute to effectiveness depend somewhat on the situation. A supervisor in a meatpacking plant and one in an information technology department will need different sets of personal characteristics. The situation includes such factors as the people being supervised, the job being performed, the company, and the cultural background of employees.

Another important perspective on the trait approach is that leadership effectiveness usually depends on the right combination of personal characteristics in a given situation.[4] For example, the leader of a group of packaging design specialists might need to be open to new ideas. At the same time the leader might need to have a good sense of humor, because packing specialists are creative enough to appreciate what is funny.

In the next several pages, we describe some of the more important traits and characteristics of leaders. Many of these traits and characteristics can be developed and refined. Figure 11-1 outlines the seven key traits.

SELF-CONFIDENCE AND COURAGE

Self-confidence is necessary for leadership because it helps assure group members that activities are under control. The confidence centers on a belief that a person

FIGURE 11-1

SEVEN KEY LEADERSHIP TRAITS

has the knowledge, skills, and abilities associated with leading others. As a result, the person has *leader self-efficacy*.[5]

Assume you are a manager in a company that is facing bankruptcy. At a meeting you attend, the chief executive officer sobs, "I'm sorry, I'm just no good in a crisis. I don't know what's going to happen to the company. I don't think I can get us out of this mess. Maybe one of you would like to try your hand at turning around the company." You would probably prefer that the CEO behave in a confident, assured manner.

In other leadership situations as well, the leader who functions best is self-confident enough to reassure others and to appear in control. But if the leader is so self-confident that he so she will not admit errors, listen to criticism, or ask for advice, that too creates problems. Being too self-confident can lead to the person to ignore potential problems, thinking, "I can handle whatever comes my way."

One of many possible examples of a self-confident leader is Oprah Winfrey, who is well-known as a show business celebrity yet is also the head of an extensive business empire, including the multimedia conglomerate Harpo Inc. and the Oprah Winfrey Network (OWN). During staff meetings, Oprah is typically quite positive about the future of her company. "This is the foundation of greater things to come," she often told her managers as she developed an array of partnerships and spinoffs.[6] Self-confidence often takes the form of the courage to face the challenges of taking prudent risks and taking initiative in general. Courage comes from the heart, as suggested by the French word for heart, *coeur*. Leaders must be able to face up to responsibility and be willing to put reputations on the line, even if this means taking a course of action others would not advise.

Being confident and courageous does not exclude a leader from also displaying humility. People who are too confident and courageous will often neglect to welcome input from others or listen to criticism. A leader with an appropriate degree of humility will also admit to having made a mistake and is therefore willing to change course, as in the following example:

The manager of an upscale restaurant was concerned that because customers were cutting back on expenses in general, it would be a good idea to offer less expensive menu items to the public. The manager's decision was to include a "budget menu" to accompany the regular menu. About 75 percent of customers shifted to the budget menu, resulting in a serious revenue drain. The manager then told his workers that he had made a dumb move. The budget menu was removed, yet one low-priced meal was left on both the dinner and lunch menu. Soon the economy picked up, and restaurant revenues returned to normal.

EMOTIONAL INTELLIGENCE

Emotional intelligence is considered a major contributor to leadership effectiveness. In review, the concept refers to managing ourselves and our relationships effectively with an emphasis on dealing with emotion. Intelligence of this type can be developed through working on some of its components, such as learning to control your temper and developing empathy by listening to people carefully. It is also important to develop the habit of looking to understand the feelings and emotions of people around you. Also ask yourself, "How do I feel about what's going on here?" When you have a hunch about people's motives, look for feedback in the future to see if you were right. Here is an example of applying emotional intelligence:

> Visualize yourself as a team leader. Vanessa, one of the team members, says to you, "I'm worried about Rick. I think he needs help. He looks like he has a drinking problem." If you have good emotional intelligence, you might think to yourself, "I wonder why Vanessa is telling me this. Is she simply being helpful? Or is she out to backstab Rick?" So you seek some tangible evidence about Rick's alleged problem before acting. You would also seek to spend more time with Vanessa so you can better understand her motives. Your investigation might reveal that Vanessa and Rick are rivals and have a personality clash.

With much less emotional intelligence, you would immediately get in touch with Rick, accuse him of having a drinking problem, and tell him to get help or get fired. With good emotional intelligence you would also be quite hesitant to accuse an employee of being alcoholic without substantial evidence.

Many business leaders encounter difficulties for what appears to be a deficit in emotional intelligence. A case in point is former Coca-Cola president Stephen J. Heyer. Despite his marketing brilliance, he was passed over for the CEO position. Among the reasons were his confrontational style, including his tendency to belittle other executives and staffers. Heyer rebounded and became the CEO of Starwood Hotels and Resorts. However, his pattern of low emotional intelligence continued at Starwood. Heyer was accused of ten instances of creating a hostile work environment for female employees and was forced to resign. (Heyer denied all charges.)[7]

TRUSTWORTHINESS AND CHARACTER

Trust

a person's confidence in another individual's intentions and motives and in the sincerity of that individual's words

Considerable evidence exists that being trustworthy or honest contributes to being an effective leader. An effective leader is supposed to *walk the talk*, thereby showing a consistency between deeds (walking) and words (talking). Group members consistently believe that leaders must display honesty, integrity, and credibility. Leaders themselves believe that honesty and integrity make a difference in their effectiveness.[8] In this context, **trust** is defined as a person's confidence in another individual's intentions and motives and in the sincerity of that individual's words. Leaders must be trustworthy, and they must also trust the group members.

It takes a leader a long time to build trust, yet one brief incident of untrustworthy behavior can destroy it. An example of untrustworthy behavior would be using company money for private purposes or sexually harassing a team member. Leaders are usually allowed a fair share of honest mistakes. In contrast, dishonest mistakes quickly erode leadership effectiveness. Meg Whitman, the former CEO of eBay, exemplifies a leader who many people—employees and members of the eBay community—trust. Part of the trust comes from her being self-effacing and low key and the fact that she responds directly to e-mail messages from buyers and sellers.[9] The small percentage of fraudulent people who prey on eBay users have not diminished trust in Whitman because the criminals are not eBay employees.

Having certain character traits contributes to being trustworthy and being perceived as a trustworthy person. **Character** in this context refers to doing the right things despite outside pressures to do the opposite. Being of good character also includes leaving enduring marks that set one apart from another.[10] To be of good character is to be moral. The U.S. Air Force has developed a list of twelve attributes that are part of its character program. Air Force leaders are expected to have many of these attributes, and leaders in other organizations will benefit as well. Figure 11-2 lists and defines these twelve traits.

> **Character**
> doing the right things despite outside pressures to do the opposite; includes leaving enduring marks that set one apart from another; being moral

STRONG WORK MOTIVATION AND HIGH ENERGY

Leadership positions tend to be both physically and mentally demanding. A successful leader must be willing to work hard and long to achieve success. Many business leaders often work seventy-hour weeks, as do a large number of business owners. Many leaders appear to be driven by a need for self-fulfillment. Another fundamental reason strong work motivation is required for effectiveness is that a person has to be willing to accept the heavy responsibility that being a supervisor entails. As one department manager said, "Whoever thought being a manager would mean that I would have to fire a single parent who has three children to feed and clothe?"

COGNITIVE SKILLS AND OPENNESS TO EXPERIENCE

Cognitive skills, as well as personality, are important for leadership success. Problem solving and intellectual skills are referred to collectively as **cognitive skills.** The term *cognition* refers to the mental process of faculty by which knowledge is gathered.

> **Cognitive skills**
> problem-solving and intellectual skills

---

1. *Integrity.* Consistently adhering to a moral or ethical code or standard. A person who consistently chooses to do the "right thing" when faced with alternate choices.
2. *Honesty.* Consistently being truthful with others.
3. *Loyalty.* Being devoted and committed to one's organization, supervisors, coworkers, and subordinates.
4. *Selflessness.* Genuinely concerned about the welfare of others and willing to sacrifice one's personal interest for others and their organization.
5. *Compassion.* Concern for the suffering or welfare of others and their organization.
6. *Competency.* Capable of performing tasks assigned in a superior fashion and excels in all task assignments. Is effective and efficient.
7. *Respectfulness.* Shows esteem for and consideration and appreciation of other people.
8. *Fairness.* Treats people in an equitable, impartial, and just manner.
9. *Responsibility and self-discipline.* Can be depended on to make rational and logical decisions and to do tasks assigned. Can perform tasks assigned without supervision.
10. *Decisiveness.* Capable of making logical and effective decisions in a timely manner. Does not "shoot from the hip" but does promptly make a good decision after considering data appropriate to the decision.
11. *Spiritual appreciation.* Values the spiritual diversity among individuals with different backgrounds and cultures and respects all individuals' rights to differ from others in their beliefs.
12. *Cooperativeness.* Willingness to work or act together with others in accomplishing a task or some common end or purpose.

Source: Copyright © 2000 by William H. Hendrix.

FIGURE 11-2

CHARACTER ATTRIBUTES OF LEADERS

To inspire people, bring about constructive changes, and solve problems creatively, leaders need to be mentally sharp. A synthesis of 151 different studies examining the relationship between intelligence and leadership performance found a slight positive relationship between the two variables. But when the leader's job emphasized playing an active role in making decisions about the work of the group (such as helping solve technical problems), intelligence showed a higher relationship with performance.[11]

A cognitive skill of major importance is *knowledge of the business*, or technical competence. An effective leader has to be technically or professionally competent in some discipline, particularly when leading a group of specialists. It is difficult for the leader to establish rapport with group members when he or she does not know what they are doing. A related damper on leadership effectiveness is when the group does not respect the leader's technical skill. Good practical intelligence (*street smarts*) is also part of an effective leader's intellectual makeup. A leader with high practical intelligence could size up a good opportunity without spending an extensive amount of time analyzing what could possibly go wrong.

Closely related to cognitive skills is the personality characteristic of **openness to experience,** a positive orientation toward learning. People who have considerable openness to experience have well-developed intellects. Traits commonly associated with this dimension of the intellect include being imaginative, cultured, curious, original, broad-minded, intelligent, and artistically sensitive.

Openness to experience
personality characteristic of positive orientation toward learning; people with considerable openness to experience have well-developed intellects

ASSERTIVENESS

Assertiveness is a widely recognized leadership trait. If you are self-confident, it is easier to be assertive with people. An assertive leader might say, "I know that the ice storm put us out of business for four days, but we can make up the time by working smart and pulling together. Within thirty days, we will have met or surpassed our goals for the quarter." This statement reflects self-confidence in leadership capabilities and assertiveness in expressing thoughts.

Assertiveness helps leaders perform many tasks and achieve goals. Among them are confronting group members about their mistakes, demanding higher performance, and setting high expectations. An assertive leader will also make demands on higher management, such as asking for equipment needed by the group. As with many personality dimensions, the right amount of assertiveness works best. Studies conducted with working business students who were asked to size up their boss found that being too low or too high on assertiveness was perceived as a leadership weakness.[12]

CHARISMA

An important quality for leaders at all levels is **charisma,** a type of charm and magnetism that inspires others and makes them loyal to the leader. Not every leader has to be charismatic, yet to be an effective leader you often need some degree of this personality quality. Being charismatic helps leaders form better relationships with workers, who might then work harder for them. A charismatic leader who inspires people therefore contributes to attaining results or being effective.

Charisma
type of charm and magnetism that inspires others; important quality for leaders at all levels

A leader's charisma is determined by the subjective perception of him or her by other people. Therefore, it is impossible for even the most effective leaders to inspire and motivate everyone. Even popular business leaders are disliked by some of their employees. For example, Steve Jobs, cofounder of Apple Computer, is regarded as charismatic and inspirational by many employees and company outsiders. Yet, he is also perceived to be arrogant and obnoxious by many others who work with him because of his explosive temper and second-guessing their decisions.

Jobs also admits to being obnoxious on occasion. Charisma encompasses many traits and characteristics. Here we focus on vision, passion, enthusiasm, excitement, and humor.

Vision

Top-level leaders need a visual image of where the organization is headed and how it can get there. The person with vision can help the organization or group establish a vision. The progress of the organization depends on the executive having a vision, or an optimistic version of the future. Effective leaders project ideas and images that excite people and therefore inspire employees to do their best. Leadership positions of lesser responsibility also call for some vision. Each work group in a progressive company might be expected to form its own vision, such as "We will become the best accounts receivable group in the entire auto replacement parts industry."

Vision, similar to other leadership characteristics, usually has the biggest impact when combined with one or more other characteristics. Marian Elen Lagomasino, the CEO of Asset Management Advisors LLC, has this to say about vision:

> Leaders need a vision of what they want to have, then they need to have the courage to make it happen. It's most important to have courage because you need to be able to communicate that vision to people in your company. As you add others to your company and they see your vision, they will want to do what needs to get done to realize that vision.[13]

Passion, Enthusiasm, and Excitement

Charismatic leaders are passionate about their work and their group members. Part of the reason charismatic leaders can readily be passionate, enthusiastic, and excited is that they tend to be extraverted. The extraversion is most strongly associated with the type of charismatic leader who brings about major changes in the organization or an organizational unit.[14] The charismatic business owner is likely to think about the company's product or service day and night. Because of their contagious excitement, charismatic leaders stimulate group members. Workers respond positively to enthusiasm, especially because enthusiasm may be perceived as a reward for good performance. Enthusiasm is also effective because it helps build good relationships with group members. Spoken expressions of enthusiasm include such statements as "great job" and "I love it." Andrea Jung, the stylish and inspirational chief executive officer of Avon Products, tells Avon representatives at company meetings that she loves them. The leader can express enthusiasm nonverbally through gestures, nonsexual touching, and so forth. The accompanying Human Relations in Practice provides a famous business leader's perspective on the importance of passion in building an enterprise.

An important positive consequence of the passion and enthusiasm of the leader is that they contribute to the emotional well-being of group members. A study with forty-eight groups of firefighters found that firefighters under the command of a charismatic officer were happier than those groups reporting to supervisors low in charisma. Both charisma and happiness were measured by questionnaires of known accuracy.[15]

The emotional state of followers (group members) is also significant for understanding how charisma works. When people are in a state of emotional arousal, such as facing a crisis or an unusual success, they are more ready to perceive a leader as being charismatic.[16] A historically important example is when Chrysler Corporation was facing bankruptcy in the late 1970s. Chairman Lee Iacocca spearheaded a federal government loan to save the company. In the process, the name Iacocca became almost synonymous with charisma. Chrysler employees, as well as suppliers and many others, were in dire need of a charismatic leader.

Human Relations in Practice

Apple Cofounder Steve Wozniak Operates with Passion

Steve Wozniak, the cofounder of Apple Computer, told a Stanford University School of Business audience, "You are not going to be too successful unless it's in your heart and is your passion. You want to be the sort of person who can create a company, who can develop a product and service, and then take it to another level." It's not easy for startups to find engineers with both broad expertise and passion for the work, said Wozniak.

To get started through their often-lean early years, leaders also need to be multiskilled and have complementary strengths, Wozniak said. He cited the example of Apple cofounder Steve Jobs, the long-time Apple CEO. "Me? I just wanted to build the best computer possible. So it was the ideal team—because what I could do he couldn't do and vice versa."

Saying he didn't want his business success to change him, Wozniak recalled important periods in life: teaching fifth-grade students for eight years and how he built his own ham radio when he was in the fifth grade.

Today he continues to connect with young entrepreneurs. "I try to find young people who remind me of Steve Jobs and me when we were starting, and I try to get involved with them and help them out with their startups, their companies, their directions," Wozniak said. "I love being around those things, not the big huge public company realms. My friends are interesting technical people working on neat little things. Sometimes, they are a little bit on the hacker side, but they're the interesting people in the world. They're the ones you'll see movies about."

Source: Michele Chandler, "Wozniak Reflects on Founding Apple Computer," *Stanford Graduate School of Business News* (www.gsh.standarford.edu/news), March 2008.

Sense of Humor

Humor is a component of charisma and a contributor to leadership effectiveness. Humor helps leaders influence people by reducing tension, relieving boredom, and defusing anger. The most effective form of humor by a leader is tied to the leadership situation. It is much less effective for the leader to tell rehearsed jokes. A key advantage of a witty, work-related comment is that it indicates mental alertness. A canned joke is much more likely to fall flat.

A sales manager was conducting a meeting about declining sales. He opened the meeting by saying, "Ladies and gentlemen, just yesterday I completed a spreadsheet analysis of our declining sales. According to my spreadsheet analysis, if we continue our current trend, by the year 2016 we will have sales of negative $3,750,000. No company can support those figures. We've got to reverse the trend." The manager's humor helped dramatize the importance of reversing the sales decline.

A caution about charisma is that it is not entirely dependent on personal characteristics but also on what a person accomplishes. Achieving outstanding results may lead to being perceived as charismatic. An example would be if an almost-forgotten coach suddenly has an outstanding season and is then described as charismatic.

Although inherited characteristics, such as energy, contribute to charisma, most people can develop some charismatic qualities. Figure 11-3 presents suggestions for becoming more charismatic.

FIGURE 11-3 SUGGESTIONS FOR BECOMING MORE CHARISMATIC

Following are a number of suggestions for behaving charismatically, all based on characteristics and behaviors often found among charismatic leaders and other charismatic persons.

1. *Communicate a vision.* A charismatic leader offers an exciting image of where the organization is headed and how to get there. A vision is more than a forecast because it describes an ideal version of the future of an entire organization or an organizational unit, such as a department. The supervisor of paralegal services might communicate a vision such as, "Our paralegal group will become known as the most professional and helpful paralegal group in Arizona."

2. *Make frequent use of metaphors and analogies.* To inspire people, the charismatic leader uses colorful language and exciting metaphors and analogies. Develop metaphors to inspire people around you. To pick up the spirits of her maintenance group, a maintenance supervisor told the group, "We're a lot like the heating and cooling system in a house. A lot of people don't give us much thought, but without us their lives would be very uncomfortable."

3. *Inspire trust and confidence.* Make your deeds consistent with your promises. As mentioned earlier in this chapter, being trustworthy is a key leadership trait. Get people to believe in your competence by making your accomplishments known in a polite, tactful way.

4. *Be highly energetic and goal oriented.* Impress others with your energy and resourcefulness. To increase your energy supply, exercise frequently, eat well, and get ample rest. You can also add to an image of energy by raising and lowering your voice frequently and avoiding a slow pace.

5. *Be emotionally expressive and warm.* A key characteristic of charismatic leaders is the ability to express feelings openly. In dealing with team members, refer to your feelings at the time, such as "I'm excited because I know we are going to hit our year-end target by mid-October." Nonverbal emotional expressiveness, such as warm gestures and frequent touching (nonsexual) of group members, also exhibits charisma.

6. *Make ample use of true stories.* An excellent way of building rapport is to tell stories that deliver a message. Storytelling adds a touch of warmth to the teller and helps build connections among people who become familiar with the same story.

7. *Smile frequently, even if you are not in a happy mood.* A warm smile seems to indicate a confident, caring person, which contributes to a perception of charisma.

8. *Be candid.* Practice saying directly what you want rather than being indirect and evasive. If you want someone to help you, don't ask, "Are you busy?" Instead, ask, "Can you help me with a problem I'm having right now?"

9. *Make everybody you meet feel that he or she is quite important.* For example, at a company social gathering, shake the hand of every person you meet. Also, thank people frequently both orally and by written notes.

10. *Stand up straight and use other nonverbal signals of self-confidence.* Practice having good posture. Minimize fidgeting, scratching, foot tapping, and speaking in a monotone. Walk at a rapid pace without appearing to be panicked. Dress fashionably without going to the extreme that people notice your clothes more than they notice you. Shake hands firmly without creating pain, and make enough eye contact to notice the color of the other person's eyes. When you take that much trouble, you project care and concern.

11. *Be willing to take personal risks.* Charismatic leaders are typically risk takers, and risk taking adds to their charisma. Risks you might take include suggesting a bright but costly idea and recommending that a former felon be given a chance in your firm.

What Are Some Behaviors and Skills of Effective Leaders?

◀ Learning Objective 2 ◀

The personal traits, skills, and characteristics just discussed help create the potential for effective leadership. A leader also has to *do* things that influence group members to achieve good performance. Workers want their leaders to be charismatic but also want competence and results.[17] The behaviors or skills of leaders described next contribute to productivity and morale in most situations. Before studying the behaviors and skills of effective leaders, do Human Relations Self-Assessment Quiz 11-1. The exercise will help you understand how ready you are to assume a leadership role. Taking the quiz will also give you insight into the type of thinking that is characteristic of leaders.

Human Relations Self-Assessment Quiz   11-1

Readiness for the Leadership Role

Indicate the extent to which you agree with each of the following statements. Use a 1 to 5 scale: (1) disagree strongly, (2) disagree, (3) neutral, (4) agree, (5) agree strongly. If you do not have leadership experience, imagine how you might react to the questions if you were a leader.

1.	It is enjoyable having people count on me for ideas and suggestions.	1	2	3	4	5
2.	It would be accurate to say that I have inspired other people.	1	2	3	4	5
3.	It's a good practice to ask people provocative questions about their work.	1	2	3	4	5
4.	It's easy for me to compliment others.	1	2	3	4	5
5.	I like to cheer up people even when my own spirits are down.	1	2	3	4	5
6.	What my team accomplishes is more important than my personal glory.	1	2	3	4	5
7.	Many people imitate my ideas.	1	2	3	4	5
8.	Building team spirit is important to me.	1	2	3	4	5
9.	I would enjoy coaching other members of the team.	1	2	3	4	5
10.	It is important to me to recognize others for their accomplishments.	1	2	3	4	5
11.	I would enjoy entertaining visitors to my firm even if it interfered with my completing a report.	1	2	3	4	5
12.	It would be fun for me to represent my team at gatherings outside our department.	1	2	3	4	5
13.	The problems of my teammates are my problems, too.	1	2	3	4	5
14.	Resolving conflict is an activity I enjoy.	1	2	3	4	5
15.	I would cooperate with another unit in the organization even if I disagreed with the position taken by its members.	1	2	3	4	5
16.	I am an idea generator on the job.	1	2	3	4	5
17.	It's fun for me to bargain whenever I have the opportunity.	1	2	3	4	5
18.	Team members listen to me when I speak.	1	2	3	4	5
19.	People have asked to me to assume the leadership of an activity several times in my life.	1	2	3	4	5
20.	I've always been a convincing person.	1	2	3	4	5

Total Score _____

Scoring and Interpretation:

Calculate your total score by adding the numbers circled. An interpretation of the scoring is as follows:

90–100	High readiness for the leadership role
60–89	Moderate readiness for the leadership role
40–59	Some uneasiness with the leadership role
39 or less	Low readiness for carrying out the leadership role

   If you are already a successful leader and you scored low on this questionnaire, ignore your score. If you scored surprisingly low and you are not yet a leader, or you are currently performing poorly as a leader, study the statements carefully. Consider changing your attitude or your behavior so that you can legitimately answer more of the questions with a 4 or 5. Studying the rest of this chapter will give you additional insight into the leader's role that may be helpful in your development as a leader.

PRACTICE STRONG ETHICS

Being trustworthy facilitates a leader practicing strong (or good) ethics, the study of moral obligation, or separating right from wrong. Ethics deals with doing the right thing by employees, customers, the environment, and the law.[18] Practicing good ethics contributes to effective leadership for several reasons. Workers are more likely to trust an ethical than an unethical leader, which helps the leader gain the support of the group. Good ethics serves as a positive model for group members, thus strengthening the organization. Also, ethical leaders help group members avoid common ethical pitfalls in the workplace. Many of these unethical practices, as listed next, can lead to lawsuits against the company:

- Lying or misrepresenting facts
- Blaming others for your mistakes
- Divulging personal or confidential information to others in the company to promote yourself
- Permitting or failing to report violations of legal requirements
- Protecting substandard performers from proper discipline
- Condoning or failing to report theft or misuse of company property
- Suppressing grievances and complaints
- Covering up accidents and failing to report health and safety hazards
- Ignoring or violating higher management's commitments to employees
- Taking credit for the ideas of others[19]

To simplify a complex issue, an effective leader practices the Golden Rule: *Do unto others as you would have others do unto you.*

A strategic way of behaving ethically as a leader according to psychologist Howard Gardner of the Harvard Graduate School of Education is to develop an *ethical mind*. It is mind-set that helps workers aspire to do good work that matters to their coworkers, employers, and society in general. You believe that maintaining an ethical compass is essential for the health of your employer. Gardner explains further:

> A person with an ethical mind asks herself, "What kind of person, worker, and citizen do I want to be? If all the workers in my profession adopted the mind-set I have, or if everyone did what I do, what would the world be like?"[20]

A leader with an ethical mind would avoid the unethical behaviors listed above, along with swindling investors with such schemes as selling them securities based on loans with very high—and undisclosed—default rates.

DIRECTION SETTING

Given that leaders are supposed to bring about change, they must point people in the right direction. Setting a direction includes the idea of establishing a vision for the organization or a smaller group. An example of direction setting by a top-level manager would be for the chief executive officer of a toy company to decide that the company should now diversify into the bicycle business. Direction setting by a team leader would include encouraging the group to strive toward error-free work from this point forward or to collaborate more with each other to form a true team.

A specific example of direction setting is the initiatives taken by high-flying Delta Airlines executive Joanne Smith.

> A one-time flight attendant herself while in college, Smith pointed Delta in the direction of sprucing up its planes to attract passengers while the airline was still in bankruptcy-court protection. Among her initiatives were to replace faded carpets, replace worn-out fabric seats with leather upholstery, have flight attendants wear designer uniforms, and empower attendants to create their own passenger greetings.[21]

DEVELOP PARTNERSHIPS WITH PEOPLE

Partnership
the leader and group members are connected in such a way that the power between them is approximately balanced

Leadership is now regarded as a long-term relationship, or partnership, between leaders and group members. According to consultant and trainer Peter Block, in a **partnership** the leader and group members are connected in such a way that the power between them is approximately balanced. To form a partnership, the leader has to allow the group members to share in decision making. Four conditions are necessary to form a true partnership between the leader and group members:

1. **Exchange of purpose.** The leader and team member should work together to build a vision.

2. **A right to say no.** In a partnership, each side has the right to say no without fear of being punished.

3. **Joint accountability.** Each person takes responsibility for the success and failure of the group.

4. **Absolute honesty.** In a partnership, not telling the truth to each other is an act of betrayal. When group members recognize that they have power, they are more likely to tell the truth because they feel less vulnerable to punishment.[22]

Another way for leaders to form partnerships with people is to pay attention to everyone who has contact with the leader or his or her group, including custodial workers. By being in touch with so many people, and soliciting their opinions, if you are a leader, you will be able to make more useful decisions.[23]

HELP GROUP MEMBERS REACH GOALS AND ACHIEVE SATISFACTION

Effective leaders help group members in their efforts to achieve goals according to the path–goal theory of leadership.[24] In a sense, they smooth out the path to reaching goals. One important way to do this is to provide the necessary resources to group members. An important aspect of a leader's job is to ensure that subordinates have the proper tools, equipment, and human resources to accomplish their objectives.

Another way of helping group members achieve goals is to reduce frustrating barriers to getting work accomplished. A leader who helps group members cut through minor rules and regulations would be engaging in such behavior. In a factory, a supervisory leader has a responsibility to replace faulty equipment, make sure unsafe conditions are corrected, and see that troublesome employees are either rehabilitated or replaced.

Another important general set of actions characteristic of an effective leader is looking out for the satisfaction of the group. Small things sometimes mean a lot in terms of personal satisfaction. One office manager fought for better beverage facilities for her subordinates. Her thoughtfulness contributed immensely to job satisfaction among them. Giving group members emotional support is another effective way of improving worker satisfaction. An emotionally supportive leader would engage in activities such as listening to group members' problems and offering them encouragement and praise. Encouragement can also take the form of asking group members to identify and fix whatever is holding them back.[25] For example, with encouragement from her head nurse, a new nurse admitted that her knowledge of calculating fractions and percentages was not good enough for dispensing certain medications. The newcomer nurse then set about to study the arithmetic she needed.

Again, basic human relations skills contribute to leadership effectiveness.

SET HIGH EXPECTATIONS

In addition to making expectations clear, it is important for leaders to set high expectations for group members. Effective leaders consistently hold group members to high standards of performance. The owner of a Toyota dealership might say, "I see that our customer satisfaction ratings have been about 80 percent. From now on, I want to hear back from regional headquarters that our ratings average 95 percent. We'll figure out together how to do it." If you as a leader expect others to succeed, they are likely to live up to your expectations. This mysterious phenomenon has been labeled the **Pygmalion effect.** According to Greek mythology, Pygmalion was a sculptor and king of Cyprus who carved an ivory statue of a maiden and fell in love with the statue. The statue was soon brought to life in response to his prayer. (Pygmalion wished so hard for the statue to become alive that the statue was transformed into a living woman to love.)

The point of the Pygmalion effect is that the leader can elevate performance by the simple method of expecting others to perform well. The manager's high expectations become a self-fulfilling prophecy. Why high expectations lead to high performance could be linked to self-confidence. As the leader expresses faith in the group members' abilities to perform well, they become more confident of their skills. Also, when a managerial leader believes that a group member will succeed, the manager communicates this belief without realizing it.

Pygmalion effect
leader's ability to elevate worker performance by the simple method of expecting them to perform well; the manager's high expectations become a self-fulfilling prophecy

GIVE FREQUENT FEEDBACK ON PERFORMANCE

Effective leaders inform employees how they can improve and praise them for things done right. Often, a simple e-mail message can be effective feedback, such as, "Sue, the financial analysis you prepared for our client today was exactly the information he needed to purchase a $300,000 variable annuity. Thanks so much." Less effective leaders, in contrast, often avoid confrontation and give limited positive feedback. An exception is that some ineffective leaders become involved in many confrontations—they are masters at reprimanding people!

MANAGE A CRISIS EFFECTIVELY

When a crisis strikes, that's the time to have an effective leader around. When things are running very smoothly, you may not always notice whether your leader is present. Effectively managing a crisis means giving reassurance to the group that problems will soon be under control, specifying the alternative paths for getting out of the crisis and choosing one of the paths. Showing compassion for those directly affected by the crisis is also quite helpful. After Hurricane Katrina, for example, managers at McDonald's made a concentrated effort to be in touch with as many employees as possible to communicate concern about their welfare and to discuss their employment situation. As implied earlier, a crisis is a key opportunity for the leader to behave charismatically because group members are probably looking for charismatic leadership.

ASK THE RIGHT QUESTIONS

Leaders do not need to know all the answers. Instead, a major contribution can be to ask the right questions. Although being knowledgeable about the group task is important, there are many times when asking group members penetrating questions is more important. In today's complex and rapidly changing business environment, the collective intelligence of group members is needed to solve problems.[26] Quite often a leader does not have the answer to a problem, so asking questions is important. Also, asking questions rather than giving answers is the natural method of helping group members become better problem solvers. Here are sample questions a leader might ask group members to help them meet their challenges:

- What are you going to do differently to reduce by 50 percent the time it takes to fill a customer order?

- Top management is thinking of getting rid of our group and subcontracting the work we do to outside vendors. What do you propose we do to make us more valuable to the company?

- Can you figure out why the competition is outperforming us?

BE A SERVANT LEADER

Servant leader

one who serves group members by working on their behalf to help them achieve their goals, not the leader's goals

A humanitarian approach to leadership is to be a **servant leader,** one who serves group members by working on their behalf to help them achieve their goals, not the leader's goals. With confidence shaken in several well-publicized corrupt leaders, interest has increased in the development of leaders who set aside self-interest for the betterment of their followers and employers.[27]

The idea behind servant leadership, as developed by Robert K. Greenleaf, is that leadership stems naturally from a commitment to service. Serving others, including employees, customers, and the community, is the primary motivation for the servant leader. The servant leader is passionate about the people he or she works with and for.[28] Servant leadership encompasses many different acts, all designed to make life easier or better for group members. Several acts or aspects of servant leadership are mentioned next.

- **Humble servant.** A good starting point is for the leader to see himself or herself as a humble servant. ("I'm here to serve you.") The leader downplays his or her ego to support the talents of others. Servant leaders also look for the opportunity to lend assistance directly to employees, such as a supermarket manager bagging groceries during an unanticipated rush of business. A servant leader would also provide the tools people needed to accomplish their work, such as fighting for enough money for the budget to purchase expensive new equipment.

- **Good listener.** A servant leader emphasizes listening to subordinates, because you cannot help people if you do not understand their concerns. Sam Palmisano, the chairman and CEO of IBM, believes strongly in the listening aspect of servant leadership. In his words:

    I've noticed that some of the most effective leaders don't make themselves the center of attention. They are respectful. They listen. This is an appealing personal quality, but it's also an effective leadership attribute. Their selflessness makes the people around them comfortable. People open up, speak up, and contribute. They give those leaders their very best.[29]

- **Realistic about what can be done.** Although a servant leader is idealistic, he or she recognizes that one individual cannot accomplish everything. So the leader listens carefully to the array of problems facing group members and then concentrates on a few. As the head of a nurses' union told the group, "I know you are hurting in many ways. Yet I think that the work overload issue is the biggest one, so we will head into negotiations working on obtaining sensible workloads. After that we will work on job security."

■ **Development of subordinates.** Another important behavior of servant leaders is that they want subordinates to grow and succeed. They demonstrate genuine concern for the career growth of group members by providing emotional support and mentoring.[30] As such, a servant leader is likely to be perceived as a good coach.

What Is Leadership Style, and What Is Style Flexibility?

◀ Learning Objective 3 ◀

Understanding the traits, behaviors, skills, and attitudes of leaders points to another major approach to explaining leadership. A **leadership style** is a leader's characteristic way of behaving in a variety of situations. Here we look at the classic dimensions of leadership style, participative leadership, and style flexibility or adaptability.

Leadership style
a leader's characteristic way of behaving in a variety of situations

THE CLASSIC DIMENSIONS OF CONSIDERATION AND INITIATING STRUCTURE

Leadership styles have been characterized in many ways, beginning in the 1950s with studies at the Ohio State University conducted with factory supervisors and military personnel.[31] Most approaches to leadership style are variations, refinements, and expansions of this pioneering work. The researchers asked group members to describe their supervisors by responding to the questionnaires. Leaders were also asked to rate themselves on leadership dimensions (activities they performed). Two main dimensions were identified that accounted for the vast majority of a leader's activity: "consideration" and "initiating structure."

Consideration is the degree to which the leader creates an environment of emotional support, warmth, friendliness, and trust. The leader creates this environment by being friendly and approachable and looking out for the welfare of the group. He or she also keeps the group informed about new developments and does small favors for the group, such as getting the break area repainted. In other words, the leader focuses on the human relations aspect of work.

Consideration
the degree to which the leader creates an environment of emotional support, warmth, friendliness, and trust

Initiating structure means organizing and defining relationships in the group by engaging in such activities as assigning specific tasks, specifying procedures to be followed, scheduling work, and making expectations clear. In other words, the leader provides structure for the group and focuses on the work.

Initiating structure
organizing and defining relationships in the group by engaging in such activities as assigning specific tasks, specifying procedures to be followed, scheduling work, and making expectations clear

Leaders have been categorized with respect to how much emphasis they place on the two dimensions of consideration and initiating structure. As implied by Figure 11-4, the two dimensions are not mutually exclusive. A leader can achieve high or low status on both dimensions. For example, an effective leader might contribute to high productivity yet still place considerable emphasis on warm human relationships. Hewlett Packard CEO Mark Hurd emphasizes initiating structure in his style, including his heavy emphasis of insisting on extreme organizational efficiency, including paring down costs. In contrast, servant leaders tend to emphasize consideration because they focus so much on concerns of group members. A leader's style could be characterized in terms of which one of the four boxes he or she fits into in Figure 11-4. Later approaches to classifying leadership style, such as the leadership grid and the path–goal theory of leadership, build on these dimensions.

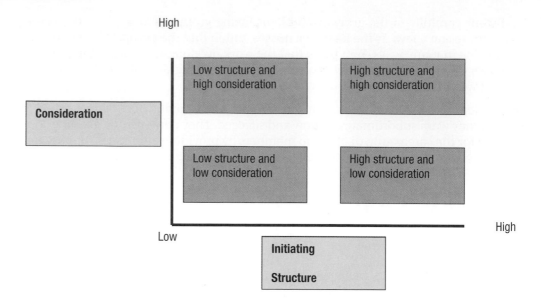

THE PARTICIPATIVE (TEAM) LEADERSHIP STYLE

For the past thirty years, the participative leadership style has received the most attention because this style enables the leader to share decisions with the group and capitalize on the talents of the group. By definition, a **participative leader** shares decision-making authority with the group. At his or her best, the participative leader motivates group members to work as a team toward high-level goals. Encouraging employees to participate in making decisions is the major approach to empowerment. Participative leadership is often favored because workers are more willing to implement decisions when they are involved in formulating the decisions. Participative leadership encompasses so many different behaviors that it is useful to divide it into three subtypes: consultative, consensus, and democratic.

Consultative Leaders

A **consultative leader** solicits opinions from the group before making a decision yet does not feel obliged to accept the group's thinking. Leaders of this type make it clear that they alone have authority to make the final decisions. A standard way to practice consultative leadership would be to call a group meeting and discuss an issue before making a decision.

Consensus Leaders

A **consensus leader** encourages group discussion about an issue and then makes a decision that reflects the consensus of the group members. Consensus-style leaders thus turn over more authority to the group than do consultative leaders. The consensus style results in long delays in decision making because every party involved has to agree.

Democratic Leaders

A **democratic leader** confers final authority on the group. He or she functions as a collector of opinion and takes a vote before making a decision. The group usually achieves its goals when working under a democratic leader. Democratic leadership has more relevance for community activities than for most work settings.

Participative leader
leader who shares decision-making authority with the group; motivates group members to work as a team toward high-level goals

Consultative leader
leader who solicits opinions from the group before making a decision, yet does not feel obliged to accept the group's thinking; this type leader makes it clear that he or she alone has authority to make the final decisions

Consensus leader
leader who encourages group discussion about an issue and then makes a decision that reflects the consensus of the group members

Democratic leader
leader who confers final authority on the group; functions as a collector of opinion and takes a vote before making a decision (in extreme sometimes referred to as a free-rein leader)

When democratic leaders turn over too much authority to the group they are referred to as laissez-faire (or free rein) leaders. Laissez-faire leadership works only with highly motivated and self-sufficient individuals. Otherwise, group members left completely on their own may become dissatisfied and unproductive. A study with over two thousand Norwegian workers found that workers managed with a laissez-faire style were likely to suffer from role ambiguity, or not knowing what is expected. As a result these workers were stressed and anxious, often guessing if they were focusing on the correct tasks and establishing the right priorities.[32]

Participative leadership is also referred to as *trickle-up* leadership because suggestions flow from workers to management. Part of trickle-up leadership is for group members to step in when they perceive that the leader is having difficulty. According to Wharton School professor of organizational behavior Michael Useem, as technology evolves and organizations decentralize, frontline workers have more independence and responsibility. They are more aware of customer demands and how to manufacture a product or provide a service. These same workers can often see what the leaders are missing and can therefore step in to help a faltering leader. In the U.S. Marines, when a superior issues a flawed order, officers are expected to point out the flaws before the order is implemented. For example, four-star general Peter Pace ends his meetings by asking subordinates to tell him what they each think. By encouraging the group members to challenge him, Pace reinforces a culture of trickle-up leadership.[33]

In contrast to the participative leader is the leader/manager who makes decisions more independently. An **autocratic leader** attempts to retain most of the authority granted to the group. Autocratic leaders make all the major decisions and assume subordinates will comply without question. Leaders who use this style give minimum consideration to what group members are likely to think about an order or decision. Group members sometimes see an autocrat as rigid and demanding.

Although the autocratic leadership style is not in vogue, many successful leaders are autocratic. Among them are *turnaround managers*—those who specialize in turning around failing organizations or rescuing them from crises. Other situations calling for autocratic crisis management include earthquakes, product recalls, and workplace violence. The autocratic style generally works best in situations where decisions have to be made rapidly or when group opinion is not needed. One situation calling for autocratic leadership would be extinguishing an oil rig fire at sea. Another would be when a company is undergoing liquidation and bankruptcy. When Carol Bartz was appointed as chief executive of Yahoo! Inc, she led in an autocratic direction by imposing *top-down management*, meaning that more decisions would now by made by her and other top executives. For example, product development and marketing that were previously spread throughout the company became consolidated into one department.[34]

Human Relations Self-Assessment Quiz 11-2 gives you the opportunity to measure your present or potential leadership style.

Autocratic leader
leader who attempts to retain most of the authority granted to the group; autocratic leaders make all the major decisions and assume subordinates will comply without question

Adapting to the Various Styles as a Subordinate

Part of understanding leadership is being able to adapt to the style of your superior. To begin, the suggestions for getting along with your manager presented in Chapter 9 should work well for leaders of any style. In addition, keep these suggestions in mind for adapting to the three styles presented next.

1. **Participative style (consultative, consensus, and collaborative).** With a participative style of leader, it is important for you to play an active role as a subordinate. Above all, be prepared to offer suggestions for improving work processes and procedures. Offer constructive feedback for building on the suggestions of your

Human Relations Self-Assessment Quiz   11-2

What Style of Leader Are You or Would You Be?

Answer the following questions, keeping in mind what you have done, or think you would do, regarding the scenarios and attitudes described.

	Mostly True	Mostly False
1. I am more likely to take care of a high-impact assignment myself than turn it over to a group member.	_____	_____
2. I would prefer the analytical aspects of a manager's job rather than working directly with group members.	_____	_____
3. An important part of my approach to managing a group is to keep the members informed almost daily of any information that could affect their work.	_____	_____
4. It's a good idea to give two people in the group the same problem and then choose what appears to be the best solution.	_____	_____
5. It makes good sense for the leader or manager to stay somewhat aloof from the group, so he or she can make a tough decision when necessary.	_____	_____
6. I look for opportunities to obtain group input before making a decision, even on straightforward issues.	_____	_____
7. I would reverse a decision if several of the group members presented evidence that I was wrong.	_____	_____
8. Differences of opinion in the work group are healthy.	_____	_____
9. I think that an activity to build team spirit, such as the team fixing up a poor family's house on a Saturday, is an excellent investment of time.	_____	_____
10. If my group were hiring a new member, I would like the person to be interviewed by the entire group.	_____	_____
11. An effective team leader today uses e-mail for about 98 percent of communication with team members.	_____	_____
12. Some of the best ideas are likely to come from the group members rather than the manager.	_____	_____
13. If our group were going to have a banquet, I would get input from each member on what type of food should be served.	_____	_____
14. I have never seen a statue of a committee in a museum or park, so why bother making decisions by a committee if you want to be recognized?	_____	_____
15. I dislike it intensely when a group member challenges my position on an issue.	_____	_____
16. I typically explain to group members what method they should use to accomplish an assigned task.	_____	_____
17. If I were out of the office for a week, most of the important work in the department would get accomplished anyway.	_____	_____
18. Delegation of important tasks is something that is very difficult for me.	_____	_____
19. When a group member comes to me with a problem, I tend to jump right in with a proposed solution.	_____	_____
20. When a group member comes to me with a problem, I typically ask that person something such as, "What alternative solutions have you thought of so far?"	_____	_____

Continued

leader. Demonstrate that you are a professional who wants to be considered a partner in the success of the organizational unit (such as a department or team).

2. **Autocratic style.** Be a good soldier. Expect to be given clear, precise, directions, and guidance. Provide input to your boss when asked, but keep in mind that even if you are quite talented, your manager has formal authority for running your organizational unit. When you become the boss, you can make the big decisions. An autocratic leader welcomes subordinates who readily accept assignments and follow through on time. Be brief and businesslike in your interactions with your boss, because he or she most likely does not like to spend lots of time in discussions with subordinates.

3. **Laissez-faire style.** Recognize that you are pretty much on your own in terms of receiving guidance, feedback, directions, and encouragement from your boss. Check in with your boss occasionally to make sure you are working on the right assignment or project. Do not hint that the lack of structure is intolerable for you. If you want guidance, consult a trusted coworker.

STYLE FLEXIBILITY AND ADAPTABILITY

Although leadership style refers to a person's characteristic approach to dealing with leadership tasks, effective leaders adapt their style to fit the situation. For example, a leader might typically use a consensus style, yet when managing a crisis he or she might become more authoritarian—giving subordinates directions in a hurry without waiting to achieve agreement among group members. A study with three thousand executives revealed that leaders who get the best results do not rely on one style. Instead, they use several different styles in one week, such as being autocratic in some situations and democratic in others.[35] Furthermore, a more recent analysis of hundreds of studies suggests that leadership should be defined as "doing the right thing at the right time."[36] The leader makes the decision or chooses the action that fits the circumstances. An example might be transferring a valuable worker to a temporary assignment rather than firing him or her because of too little work for that individual at the moment.

Rule of Thumb for Style Flexibility

A rule of thumb for attaining style flexibility is to give considerable guidance, direction, and coaching to a worker who has low motivation or capability in terms of accomplishing the task. In contrast, give less guidance, direction, and coaching to a worker with high motivation and capability. The preceding is perhaps the best established finding about providing leadership to others.

Avoiding Leadership Lopsidedness

A recent perspective on being an adaptable leader is to avoid being lopsided, or going too far in one direction as a leader. Leadership specialist Bob Kaplan has developed a theory of leadership behavior based on two polarities (or end-points): forceful and enabling behaviors, and strategic and operational behaviors.[37] Many leaders go too far in one direction or another.

1. **Forceful versus enabling.** One error is for leaders to be too forceful in asserting themselves, not allowing subordinates to influence them, and being insensitive. In the other extreme, the leader is too enabling by giving subordinates too much leeway, putting kindness over results, and not holding subordinates accountable.

2. **Strategic versus operational.** The leader who is too strategic errs on the side of being out of touch with everyday realities, too conceptual (big-picture thinking), and too ambitious. The leader who is too operational (getting work on hand accomplished) is too detail oriented, not bold enough, and inflexible.

To avoid being lopsided, the leader has to be sensitive enough to observe if he or she is moving too far on the two poles of forceful versus enabling and strategic versus operational. Your role as a subordinate would be to offer your leader constructive feedback (unless your leader is a total autocrat).

Adapting Leadership Style to Cultural Values

Another way in which leadership style flexibility can be important is when it has to be adapted to fit cultural values. (Chapter 13 provides more information about these values.) Visualize an autocratic manager from France being sent to a Swedish subsidiary where Swedes strongly value democracy and status equality. The Swedish workers might not take too kindly to the French manager's autocratic behavior. And the French manager might dislike not being treated with great respect. The study summarized next illustrates how cultural values can influence which leadership style is the most effective.

> The participants in the study were over 800 bank employees in China, India, Kenya, and the U.S. These countries represented both collectivistic (group-oriented) and individualistic cultures, with China and India being more collectivistic. The major finding was that workers who embrace group-oriented, collectivistic values responded positively to transformational leadership as opposed to transactional leadership. (Transformational leaders focus on major changes, and inspire workers by emphasizing the importance of group values and focusing on collective interests, of the common good. Transactional leaders focus more on clarifying roles and tasks, while offering rewards based on task accomplishment.) In contrast, employees who embrace individual goals and accomplishments responded more favorably to transactional than transformational leadership.[38]

How Does a Leader Get Along Well with Subordinates?

◀ Learning Objective 4 ◀

The concepts already mentioned in this chapter, as well as other information you have studied about getting along with people, apply to a leader getting along well with subordinates. We spotlight this topic by presenting a well-documented theory about leader–member relationships, as well as a few illustrative principles.

THE LEADER–MEMBER EXCHANGE MODEL

George Graen, a professor of organizational behavior at the University of Illinois, Champaign–Urbana, and his associates have developed a leadership model that focuses on the quality of leader–member relations. The **leader–member exchange (LMX) model** recognizes that leaders develop unique working relationships with each group member.[39] A leader might be considerate and compassionate toward one team member yet rigid and unfeeling toward another.

Each relationship between the leader/manager and employees differs in quality. One subset of employees, the in-group, is given additional rewards, responsibility, and trust in exchange for their loyalty and performance. In contrast, another subset of employees (the out-group) is treated in accordance with a more formal understanding of the supervisor–subordinate relationship. The leader's first impression of a group member's competency heavily influences whether he or she becomes a member of the in-group or out-group.

In-group members have attitudes and values similar to the leader and interact frequently with the leader. Out-group members have less in common with the leader and operate somewhat detached from the leader. The one-to-one relationships have a major influence on the subordinate's behavior in the group. Members of the in-group become part of a smoothly functioning team headed by the formal leader. Out-group members are less likely to experience good teamwork. Being a member of the in-group facilitates achieving high productivity and satisfaction. Out-group members receive less challenging assignments and are more likely to quit because of job dissatisfaction.[40]

The specific relevance of the LMX model for getting along with group members is that if the leader establishes good relationships with group members, higher productivity and satisfaction is likely to occur.

> **Leader–member exchange (LMX) model**
> leadership model that focuses on the quality of leader–member relations; recognizes that leaders develop unique working relationships with each group member

SUGGESTIONS FOR ATTAINING GOOD RELATIONSHIPS WITH SUBORDINATES

A key part of leadership is forming good relationships with people, so getting along with subordinates is essential. If you are a leader and your subordinates do not like you, it will be difficult for the group to achieve high productivity and satisfaction. A sampling follows of time-tested principles for attaining good relationships with subordinates.

1. **Solicit opinions before taking action.** In the spirit of participative leadership, find out what group members think of your potential action, even on relatively small matters such as selecting a restaurant for a department banquet. Subordinates will be pleased that their input matters, and they will be more cooperative in implementing your decision.

2. **Ask how you can make their jobs better.** An excellent relationship builder with subordinates is playing an active role in facilitating the jobs of subordinates

running more smoothly. Toward this end, ask such questions as, "What drives you the craziest about the processes around here?" and "If you could have a fantasy tool that made your job easier, what would it be?"[41]

3. Fight for their demands. An axiom of effective management is for the supervisor to bring forth the demands of group members to higher management and then fight for these demands, such as needing new equipment. Carrying out this principle enhances your stature among group members and helps you win their support.

4. Give out recognition. Most people are recognition deprived, so being a boss who recognizes the contributions of subordinates goes a long way toward building positive relationships with them. Effective forms of recognition include thank-you notes and face-to-face comments, such as, "You really helped us out in a jam, and I appreciate it." You will learn more about recognition in your study of motivation.

5. Listen to the problems and suggestions of group members. Listening is an essential tool of the participative leader or manager, and it is also an excellent way of cultivating subordinates. You will recall that listening is an important component of servant leadership. To be listened to is to be respected and considered important.

6. Be courteous. Many managers are rude to subordinates, so showing courtesy will help you build relationships with your direct reports. Being courteous to subordinates would include such acts as responding quickly to e-mail messages, returning phone calls, not multitasking when subordinates are talking to you, not keeping people waiting for you, and not belittling them.

7. Look for opportunities to say yes to requests. Repeated refusals on requests can be demoralizing and demotivating for employees, especially when the request is feasible. Some requests, such as asking for a cash bar in the lunchroom, must be refused. But look for opportunities to say yes. A useful guideline is when a group member makes a request, avoid automatically replying, "We cannot do that." Instead, ask yourself, "Can we do that?"[42]

In short, getting along well with subordinates involves the practice of good human relations, in addition to recognizing that you need the support of your subordinates as much as they need you.

▶ Learning Objective 5 ▶

How Do You Develop Your Leadership Potential?

How to improve your potential for becoming a leader is a topic without limits. Developing your leadership potential is possible because both nature and nurture contribute to leadership effectiveness. Just as in playing music or sports, you need certain talents to begin with, such as good eye–hand coordination, but with practice you can improve. John Wooden, perhaps the most successful college basketball coach in history, later became a leadership specialist. At age ninety-three, Wooden offered this opinion about leadership development:

> In my opinion, you can be taught leadership. You have to have certain qualities that demand respect, but the things that are so important in leadership can be taught. Not everyone can become a leader, though.[43]

Almost anything you do to improve your individual effectiveness will have some impact on your ability to lead others. If you strengthen your self-confidence, improve your memory for names, study this book carefully, read studies about leadership, or improve your physical fitness (giving you more energy), you stand a good chance of improving your leadership potential. Eight modes of advancement might be kept in mind if you are seeking to improve your leadership potential:

1. **General education and specific training.** Almost any program of career training or education can be considered a program of leadership development. Courses in human relations, management, or applied psychology have obvious relevance for someone currently occupying or aspiring toward a leadership position. Many of today's leaders in profit and nonprofit organizations hold formal degrees in business. Specific training programs will also help you improve your leadership potential. Among them might be skill development programs in interviewing, employee selection, listening, cross-cultural training, budgeting, planning, improving work habits, resolving conflict, and communication skills. After acquiring knowledge through study, you then put the knowledge into practice as a leader.

Pioneering leadership scholar and University of Southern California professor Warren G. Bennis emphasizes that becoming a leader involves continual learning, development, and the reinvention of the self.[44] "Reinvention" in this sense could mean rethinking your assumptions about people or even changing careers into one you found that was a better fit with your values.

2. **Leadership development programs.** A focused way of improving your leadership potential is to attend development programs designed specifically to improve your ability to lead others and develop self-confidence. A popular type of leadership development program called *outdoor training* (or *offsite training*) places people in a challenging outdoor environment for a weekend or up to ten days. Participants are required to accomplish physical feats, such as climbing a mountain, whitewater canoeing, building a wall, or swinging between trees on a rope. Participants in these outdoor programs learn such important leadership skills and attitudes as teamwork and trusting others and gain confidence in their abilities to accomplish the seemingly impossible.

3. **Acquire broad experience.** Because leadership varies somewhat with the situation, a sound approach to improving leadership effectiveness is to attempt to gain supervisory experience in different settings. A person who wants to become an executive is well advised to gain supervisory experience in at least two different organizational functions, such as customer service and finance. Support for this viewpoint can be found from the work of Personnel Decisions International, a firm that specializes in leadership development. A long-term study found that first-level supervisors are more likely to succeed if they have cross-functional (having worked in different departments) experience.[45]

First-level supervisory jobs are an invaluable starting point for developing your leadership potential. It takes considerable skill to manage a fast-food restaurant effectively or to direct a public playground during the summer. First-level supervisors frequently face situations in which subordinates are poorly trained, poorly paid, and not well motivated to achieve company objectives. Taking a turn as a team leader is also valuable experience for developing leadership skills.

4. **Modeling effective leaders.** Carefully observe a capable leader in action and incorporate some of his or her approaches into your own behavior. You may not be able to or want to become that person's clone, but you can model (imitate) what the person does. For instance, most inexperienced leaders have a difficult time confronting others with bad news. Observe a good confronter handle the situation and try his or her approach the next time you have some unfavorable news to deliver. The biography or autobiography of a leader whom you admire is another source of ideas for modeling an effective leader.

5. **Self-development of leadership characteristics and behavior.** Study the leadership characteristics and behaviors described in this chapter. As a starting point, identify several attributes you think you could strengthen within yourself, given some

self-determination. For example, you might decide that with effort you could improve your passion and enthusiasm. You might also believe that you could be more emotionally supportive of others. It is also helpful to obtain feedback from reliable sources, such as a trusted manager, about which traits and behaviors you particularly need to develop.

6. Practice a little leadership. An effective way to develop your leadership skills is to look for opportunities to exert a small amount of helpful leadership in contrast to waiting for opportunities to accomplish extraordinary deeds.[46] A "little leadership" might involve such behaviors as mentoring a struggling team member, coaching somebody about how to use a new high-tech device, or making a suggestion about improving a product.

7. Practice self-leadership. One of the most effective ways of becoming a leader is to begin by leading yourself, or practicing **self-leadership.** According to this concept, all organizational members are capable of leading themselves to some extent. You influence yourself without waiting for an external leader to lead you, much like taking the initiative to accomplish something worthwhile or being a good organizational citizen. According to Charles C. Manz, a professor of business leadership at the University of Massachusetts, self-leadership extends as far as setting your own standards and objectives. "It addresses what should be done, and why it should be done, in addition to how to do it." Recognize, however, that you still have to accomplish what your leader wants you to accomplish, but you can go beyond the minimum required in your job.[47]

8. Become an integrated human being. A philosophical approach to leadership suggests that the model leader is first and foremost a fully functioning person. According to this belief, the type of person you are determines whether you will be an effective leader. According to consultant William D. Hitt, mastering the art of leadership comes with self-mastery. Leadership development is the process of self-development. As a result, the process of becoming a leader is similar to the process of becoming an integrated human being. For example, you need to develop values that guide your behavior before you can adequately guide the behavior of others, and you also need courage.[48]

Self-leadership

leading oneself; influencing oneself without waiting for an external leader to lead; all organizational members are capable of leading themselves to some extent

▶ Learning Objective 6 ▶

What Are Several Key Challenges of Being a First-Time Leader?

Another way of preparing for becoming a leader for the first time is to think through some of the inevitable challenges in the first-time leader faces, as described next.

1. **Uncertainty about how much time to spend leading versus doing individual tasks.** From the first-level supervisor of entry-level workers to the chairperson of the board, leaders spend some time as individual contributors, including preparing budgets, thinking of ideas for new products, and making financial deals. As a new leader you have to work with your manager and perhaps your direct reports to find the right balance between doing and leading.

2. **Assuming that you have the authority and freedom to do what you think is best.** First-time leaders usually have much less authority and autonomy than they thought they would have. You are most likely to find yourself in a web of relationships with subordinates, bosses, coworkers, and perhaps customers. Many of these people make demands on you and question your judgment. "You are not really in control of anything," said one new manager.[49]

3. **Overcoming the resentment of the people in the group who wanted your leadership position.** If you are selected from among the group to be the new leader, you will have to deal with the resentment and envy of several direct reports who wanted your position. It can be helpful to deal openly with the issue with such statements as, "I know that other people would be equally qualified to be the leader of the group. Yet management has chosen me for this position, at least for now. I respect your expertise and I need your contribution. I also want your respect for me in my job as the chosen leader."

4. **Building relationships and fostering teamwork quickly enough.** As a new leader, a high priority is to build constructive relationships with subordinates as quickly as possible, using many of the techniques described earlier in this chapter. Several direct reports who were your former coworkers may attempt to manipulate you and take advantage of prior friendships to receive special treatment. It is essential to build a professional, merit-based team climate as soon as possible. In the words of career coach Aya Fubara Eneli, "Friendships work best between equals. If you were already friends with some of the staff, expect those relationships to change. It's difficult to be a friend while giving orders and judging performance."[50]

5. **Overcoming the need to be liked by everybody.** The most admired leaders at every level are rarely liked by everybody. By the nature of their roles, leaders make decisions that not everybody agrees with. The changes you bring about may hurt the feelings of some people and jeopardize their positions. Your role is to establish and implement goals that will result in the greatest good.

Concept Review and Reinforcement

Leadership, 312
Leadership effectiveness, 312
Trust, 314
Character, 315
Cognitive skills, 315
Openness to experience, 316
Charisma, 316

Partnership, 322
Pygmalion effect, 323
Servant leader, 324
Leadership style, 325
Consideration, 325
Initiating structure, 325
Participative leader, 326

Consultative leader, 326
Consensus leader, 326
Democratic leader, 326
Autocratic leader, 327
Leader–member exchange (LMX) model, 331
Self-leadership, 334

Summary and Review

Leadership is the process of bringing about positive changes and influencing others to achieve worthwhile goals and coordinating the pursuit of these goals. Effective leadership is needed at the top of organizations, but supervisors and team leaders also need to provide effective leadership. Effective leaders have the "right stuff." Certain traits and characteristics contribute to leadership effectiveness in many situations. Among them are the following:

- Self-confidence and courage
- Emotional intelligence
- Trustworthiness and character
- Strong work motivation and high energy
- Cognitive skills and openness to experience
- Assertiveness
- Charisma (vision, passion, enthusiasm, excitement, and humor)

Behaviors and skills of an effective leader (one who maintains high productivity and morale) include these:

- Practicing strong ethics
- Direction setting
- Developing partnerships with people (emphasizing power sharing)
- Helping group members reach goals and achieve satisfaction
- Setting high expectations (the Pygmalion effect)
- Giving frequent feedback on performance
- Managing a crisis effectively
- Asking the right questions
- Being a servant leader

Leadership style is a leader's characteristic way of behaving in a variety of situations. Most approaches to understanding leadership style stem from the two dimensions of consideration and initiating structure. Leaders can be characterized with respect to how much emphasis they place on these two dimensions.

Participative leaders share decisions with the group and capitalize on the talents of the group. The subtypes of participative leadership are consultative, consensus, and democratic. In contrast to the participative leader is the autocratic leader/manager who makes decisions more independently. Part of understanding leadership is being able to adapt to the style of your superior. For example, with a participative style of leader, play an active role as a subordinate, and be prepared to offer input into decisions.

Effective leaders tend to adapt their style to the situation, such as a consensus leader becoming authoritarian during a crisis. The effective leader does the right thing at the right time. In general, workers with low motivation and capability need more guidance, direction, and coaching. Cultural values, such as a belief in collectivism, can influence which style is best.

According to the leader–member exchange (LMX) model, leaders develop unique working relationships with each group member. If the leader establishes good relationships with group members, higher productivity and satisfaction are likely to occur.

Time-tested principles for attaining good relationships with subordinates include:

- Soliciting opinions before taking action
- Fighting for their demands
- Giving out recognition

- Listening to the problems and suggestions of group members
- Being courteous
- Looking for opportunities to say yes to requests

Many activities in life can in some way contribute to the development of a person's leadership potential. Eight recommended avenues for improving your leadership potential or leadership skills are as follows:

- General education and specific training
- Participating in leadership development programs
- Acquiring broad experience
- Modeling effective leaders
- Self-developing leadership characteristics and behavior

- Practicing a little leadership
- Practicing self-leadership
- Becoming an integrated human being

First-time leaders face key challenges, such as:

- Uncertainty about how much time to spend on leading versus doing individual tasks
- Assuming you have the authority and freedom to do what you think is best
- Overcoming the resentment of the people in the group who wanted your leadership position
- Building relationships and fostering teamwork quickly enough
- Overcoming the need to be liked by everybody

Check Your Understanding

1. Provide an example of something a leader motivated or inspired you to do that you would not have done without his or her presence.
2. A business author said that during a recession the last thing the business world is concerned with is once-popular terms such as "emotional intelligence" and "corporate social responsibility." What might be the downside of forgetting about emotional intelligence when a business organization is struggling?
3. Why does being charismatic often make a leader more effective?
4. Rate the charisma of the current president of the United States on a scale of 1 to 10. Explain the basis for your rating.
5. Provide an example of how you might use the Pygmalion effect in working with subordinates or with a child you have or might have.

6. In what way is the professor in this course a *servant leader* in his or her relationship with the students in the class?
7. Some organizational leaders continue to say, "I don't want to be loved. I want to be feared." How effective do you think such an attitude is for being a leader in today's world?
8. Give an example of a specific action taken by a present or former boss that helped cultivate good relationships with subordinates. Also identify an action that hurt relationships with subordinates.
9. Imagine yourself in either your present job or a job of your choice. How would you practice self-leadership in this job?
10. In what way does your program of study contribute to your development as a leader?

Web Corner

Overview of leadership:
www.ccl.org

Leadership development programs:
www.academyleadership.com/

Servant leadership:
http://greenleaf.org

INTERNET SKILL BUILDER

You have already received suggestions in this chapter for developing your charisma. Visit www.core-edge.com to

search for additional ideas for charisma development. Go to the section on charisma, and read a couple of the case histories to uncover ideas you might try to enhance your charisma. Watch the video "A Conversation on Charisma." After digging through core-edge.com, list two concrete ideas you might implement to enhance your charisma.

Also answer these questions: (a) What is charismatology? and (b) What is your rating of the charisma of the presenter in the video?

Developing Your Human Relations Skills

Human Relations Application Exercises

Applying Human Relations Exercise 11-1

Developing Your Charisma

An effective way of developing your leadership potential is to project a more charismatic image, even if you do not truly make over your personality. If you appear more charismatic to others, they are more likely to respond to your leadership. Also, if you project a more charismatic image, you are more likely to be nominated for leadership positions and assignments. Following is a checklist of the suggestions for becoming more charismatic as presented in Figure 11-3. As you go through the list, select two or three ideas that you would be willing to try in the next two weeks. Note that some of the suggestions are much easier than others to implement in the short range.

Charisma Suggestions (see Figure 11-3 for explanations)	Yes, I will try it
1. Communicate a vision.	❏
2. Make frequent use of metaphors and analogies.	❏
3. Inspire trust and confidence.	❏
4. Be highly energetic and goal oriented.	❏
5. Be emotionally expressive and warm.	❏
6. Make ample use of true stories.	❏
7. Smile frequently, even if not in happy mood.	❏
8. Be candid.	❏
9. Make everybody you meet feel that he or she is important.	❏
10. Multiply the effectiveness of your handshake.	❏
11. Stand up straight and use other nonverbal signals of self-confidence.	❏
12. Be willing to take personal risks.	❏
13. Be self-promotional.	❏

Now that you have made your choice of suggestions, try them out with other people, including students, athletic team members, coworkers, or members of a community group. After your experience, answer the following questions:

1. How did people react to me when I attempted to be more charismatic?
2. How can I use this approach more effectively next time? (How should I fine-tune my approach?)
3. Are these approaches to charisma enhancement making any contribution to my development as a leader?

Applying Human Relations Exercise 11-2

My Personal Leadership Journal

A potentially important tool in your development as a leader is to maintain a journal or diary of your leadership experiences. Make a journal entry within twenty-four hours after you carried out a leadership action of any kind, or failed to do so when the opportunity arose. You will, therefore, have entries dealing with leadership opportunities both capitalized on and missed. An example: "A few of my neighbors were complaining about trash flying around the neighborhood on trash pick-up days, particularly when the wind was strong. I took the initiative to send e-mails and flyers to neighborhood residents discussing what could be done about the problem. I suggested that people pack their recycling boxes more tightly. I also suggested ever so politely that people should pick up their own flying trash. Soon the problem nearly disappeared."

Also include in your journal such entries as comments you receive on your leadership ability, leadership traits that you appear to be developing, and leadership ideas about which you learn. Also, keep a list of leadership articles and books you intend to read. You might also want to record observations about significant acts of leadership or leadership blunders that you have observed in others, either firsthand or through the media.

Review your journal monthly, and make note of any progress you think you have made in developing your leadership skills. Also consider preparing a graph of your progress in developing leadership skills. The vertical axis can represent skill level on a 1 to 100 scale, and the horizontal axis might be divided into time intervals, such as calendar quarters.

"Some Good Leadership Advice I Received."

Here is an opportunity for you to obtain some potentially useful information for your present or future career as a leader. Each class member contacts an experienced person in his or her network to get one brief piece of advice about his or her leadership development. Among the potential experienced people are business executives, business owners, human resource professionals, public officials, former instructors, athletic coaches, parents, or other family members. You might contact the person through an e-mail, text message, phone call, blog, or social networking Web site. Try an approach of this nature: "I'm doing a class activity for a unit on leadership in a human relations course. Would you be willing to give me about two sentences of advice for helping me become a leader or develop my present leadership skills?" (You will most likely encounter a strong willingness to help by almost anybody you contact.)

Record the advice you receive in written form. During class, each student, or a number of volunteers, will make about a one-minute presentation sharing the leadership advice received. After all the presentations, hold a class discussion centering on these points:

- What was the most frequent advice offered?
- What was the most useful advice offered?
- What advice would most likely backfire?
- How helpful for my leadership development was this activity?

Charismatically Challenged Colleen

Twenty-seven-year-old Colleen worked as a merchandising specialist for ValuMart, one of the largest international retail chains. Based in the United States, ValuMart also has a strong presence in Canada, Europe, Japan, and Hong Kong. Colleen began her employment with ValuMart as a cashier and two years later was invited into the training program for merchandising specialists.

Colleen performed well as a merchandising trainee in the soft-goods line. Her specialty areas included linens and bedding, men's and women's jewelry, home decorations, and men's, women's and children's clothing. For several years in a row, Colleen received performance evaluation ratings of above average or outstanding. Among the write-in comments made by her supervisors were "diligent worker," "knows the tricks of merchandising," "good flair for buying the right products at the right price," and "fits right into the team."

Despite the positive performance evaluation ratings supported with positive comments, Colleen had a gnawing discontent about her career at ValuMart. Despite five years of good performance, she was still not invited to become a member of the group called "ValuTrackers." The ValuTrackers are a group of merchandising and operations specialists who are regarded as being on the fast track to become future ValuMart leaders. The leaders hold high-level positions such as head merchandiser, regional vice president, and store manager.

Several times when Colleen inquired as to why she was not invited to join the ValuTrackers, she was told something to the effect that she was not quite ready to be included in this elite group. She was also told not to be discouraged, because the company still valued her contribution.

One day Colleen thought, "I'm headed toward age thirty, and I want a great future in the retail business now." So she convinced her boss, the merchandising supervisor (Evan), to set up a career conference with three people: Colleen, the boss, and her boss's boss (Heather), the area merchandising manager. She let Evan know in advance that she wanted to talk about her potential for promotion.

Evan started the meeting by saying, "Colleen, perhaps you can tell Heather and me again why you requested this meeting."

Colleen responded, "Thanks for asking, Evan. As I mentioned before, I'm wondering what you think is wrong with me. I receive a lot of positive feedback about my performance, but I'm not a ValuTracker. Also, you seem to change the subject when I talk about wanting to become a merchandising supervisor, and eventually a merchandising executive. What am I doing wrong?"

Heather responded, "Evan and I frequently talk about the performance and potential of all our merchandising specialists. You're a good performer, Colleen, but you lack that little spark that makes a person a leader. You go about your job efficiently and quietly, but that's not enough. We want future leaders of ValuMart to make an impact."

Evan added, "I go along with Heather's comments. Another point, Colleen, is that you rarely take the initiative to suggest ideas. I was a little shocked by your request for a three-way career interview, because it's one of the few initiatives you have taken. You're generally pretty laid-back."

"Then what do I have to do to convince you two that I should be a ValuTracker?" asked Colleen?

Heather replied, "Start acting more like a leader. Be more charismatic." Evan nodded in agreement.

Questions

1. What career advice can you offer Colleen?

2. What might Colleen do to develop more charisma?

3. What is your opinion of the fairness of the ValuTracker program?

Human Relations Role-Playing Exercise

Colleen Attempts to Project Charisma During a Videoconference

The case study about Colleen serves as the background and the story line for this role-play. One person plays the role of Colleen, who is serious about wanting to appear and act more charismatic in interactions with work associates. Suddenly, Colleen gets a bright idea. Key members of her store are scheduled for a videoconference with the corporate group about upcoming improvements in the stores, including both refurbishing the stores and upgrading the merchandise. Colleen recognizes that key people from corporate will be observing store employees who attend the conferences.

The student playing the role of Colleen, who will both listen to what is being presented, will also have the opportunity to interact with the corporate presenters. Colleen wants to impress the corporate group, all the time demonstrating that she has the kind of charisma that would make her a strong candidate for being a Valu-Tracker.

Another two students play the roles of two presenters from corporate, who react to the comments by Colleen between parts of their presentation about upgrading the stores. The presenters can make up their own suggestions for upgrading ValuMart, to give Colleen something specific to which she can react.

Observers rate the role-players on two dimensions, using a 1 to 5 scale from very poor to very good. One dimension is "effective use of human relations techniques." For Colleen, focus on how well she projects charisma. The second dimension is "acting ability." A few observers might voluntarily provide feedback to the role-players in terms of sharing their ratings and observations. The course instructor might also provide feedback.

Human Relations Case Study 11-2

So, Is This How You Learn Leadership?

Len Olsen, age twenty-three, was proud to be selected as part of the leader's program at a national chain of family restaurants. Workers selected for the leadership program are considered to be in line for running individual restaurants and as potential candidates in the long run for leadership positions in corporate headquarters. Before entering the key phase of the leadership program, all candidates must first work a minimum of one year as a server or bartender at one of the company stores (restaurants).

Olsen worked one year as a server in a downtown Chicago restaurant and then was assigned to another Chicago restaurant to begin his formal leadership training as an assistant manager. Olsen's assignments as an assistant manager included scheduling the wait staff, conducting preliminary screening interviews of job applicants, and resolving problems with customers. After three months on the job, Olsen was asked by a member of the corporate human resources staff how his leadership training program was going. Olsen replied,

"I'm a little bit skeptical. I don't think I'm learning much about leadership."

When asked why he didn't think he was learning much about leadership, Olsen listed what he considered three recent examples of the type of responsibilities he faced regularly:

- At eleven yesterday morning, I received a phone call from Annie, one of the servers. She told me she wouldn't be in to work that afternoon because her Labrador retriever had become quite ill and she had to take it to the vet. I told Annie that we desperately needed her that afternoon because of a large luncheon party. Annie told me her dog was more important to her than the job.
- Two weeks ago, Gus, one of our salad chefs, showed up to work absolutely drunk. I told him that working while drunk was completely against company rules. He got a little belligerent, but I did get him to take a taxi home at company expense.
- Two days ago a customer in the restaurant spilled a cup of hot coffee on herself while answering a call on her cell phone. She told me that the coffee was too hot and that she was going to sue the restaurant. I explained to her tactfully that unless she was truly burned, she had no claim. I offered to have the restaurant pay for her dry cleaning, and then she calmed down.

Olsen then said to the human resources manager, "What has stuff like this got to do with leadership? I mean, I'm not creating great visions or inspiring hordes of people. In what way am I becoming a leader?"

Questions

1. What is your opinion of the contribution of Olsen's representative experiences to his development as a leader?

2. What else can the restaurant chain do to help Olsen, and others in the leadership program, develop as leaders?

REFERENCES

1. Michael R. Crittenden, "1: Sheila Bair, Chairman, Federal Deposit Insurance Corp." *Wall Street Journal*, November 10, 2008, p. R3.

2. Mark Van Vugt, Robert Hogan, and Robert B. Kaiser, "Leadership, Followership, and Evolution, *American Psychologist*, April 2008, pp. 182–183.

3. Joseph A. Raelin, *Creating Leaderful Organizations: How to Bring out Leadership in Everyone* (San Francisco: Berrett-Koehler, 2003).

4. Stephen J. Zaccaro, "Trait-Based Perspectives of Leadership," *American Psychologist*, January 2007, p. 6.

5. Sean T. Hannah, Bruce J. Avolio, Fred Luthans, and P. D. Harms, "Leadership Efficacy: Review and Future Directions," *Leadership Quarterly*, December 2008, p. 669.

6. Sonia Alleyne, "Oprah Means Business," *Black Enterprise*, June 2008, p. 117.

7. Dean Foust, "Coke: Time for a Shakeup," *Business Week*, March 8, 2004, p. 40; "Starwood to Open More than 70 Hotels in the Next Two Years." Retrieved February 22, 2005, from: Hotel-Online.com; Peter Sanders and Joann S. Lublin, "Starwood CEO's Ouster Followed Battle with Board over His Conduct," *Wall Street Journal*, April 7–8, 2007, pp. A1, A2.

8. Gareth R. Jones and Jennifer M. George, "The Experience and Evolution of Trust: Implications for Cooperation and Teamwork," *Academy of Management Review*, July 1998, pp. 531–546; Jenny C. McCune, "That Elusive Thing Called Trust," *Management Review*, August 1998, pp. 10–16.

9. Chris Taylor, "Builders & Titans," *Time*, April 26, 2004, pp.74–75.

10. Cassie R. Barlow, Mark Jordan, and William H. Hendrix, "Character Assessment: An Examination of Leadership Levels," *Journal of Business and Psychology*, Summer 2003, p. 563.

11. Timothy A. Judge, Amy E. Colbert, and Remus Ilies, "Intelligence and Leadership: A Quantitative Review and Test of Theoretical Positions," *Journal of Applied Psychology*, June 2004, pp. 542–552.

12. Daniel R. Ames and Francis J. Flynn, "What Breaks a Leader: The Curvilinear Relation between Assertiveness and Leadership," *Journal of Personality and Social Psychology*, Volume 92, 2007, pp. 307–324.

13. Luisa Beltran, "Standout Performer: Cuban-Born Maria Elena Lagomasino Managed to Ascend Wall Street without Blending In," *Hispanic Business*, April 2007, p. 26.

14. Joyce E. Bono and Timothy A. Judge, "Personality and Transformational and Transactional Leadership: A Meta-Analysis," *Journal of Applied Psychology*, October 2004, pp. 901–910.

15. Amir Erez et al., "Stirring the Hearts of Followers: Charismatic Leadership as the Transferal of Affect," *Journal of Applied Psychology*, May 2008, pp. 602–613.

16. Juan Carlos Pastor, Margarita Mayo, and Boas Shamir, "Adding Fuel to the Fire: The Impact of Followers' Arousal on Ratings of Charisma," *Journal of Applied Psychology*, November 2007, pp. 1584–1596.

17. Tom Bateman, "Leading for Results: Brief but Powerful Lessons from Katrina and Iraq," *Organizational Dynamics*, October–December 2008, p. 301.

18. "Ethics—Business Educators Teach Students to . . . Do the Right Thing!" *Keying In*, January 1997, p. 1.

19. Robert B. Maddux and Dorothy Maddux, *Ethics in Business: A Guide for Managers* (Los Altos, CA: Crisp, 1994).

20. "The Ethical Mind: A Conversation with Psychologist Howard Gardner," *Harvard Business Review*, March 2007, pp. 51–56.

21. Paulo Prada, "50: Joanne Smith: Senior Vice President of In-Flight Service and Global Product Development," *Wall Street Journal*, November 10, 2008, p. R8.

22. Peter Block, *Stewardship: Choosing Service over Self-Interest* (San Francisco: Berrett-Koehler, 1993), pp. 27–32.

23. Umesh Ramakrishnan, *There's No Elevator to the Top* (New York: Portfolio/Penguin, 2008).

24. Robert T. Keller, "A Test of the Path–Goal Theory of Leadership with Need for Clarity as a Moderator in Research and Development Organizations," *Journal of Applied Psychology*, April 1989, pp. 208–212.

25. "Carrot & Stick Failing? Try Encouragement," *Executive Leadership*, July 2007, p. 4.

26. Ronald A. Heifetz and Donald L. Laurie, "The Work of Leadership," *Harvard Business Review*, January–February 1997, p. 124.

27. Robert C. Liden, Sandy J. Wayne, Hao Zhao, David Henderson, "Servant Leadership: Development of a Multidimensional Measure and Multi-Level Assessment," *Leadership Quarterly*, April 2008, pp. 161–177.

28. Robert K. Greenleaf, *The Power of Servant Leadership: A Journey into the Nature of Legitimate Power and Greatness* (San Francisco: Berrett-Koehler, 1998); James C. Hunter, *The World's Most Powerful Leadership Principle: How to Become a Servant Leader* (New York: Crown Business, 2004).

29. "The Best Advice I Ever Got," *Fortune*, May 12, 2008, p. 74.

30. Liden, et al, "Servant Leadership," p. 162.

31. Ralph M. Stogdill and Alvin E. Coons, eds., *Leader Behavior: Its Description and Measurement* (Columbus: The Ohio State University Bureau of Business Research, 1957); Carroll L. Shartle, *Executive Performance and Leadership* (Upper Saddle River, NJ: Prentice Hall, 1956).

32. Anders Skogstad, Ståle Einarsen, Torbjorn Torscheim, Merethe Sschanke Assland, and Hilde Hetland, "The Destructiveness of Laissez-Faire Leadership Behavior," *Journal of Occupational Health Psychology*, Number 1, 2007, pp. 80–92.

33. Cited in Bill Breen, "Trickle-Up Leadership," *Fast Company*, November 2001, p. 90.

34. Jessica E. Vascellaro, "Yahoo CEO Set to Install Top-Down Management," *Wall Street Journal*, February 23, 2009, p. B1.

35. Richard Pascale, "Change How You Define Leadership, and You Change How You Run a Company," *Fast Company*, April–May 1988, pp. 114–120.

36. Gary Yukl and Richard Lepsinger, *Flexible Leadership: Creating Value by Balancing Multiple Challenges and Choices* (San Francisco: Jossey-Bass, 2004).

37. Bob Kaplan with Rob Kaiser, *The Versatile Leader: Make the Most of Your Strengths—Without Overdoing It* (San Francisco: Pfeiffer, 2006).

38. Yunxia Zhu, "Do Cultural Values Shape Employee Receptivity to Leadership Styles?" *Academy of Management*

Perspective, August 2007, pp. 89–90; Fred O. Walumbwa, John. J. Lawler, and Bruce J. Avolio, "Leadership, Individual Differences, and Work-Related Attitudes," *Applied Psychology: An International Review*, no. 2, 2007, pp. 212–230.

39. George Graen and J. F. Cashman, "A Role-Making Model of Leadership in Formal Organizations: A Developmental Approach," in J. G. Hunt and L. I. Larson, eds., *Leadership Frontiers* (Kent, OH: Kent State University Press, 1975), pp. 143–165; Robert P. Vecchio, "Leader–Member Exchange, Objective Performance, Employment Duration, and Supervisor Ratings: Testing for Moderation and Mediation," *Journal of Business and Psychology*, Spring 1998, pp. 327–341.

40. Robert P. Vecchio, "Are You In or Out with Your Boss?" *Business Horizons*, vol. 29, 1987, pp. 76–78.

41. "Personalize Your Management Style," *Manager's Edge*, June 2007, p. 3.

42. "Motivate by Telling Staffers 'Yes,'" *Manager's Edge*, May 2007, p. 4.

43. Quoted in Casey Feldman, "Game Changers," *Fortune*, July 21, 2008, p. 54.

44. "Warren G. Bennis, Leadership Guru," in *Business: The Ultimate Resource* (Cambridge, MA: Perseus Publishing, 2002), p. 969.

45. Donna M. Owens, "Success Factors: The Right Experience Can Increase Your Leadership Potential," *HR Magazine*, August 2008, pp. 87–88.

46. Michael E. McGill and John W. Slocum Jr., "A Little Leadership Please?" *Organizational Dynamics*, Winter 1998, p. 48.

47. Craig L. Pearce and Charles C. Manz, "The New Silver Bullet of Leadership: The Importance of Self- and Shared Leadership in Knowledge Work," *Organizational Dynamics*, no. 2, 2005, p. 133. The quote is from the same source.

48. William D. Hitt, *The Model Leader: A Fully Functioning Person* (Columbus, OH: Battelle Press, 1993).

49. Linda Hill, "Becoming the Boss," *Harvard Business Review*, January 2007, pp. 51–52.

50. Quoted in Sonja D. Brown, "Congratulations, You're a Manager, Now What?" *Black Enterprise*, April 2006, p. 104.

12

Motivating Others and Developing Teamwork

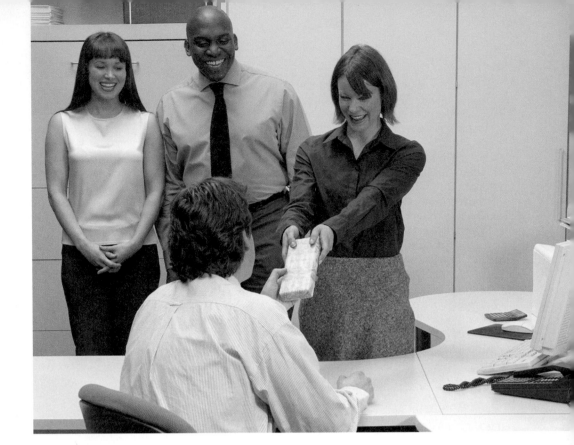

Outline

1 How Do You Diagnose What Motivates Others Toward Good Performance?

2 What Are Two Classic Approaches to Understanding Work Motivation?

3 How Do You Motivate Through Empowerment, Job Design, and Various Forms of Positive Reinforcement?
Empowerment
Motivation through Job Design and Interesting Work
Motivation through Positive Reinforcement
Financial Incentives as Positive Reinforcement
Motivation through Recognition and Praise

4 What Are Some Strategies and Tactics for Building Teamwork?

5 How Does Understanding Group Dynamics Contribute to Teamwork Development?
Stages of Group Development
Team Member Roles
The Problem of Groupthink (Too Much Consensus)

6 What Are the Characteristics of an Effective Work Group?

F rank Blake, the chief executive of Home Depot, explained during an interview what he had learned from his former bosses. Part of his answer was as follows:

"Vice President Bush (father of President George W. Bush) took an hour and a half every morning to write notes to people, including his staff. The power of connecting to people and expressing that they're doing a good job is invaluable. Every Sunday I have everybody in the field roll up their examples of the associates (store employees) who have done extraordinary things, and then I send them handwritten notes—about 40 to 50 a week—and just say that I appreciate them."[1]

The words of the CEO of one of the world's best-known retailers illustrate the importance of appreciation and recognition for motivating a workforce. In this chapter we describe a variety of theories and practices for motivating others, including recognition. We also describe the closely related topic of developing teamwork because a group of people working together as a team are motivated to perform well. Furthermore, one of the biggest motivational challenges facing managers and team leaders is to get the team working together smoothly.

After studying the information and doing the exercises in this chapter, you should be able to:

1 Understand how to diagnose what motivates people to perform well.

2 Recognize the contribution of two classical motivation theories to understanding work motivation.

3 Understand how to motivate others through empowerment and job design, including interesting work.

4 Understand how positive reinforcement, including financial incentives, recognition, and praise, are used for employee motivation.

5 Describe strategies and tactics for developing teamwork.

6 Understand group dynamics in terms of the development of groups and group roles.

7 Identify the characteristics of effective work groups, and be aware of the problem of groupthink.

▶ Learning Objective 1 ▶

How Do You Diagnose What Motivates Others Toward Good Performance?

Motivation
concept with two widely used meanings: (1) an internal state that leads to effort expended toward objectives and (2) an activity performed by one person to get another to accomplish work

An eternal challenge for people responsible for the work of others is to get them to perform at a high level. **Motivation** has two widely used meanings: (1) an internal state that leads to effort expended toward objectives and (2) an activity performed by one person to get another to accomplish work. Usually the manager is doing the motivating, yet many people in the workplace have a need to motivate others. To accomplish their work, people must motivate individuals who report to them, coworkers, supervisors, and customers. Understanding how to motivate others, therefore, is essential to your success. Keep in mind also that it is often important to motivate groups of people, such as a team, in addition to motivating people one at a time.

Knowledge of motivation is particularly important in the current era because so many workers do not feel identified with their work or their employers. According to one large study, about 70 percent of the U.S. workforce show up and do what is expected of them but do not invest the additional energy necessary to excel. Often these workers would like to contribute more, but they feel there is a disconnect with an immediate supervisor or that the organization does not care about them.[2] Note here that satisfaction is thought to be tied in with motivation, because if these disengaged workers were more satisfied with the supervisor and company, they might be more motivated.

A starting point in being able to motivate people and groups is to understand what outcomes or payoffs they want from their work. If you know what a person wants—and the person knows what he or she wants—you are in a better position to motivate that person. Questions can be asked in person or through a survey.[3] Basic questions might include:

■ What could this job offer you that would make you work at your best?

■ What factors about this job would bring out your best?

■ What might the company do to make you excited about your job?

■ How can I (or we) make your job a wonderful experience for you?

■ What would make you feel really good about your job?

A person's behavior is often more revealing than what he or she says. You might, therefore, also gain some diagnostic insights by observing what elements of the job or work situation strongly interest the subordinate. For example, one group member might display enthusiasm primarily when there is an opportunity to do exciting work. Another group member might be excited primarily when a weekend or holiday approaches. You could tentatively conclude that the first person is motivated by exciting work and the second by time off from work.

▶ Learning Objective 2 ▶

What Are Two Classic Approaches to Understanding Work Motivation?

As described in Chapter 3, Maslow's hierarchy of needs arranges human needs into a pyramid-shaped model with basic physiological needs at the bottom and self-actualization needs at the top. Maslow's needs hierarchy provided an exciting beginning to recognizing the importance of understanding human needs to better motivate others. A practical application of the needs hierarchy is that when a manager wants to motivate a group member, he or she must offer the individual a reward that will satisfy an important need.

The study of the needs hierarchy led to the **two-factor theory of work motivation.** According to the research of late industrial psychologist Frederick Herzberg, there are two different sets of job factors.[4] One set, the motivators (or satisfiers), can motivate and satisfy workers. The other set, dissatisfiers (or hygiene factors), can only prevent dissatisfaction. Motivators relate to higher-order needs, whereas hygiene factors relate to lower-order needs.

The two-factor theory explains how to design jobs to make them motivational. The motivational elements are the intrinsic, or job content, factors that make a job exciting. Motivator factors include achievement, recognition, advancement, responsibility, the work itself, and personal growth possibilities. The extrinsic, or job context, factors are hygienic. Although they are health maintaining and desirable, they are not motivational. Examples of hygiene factors are pay, status, job security, working conditions, and quality of leadership. Herzberg believed that motivation increases when one combines pay with a motivator such as challenging work.

According to the two-factor theory, only the presence of motivator factors leads to more positive energized behavior. For example, challenging work will motivate many people to exert increased effort. If intrinsic factors, such as challenging work, are not present, the result is neutral rather than negative, and the worker will feel bland rather than angry or unhappy. Although the presence of hygiene (or extrinsic) factors is not motivational, their absence can cause dissatisfaction, as in the following illustration. A police captain reported that when officers were assigned old patrol cars, they complained frequently, but when assigned brand new patrol cars, they did not express much appreciation. Nor did they increase their productivity as measured by the number of citations issued.

The two-factor theory has made two lasting contributions to work motivation. First, it has helped managers realize that money is not always the primary motivator. Second, it has spurred much of the interest in designing jobs to make them more intrinsically satisfying, as described later in this chapter.

A Modern Look at the Two-Factor Theory

A major problem with the two-factor theory is that it de-emphasizes individual differences and glosses over the importance of hygiene factors in attracting and retaining workers. Hygiene factors such as good benefits and company management satisfy and motivate many people. Many working parents will work extra hard to keep their jobs at a company that offers on-site child care or flexible working hours. Furthermore, benefits such as company-subsidized health insurance, dental insurance, and a retirement pension would motivate many workers today to work hard and stay with a firm. The reason is that some private and public employers have drastically reduced benefits in recent years. Also, time off and flexible hours are particularly appealing to younger workers and will motivate them to work harder and stay with their employer.[5]

Because of their historical importance, and the fact that the theories of Maslow and Herzberg still influence modern thinking, the two theories are compared in Figure 12-1.

How Do You Motivate Through Empowerment, Job Design, and Various Forms of Positive Reinforcement?

◀ Learning Objective 3 ◀

Among the standard practices for employee motivation are empowerment, job design, and various forms of positive reinforcement, including financial incentives, recognition, and praise.

Two-factor theory of work motivation
two different sets of job factors—one set, the motivators, or satisfiers, can motivate and satisfy workers; the other set, dissatisfiers, or hygiene factors, can only prevent dissatisfaction

FIGURE 12-1 COMPARISON OF THE HIERARCHY OF NEEDS AND TWO-FACTOR THEORY

Maslow's Hierarchy of Needs	Herzberg's Two-Factor Theory *Satisfiers or Motivators*	Managerial Action
Self-actualization Self-esteem	Achievement Recognition Work itself Responsibility Advancement Growth	Allow these factors to be present to increase satisfaction and motivation.
	Dissatisfiers or Hygiene Factors	
Social (love, affection, or belonging) Safety and security Physiological	Company policy and administration Supervision Working conditions Salary Relationship with coworkers Personal life Status Job security	Keep these factors at adequate levels to prevent dissatisfaction and de-motivation.

EMPOWERMENT

A comprehensive strategy for employee motivation is to grant workers more power by enabling them to participate in decisions affecting themselves and their work. Empowerment basically involves passing decision-making authority and responsibility from managers to employees. A key point is that the leader shares power with group members. Because group members have some power, they can influence the manager, such as giving him or her guidance.

Empowerment
process by which a manager shares power with team members, thereby enhancing their feelings of self-efficacy

Workers experience a greater sense of self-efficacy and ownership of their jobs when they share power. According to this logic, **empowerment** is the process by which a manager shares power with team members, thereby enhancing their feelings of self-efficacy. Because the worker feels more effective, empowerment contributes to intrinsic motivation. The individual has a choice in initiating and regulating actions, such as in deciding how to perform a particular task.[6] Sharing power with team members enables them to feel better about themselves and perform at a higher level. Teams as well as individuals can be empowered. An example of empowering a team would be to give it responsibility for developing a new product.

Empowerment as Shared Leadership

Shared leadership
the leader granting group members authority to carry out some of the leadership activities

Another way of understanding empowerment is that it involves **shared leadership,** or the leader granting group members authority to carry out some of the leadership activities. Instead of relying exclusively on the designated head of the group for leadership, the group members guide and influence themselves. The shared leadership is particularly useful when group members have certain technical knowledge they need to accomplish the work and the leader lacks this knowledge. But the leader of the group plays an important role in coaching the team members in how to assume leadership responsibility.[7]

Visualize a group of environmental specialists seeking ways to make an existing office building environmentally friendly. All group members have specialized knowledge of their own that they want to share with coworkers and influence them with. The leader steps back to allow this shared leadership take place, such as one group member influencing others to plant a garden on the roof to help moderate temperature and absorb carbon dioxide.

Several Forms of Empowerment

Employee empowerment often takes the form of giving customer contact employees more freedom in making decisions. At the same time, the employees are encouraged to exercise initiative and imagination (such as figuring how to satisfy an unusual customer demand), and they are rewarded for doing so.

Package carrier UPS empowers its managers to deal with crises at the local level so they can respond quickly. Immediately following the 9/11 terrorist attacks, UPS in lower Manhattan was left with thousands of undeliverable packages to World Trade Center addresses. The UPS managers decided on their own to first sort out all those packages containing medical and pharmaceutical supplies, so the supplies would be available immediately to treat the wounded. Decisions were made later about what to do with packages addressed to demolished addresses.

Although customer-contact employees are empowered, they are still given overall direction and limits to the extent of their authority. For example, a customer service worker cannot overturn a company rule, thereby creating a health or safety hazard. At a New York City hotel, a young woman wanted to check in with a boa constrictor draped around her shoulders. The snake lover insisted that her boa did not fit the ordinary pet category such as a dog, cat, or bird. The hotel associate replied firmly, "Sorry, I'm not empowered to allow boa constrictors into our hotel."

An extreme form of empowerment is when workers establish their own priorities and choose which projects they would like to pursue. Although there may not be loads of workplaces that can grant so much freedom to employees, it can be done, as illustrated by Meetup.

The company offers a Website to facilitate establishing local groups for such purposes as pulling together volunteers for political campaigns. Based on employee complaints about the layout of the organization, the traditional organization chart was replaced with a dispersion of power to the staff professionals. Employees are empowered to decide which projects get tackled first and organize themselves into teams to work on the projects. Management still reserves the right to regain control if the extreme empowerment approach does not work. Also, not all workers at Meetup, or other companies, are comfortable with so little structure and guidance.[8]

MOTIVATION THROUGH JOB DESIGN AND INTERESTING WORK

Many management experts contend that if you make jobs more interesting there may be less need for motivating people with external rewards. Also, attempting to motivate people by external rewards may not be sufficient. Motivating people through interesting work is based on the principle of **intrinsic motivation,** which refers to a person's beliefs about the extent to which an activity can satisfy his or her

Intrinsic motivation
a person's beliefs about the extent to which an activity can satisfy his or her needs for competence and self-determination; instead of looking to somebody else for rewards, a person is motivated by the intrinsic, or internal, aspects of the task

needs for competence and self-determination. Instead of looking to somebody else for rewards, a person is motivated by the intrinsic, or internal, aspects of the task.

Prosocial motivation
the desire to expend effort to help other people

Intrinsic motivation contributes even more to productivity when combined with **prosocial motivation,** the desire to expend effort to help other people. People who are agreeable by nature are more likely to have strong prosocial motivation. A study was conducted with fundraising callers whose task was to telephone alumni to raise money for the university. A major finding was that those callers who experienced both intrinsic and prosocial motivation tended to have high productivity in terms of calls made and funds raised.[9]

Job enrichment
making a job more motivating and satisfying by adding variety and responsibility

Job enrichment refers to making a job more motivating and satisfying by adding variety and responsibility. A job is considered enriched to the extent that it demands more of an individual's talents and capabilities. As the job becomes more meaningful to you, you become better motivated and, it is hoped, more productive. Unless you want an enriched job, these positive results may not be forthcoming. Substantial research and practical experience has gone into enriching jobs. Three noteworthy characteristics of an enriched job are direct feedback, client relationships, and new learning.[10]

Direct feedback occurs when a worker receives immediate knowledge of the results he or she is achieving. This evaluation of performance can be built into the job (such as a highway patrol officer catching a speeder) or provided by a supervisor. *Client relationship* refers to an employee having a client or customer to serve, whether that client is inside or outside the organization. In this regard, both a customer service representative and a hairstylist have enriched jobs. *New learning* takes place when a job incumbent feels that he or she is growing psychologically. In contrast, an impoverished job allows for no new learning. The information technology component built into most jobs provides ample opportunity for new learning, as would learning a second language to relate better to customers in another country. A basic example of job enrichment is as follows: Instead of simply putting an accounts payable specialist in charge of more accounts, put the person in charge of following up on the calls, talking with collection agencies, and redesigning the workflow.[11]

Going beyond the formal theory of job enrichment, interesting work also includes having a sense of purpose as you may have studied in relation to self-motivation and goal setting. The interesting work is often at the team level. Jack Welch, the former chair of GE, and his wife, Suzy Welch, a former *Harvard Business Review* editor, say that a bold mission allows bosses to say, "There's the hill. Let's take it together."[12] An example of a bold mission leading to interesting work for most people would be working on a community redevelopment project or finding a cure for childhood leukemia.

MOTIVATION THROUGH POSITIVE REINFORCEMENT

Positive reinforcement
increasing the probability that behavior will be repeated by rewarding people for making the desired response; improves learning and motivation

Rewarding a worker for achieving a certain result or behaving in a particular way is a widely used motivational tactic. **Positive reinforcement** means increasing the probability that behavior will be repeated by rewarding people for making the desired response. The phrase *increasing the probability* means that positive reinforcement improves learning and motivation but is not 100 percent effective. The phrase *making the desired response* is also noteworthy. To use positive reinforcement properly, a reward must be contingent on doing something right. Simply paying somebody a compliment or giving the person something of value is not positive reinforcement. Because financial incentives, recognition, and praise are given for attaining a given goal, they function as positive reinforcement.

Positive reinforcement is easy to visualize with well-structured jobs, such as data entry or producing parts. Yet positive reinforcement is also used to encourage desired behavior for those in highly paid, complex jobs. An accountant who developed a new method of the company getting paid faster might be rewarded with two extra days of vacation.

Rules for the Effective Use of Positive Reinforcement

To use positive reinforcement effectively, certain rules and procedures must be followed. Although using rewards to motivate people seems straightforward, positive reinforcement requires a systematic approach. The rules are specified from the standpoint of the person trying to motivate another individual, such as a group member, coworker, supervisor, or customer. The same rules also apply to motivating a work group.

Rule 1: State Clearly What Behavior Will Lead to a Reward. The nature of good performance, or the goals, must be agreed on by the manager and group member. Clarification might take this form: "We need to decrease by 40 percent the number of new credit card customers who have delinquent accounts of sixty days or more."

Rule 2: Choose an Appropriate Reward. An appropriate reward is effective in motivating a given person and feasible from the standpoint of the individual or the company. If one reward does not motivate the person, try another. One person might be motivated by time off from work, another by an interesting assignment, and a third by an e-mail note of praise with a copy to a high-ranking executive. Many employees are strongly motivated by the possibility of receiving a promotion, especially because promotions offer the prospect of more status and higher pay.[13] The importance of choosing the right reward underscores the fact that not all rewards are reinforcers. A reward is something of perceived value by the person giving the reward, but if the reward does not strengthen the desired response (such as wearing safety goggles), it is not a true reinforcer.[14]

Rule 3: Supply Ample Feedback. Positive reinforcement cannot work without frequent feedback to individuals. Feedback can take the form of simply telling people they have done something right or wrong. Brief e-mail messages or handwritten notes are other forms of feedback. As described at the outset of the chapter, effective motivators make extensive use of handwritten thank-you notes.

Rule 4: Schedule Rewards Intermittently. Rewards should not be given on every occasion of good performance. **Intermittent rewards** sustain desired behaviors longer and also slow down the process of behaviors fading away when they are not rewarded. If each correct performance results in a reward, the behavior will stop shortly after a performance in which the reward is not received. Another problem is that a reward given continuously may lose its impact. A practical value of intermittent reinforcement is that it saves time. Few managers or team leaders have enough time to dispense rewards for every correct action by group members.

Intermittent rewards
sustaining desired behaviors longer and slowing down the process of behaviors fading away when they are not rewarded

Rule 5: Make the Rewards Follow the Observed Behavior Closely in Time. For maximum effectiveness, people should be rewarded soon after doing something right. A built-in, or intrinsic, feedback system, such as software working or not working, capitalizes on this principle. E-mail and instant messaging are again useful here because it would be difficult for the manager or team leader to congratulate in person team members who work in another location.

Rule 6: Make the Reward Fit the Behavior. People who are inexperienced in applying positive reinforcement often overdo the intensity of spoken rewards. When an employee does something of an ordinary nature correctly, a simple word of praise such as "Good job" is preferable to something like "Fantastic performance." A related idea is that the magnitude of the reward should vary with the magnitude of the accomplishment.

Rule 7: Make the Rewards Visible. Another important characteristic of an effective reward is the extent to which it is visible, or noticeable, to other employees.

When other workers notice the reward, its impact multiplies because other people observe what kind of behavior is rewarded.[15] Rewards should also be visible, or noticeable, to the employee. A reward of five dollars per week added to a person's paycheck might be hardly noticeable, after payroll deductions. However, a bonus check for $200 might be very noticeable. A dramatic technique for making rewards visible is to offer workers something luxurious, exotic, or self-indulgent they would most likely not purchase for themselves even if they could afford it. Examples include a luxury vacation, or gift certificates for a series of massages.[16]

Rule 8: Change the Reward Periodically. Rewards do not retain their effectiveness indefinitely. Employees and customers lose interest in striving for a reward they have received many times in the past. This is particularly true of a repetitive statement such as "Nice job" or "Congratulations." It is helpful for the person giving out the rewards to study the list of potential rewards and try different ones from time to time.

FINANCIAL INCENTIVES AS POSITIVE REINFORCEMENT

Money is a natural motivator, and no program of motivation can exclude the role of financial compensation. Even the most ardent critics of the motivational power of money recognize that nonfinancial motivators are effective only when compensation is considered to be fair and adequate. When workers are preoccupied with not being paid fairly, they are less likely to respond to other approaches to motivation. When money is used as a motivator, it becomes a positive reinforcer because a person receives more money for performing well.

A challenge in understanding the role of money and other forms of compensation is that they are not pure concepts. High pay is also closely associated with other outcomes such as status and recognition. Thus, a person may work hard to earn more money as a way of achieving more status and recognition. Here we describe programs making pay partially contingent on performance, individual factors that influence the effectiveness of financial incentives, and problems with financial incentives.

Linking Compensation to Performance

Variable pay
incentive plan that intentionally pays good performers more money than poor performers

Many employers make a systematic effort to link some portion of pay to performance to make pay more motivational. **Variable pay** (or *merit* pay) is an incentive plan that intentionally pays good performers more money than poor performers. Employees receive more money by excelling on performance measures such as number of sales or number of computer programs completed. Whatever the specific plan, employees receive a base level of pay along with a bonus related to performance. The better your performance as measured by your employer, the higher your pay. Linking salary increases to good performance helps employers spare the cost of giving too many workers a pay boost. At the same time such plans are perceived to be useful in retaining valuable employees.[17]

Another approach to relating pay to performance is to link bonuses to results obtained by the work group or the entire company. A companywide bonus plan ties individual merit pay to overall company or division performance, such as a year-end bonus based on company profits. The financial results on which the bonuses are determined can be measured at the division, group, business unit, or company level. Sometimes the bonus is based on a combination of the levels mentioned.[18] Here is a successful example of using a bonus plan to motivate employees:

David Hayes, the founder and CEO of Skyline Construction in San Francisco, offered his employees a bonus plan. Seventy-five percent of the eligible workers opted for the lowest salary combined with the highest bonus. After two years, sales grew from $36 million to $71 million, while costs as a percentage of sales shrank.[19]

Personal Factors Influencing the Power of Financial Incentives

Individual differences profoundly influence the motivational power of financial incentives. Workers who attach a high value to financial incentives will be more motivated by money than those who attach a low value. A major influencing factor is that money is a good motivator when you need it badly enough. Money has a motivational pull for most people who perceive themselves to have a strong need for money. Once people have enough money to pay for all those things they think are important in life, money may lose its effectiveness. There are tremendous individual differences in what people classify as necessities. If, for example, somebody thinks owning three cars and having two residences is a necessity, that person will be motivated by money for a long time.

Problems Created by Financial Incentives

Despite their effectiveness as motivators, financial incentives also create human problems. A major concern is that financial rewards can lead a person to focus on rewards rather than the joy built into exciting work. Another problem is that after people receive several increases based on performance, merit pay comes to be perceived as a right or entitlement. A person who does not receive a merit increase one quarter often feels that he or she has been punished. Another problem with cash awards is that they sometimes interfere with teamwork as employees concentrate on individual financial rewards. Also, pay-for-performance plans can prompt executives, corporate professionals, and sales representatives to focus on achieving exceptional financial results, sometimes by unethical means. Many of the Wall Street financial scandals in recent years came about because investment specialists invented complex investment instruments to sell to the public. Often these instruments, such as "collateralized debt obligations," were derived from very high-risk loans.

MOTIVATION THROUGH RECOGNITION AND PRAISE

The workplace provides a natural opportunity to satisfy the **recognition need**—the desire to be acknowledged for one's contributions and efforts and to feel important. A manager can thus motivate many employees by making them feel important. Employee needs for recognition can be satisfied both through informal recognition and by establishing formal recognition programs. If the recognition prize is made contingent on achievement, the recognition program functions like positive reinforcement.

Recognition need
the desire to be acknowledged for one's contributions and efforts and to feel important

Praise as Recognition

Praising workers for good performance is closely related to informal recognition. An effective form of praise describes the worker's performance rather than merely making an evaluation. Describing good performance might take this form: "You turned an angry customer into an ally who referred new business to us." A more general evaluation would be "You are great with angry customers."

Although praise costs no money and requires only a few minutes of time, many workers rarely receive praise. According to a survey of 1,003 adults, only 43 percent agreed that they were consistently recognized in ways they perceived as meaningful.[20] Data from a decade-long study suggest that 79 percent of employees who quit their job contend that a key reason they left was lack of appreciation.[21] Managers and team leaders therefore have a good opportunity to increase motivation by the simple act of praising good deeds. Other informal approaches to recognizing good performance include taking an employee to lunch, a handshake from the manager or team leader, and putting flowers on an employee's desk.

Tailor Praise to Individual Preferences

An advanced use of praise is to tailor the praise to the needs of the person being praised, much like the diagnostic approach to motivation. A study with 103 working adults found that people who perceived themselves to be technically oriented have a more negative attitude toward being flattered (a strong form of praise). Instead, they prefer a laid-back, factual statement of how they made a contribution. (An example: "Your solution to the problem saved us 30 percent in raw material costs.") Conversely, people who perceived themselves to be less technically oriented were more positively disposed toward being flattered. (An example: "I love it. What a fantastic solution to our problem.") Also, women had a more positive attitude toward being flattered than did men.[22] So it would appear that non-technically oriented women would be the most receptive to praise and flattery!

Another example of differences in response to recognition and praise is that not every employee wants to receive the accolade of "employee of the month" or to receive public recognition. A cultural difference is that many Asian workers prefer that praise be given privately or shared with the team publicly.[23] Team recognition rather than individual recognition is often more effective in Japan. Another cultural difference is that recognition of individuals is preferred in Bangalore, India.[24]

Company Recognition Programs

Formal recognition programs are more popular than ever as companies attempt to retain the right employees and keep workers productive who worry about losing their jobs or having no private work area. Company recognition programs include awarding watches and jewelry for good service, plaques for good performance, and on-the-spot cash awards (about $25 to $50) for good performance. Because so many workers are not in face-to-face contact with their managers, managers often deliver verbal recognition by e-mail or telephone. Furthermore, some recognition programs are administered through Web sites in which the employee can choose from among a list of possible awards.[25]

The accompanying Human Relations in Practice insert illustrates the effective use of a company recognition program.

▶ **Learning Objective 4** ▶

What Are Some Strategies and Tactics for Building Teamwork?

So far in this chapter we have studied how leaders and managers can influence subordinates by direct use of motivational techniques. Team leaders, as well as other managers, also need to use techniques that influence subordinates to work well together in a team. Influencing others is similar to motivating them. In this section we describe methods for building **teamwork**—work done with an understanding and commitment to group goals on the part of all team members.[26] In the following sections we describe more about how groups function because such knowledge can indirectly help the manager or leader do a better job of developing teamwork. An analogy is that if a professor understands how people learn, he or she can be more effective at teaching.

Good teamwork enhances, but does not guarantee, a successful team. For example, a group with excellent teamwork might be working on improving a product or service no longer valued by the company or customers. No matter what the output of the team, it will probably be ignored. A list of strategies and tactics for building teamwork follows.

1. Get qualified members. A starting point in developing good teamwork is to select members for the team who are interested in and qualified to be strong team

Teamwork

work done with an understanding and commitment to group goals on the part of all team members

"Teamwork is the ability to work together toward a common vision; the ability to direct individual accomplishments toward organizational objectives. It is the fuel that allows common people to attain uncommon results."

—Andrew Carnegie, steel manufacturer and philanthropist, 1835–1919

Human Relations in Practice

Sports Medicine Center Motivates its Employees Through Recognition

Lynn Fraser is the director of the physical therapy unit within the Center of Sports Medicine at a large private hospital. Sports injuries have surged in recent years as more students and full-time workers alike participate in sports. For example, there is a long waiting list for men and women and boys and girls who want treatment for a torn anterior cruciate ligament (ACL). Fraser says, "There is a boom in demand for physical therapy for sports injuries. Our group is under continuous pressure. We could easily find productive work for another five physical therapists and aides, but budget restrictions have placed a lid on hiring for now. Yet even with a bigger budget for staffing it would be difficult to hire five new therapists because there is such a shortage of these people."

To help deal with the problem of an overworked staff, all of whom could find employment elsewhere, Fraser decided to start an employee recognition program. She enlisted the services of a human resources specialist within the hospital to help launch the program. Both Fraser and the HR specialist, Alex Garcia, agreed that the physical therapy group needed a recognition program more sophisticated than a plaque celebrating the employee of the month.

The data for giving recognition awards stem from three sources. First are comment cards given to patients of the physical therapy unit as they leave the facility, asking them questions about their experience at the unit. A second, and related, source of data are e-mail inquiries sent to a random sample of patients. Both sources of information invite patients to explain what they liked and disliked about their experiences, including the opportunity to identify the names of staff members who were particularly helpful.

A third source of data is spontaneous comments about staff members made to the receptionists at the desk. The receptionists are invited to record, by computer, any positive comments made about therapists and other staff members. For example, a patient might comment while paying the bill, "That Holly [one of the physical therapists] is a miracle worker."

The recognition committee consists of Fraser, Garcia, and the chief sports medicine physician. The committee meets once a month to evaluate the three sources of data to see which two staff members—professional workers and support workers included—merit a recognition award. The recognition rewards consist of (a) a written statement of appreciation that is included in the staff member's human resource filed, (b) gift certificates for two to an upscale restaurant, and (c) a two-year subscription to a health magazine.

When asked how the recognition program was working, Fraser replied, "The subjective results are that our professionals and support staff make quite positive comments about the program. The objective results are that after two years our turnover of the professional and support staff is much lower than the national and regional averages."

Source: Case history collected at a large private hospital in the northeastern United States.

members. The hiring manager or team leader should look for individuals who have enjoyed and performed well on teams in the past, both on and off the job. A study conducted in a manufacturing organization with highly interdependent teams found that being conscientious, extraverted, and having knowledge about teamwork were positively related to good job performance as a team member.[27]

2. Agree on what constitutes success. Gordon Bethune, the CEO who helped rebuild Continental Airlines from "worst to first," offers a good early step for building teamwork. He maintains that the entire team must agree on what constitutes success. Every team member has to say, "Yes, that's it."[28]

3. Have urgent, constructive purpose. Another early step is to help team members believe they have an urgent, constructive purpose. An example would be, "If we don't patch this software problem, we will get 95 percent returns." A demanding performance challenge helps create and sustain the team. Rewards should stem from meeting the challenge.

4. Compete against common enemy. Competing against a common enemy is one of the best-known methods of building team spirit. It is preferable that the adversary is external, such as an independent diner competing against franchised family restaurants.

5. Have a culture of teamwork. A primary strategy for teamwork promotes the attitude that working together effectively is an expected norm. Developing such a culture of teamwork generally proves difficult when a strong culture of individualism exists within the firm. The team leader can communicate the norm of teamwork by making frequent use of words and phrases that support teamwork. Emphasizing the words *team members* or *teammates*, and de-emphasizing the words *subordinates* and *employees*, helps communicate the teamwork norm. The norm of teamwork is also fostered by having a code of conduct to which members agree. Provisions of the code might include, "Never abandon a teammate" and "Never humiliate a teammate."

As a team leader, you can contribute to a culture of teamwork by remembering to share credit with teammates whenever you receive a compliment for what the group has accomplished. Tell the group directly about the praise. Or if the praise is given publicly, make a statement in front of the team, such as, "I appreciate the compliment, but I could not have done it without Gus, Jennifer, Fred, and Hillary."[29] Although, this sentiment is widely expressed, it still has a positive impact on teamwork.

6. Use consensus decision-making style. Using the consensus decision-making style provides another way to reinforce teamwork. A sophisticated approach to enhancing teamwork, it feeds team members valid facts and information that motivate them to work together. New information prompts the team to redefine and enrich its understanding of the challenge it is facing, thereby focusing on a common purpose. The consensus decision-making style helps develop teamwork also because the team members feel empowered because they feel involved in decision making. As the team members share in decision making, they are likely to develop a cooperative spirit.

7. Use teamwork language. A subtle yet potent method of building teamwork emphasizes the use of language that fosters cohesion and commitment. In-group jargon bonds a team and sets the group apart from others. For example, a team of computer experts says, "Give me a core dump" to mean "Tell me your thoughts." The culture at Microsoft heavily emphasizes using hip jargon to build teamwork. Using the term *bandwidth* as a synonym for *intelligence* appears to have been invented by former CEO and chairman Bill Gates.

8. Minimize micromanagement. To foster teamwork, the manager should minimize micromanagement, or supervising group members too closely and second-guessing their decisions. Micromanagement can hamper a spirit of teamwork (potency) because team members do not feel in control of their own work. A relatively frequent example of a team leader being a micromanager (or *control freak*) is dictating which font should be used on team reports.

9. Reward the team as well as individuals. One high-impact strategy for encouraging teamwork rewards the team as well as individuals. The most convincing team incentive is to calculate compensation partially on the basis of team results. For a more general reward strategy, managers apply positive reinforcement whenever the group or individuals engage in behavior that supports teamwork. For example, team members who took the initiative to have an information-sharing session can be singled out and praised for this activity. The use of team-based incentives began in manufacturing, but it has spread to hospitals and health systems. Rewards are typically tied to specific goals, such as increased patient satisfaction or a reduction in accounts receivables.[30]

10. Publish a team book. To enhance team spirit, the manager can publish a team book containing a one-page biography of each team member. The biography can include a photo, a list of hobbies, personal interests, and family information. As team members look through the book, they become better acquainted with each other, leading to feelings of closeness.

11. Show respect for team members. Showing respect for team members is a general technique for building teamwork. Respect can be demonstrated in such ways as asking rather than demanding something be done—for example, "Jason, could you investigate developing a Web site for the team?" Giving team members your undivided attention when they come to you with a problem is another demonstration of respect, as are making positive comments about other team members and not talking behind their backs.

12. Send members to offsite training. Another option available to organizations for enhancing teamwork comes through experiential learning, such as sending members to offsite (or outdoor) training. Participants acquire teamwork skills by confronting physical challenges and exceeding their self-imposed limitations. (As mentioned in Chapter 11, offsite training is also used for leadership development.) In rope activities, which are typical of outdoor training, participants attached to a secure pulley with ropes climb ladders and jump off to another spot.

A day at an auto-racing track, another form of outdoor training for elite teams, provides team members with an opportunity to drive at racecar speeds in some kind of cooperative venture. Getting the team to work together in doing a social good, such as repairing a rundown house in a poor neighborhood, is another popular form of team building. A recent entrant to team-building activities is for businesspeople to engage in cooperative activities in indoor inflatable playgrounds—the type of inflatable structure typically reserved for young children. Among the activities are "Tag Team Climbing" to improve cooperation.[31]

All of these challenges require teamwork rather than individual effort, hence their contribution to team development. Offsite training generally offers the most favorable outcomes when the trainer helps the team members comprehend the link between such training and on-the-job behavior.

13. Encourage communication among virtual team members. A special challenge in developing good teamwork is when the members are geographically dispersed, as in a virtual team. Because the members communicate with each other mostly by e-mail and group software, they lose out on the face to-face interaction useful for building teamwork. A technologically advanced approach is for the virtual team members to use online team rooms where everyone can see the state of work in progress and interact with each other simultaneously.[32] (The setup is much like a blog for team member use.) Bringing the group together for an occasional face-to-face meeting is also helpful in building teamwork.

A study showed that virtual teams profit from norms that describe how communication technology will be used. After these norms are accepted, trust—and therefore teamwork—is likely to be enhanced. These norms include such actions as how often to check the team's knowledge repository (e.g., the team intranet) and how to use the repository for useful discussions rather than as a place to store documents. Norms also need to be established regarding what information should be posted, when to post it, and how to comment. Rules of etiquette should also be established, such as only using all capitals to communicate urgent messages.[33]

14. **Make appropriate use of a team slogan, logo, and clothing.** Many teams and groups in the workplace will develop closer ties among each other when they identify with a team logo and slogan that might be emblazoned on T-shirts, coffee mugs, pencils, and pens. The purpose of the symbols is to remind the group that they are part of a greater whole.[34] For some work situations, such as a group of financial planners or tax consultants, such gimmicks might be inappropriate. Yet for many groups, such as manufacturing employees, call center workers, and distribution center specialists, the team slogan, logo, and clothing might work well. The team members should be encouraged to develop the slogan and logo. For example, a group of dog and cat groomers might label themselves the Proud Pet Champions and use a logo of a cartoon dog and cat next to "PPC." in large letters.

15. **Step in to resolve conflict.** Conflict often arises in teams, especially when team members believe that they the authority to decide on which work procedure or process to use.[35] Based on this freedom, the team members might squabble about which procedure or process is the most effective. Too much conflict lowers the team spirit, so the team leader should encourage the team members to resolve the conflict themselves or step in to facilitate conflict resolution. The techniques described in Chapter 10 should work well for resolving conflict within the team.

Effective managers and team leaders pick and choose from strategies as appropriate to build teamwork. Relying too heavily on one tactic, such as establishing a mission statement or outdoor training, limits the development of sustained teamwork.

▶ Learning Objective 5 ▶

How Does Understanding Group Dynamics Contribute to Teamwork Development?

Group dynamics
the forces operating in groups that affect how members work together

An indirect way of a leader being effective at developing teamwork is to be knowledgeable about how groups operate. **Group dynamics** refers to the forces operating in groups that affect how members work together. To help zero in on this vast body of knowledge, we feature three practical topics: the stages of group development, team member roles, and the characteristics of an effective work group, including the problem of groupthink.

STAGES OF GROUP DEVELOPMENT

Key to understanding the nature of work groups is to know what the group does (the content) and how it proceeds (the process). A key group process is the group's development over time. To make this information more meaningful, relate it to any group to which you have belonged for at least one month. Understanding the

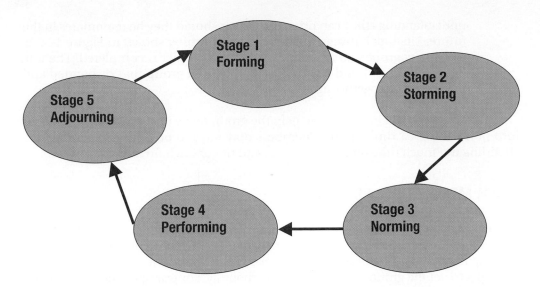

FIGURE 12-2

THE STAGES OF GROUP DEVELOPMENT: MOST GROUPS FOLLOW A PREDICTABLE SEQUENCE OF STAGES

stages of group development can lead to more effective group leadership or membership. The five group stages are shown in Figure 12-2 and described next.[36]

Stage 1. Forming. At the outset, members are eager to learn what tasks they will be performing, how they can benefit from group membership, and what constitutes acceptable behavior. Members often inquire about rules they must follow. Confusion, caution, and communality are typical during the initial phase of group development.

Stage 2. Storming. During this "shakedown" period, individual styles often come into conflict. Hostility, infighting, tension, and confrontation are typical. Members may argue to clarify expectations of their contributions. Coalitions and cliques may form within the group, and one or two members may be targeted for exclusion. Subgroups may form to push for an agenda of interest to them. (Despite the frequency of storming, many workplace groups work willingly with one another from the outset, thus skipping stage 2.)

Stage 3. Norming. After storming comes the quieter stage of overcoming resistance and establishing group standards of conduct (norms). Cohesiveness and commitment begin to develop. The group starts to come together as a coordinated unit, and harmony prevails. Norms stem from three sources. First, the group itself quickly establishes limits for members, often by effective use of glares and nods. For example, the team member who swears at the leader might receive angry glances from other members. Second, norms may also be imposed that are derived from the larger organization and from professional codes of conduct. A third source of norms might be an influential team member who inspires the group to elevate its performance or behavior. The head of an audit team might say, "Let's develop the reputation of an audit team that is the most professional and objective in the industry."

Stage 4. Performing. When the group reaches the performing stage, it is ready to focus on accomplishing its key tasks. Issues concerning interpersonal relations and task assignment are put aside as the group becomes a well-functioning unit. Intrinsic motivation and creativity are likely to emerge as the group performs. At their best, members feel they are working "for the cause," much like a political campaign team or a team bringing a breakthrough product to market.

Stage 5. Adjourning. Temporary work groups are abandoned after their task has been accomplished, much like a project team to erect an office tower. The same group members, however, have developed important relationships and understandings they can bring with them should they be teammates in the future. The link between adjourning and forming shown in Figure 12-2 is that many groups do reassemble after one project is completed. The link between stages 1 and 5 would not apply for a group that disbanded and never worked together again.

A key managerial challenge is to help the group move past the first three stages into performing. At times, group members may have to be notified that they are spending too much time on process issues and not enough on the task at hand.

TEAM MEMBER ROLES

A major challenge in learning to become an effective team member is to choose the right roles to occupy. A **role** is a tendency to behave, contribute, and relate to others in a particular way. It is helpful for the leader to understand these roles as he or she attempts to get the group working together smoothly. For example, the leader might want to make sure that all positive roles are filled. If you carry out positive roles, you will be perceived as a contributor to team effort. If you neglect carrying out these roles, you will be perceived as a poor contributor. Human Relations Self-Assessment Quiz 12-1 will help you evaluate your present inclinations toward occupying effective roles as a team member. In this section we describe a number of the most frequently observed positive roles played by team members. We also mention a group of negative roles.

According to the role theory developed by Meredith Belbin and his group of researchers at Belbin Associates, there are nine frequent roles occupied by team members.[37] All of these roles are influenced to some extent by an individual's personality.

1. **Creative problem solver.** The creative problem solver is creative, imaginative, and unorthodox. Such a person solves difficult problems. A potential weakness of

Role
tendency to behave, contribute, and relate to others in a particular way

Human Relations Self-Assessment Quiz   12-1

Team Player Roles

For each of the following statements about team activity, check mostly agree or mostly disagree. If you have not experienced such a situation, imagine how you would act or think if placed in that situation. In responding to the statements, assume that you are taking the questionnaire with the intent of learning something about yourself.

	Mostly Agree	Mostly Disagree
1. It is rare that I ever miss a team meeting.	_____	_____
2. I regularly compliment team members when they do something exceptional.	_____	_____
3. Whenever I can, I avoid being the note taker at a team meeting.	_____	_____
4. From time to time, other team members come to me for advice on technical matters.	_____	_____
5. I like to hide some information from other team members so I can be in control.	_____	_____
6. I welcome new team members coming to me for advice and learning the ropes.	_____	_____
7. My priorities come first, which leaves me with very little time to help other team members.	_____	_____
8. During a team meeting, it is not unusual for several other people at a time to look toward me for my opinion.	_____	_____

Continued

9. If I think the team is moving in an unethical direction, I will say so explicitly.   _____   _____

10. Rarely will I criticize the progress of the team even if I think such criticism is deserved.   _____   _____

11. It is not unusual for me to summarize the progress in a team meeting, even if not asked.   _____   _____

12. To conserve time, I attempt to minimize contact with my teammates outside of our meetings.   _____   _____

13. I intensely dislike going along with a consensus decision if the decision runs contrary to my thoughts on the issue.   _____   _____

14. I rarely remind teammates of our mission statement as we go about our work.   _____   _____

15. Once I have made up my mind on an issue facing the team, I am unlikely to be persuaded in another direction.   _____   _____

16. I am willing to accept negative feedback from team members.   _____   _____

17. Simply to get a new member of the team involved, I will ask his or her opinion.   _____   _____

18. Even if the team has decided on a course of action, I am not hesitant to bring in new information that supports another position.   _____   _____

19. Quite often I talk negatively about one team member to another.   _____   _____

20. My teammates are almost a family to me because I am truly concerned about their welfare.   _____   _____

21. When it seems appropriate, I joke and kid with teammates.   _____   _____

22. My contribution to team tasks is as important to me as my individual work.   _____   _____

23. From time to time I have pointed out to the team how we can all improve in reaching our goals.   _____   _____

24. I will fight to the last when the team does not support my viewpoint and wants to move toward consensus.   _____   _____

25. I will confront the team if I believe that the members are thinking too much alike.   _____   _____

Total Score   _____

Scoring and Interpretation:

Give yourself one point (+1) for each statement you gave in agreement with the keyed answer. The keyed answer indicates carrying out a positive, as opposed to a negative, role.

1. Mostly agree	10. Mostly disagree	19. Mostly disagree
2. Mostly agree	11. Mostly agree	20. Mostly agree
3. Mostly disagree	12. Mostly disagree	21. Mostly agree
4. Mostly agree	13. Mostly disagree	22. Mostly agree
5. Mostly disagree	14. Mostly disagree	23. Mostly agree
6. Mostly agree	15. Mostly disagree	24. Mostly disagree
7. Mostly disagree	16. Mostly agree	25. Mostly agree
8. Mostly agree	17. Mostly agree	
9. Mostly agree	18. Mostly agree	

20–25   You carry out a well above average number of positive team roles. Behavior of this type contributes substantially to being an effective team player. Study the roles in this chapter to further build your effectiveness as a team member.

10–19   You carry out an average number of positive team roles. Study carefully the roles described in this chapter to search for ways to carry out a greater number of positive roles.

0–9   You carry out a substantially above average number of negative team roles. If becoming an effective team player is important to you, you will have to diligently search for ways to play positive team roles. Study the information about roles in this chapter carefully.

this role is that the person tends to ignore fine details and becomes too immersed in the problem to communicate effectively.

2. **Resource investigator.** The resource investigator is extroverted, enthusiastic, and communicates freely with other team members. He or she will explore opportunities and develop valuable contacts. A potential weakness of this role is that the person can be overly optimistic and may lose interest after the initial enthusiasm wanes.

3. **Coordinator.** The coordinator is mature, confident, and a natural team leader. He or she clarifies goals, promotes decision making, and delegates effectively. A downside to occupying this role is that the person might be seen as manipulative and controlling. Some coordinators delegate too much by asking others to do some of the work they (the coordinators) should be doing.

4. **Shaper.** The shaper is challenging, dynamic, and thrives under pressure. He or she will use determination and courage to overcome obstacles. A potential weakness of the shaper is that he or she can be easily provoked and may ignore the feelings of others.

5. **Monitor–evaluator.** The monitor–evaluator is even tempered, engages in strategic (big picture and long-term) thinking, and makes accurate judgments. He or she sees all the options and judges accurately. A potential weakness of this role occupant is that he or she might lack drive and the ability to inspire others.

6. **Team worker.** The team worker is cooperative, focuses on relationships, and is sensitive and diplomatic. He or she is a good listener who builds relationships, dislikes confrontation, and averts friction. A potential weakness is that the team worker can be indecisive in a crunch situation or crisis.

7. **Implementer.** The implementer is disciplined, reliable, conservative, and efficient. He or she will act quickly on ideas and convert them into practical actions. A potential weakness is that the implementer can be inflexible and slow to see new opportunities.

8. **Completer–finisher.** The completer–finisher is conscientious and eager to get the job done. He or she has a good eye for detail and is effective at searching out errors. He or she can be counted on for finishing a project and delivering on time. A potential weakness is that he or she can be a worrier and reluctant to delegate.

9. **Specialist.** The specialist is a single-minded self-starter. He or she is dedicated and provides knowledge and skill in rare supply. A potential weakness of the specialist is that he or she can be stuck in a niche with little interest in other knowledge and may dwell on technicalities.

The weaknesses in the first nine roles point to problems the team leader or manager can expect to emerge, and therefore allowances should be made. Belbin refers to these potential problems as *allowable weaknesses*, because allowances should be made for them. To illustrate, if a team worker has a tendency to be indecisive in a crisis, the team should not have high expectations of the team worker when faced with a crisis. Team workers will be the most satisfied if the crisis is predicted and decisions involving them are made before the pressure mounts.[38]

Another perspective on team roles is that team members will sometimes engage in *self-oriented roles*. Members will sometimes focus on their own needs rather than those of the group. The individual might be overly aggressive because of a personal need, such as wanting a bigger budget on his or her project. The individual might hunger for recognition or power. Similarly, the person might attempt to dominate the meeting, block others from contributing, or serve as a distraction. One of the ploys used by distracters recently is to engage in cell phone conversations during a meeting and blaming it on "those people who keep calling me."

The many roles just presented overlap somewhat. For example, the implementer might engage in specialist activities. Do not be concerned about the overlap. Instead, pick and choose from the many roles as the situation dictates—regardless of whether overlap exists.

The behavior associated with the roles just described is more important than remembering the labels. For example, remembering to be creative and imaginative is more important than remembering the specific label *creative problem solver*.

THE PROBLEM OF GROUPTHINK (TOO MUCH CONSENSUS)

For a team to be truly effective, somebody has to step forth and say, "The emperor has no clothes" when the group is making an outrageously bad decision. Often the shaper or monitor–evaluator plays this role. **Groupthink** is a deterioration of mental efficiency, reality testing, and moral judgment in the interest of group solidarity. Simply put, groupthink is an extreme form of consensus. The group atmosphere values getting along more than getting things done.[39] The group thinks as a unit, believes it is impervious to outside criticism, and begins to have illusions about its own invincibility. As a consequence, the group loses its powers of critical analysis.

One historically important example of groupthink took place in relation to the explosion of the space shuttle *Challenger*. According to several analyses of the incident, NASA managers were so committed to reaching space program objectives that they ignored safety warnings from people both within and outside the agency. As reported in an internal NASA briefing paper dated July 20, 1986, both astronauts and engineers expressed concern that the agency's management had a groupthink mentality. Of related significance, the management style of NASA managers is characterized by a tendency not to reverse decisions and not to heed the advice of people outside the management group. The analysis of their styles was conducted by a series of management-style tests administered several years prior to the *Challenger* explosion.[40]

A high-level business example of groupthink took place during 2001 when a group of top executives at the energy company Enron Corporation created an artificial shortage of electricity in order to raise prices.[41] Ultimately, the scam was publicly exposed. We can assume that such a large decision was a group decision and that nobody on the executive team attempted to stop the outrageous scheme or to inform the federal government.

Groupthink might also take place in the classroom to produce a result that could backfire, as described in the following example:

Five students in a marketing course were assigned to a team to develop a plan for a new business. Students were instructed to use the guidelines for developing a business plan discussed in class and described in the course textbook. However, the requirements were to develop an original idea for a business, one that was not already known to be described in print or electronically. After a couple of late-night meetings, the group became discouraged because most of the ideas they developed seemed either to be already in existence or too ordinary.

Suddenly one of the students made a comment about copying a business plan from the Internet. Eyes rolled at first, but the idea quickly gained traction. Within two hours the group found a business plan that had been used in Nevada for reselling and recycling small items that airport security would not allow on the plane. These included scissors, manicure sets, shampoos, and bottled water. Spontaneously the group thought "Great idea. We'll save lots of time and get an A for the project. Our instructor will never have the time to check out the originality of the idea." The group went out for a late-night snack to celebrate their creativity.

Unfortunately for the students, the professor did a thorough Internet search of every business plan submitted by students. The great idea from Nevada was uncovered on the Internet, and the team grade was F, along with

Groupthink

a deterioration of mental efficiency, reality testing, and moral judgment in the interest of group solidarity; extreme form of consensus the possibility of being disciplined further for cheating. As the team leader said, "How could people as sharp as us be so stupid?" [They weren't stupid—they were victims of groupthink.]

The negative aspects of groupthink can often be prevented if the team leader, or a member, encourages all team members to express doubts and criticisms of proposed solutions to the problem or suggested courses of action. It is also helpful to periodically invite qualified outsiders to meet with the group and provide suggestions.

▶ Learning Objective 6 ▶

What Are the Characteristics of an Effective Work Group?

Groups, like individuals, have characteristics that contribute to their uniqueness and effectiveness. Effectiveness includes such factors as objective measures of production (e.g., units produced), favorable evaluations by the manager, and worker satisfaction. For a group to be effective, the members must strive to act like a group or team. Also, the task given to the group or team should require collective effort instead of being a task that could be better performed by individuals. For example, many customers would prefer to be called on by an individual sales representative rather than by a sales team, so for some customers the rep should work individually rather than in a team effort. As shown in Figure 12-3, and based on dozens of different studies, effective work group and team characteristics can be grouped into twelve characteristics or factors.

FIGURE 12-3 KEY CHARACTERISTICS OF EFFECTIVE TEAMS AND WORK GROUPS

1. The team has clear-cut goals linked to organizational goals so that group members feel connected to the entire organization. Group members are empowered so they learn to think for themselves rather than expecting a supervisor to solve all the difficult problems. At the same time, the group believes it has the authority to solve a variety of problems without first obtaining approval from management.
2. Group members are assigned work they perceive to be challenging, exciting, and rewarding. As a consequence, the work is self-rewarding.
3. Members depend on one another to accomplish tasks and work toward a common goal. At the same time, the group believes in itself and that it can accomplish an interdependent task.
4. Members learn to think "outside the box" (are creative).
5. Members receive extensive training in technical knowledge, problem-solving skills, and interpersonal skills.
6. Group size is generally about six people, rather than ten or more.
7. Team members have good intelligence and personality factors, such as conscientiousness and pride, that contribute to good performance.
8. There is honest and open communication among group members and with other groups in the organization.
9. Members have the philosophy of working as a team—twenty-five brains, not only fifty hands.
10. Members are familiar with their jobs, coworkers, and the work environment. This experience adds to their expertise. The beneficial effects of experience may diminish after a while because the team needs fresh ideas and approaches.
11. The team has emotional intelligence in the sense that it builds relationships both inside and outside the team. Included in emotional intelligence are norms that establish mutual trust among members, a feeling of group identity, and group efficacy.
12. Stronger performing group members assist weaker performing group members accomplish their task, particularly when the performance of the "weakest link" in the group is key for group performance.

Sources: Michael A. Campion, Ellen M. Papper, and Gina Medsker, "Relations between Work Team Characteristics and Effectiveness: A Replication and Extension," *Personnel Psychology*, Summer 1996, p. 431; Stanley M. Gulley, Kara A. Incalcaterra, Aparna Joshi, and J. Matthew Beaubien, "A Meta-Analysis of Team Efficacy, Potency, and Performance: Interdependence and Level of Analysis as Moderators of Observed Relationships," *Journal of Applied Psychology*, October 2002, pp. 819–832; Vanessa Urch Druskat and Steven B. Wolff, "Building the Emotional Intelligence of Groups," *Harvard Business Review*, March 2001, pp. 80–90; Clause W. Langred, "Too Much of a Good Thing? Negative Effects of High Trust and Individual Autonomy in Self-Managing Work Teams, "*Academy of Management Journal*, June 2004, pp. 385–399; Bernhard Weber and Guido Hertel, "Motivation Gains of Inferior Group Members: A Meta-Analytical Review," *Journal of Personality and Social Psychology*, No. 6, 2007. pp. 973–993.

Concept Review and Reinforcement

Key Terms

Motivation, 346
Two-factor theory of work
    motivation, 347
Empowerment, 348
Shared leadership, 348
Intrinsic motivation, 349

Prosocial motivation, 350
Job enrichment, 350
Positive reinforcement, 350
Intermittent rewards, 351
Variable pay, 352
Recognition need, 353

Teamwork, 354
Group dynamics, 358
Role, 360
Groupthink, 363

Summary and Review

Motivating others toward good performance begins with the diagnosis of motivation. Diagnostic questions might include, "What could this job offer you that would make you work at your best?" Diagnosis should also include observing the subordinate's behavior in terms of what interests him or her.

Two classic theories of worker motivation are Maslow's hierarchy of needs and Herzberg's two-factor theory of motivation.

- A practical application of the needs hierarchy is that when a manager wants to motivate a group member, he or she must offer the individual a reward that must satisfy an important need.
- According to the two-factor theory of work motivation, one set of factors, the motivators or satisfiers, can motivate and satisfy workers. The other set, dissatisfiers, or hygiene factors, can only prevent dissatisfaction.

Empowerment is a comprehensive motivational strategy that grants workers more power by enabling them to participate in decisions affecting them and their work.

- Empowerment contributes to intrinsic motivation.
- Empowerment is commonplace in the service industry.
- Empowered employees must still be given overall direction and limits to the extent of their authority.

Motivation can take place through job design and interesting work, based on the principle of intrinsic motivation. Job enrichment makes a job more motivating and satisfying through means such as the following:

- Direct feedback to the job incumbent
- The opportunity for client relationships
- New learning

Rules for effectively using positive reinforcement to motivate employees include the following:

- State clearly what behavior will lead to a reward.
- Choose an appropriate reward.
- Supply ample feedback.
- Schedule rewards intermittently.
- Make the rewards follow the observed behavior closely in time.
- Make the reward fit the behavior.
- Make the rewards visible.
- Change the reward periodically.

Financial incentives are a natural motivator and are a form of positive reinforcement. Such incentives have multiplied in importance as companies struggle to stay afloat in worldwide competition. Money is also tied in with recognition. Key issues about financial incentives include the following:

- To make pay more motivational, many employers link pay to performance such as in variable pay and financial bonuses.
- Personal factors influence the power of financial incentives, including the value the worker attaches to money and the need for money.
- Financial incentives can cause problems, including a focus more on rewards than the joy built into exciting work and workers attaining good financial results by unethical means.

Motivation through recognition and praise is an important motivational strategy because the workplace provides a natural opportunity to satisfy the recognition need. Praising workers for good performance is closely related to informal recognition. Many workers rarely receive praise. An advanced use of praise is to tailor the praise to the needs of the person. Formal recognition programs are important for employee retention as well as motivation.

Team leaders as well as other managers need to use techniques that influence subordinates to work well together as a team. Among the many suggestions presented in the chapter for building teamwork are the following:

- Select members for the team who are interested in being and qualified to be strong team members.
- Help team members believe they have an urgent, constructive purpose.
- Use the consensus decision-making style.
- Reward the team as well as individuals.
- Show respect for team members.

Understanding how groups operate (group dynamics) helps a leader effectively build teamwork. One useful concept is the stages of group development: forming, storming, norming, performing, and adjourning. Team members occupy various roles, including the following:

- Resource investigator
- Coordinator
- Monitor–evaluator
- Completer–finisher
- Specialist

A key potential problem with group effort is groupthink, or extreme consensus. The problem can be lessened by team members occupying a critical role.

An effective work group has characteristics that contribute to its uniqueness and effectiveness, as outlined in Figure 12-3. For a group to be effective, the members must strive to be a team and work on a task that requires collective effort.

Check Your Understanding

1. How could diagnosing the motivational wishes and needs of employees save a company a lot of money when launching motivational programs?
2. What objection might some employees have to being empowered?
3. In what way might a program of job enrichment help reduce turnover?
4. To what extent do you think positive reinforcement is useful in motivating high-level workers, such as accountants and information technology specialists?
5. What type of recognition on the job would be motivational for you? How do you know?
6. Assume that Jennifer from the tech support center gets rid of a nasty virus in your desktop computer.

What is likely to be an effective statement of praise for her?

7. Assume that your employer sent you to an offsite team-building exercise that you thought was a waste of time and money. How would you deal with the situation?
8. Reflect on any group you currently belong to or were a member of in the past. Describe how the group went through the stages of group development.
9. What are several group norms that exist in the class for which you are studying this text?
10. Identify several of the characteristics of an effective work group that one of your favorite athletic team possesses. Justify your reasoning the best you can.

Web Corner

Tips for motivating a cleaning crew (or other basic workers):
www.custodian.info/crew.html

Gourmet cooking as a team building exercise:
www.recipeforsuccess.com/teamcuisine.html

Teamwork quotes and proverbs:
www.heartquotes.net/teamwork-quotes.html

INTERNET SKILL BUILDER

Visit www.nelson-motivation.com to watch a five-minute video clip of one of Bob Nelson's talks. After watching the video, answer the following questions:

1. What have I learned that I could translate into a skill for motivating employees?
2. Which theory, or approach, to motivation does Nelson emphasize in his presentation?

Developing Your Human Relations Skills

Applying Human Relations Exercise 12-1

The Job Enrichment Squad

Work individually or in small groups to develop skill in enriching several standard jobs by making them more interesting, challenging, and responsibility oriented. As part of your analysis, see if you can find someone who has held such a job (either you or a group member), and interview the job incumbent for some ideas. You might use e-mail or instant messaging as an alternative or supplement to telephone or face-to-face interviews. Choose three from among the following positions:

- Supermarket cashier
- Highway toll collector
- Custodial worker at an educational institution
- Home health aide
- Car wash attendant
- Call center operator for service with desktop and personal computers

In your problem-solving activity and in your interviews, seek answers to these basic questions: (1) What is the most boring part of this job? (2) What is the most exciting part of this job? (3) What is the most de-motivating part of the job? (4) What is the most motivating part of the job? (5) Find an answer to any other questions or issues you think are relevant.

After you have completed your analysis, prepare a report of about two brief paragraphs as to how the specific job can be more motivational through job design.

Applying Human Relations Exercise 12-2

Team Member Roles

A team of approximately six people is formed to conduct a twenty-minute meeting on a significant topic of their choosing. The possible scenarios follow:

Scenario A: Management Team. A group of managers is pondering whether to lay off one-third of the workforce to increase profits. The company has had a tradition of caring for employees and regarding them as the company's most precious asset. But the CEO has said privately that times have changed in our competitive world, and the company must do whatever possible to enhance profits. The group wants to think through the advisability of laying off one-third the workforce and explore other alternatives.

Scenario B: Group of Sports Fans. A group of fans has volunteered to find a new team name to replace "Redskins" for the local basketball team. One person among the group of volunteers believes that the name "Redskins" should be retained because it is a compliment, rather than an insult, to Native Americans. The other members of the group believe that a name change is in order, but they lack any good ideas for replacing a mascot team name that has endured for more than fifty years.

Scenario C: Community Group. A community group is attempting to launch an initiative to help battered adults and children. Opinions differ strongly as to what initiative would be truly helpful to these people. Among the alternatives are establishing a shelter for battered people, giving workshops on preventing violence, and self-defense training. Each group member with an idea strongly believes that he or she has come up with a workable possibility for helping with the problem of battered people.

While the team members are conducting their heated discussion, other class members make notes on which team members carry out which roles. Watching for the nine different roles, as well as the self-oriented roles, can be divided among class members. For example, the people in the first row might look for examples of the creative problem solver. Use the role worksheet that follows to help make your observations. Summarize the comment that is indicative of the role. An example would be noting in the shaper category: "Linda said naming the team the 'Washington Rainbows' seems like too much of an attempt to be politically correct."

Creative problem solver _____

Team worker _____

Resource investigator _____

Implementer _____

Coordinator _____

Completer–finisher _____

Shaper _____

Specialist _____

Monitor–evaluator _____

Self-oriented roles _____

Human Relations Class Activity

A Survey of Positive Motivators

As explained in Chapter 12, positive reinforcement only works well as a motivational technique when the right (effective) motivators (or reinforcers) are used. Plenty of written information is available about what constitutes effective motivators, including recognition. For this class activity, you will collect fresh data about effective motivators. The steps are as follows:

1. Each student completes the following sentence: "The most effective form of positive reinforcement I ever received on the job (or in school, sports, or community activity) was _____."
2. Each student submits his or her answer to a class database. If the class has a Website, intranet, or similar centralized method of collecting input, simply submit your answer using that medium. If you do not have such a system, simply send an e-mail or instant message to every class member with your answer.
3. Each student, or a few volunteers, will them compile a list of the five most effective motivators, based on how frequently the motivator was mentioned. For example, perhaps four class members completed the sentence with a response such as, "I was given a gift certificate for having been an outstanding performer."
4. If the class size is large enough, look for possible sex differences in preference for motivators.
5. Hold a class discussion of (a) how well you think the class findings might fit many different work settings and (b) how useful this activity has been in giving you ideas for motivating workers.

Human Relations Case Study 12-1

The Car Wash Blues

Pedro Ramirez was so proud. After years of saving money and building up his credit rating, Ramirez bought a car wash in St. Paul, Minnesota, that had been closed for several months. After redecorating and repainting the shop, Pedro renamed the car wash Sparkle Car Wash. Pedro reasoned that his car wash had an above-average opportunity to be successful because the many snowy fall and winter days in St. Paul helped keep autos and small trucks in need of washing.

Before opening, Pedro decided to staff the car wash. He hired an uncle as a part-time bookkeeper, along with five car wash attendants. To help promote business at Sparkle Car Wash, Pedro placed thousands of flyers tucked under the windshield wipers of cars parked in mall parking lots and on the street. The flyers along with the fact that the neighborhood needed another car wash helped bring business to an acceptable level. Pedro's uncle told him that if the present volume of car washes held up and labor costs remained stable, the car wash business would be a financial success.

Within two months, Pedro began to experience some labor problems. Three of the car wash attendants quit, with two just not coming back after they were paid. These two car wash attendants who quit were replaced, but one had to be fired. Instead of paying attention to customers, he remained distracted by his iPod and often ignored customer requests. These included customers asking for help closing a vehicle window or asking about how to operate the auto vacuum cleaners.

Two weeks later, two more car was attendants quit, both offering the excuse that they had found a "real job" somewhere else. One of the attendants said customers were making crude remarks toward her. The other attendant complained that almost nobody gave him a tip.

Pedro developed a motivational program to help keep his attendants on the job, as well as playing more careful attention to customers. He would allow them one free car wash a week, along with a paid-for lunch at McDonald's if they performed well for the entire week. Two weeks later, one more car was attendant quit, and more careful attention was not being paid to customer requests.

Questions

1. How effective do you think the rewards of a weekly car wash and a meal at McDonald's will be in motivating the car wash attendants to stay on the job and treat customers better?

2. What other approach to employee motivation might work for reducing turnover and providing better customer service?

3. To what extent do you think it might be hopeless to motivate car wash attendants to stay on the job longer and provide better customer service?

Human Relations Role-Playing Exercise

Pedro Conducts a Motivational Interview with Bubba

The case, "The Car Wash Blues," provides the setting for this role-play but takes the storyline further. One student plays the role of Pedro, who decides he must be more professional in his attempt to motivate the car wash attendants. He decides to conduct a diagnostic interview with Bubba, one of the newly hired car wash attendants. Among the questions he will ask Bubba are:

- What can management at Sparkle Car Wash offer you that would make you want to stick around as well as do your best to make our customers happy?
- How important is money to you?
- What are your career plans?

Another student plays the role of Bubba, who was not expecting a diagnostic interview. In fact, no boss in previous jobs has paid serious attention to him other than to reprimand him for poor performance. But because the interview is being conducted on company time, Bubba welcomes the change of pace from wiping down cars with a chamois cloth. (If a woman plays the role of Pedro or Bubba, she is free to use a name other than Pedro or Bubba.)

Observers rate the role-players on two dimensions, using a 1 to 5 scale from very poor to very good. One dimension is "effective use of human relations techniques." For Pedro, focus on how well he shows a sincere interest in attempting to motivate Bubba. The second dimension is "acting ability." A few observers might voluntarily provide feedback to the role-players in terms of sharing their ratings and observations. The course instructor might also provide feedback.

Human Relations Case Study 12-2

Carol Bartz at Yahoo! Wants to Build a Team

A couple of years ago, Carol Bartz, the newly appointed CEO of Yahoo!, had a long to-do list. She needed to chart the company's strategy, weigh a potential search partnership with Microsoft, boost morale, and round out her management team. Bartz didn't have much time to deliver because of a weak economy that was hurting online advertising.

Before joining Yahoo!, Bartz, 60, was the executive chairman of Autodesk, a computer-aided design software firm, where she was CEO for 14 years before stepping down in April 2006. Bartz also worked at Sun Microsystems, Digital Equipment, and 3M.

Wharton observers say Bartz could infuse Yahoo! with a trait much needed at the company: decisiveness. Yahoo!'s biggest problem, they contend, is lack of focus. Is Yahoo! a media company? Is it a technology outfit? Does it need to be in search? Who are Yahoo!'s biggest competitors—Google or established media companies? Bartz's job will be to answer those questions.

Bartz said her immediate goal was to meet with Yahoo! employees and gather information for future moves. "Its' no secret that Yahoo! has had challenges over the past year, but as I look around I see a powerful global brand with a great collection of assets, strong technology, good cash flow, and talented employees," said Bartz. "I have a lot of ideas on the subject of strategy, but it would be very presumptuous to discuss them on my first day on the job. I'm first going to do a deep dive to meet the great people of Yahoo! before I start speaking about how I plan to lead the company," she stated.

Observers thought that Bartz's first mission was to calm the water at Yahoo!. At the time the company had angry shareholders, a restive board member, Carl Ichan, who was itching for a search deal with Microsoft, and employees in need of a leader. In addition, employees had to endure a year of dour media reports about Yahoo!'s future. And there was the financial crisis that was hurting online advertising—the mainstay of Yahoo!'s business.

As Bartz addressed business strategy and short-term challenges, she also needed to build a management team, according to Wharton observers. They also thought that she needed a mix of insiders and long-time colleagues she can trust. From there, she could focus on rebuilding Yahoo!'s management talent, which had eroded due to turnover and layoffs.

Questions

1. How much were Bartz's preliminary statements of what she would do at Yahoo! conducive to building teamwork?

2. Give Bartz a few recommendations for building teamwork among the most likely group of highly paid and talented executives.

3. To what extent should Carol Bartz have gone into the crisis mode as a leader?

4. Based on media reports, how well is Yahoo! doing today under the leadership of Bartz?

Source: "Carol Bartz's Challenge at Yahoo: Choose a Path, Build a Team, and Do It Fast," *Knowledge@Wharton* (www.knowledge.wharton.upenn.edu), January 21, 2009.

REFERENCES

1. Ann Zimmerman, "Home Depot Chief Renovates," *Wall Street Journal*, June 5, 2008, p. B1.
2. Steve Bates, "Getting Engaged," *HR Magazine*, February 2004, pp. 44–46.
3. John Sullivan, "Personalizing Motivation," *Workforce Management*, March 27, 2006, p. 50.
4. Frederick Herzberg, Bernard Mausner, and Barbara Synderman, *The Motivation to Work*, 2nd ed. (New York: Wiley, 1959); Herzberg, *Work and the Nature of Man* (Cleveland: World Publishing, 1966).
5. Cindy Krischer Goodman, "Managers Use Perks for Young Workers," McClatchy Newspapers, September 24, 2006.
6. Gretchen M. Spreitzer, "Psychological Empowerment in the Workplace: Dimensions, Measurement, and Validation," *Academy of Management Journal*, October 1995, pp. 1443–1444.
7. Jay B. Carson, Paul. E. Tesluk, and Jennifer A. Marrone, "Shared Leadership in Teams: An Investigation of Antecedent Conditions and Performance," *Academy of Management Journal*, October 2007, pp. 1217–1234.
8. Heather Green, "How Meetup Tore Up the Rule Book," *Business Week*, June 16, 2008, pp. 88–89.
9. Adam M. Grant, "Does Intrinsic Motivation Fuel the Prosocial Fire? Motivational Synergy in Predicting Persistence, Performance, and Productivity," *Journal of Applied Psychology*, January 2008, pp. 48–58.
10. Frederick Herzberg, "The Wise Old Turk," *Harvard Business Review*, September–October 1974, pp. 70–80.
11. David Javitch, "Getting Your Employees Excited Again," *Entrepreneur*, August 7, 2006.
12. Jack and Suzy Welch, "Keeping Your People Pumped," *Business Week*, March 27, 2006, p. 122.
13. Philip Moss, Harold Salzman, and Chris Tilly, "Under Construction: The Continuing Evolution of Job Structures in Call Centers," *Industrial Relations*, Vol. 47, 2008, pp. 173–208.
14. Fred Luthans and Alexander Stajkovic, "Reinforce for Performance: The Need to Go Beyond Pay and Even Rewards," *Academy of Management Executive*, May 1999, p. 52.
15. Steven Kerr, *Ultimate Rewards: What Really Motivates People to Achieve* (Boston: Harvard Business School Publishing, 1997).
16. Mark Henricks, "Start Their Engines," *Entrepreneur*, January 2008, p. 85.
17. Joseph De Avila, "More Firms Base Raises on Performance," *Wall Street Journal*, August 15, 2007, p. D5.
18. Patricia K. Zingheim and Jay R. Schuster, "Value Is the Goal," *Workforce*, February 2000, p. 57.
19. Mark Henricks, "Pay for Performance," *Entrepreneur*, November 2008, pp. 77–78.
20. Adrian Costick and Chester Elton, *The Carrot Principle* (New York: The Free Press, 2007).
21. Charlotte Huff, "Risk of Creating 'Soft' Employees," *Workforce Management*, September 24, 2007, p. 28.
22. Andrew J. DuBrin, "Self-Perceived Technical Orientation and Attitudes toward Being Flattered," *Psychological Reports*, Vol. 96, 2005, pp. 852–854.
23. Charlotte Garvey, "Meaningful Tokens of Appreciation: Cash Awards Aren't the Only Way to Motivate Your Workforce," *HR Magazine*, August 2004, p. 103.
24. Charlotte Huff, "Motivating the World," *Workforce Management*, September 24, 2007, p. 31.
25. Bob Nelson, "Long-Distance Recognition," *Workforce*, August 2000, pp. 50–52.
26. Jon R. Katzenbach and Douglas K. Smith, "The Discipline of Teams," *Harvard Business Review*, March–April 1993, p. 112; Gilad Chen et al., "A Multilevel Study of Leadership, Empowerment, and Performance in Teams," *Journal of Applied Psychology*, March 2007, pp. 331–346; Regina Fazio Maruca, ed., "Unit of One: What Makes Teams Work?" *Fast Company*, November 2000, pp. 109–114; "Improve Teamwork with a 'Code of Conduct,'" *Manager's Edge*, February 2005, p. 1.
27. Frederick P. Morgeson, Matthew H. Reider, and Michael A. Campion, "Selecting Individuals in Team Settings: The Importance of Social Skills, Personality Characteristics, and Teamwork Knowledge," *Personnel Psychology*, Autumn 2005, pp. 583–611.
28. Sheila M. Puffer, "Continental Airlines' CEO Gordon Bethune on Teams and New Product Development," *Academy of Management Executive*, August 1999, p. 30.
29. "Share the Wealth When It Comes to Praise," *Manager's Edge*, September 2007, p. 3.
30. Matt Bolch, "Rewarding the Team" *HR Magazine*, February 2007, p. 92.
31. Belinda Luscombe, "Getting Jumpy at Work" *Time*, February 23, 2009, p. 93.
32. Ann Majchrzak, Arvind Malhgotra, Jeffrey Stamps, and Jessica Lipnack, "Can Absence Make a Team Grow Stronger?" *Harvard Business School*, May 2004, pp. 131–137.
33. Arvind Malhotra, Ann Majchrzak, and Benson Rosen, "Leading Virtual Teams," *Academy of Management Perspectives*, February 2007, pp. 61–62.
34. "5 Ways to Create Team Motivation," *Manager's Edge*, November 2007, p. 4.
35. Claus W. Langfred, "The Downside of Self-Management: A Longitudinal Study of the Effects of Conflict on Trust, Autonomy, and Task Interdependence in Self-Managing Teams," *Academy of Management Journal*, August 2007, pp. 885–900.
36. J. Steven Heinen and Eugene Jacobsen, "A Model of Task Group Development in Complex Organizations and a Strategy of Implementation," *Academy of Management Review*, October 1976, pp. 98–111.
37. "R. Meredith Belbin," in *Business: The Ultimate Resource* (Cambridge, MA: Perseus Publishing, 2002), pp. 966–967; Belbin Team-Roles. Retrieved March 12, 2005, from: http://www.belbin.com/belbin-teamroles.htm.
38. From a review of Meredith Belbin, *Management Teams: Why They Succeed or Fail*, 2nd ed. (London: Butterworth Heinemann, 2004), by Colin Thomson appearing at http://www.accountingweb.co.uk. Retrieved March 13, 2005.
39. Irving L. Janis, *Victims of Groupthink: A Psychological Study of Foreign Policy Decisions and Fiascos* (Boston: Houghton Mifflin, 1972), 39–40; Glenn Whyte, "Groupthink Reconsidered," *Academy of Management Review*, January 1989, pp. 40–56.
40. Kenneth A. Kovach and Barry Bender, "NASA Managers and *Challenger*: A Profile of Possible Explanations," *Personnel*, April 1987, p. 40.
41. Paul Kienitz, "Enron and Friends." Retrieved April, 15, 2006, from: www.paulkienitz.net/enron.

13

Diversity and Cross-Cultural Competence

Outline

1 What Are the Major Dimensions of Differences in Cultural Values?
Multicultural Identities and the Cultural Mosaic
Applying Knowledge of Cultural Differences in Values

2 What Are Some Barriers to Good Cross-Cultural Relations?
Perceptual Expectations
Ethnocentrism
Stereotypes in Intergroup Relations
Different Norms and Codes of Conduct
Micro-Inequities

3 What Are Some Approaches to Improving Cross-Cultural Relations?
Develop Cultural Sensitivity and Cultural Intelligence
Focus on Individuals Rather than Groups
Respect All Workers and Cultures
Value Cultural Differences
Minimize Cultural Bloopers
Participate in Cultural Training
Participate in Diversity Training

4 How Do You Overcome Cross-Cultural Communication Barriers?

5 Why Are Gender Differences in Leadership Style Regarded as Cultural Differences?

6 What Are Some of the Legal Aspects of Working in a Culturally Diverse Environment?

Federal Laws Prohibiting Job Discrimination

Additional Examples of Legislation and Court Rulings to Ensure Equal Rights

Affirmative Action

Learning Objectives ▶

After studying the information and doing the exercises in this chapter, you should be able to:

1 Explain some of the major ways in which cultures differ from one another.

2 Pinpoint barriers to cross-cultural relations.

3 Describe techniques for improving cross-cultural relations.

4 Be sensitive to potential cultural bloopers.

5 Be prepared to overcome cross-cultural communication barriers.

6 Recognize and understand gender differences in leadership style.

7 Be aware of some of the legal aspects of working in a culturally diverse environment.

O n a steamy July afternoon, Antonia Diaz makes her way to a worktable in the bowels of a dusty construction pit outside Washington, DC, and heaves a circular saw onto a plywood sheet. With her eyes fixed on the wood, she painstakingly makes the first cut in her latest project—construction of a handrail for a dangerous open stairwell her coworkers use to move supplies. "My work makes it safe for everyone," she says in accented English. "Otherwise, someone could fall and break a foot or leg. I'm so proud of what I do."

It's a claim she could not have made five years ago, when she immigrated to the United States from Honduras, speaking only Spanish and not knowing a miter box from a whipsaw. Diaz, a brawny one-time truck driver, landed a job as a laborer at Miller & Long, a Maryland construction company, shortly after arriving in the country. Within a few weeks, she began attending the English classes that the company offered to its mostly Spanish-speaking workers on Saturdays.

She also entered Miller & Long's carpentry apprenticeship, where she was required to study textbooks and other technical materials available only in English. "The teacher would say, 'I'm sorry guys, but this is the U.S., and we speak English," she recalls.

Three years later, her studies paid off. She passed her carpentry certification exam—offered only in English—and was promoted to Miller & Long's safety team at nearly twice her starting salary. She began dating a coworker who speaks only English. The couple is now raising their two-year-old daughter.[1]

The story about the safety team member who worked her way up in a construction company illustrates how welcoming diversity can strengthen a company as well as uplift an individual. Being able to work well with people from diverse groups, including other cultures both outside and inside your own country, is important for career success.

Being able to relate to a culturally diverse customer base is also necessary for success. Not only is the workforce becoming more diverse, but also business has become increasingly international or globalized. Small and medium-size firms, as well as corporate giants, are increasingly dependent on trade with other countries. Furthermore, as an increasing number of jobs are sent overseas, more U.S. workers will have contact with personnel in foreign countries. Retailers are also involved in globalization because so many store customers are immigrants. Many companies are using bilingual Web sites to convert online browsers into in-store customers. Similarly, other retailers are hiring store associates with foreign language skills and updating store signs and displays to appeal to immigrants.[2] The globalization of business therefore increases the relevance of cross-cultural skills.

This chapter presents ideas and techniques you can use to sharpen your ability to work effectively with people from diverse backgrounds. The buzzword for this activity is to be *inclusive* in your relationships with people. We also include a discussion of antidiscrimination legislation that protects the rights of workers.

▶ Learning Objective 1 ▶

What Are the Major Dimensions of Differences in Cultural Values?

Everything we do in work and personal life is influenced by a combination of heredity and culture, or nature and nurture. You might be thirsty at this moment because a genetically produced mechanism in your brain tells you it is time to ingest fluid. But if you choose to drink a Diet Pepsi or papaya juice with a coworker, you are engaging in culturally learned behavior. **Culture** is a learned and shared system of knowledge, beliefs, values, attitudes, and norms. As such, culture includes an enormous amount of behavior. Here we describe seven dimensions (or facets) of cultural values that help us understand how cultures differ from each other.[3] In other words, various cultures value different types of behavior.

Recognize that these dimensions are stereotypes, representing a typical value for a person in a given culture. You might find, for example, that most Chinese people are oriented more toward the group than seeking individual recognition, but you might meet some Chinese people who are egotistical and self-centered.

Culture
a learned and shared system of knowledge, beliefs, values, attitudes, and norms

1. **Individualism versus collectivism.** At one end of the continuum is individualism, a mental set in which people see themselves first as individuals and believe that their own interests take priority. Members of a society who value individualism are more concerned with their careers than with the good of the firm. Members of a society who value collectivism, in contrast, are typically more concerned with the organization or the work group than with themselves. An example of individualistic behavior would be to want to win an "employee of the month" award; an example of collectivistic behavior would be to want to win an award for the team. Highly individualistic cultures include the Unites States, Canada, and the Netherlands. Japan and Mexico are among the countries that strongly value collectivism. But with the increasing emphasis on teamwork in American culture, more U.S. workers are becoming collectivistic.

2. **Acceptance of power and authority.** People from some cultures accept the idea that members of an organization have different levels of power and authority. In a culture that believes in concentration of power and authority, the boss makes many decisions simply because he or she is the boss. Group members readily comply because they have a positive orientation toward authority, including high respect for elders. In a culture with less acceptance of power and authority, employees do not

recognize a power hierarchy. They accept directions only when they think the boss is right or when they feel threatened. Cultures that readily accept power and authority include France, China, Malaysia, and India. Countries that have much less acceptance of power and authority are the United States and, particularly, the Scandinavian countries (e.g., Sweden).

3. **Materialism versus concern for others.** In this context, materialism refers to an emphasis on assertiveness and the acquisition of money and material objects. It also means de-emphasizing caring for others. At the other end of the continuum is concern for others, an emphasis on personal relations, and a concern for the welfare of others. Materialistic countries include Japan and Italy. The United States is considered to be moderately materialistic. For example, the high participation rates in charities suggest that Americans are somewhat interested in the welfare of others, and therefore not totally materialistic. Scandinavian countries all emphasize caring as a national value.

4. **Formality versus informality.** A country that values formality attaches considerable importance to tradition, ceremony, social rules, and rank. At the other extreme, informality refers to a casual attitude toward these same aspects of culture. Workers in Latin American countries highly value formality, such as lavish public receptions and processions. Americans, Canadians, and Scandinavians are much more informal. Casual observation suggests that most of the industrialized world is becoming more informal through such practices as an emphasis on using the first name only during business introductions and talking with customers over the phone.

5. **Urgent time orientation versus casual time orientation.** Individuals and nations attach different importance to time. People with an urgent time orientation perceive time as a scarce resource and tend to be impatient. People with a casual time orientation view time as an unlimited and unending resource and tend to be patient. Americans are noted for their urgent time orientation. They frequently impose deadlines and are eager to get started doing business. Asians and Middle Easterners, in contrast, are patient negotiators. Many corporate workers and entrepreneurs engaged in international business recognize the importance of building relationships slowly overseas.

6. **Work orientation versus leisure orientation.** A major cultural difference is the number of hours per week and weeks per year people expect to invest in work versus leisure or other nonwork activities. American corporate professionals typically work about fifty-five hours per week, take forty-five-minute lunch breaks, and take two weeks of vacation. Japanese workers share similar values with respect to time invested in work. In contrast, many European countries have steadily reduced the workweek in recent years while lengthening vacations.

7. **High-context versus low-context cultures.** Cultures differ in how much importance they attach to the surrounding circumstances, or context, of an event. People from a high-context culture place more emphasis on *how* something is said rather than *what* is said. (They emphasize nonverbal communication.) For example, a person from a high-context culture is not likely to take you seriously if you smile when you say that you do not like his or her service.

High-context cultures make more extensive use of body language as part of their emphasis on nonverbal communication. Some cultures, such as the Hispanic and African American cultures, are high context. In contrast, Northern European cultures are low context and make less use of body language. The Anglo American culture is considered to be medium-low context. People in low-context cultures seldom take time in business dealings to build relationships and establish trust.

MULTICULTURAL IDENTITIES AND THE CULTURAL MOSAIC

Multicultural identities
individuals who incorporate the values of two or more cultures because they identify with both their primary culture and another culture or cultures

Another complexity about understanding cultural differences is that many people have **multicultural identities** because they identify with both their primary culture and another culture or cultures. As a consequence, these people may incorporate the values of two cultures. Young people develop a global identity that gives them a feeling of belonging to a worldwide culture. The feeling of belongingness enables them to communicate with people from diverse places when they travel, when others travel to where they live, and when they communicate globally using e-mail and the telephone. Television and movies also help us develop a global identity.

Further, according to this theory, people retain a local identity along with their global identity. Young people in India provide an apt example. The country has a rapidly growing high-tech sector led mostly by young people. Yet most of these well-educated young people still cling to local traditions, such as a marriage arranged by the parents and the expectation that they will care for their parents in old age.[4]

Another complexity of culture is that a person's country is but one cultural influence. For example, people from the upper socioeconomic group within one country or ethnic group might value education and the use of grammatically correct speech more than people from a lower socioeconomic group.

The Cultural Mosaic

Cultural mosaic
an individual's unique mixture of multiple cultural identities that yields a complex picture of the cultural influences on that person

The fact of multicultural identities and different values among people from the same country and ethnic groups has recently been labeled the cultural mosaic by management professors Georgia T. Chao from Michigan State University and Henry Moon of Emory University. The **cultural mosaic** refers to an individual's unique mixture of multiple cultural identities that yields a complex picture of the cultural influences on that person. Rather than choosing a particular "tile" such as race, gender, or country of origin, people develop an identity based on a mix of smaller tiles.[5] Every reader of this book is probably an example of a cultural mosaic. One of thousands of possible examples is that one person could derive a cultural identity from being a (1) U.S. citizen, (2) African American, (3) Baptist, (4) male, (5) musician, (6) football player, (7) accountant, and (8) Southerner.

Religious Values

The religious value part of the cultural mosaic often affects when people are willing to work or not work. One potential cultural clash is that the rights of an individual to freely practice and observe religious beliefs sometimes collide with company goals. Differences in religious practices must be recognized because the number of religions in the workplace has increased substantially.

Religious diversity can create problems as more companies move to 24/7 (around-the-clock, seven-days-per-week) schedules. Employers therefore need more flexibility from employees, yet religious beliefs often limit times at which employees are willing to work. The message for improved understanding is that employers must recognize workers' religious beliefs. At the same time, workers must understand the importance of a company meeting the demands of the marketplace, such as having 24-hour customer service support. Workers, for example, can trade off working on each others' religious holidays.

APPLYING KNOWLEDGE OF CULTURAL DIFFERENCES IN VALUES

How might you use this information about cultural differences to improve interpersonal relationships on the job? A starting point would be to recognize that a person's national values might influence his or her behavior. Assume that you wanted to establish a good working relationship with a person from a high-context culture. Make sure your facial expression fits the content of your words. For example, do not smile when, as a supervisor, you say, "No, you cannot take off tomorrow afternoon to have your French poodle groomed." You would also want to emphasize body language when communicating with that individual. A related point is that people from high-context cultures are more likely to touch and kiss strangers. As Fernando, who was raised in the Dominican Republic and is studying in the United States, said, "In my country, I hug people I meet for the first time. When I do it here, they think I'm very rude."

What Are Some Barriers to Good Cross-Cultural Relations?

◀ Learning Objective 2 ◀

Many logical reasons exist as to why people often encounter difficulties in developing good relations and communicating with people from different cultures. The fact that cultures differ in key dimensions creates some friction in cross-cultural relations. A go-getter from Brooklyn, New York, might say to himself, "Why do I have to spend three days here in Hong Kong wining and dining customers just so I can sell them an enterprise software system?"

Here we look at several of the underlying factors that create problems in developing smooth cross-cultural relations. Not being aware of the type of barriers presented next blocks effective cross-cultural relations because such lack of awareness often leads to misunderstandings. The techniques presented in the following section of the chapter are designed to overcome some these barriers. To get you started thinking about your readiness to work in a culturally diverse environment, as well as to minimize cross-cultural barriers, take Human Relations Self-Assessment Quiz 13-1.

PERCEPTUAL EXPECTATIONS

Achieving good cross-cultural relations is hampered somewhat by people's predisposition to discriminate. They do so as a perceptual shortcut, much like stereotyping. A bank customer, for example, might be communicating with a 24-year-old man about a mortgage application. Dissatisfied with his concerns about her creditworthiness, the customer might say, "Let me speak to a mortgage officer." In reality, the man *is* a mortgage officer, but the woman expects an older person to be occupying such a position. The message in this anecdote about perceptual expectations is important. We have to overcome this form of discrimination to enhance cross-cultural relations.

Positive expectations or stereotypes can also create some barriers to cross-cultural relations. Two company representatives were entertaining Sophie, a work associate from Jamaica. They assumed that because Sophie was black and Jamaican, she enjoyed dancing, so they invited her to a dance club. Sophie was a little taken aback and said, "What makes you think I like to dance? Not every Jamaican lady has natural rhythm." Similarly, on the job, we sometimes think that everybody from a certain national group has the characteristics of that group. For example, not all Chinese workers are methodical or precise or have good eye–hand coordination and exceptional math skills.

ETHNOCENTRISM

A key barrier to good cross-cultural relations is **ethnocentrism,** the assumption that the ways of one's culture are the *best* ways of doing things. Another part of ethnocentrism is to believe that our own way of living is essentially the only way. Most cultures

"Business needs to change with the demographics. Those companies that embrace diversity and make sure it is represented throughout their organization have a much better bottom line. It mirrors what's going on in the world."

—Miriam Brewer, director of diversity at the International Franchise Association Education Foundation. Quoted in *Hispanic Business*, March 2008, p. 36.

Ethnocentrism
the assumption that the ways of one's culture are the *best* ways of doing things

Human Relations Self-Assessment Quiz 13-1

Cross-Cultural Skills and Attitudes

Following are skills and attitudes that various employers and cross-cultural experts think are important for relating effectively to coworkers in a culturally diverse environment.

	Applies to Me Now	Not There Yet
1. I have spent some time in another country.	_____	_____
2. At least one of my friends is deaf or blind or uses a wheelchair.	_____	_____
3. Currency from other countries is as real as the currency from my own country.	_____	_____
4. I can read in a language other than my own.	_____	_____
5. I can speak in a language other than my own.	_____	_____
6. I can write in a language other than my own.	_____	_____
7. I can understand people speaking in a language other than my own.	_____	_____
8. I use my second language regularly.	_____	_____
9. My friends include people of races different from my own.	_____	_____
10. My friends include people of different ages.	_____	_____
11. I feel (or would feel) comfortable having a friend with a sexual orientation different from mine.	_____	_____
12. My attitude is that although another culture may be very different from mine, that culture is equally good.	_____	_____
13. I would be willing to (or already do) hang art from different countries in my home.	_____	_____
14. I would accept (or have already accepted) a work assignment of more than several months in another country.	_____	_____
15. I have a passport.	_____	_____

Interpretation:

If you checked "Applies to Me Now" for ten or more of the preceding items, you most likely function well in a multicultural work environment. If you answered "Not There Yet" to ten or more of the preceding items, you need to develop more cross-cultural awareness and skills to work effectively in a multicultural work environment. You will notice that being bilingual gives you at least five points on this quiz.

Source: Several ideas for statements on this quiz are derived from Ruthann Dirks and Janet Buzzard, "What CEOs Expect of Employees Hired for International Work," *Business Education Forum,* April 1997, pp. 3–7; Gunnar Beeth, "Multicultural Managers Wanted," *Management Review,* May 1997, pp. 17–21.

consider themselves to be the center of the world, such as the French believing that any cultivated person must appreciate French painters and French wine. One consequence of ethnocentrism is that people from one culture prefer people from other cultures similar to themselves. English people, therefore, would have more positive attitudes toward Australians than they would toward Mexicans. Despite this generalization, some countries that appear to have similar cultures are intense rivals. Many Japanese and Korean people dislike each other, as do the French and Belgians. In what way do you feel your country's way of doing something is the best?

STEREOTYPES IN INTERGROUP RELATIONS

We described perceptual expectations as a form of stereotype that could interfere with effective cross-cultural relations. Stereotypes, in general, create some problems.

As a result of stereotypes, people overestimate the probability that a given member of a group will have an attribute of his or her category. People tend to select information that fits the stereotype and reject inconsistent information. As a consequence, we readily draw conclusions about people from another cultural group without carefully listening and observing. As an Indian American business graduate reports,

> I took a job with a systems consulting company. The job was supposed to involve a lot of contact with users. But because I look and sound Indian, the managers just assumed that I'm heavy into information technology. Writing code all day gives me a headache. I try to explain my preferences, but all I get is a puzzled look from my manager. [The problem here is that being placed in the wrong job can lead to dissatisfaction and costly turnover.]

DIFFERENT NORMS AND CODES OF CONDUCT

Various cultural groups have norms of their own, such as in some countries men walking ahead of the women. Also, what is permissible conduct in one group may be frowned on and even punished in another group. In the United States it is permissible for people to publish nasty (even X-rated) cartoons about political leaders without fear of reprisal by the government. In some countries such behavior will lead to long-term imprisonment. In some countries copying the products and ideas of others is an accepted business strategy, but it is considered piracy in another country.

At times, we may make the mistake that others are similar to us and become confused when they act differently from our expectations. We may unknowingly insult others from a different culture, or they many unknowingly insult us. If you are from a culture that highly values time, such as the Americans and the English (James Bond is always on time), you may be angry when your new Brazilian acquaintance arrives thirty minutes late for a party. Because most Brazilians do not adhere to rigid time schedules for social events, you have just experienced a clash of different cultural norms.

Business practices are also subject to cultural norms. As a result, sometimes a practice in another country might seem bizarre to a foreigner. A case in point is that Americans and Europeans generally prefer to shop in clean and quiet stores where products are carefully arranged. In contrast, lower-middle-class shoppers in India are more comfortable in tiny, cramped stores, often filled with haggling customers.

> Kishore Biyani, an Indian entrepreneur, made the mistake of opening Western-style supermarkets in India. Too many customers walked down the wide isles, past neatly stocked shelves, without buying anything. So Biyani redesigned his stores to make them messier, noisier, and more cramped. "The shouting, the untidiness, and the chaos are part of the design," he says. Even dirty, spotted onions serve the function of appearing farm fresh, which appeals to Indians. (Biyani's company, Pantaloon Retail, Ltd., has become India's largest retailer.)[6]

MICRO-INEQUITIES

Many barriers to effective cross-cultural relations surface because a person is unaware that he or she is slighting another individual, according to Mary Row, a researcher on gender and racial differences. These slights are referred to as micro-inequities, as you have studied in relation to interpersonal conflict. Understanding micro-inequities can lead to changes in one-on-one relationships that may profoundly irritate others.[7] For example, a manager was introducing a new office assistant to the group, mentioning the name of each member one by one. However, the manager omitted mentioning the name of the one Philippine American group member.

As part of a training program in understanding micro-inequities, the people who are slighted are taught to confront the issue rather than let resentment build. The Philippine American worker might say tactfully to the manager, "Diane, the new assistant, was introduced to everybody but me. And I am the only Philippine in the department. Was this a coincidence?"

▶ **Learning Objective 3** ▶

What Are Some Approaches to Improving Cross-Cultural Relations?

By now you are probably aware of how to improve cross-cultural relations by avoiding some of the mistakes already mentioned or implied, such as relying too heavily on group stereotypes. In this section, we take a systematic look at approaches you can use on your own along with training programs designed to improve cross-cultural relations.[8] The methods and techniques for such improvement are outlined in Figure 13-1.

DEVELOP CULTURAL SENSITIVITY AND CULTURAL INTELLIGENCE

To relate well to someone from a foreign country, a person must be alert to possible cultural differences. When working in another country, one must be willing to acquire knowledge about local customs and learn how to speak the native language, at least passably. When working with people from different cultures, even from one's own country, the person must be patient, adaptable, flexible, and willing to listen and learn.

Cultural sensitivity

an awareness of and a willingness to investigate the reasons why people of another culture act as they do

These characteristics mentioned are part of **cultural sensitivity,** an awareness of and a willingness to investigate the reasons why people of another culture act as they do.[9] A person with cultural sensitivity will recognize certain nuances in customs that will help build better relationships with people from cultural backgrounds other than his or her own. A culturally sensitive person will also recognize that humor does not easily translate from one culture to another and that some types of humor might be offensive in another culture. Assume, for example, you are

FIGURE 13-1

IMPROVING CROSS-CULTURAL RELATIONS

Methods and techniques

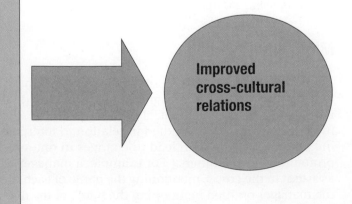

1. Develop cultural sensitivity and cultural intelligence.
2. Focus on the individual rather than groups.
3. Respect all workers and cultures.
4. Value cultural differences.
5. Minimize cultural bloopers.
6. Participate in cultural training.
7. Participate in diversity training.

Improved cross-cultural relations

having lunch with a group of Japanese workers on a trip to Japan. You begin your joke with, "This old guy walks into a bar. . . ." The Japanese workers might take offense because older people are highly respected in Japan.

One approach to enhancing cultural sensitivity is to keep in mind the types of cultural differences mentioned throughout this chapter, even down to such details as holding a fork in your left hand when dining in England and India. Another approach is to raise your antenna and observe carefully what others are doing. Suppose you are on a business trip to a different region of your country and are invited to have dinner at the plant general manager's house. You notice that she takes off her street shoes on entering the house. You do likewise to establish better rapport, even if your host says, "Oh, please don't bother." It is obvious from your host's behavior that she observes a "shoe code" in her house.

An advanced aspect of cultural sensitivity is to be able to fit in comfortably with people of another culture by observing the subtle cues they give about how a person should act in their presence. **Cultural intelligence, or CQ,** is an outsider's ability to interpret someone's unfamiliar and ambiguous behavior the same way that person's compatriots would.[10] (CQ refers to a cultural quotient.) With high cultural intelligence a person would be able to figure out what behavior would be true of all people and all groups, such as rapid shaking of a clenched fist to communicate anger. Also, the person with a high CQ could figure out what is peculiar to this group and those aspects of behavior that are neither universal nor peculiar to the group. These ideas are abstract, so an example will help clarify.

Cultural intelligence (CQ)
an outsider's ability to interpret someone's unfamiliar and ambiguous behavior the same way that person's compatriots would

An American expatriate manager served on a design team that included two German engineers. As other team members floated their ideas, the engineers condemned them as incomplete or underdeveloped. The manager concluded that the Germans in general are rude and aggressive.

With average cultural intelligence, the American would have realized he was mistakenly equating the merit of an idea with the merit of the person presenting it. The Germans, however, were able to make a sharp distinction between the two. A manager with more advanced cultural intelligence might have tried to figure out how much of the two German's behavior was typically German and how much was explained by the fact that they were engineers.

Similar to emotional intelligence, cultural intelligence encompasses several different aspects of behavior. The three sources of cultural intelligence relate to the cognitive, emotional/motivational, and the physical, explained as follows:[11]

1. **Cognitive (the head).** The cognitive part of CQ refers to what a person knows and how he or she can acquire new knowledge. Here you acquire facts about people from another culture, such as their passion for football (soccer in North America), their business practices, and their promptness in paying bills. Another aspect of this source of cultural intelligence is figuring out how you can learn more about the other culture.

2. **Emotional/motivational (the heart).** The emotional/motivational aspect of CQ refers to energizing one's actions and building personal confidence. You need both confidence and motivation to adapt to another culture. A man on a business trip to the Ivory Coast in Africa might say to himself, "When I greet a work associate in a restaurant, can I really pull off kissing him on both cheeks. What if he thinks I'm weird?" With strong motivation, the same person might say, "I'll give it a try. I kind of greet my grandfather the same way back in the United States."

3. **The body (physical).** The body aspect of CQ is the action component. The body is the element for translating intentions into actions and desires. Kissing the same-sex African work associate on both cheeks is the *physical* aspect previously

mentioned. We often have an idea of what we should do, but implementation is not so easy. You might know, for example, that when entering an Asian person's home you should take off your shoes, yet you might not actually remove them—thereby offending your Asian work (or personal life) associate.

To practice high cultural intelligence, the mind, heart, and body have to work together. You have to figure out how you have to act with people from another culture, you need motivation and confidence to change, and you have to translate your knowledge and motivation into action. So when you are on a business trip to South Korea, go ahead and bow when you are introduced to the plant manager.

FOCUS ON INDIVIDUALS RATHER THAN GROUPS

Understanding broad cultural differences is a good starting point in building relationships with people from other cultures. Nevertheless, it is even more important to get to know the individual rather than relying exclusively on an understanding of his or her cultural group. Instead of generalizing about the other person's characteristics and values (such as assuming that your Mexican American coworker chooses to be late for meetings), get to know his or her personal style. You might find that this particular Mexican American values promptness and becomes anxious when others are late for a meeting. A consultant in the area of cross-cultural relations suggests that the best way to know individuals is to build personal relationships with people and not to generalize.[12]

Focusing on individuals rather than groups is sometimes difficult because people tend to hold on strongly to cultural stereotypes. Evidence that these stereotypes are strong comes from an experiment with college students who were purposely presented with stereotype-busting strangers. One of these stereotype busters was a young Asian American woman with a thick Southern drawl. (She was really a hired actress trained by a voice coach to learn an accent specific to Charleston, South Carolina.) Students worked in pairs with either a stereotype buster or a person whose behavior was consistent with the stereotype. Students paired with a stereotype buster performed less well on a word-finding game, showed more physical signs of stress, and smiled less frequently. Watching a participant's initial meeting with one of the surprising partners was revealing according the experimenter, Wendy Berry Mendes of Harvard University: "She'd begin the introduction with, 'Hi, I'm Jenny and I'm from Charleston, South Carolina,' and our participants just froze and stared at this truly surprising person. Their body posture stayed closed and more defensive during the interaction."[13]

One lesson for cross-cultural relations to be learned from this experiment is to focus on the individual's characteristics and try not to be upset because the person's behavior is not consistent with your stereotype of how he or she is supposed to behave. For example, many Americans find it strange when they meet a black businessperson with an English or French accent. As one American tourist said when visiting Paris, "I didn't know black people spoke French." (The same tourist never took her study of geography seriously.)

RESPECT ALL WORKERS AND CULTURES

An effective strategy for achieving cross-cultural understanding is to simply respect all others in the workplace, including their cultures. An important component of respect is to believe that although another person's culture is different from yours, it is equally good. Respect comes from valuing differences, such as one person speaking standard English and the other favoring American Sign Language. Respecting other people's customs can translate into specific attitudes, such as respecting one coworker for wearing a yarmulke on Friday or another for wearing an African outfit to celebrate Kwanzaa. Another way of being respectful would be to listen carefully to the opinion of a senior worker who says the company should never have converted to voice mail in place of assistants answering the phone (even though you disagree). An aspect of respecting all workers is the importance of respecting the rights of majorities, including white males.

Another way of showing respect for all workers and cultures is to develop supportive peer relations in the workplace with people from different cultural groups. A supportive relationship includes a feeling of closeness and trust, the sharing of thoughts and feelings, and the feeling that one is able to seek assistance from another. Such respect in the form of support doubles in importance because the creativity advantage of a diverse group is more likely to surface when there is a supportive relationship among coworkers who differ demographically.

Another way of respecting all workers and cultures is to practice **sexual equity**—parity among heterosexual, gay, lesbian, bisexual, and transgender employees. The last four groups have come to be referred to collectively as GLBT. Sexual equity most frequently takes the form of an employer offering health-care coverage for same-sex domestic partners.[14] Less typical is the initiative of IBM, which has developed an accreditation program for GLBT suppliers to help GLBT-friendly companies identify accommodating companies as business partners.

True respect of any group goes beyond company policies and extends to informal social behavior. A group of workers who invited a transgender coworker (one who had switched sexes) would be showing total respect by inviting him or her to join them for an after-work drink. (For some people, however, religious beliefs would make showing such respect difficult.)

> **Sexual equity**
> parity among heterosexual, gay, lesbian, bisexual, and transgender employees

VALUE CULTURAL DIFFERENCES

Recognizing cultural differences is an excellent starting point in becoming a **multicultural worker**—one who can work effectively with people of different cultures. More important, however, is to *value* cultural differences. The distinction goes well beyond semantics. If you place a high value on cultural differences, you will perceive people from other cultures to be different but equally good. Gunnar Beeth, an executive placement specialist in Europe, notes that you cannot motivate anyone, especially someone of another culture, until that person first accepts you. A multilingual sales representative has the ability to explain the advantages of a product in other languages. In contrast, a multicultural sales rep can motivate foreigners to make the purchase. The difference is substantial.[15]

A challenge in showing respect for other cultures is not to act revolted or shocked when a member of another culture eats something that lies outside your area of what is acceptable as food. Some Westerners are shocked and repelled to find that some Easterners eat insects, cats, dogs, sheep's eyeballs, chicken soup containing the feet, and rattlesnakes. Some Easterners are shocked and repelled to find that Westerners eat a sacred animal such as cow and are surprised about popcorn.[16]

Other cross-cultural differences in customs also represent a challenge when trying to respect another culture. An American might find it difficult to respect the Pakistani practice of having young children work in factories. In contrast, the Pakistani might find it difficult to respect the American practice of putting old relatives in nursing homes and hospices. Sometimes it takes careful reflection on one's own culture to be able to respect another culture.

A well-documented advantage stemming from valuing cultural differences is creative problem solving. The diversity of viewpoints within the group can enhance group creativity. Another perspective on the contribution of cultural

> **Multicultural worker**
> one who can work effectively with people of different cultures

differences to creativity is that multicultural experience helps us become more creative.[17] In practice, this finding could mean that working with different cultural groups within the same company, or outside the company, would facilitate workers becoming more creative problem solvers. Broadening your perspective helps develop your flexible thinking. A more specific advantage is that exposure to different cultures might trigger a profitable idea that you could transport to your own culture. For example, cottages of about 500 square feet found in many cultures outside the United States now have a small but growing market in the United States.

MINIMIZE CULTURAL BLOOPERS

An effective way of being culturally sensitive is to minimize actions that are likely to offend people from another culture based on their values and customs. Cultural bloopers are most likely to take place when you are visiting another country. The same bloopers, however, can also be committed with people from a different culture within your own country. To avoid these bloopers, you must carefully observe persons from other cultures. Studying another culture through reading is also helpful. Even small behaviors, such as while in France asking for ketchup to accompany an omelet, can strain a business relationship.

E-commerce and other forms of Internet communication have created new opportunities for creating cultural bloopers. Web site developers and the workers responsible for adding content must have good cross-cultural literacy, including an awareness of how the information might be misinterpreted. Here is a sampling of potential problems:

- Numerical date formats can be readily misinterpreted. To an American, 4/9/11 would be interpreted as April 9, 2011 (or 1911!). But many Europeans would interpret the same numerical expression as September 4, 2011.

- Colors on Web sites must be chosen carefully. For example, in some cultures purple is the color of royalty, whereas in Brazil purple is associated with death.

- Be careful of metaphors that may not make sense to a person for whom your language is a second language. Examples include "We've encountered an ethical meltdown" and "Our biggest competitor is over the hill."

International business specialist Rick Borelli recommends that being able to communicate your message directly in your customer's mother tongue provides a competitive advantage.[18] Consumers are four times more likely to purchase from a Web site written in their native language. The translator, of course, must have good knowledge of the subtleties of the language to avoid a blooper. An English-to-French translator used the verb *baiser* instead of *baisser* to describe a program of lowering prices. *Baisser* is the French verb "to lower," whereas *baiser* is the verb "to kiss." Worse, in everyday language, *baiser* is a verb that refers to having an intimate physical relationship!

Keep two key facts in mind when attempting to avoid cultural mistakes. One is that members of any cultural group show individual differences. What one member of the group might regard as an insensitive act another might welcome. Recognize also that one or two cultural mistakes will not peg you permanently as a boor. Figure 13-2 will help you minimize certain cultural bloopers.

Avoiding cultural bloopers might also be framed as being *politically correct*. The point of political correctness is to avoid offending anybody. As an American when visiting India, you would therefore not say to your guests that "Eating with your hands is disgusting." Nor would you say to an Inuit (aka Eskimo), "Killing seals is barbaric."

FIGURE 13-2 CULTURAL MISTAKES TO AVOID WITH SELECTED CULTURAL GROUPS

Western Europe

Great Britain
- Asking personal questions. The British protect their privacy.
- Thinking that a businessperson from England is unenthusiastic when he or she says, "Not bad at all." English people understate positive emotion.
- Gossiping about royalty.

France
- Expecting to complete work during the French two-hour lunch.
- Attempting to conduct significant business during August—*les vacances* (vacation time).
- Greeting a French person for the first time and not using a title such as *sir* or *madam* (or *monsieur*, *madame*, or *mademoiselle*)

Italy
- Eating too much pasta, as it is not the main course.
- Handing out business cards freely. Italians use them infrequently.

Spain
- Expecting punctuality. Your appointments will usually arrive twenty to thirty minutes late.
- Make the American sign for "okay" with your thumb and forefinger. In Spain (and many other countries) this is vulgar.

Scandinavia (Denmark, Sweden, Norway)
- Being overly conscious of rank in these countries. Scandinavians pay relatively little attention to a person's place in the hierarchy.
- Introducing conflict among Swedish work associates. Swedes go out of their way to avoid conflict.

Greece
- Saying good-bye by using the American handshake. Greeks regard this practice to be an insult.

Asia

All Asian countries
- Pressuring an Asian job applicant or employee to brag about his or her accomplishments. Asians feel self-conscious when boasting about individual accomplishments and prefer to let the record speak for itself. In addition, they prefer to talk about group rather than individual accomplishments.

Japan
- Shaking hands or hugging Japanese (as well as other Asians) in public. Japanese consider the practices to be offensive.
- Looking directly in the eye of a business acquaintance for more than a few seconds.
- Not interpreting "We'll consider it" as "no" when spoken by a Japanese businessperson. Japanese negotiators mean "no" when they say, "We'll consider it."
- Not giving small gifts to Japanese when conducting business. Japanese are offended by not receiving these gifts.
- Giving your business card to a Japanese businessperson more than once. Japanese prefer to give and receive business cards only once.

China
- Using black borders on stationary and business cards, because black is associated with death.
- Giving expensive gifts, because this may obligate the person to reciprocate with something of equal value to you.
- Making cold calls on Chinese business executives. An appropriate introduction is required for a first-time meeting with a Chinese official.

Korea
- Saying no. Koreans feel it is important to have visitors leave with good feelings.

India
- Telling Indians you prefer not to eat with your hands. If the Indians are not using cutlery when eating, they expect you to do likewise.

Thailand
- Pointing the soles of your shoes toward another person. Be aware of this potential mistake when sitting.

Mexico and Latin America

Mexico
- Flying into a Mexican city in the morning and expecting to close a deal by lunch. Mexicans build business relationships slowly.

Most Latin American countries
- Attempting to impress Brazilians by speaking a few words of Spanish. Portuguese is the official language of Brazil.
- Wearing elegant and expensive jewelry during a business meeting. Most Latin Americans think people should appear more conservative during a business meeting.

Note: A cultural mistake for Americans to avoid when conducting business in most countries outside the United States and Canada is to insist on getting down to business quickly. Other stereotyped American traits to avoid are aggressiveness, impatience, and frequent interruptions to get your point across. North Americans in small towns also like to build a relationship before getting down to business. Another general mistake for Americans is to use a familiar, laid-back style in locales where "business casual" is unacceptable and first names are reserved for family and friends.[19]

PARTICIPATE IN CULTURAL TRAINING

Cultural training

set of learning experiences designed to help employees understand the customs, traditions, and beliefs of another culture

For many years companies and government agencies have prepared their workers for overseas assignments. The method most frequently chosen is **cultural training,** a set of learning experiences designed to help employees understand the customs, traditions, and beliefs of another culture. In today's diverse business environment and international marketplace, learning about individuals raised in different cultural backgrounds has become more important. Many industries therefore train employees in cross-cultural relations. Cultural training is considered essential for international workers involved with people from other cultures because negotiating styles differ across cultures. For example, the Japanese prefer an exchange of information to confrontation. Russians, in contrast, enjoy combat in negotiations.[20] (Again, we are dealing with cultural stereotypes.)

Much of the information presented in this chapter, such as understanding cultural values and bloopers, is often incorporated into cultural training. Here we describe some of the learning skills emphasized in cultural training as well as one of its frequent components, language training.

Learning Skill Dimensions of Cross-Cultural Training Program

Cultural training includes a wide variety of information and skill development, and cultural training programs vary considerably in terms of what knowledge and skills they teach. Two professors of organizational behavior, Yoshitaka Yamazaki of the International University of Japan and D. Christopher Kayes of the George Washington University, have synthesized what goes into cultural training. They identified seventy-three skills that are useful for expatriates (those people who live in a foreign land) in adapting to another culture. As part of their analysis, the researchers organized the seventy-three skills into five learning skill dimensions.[21] Figure 13-3 highlights and summarizes some of the competencies and knowledge or skill associated with the five dimensions. You will observe that much of cultural training relates to the development of human relations skills, including cultural sensitivity and cultural intelligence.

Foreign Language Training

Learning a foreign language is often part of cultural training or can also be a separate activity. Knowledge of a second language is important because it builds better connections with people from other cultures than does relying on a translator. Many workers aside from international business specialists also choose to develop skills in a target language. Speaking another language can help build rapport with customers and employees who speak that language. Almost all language training has elements similar to taking a course in another language or self-study. Companies invest heavily in helping employees learn a target language because it facilitates conducting business in other countries. Medical specialists, police workers, and firefighters also find second-language skills to be quite helpful. Clients under stress, such as an injured person, are likely to revert to their native tongue.

Many multinational companies have downplayed the importance of American workers being fluent in a second language because English has become the standard language of commerce.[22] Despite the merits of this observation, speaking and writing well in the language of your target can help establish rapport. Furthermore, from the standpoint of career management it is worth noting that more and more highly placed managers in large companies are bilingual. Another value of foreign-language training is to better communicate with subordinates, coworkers, and customers. For example, it is estimated that in the United States, nearly two-thirds of construction workers do not speak English as

FIGURE 13-3

COMPETENCIES FOR SUCCESSFUL CROSS-CULTURAL ADAPTATION OF EXPATRIATES

Source: Abridged from Yoshitaka Yamazaki and D. Christopher Kayes, "An Experiential Approach to Cross-Cultural Learning: A Review and Integration of Competencies for Successful Expatriate Adaptation," *Academy of Management Learning and Education*, December 2004, p. 372.

Learning Skill Dimension	Cross-Cultural Competency Cluster	Knowledge or Skill Required
Interpersonal	Building relationships	Ability to gain access to and maintain relationships with members of host culture
	Valuing people of different cultures	Empathy for differences; sensitivity to diversity
Information	Listening and observation	Awareness of cultural history and reasons for cultural actions and customs
	Coping with ambiguity	Ability to recognize and interpret implicit behavior, especially nonverbal cues
Analytical	Translating complex information	Knowledge of local language, symbols, or other forms of verbal language and written language
Action	Taking action and initiative	Understanding of intended and potentially unintended consequences of actions
	Managing others	Ability to manage details of a job, including maintaining cohesion in a group
Adaptive	Adaptability and flexibility	Ability to view change from multiple perspectives
	Managing stress	Understanding of own and other's moods, emotions, and personality

their primary language. Construction supervisors who speak Spanish can prevent many accidents.[23]

As with any other skill training, these investments can only pay off if the trainee is willing to work hard developing the new skill outside the training session. It is unlikely that almost anyone can develop conversational skills in another language by listening to foreign language cassette tapes or taking classes for thirty days. The quick training program, however, helps you develop a base for further learning. Allowing even ten days to pass without practicing your target language will result in a sharp decline in your ability to use that language.

PARTICIPATE IN DIVERSITY TRAINING

The general purpose of cultural training is to help workers understand people from other cultures. Understanding can lead to dealing more effectively with them as work associates or customers. **Diversity training** has a slightly different purpose. It attempts to bring about workplace harmony by teaching people how to get along with diverse work associates. Quite often the program is aimed at minimizing open expressions of racism and sexism. Diversity training takes a number of forms. Nevertheless, all training programs center on increasing awareness of and empathy for people who are different in some noticeable way from oneself.

Diversity training program that attempts to bring about workplace harmony by teaching people how to get along with diverse work associates; often aimed at minimizing open expressions of racism and sexism

Recognizing Differences

A starting point in diversity training is to emphasize that everybody is different in some way and that all these differences should be appreciated. The subtle point here is that cultural diversity does not refer exclusively to differences in race, ethnicity, age, and sex. As the United States Office of Civil Rights explains, "Diversity is a term used broadly to refer to many demographic variables, including but not limited to race, religion, color, gender, national origin, disability, sexual orientation, age, education, geographic origin, and skill characteristics."[24]

Diversity training emphasizes *inclusion*, or including everybody when appreciating diversity. The accompanying Human Relations in Practice illustrates both the scope of diversity and how much importance companies attach to having a diverse workforce. Figure 13-4 presents a broad sampling of the ways in which workplace associates can differ from one another. All these differences are tucked under the welcoming *diversity umbrella*. Studying this list can help you anticipate the type of differences to understand and appreciate in a diverse workplace. The differences include cultural as well as individual factors. Individual factors are also important because people can be discriminated against for personal characteristics as well as group characteristics. Many people who are disfigured, for example, believe they are held back from obtaining a higher-level job because of their disfigurement, such as a facial birthmark.

Another important part of diversity training is to develop empathy for diverse viewpoints. To help training participants develop empathy, representatives of various groups explain their feelings related to workplace issues. In one segment of such a program, a minority group member was seated in the middle of a circle. The other participants sat at the periphery of the circle. First, the coworkers listened to a Vietnamese woman explain how she felt excluded from the in-group composed of whites and African Americans in her department. "I feel like you

FIGURE 13-4

THE DIVERSITY UMBRELLA

- Race
- Sex or gender
- Religion
- Age (young, middle aged, and old)
- Generation differences, including attitudes (e.g., baby boomers versus the Net generation)
- Ethnicity (country of origin)
- Education
- Abilities
- Mental disabilities (including attention deficit disorder)
- Physical status (including hearing status, visual status, being able-bodied, wheelchair user)
- Values and motivation
- Sexual orientation (heterosexual, homosexual, bisexual, transsexual)
- Marital status (married, single, cohabitating, widow, widower)
- Family status (children, no children, two-parent family, single parent, grandparent, opposite-sex parents, same-sex parents)
- Personality traits
- Functional background (area of specialization, such as marketing, manufacturing)
- Technology interest (high tech, low tech, technophobe)
- Weight status (average, obese, underweight, anorexic)
- Hair status (full head of hair, bald, wild hair, tame hair, long hair, short hair)
- Style of clothing and appearance (dress up, dress down, professional appearance, casual appearance, tattoos, body piercing including multiple earrings, nose rings, lip rings)
- Tobacco status (smoker versus nonsmoker, chewer versus non-chewer)
- Your creative suggestion

Human Relations in Practice

The Corporate Diversity Policy of Alliant Energy

A core corporate value of Alliant Energy is to be a responsible corporate citizen, caring for the environment and the communities where we do business and encouraging diversity in our employee and supplier ranks.

Diversity includes, but is not limited to, race, gender, age, physical and mental abilities, lifestyles, culture, education, ideas and background.

At Alliant Energy we recognize, respect, and appreciate the valuable and different perspectives that each of us bring to the work environment, our company and our customers.

Our goal is to break down barriers and create an environment that maximizes the contributions of all employees.

Recognizing the work that needs to be done to improve diversity attitudes, behaviors and outcomes, Alliant Energy helped form the Diversity Focus organization. Diversity Focus seeks to work with businesses, government, education and all individuals and groups who embrace diversity to improve the welcoming nature of the Cedar Rapids and Iowa City corridor.

Source: "Corporate Diversity Policy." Retrieved March 27, 2009, from: www.alliantenergy.com (Madison, Wisconsin).

simply tolerate me. You do not make me feel that I am somebody important. You make me feel that because I am Vietnamese I don't count." The next person to sit in the middle of the circle was Muslim. He complained about people wishing him Merry Christmas. "I would much prefer that my coworkers would stop to think that I do not celebrate Christian holidays. I respect your religion, but it is not my religion."

Concerns about Diversity Training

A criticism of many diversity training programs is that too many angry feelings are expressed and that negative stereotypes are reinforced, leading to strained relationships. Another criticism is that the program might be considered patronizing because the majority of participants are already respectful of people different from themselves and know how to work harmoniously with a wide variety of people.

Support for the importance of diversity training comes from a five-year study of the impact of diversity on business results conducted by Thomas A. Kochan, a professor of both management and engineering systems at the Massachusetts Institute of Technology. He concludes that a culturally diverse workforce enhances business performance only when proper training is provided to employees. An organizational culture that supports diversity, meaning that the values and atmosphere of the firm welcome inclusion, is also required.[25]

Even when diversity training attains its goal of enhanced cross-cultural understanding, the training may not lead to enhanced promotional opportunities for women and minorities. An analysis of decades of federal employment statistics provided by business firms found no real change in the number of women and minority managers after diversity training began. In contrast, mentoring programs did facilitate the promotion of women and minorities.[26]

▶ Learning Objective 4 ▶

How Do You Overcome Cross-Cultural Communication Barriers?

A key part of developing good cross-cultural relations is to overcome or prevent communication barriers stemming from cultural differences. Personal life, too, is often more culturally diverse today than previously, leading to culturally based communication problems. The information about avoiding cultural bloopers presented in this chapter might also be interpreted as a way to prevent communication barriers. Here we describe ten additional strategies and tactics to help overcome cross-cultural communication barriers.

1. **Be alert to cultural differences in customs and behavior.** To minimize cross-cultural communication barriers, recognize that many subtle job-related differences in customs and behavior may exist. For example, Asians typically feel uncomfortable when asked to brag about themselves in the presence of others. From their perspective, calling attention to oneself at the expense of another person is rude and unprofessional.

2. **Use straightforward language and speak slowly and clearly.** When working with people who do not speak your language fluently, speak in an easy-to-understand manner. Be patient for many reasons, including the fact that your accent in your native tongue may not be the same as the person from whom your target learned your language. (For example, English as learned in India is quite different from English as learned in Ohio.) Minimize the use of idioms and analogies specific to your language. For example, in North America the term "over the hill" means outdated or past one's prime. A person from another culture may not understand this phrase yet be hesitant to ask for clarification. Speaking slowly is also important because even people who read and write a second language at an expert level may have difficulty catching the nuances of conversation. Facing the person from another culture directly also improves communication because your facial expressions and lips contribute to comprehension.

Speaking slowly and clearly is more effective at overcoming communication barriers than shouting at a person who does not understand your language well. For example, some Americans visiting other countries will shout at a restaurant server, "DON'T YOU SPEAK ENGLISH?" Shouting makes people defensive, including shouting at blind people to enhance comprehension. (Because the blind person cannot see a person's lips to enhance understanding, speaking clearly and not murmuring is helpful.) Also, a deaf person who reads lips will usually not understand words better when the speaker shouts. The vibrations given off by the shouting might be considered offensive.

3. **When the situation is appropriate, speak in the language of the people from another culture.** Americans who can speak another language are at a competitive advantage when dealing with businesspeople who speak that language. The language skill, however, must be more advanced than speaking a few words and phrases. A new twist in speaking another language has surged recently: As more deaf people have been integrated into the workforce, knowing American Sign Language can be a real advantage to a worker when some of his or her coworkers or customers are deaf.

4. **Observe cultural differences in etiquette.** Violating rules of etiquette without explanation can erect immediate communication barriers. A major rule of etiquette is that in most countries people in high-status positions expect to be treated with respect. Formality is important, unless invited to act otherwise. When visiting a company in Asia, for example, it is best to be deferent to (appeal to the authority of) company dignitaries. Visualize yourself as a company representative of a high-tech American firm that manufactures equipment for legally downloading music over

the Internet. You visit Sony Corporation in Japan to speak about a joint venture. On meeting the marketing vice president, bow slightly and say something to the effect of, "Mr. _____, it is my honor to discuss doing business with Sony." Do not commit the etiquette mistake of saying something to the effect of, "Hi, Charlie. How's the wife and kids?" (An American actually said this at a Japanese company shortly before being escorted out the door.)

5. Be sensitive to differences in nonverbal communication. Stay alert to the possibility that a person from another culture may misinterpret your nonverbal signal. To use positive reinforcement, some managers will give a sideways hug to an employee or will touch an employee's arm. People from some cultures resent touching from workmates and will be offended. Koreans in particular dislike being touched or touching others in a work setting. (Refer to the discussion of cultural bloopers.) Another example of a potential nonverbal communication problem is "thumbs up" indicator used frequently in North America to convey the thought "Good job." Yet in some geographic areas such as Australia and Nigeria, the gesture is considered offensive.[27]

6. Do not be diverted by style, accent, grammar, or personal appearance. Although all these superficial factors are related to business success, they are difficult to interpret when judging a person from another culture. It is therefore better to judge the merits of the statement or behavior.[28] A brilliant individual from another culture may still be learning your language and thus make basic mistakes in speaking your language. He or she might also not have developed a sensitivity to dress style in your culture.

7. Listen for understanding, not agreement. When working with diverse teammates, the differences in viewpoints can lead to conflict. To help overcome such conflict, follow the LUNA rule: Listen for Understanding, Not Agreement. In this way you gear yourself to consider the viewpoints of others as a first resort. For example, some older workers may express some intense loyalty to the organization, whereas their younger teammates may speak in more critical terms. By everyone listening to understand, they can begin to appreciate each others' paradigms and accept differences of opinion.[29] Listening is a powerful tool for overcoming cross-cultural communication barriers.

8. Be attentive to individual differences in appearance. A major cross-cultural insult is to confuse the identity of people because they are members of the same race or ethnic group. Psychological research suggests that people have difficulty seeing individual differences among people of another race because they code race first, such as thinking, "He has the nose of an African American." However, people can learn to search for more distinguishing features, such as a dimple or eye color.[30]

9. Ask lots of questions to clarify potential misunderstandings. Many cross-cultural communication barriers can be avoided by asking questions to clarify potential misunderstandings. Even when speaking the same language, cultural traditions might lead to misunderstanding. For example, a representative from a foreign company might say that he or she "would be honored to try your product." However, "being honored" might imply that the person wants to try the products for free.

10. Do not misinterpret a formal communication style during a multicultural team meeting. Business consultant Sangeeta Gupta reminds us that workers from many Asian, Middle Eastern, and Latin countries, as well as those from the American South, will often use a formal communication style during a meeting. Formal communicators are likely to take their turn to speak and will often wait to hear what their manager has to say before expressing an opinion. In a U.S. environment, this formality might be interpreted as the team member not having much to contribute.[31] To overcome the barrier, encourage the more formal communicators to contribute in a polite, nonintimidating manner.

Many of the cross-cultural communication barriers mentioned in the preceding list take place between customers and call centers located in other countries, especially those located in India and the Philippines. At times the communication problems are a question of understanding the other person's pronunciation. At other times the problems stem from the hostility of American customers who perceive the overseas call center operators to be taking their jobs away.

A major cross-cultural communication problem arises when the American who called cannot understand the version of English spoken by the customer service or technical support representative. Americans who can understand people well only from their own geographic region are likely to have the most difficulty in understanding the overseas technical support or customer service representative. The problem has been particularly acute with customers seeking technical assistance for prepaid cell phones. For example, the rep from India might ask the American to enter a long series of numerals—a challenging task even if you are familiar with the other person's accent.

Overseas agents typically receive training in American culture and even keep track of weather in different regions in the United States, so they can make some introductory small talk. Also, the overseas agents call themselves by American first names, such as "Jack" or "Jennifer," and keep abreast of major American television shows and sporting events to help break communication barriers. Despite these initiatives, unless the customer seeking help is accustomed to speaking with people with a variety of accents, the communication barriers remain.

In recognition of the potential cross-cultural communication barriers that occur with overseas call centers, the trend toward such outsourcing is slowing down. One compromise is to offer technical support and customer service from American centers during daytime working hours and overseas service during the night.

▶ Learning Objective 5 ▶

Why Are Gender Differences in Leadership Style Regarded as Cultural Differences?

Differences in the way men and women lead can be interpreted as cultural differences because gender is one of the factors contributing to the cultural mosaic. A number of factors may contribute to a person's cultural identity, with maleness or femaleness being one contributor. Several researchers and writers have argued that women have certain acquired traits and behaviors that suit them for a people-oriented leadership style.[32] Consequently, women leaders frequently exhibit a cooperative, empowering style that includes nurturing team members. According to this same perspective, men are inclined toward a command-and-control, somewhat militaristic leadership style. Women find participative management more natural than do men because they feel more comfortable interacting with people. Furthermore, it is argued that women's natural sensitivity to people gives them an edge over men to encouraging group members to participate in decision making.

The gender differences in leadership style that do exist could be attributable in part to differences in communication style between men and women. Men are more concerned about transmitting information and gaining status while they communicate, whereas women are more concerned about building social connections.

Assume that these differences in the preferred leadership style between men and women were generally true. Women managers, therefore, would be better suited for organizations that have shifted to participation and empowerment. It may be true that more women than men gravitate naturally toward the consultative, consensus, and democratic leadership styles, and men toward the autocratic. Nevertheless, there are many male leaders who find the participative style to be a good fit and many women who are autocratic.

Even if gender differences in leadership style exist, this type of cultural difference requires a minimum of adaptation by most people. Fewer and fewer people in the workforce find it unusual or difficult to work with members of the opposite sex, even if they have a preference for working with members of their own sex.

What Are Some of the Legal Aspects of Working in a Culturally Diverse Environment?

◀ Learning Objective 6 ◀

In this chapter we have emphasized the interpersonal aspects of building good relationships with work associates who are demographically and culturally diverse. The legal side of diversity focuses on such matters as protecting workers from being discriminated against, such as not being denied a job you are qualified for because of race, gender, age, or physical disability. A recent analysis concludes that the groups disadvantaged in the U.S. workplace are women, people of color, sexual minorities, and people with disabilities.[33] Note that not all members of these groups are disadvantaged, including the reality that in 2009 the CEO of American Express was an African American man, the CEO of Xerox Corp. was an African American woman, and the CEO of Yahoo! was a women also.

Legislation may help advance the rights of many workers, but it does not require workers to develop constructive relationships with each other or to develop cultural intelligence. Here we look briefly at relevant employment legislation, as well as affirmative action.

FEDERAL LAWS PROHIBITING JOB DISCRIMINATION

Workers are protected by a series of federal laws that prohibit job discrimination. In addition, states, provinces (Canada), and municipalities have their own laws governing fair treatment of employees. Furthermore, many employment lawyers bring forth lawsuits for discrimination not specifically mentioned in federal laws. For example, a job candidate might claim that he was denied a position for which he was qualified because he was obese. A state or local judge could then decide whether the claim was justified. The general purpose of job discrimination laws is to protect individuals who have been disadvantaged in the past because of demographic (not cultural) characteristics. Employment legislations began with prohibiting employment discrimination based on race, color, religion, sex, or national origin. Figure 13-5 summarizes Federal Equal Employment Opportunity (EEO) laws. These laws apply to all private employers, state and local governments, and educational institutions that employ fifteen or more individuals.

An effective way of understanding how these laws might affect the individual is to specify the discriminatory practices prohibited by these laws. Under Title VII, the ADA, and the ADEA, it is illegal to discriminate in any aspect of employment, including hiring and firing; compensation, assignment, or classification of employees; transfer, promotion, layoff, or recall; job advertisements; recruitment; testing; use of company facilities; training and apprenticeship programs; fringe benefits; pay, retirement plans, and disability leave; or other terms and conditions

FIGURE 13-5

FEDERAL LAWS PROHIBITING JOB DISCRIMINATION

- Title VII of the Civil Rights Act of 1964 (Title VII) prohibits employment discrimination based on race, color, religion, sex, or national origin.
- The Equal Pay Act of 1963 (EPA) protects men and women who perform substantially equal work in the same establishment from sex-based wage discrimination.
- The Age Discrimination in Employment Act of 1967 (ADEA) protects individuals who are forty years of age or older.
- Title I and Title V of the Americans with Disabilities Act of 1990 (ADA) prohibits employment discrimination against qualified individuals with disabilities in the private sector and in state and local governments.
- Sections 501 and 505 of the Rehabilitation Act of 1973 prohibit discrimination against qualified individuals with disabilities who work in the federal government.
- The Civil Rights Act of 1991 provides, among other things, monetary damages in cases of intentional employment discrimination.

The U.S. EEOC enforces all of these laws. EEOC also provides oversight and coordination of all federal equal employment opportunity regulations, practices, and policies.

Source: Available at www.eeoc.gov/facts/ganda.html.

of employment. Discriminatory practices under these laws also include the following:

1. Harassment on the basis of race, color, religion, sex, national origin, disability, or age.

2. Retaliation against an individual for filing a charge of discrimination, participating in an investigation, or opposing discriminatory practices.

3. Employment decisions based on stereotypes or assumptions about the abilities, traits, or performance of individuals of a certain sex, race, age, religion, or ethnic group or individuals with disabilities.

4. Denying employment opportunities to a person because of marriage to, or association with, an individual of a particular race, religion, national origin, or an individual with a disability. Title VII also prohibits discrimination because of participation in schools or places of worship associated with a particular racial, ethnic, or religious group.

Although all of these forms of discrimination may appear clear-cut, a good deal of interpretation is required to decide whether a given employee is the subject of discrimination. For example, assume that a woman files a charge of sexual harassment. Later, she is bypassed for promotion. She claims she is now the victim of discrimination, yet the company claims that she did not have the appropriate interpersonal skills to be promoted to a supervisory position.

Among the remedies awarded to individuals judged to be discriminated against are back pay, promotion, reinstatement, and the employer paying attorney's fees and court costs. Compensatory and punitive damages are also possible.

ADDITIONAL EXAMPLES OF LEGISLATION AND COURT RULINGS TO ENSURE EQUAL RIGHTS

The federal legislation described above set the stage for a wide variety of laws and judicial rulings to prevent employment discrimination and thereby protect the rights of workers. Similar legislation is found in Canada, as well as European and some Asian countries. Here we highlight a few representative examples of how the rights of workers against discrimination are protected beyond major federal legislation summarized in Figure 13-5.[34]

- **Unconscious bias.** Several court rulings have recognized that unconscious prejudice and bias can prevent women and people of color from achievement and advancement after they have joined an employer. One example is a class-action suit against Wal-Mart involving more than 2 million women (*Dukes et al. v. Wal-Mart Stores Inc.*, 2004).

- **Protection for people with disabilities.** The Ticket to Work and Work Incentives Improvement Act of 1999 and the Workforce Investment Act of 1998 both focus on increased workforce participation for people with disabilities. For example, the 1998 act mandates state attention to developing employment programs, including career centers to help the disabled. (A problem remains in implementing disability legislation in unambiguously defining the meaning of *disability*. For example, one worker was fired for downloading pornography on his desktop computer. He sued, claiming he had a *disability* of pornography addiction. The judge supported the company.)

- **Protection against genetic discrimination.** The Genetic Anti-Discrimination Bill of 2008 protects workers from losing their jobs or health insurance and gaining promotions when genetic testing reveals they are susceptible to diseases that are costly to treat, such as cancer, heart disease, or other ailments.

AFFIRMATIVE ACTION

A key aspect of implementing the spirit and letter of antidiscrimination law in the United States has been affirmative action programs. **Affirmative action** consists of complying with antidiscrimination laws and correcting past discriminatory practices. Under an affirmative action program, employers actively recruit, employ, train, and promote minorities and women, groups who have been discriminated against by an employer in the past. As a result, women and minority group members have been underrepresented in certain positions. Part of an affirmative action plan might be to actively recruit Latino business graduates to place them in a company management training program.

Affirmative action
programs that comply with antidiscrimination laws and attempt to correct past discriminatory practices

Affirmative action has been the subject of continuing debate. Proponents of affirmative action believe that it provides the opportunity many people need to prove their capability and earn just rewards. Opponents of affirmative action believe that it provides preferential treatment for certain groups and winds up discriminating against workers who are qualified but do not fit an affirmative action category. The National Leadership Network of Black Conservatives is an example of a group strongly opposed to affirmative action. The National Leadership Network supports the position that affirmative action is wrong because it is "a system rooted in the belief that blacks and certain other minorities cannot hope to win if they have to compete on a level playing field."[35] What is your opinion about the merits of affirmative action?

Concept Review and Reinforcement

Summary and Review

Being able to work well with people from other cultures, both outside and inside your own country, is important for career success. Seven dimensions of cultural values that help us understand how cultures differ from one another are as follows:

- Individualism versus collectivism
- Acceptance of power and authority
- Materialism versus concern for others
- Formality versus informality
- Urgent time orientation versus casual time orientation
- Work orientation versus leisure orientation
- High-context versus low-context cultures (with an emphasis on body language)

Many people have multicultural identities because they identify with their own culture as well as other cultures. Similarly, according to the cultural mosaic, people have a rich mixture of cultural identities. The religious value part of the cultural mosaic often affects when people are willing to work or not work. It is important to be alert to possible cultural differences.

Certain underlying factors create problems in developing smooth cross-cultural relations, including communication problems.

- Perceptual expectations are much like stereotypes that lead to misunderstandings.
- Ethnocentrism, or thinking that one's culture is best, leads to misunderstandings.
- Misunderstandings also come about from stereotypes in intergroup relations.
- Different cultural norms and codes of conduct can lead to confusion.
- Micro-inequities also create problems.

Six specific methods and techniques for improving cross-cultural relations are as follows:

- Develop cultural sensitivity (be aware of differences) and cultural intelligence (cognitive, emotional, and body components).
- Focus on individuals rather than groups.
- Respect all workers and cultures (including practicing sexual equity).
- Value cultural differences (this also involves showing respect).
- Minimize cultural bloopers (embarrassing mistakes).
- Participate in cultural training, including language training. (The skill dimensions of cross-cultural training are interpersonal, information, analytic, action, and adaptive.)
- Participate in diversity training, or learning to get along with diverse work associates.

Cross-cultural communication barriers can often be overcome by the following:

- Being alert to cultural differences in customs and behavior
- Using straightforward language and speaking slowly and clearly
- Speaking in the language of the other group
- Observing cultural differences in etiquette
- Being sensitive to differences in nonverbal communication
- Not being diverted by style, accent, grammar, or personal appearance
- Listening for understanding, not agreement
- Being attentive to individual differences in appearance

- Asking lots of questions to clarify potential misunderstandings
- Correctly interpreting a formal communication style during a multicultural team meeting

Gender differences in leadership style have been observed that could be interpreted as cultural differences between men and women. Women tend toward a cooperative, empowering style that includes nurturing team members. It is argued that men lean toward a command-and-control autocratic style.

The legal side of diversity focuses on such matters as protecting workers from discrimination, but it is not part of developing cross-cultural competence. Workers are protected by a series of federal, state, and municipal laws that govern fair treatment of employees. It is illegal to discriminate in any aspect of employment including hiring and firing, compensation, and recruitment. Legislation and court rulings continue to emerge to ensure the equal rights of workers. Affirmative action programs consist of complying with antidiscrimination laws and correcting past discriminatory practices.

Check Your Understanding

1. Imagine an American worker sent on assignment to Malaysia, a country that highly values respect for authority. How might the American adapt to this belief in respect for authority?
2. In what way might having a high acceptance for power and authority make it difficult for a person to work well on a team that has very little supervision?
3. Identify three positive stereotypes about cultural groups that are related to job behavior. (An example would be the observation that Mexican laborers are known for their hard work and dependability.)
4. When you meet someone from another culture, what can you do to demonstrate that you respect that person's culture?
5. Provide an example of cultural insensitivity of any kind that you have seen, read about, or could imagine.
6. Imagine that you are trying hard to "Do as Romans do when in Rome" in a foreign country. You are attending a business dinner and your host invites you to eat a meal that is composed of an animal you consider to be a household pet. How would you handle this situation?
7. In an era of welcoming cultural diversity, does a company have the right to exclude employees with visible body piercings from any type of positions?
8. Suppose a company wants to promote cross-cultural understanding. Should the executives then discourage employees from one racial or ethnic group from forming a club or sitting together in the company cafeteria? Explain your position.
9. Many people speak loudly to deaf people, blind people, and those who speak a different language. Based on the information presented in this chapter, what mistakes are these people making?
10. How might you be able to convert cross-cultural skills into higher income and job status for yourself?

Web Corner

Cultural training:
www.berlitz.com; www.culturalsavvy.com (Click on "Tips & Info.")

Cultural diversity:
www.diversityinc.com

INTERNET SKILL BUILDER

Developing Your Multicultural Skills

A useful way of developing skills in a second language and learning more about another culture is to use as a home page (the page that appears when you open the Internet) a page written in your target language. In this way, each time you go the Internet on your own computer, your home page will contain fresh information in the language you want to develop.

Assume that your target language is French. Enter a phrase such as "French language newspaper" or "French current events" in the search box. Once you find a suitable choice, insert that newspaper as your cover page. The search engine might have brought you to www.france2.fr or www.cyberpresse.ca. These Web sites keep you abreast of French and French Canadian international news, sports, and cultural events—written in French. Now every time you access the Internet, you can spend a few minutes becoming multicultural. You can save lot of travel costs and time using the Internet to help you become multicultural.

Developing Your
Human Relations Skills

Human Relations Application Exercises

Applying Human Relations Exercise 13-1

Avoiding Cultural Mistakes

Refer to Figure 13-2, Cultural Mistakes to Avoid with Selected Cultural Groups. Review the list of cultural groups listed. After you have chosen one or two cultural groups, imagine how and where you might have an opportunity to relate to someone from one of these culture groups. During the next thirty days, look for an opportunity to relate to a person from another culture in the way described in these suggestions. You may have to be creative to find a target with whom you can practice your cross-cultural skills. Before approaching your target, answer these questions:

1. What would be my usual approach to dealing with a person from that culture? (An example here would be as follows: "Usually when I visit the neighborhood convenience store operated by a Korean family, I attempt to place the money for purchases directly in the hands of the cashier.)
2. What will I do differently after studying the suggestions in Figure 13-2? (Because touching a Korean's hand might be uncomfortable for him or her, I will lay the money on the counter and let the cashier pick it up.)

Observe the reaction of the other person for feedback on your cross-cultural effectiveness. Then assess whether your approach to improving cross-cultural relations had any effect on your target.

Applying Human Relations Exercise 13-2

Developing Empathy for Differences

Class members go up to the front of the room one by one and give a brief presentation (perhaps two or three minutes) of any way in which they have been perceived as different and how they felt about this perception. The difference can be of any kind, relating to characteristics such as ethnicity, race, major field of study, physical appearance, height, weight, hair color, or body piercing. Here is an example repeatedly heard from very tall people: "I am so tired of the same old stupid comment, 'How's the weather up there?' It also annoys me that so many people ask me to change a lightbulb in a highly placed fixture. Even worse, because I'm tall, people think I would want to help them move furniture." An example heard frequently from information technology students is as follows: "When I'm out socially, people are forever asking me about some software problem they are facing. They think I know all about every software package ever written. Even worse, they think I have no life outside of computers. Why should I want to talk about computer problems when I'm partying?"

After each member of the class has presented (perhaps even the instructor), class members discuss what they learned from the exercise. Points to look for include the following:

- What pattern do you see in the ways people perceive themselves to be different?
- What is the most frequent difference reported by class members?
- What kind of perceptions by others seem to hurt the most?

It is also important to discuss how this exercise can improve relationships on the job. What would be at least one takeaway from the exercise?

Human Relations Class Activity

Cultural Gaffes in Both Directions

Many analyses of cross-cultural relations emphasize the mistakes American make in dealing with people from other cultures, as described in Figure 13-2. But people from non-American cultures also make mistakes in dealing with Americans. An example would be a Japanese businessperson who did not take an American company manager seriously because she was a woman.

The class assignment here is for student to collect two cross-cultural gaffes (or mistakes): one made by an American in relation to a person from another culture and one made by a foreigner in relation to an American. Use any method of gaffe collection you want, including conversations with people you know, your own observations, e-mails, blogs, or Internet search engines.

At a time designated by the instructor, each student or a number of volunteers present their gaffes in front of class. The gaffes can be presented in about two minutes. As class members listen to the gaffes, look for (a) frequently occurring gaffes and (b) lessons to be learned from these gaffes. An example of a lesson would be how to use this information about gaffes to improve cross-cultural relations.

Human Relations Case Study 13-1

Dunkin' Donuts Patches an Unintended Blooper

Dunkin' Donuts pulled an online ad featuring Rachael Ray after bloggers said the scarf she was wearing in the commercial looked like a *kaffiyeh*, a traditional Arab scarf. Conservative columnist Michelle Malking wrote about the ad: "The kaffiyeh, for the clueless, is the traditional scarf of Arab men that has come to symbolize murderous Palestinian jihad."

In the ad, the popular cook was wearing a black and white silk scarf with a paisley design. It was selected by a stylist for the ad shoot, says the coffee chain. "Absolutely no symbolism was intended," said a statement from Margie Myers, senior vice president of communications for Dunkin' Brands. "We are no long using the online ad because the possibility of misperception detracted from its original intention to promote our iced coffee."

Questions

1. What does this brief story illustrate about the importance of a business firm (or its advertising agency) understanding other cultures in depth?

2. How justified are the complaints of the bloggers that a scarf should not be used in a commercial because it resembles a kaffiyeh?

3. If you were the Dunkin' Donuts official in charge, would you have pulled the ad in question?

Source: Suzanne Vranica, "Dunkin' Donuts Pulls Ray Ad over Scarf," *Wall Street Journal*, May 29, 2008, p. B7.

Human Relations Case Study 13-2

The Multicultural Dealership

Manuel Ortiz is the owner and operator of Futura Motors, a large automobile and small-truck dealership in Brooklyn, New York. The dealership represents several Japanese and Korean vehicle manufacturers. For more than a decade, Ortiz and his management team have invested time, effort, and money into building culturally diverse sales and service staffs to better serve the many ethnic, cultural, and racial groups that make up the dealership's customer base. Ortiz brags that in total his sales staff speaks thirteen different languages. "In this way we can communicate in the native tongue of almost any customer or sales prospect who shows up on the floor," says Ortiz. (A *sales prospect* is anyone who visits Futura without the full intention of purchasing a vehicle from the dealership, including the people who are "just looking.")

The culturally diverse sales and service staffs apparently have contributed to the growth and profitability of Futura, although such an assertion would be difficult to prove. For example, Ortiz has not been able to compare the dollar volume of Futura to a comparable-sized foreign dealership in Brooklyn that has a more homogeneous workforce.

Penny Shakelford, the office manager at Futura, has recently brought a potential problem to Ortiz's attention that has caused him some concern about how well he and his staff are managing diversity. According to Shakelford, the multicultural sales staff appears to be well accepted by most customers and prospects, yet some problems are surfacing. Based on direct concerns expressed by both customers and prospects, Shakelford believes that they are being patronized on the basis of their demographic group. She explains:

"My impression is that some customers think we are bending over backwards to make them feel at home. If a person who walks on the floor appears to be an African American, immediately an African American sales rep walks up to him or her. The same goes for several other visible ethnic or racial groups. Two different Asiatic Indians wrote down on customer service survey cards that they thought it was too obvious that an Indian rushed out on the floor as soon as they appeared.

"A Mexican American woman said she thought it was a little bit much that three minutes after she and her husband walked into the dealership, a young sales rep introduced himself in Spanish. The customer said she was in Brooklyn, not Mexico City, and wanted to be treated like an American."

Ortiz said that it appears that the vast majority of customers and prospects find no problem with their attempt to make a direct appeal to their racial or ethnic group but that maybe some adjustment needs to be made.

"We need to give this problem some thought. We don't want to insult anybody, but neither do we want to lose our competitive edge of having a multicultural workforce."

Questions

1. What is your opinion of the merits of a vehicle dealership attempting to match the demographic group of a customer with a sales rep of the same demographic group?

2. What do you recommend Ortiz and his management team do about the complaints the Futura dealership has received.

3. To help you analyze this case, get the input from a few people in your network about how they would feel about having a person from their demographic group approach them when they visited a dealership. (Perhaps a few classmates representing different ethnic groups can provide useful input.)

Human Relations Role-Playing Exercise

Demographic Match-Ups at Futura Motors

The case study about the multicultural dealership serves as the background and the story line for this role-play.

For the first scenario, one person plays the role of Wanda, a Latino sales rep at Futura Motors. A Latino-appearing man appears on the sales lot, and he is carefully looking at a new Jaguar. Wanda wants to use her Latino roots to give her an edge in helping make a sale to the potential buyer. Another person plays the role of the Latino-appearing sales prospect. His mind right now is on the dark green Jaguar, not on the demographic characteristics of the sales rep. Run the role-play for about six minutes.

For the second scenario, a black woman comes on the lot and is seriously eying a Lexus. The woman could be African American, African, Jamaican, or perhaps from Europe. Nevertheless, Jeff, an African American, is assigned to help the sales prospect. Jeff, who can get carried away sometimes, decides that he is going to greet the prospect with a high-five as a means of establishing rapport. The woman, who is really from Ghana, Africa, wonders why she is receiving this rather informal and sports-like greeting. She is also wondering if the sales rep might have some stereotypes about how to greet a black person. The woman has some questions about the gas economy and the safety of the Lexus she is considering. Run the role-play for about six minutes.

Observers rate the role-players on two dimensions, using a 1 to 5 scale from very poor to very good. One dimension is "effective use of human relations techniques." The second dimension is "acting ability." A few observers might voluntarily provide feedback to the role-players in terms of sharing their ratings and observations. The course instructor might also provide feedback.

REFERENCES

1. Rita Zeidner, "One Workforce—Many Languages," *HR Magazine,* January 2009, pp. 33–34.
2. Tiffany Hsu, "Retailers Catch On to the Buying Power of Immigrants," *Los Angeles Times* (www.latimes.com), December 24, 2008.
3. Geert Hofstede, *Culture's Consequences: International Differences in Work-Related Values* (Beverly Hills, CA: Sage, 1980). Updated and expanded in "A Conversation with Geert Hofstede," *Organizational Dynamics,* Spring 1993, pp. 53–61; Harry Triandis, The Many Dimensions of Culture," *Academy of Management Executive,* February 2004, pp. 88–93; Manasour Javidan, Peter W. Dorfman, May Sully de Luque, and Robert J. House, "In the Eye of the Beholder: Cross-Cultural Lessons in Leadership from Project GLOBE," *Academy of Management Perspectives,* February 2006, pp. 69–70.
4. Jeffrey Jensen Arnett, "The Psychology of Globalization," *American Psychologist,* October 2002, pp. 777–778.
5. Georgia T. Chao and Henry Moon, "The Cultural Mosaic: A Methodology for Understanding the Complexity of Culture," *Journal of Applied Psychology,* November 2005, pp. 1128–1140.
6. Eric Bellman, "In India, a Retailer Finds Key to Success Is Clutter," *Wall Street Journal,* August 8, 2007, pp. A1, A10.
7. Gary M. Stern, "Small Slights Bring Big Problems," *Workforce,* August 2002, p. 17.
8. Based on the contribution of Terri Geerinck in Andrew J. DuBrin and Terri Geerinck, *Human Relations for Career and Personal Success,* 2nd Canadian ed. (Toronto: Prentice Hall, 2001), p. 201. Geerinck also contributed the idea of a separate chapter on cross-cultural competency.
9. Arvind V. Phatak, *International Dimensions of Management* (Boston: Kent, 1983), p. 167.
10. P. Christopher Earley and Elain Mosakowski, "Cultural Intelligence," *Harvard Business Review,* October 2004, p. 140. The example is from the same source, same page.
11. Earley and Mosakowski, "Toward Cultural Intelligence: Turning Cultural Differences into Workplace Advantage," *Academy of Management Executive,* August 2004, pp. 154–155.
12. Todd Raphael, "Savvy Companies Build Bonds with Hispanic Employees," *Workforce,* September 2001, p. 19.
13. Experiment reported in Christopher Munsey, "Stereotype-Busting Can Spur Stress, Reduce Cognitive Performance," *Monitor on Psychology,* June 2007, p. 11.
14. Diane Cadrain, "Sexual Equity in the Workplace," *HR Magazine,* September 2008, pp. 44–50.
15. Gunnar Beeth, "Multicultural Managers Wanted," *Management Review,* May 1997, p. 17.
16. A few of these tasty morsels are from Lillian H. Chaney and Jeannette S. Martin, *Interpersonal Business Communication,* 3rd ed. (Upper Saddle River, NJ: Pearson Prentice Hall, 2004), p. 190.
17. Angela Ka-yee Leung, William W. Maddux, Adam G. Galinsky, and Chi-yue Chiu, "Multicultural Experience Enhances Creativity: The When and How," *American Psychologist,* April 2008, pp. 169–181.
18. Rick Borelli, "A Worldwide Language Trap," *Management Review,* October 1997, pp. 52–54.
19. The comment about informality is credited to Jacqueline Whitmore as cited in Michael Peltier, "Etiquette Lessons," *Time,* January 31, 2005, p. A4.
20. Marc Diener, "Culture Shock," *Entrepreneur,* July 2003, p. 77.
21. Yoshitaka Yamazaki and D. Christopher Kayes, "An Experiential Approach to Cross-Cultural Learning: A Review and Integration of Competencies for Successful Expatriate Adaptation," *Academy of Management Learning & Education,* December 2004, pp. 362–379.
22. Gretchen Weber, "English Rules," *Workforce Management,* May 2004, p. 48.
23. Donna M. Owens, "Multilingual Workforces," *HR Magazine,* September 2005, p. 127.
24. Definition from the U.S. Department of the Interior, Office of Civil Rights, as quoted in Janet Perez, "Diversity Inside-Out," *Hispanic Business,* April 2006, p. 64.
25. Research reported in Fay Hansen, "Diversity's Business Case Doesn't Add Up," *Workforce,* April 2003, pp. 28–32.
26. Study reported in Lisa Takuchi Cullen, "The Diversity Delusion," *Time,* May 7, 2007, p. 74.
27. "Escape these Cross-Cultural Traps," *Communication Briefings,* Volume XXII, Number 1, Condensed Issue, 2008.
28. David P. Tulin, "Enhance Your Multi-Cultural Communication Skills," *Managing Diversity,* 1, 1992, p. 5.
29. "Use Team's Diversity to Best Advantage," *Executive Strategies,* April 2000, p. 2.
30. Siri Carpenter, "Why Do 'They All Look Alike'?" *Monitor on Psychology,* December 2000, p. 44.
31. Sangeeta Gupta, "Mine the Potential of Multicultural Teams," *HR Magazine,* October 2008, p. 80.
32. One example of this research is Robert J. Kabacoff, *Gender Differences in Organizational Leadership* (Portland, ME: Management Research Group), as reported in "Do Men and Women Lead Differently?" *Leadership Strategies,* Premier Issue (2001).
33. Ruth E. Fassinger, "Workplace Diversity and Public Policy," *American Psychologist,* May–June 2008, p. 252.
34. Fassinger, "Workplace Diversity," pp. 262–265; "Bush Signs Genetic Anti-Discrimination Bill," Associated Press, May 21, 2008.
35. Interview with Ward Connerly, "A Poison Divides Us," The National Leadership Network of Black Conservatives, Affirmative Action Information Center. Retrieved April 23, 2006, from: www.nationalcenter.org/AA.html; Jeff Jacoby, "On Flattering Minorities," www.townhall.com, May 19, 2004.

14

Getting Ahead in Your Career

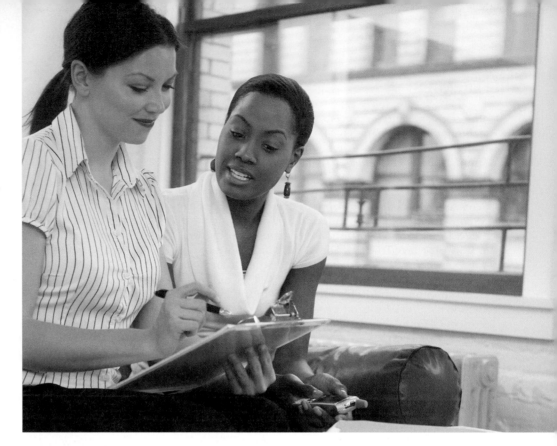

Outline

1 What Are the Basics of Conducting a Job Search?
Target Your Job Search
Finding Jobs through Networking and the Internet
Job Hunting during Difficult Economic Times

2 What Are Some Effective Career Advancement Strategies and Tactics?
Taking Control of Yourself
Exerting Control over the Outside World

3 Developing Your Networking Skills

T wo years after Brian Padworski began his career as an audit associate, he asked a colleague at KPMG to be his career: "The economy is not where it was a year ago, especially in the last three months, and having a mentor helps you," says Padworski, 23, who was looking for ways to shore up his future.

Padworski's mentor has encouraged him to become more aggressive, volunteer for extra assignments, and to earn his CPA designation. "He helps me to assess my skills and gives me a better idea of how to get the next level," says Padworski.[1]

The audit associate might be a newcomer in his field, but he demonstrates a wise approach to moving forward in his career—taking the initiative to find a mentor and then taking the mentor's advice seriously. Finding a mentor is but one of many useful approaches to career advancement, but our discussion of career advancement is preceded by the necessary first step of conducting a job campaign.

We have divided the vast information about career advancement into three sections. The first section deals with approaches to managing or taking control of your own behavior to advance or retain a good position. The second section deals with approaches to exerting control over your environment to improve your chances for success. The third section deals with networking, the most widely accepted career advancement strategy. To begin relating career development to yourself, do Human Relations Self-Assessment Quiz 14-1.

Human Relations Self-Assessment Quiz 14-1

The Career Development Inventory

Career development activities inevitably include answering some penetrating questions about yourself, such as the twelve questions that follow. You may need several hours to do a competent job answering these questions. After individuals have answered these questions by themselves, it may be profitable to hold a class discussion about the relevance of the specific questions. A strongly recommended procedure is for you to date your completed inventory and put it away for safekeeping. Examine your answers in several years to see (a) how well you are doing in advancing your career and (b) how much you have changed.

Keep the following information in mind in answering this inventory: People are generous in their self-evaluations when they answer career development inventories, so you might want to discuss some of your answers with somebody who knows you well.

1. How would you describe yourself as a person?
2. What are you best at doing? Worst?
3. What are your two biggest strengths or assets?
4. What skills and knowledge will you need to acquire to reach your goals?
5. What are your two biggest accomplishments?
6. Write your obituary as you would like it to appear.
7. What would be the ideal job for you?
8. What career advice can you give yourself?
9. Describe the two peak work-related experiences in your life.
10. What are your five most important values (the things in life most important to you)?
11. What goals in life are you trying to achieve?
12. What do you see as your niche (spot where you best fit) in the modern world?

▶ Learning Objective 1 ▶

What Are the Basics of Conducting a Job Search?

The purpose of this section is to provide a review of a few key ideas you need to conduct a successful job search, including sources of job leads, preparation of a cover letter and job résumé, and performing well in a job interview. You are probably already convinced that finding a job is a valuable investment in time. A recent analysis suggests that people have come to appreciate having a job more than ever. Holding a job is once again respected as the best source of revenue for most families. A decade ago, many people had a different attitude, as explained by money manager David Ellison: "Land was valuable, and capital was valuable, and labor—who cared? The attitude was, 'As long as I buy a few homes and invest in a hedge fund, I'm done. I can sit in my chair and watch football games.'"[2]

Although job search knowledge is readily available, this concise information can be used as a refresher and a reminder to be systematic in finding a new position. We also present a few fine points to help give you an edge over those who do the minimum necessary to find a new position.

TARGET YOUR JOB SEARCH

A job search begins with a reasonably flexible description of the type of job or jobs for which you are looking. Flexibility is called for because, with so many different jobs available, it is difficult to be too specific. Also, flexibility with respect to the type of employer is important. For example, many job seekers overlook the possibilities of working for the U.S. government. The federal government hires graduates in dozens of fields, and the starting pay is competitive with similar private-sector jobs. Your chances of finding suitable employment are directly proportional to the number of positions that will satisfy your job objectives. One person with a degree in information technology might be interested exclusively in working in the information systems division of a major corporation. Another person with the same background is willing to work in the information technology field for a large company, a small company, a high-tech start-up, a government agency, a hospital, or an educational institution. The second person has a better chance than the first of finding a job in a geographic location he or she wants.

Closely tied in with the type of work you are seeking is the type of organization in which you would prefer to work. You are much more likely to be successful in your new job and your career when you find a good **person–organization fit**—the compatibility of the individual and the organization. In other words, what type of organization culture (or atmosphere) would fit you best? Your job satisfaction will be higher, and you are likely to stay longer with an employer, when there is a good person–organization fit. In addition to fitting in well with the organization, it is also important to fit your job, group, and supervisor.[3]

A study with business interns suggested that the importance of a good person–organization fit increases when the job holder does not feel that the job is a strong fit for his or her psychological needs. One of the statements used to measure fit with needs was, "I feel that this internship enables me to do the kind of work I want to do."[4] The implication is that if you find a job where you fit into the organization, it can compensate a little for not having a job that strongly satisfies your needs.

Unless you have had exposure to different types of organizations, you may have only tentative ideas about a good person–organization fit for you. Questioning people who work at different places can provide you with some useful clues. A vital source of input about a prospective employer is present and past employees. Further, plant tours open to the public can provide valuable tips about what it is like to work in a particular firm.

Visits to stores, restaurants, and government agencies will provide informal information about the general nature of working conditions in those places. Using the Internet to find facts about a company has become standard practice. The Internet search includes the firm's Web site as well as news stories about the company. Also, the time spent talking to your prospective supervisor and coworkers is time well spent.

Person–organization fit
the compatibility of the individual and the organization

FINDING JOBS THROUGH NETWORKING AND THE INTERNET

Two cornerstone principles of conducting a job campaign are to use several different methods and keep trying. These two principles should be applied because most approaches to job finding are inefficient yet effective. *Inefficient* refers to the fact that a person might have to make many contacts to find only one job. Yet the system is *effective* because it does lead to a desired outcome—finding a suitable position. Here we look at two of dozens of possible routes for conducting a job search—social networking and the Internet.

Networking (Contacts and Referrals)

The most effective method of finding a job is through personal contacts who might then refer you to a potential employer. **Networking** is the process of establishing a group of contacts who can help you in your career. Networking is particularly helpful because it taps you into the *internal job market*. This market is the large array of jobs that haven't been advertised and are usually filled by word of mouth or through

Networking
the process of establishing a group of contacts who can help you in your career; establishing contacts to find a better position, become a customer, become a valuable supplier, solve difficult problems, or find a mentor; people in a network also offer emotional support

friends and acquaintances of employees. More jobs are found by a referral from a personal contact than through any one more formal sources such as recruitment sites on the Internet or print advertising. A Right Management survey found that 42 percent of job seekers found their job through a networking contact.[5]

The best way to reach the jobs in the internal market is by getting someone to recommend you for one. When looking for a job, it is therefore important to tell every potential contact of your job search. Be able to tell your story briefly, in terms of your experience, strengths, and the type of work you are seeking.[6] The more influential the person, the better. Be specific about the type of job you are seeking. When workers are in short supply, some companies give cash bonuses and prizes to employees for referring job candidates to them. To use networking effectively, it may be necessary to create contacts aside from those you already have. Networking is time-consuming yet is usually well worth the effort.

Potential sources of contacts for your network include the following: friends, family members, faculty and staff, athletic team members, professional associations, and career and job fairs. Attending job fairs also illustrates the point that every feasible method of job finding should be attempted. Recruiters who are looking to fill specific positions might be present at the job fair, along with those recruiters who are looking only to build relationships for the future.

Joining online networking sites, such as LinkedIn.com, Twitter.com, and Friendster.com has become standard practice for conducting a job search. A major purpose of these sites is for members to help each other find jobs. Some sites emphasize professional contacts, whereas others focus on developing friendships. Many employers recruit directly through these sites, such as a company having a Facebook site. The usefulness of online networking increases when you meet face-to-face a few of the most promising contacts. Another benefit of being active with social networking sites is that recruiters often search these sites for possible candidates to fill a position.

An important caution about networking: Too many people are consuming too much of other people's time to help them with their job searches. Keep your request for assistance brief and pointed. Ask to reciprocate in any way you can. For example, you might prepare a chart or conduct research for a manager who gave you a job lead. Bothering influential network members too frequently can lead to your being ignored as a pest or high-maintenance person.

The Internet and Résumé Database Services

Using the Internet, for little or no cost, the job seeker can post a résumé or scroll through hundreds of job opportunities. Web sites such as Career Mosaic and E-Span are résumé database services that give employers access to résumés submitted by job hunters. It is also helpful to look for job Web sites for a specific field, such as information technology, finance, or sales. The employment section of company Web sites can be as effective as general job boards in finding job leads. Another Web approach to finding jobs is to simply insert the position you are seeking, such as "accounts payable specialist," "banquet manager," or "surgical technician" into a search engine. You are likely to find recruiters and employers claiming to have such a position open.[7] Job hunting on the Internet can lead to a false sense of security. Using the Internet, a résumé is cast over a wide net, and hundreds of job postings can be explored. As a consequence, the job seeker may think that he or she can sit back and wait for a job offer to come through e-mail, your niche on a social networking site, or into your Web site. In reality, the Internet is only one source of leads that should be used in conjunction with other job-finding methods. Thousands of other job seekers can access the same job openings, and many of the positions listed have already been filled.

A major challenge of job hunting through the Internet is finding a way to speak to a company representative about your application. Telephoning the human resources department of a large company usually leads to a voice mail system with a lengthy menu and rarely a return call. A plausible approach to making a personal contact is to call the main number of your target company and get connected to the operator. Ask for the department where you hope to work, and you may be able to establish a personal contact—provided that you do not encounter another lengthy menu. Marc Cenderella, the president of Ladders.com, offers this advice: "Hitting 'send' is not the end. You still need to get on the phone, take people to lunch, and work your way to the top of the résumé pile the old-fashioned way.[8]

The T-Form Cover Letter

We all know that a cover letter must accompany a résumé sent online or through the mail. The cover letter helps link the job seeker to the potential employer. A novel format for a cover letter to consider is one that systematically outlines how the applicant's qualifications match up against the job requirements posted in the position announcement. The T-form (or column) approach gives the reader a tabular outline of how the applicant's background fits the position description. The T-form cover letter, presented in Figure 14-1, is also recommended because it has an attention-getting format.[9]

Preparing an Effective Job Résumé

The major purpose of a résumé is to market yourself to a prospective employer. The résumé therefore presents a targeted message that will help you obtain a job interview, not a job. You need a résumé both as an outside candidate and often when seeking a transfer within a large firm. Effective résumés are straightforward, factual presentations of a person's experiences, education, skills, and accomplishments. The word *factual* is important because employers frequently verify facts presented on résumés, and gross inaccuracies lead to immediate rejection of the candidate. A challenge in preparing an effective résumé is to suit many different preferences—e.g., some people spell *résumé* with the acute accents (*résumé* is a French word) and some without. Résumé preparation is a broad topic, yet many of the major points are described in the following list.

   1. Length. Résumé length illustrates how employers hold different opinions about the best résumé format. For people of limited job experience, a one-page

FIGURE 14-1

THE T-FORM COVER LETTER

Dear Sales Manager:

In response to your recent advertisement in the *Atlanta Gazette* and on the Monster.com board for telemarketing sales professionals, please consider the following:

Requirements	My Qualifications
Prior sales experience a must	Two years of full-time and part-time selling, including retail and magazine subscription renewals
Great communicator	Two different managers praised my communication skills; received an A in two communication skills courses
Self-motivated	Work well without supervision; considered to be a self-starter
Reliable	Not one sick day in two years; never late with a class assignment

   Your opportunity excites me, and I would be proud to represent your company. My résumé is enclosed for your consideration.

Sincerely,

résumé is usually sufficient. For candidates with more experience, two pages may suffice. A *curriculum vitae* (CV) is used to provide a more comprehensive work and education history of the sender and can easily run to more than six pages. A CV is used primarily by professors and scientists and would include such detailed information as publications, patents, and committee experience.

2. General construction. Information about résumé construction is readily available. For example, Microsoft Word includes job résumé templates under File/New/Other Documents. You will find there templates for contemporary, elegant, and professional résumés, plus a résumé wizard that helps you construct an individualized résumé. Done properly, a résumé can lead to an interview with a prospective employer. Done poorly, it will block you from further consideration. *Poor* refers to such features as misspellings, misuse of words, disorganization, lack of accurate contact information, too many abbreviations and acronyms, and too much unaccounted for blocks of time. Job candidates who are found to have misrepresented facts (such as pretending to have graduated from a particular school) on a résumé are immediately disqualified. According to the Society for Human Resource Management, approximately 75 percent of employers reject applicants if their résumés contain spelling errors or contain major grammatical errors.[10]

3. Keyword importance. Keywords are an essential part of résumé construction because prospective employers screen for these words both visually and electronically. **Keywords** are terms for skills, certifications, job activities, and other qualifications sought for a particular job.[11] Although keywords vary according to the position in question, here is a sampling: *cost reduction, revenue enhancement, customer delight, enterprise software, Google optimization, business process improvement*, and *diversity skills*.

Keywords
terms for skills, certifications, job activities, and other qualifications sought for a particular job

4. Customization. Your résumé should be customized somewhat to fit the position under consideration, rather than sending a generic version to all prospective employers. The cover letter, as mentioned earlier, makes the major contribution to customization. Customizing your résumé could mean emphasizing your sales accomplishments of any type if you were applying for a sales position or highlighting your community activities when applying for a position as an administrator at a nonprofit organization.

5. Skills and accomplishments. Whichever style of résumé you choose, it should include a section about your job-related skills and accomplishments. A *skill* is an activity, such as preparing a PowerPoint presentation, compiling a research report on consumer preferences, or translating documents from Spanish to English. Most employers hire for skills, so being specific about your skills in a résumé is essential. (Skill description is also quite important during a job interview.) Skills can be based on academic pursuits, paid work, volunteer work, and sometimes sports, such as a team captain mentioning "activity scheduling" as a skill. Remember, though, that a skill is something you can do now and does not refer to a course you once took, unless you have practiced the skill learned in the course.

The skills mentioned on your résumé might be incorporated into the summary section. Jeevan DeVore, vice president of operations for Career-Perfect.com, writes that a résumé should have a brief but compelling summary to catch the potential employer's eye within the first ten seconds. After that, enough depth and detail can be presented to hold the reader's interest.[12]

6. The video résumé. Another challenge when job hunting is whether to send a video résumé. Done professionally, a video résumé can be an asset, but some employers do not want to bother downloading and watching a video. Also, some employers are concerned that a video clearly reveals demographic factors about the candidate, such as sex, race, and approximate age. Rejecting the candidate might therefore lead to charges of discrimination. A sensible approach is to ask whether the employer would like to receive your video résumé in addition to the traditional version. Attaching a copy of the video will often be more welcome than expecting the employer representative to track down your video on the Internet.

7. Additional information about you. To provide prospective employers with information about yourself beyond the résumé, you might provide a link to your personal Web site or page on LinkedIn or similar social networking site. The site becomes a permanent online home for your credentials. In this way, the employer has a choice about obtaining additional information, but you are not forcing the representative to obtain the information to review your credentials.

8. Your online reputation. It is essential to not have embarrassing information about or photographs of you accessible through search engines. Alert prospective employers if someone with the same name as yours has a negative online presence. The problem is that an Internet search has become part of the employer's background investigation. Negative information about oneself on the Web can sometimes be removed by asking or hiring a service for such purposes. Another aspect of your online reputation is that you might need to distance yourself from others who share your name. If you have a LinkedIn profile, insert a clear photo of yourself. When you send you résumé, by either a hard copy or online, provide a link to your profile.[13]

The Successful Job Interview

A successful job campaign results in one or more employment interviews. Screening interviews are often conducted by telephone, particularly for customer service positions requiring telephone skills. An effective way of preparing for a telephone interview is to prepare a thirty-second presentation of yourself including your name, your schooling, job experience, and the type of job you want. Keep working at your presentation until you reduce it to thirty seconds of clear, useful information.

More extensive interviews are usually conducted in person. Being interviewed by one person at a time is still standard practice. Many firms, however, also conduct panel (or group) interviews in which the job candidates speak to several prospective work associates at the same time. Often the group interview is conducted in a casual environment, such as a restaurant or company cafeteria. The candidate may not be aware that meeting with the group is actually an interview and that he or she is being judged. The accompanying Human Relations in Practice illustrates how a candidate might display strength during a panel interview.

Another approach to employment interviewing is the **behavioral interview,** in which a candidate is asked how he or she handled a particular problem in the past. Such an interview is essentially a job sample because the interviewee is asked how a previous problem was dealt with. An example of a behavioral interview questions is as follows: "Tell me how you dealt with an angry customer. What was the problem, and what was the outcome?" Behavioral interviews are used frequently because they seem more related to job behavior than personal characteristics, general interview impressions, or test scores. Of course, this assertion neglects the important fact that a person with strong potential may never have handled the type of job situation presented yet could do so in the future.

> **Behavioral interview**
> a candidate is asked how he or she handled a particular problem in the past

Becoming a skillful interviewee requires practice. You can acquire this practice as you go through the job-finding process. In addition, you can rehearse simulated job interviews with friends and other students. Practice answering the questions posed in Figure 14-2. You might also think of several questions you would not like to be asked and develop answers for them. Think through how you have handled difficult job situations, such as dealing with a tight deadline or resolving conflict with a customer, so you can describe these situations during an interview.

Preparing a video of the practice interviews is especially helpful because it provides feedback on how you presented yourself. In watching the playback, pay particular attention to your spoken and nonverbal communication skills. Then make

FIGURE 14-2

TWELVE QUESTIONS FREQUENTLY ASKED OF JOB CANDIDATES

The following questions are of the same basic type and content encountered in most employment interviews. Practice answering them in front of a friend, camcorder, or mirror.

1. Why did you apply for this job?
2. What are your short-term and long-term goals?
3. What are your strengths? Areas for improvement?
4. Why should we hire you?
5. What do you know about our firm?
6. Describe how well you work under pressure.
7. Here's a sample job problem. How would you handle it?
8. Why did you leave your last job?
9. What negative information about you is likely to show up when we conduct a background check of you?
10. Why would hiring you make us more profitable (or stay within budget)?
11. What are your accomplishments?
12. Give me an example of a time in which you took the initiative on the job.

Note: Questions 6 and 7 are often asked as part of a behavioral interview.

Skill–benefit statements
brief explanations of how an individual's skills can benefit the company

adjustments as needed. Many colleges of business and career schools require students to be videotaped before they go out on job interviews.

A general guide for performing well in the job interview is to present a positive but accurate self-picture. Your chances of performing well in a job increase if you are suited for the job. An effective job-getting tactic is to explain to a prospective employer what you think you can do to help the company. Look for opportunities to make **skill–benefit statements**—brief explanations of how your skills can benefit the company. If you were applying for a billing specialist position in a company that you knew was having trouble billing customers correctly, you might make this skill–benefit statement: "Here is how I would apply my skill and experience in setting up billing systems to help develop a billing system with as few glitches as possible." Or you might state that your previous employer had a billing problem and then explain how you helped solve the problem.

Attempt to be alert to any behavior on your part that could create the difference between a good impression and a poor impression. Showing up late for the interview is an obvious taboo. Arriving at the company office way too early also creates a poor impression. Employees at the hiring company will often feel uncomfortable having a candidate seated in the waiting room for an hour or more. A guideline is to present yourself about ten minutes before the interview, thereby giving the impression of a candidate who is prompt yet respectful of the interviewer's time.[14]

The thank-you note, whether by e-mail or handwritten, should briefly mention your interest in the position and perhaps reinforce an important point, such as your confidence in your ability to make a contribution. If necessary, follow up again, but avoid being perceived as desperate or as a pest by making repeated follow-ups.

JOB HUNTING DURING DIFFICULT ECONOMIC TIMES

Difficult economic times surface about every ten years, so it is likely that during one of these downturns you will be conducting a job search. The most important general principle to keep in mind is to be even more conscientious in following standard job-hunting suggestions when jobs are in short supply. You might have to attempt more approaches to finding a job, and the hunt could take longer. Also, be prepared to tolerate frustration because so many people are competing for the

Human Relations in Practice

Job Candidate Deals Successfully with a Panel Interview

Frederick Shack, executive director of Urban Pathways, a New York nonprofit organization that offers transition housing for the homeless, says, "You're not always going to be on the same page with everyone in the room. But you can disagree without being offensive."

That's what Shack did after he donned a suit for his Urban Pathway interview with its board's seven-person search panel. "You're dressed better than I have ever dressed in my life," complained one member, a retiree attired in jeans and a tattered T shirt. "This is how I dress," Shack replied. Everyone laughed.

Shack politely differed with another panelist's praise of stability at Urban Pathways, where many staffers enjoyed long tenure. "I said, 'Not necessarily. It may be there's a real turnover need for the organization to grow and move forward.'" The board member "reacted well," according to Shack.

He was appointed to the position of executive director in January 2005, has held on to the position, and still wears a suit to work every day.

Source: Joann S. Lublin, "For Job Hunters, the Big Interview Is Getting Bigger," *Wall Street Journal*, June 3, 2008, p. D1.

same jobs. For example, recruiters at career fairs may appear physically and emotionally exhausted. Five more specific guidelines are presented next.

1. **Go where the jobs are.** Even when times are bad, there are still some jobs available. At times a job seeker may have to be willing to relocate to a more prosperous region to find a job. Another approach is to look for industries and sectors that are prospering even when the economy is down. During the recession of 2007–2010, the fields of education, health care, farming, discount stores, and veterinary medicine continued to expand.[15] (And, of course, if you are a paralegal, seek employment at a law firm specializing in bankruptcy.) During the same period many *eco-friendly* jobs, or those related to sustaining the environment, were opening. So the bookkeeper looking for a job might have contacted such enterprises as a hospital, discount chain, veterinary clinic, or company creating alternative energy.

2. **If you have been laid off, get over the emotional hurdle before plunging into the job search.** A reality of conducting a job search during a recession is that the person may have been laid off. Before starting a search for new employment, the person has to overcome the emotional shock of having been laid off—essentially fired. The person should spend about two days ruminating about the problem and describing his or her hurt feelings to friends and family members. The danger of not getting past the emotional shock is that the person will engage in self-pity and bitterness during interviews or contact with network members.[16] People angered about job loss have also been known to write angry blogs that will be perceived negatively by prospective employers and network members who might want to help with the job search.

3. **Minimize defensiveness about having been laid off during a downsizing.** Many job seekers during a business downturn are those who have been laid off because their employer has downsized. Many recruiters and hiring managers recognize

that having been laid off is therefore not necessarily related to poor job performance. Consequently, you can make matter-of-fact statements such as, "I am job hunting because our entire unit was downsized due to a drop in business," or "Our CEO decided to eliminate the marketing department as a survival measure."

4. **Intensify your efforts at meeting people face-to-face.** When fewer jobs are available, personal contact with people who might be able to help you multiplies in value. Perhaps working online can help you arrange a few contacts to meet in person, but spending too much time online can be self-defeating.

5. **Be quite flexible when you do receive an offer.** An unemployed person has very little bargaining power, so do not attempt to negotiate for a higher starting salary or additional benefits when you receive an offer. Instead, perform so well in the new position that higher compensation will be forthcoming.[17]

A final note here about finding a job in good or bad times is to avoid widely practiced tactics that disqualify candidates. Executive coach and corporate trainer Jim Pawiak spoke to a panel of HR specialists and hiring managers on how *not* to get a job. His findings encompass much wisdom:

> Being rude to the receptionist or administrative assistant, "cute" e-mail account names (e.g., babygirl44@, and bookworm@); busy signals (use voice mail rather than an answering machine); taking a call waiting interruption while talking with an employer; smelling like tobacco smoke; wearing perfume or aftershave lotion when interviewing; the dead-fish handshake; not making eye contact; not asking questions; not knowing anything–asking anything about the company; not saying "Thank you" at the end of the interview.[18] [Also, complaints are surfacing of job candidates who receive cell-phone calls and text messages while being interviewed.]

▶ Learning Objective 2 ▶

What Are Some Effective Career Advancement Strategies and Tactics?

As you look to advance your career, it is helpful to divide your approach into developing your personal qualities and developing qualities that focus more on your interaction with the environment.

TAKING CONTROL OF YOURSELF

The unifying theme to the strategies, tactics, and attitudes described in this section is that you must attempt to control your own behavior. You can advance your career by harnessing the forces under your control. Such a perspective is important because individuals have the primary responsibility for managing their own careers. Some companies have career development programs, but the individual is still responsible for achieving his or her goals.

Develop Expertise, Passion, and Pride

A starting point in getting ahead is to develop a useful job skill. This tactic is obvious if you are working as a specialist, such as an insurance underwriter. Being skilled at the task performed by the group is also a requirement for being promoted to a supervisory position. After being promoted to a supervisory position or another managerial job, expertise is still important for further advancement. It helps a manager's reputation to be skilled in such things as developing business strategy, computer applications, preparing a budget, and interviewing job candidates.

The subject of expertise has received considerable attention lately. Two major conclusions of these studies are that expertise takes a long time to develop and that hard work combined with coaching is more important than raw talent in attaining expertise. *Long time* refers to about ten years in a complex endeavor such as research, writing, music, or charismatic leadership.[19] The hard work should focus on overcoming a specific problem, such as not being able to make presentations.

Malcolm Gladwell, an author who has popularized research about human behavior, has developed the 10,000 Hour Rule. It states that the key to success in any field is not talent but to simply practice 10,000 hours, or twenty hours a week for ten years. What Gladwell and several other researchers gloss over is that practice has to be combined with a minimum of natural talent to achieve success.[20] Some people, for example, cannot learn a second language (or how to dunk a basketball) no matter how hard they try. Another exception to the 10,000 Hour Rule is that many people in their late teens and early twenties are world-class experts or performers, especially in the fields of information technology and sports.

Although expertise is highly recommended, the workplace also demands that a person perform a variety of tasks as is required in working on a team. A finance specialist assigned to a product development team would also be expected to know something about marketing, such as how to analyze a marketing survey. A recommended approach is to have depth in your primary field but also have breadth by having several lesser areas of expertise. A widespread example is that no matter what your specialty field, you are also expected to have information technology skills.

Passion goes hand in hand with expertise; it contributes to problem solving and is a major requirement for being an effective leader. It is difficult to sustain expertise if you are not passionate about your specialty field. The phrase "following your passion" often refers to turning a hobby or intense interest into a career, but corporate employees can also be passionate about work. A work-passionate person, for example, would regularly read information about his or her specialty. In support of job passion, career coach and author Cynthia Shapiro advises that "Companies are running scared. They're looking for the kind of passion that creates a competitive edge. Employers rarely get rid of cheerleaders. Even in a drastic layoff, their jobs are safe."[21]

Developing expertise and being passionate about your work leads naturally to being proud of what you produce. People who take pride in their work are likely to achieve higher quality and a good reputation. From the standpoint of management, proud workers are major contributors because their pride motivates them to excel.

Develop a Code of Professional Ethics

Another solid foundation for developing a career is to establish a personal ethical code. An ethical code determines what behavior is right or wrong, good or bad, based on values. The values stem from cultural upbringing, religious teachings, peer influences, and professional or industry standards. A code of professional ethics helps a worker deal with such issues as accepting bribes, backstabbing coworkers, and sexually harassing a work associate.

Perform Well, Including Going beyond Your Job Description

Good job performance is the bedrock of a person's career. In rare instances, a person is promoted on the basis of favoritism alone. In all other situations, an employee must have received a favorable performance evaluation to be promoted. Before an employee is promoted, the prospective new boss asks, "How well did this person perform for you?" To be an outstanding performer, it is also necessary to go outside your job description by occasionally taking on tasks not expected of you. Going beyond your job description is part of being a good organizational citizen. During a prolonged business downturn, workers at all levels are likely to work harder, thereby raising the bar on what constitutes good performance. A paralegal

"Nothing is more important than your reputation. You can't build a reputation on what you say you are going to do—you have to build it on what you do. I learned early on in this business that I was going to live or die by my reputation."

—Jerome Henderson, team leader at HomeBanc Mortgage Corp, Raleigh, North Carolina, and defensive back for nine years in the NFL who performed well by doing the preparation work for three house closings in one day might now get four accomplished.

Performing well on all your assignments is also important because it contributes to the **success syndrome,** a pattern in which the worker performs one assignment well and then has the confidence to take on an even more difficult assignment. Each new assignment contributes to more self-confidence and more success. As you succeed in new and more challenging assignments, your reputation grows within the firm.

Continue to Hone Your Interpersonal Skills

Interpersonal skills, such as those you have been studying in this book, help propel you forward in most careers. To take an extreme example, most people do not think that morticians need good interpersonal skills. But funeral directors insist that an effective mortician must be able to project empathy and compassion without appearing artificial.

Among the many ways in which interpersonal skills help advance your career is to gain you the cooperation of coworkers. A study by Brent A. Scott of Michigan State University and Timothy A. Judge of the University of Florida found that popular workers (those with good interpersonal skills) drew more coworker support regardless of their place on the organization chart.[22] Getting along well with coworkers, in turn, will often facilitate being promoted.

Develop a Proactive Personality

If you are an active agent in taking control of the forces around you, you stand a better chance of capitalizing on opportunities. Also, you will seek out opportunities, such as seeing problems that need fixing. A **proactive personality** is a person relatively unconstrained by forces in the situation and who brings about environmental change. People who are highly proactive identify opportunities and act on them, showing initiative, and keep trying until they bring about meaningful change. Jeffery A. Thompson, a professor of organizational behavior at Brigham Young University, found that one reason proactive personalities perform better is that they develop the social networks they need to help them achieve their goals. For example, the person with a proactive personality would know who to contact for help with a specific business or technical problem.[23]

A health and safety specialist with a proactive personality might identify a health hazard others had missed. She would identify the nature of the problem and urge management for funding to control the problem, making use of her network. Ultimately, her efforts in preventing major health problems would be recognized. Having a proactive personality makes it easier for a person to be a good corporate citizen because such behavior is "built into your DNA."

Managers prefer workers with a proactive personality because these workers become proactive employees, or those who take the initiative to take care of problems. Today's employee is supposed to be enterprising. Instead of relying solely on the manager to figure out what work needs to be accomplished, he or she looks for projects to undertake. The proactive employee, however, may clash with an old-fashioned manager who believes that an employee's job is strictly to follow orders. It may not be easy to develop a proactive personality, but a person can get started by taking more initiative to fix problems and attempt to be more self-starting.

Create Good First Impressions and a Favorable Appearance

Every time you interact with a new person inside or outside your company, you create a first impression. Fair or not, these first impressions have a big impact on your career. If your first impression is favorable, you will often be invited back by an internal or external customer. Your first impression also creates a halo that may influence

Success syndrome
pattern in which the worker performs one assignment well and then has the confidence to take on an even more difficult assignment

Proactive personality
characteristic of a person who is relatively unconstrained by forces in a situation and who brings about environmental change; highly proactive people identify opportunities and act on them, showing initiative, and keep trying until they bring about meaningful change

perceptions about the quality of your work in the future. If your first impression is negative, you will have to work extra hard to be perceived as competent later on.

Looking Successful. Looking successful contributes to a positive first impression. Your clothing, your desk and cubicle or office, and your speech should project the image of a successful, but not necessarily flamboyant, person. Appearing physically fit is also part of the success image. Your standard of dress should be appropriate to your particular career stage and work environment. The best guideline for dressing successfully is to carefully observe the dress code of your firm. Another guideline to consider is to dress for the job you want next, not the job you have now.

An extreme standard is that highly placed business executives often dress as if they were walking advertisements for the beauty and fashion industry. Appropriate dress for an inventory specialist is not the same as that for an outside salesperson dealing with industrial customers. Yet in the past few years, more formal business attire, such as suits for men and women, is making a comeback. Formal business attire is also referred to as *power dressing*, a term from the 1980s that has crept back into use. Some fashion advisors contend that pantyhose are more professional than bare legs for professional women, yet this advice arouses controversy.[24]

Many salespeople and managers today maintain a flexible clothing style by such means as keeping a jacket and extra jewelry in the car or office. When an unanticipated meeting with a customer or some other special occasion arises, a quick modification of clothing style is possible.

Looking successful does not always mean sinking considerable money into clothing and accessories. Many discount stores offer stylish clothing, and physical fitness can be attained without belonging to an athletic club.

Appearing to Be in Control. Projecting a sense of control is another key factor contributing to a positive first impression. Show that you are in control of yourself and the environment and that you can handle job pressures. Avoid letting your body language betray you—fidgeting or rubbing your face sends negative nonverbal messages. Make your gestures project self-assurance and purpose. A verbal method of appearing in control is to make a positive assertion such as, "This is a demanding assignment, and I welcome the challenge."

Tattoos and Body Piercing. Body art in the form of tattoos and piercing often figures into physical appearance. More companies today accept such decorations as a fact of modern culture. Despite this general acceptance of body art, excessive decoration in visible places could be a career deterrent.[25] Many cities and school districts across the United States have forced their employees to cover up their tattoos in order to retain their jobs.[26] (Hidden tattoos are not restricted.)

Document Your Accomplishments and Be Visible

Keeping an accurate record of your job accomplishments can be valuable when you are being considered for promotion, transfer, or assignment to a team or project. Documenting your accomplishments can also be used to verify new learning. In addition, a record of accomplishments is useful when your performance is being evaluated. You can show your manager what you have done for the company lately. Many professional-level workers maintain a portfolio of their accomplishments, such as samples of work accomplished. The portfolio is much like that used by photographers, artists, and models when applying for a job. Here are two examples of documented accomplishments from different types of jobs:

1. A bank teller suggested that at least one person in the bank should be fluent in American Sign Language to facilitate serving deaf customers. After implementing the idea, the bank attracted many more deaf customers.

2. A maintenance supervisor decreased fuel costs in the office by 27 percent in one year by installing ceiling fans.

After documenting your accomplishments, it pays to advertise, therefore being visible to key people. A key part of being visible is to get others to appreciate your good work.[27] Let key people know in a tasteful way of your tangible accomplishments, and focus on how these accomplishments helped the organization. You might request an opportunity to make a presentation to your boss to review the status of one of your successful projects. Or you could use e-mail for the same purpose if it would be presumptuous for you to request a special meeting to discuss your accomplishments.

Keep Growing through Continuous Learning and Self-Development

Many employers expect employees to keep learning, either through company-sponsored programs or on their own. It is particularly important to engage in new learning in areas of interest to the company, such as developing proficiency in a second language if the company has customers and employees in other countries. Continuous learning can take many forms, including formal schooling, attending training programs and seminars, and self-study. To engage in continuous learning, it is essential to remain open to new viewpoints on your established beliefs. A belief (or stereotype) that has been true for a long time may no longer hold true. A person might think, for example, that almost all workers older than sixty are simply putting in time until they reach the traditional retirement age of sixty-five. In reality, many workers plan to continue to work well into their seventies and eighties.

Observe Proper Etiquette

Business etiquette
special code of behavior required in work situations

Proper etiquette is important for career advancement because such behavior is considered part of acting professionally. **Business etiquette** is a special code of behavior required in work situations. Both *etiquette* and *manners* refer to behaving in an acceptable and refined way. In the digital era, etiquette is just as important as ever because of the new challenges that high-tech devices bring. For example, is it good etiquette to read the information on a coworker's computer screen when visiting his or her cubicle? Or should you multitask when on the phone with your boss or coworker? The globalization of business also creates challenges, such as figuring out when visiting another country whether handshakes are acceptable.

Deciphering what constitutes proper etiquette and business manners requires investigation. One approach is to use successful people as models of behavior and sources of information. Another approach is to consult a current book about business etiquette. The basic rules of etiquette are to make the other person feel comfortable in your presence, be considerate, and strive not to embarrass anyone. Also, be cordial to all, remembering that everyone deserves our respect. Specific guidelines for practicing etiquette stem from these basic rules. Figure 14-3 presents examples of good business etiquette and manners.

Develop Your Personal Brand

Personal brand
your distinctive set of strengths, including skills and values

Another important component of career development is to develop your **personal brand,** or your distinctive set of strengths, including skills and values. A personal brand is also referred to as the "brand called you."[28] (Your expertise usually represents your distinctive set of strengths.) Your personal brand makes you unique, thereby distinguishing you from the competition. Although the analogy of each person becoming a recognizable brand name, such as Nike or Tiffany, is far-fetched, the idea of becoming a trusted person of value is sound. Your identity as shown on the Internet, including on social networking sites, is also part of your

FIGURE 14-3 BUSINESS ETIQUETTE AND MANNERS

Following are fifteen specific suggestions about business etiquette and manners that should be considered in the context of a specific job situation. For example, "Make appointments with high-ranking people" is not so relevant in a small, informal company when the company places less emphasis on formality.

1. *Be polite to people in person.* Say "good morning" and "good evening" to work associates at all job levels. Smile frequently. Offer to bring coffee or another beverage for a coworker if you are going outside to get some for yourself. When somebody shakes your hand, stand up instead of remaining in your chair.

2. *Write polite letters and e-mail messages.* An important occasion for practicing good etiquette is the writing of business and personal letters and e-mail messages. Include the person's job title in the inside address and spell the person's name correctly. Use supportive rather than harsh statements. (For example, say "It would be helpful if you could" rather than "You must.") When writing a hard-copy letter, avoid block writing because it is much harsher than indented lines.

3. *Practice good table manners.* Avoid smacking your lips or sucking your fingers. If someone else is paying the bill, do not order the most expensive item on the menu (such as a bottle of Dom Pérignon champagne). Offer to cut bread for the other person, and do not look at the check if the other person is paying. A pet peeve of many people is dining with others who eat with their mouths open.

4. *Names should be remembered.* It is good manners and good etiquette to remember the names of work associates, even if you see them only occasionally. If you forget the name of a person, it is better to admit this rather than guessing and coming up with the wrong name. Just say, "I apologize, but I have forgotten your name. Tell me once more, and I will not forget it again."

5. *Males and females should receive equal treatment.* Amenities extended to females by males in a social setting are minimized in business settings. During a meeting, a male is not expected to hold a chair or a door for a woman, nor does he jump to walk on the outside when the two of them are walking down the street. Many women resent being treated differently from males with respect to minor social customs. In general, common courtesies should be extended by both sexes to one another. A handshake and a smile are a better greeting than a kiss on the cheek of the opposite-sex person. Yet if a client or customer initiates the light kiss, it is acceptable to follow suit.

6. *Shouting is out.* Emotional control is an important way of impressing superiors. Following the same principle, shouting in most work situations is said to detract from your image.

7. *The host or hostess pays the bill.* An area of considerable confusion about etiquette surrounds business lunches and who should pay the check—the man or the woman. The rule of etiquette is that the person who extends the invitation pays the bill.

8. *Introduce the higher-ranking person to the lower-ranking person.* Your boss's name will be mentioned before a coworker's, you introduce the older person to the younger person, and a client is introduced first to coworkers. ("Ms. CEO, I would like you to meet our new custodial assistant.")

9. *Address superiors and visitors in their preferred way.* As the modern business world has become informal, a natural tendency has developed to address people at all levels by their first names. It is safer to first address people by a title and their last names and then wait for them to correct you if they desire. You will probably find that over 90 percent of people want to be addressed by their first name. But important exceptions exist. For example, many Asian executives prefer to be referred to by a title such as Mr., Mrs., Ms., or Dr.

10. *Make appointments with high-ranking people rather than dropping in.* Although the business world has become increasingly informal, it is taboo in most firms for lower-ranking employees to casually drop in to the office of an executive. Use e-mail instead to contact higher-ranking managers directly.

11. *When another person is opening a door to exit a room or building, do not jump in ahead of him or her.* Many people have developed the curious habit of quickly jumping in past another person (moving in the opposite direction) who is exiting. Not only is this practice rude, but it can also lead to an uncomfortable collision.

12. *Minimize annoying, irritating, and interrupting work associates with your cell phone.* It is best to stick with a standard ringtone, rather than a bizarre noise or parts of a song. Do not yell into the phone. In most organizations it is best to put your phone away during a meeting and turn it off, including vibration mode. Check your phone before the meeting. If you are expecting a medical or another emergency call during the meeting, inform others of your problem before the meeting. Minimize receiving or making phone calls and text messages while talking to a work associate.

13. *Follow company etiquette about using laptop computers during a meeting.* Managers at some companies encourage the use of laptop and tablet computers at meetings because participants can readily take notes and access data that contribute to the meeting. Managers at other companies might find the use of laptop computers during meetings to be rude and discourteous behavior. The major reason is that the laptop user often focuses on matters that are not related to the meeting, such as reading e-mail and doing other work.

Continued

FIGURE 14-3 BUSINESS ETIQUETTE AND MANNERS (CONTINUED)

14. *Be sensitive to cross-cultural differences in etiquette.* When dealing with people from different cultures, regularly investigate possible major differences in etiquette, as described in Chapters 7 and 13.

15. *Minimize social kissing in an American workplace, but welcome it in Europe.* Kissing in business is generally regarded as rude except among close acquaintances, yet it is more frequent in Europe. However, European kissing amounts to pecks on both cheeks or the top of the hand, never on the lips.

Caution: Although all the above points could have some bearing on the image you project, violation of any one of them would not necessarily have a negative impact on your career. It is the overall image you project that counts the most. Therefore, the general principle of being considerate of work associates is much more important than any one act of etiquette or manners.

Source: Jim Rucker and Jean Anna Sellers, "Changes in Business Etiquette," *Business Education Forum,* February 1998, p. 45. Compilation from other sources in Andrea Sachs, "Corporate Ps and Qs," *Time,* November 1, 1999, p. 23; Sachs, "Learn How to Behave," *Time,* August 2005, p. A5; Letitia Baldrige, *The Executive Advantage* (Washington, DC: Georgetown Publishing House, 1999); Dean Hachamovitch, "Minding the Meeting, or Your Computer?" *New York Times* (www.nytimes.com), August 26, 2007; Louise Lee, "Cell? Well . . . Use Your Phone for Good, Not Evil," *Business Week Small Biz,* February/March 2009, p. 22.

personal brand. A major value that contributes to your brand is your consistency, because an employer wants employees to consistently deliver results.

Your personal brand will be more effective if it is authentic in the sense of accurately reflecting who you are. You might add a little drama to your strengths, but the strengths should still be true. For example, if Mike regularly volunteers to feed people at a mission for the homeless, he might describe himself as having "enduring humanitarian values." Yet it would be a stretch for him to say he is "committed to ending world hunger." Notice that Mike's personal brand would include a deep concern for human welfare.

You begin developing your personal brand by identifying the qualities or characteristics that distinguish you from coworkers. What have you done recently to make you stand out? What benefits do you offer? Do you deliver high-quality work on time? Are you a creative problem solver? Next, you would make yourself visible so you can cash in your uniqueness (your brand). Almost all the ideas in this chapter will help you develop your personal brand. Three useful questions to ask in formulating your personal brand are as follows:[29]

- What am I passionate about—what do I really love?
- What are my greatest strengths?
- How can I use my strengths to fuel my passion?

Developing a personal brand statement requires considerable work and might require some professional coaching. Here is the personal brand statement Mike developed:

I am a hard-hitting package of strengths who can be a real asset to an employer. Few people combine superb analytical, information technology, and people skills the way I do. The help I give the homeless shows that I really care about the welfare of others. In school, as well as on the job, I have established a record of high performance and dependability.

EXERTING CONTROL OVER THE OUTSIDE WORLD

In this section we emphasize approaches that require you to exert some control over the outside environment. If you do not control it, at least you can try to juggle it to your advantage. For example, the "Find a Mentor" section suggests that you search out a friendly and supportive person in your field who can help you advance in your career.

Develop a Flexible Career Path

Planning your career inevitably involves some form of goal setting. If your goals are laid out systematically to lead to your ultimate career goal, you have established a **career path,** a sequence of positions necessary to achieve a goal. Here we describe two types of career paths. One type emphasizes climbing up the ladder in a traditional organization. The other emphasizes the horizontal movements that better fit the new model of career advancement.

The Traditional Career Path. A traditional career path is based on the assumption that a person will occupy a series of positions, each at a higher level of responsibility than the previous one. A person thus climbs the organizational ladder or hierarchy. If a career path is laid out in one firm, it must be related to the present and future demands of that firm. If you aspire toward a high-level manufacturing position, you would need to know the future of manufacturing in that company. Many U.S. firms, for example, continue to conduct more of their manufacturing in China. If you were really determined, you might study the appropriate language and ready yourself for a global position.

Goals and Values. Before establishing the goals on the career path, it is helpful to clarify your values, as described in Chapter 5. These are probably the same values that enabled you to choose a career in the first place. While sketching out a career path, you should also list your personal goals. They should mesh with your work plans to help avoid major conflicts in your life. Some lifestyles, for example, are incompatible with some career paths. You might find it difficult to develop a stable home life (spouse, children, friends, community activities, garden) if you aspire to holding field positions in international marketing.

Fine-Tune as Necessary. Your career path is a living document and may need to be modified as your circumstances change. Keep in mind changes in your company and industry. If becoming a branch manager is an important step in your career path, check to see if your company or industry still has branch managers. The changing preferences of your family can also influence your career path. A family who wanted to stay put may now be willing to relocate, which could open up new possibilities on your career path.

Contingency ("what if?") plans should also be incorporated into a well-designed career path. For instance, "If I don't become an agency supervisor by age thirty-five, I will seek employment in the private sector." Or "If I am not promoted within two years, I will enroll in a business school program."

Graphing the Career Path. Career paths can be laid out graphically, as shown in Figure 14-4. One benefit of a career path laid out in chart form is that it gives a clear perception of climbing steps toward your target position. As each position is attained, the corresponding step can be shaded in color or crosshatched.

Most goals in a career path include a time element, which is crucial to sound career management. Your long-range goal might be clearly established in your mind (such as owner and operator of a health spa). At the same time you must establish short-range goals (get any kind of job in health spa) and intermediate-range goals (manager of a health spa by age 30). Goals set too far in the future that are not supported with more immediate goals may lose their motivational value. The career path in Figure 14-4 features a steady progression of promotions yet a reasonable number of years in each position. Such planning is realistic because promotions often take a long time to achieve.

The Horizontal Career Path. Many organizations today have no fixed career paths. Instead of plotting a series of moves over a long time period, many individuals

Career path
sequence of positions necessary
to achieve a goal

FIGURE 14-4

A VERTICAL CAREER PATH

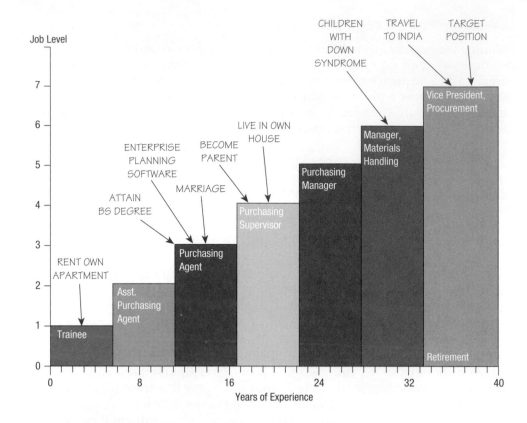

can only make predictions about the type of work they would like to be doing rather than target specific positions. A significant feature of the horizontal career path is that people are more likely to advance by moving sideways than moving up. Or at least people who get ahead will spend a considerable part of their careers working in different positions at or near the same level. In addition, they may occasionally move to a lower-level position to gain valuable experience. With a horizontal career path, the major reward is no longer promotion but the opportunity to gain more experience and increase job skills. Figure 14-5 presents a horizontal career path. A horizontal career path, as well as a traditional (or vertical) career path, does not necessarily mean the person stays with the same firm. Instead, the experiences are accumulated in different firms.

Achieve Broad Experience

Most people who land high-ranking positions usually have broad experience. Therefore, a widely accepted strategy for advancing in responsibility is to strengthen your

FIGURE 14-5

A HORIZONTAL CAREER PATH

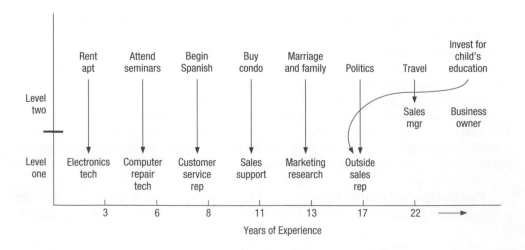

credentials by broadening your experience. Workers who follow the alternative model of career advancement, as illustrated by the horizontal career path, are automatically achieving broad experience. It is best to achieve breadth early in your career because it is easier to transfer when an individual's compensation is not too high. Broadening can come about by performing a variety of jobs or sometimes by performing essentially the same job in different organizations. You can also achieve breadth by working on committees and special assignments.

Breadth can also be attained through self-nomination. Have the courage and assertiveness to ask for a promotion or a transfer. Your manager or team leader may not know that you are actually seeking more responsibility. An effective method of convincing him or her is to volunteer for specific job openings or for challenging assignments. A boss may need convincing because many more people will be seeking advancement than are actually willing to handle more responsibility.

A major benefit of broad experience is that you achieve more career portability, allowing you to move to another employer should the need exist. The employability derives from being a more flexible person with a broader perspective. For example, a person who has worked in both the underwriting (setting rates for risks) and the claims aspects of insurance would be well regarded by insurance companies.

Find a Mentor

The vast majority of successful people have had one or more mentors during their careers. A **mentor** is a more experienced person who guides, teaches, and coaches another individual. In years past, mentors were almost always higher-ranking people. Today mentors can be peers and even lower-ranking individuals. A lower-ranking individual, for example, can educate you on how other parts of the organization work—something you may need to know to advance. Under a **buddy system,** the company assigns a new employee a coworker who looks out for his or her welfare, such as explaining company etiquette.[30] The buddy acts somewhat like a mentor, yet the relationship with the buddy may be for a shorter term.

Many organizations assign a mentor to a company newcomer, yet you might want to supplement company-assigned mentoring with a mentor you find on your own. Sometimes you are able to develop a mentor from the contacts you make on the Internet. After the person becomes your mentor, much of the mentoring can take place through e-mail and messaging. (Busier mentors may prefer e-mail and text messages because they can respond at their leisure.) E-mentoring will sometimes increase the pool of potential mentors and allow relationships to develop without social bias, such as people being suspicious of the nature of a mentoring relationship between a middle-age man and a young woman.[31]

Mentorship is an important development process in many occupations: master–apprentice, physician–intern, teacher–student, and executive–junior executive. An emotional tie exists between the less experienced person (the protégé) and the mentor. The mentor serves as a positive model and a trusted friend. A mentor can also offer candid advice, not otherwise available. Tim Kruse, co-founder of a company that produces voice-recognition software, made this comment about his mentor: "He doesn't just tell me I'm great. I can call my mom if I want that."[32]

A variation of traditional one-on-one mentoring is to establish a group of mentors who might help you with different types of problems. Having multiple mentors is often necessary because an individual mentor may not have all the skills, or time, to provide all the guidance you need. One mentor might be quite good at helping you deal with human relations problems, another with communication technology problems, and another with the financial aspects of your job. Having multiple mentors is asking to have a personal board of directors, or a small group of people who serve as your advisors.[33]

In return, the person being mentored expresses appreciation, gives positive feedback to the mentor, and shares victories. It is also important to offer a concrete service in return for the mentor's advice. Possibilities include offering to collect

Mentor
a more experienced person who guides, teaches, and coaches another individual

Buddy system
the company assigns a new employee a coworker who looks out for his or her welfare, such as explaining company etiquette

information, prepare computer graphics, or run a few errands. Many mentors believe that they have much to learn from their protégés. David C. Pease, an HR executive, wrote that his wife had a stroke while he was a mentor to Linda Woolley, a manager at a homecare facility. Woolley gave him suggestions on being a caregiver because her mother had recently suffered a stroke.[34]

Finding a mentor involves the same process as networking. You might ask people in your network if they could think of a possible mentor for you. With e-mentoring, geographic distance does not create a substantial barrier. With any prospective mentor, it is best to begin gradually by asking for some advice and then see how the relationship develops.

Deal Constructively with Having a Subordinate Older than You or a Younger Boss

In the modern workplace, chronological age does not govern who is likely to be the subordinate or the boss. Two challenges that must be dealt with effectively to help advance one's career are dealing with a subordinate older than you or having a boss younger than you.

Older Subordinate. A tricky workplace issue is developing a constructive relationship with a subordinate considerably older than you. An effective starting point in building the relationship is to show respect for the subordinate's experience and wisdom. Ask for his or her input based on experience, but avoid phrases such as, "As an old-timer, you must know . . ." Listening carefully to the older subordinate will help develop a good working relationship.

If the subordinate brings up the problem of age differences, point out that the company appointed you to the position of administrative boss despite the age difference and that you did not create the situation. Working to create teamwork, as described in Chapter 12, will help break down age barriers because the focus will be on team accomplishment rather than a boss–subordinate rivalry. Include the older subordinate when asking for input about topics often thought to be of more interest to younger workers, such as communication technology.[35]

Younger Boss. Many workers face an ego problem when reporting to a person younger in age, even if the age difference is slight. A starting point in building a constructive relationship is to recognize that having a younger boss is part of the modern world, just like having a doctor or lawyer younger than you. Do not assume that because your boss is younger, he or she is not qualified for the position. Take the initiative to communicate frequently with your boss in a open way that focuses on work issues rather than the age difference. Communicate with your boss as readily as you would with a boss older than you, and you will quickly break down communication barriers.

Look for the learning opportunities that working for a younger boss might bring, such as new ideas based on his or her recent education and fascination with technology. Express your interest in learning new technologies and business processes. Perhaps the younger boss can help you bring other young people into your network, thereby expanding your learning opportunities. Take the opportunity to show that you embrace change, because the negative stereotype about older workers is that they resist change. Unless absolutely necessary, avoid statements such as, "We tried that in the past, and it won't work." Show that you are willing to challenge the status quo by making statements such as, "So far our process has worked, but maybe it can work better if we make some changes."

Express enthusiasm for being part of the team, because the majority of younger bosses believe that teamwork is a major contributor to success. But be willing to express disagreement, but in a diplomatic, collaborative way. A quick way to irritate a younger boss is for you to act in the role of a finger-wagging parent.[36]

Balance Your Life

Balancing your life among the competing demands of work, social life, and personal interests can help you advance your career. Having balance gives you additional energy and vitality that will help you in your career. Having something exciting to look forward to outside of work can sometimes provide a spark that will help you perform well. Also, outside interests, including raising a family, are expensive, giving you another incentive to be an outstanding performer.

Without balance, a career person runs the risk of burnout and feeling that work is not worthwhile. Stephen Covey writes, "Always being the last to leave the office does not make you an indispensable employee. In fact, those who work long hours for extended periods are prone to burnout. The trick is to have your priorities clear, honor your commitments, and keep a balance in life."[37]

Developing Your Networking Skills

◀ Learning Objective 3 ◀

Developing a network of contacts is important for finding a job. As a career advancement tactic, networking serves several purposes. The contacts you establish can help you find a better position, offer you a new position, become a customer, become a valuable supplier, help you solve difficult problems, or find a mentor. People in your network can also offer you emotional support during periods of adversity.

A recommended approach to networking is to keep a list of at least twenty-five people whom you contact at least once a month. The contact can be as extensive as a luncheon meeting or as brief as an e-mail or text message. The starting point in networking is to obtain an ample supply of business cards, and introduce yourself to as many potentially valuable network members as feasible. You then give a card to any person you meet who might be able to help you now or in the future. While first developing your network, be inclusive. Later, as your network develops, you can strive to include a greater number of influential and successful people. People in your network can include relatives, classmates, and people you meet while traveling, vacationing, or attending trade shows.

Community activities and religious organizations can also be a source of contacts. Golf is still considered the number one sport for networking because of the high-level contacts the sport generates. In the words of PFI Tech founder Cesar Sosa, "Golf is primarily a tool to get people in a non-working environment so you can speak a little more freely."[38] The range of potential people in your network is much greater over the Internet than if networking is done locally and in person. Some of the people in these groups can become valuable business contacts, although many relationships with your "friends" or "followers" are weak associations. Online networking includes newsgroups, mailing lists, chat rooms, and e-mail. Figure 14-6 offers some additional networking suggestions, and Exercise 14-1 provides a worksheet for networking.

Networking is obviously beneficial in a field such as direct selling, in which you contact people you know to purchase your goods or services. For example, if you sell products such as financial services, Avon, or Tupperware, you are expected to capitalize on personal contacts. Almost any successful businessperson you meet uses networking, at least to some extent. A study conducted in Germany over a three-year period with over two hundred workers in several fields demonstrates that networking really does enhance career success. Networking was shown to enhance current salary as well as growth of salary over time. Furthermore, workers who engaged in more networking had higher job satisfaction. The researchers concluded that networking has a good return on investment.[39] We caution again to be selective about your networking. Overreliance on networking, such as contacting people who probably have no interest in hearing from you, can be annoying to the recipient.

FIGURE 14-6

NETWORKING SUGGESTIONS

The following networking suggestions are gathered from a number of career counselors and business writers. Select and choose from among the list those ideas that appear to best fit your personality and circumstances.

- *Expand and diversify your network.* Everyone you come in contact with is a potential resource to help you in your career. Even someone whose sole purpose is to cheer you on during downturns can be a valuable ally. Keep filling your network with new contacts, because older contacts may fade away. Retired people who have had successful careers can be a valuable source of contacts, and they typically enjoy assisting people at earlier stages in their careers.
- *Add value as well while asking for assistance.* Consider how you can help the other person, and listen as much as talk.
- *When networking by e-mail, include your telephone number and address.* The other person may want to contact you by means other than an e-mail. Don't give up—e-mail messages may get deleted by accident or disappear because of technical problems.
- *Join groups whose purpose and members fit your field of interest,* such as groups of accountants, health-care professionals, or automobile and truck dealers.
- *When approaching someone to be part of your network, explain how you received his or her name,* or refresh the person's mind as to how you met previously.
- *If you attend a formal networking event (such as a professional meeting), "work the room."* Engage in professional conversations with as many people as feasible.
- *Create good relationships with your peers and fellow students.* Some of them may occupy influential positions in the future.
- *Strive to develop a personal relationship with at least two people at higher levels in your place of work.* Keep these people informed of what you are doing, and ask for their advice.
- *Be memorable for positive reasons.* Making a lasting positive impression is a promising way of keeping a network alive.
- *When you have a change of status, such as accepting a new position, notify network members.* Notify everyone when your contact information changes, and monitor your contacts to keep their information current. Social networking sites are particularly useful for this task.
- *Pursue further possible network members you encounter on social networking Web sites.* Having a "follower" or a "friend" on such a site does not necessarily mean that he or she is a valuable professional contact. Especially with LinkedIn, communicate with people you know. Do not send invitations to people who do not know you. LinkedIn is supposed to be a vehicle for strengthening relationships with people you already know. (Also, LinkedIn members are typically busy professionals.)

Source: Anita Bruzzese, "Restrain Yourself and Think When Networking by E-Mail," Gannett News Service, June 30, 2003; Anne Fisher, "How Do I Network When I Don't Even Know Anyone?" *Fortune,* July 22, 2002, p. 226; Heather Huhman, "Getting the Net Worth out of Your Network," *San Francisco Examiner* (www.examiner. com), December 22, 2008; Julia Angwin, "How to Twitter," *Wall Street Journal,* March 7–9, 2009, p. W3. Niala Boodhoo and Bridget Carey, "LinkedIn CEO Shares Advice on Social Network, Careers," *Miami Herald* (www. miamiherald.com), May 12, 2009.

Concept Review and Reinforcement

Key Terms

Person–organization fit, 405
Networking, 405
Keywords, 408
Behavioral interview, 409

Skill–benefit statements, 410
Success syndrome, 414
Proactive personality, 414
Business etiquette, 416

Personal brand, 416
Career path, 419
Mentor, 421
Buddy system, 421

Summary and Review

The job search begins with a reasonably flexible statement of the type of job you are seeking (your job objective). Knowing what type of organization you would prefer to work for will help focus your job search. Use different methods of job searching and keep trying.

- The most effective method of finding a job is through personal contacts, or networking. Getting someone on the inside to recommend you for a job is the best way to reach the internal job market.
- Job hunting on the Internet can be done through social networking sites, job boards, company Web sites, and direct entry into a search engine of the job you are seeking. Despite using the Internet, it is important to speak to a person to conclude your job search.

A novel format for a cover letter is the T-form approach, which systematically outlines how the applicant's qualifications match up against the job requirements.

The major purpose of a résumé is to market yourself to a prospective employer. Effective résumés are straightforward, factual presentations of a person's experiences, skills, and accomplishments. Avoid making untrue statements on your résumé. There is no one best way to prepare a résumé, but keywords are important, and so is customizing your résumé for a specific position. A résumé should include a section about your job-related skills and accomplishments.

Rehearse being interviewed and then present yourself favorably but accurately in the interview. Behavioral interviews have become important.

- To perform well in an interview, present a positive but accurate self-picture.
- Look for opportunities to make a skill–benefit statement about how your skills can help the company.

Job hunting during difficult economic times includes such considerations as (a) going where the jobs are, (b) getting over the emotional hurdle of having been laid off, (c) minimizing defensiveness about having been laid off, (d) intensifying your efforts at meeting people face-to-face, and (e) being quite flexible when you do receive an offer.

One set of strategies and tactics for getting ahead can be classified as taking control of your own behavior. Included are these approaches:

- Develop expertise, passion, and pride.
- Develop a code of professional ethics.
- Perform well, including going beyond your job description.
- Develop a proactive personality.
- Create good first impressions and a favorable appearance.
- Document your accomplishments.
- Keep growing through continuous learning and self-development.
- Observe proper etiquette.
- Develop your personal brand.

Another set of strategies and tactics for career advancement centers on taking control of your environment, or at least adapting it to your advantage. Included are the following:

- Develop a flexible career path (including the traditional and horizontal types).
- Achieve broad experience.
- Find a mentor (also use the buddy system if offered by the company).
- Deal constructively with having a subordinate older than you or a younger boss.
- Balance your life.

Developing networking skills is a major career advancement tactic that can help you find a new position, become a customer, become a valuable supplier, solve difficult problems, find a mentor, and receive emotional support. Keep a list of at least twenty-five people whom you contact monthly. With mentors, add value while asking for assistance. Social networking sites can be useful in building your network.

Check Your Understanding

1. During times when there is a shortage of skilled workers, why is it still important to study how to conduct a job campaign?
2. During a period in which there is a dire shortage of jobs available, which job-hunting tactics do you think would be the most relevant?
3. What can you do today to help you develop a contact that could someday lead to a job?
4. Make up a behavioral interview question that you might be asked, and develop a good answer.
5. Bill Gates and Steve Jobs dropped out of college, so why does completing your degree enhance your chances for career success?
6. Which expertise would you like to have that would probably take ten years to develop?
7. Identify several jobs for which observing good business etiquette would be particularly important.
8. Identify several tactics you would be willing to use to attract a mentor in a large company.
9. How might a person go about networking for career advancement in an airport or on an airplane?
10. Which criteria are you using, or will you use, to know if your career is successful?

Web Corner

Personal brand building:
www.personalbrandcoaching.com

Career advice, including job search and salaries:
www.vault.com.

Career advancement suggestions from the Wall Street Journal:
www.careerjournal.com.

Find a mentor:
www.advancementoring.com

INTERNET SKILL BUILDER

So many job boards exist on the Internet that conducting a Web-based job search can be baffling. A direct approach is to visit Yahoo! Hot Jobs (on the front page of www.yahoo.com) and enter three specific job titles of interest to you. You will be directed to lots of job opportunities closely matching the job titles you entered. It may be helpful to enter variations of the same job title, such as both "administrative assistant" and "executive assistant." Your assignment is to identify five jobs for which you appear to be qualified. Even if you have no interest in conducting a job search, it is informative to be aware of job opportunities in your field. Seek answers to the following questions:

1. Do I appear to have the qualifications for the type of job I am seeking?
2. Is there a particular geographic area where the job or jobs I want are available?
3. How good are opportunities in my chosen field?

Developing Your Human Relations Skills

Applying Human Relations Exercise 14-1

Building Your Network

Networking can be regarded as the process of building a team that works with you to achieve success. You can start the following exercise now, but it will probably take your entire career to implement it completely. To start networking or make your present networking more systematic, take the following steps:

Step 1: Jot down your top three goals or objectives for the following three months, such as obtaining a new job or promotion, starting a small business, or doing a field research study.

1. _____

_____

2. _____

_____

3. _____

_____

Step 2: List family members, friends, and acquaintances who could assist you in meeting your goals or objectives. Prepare a contact card or database entry for each person on your list, including as many details as you can about the person and the person's family, friends, employers, and contacts. Include in your contacts members of your online network, assuming they are more than people who do not really know you but simply list you as a "friend" or "favorite."

Step 3: Identify what assistance you will request of your contact or contacts. Be realistic in light of your prior investment in the relationship. Remember, you have to be a friend to have a friend.

Step 4: Identify how you will meet your contact or contacts during the next month. Could it be for lunch or at an athletic field, nightclub, sports club, recreational facility on campus, cafeteria, and so forth? Learn more about your contacts during your face-to-face meetings. In some cases you may have to use the telephone or e-mail to substitute for an in-person meeting. Look for ways to mutually benefit from the relationship. At the beginning of each week, verify that you have made a small investment in building these relationships.

Step 5: Ask for the help you need. A network must benefit you. Thank the contact for any help given. Jot down on your planner a reminder to make a follow-up call, letter, or e-mail message to your contacts. In this way, you will have less work to do before you make another request for help.

Step 6: For each person in your network, think of a favor, however small, that you can return to him or her. Without reciprocity, a network fades rapidly.

Source: Adapted and expanded from Cheryl Kitter, "Taking the Work out of Networking," *Success Workshop*, supplement to *The Pryor Report*, March 1998, pp. 1–2.

Applying Human Relations Exercise 14-2

Career Pathing

1. Each class member will develop a tentative career path, perhaps as an outside assignment. About six volunteers will then share their paths with the rest of the class. Feedback of any type will be welcomed. Class members studying the career paths of others should keep in mind such issues as the following:

   a. How logical does it appear?
   b. Is this something the person really wants, or is it simply an exercise in putting down on paper what the ambitious person is supposed to want?
   c. How well do the individual's work plans mesh with personal plans?

2. Each class member will interview an experienced working person outside of class about his or her career path. Most of the people interviewed will have already completed a portion of their path. Therefore, they will have less flexibility (and perhaps less idealism) than people just getting started in their careers. The conclusions reached about these interviews will make a fruitful class discussion. Among the issues raised might be the following:

a. How familiar were these people with the idea of a career path?
b. How willing were they to talk about themselves?

c. Were many actual "paths" discovered, or did a series of jobs simply come about by luck or "fate"?

Human Relations Class Activity

Overcoming Barriers to Career Success

To assist in achieving your career goals, answer the following questions. Keep in mind, however, that you might want to confine your answers to information that you would be willing to share with fellow students:

1. What is the biggest potential barrier to my career success?
2. How do I plan to overcome or deal with this barrier?

Possible answers to these two questions are almost unlimited, yet here is a sample answer: "My biggest barrier to career success is that I want to become a certified financial planner, but I don't have a big enough family or network of friends to develop a client base. My plan is to get started networking now, including becoming much more active in online networking."

Each class member, or a group of volunteers, will address the class one by one with answers to the two questions. Perhaps answers to the questions can be distributed electronically to all class members before the day of presentations. After the presentations, hold a brief class discussion about (a) the barriers most commonly cited and (b) the most likely effectiveness of the plans for overcoming the barriers.

Human Relations Role-Playing Exercise

Cheryl Seeks a Mentor

Marketing assistant Cheryl works for a large pharmaceutical company. She would like to advance her career, perhaps someday becoming a marketing executive. Cheryl has read and heard frequently that one of the best ways to advance one's career in a large company is to find a successful mentor, but the company she works for does not have a formal mentoring program. Cheryl therefore decides to find a mentor on her own. She sends an e-mail to Meg Aspen, the director of marketing for health products (such as vitamins and food supplements), wanting to know if Meg would be interested in becoming her mentor. Already overloaded with work, Aspen responds that she will give Cheryl a fifteen-minute interview next Thursday at 4:45 p.m. to discuss her request.

One student plays the role of eager Cheryl, who wants to make a good connection with Meg immediately. Another student plays the role of Meg Aspen, who is not thrilled about taking on addition responsibility, but she wants to be at least a little helpful. Run the role-play for about eight minutes.

Observers rate the role-players on two dimensions, using a 1 to 5 scale from very poor to very good. One dimension is "effective use of human relations techniques." For Cheryl, focus on how well she projects a genuine interest in learning from a mentor. The second dimension is "acting ability." A few observers might voluntarily provide feedback to the role-players in terms of sharing their ratings and observations. The course instructor might also provide feedback.

Human Relations Case Study 14-1

Stacy Sings the Blues

Stacy, age twenty-seven, was proud to be an architectural technician student. She liked the idea of combining her interest in art with being part of something important. As she reasoned, "I will be helping architects erect skyscrapers, small office buildings, and houses that will last for a century. I will help provide beautiful environments in which fellow human beings will work and live."

To help fund her schooling and pay her living expenses while at career school, Stacy tended bar at the Big Boar Inn, a trendy bar frequented mostly by young people. Stacy had worked on and off as a bartender before attending career school. For several years after high school, she traveled around the world finding work at bars and resorts wherever she could. During her travels, Stacy made notes of the designs of buildings and prepared many sketches of her own ideas about building designs. She knew that she wanted someday to work in the field of architecture.

Several months before graduation, Stacy's father and several friends asked her when she would be starting her job hunt. Stacy explained that she was too busy finishing her studies at school and working at the Big Boar to get seriously involved in a job hunt. "After graduation in May, I'll take a couple of months to unwind and then begin searching for a job. Besides, most architectural firms don't get serious about hiring recent graduates until after Labor Day." Stacy's dad thought she was being a little laid-back in her job-hunting approach but did not think he was in a position to tell her what to do.

After graduation, Stacy continued to work at the Big Boar about twenty-five hours per week. She spent a lot of time at the beach and developed a deep tan. One day she ran into her mentor, Professor Bill Byron, at the supermarket. Byron asked Stacy how her job search was going.

Stacy replied, "I will be getting to working on my résumé soon. With the job market for architectural technicians being soft right now, I didn't see any need to rush. Would it be okay to drop by your office to get some advice on my résumé?"

Stacy met with Mr. Byron a week later. He gave Stacy a few suggestions about résumé construction and also noted that her portfolio of architectural renderings needed more work before she could present the portfolio to prospective employers. Stacy then decided to sharpen her portfolio before beginning her job search.

At the urging of a friend, Stacy began an Internet search for a position as an architectural technician. She focused on openings in Atlanta, Miami, and Washington, DC, because of their warm climates. Stacy spotted a total of three openings for architectural technicians and sent a résumé and cover letter to the addresses indicated in the ads. Stacy also posted her résumé on two general job boards, as well as on Facebook.

Two months passed, and Stacy had not heard back from any of the firms to which she sent letters. Stacy's next approach was to give a copy of her résumé to a friend who sold furniture to an architectural firm in New Jersey. The friend said he would give the résumé to a personal contact he had at the firm.

During a work break at the Big Boar, a server asked Stacy how her job hunt was proceeding. Stacy replied, "Right now, I'm just sitting back and waiting to hear. There's not much else I can do."

Questions

1. What is your evaluation of the effectiveness of Stacy's job campaign?

2. What recommendations can you make to Stacy to help her find a position as an architectural technician?

3. You be the career counselor. Does Stacy really want to leave her job as a bartender at the Big Boar Inn and become an architectural technician?

Human Relations Case Study 14-2

Jim Works the Airports and the Flights

Jim is a co-owner of a firm that supplies tech support to companies that are either not big enough to have their own tech support staff or choose to outsource all or part of such support. As Jim sees it, his number of potential customers is almost unlimited. In addition to being on the outlook for new customers, Jim says, "If the right job offer came along, I might sell my half of the firm to my partner and collect a great salary for the foreseeable future."

Several years ago Jim developed a few contacts during a seven-hour layover at Chicago O'Hare Airport who shortly thereafter became major customers. His early good luck at the airport in developing contacts gave him the idea of visiting airports and taking flights purposely for business development, and perhaps finding the ideal job.

Jim searches a few travel Web sites to find low-price flights to major cities. When he can fly business class at a reasonable price, Jim dresses in his best business attire and carries a luxurious briefcase and a flashy Black-Berry. He also carries dozens of impressive-looking business cards. Jim arrives a few hours before flight time and then clears the security gate. He believes that the best contacts are made in the seating areas near the boarding gates. In Jim's words, "You get the serious types near the gates. Even the restaurants and bars near the gates are a better source of contacts than the areas outside the security area."

When Jim spots a person who looks prosperous seated near the boarding gate, he looks to sit down near the person. If his prospect is on the cell phone or reading a newspaper, Jim waits for a logical pause before making his approach. One of his most effective approaches is to smile and then say, "Hi, I'm Jim Baxter, and my firm does tech support. I sure hope the flight leaves on time." If the stranger shows no interest in starting a conversation, Jim tries another attempt a few minutes later. If still no interest on the stranger's part, Jim gets up from his seat, and says, "Have a nice flight."

During a flight, Jim approaches only a person seated next to him. With a flight of even one hour, Jim has plenty of time to make a soft sales pitch or discuss possible job openings in tech-support management at the prospect's firm.

Jim notes that his approach to developing contacts and new business is much less expensive than advertising in trade magazines or on Web sites. "And besides," he says, "my method is much more personal."

Questions

1. What is your evaluation of the effectiveness of using airports and flights as a method of prospecting for customers and a possible new position?

2. What is your evaluation of the ethics of Jim's approach to developing customers and looking for a new position?

3. How would you react to Jim if he approached you while you were seated next to him in-flight or in the waiting area?

REFERENCES

1. Toddi Gutner, "Finding Anchors in the Storm: Mentors," *Wall Street Journal*, January 27, 2009, p. D4.
2. Quoted in Barbara Kiviat, "#1: Jobs Are the New Assets," *Time*, March 23, 2009, p. 46.
3. Amy L. Kristof-Brown, Ryan D. Zimmerman, and Erin C. Johnson, "Consequences of Individuals' Fit at Work: A Meta-Analysis of Person–Job, Person–Organization, Person–Group, and Person–Supervisor Fit," *Personnel Psychology*, Summer 2005, p. 310.
4. Christain J. Resick, Boris B. Baltes, and Cynthia Walker Schantz, "Person–Organization Fit and Work-Related Attitudes and Decisions: Examining Interactive Effects with Job Fit and Conscientiousness," *Journal of Applied Psychology*, September 2007, pp. 1446–1455.
5. Survey cited in Toddi Gutner, "Dealing with Job Search When You Least Expect It," *Wall Street Journal*, September 16, 2008, p. D6.
6. Alina Tugend, "When Job Hunting, Be Your Own Salesman," *New York Times* (www.nytimes.com), October 11, 2008, p. 2.
7. Sarah E. Needleman, "Recruiters Use Search Engines to Lure Job Hunters," *Wall Street Journal*, March 9, 2009, p. B4.
8. Quoted in Anne Fisher, "How to Run an Online Job Hunt," *Fortune*, June 28, 2004, p. 43.
9. Based on form used by Garrett Associates, Alexandria, Virginia.
10. Survey reported in Tiffany Hau, "Crafting a Résumé That Will Grab Recruiters," *Los Angeles Times* (www.latimes.com), March 29, 2009.
11. Laura Smith Proulx, "Who (or What) Is Really Reading Your Resume—and Why Should You Care?" *San Francisco Examiner* (www.examiner.com), March 17, 2009.
12. Laura Egodigwe, "Extreme Makeover," *Black Enterprise*, September 2004, p. 106.
13. Bridget Carey and Niala Boodhoo, "How to Deal with What Feels like Online Identity Theft," *Miami Herald* (www.miamiherald.com), April 14, 2009.
14. Sara E. Needleman, "The Interview That'll Bag a Job," *Wall Street Journal*, April 14, 2009, p. D4.
15. Victoria Barret et al., "Pockets of Prosperity," *Forbes*, October 27, 2008, pp. 36–42; Teresa Odle, "Eco-Friendly Jobs in High Demand," *CTW Features*, April 22, 2008.
16. Sarah E. Needleman, "Explaining Your Layoff to a Job Recruiter," *Wall Street Journal*, December 9, 2008, p. D4.
17. Martha I. Finney, *Rebound* (Upper Saddle River, NJ: FT Press, 2009).
18. Jim Pawlak, "Interviewing 101: How Not to Get a New Job," *Detroit News*. Retrieved September 30, 2005, from: www.detnews.com.
19. K. Anders Ericsson, Michael J. Prietula, and Edward T. Cokely, "The Making of an Expert," *Harvard Business Review*, July–August 2007, pp. 114–121; Geoff Colvin, *Talent Is Overrated* (New York: Portfolio, 2008).
20. Malcolm Gladwell, *Outliers: The Story of Success* (New York: Little Brown, 2008).
21. Quoted in Anne Fisher, "Disaster-Proofing Your Career," *Fortune*, October 3, 2005, p. 174.
22. Brent A. Scott and Timothy A. Judge, "The Popularity Contest at Work: Who Wins, Why, and What Do They Receive?" *Journal of Applied Psychology*, January 2009, pp. 20–33.
23. Jeffery A. Thompson, "Proactive Personality and Job Performance: A Social Capital Perspective," *Journal of Applied Psychology*, September 2005, pp. 1011–1017.
24. Christina Binkley, "Dress-Code Politics: Who Wears the Pants?" *Wall Street Journal*, June 19, 2008, p. D8.
25. Karen Dybis, "While No Longer Taboo, Body Art Still Can Be a Sticky Issue at Work," *Detroit News*, June 21, 2005. Available at www.detnews.com.
26. Oren Dorell, "Want a Job? Cover Up Those Tattoos," *USA Today*, November 3, 2008.
27. Beth Kowitt, "Tips for Keeping Your Job," *Fortune*, December 8, 2008, p. 14.
28. Tom Peters, "The Brand Called You: You Can't Move up if You Don't Stand Out," *Fast Company*, August–September 1997, pp. 83–94.
29. Judy Martin, "Aligning Your Passion with Your Personal Brand," *San Francisco Examiner* (www.examiner.com), March 7, 2009.
30. Vicki Neal, "What Is the Advantage of a Buddy System?" *HR Magazine*, March 2009, p. 27.
31. Betti A. Hamilton and Terri A. Scandura, "E-Mentoring: Implications for Organizational Learning and Development in a Wired World," *Organizational Dynamics*, 32, no. 4, 2003, p. 388; Donna M. Owens, "Virtual Mentoring," *HR Magazine*, March 2006, pp. 105–107.
32. Quoted in Amy Barrett, "Why You Need a Mentor," *Business Week Small Biz*, February/March 2007, p. 72.
33. Kathy E. Kram and Monica C. Higgins, "A New Approach to Mentoring," *Wall Street Journal*, September 22, 2008, p. R10.
34. David C. Pease, "Making Mentoring Memorable," *HR Magazine*, May 2009, p. 65.
35. A few of the ideas are based on "Managing a Staff of Older Employees," *All Business*. Retrieved April 5, 2009, from: www.allbusiness.com. © 1999–2009.
36. "Is Your Boss Younger than You? Tricks to Make It Work," www.preretirementlife.com, January 7, 2008; "Dealing with a Younger Boss," www.abclocal.go.com, January 8, 2009.
37. Stephen Covey, "How to Succeed in Today's Workplace," *USA Weekend*, August 29–31, 1997, pp. 4–5.
38. Quoted in Mark Henricks, "The Business of Golf," *Entrepreneur*, December 2007, pp. 43–44.
39. Hans-Georg Wolff and Klaus Moser, "Effects of Networking on Career Success: A Longitudinal Study," *Journal of Applied Psychology*, January 2009, pp. 196–206.

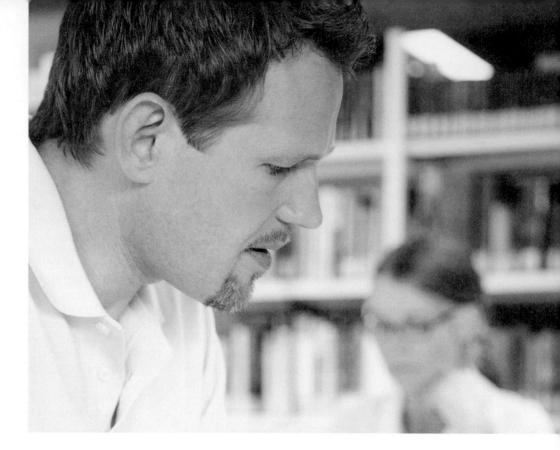

15

Learning Strategies, Perception, and Life Span Changes

Outline

1 What Are the Major Learning Strategies and Processes?
Classical Conditioning: Learning Simple Habits and Reflexes
Operant Conditioning: Learning through the Consequences of Our Behavior
Modeling and Informal Learning: Learning Complicated Skills
E-Learning
Group Learning

2 What Are Several Different Learning Styles?
Visual, Auditory, and Kinesthetic Learning Styles
Learning Styles Associated with Personality as Measured by the Golden
Personality Type Profiler
Improving Learning and Brain Functioning through Rest
Continuous Learning during Your Career

3 How Does Perception Influence How People Interpret the World?
Why Perceptual Problems Exist
Perceptual Congruence
Attribution Theory: How We Perceive the Causes of Behavior

4 How Do We Respond to Life Span Changes and Challenges?
Stages of the Lifecycle
Responding to Challenges in Adolescence
Responding to Adult Life Challenges
Responding to Late Life Challenges
Life and Job Satisfaction throughout the Life Span

5 What Are Some Basic Concepts about Changing Careers?
Factors Influencing a Career Change
Changing Careers without Changing Employers
Self-Employment as a Career Change

6 What Are Some Tactics for Coping with Change?

Learning Objectives ▶

After studying the information and doing the exercises in this chapter, you should be able to:

1 Understand the basic learning processes, three advanced learning processes, and e-learning.

2 Explain the meaning of learning styles, and develop insight into your own style.

3 Explain the importance of continuous learning.

4 Explain how perception influences behavior.

5 Identify the stages of the lifecycle.

6 Understand the challenges of responding to changes in adolescence, adulthood, and late adulthood.

7 Describe the impact of the life span on life and job satisfaction.

8 Recognize the realities of dealing with a career change.

9 Be better prepared to cope with change.

One year Christopher Pearsall earned $170,000, a sizeable sum for a blue-collar millwright at a Ford Motor truck plant in Norfolk, Va. But he toiled 12-hour days, seven days a week most of the year in the noisy and dirty factory. He sometimes dreaded going to work.

Four years later, the 34-year-old Pearsall was a $60,000-a-year product manager for Concursive, a business-software developer, also in Norfolk. He wears slacks and polo shirts on the job rather than coveralls. Despite the lower pay, he says he is much happier at the desk job in a small firm. "He has effectively done a career do over," observes Michael Harvey, the Concursive executive who hired him soon after his December 2006 layoff.

During his decade at Ford, Pearsall often lacked sleep but not ambition. He completed his millwright apprenticeship in just over half the usual four years and also got a community college degree. The finance and economics major was attending Old Dominion University part-time when he lost his job just before the plant closed. Pearsall became a full-time student, assisted by a severance package and $30,000 partial salary for up to four years.

Pearsall sought a summer internship at Concursive after his Internet research suggested that product managers often advance to senior management. A résumé sprinkled with misspelled words, however, nearly killed his candidacy. After receiving a stern letter about his résumé, Pearsall sent a revised résumé, letters of references, and an apologetic note. During the interview, Pearsall pledged to work twice as hard as someone from a white-collar background. On the job he arrived early and stayed late.

Pearsall eventually proved to be a "really good utility player" who adapted well to a completely different environment, says Harvey. Concursive made Pearsall a product manager two years after he was hired and pays his tuition until Pearsall graduates.[1]

Perhaps no reader of this book is in the same boat as Christopher Pearsall, but his story illustrates an important point about the world of work. It is possible that at any stage of our life cycle that we may be required to make major adaptations and changes. In this chapter we deal with a series of issues and topics that enable a person to develop career thrust and stay on track: how people learn, how perception influences their behavior, and the major challenges people face at different stages of their life, including a career change.

▶ Learning Objective 1 ▶

What Are the Major Learning Strategies and Processes?

Learning
generally considered a lasting change in behavior based on practice and experience

Much learning takes place on the job simply because people spend such a large proportion of their lives at work. Furthermore, workers at all levels are expected to learn new job skills and technology continuously. **Learning** is generally considered to be a lasting change in behavior based on practice and experience. Yet it is possible to learn something and store it in your mind without changing your behavior.[2] For example, you read that if you press "F12" in Windows XP you open the "Save As" function. You keep it in your mind but do not use the command yet. The new knowledge is stored in your upper brain but is not yet put into action.

Here we describe several different methods of learning, beginning with classical conditioning, the simplest type. Then we describe learning of intermediate complexity, operant conditioning, followed by two ways in which more complicated skills are learned: modeling and informal learning. We conclude with e-learning because of its widespread use in delivering content for learning. Although we describe different methods of learning, most learning depends on several methods. For example, in learning to operate a new vehicle you might need to develop simple reflexes to adjust to getting into the car. You would also use higher-level learning to understand how to use the computerized map.

CLASSICAL CONDITIONING: LEARNING SIMPLE HABITS AND REFLEXES

Classical conditioning
principles stemming from Ivan Pavlov's digestion experiments that help people understand the most elementary type of learning—how people acquire uncomplicated habits and reflexes

In the late 1890s, Russian physiologist Ivan Pavlov conducted a long series of experiments about digestion. While studying a dog, he noticed that the dog salivated not only with the presence of food in the mouth but also at the sight of the food, the sound of the food trays, and even the footsteps of the experimenter. The principles of **classical conditioning** stemming from his experiments help us to understand the most elementary type of learning—how people acquire uncomplicated habits and reflexes. The basic principles and concepts are included in more complicated forms of learning.

How Classical Conditioning Takes Place

Classical conditioning works in this manner. Kurt takes an entry-level, unskilled job in a factory. His first day on the job a bell rings in his department at 11:34 a.m. Suddenly, every other worker stops working and opens a lunchbox or heads out to the company cafeteria. Kurt says to himself, "The bell must mean it's time for lunch." By the third day on the job, Kurt develops stomach pangs and begins to salivate as soon as the bell rings. Prior to this job, Kurt was in the habit of eating lunch at 1 p.m. and did not begin to have stomach pangs until that time.

Classical conditioning helps explain such elementary job behavior as how people learn to avoid being conked on the head by cranes and low-hanging pipes. With classical conditioning, people also learn to avoid being burned twice by a hot pipe or not turning off a computer before saving a file.

Habits in Everyday Life

Although habits may appear to be simple mechanisms, they are a major part of everyday life on and off the job. According to several studies, as much as 45 percent of what we do everyday is habitual. In this sense, *habitual* refers to performing the same act almost without thinking in the same location or at the same time each day, based on subtle cues.[3] Among these many habits might be locking your car doors as you exit the car, putting one hand on your head each time you are asked a question, and going for a beverage when the clock indicates 10 a.m. Another habit, the e-mail urge, often occurs after a person has finished reading a document, completed a certain type of task, or returned to his or her cubicle after some other activity.

OPERANT CONDITIONING: LEARNING THROUGH THE CONSEQUENCES OF OUR BEHAVIOR

Operant conditioning is learning that takes place as a consequence of behavior. In other words, a person's actions are instrumental in determining whether learning takes place. Operant conditioning is the cornerstone of behaviorism, as reflected first in the work of John B. Watson and then later by B. F. Skinner. The process by which a person learns the correct way to make an overseas phone call illustrates operant conditioning. At first the instructions may seem confusing, such as whether to first enter 1 or 9 before entering the other numbers. After a few tries, the person chooses the proper sequence of numbers and then has learned how to enter an overseas number.

> **Operant conditioning**
> learning that takes place as a consequence of behavior; a person's actions are instrumental in determining whether learning takes place

Reinforcement Strategies

The term *reinforcement* in general refers to the means by which behaviors are selected and retained. It gets at the idea that a response, such as shifting your weight on a snowboard to make a turn, is strengthened. The four reinforcement strategies are positive reinforcement, negative reinforcement (avoidance learning or motivation), punishment, and extinction.

Positive Reinforcement and Negative Reinforcement. The distinction between positive and negative reinforcement is very important. Positive reinforcement adds something rewarding to a situation, such as praise or a gift certificate. Positive reinforcement is thus receiving a reward for making a desired response. **Negative reinforcement** is effective because it takes away something unpleasant from a situation. It is a form of avoidance learning or motivation. Negative reinforcement is thus being rewarded by being relieved of discomfort. The international telephone call described above included negative reinforcement. Getting the sequence of numbers correct avoided the unpleasant situation of hearing a voice say "The number that you entered is incorrect or is no longer in service."

> **Negative reinforcement**
> taking away something unpleasant from a situation; being rewarded by being relieved of discomfort; form of avoidance learning or motivation

Negative reinforcement is not the same thing as punishment. Negative reinforcement is pleasant and, therefore, a reward. Punishment, by definition, is something unpleasant, unless the person involved likes to be punished. With masochists, the reward is to be punished!

Punishment. Being punished for your mistakes can be an important part of learning. **Punishment** is the introduction of an unpleasant stimulus as a consequence of the learner having done something wrong (in the eyes of the person in control of the situation). Or the threat of punishment can be used instead of actually punishing people for the wrong response in a learning or motivational situation. Punishment assists the operant conditioning process because it weakens the particular response. You tend not to repeat a response because of its negative consequences.

> **Punishment**
> the introduction of an unpleasant stimulus as a consequence of the learner having done something wrong

Extinction

the weakening or decreasing of the frequency of undesirable behavior by removing the reward for such behavior

Extinction. The purpose of punishment is to eliminate a response. The same result can often be achieved through the reinforcement strategy of **extinction.** It refers to the weakening or decreasing of the frequency of undesirable behavior by removing the reward for such behavior. It is the absence of reinforcement. One way to stop the office clown from acting up is for coworkers to ignore that person's antics. The clown's behavior is said to be *extinguished.*

Schedules of Reinforcement

An important issue in operant conditioning (and in motivation) is how frequently to reward people when they make the correct response. Two broad types of schedules of reinforcement are in use—continuous and intermittent.

Under a *continuous schedule*, behavior is reinforced each time it occurs, such as saying "good job" every time a bank teller has exactly the right amount of money in terms of withdrawals and deposits at the end of the day. Continuous schedules usually result in the fastest learning, but the desired behavior quickly diminishes when the reinforcement stops. Under an *intermittent schedule* the learner receives a reward after some instances of engaging in the desired behavior but not after each instance. Intermittent reinforcement is particularly effective in sustaining behavior because the learner stays mentally alert and interested. At any point, the behavior might lead to the desired reward. Lottery tickets that occasionally pay small rewards, such as seven dollars, operate on this principle.

MODELING AND INFORMAL LEARNING: LEARNING COMPLICATED SKILLS

Classical and operant conditioning provide only a partial explanation of how people learn on the job. When you acquire a complicated skill, such as speaking in front of a group, preparing a budget, or designing a store display, you learn much more than simply a single stimulus–response relationship. You learn a large number of these relationships, and you also learn how to put them together in a cohesive, smooth-flowing pattern. Two important processes that help in learning complicated skills are modeling and informal learning. Both are based on processes that are inferred to take place in the brain.

Modeling

learning a skill by observing another person perform the skill; considered a form of social learning because it is learned in the presence of others

Modeling occurs when you learn a skill by observing another person perform the skill. Modeling is considered a form of social learning because it is learned in the presence of others. Many apprentices learn part of their trade by modeling an experienced craftsperson who practices the trade. Modeling is widely used in teaching sports through videotapes that give the viewer an opportunity to observe the skill being performed correctly. Although modeling is an effective way of learning, the learner must also have the proper capabilities and motivation.

Informal learning

planned or unplanned learning that occurs without a formal classroom, lesson plan, instructor, or examination; a way of learning complex skills in the workplace

Informal learning is another way of learning complex skills in the workplace. It is planned or unplanned learning that occurs without a formal classroom, lesson plan, instructor, or examination.[4] The central premise of such learning is that employees acquire important information outside of a formal learning situation. The learning can be spontaneous, such as getting a tip on retrieving information from the intranet while waiting in line at the cafeteria. Or the company might organize the work area to encourage such informal learning. The employees capitalize on a learning situation in an unstructured situation where the rewards stemming from the learning are not explicit.

Implicit learning

learning that takes place unconsciously and without an intention to learn

Informal learning can be regarded as a variation of **implicit learning,** or learning that takes place unconsciously and without an intention to learn.[5] Perhaps you have not been attempting to learn the Spanish word for *danger,* but after seeing the word *peligro* adjacent to the English word *danger* many times (such as near electric wires), you learn the Spanish word.

E-LEARNING

Important innovations in learning have taken place in both schools and industry through the use of e-learning or distance learning. Here, the learner studies independently outside of a classroom setting and interacts with a computer in addition to studying course material. **E-learning** is a Web-based form of computer-based training. Some learning programs are computer based without being delivered over the Internet. For example, the tutorials included in some software packages are a form of computer-based training. An e-learning course usually is carefully structured, with specific lesson plans for the student. E-learning is more of a method of delivering content than a method of learning, yet the process helps us understand more about learning.

A major impetus behind e-learning is that so many employees are geographically dispersed, making it difficult to gather them in one place for learning. Although e-learning is technologically different from more traditional forms of learning, it still is based on basic methods of learning. For example, the learner will often need reinforcement to keep going. Trainers at GE Capital found that when managers gave reinforcement to employees on attendance, made them feel important, and tracked their progress, they were more likely to complete the course.[6]

E-learning
studying independently outside of a classroom setting and interacting with a computer in addition to studying course material; Web-based form of computer-based training

Traits and Attitudes of the Learner

Another relevant aspect of e-learning here is that its success depends on self-motivation and self-discipline. Self-motivation is important because an assignment to take an e-learning course by the company often is not motivation enough to work independently. Self-discipline is necessary to create a regular time for performing class work, and it prevents distractions by work or home activities. In educational settings, successful distance learning also requires high motivation. Some students may not take e-learning seriously. Corporate e-learning programs have a high dropout rate; most students need the structure of a face-to-face instructor, a classroom, and other students to keep them focused on the course.[7] Other data suggest that workers are more likely to apply information acquired in an instructor-led program. One explanation offered is that a commitment will more probably develop between the instructor and the learner than between a computer and a learner.[8]

Strengths and Limitations of E-Learning

E-learning has gained momentum, yet most companies prefer to use blended learning (Web and classroom) because it combines the personal nature of classroom training with the cost efficiencies of learning via the Internet. The cost efficiencies include decreases in travel and lodging costs and payments to classroom instructors. But classroom training provides the difficult-to-measure benefit of employees spontaneously exchanging ideas that could lead to a creativity breakthrough. A survey of nearly one thousand British managers found that resistance to e-learning was caused by the loss of human touch. Approximately 75 percent preferred face-to-face conversations for learning, and over 33 percent suggested that tutor-led learning and development was more effective than e-learning.[9]

In general e-learning is most effective in delivering conceptual subject matter, such as product information, whereas classroom training is more effective for learning interpersonal skills.[10] The human touch is important for learning human relations! E-learning does provide some guidance, but an instructor adds an extra touch, such as answering questions and clarifying concepts.

GROUP LEARNING

Although true learning requires a brain, groups can learn in the sense that members come to adapt their behavior collectively in response to experience. How

Group learning
A change in the group's repertoire of potential behavior

groups learn has been studied by three professors of organizational behavior: Jeanne M. Wilson of the College of William & Mary, Paul S. Goodman of Carnegie Mellon University, and Matthew A. Cronin of George Mason University. According to their definition, **group learning** is a change in the group's repertoire of potential behavior. For example, a group of hospital workers might rehearse how to deal with a major health attack such as poisoning of the water supply and then implement the learning should the attack occur. According to the same researchers, group learning has three basic features: sharing, storage, and retrieval.[11]

1. *Sharing* is the process by which new knowledge, routines, or behaviors becomes distributed among group members. At the same time, group members must understand that others in the group possess that learning. With our emergency response workers in the hospital, each person shares new insights with the others, such as where to house all the people that might need treatment.

2. *Storage* is the process of storing in memory what has been learned. Similar to learning at the individual level, the change in behavior must be recorded for it to be most useful. If you get stung by a hive of bees once when painting a house because you poked a beehive, you must remember not to make the same mistake again. The hospital emergency response team should remember what worked and what didn't work in handling one crisis so they can better deal with the next crisis. In addition to memory, a group could store knowledge in a database.

3. *Retrieval* is the ability of group members to find and access the knowledge for subsequent inspection and use. As with individual learning, the group has to be able to access the information when needed. An individual within the group might help the group retrieve the information by stating, "Here's how we dealt with hysterical people during the last emergency."

▶ Learning Objective 2 ▶

What Are Several Different Learning Styles?

Learning style
the idea that different people learn best in different ways

Another important concept in understanding learning is **learning style,** the idea that people learn best in different ways. For example, some people acquire new material best through passive learning. Such people quickly acquire information through studying texts, manuals, magazine articles, and Web sites. They can juggle images in their mind as they read about abstract concepts such as supply and demand, cultural diversity, or customer service. Others learn best by doing rather than by studying—for example, learning hands-on about customer service by dealing with customers in many situations.

Another key dimension of learning styles is whether a person learns best by working alone or cooperatively, such as in a study group. Learning by oneself allows for more intense concentration, and one can proceed at one's own pace. Learning in groups and through classroom discussion allows people to exchange viewpoints and perspectives. Considerable evidence has been accumulated that peer tutoring and cooperative learning are effective for acquiring knowledge.[12] Another advantage of cooperative learning is that it is more likely to lead to changes in behavior. Assume that a manager holds group discussions about the importance of achieving high customer satisfaction. Employees participating in these group discussions are more likely to assertively pursue high customer satisfaction on the job than those who only read about the topic. Learning styles have also been studied more scientifically, and one such approach is described next.

VISUAL, AUDITORY, AND KINESTHETIC LEARNING STYLES

According to the visual, auditory, and kinesthetic (VAK) learning style categorization, people learn best using one of three main sensory receivers.[13] *Visual learners* learn best by seeing, and they have two subchannels—linguistic and spatial. Learners who are *visual linguistic* prefer to learn through written language, such as reading and writing assignments. This type of learner would carefully pore over an instruction manual before using a new electronic device. Learners who are *visual spatial* prefer graphics, demonstrations, and videos over written information.

Auditory learners prefer to learn by hearing, and they tend to move their lips and read out loud. An auditory learner would much prefer a spoken explanation of how to do something, such as using a new electronic device, than reading a manual. The same learners would prefer the interaction of a classroom over e-learning. *Kinesthetic learners* learn best while touching and moving and rely on two subchannels: kinesthetic (movement) and tactile (touch). These learners like to take notes while listening to lectures, tend to use highlighters, and frequently doodle while listening. When reading, the kinesthetic learner prefers to overview the material first to obtain the big picture and focus on details later.

Most learners combine all three styles to some degree while being dominant in one. For example, the visual learner might want to read the manual first to learn how to use a new electronic device. Yet the same learner might welcome a discussion about using the device and would also like to handle the device while reading the manual. Human Relations Self-Assessment Quiz 15-1 gives you an opportunity to measure your standing on the VAK dimensions.

LEARNING STYLES ASSOCIATED WITH PERSONALITY AS MEASURED BY THE GOLDEN PERSONALITY TYPE PROFILER

Another way of understanding learning styles is to recognize that your personality can influence your learning style. You may have observed, for example, that when an impulsive person needs to learn how to use an electronic device, that person will often grab the device and start hitting the various buttons. A more reflective person will often first read the manual or look over the device carefully before attempting to get it to function.

One of the best-known methods of measuring personality types is the MBTI, is a self-report questionnaire designed to make the theory of psychological types developed by psychoanalyst Carl Jung applicable to everyday life.[14] Another leading method of measuring types is the Golden Personality Type Profiler.[15] Jung developed the theory of psychological types, but he did not develop the two measuring instruments just mentioned. As measured by the Golden instrument, four separate dichotomies direct the typical use of perception and judgment by an individual.

1. **Energy flow: Extraversion versus introversion.** Extraverts direct their energy primarily toward the outer world of people and objects. In contrast, introverts direct their energy primarily toward the inner world of experiences and ideas.

2. **Information gathering: Sensation versus intuition.** People who rely on sensing focus primarily on what can be perceived by the five primary senses of vision, touch, sight, sound, and smell. People who rely on intuition focus primarily on perceiving patterns and interrelationships.

3. **Decision making: Thinking versus feeling.** People who rely primarily on thinking base conclusions on logical analysis and emphasize objectivity and detachment. People who rely on feelings base conclusions on personal or social values and focus on understanding and harmony.

Human Relations Self-Assessment Quiz 15-1

Visual, Auditory, and Kinesthetic Survey

Read each statement carefully. To the left of each statement, write the number that best describes how each statement applies to you by using the following guide:

1	2	3	4	5
Almost never applies	Applies once in a while	Sometimes applies	Often applies	Almost always applies

Answer honestly, as there are no correct or incorrect answers. It is best if you do not think about each question too long, as this could lead you to the wrong conclusion. Once you have completed all thirty-six statements (twelve statements in three sections), total your score in the spaces provided.

Section 1: Visual

____ **1.** I take a lot of notes and I like to doodle.

____ **2.** When talking to someone else I have the hardest time handling those who do not maintain good eye contact with me.

____ **3.** I make lists and notes because I remember things better if I write them down.

____ **4.** When reading a novel I pay a lot of attention to passages picturing the clothing, description, scenery, setting, etc.

____ **5.** I need to write down directions so I remember them.

____ **6.** I need to see the person I am talking to in order to keep my attention focused on the subject.

____ **7.** When meeting a person for the first time I notice the style of dress, visual characteristics, and neatness first.

____ **8.** When I am at a party, one of the things I love to do is stand back and "people-watch."

____ **9.** When recalling information I can see it in my mind and remember what I saw.

____ **10.** If I had to explain a new procedure or technique, I would prefer to write it out.

____ **11.** During my free time I am most likely to watch television or read.

____ **12.** If my boss has a message for me, I am most comfortable when he or she sends an e-mail or hard copy memo.

Total for Visual _____ (The minimum score is 12 and the maximum score is 60.)

Section 2: Auditory

____ **1.** When I read, I read out loud or move my lips to hear the words in my head.

____ **2.** When talking to someone else I have the hardest time handling those who do not talk back with me.

____ **3.** I do not take a lot of notes, but I still remember what was said. Taking notes distracts me from the speaker.

____ **4.** When reading a novel I pay a lot of attention to passages involving conversations, talking, speaking, dialogues, etc.

____ **5.** I like to talk to myself when solving a problem or writing.

____ **6.** I can understand what a speaker says, even when I am not focused on the speaker.

____ **7.** I remember things easier by repeating them again and again.

____ **8.** When I am at a party, one of the things I love to do is talk in-depth about a subject that is important to me with a good conversationalist.

____ **9.** I would rather receive information from the radio, rather than from a newspaper (or online newspaper).

____ **10.** If I had to explain a new procedure or technique, I would prefer telling about it.

____ **11.** During my free time I am most likely to listen to music.

____ **12.** If my boss has a message for me, I am most comfortable when he or she calls on the phone.

Total for Auditory _____ (The minimum score is 12 and the maximum score is 60.)

Continued

Section 3: Kinesthetic

____ **1.** I am not good at reading or listening to directions. I would rather just start working on the task or project at hand.

____ **2.** When talking to someone else I have the hardest time handling those who do not show any kind of emotional support.

____ **3.** I take notes and doodle, but I rarely go back and look at them.

____ **4.** When reading a novel I pay a lot of attention to passages revealing feelings, moods, action, drama, etc.

____ **5.** When I am reading, I move my lips.

____ **6.** I will use my hands a lot when I can't remember the right things to say.

____ **7.** My desk appears disorganized.

____ **8.** When I am at a party, one of the things I love to do is enjoy the activities such as dancing, games, and totally losing myself in the action.

____ **9.** I like to move around. I feel trapped when seated at a meeting or a desk.

____ **10.** If I had to explain a new procedure or technique, I would prefer actually demonstrating it.

____ **11.** During my free time I am most likely to exercise.

____ **12.** If my boss has a message for me, I am most comfortable when he or she talks to me in person.

Total for Kinesthetic _____ (The minimum score is 12 and the maximum score is 60.)

Total each section: Visual _____ Auditory _____ Kinesthetic _____

The area in which you have the highest score represents your best learning style. Note that you learn in *all* three styles, but you typically learn best using one of the three styles.

Source: "Learning Styles" (donclark@nwlink.com), formerly available at http:www.nwlink.com/~donclark/hrd/vak.html. Updated October 24, 2000; retrieved March 20, 2005.

4. Lifestyle orientation: Judging versus perceiving. Individuals high on Judging tend to orient their lives in a deliberate and planned manner. Individuals high on Perceiving tend to orient their lives in a spontaneous and open-ended manner.[16]

Combining the four types with each other results in sixteen personality types, such as the ESFP, or "The Entertainer." ESFP refers to extraverted/sensing/feeling/perceiving. It is believed that approximately 13 percent of the population can be classified as the ESFP type. People of this type are optimistic and are skilled at living joyfully and entertaining others. ESFPs are effective at communicating their good-natured realism to others.

You might want to take the Golden Personality Type Profiler (see the Appendix to this book). Here our concern is with how your personality influences your learning style. Figure 15-1 presents four of the sixteen personality types along with the implications for each one with respect to learning style. You will observe that the learning styles are complex rather than focusing on specific factors, such as preferring observing over reading.

Far too many people overinterpret personality types as being definitive indicators of an individual's personality and therefore pigeonhole that person. The developers of the Golden instrument point out that it is an accurate and dependable measure of the aspects of personality measured, but it is up to the person taking the Golden profiler to determine if the report's description of him or her is accurate.[17] If the results are completely out of line with what you believe to be true about yourself, or what others have told you about your personality type, the results of the Golden indicator (other type indicator) should not be a cause for concern.

FIGURE 15-1 THE LEARNING STYLES ASSOCIATED WITH FOUR DIFFERENT GOLDEN PERSONALITY TYPES

Personality Type	Highlights of Type	Learning Style Features, Including Preference for Type of Instructor
ENFP (The Proponent) Extraverted/iNtuitive/Feeling/Perceiving	Lives continually in the realm of the possible. When absorbed in their latest project, they think of little else. Filled with energy, they are tireless in their pursuit of goals. Have an almost magnetic quality that enables them to have fun in almost any setting. The combination of Extraversion, Intuition, and Perceiving is well suited for leadership.	• A preference for lessons that involve adventuresome and creative experiences • A need for time to explore possibilities, ask questions, and use imagination • Learning through a variety of methods: reading, writing, listening, observing, and interacting with others • A dislike of narrow structures or straight lectures • Excelling when the instructor takes a personal interest in him or her
ENFJ (The Communicator) Extraverted/iNtuitive/Feeling/Judging	Chief concern is fostering harmony and cooperation between self and others. Has strong ideals and a potent sense of loyalty, whether to a mate, a school, a hometown, or a favorite cause. Usually good at organizing people to get things done while keeping everyone happy. At work, well armed to deal with both variety action. Typically patient and conscientious, make a concerted effort of sticking with a job until finished.	• Performing best in a structured learning environment • Believing interaction with others and discussion of the lesson to be very important • Learning best when he or she understands how the material is connected to helping people • Liking theories and abstractions • Resisting instructors who are not warm and personable
INFP (The Advocate) Introverted/iNtuitive/Feeling/Perceiving	Capable of immense sensitivity and has an enormous emotional capacity, which is guarded closely. Has to know people well before, letting down the guard, and displaying warmth. Interpersonal relationships are a crucial focus. Has powerful sense of faithfulness, duty, and commitment to the people and causes he or she is attracted to. Able to express emotion and move people through communication. A perfectionist on the job. Prefers a quiet working environment and, despite attraction for of human companionship, will often work best alone. Will work at best only in job he or she truly believes in.	• A preference for flexible environments where you can use imagination and creativity can be used. • Learning best from lectures and written work rather than rote methods. • Enjoyment of abstraction and the world of ideas. • A preference for instructors who are personally interested in him or her.
INFJ (The Foreseer) Introverted/iNtuitive/Feeling/Judging	Imaginative, inspired, tenacious, creative, and inward looking. Also stubborn, easily bored by routine work, and often pays little attention to obstacles. Makes decisions easily. Lives in a world of ideas and will have a unique vision. Pours all own energy into achieving goals. Trusts own intuition. Can express emotion and move people through written communication. Although the companionship of people is cherished, prefers a quiet working environment and working alone. Perfectionist about quality. Creativity is his or her hallmark.	• A value for lifelong learning by interacting with others or through reading and writing • Preference for tools and materials that are organized • Enjoyment of future-oriented concepts, theories, abstractions, and ideas • Avoiding dictatorial educational settings, as well as either/or thinking

Source: Karen A. Deitz and John P. Golden, *Boundless Diversity: An Introduction to the Golden Personality Type Profiler* (San Antonio, TX: Pearson TalentLens, 2004).

Code: E = Extraverted, N = iNtuitive, F = Feeling, P = Perceiving, I = Introverted, J = Judging

IMPROVING LEARNING AND BRAIN FUNCTIONING THROUGH REST

Interest has escalated in recent years for everyday approaches to improving a person's ability to learn and solve problems. We will return to this topic again in our discussion of cognitive challenges throughout the life span when we discuss the role of mental and physical activity to enhance learning. Here we look at the importance of *inactivity* to improve brain functioning and learning. Common wisdom suggests that it is easier to learn when you are rested, and scientific evidence supports this contention.

The potential benefits of sleep include stronger memory and better attention spans. According to James B. Maas, a psychology professor at Cornell University, good sleep is a necessity rather than a luxury: "Your alertness, energy, performance, thinking, productivity, creativity, safety, and health will be affected by how much you sleep."[18] Besides enhancing alertness, sleep is a way for the brain to store new information into long-term memory. The benefits are most likely to take place from rapid eye movement (REM) sleep that usually takes place during the sixth and eighth hour of sleep, when people are most likely to dream.

During REM sleep the brain typically replenishes neurotransmitters, the chemical substances that transmit chemical impulses across synapses. The neurotransmitters are important because they organize the neural networks essential for remembering, learning, performance, and problem solving. So a catnap, or power nap, may boost productivity, but an ample amount of deep sleep is a bigger contributor to better learning and brain functioning. Sleep spindles—spikes of activity that surface during REM sleep—help people learn and remember how to perform physical tasks, such as playing golf, tennis, and basketball.

The various approaches to learning, including learning styles, help us understand how people learn. How *much* people learn is another important consideration in understanding learning in the workplace. In general, people with higher mental ability and personality traits that allow them to concentrate better (such as emotional stability and conscientiousness) acquire knowledge and skills more readily.

CONTINUOUS LEARNING DURING YOUR CAREER

A reality of almost all professional, technical, and sales occupations is that career success, and even survival, depends on continuous learning. A commonplace example is that we all have to keep learning how to use new software and hardware just to perform a job. The CEO may need to understand how enterprise-level software helps the different divisions in a firm work together, and the auto-supply store associate has to learn how to track parts by computer. Acquiring human relations skills, such as working well with coworkers from different cultures, is another area of continuous learning facing many workers.

> "Keeping up with the effects of globalization takes both openness and work—openness to learning, reading, and seeing the world, and work to adapt to the competitive, intellectual, and cultural shifts before they bite you in the rear."
> —Kerry L. Sulkowicz, career advisor and founder of the Boswell Group LLC. Quoted in "The Corporate Shrink," *Fast Company*, March 2006, p. 140.

How Does Perception Influence How People Interpret the World?

◀ Learning Objective 3 ◀

Understanding learning strategies helps us cope better with the world of work, and understanding how we interpret information we receive is also important. Most of us interpret what is going on in the world outside us as we perceive it, not as it really is. You do not usually experience a mass of colors; instead, you experience a color photograph. You do not experience a thousand different vibrations in the air; instead, you hear a favorite CD. When we answer a question, we answer in terms of our interpretation of what we hear.

An everyday happening, such as a change in air temperature, helps to illustrate the nature of human perception. Assume that you live in Vermont. A temperature of 52°F (11.1°C) would seem warm in January. The same temperature would seem cold in July. Our perception of temperature depends on many things going on inside our mind and body.

Perceptions on the job are very important. Many studies, for example, have investigated the consequences of employee job perceptions. The results show that employees who perceive their job to be challenging and interesting have high job satisfaction and motivation. In addition, these favorable perceptions lead to better job performance.[19]

In summary, **perception** deals with the various ways in which people interpret things in the external world and how they act on the basis of these perceptions. The aspects of perception described here are (a) why perceptual problems exist, (b) agreement about perceived events, and (c) how people perceive the causes of behavior. Our discussion focuses on the social rather than the physical aspects of perception, such as taste, sound, and touch.

Perception

the various ways in which people interpret things in the external world and how they act on the basis of these perceptions

WHY PERCEPTUAL PROBLEMS EXIST

Under ideal circumstances, people perceive information as it is intended to be communicated or as it exists in reality. Suppose a company promotes a specialist to a team leader position because he or she is thought to have good potential for advancement. The manager offering the promotion hopes the specialist does not see the promotion as a plot to have the person work extra hours without being paid overtime. (Team leaders usually do not receive overtime pay.) Both characteristics of the stimulus (the idea or thing to be perceived) and the mental processes of people can lead to distorted perceptions. Figure 15-2 outlines why perceptual problems exist.

FIGURE 15-2

CONTRIBUTORS TO PERCEPTUAL PROBLEMS

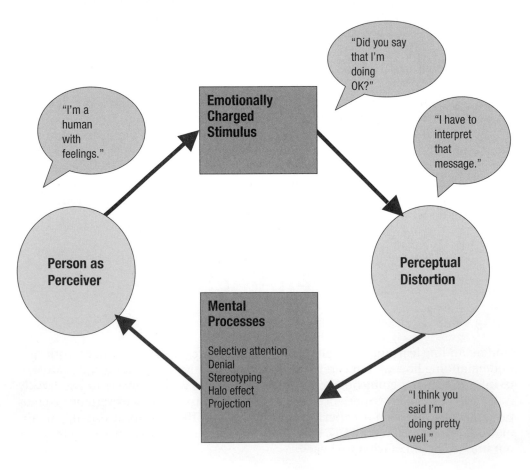

Characteristics of the Stimulus

Perceptual problems are most likely to be encountered when the stimulus or cue to be perceived has an emotional meaning. Assume that Brian, an office supervisor, announces to his staff, "I would like you to meet Brenda. She's a temporary worker here to help us out this week." Announcing the presence of an office temporary could trigger several different perceptions. The specific perceptions would depend on many motives, needs, and the knowledge of department employees. Among the possible interpretations are these:

"An office temp? I wonder if this means the company is going to cut down the regular workforce and use temps to help us through peak loads."

"This seems to be a sure sign that business has picked up. The front office would never authorize extra help unless business was booming. Things look good for getting a decent raise this year."

"I wonder if Brian has brought in a temporary worker to show us we had better get hustling or we could be replaced. I've heard a lot of these so-called temps usually wind up with full-time jobs if they like the temporary assignment."

To help reduce misperceptions, Brian should provide more complete information on why Brenda is being hired, such as pointing to a surge in orders. Reducing ambiguity helps minimize perceptual errors.

Mental Processes of People

The devices people use to deal with sensory information play a major role in creating perceptual problems. Several of these can also be classified as defensive behavior.

Selective Attention. The major contributor to perceptual distortions is the tendency for us to attend to the stimuli that are most relevant to our needs. Giving exclusive attention to something at the expense of other aspects of the environment is referred to as **selective attention.** If a stimulus fits our needs, desires, or interests we are likely to give it our attention. At the same time, we are likely to pay only minor attention to the surrounding stimuli. Thus, Joe Homeowner hears the wonderful news from the telemarketer that he is eligible to "cash out" on the equity on his home and pay off all those high-interest debts. Only after going forward with the "cashing out" does it sink in for Joe that he now has incurred a new long-term second mortgage on top of his existing mortgage.

Selective attention
giving exclusive attention to something at the expense of other aspects of the environment

Denial. If the sensory information is particularly painful to us—for example, if it hurts our self-esteem—we tend to go one step beyond selective attention. Denial is the process of excluding from awareness an important aspect of reality. This mental process is often found in the workplace, especially when people face such threats as job loss. As part of a downsizing, a woman was told by her manager that she would be terminated in thirty days unless somehow she could find another position in the company. That evening she informed her husband, "Our company is going through a downsizing, so it looks like I will be transferred to a different department in thirty days." By denying the reality of the message, the woman failed to search actively for another job within the company. She finally perceived the message correctly when handed her severance check.

Stereotyping. A common method of simplifying perception is to evaluate an individual or thing based on our perception of the group or class to which the person or object belongs. A perceptual disadvantage of stereotyping is that you do not look for the way in which somebody or something might be different from others in the same group. For example, a job seeker might say, "I won't look for a job in the retail field because retailing jobs have such low pay." Such stereotyping might result in the person's neglecting to investigate high-paying opportunities within the retail field based on the rapid promotions possible. Stereotypes can be positive as well as negative. For example, you might have the stereotype that all accountants are thorough and accurate. As a result, you fail to carefully review the tax return prepared by your accountant.

Halo Effect. We have a tendency to color everything that we know about a person because of one recognizable favorable or unfavorable trait. When a company does not insist on the use of objective measures of performance, it is not uncommon for a supervisor to give a favorable performance rating to people who dress well or smile frequently. The fine appearance or warm smile of these people has created a halo around them. Employees often create a negative halo about a supervisor simply because he or she is gruff or stern in manner or speech.

Projection. Another shortcut in the perceptual process is to project our own faults onto others instead of making an objective appraisal of the situation. Our feelings and thoughts are unacceptable to us, so we attribute them to another person. In this way we feel less anxious about ourselves. A manager who has a self-discipline problem himself might respond negatively to an employee's request to work at home one day per week. The manager might say, "Sorry, can't let you work at home. You would probably goof off half the day before you got down to work."

PERCEPTUAL CONGRUENCE

Perceptual congruence
the degree to which people perceive
things the same way

The discussion of perception so far has focused on perceptual errors. At times, most people in the organization perceive an event in the same way. **Perceptual congruence** refers to the degree to which people perceive things the same way. High congruence generally implies valid perception, but people can also agree on a distorted perception. For example, four members of a work team might have the authority to choose a fifth team member. All four might share the same inaccurate perception that a particular candidate is a good fit. After one month, they learn that the individual is a loner who functions poorly in a team environment.

Despite the reservation cited, high congruence generally leads to more positive consequences for the organization than low congruence. A case in point is that it is beneficial for managers and group members to perceive the group members' tasks in the same manner.

ATTRIBUTION THEORY: HOW WE PERCEIVE THE CAUSES OF BEHAVIOR

Attribution theory
the study of the process by which
people ascribe causes to the behaviors
they perceive

An important aspect of perception is our explanation for the causes of behavior. Stated differently, to what do we *attribute* a given behavior? **Attribution theory** is the study of the process by which people ascribe causes to the behavior they perceive. A major finding of attribution theory is that most people give relatively little weight to the circumstances in making judgments about a person's behavior. We are more likely to attribute a person's actions or results to personal characteristics than to outside forces. A supervisor who presses us to finish a project is more likely to be perceived as being impatient than as caught up in a highly competitive environment.

Another finding of attribution theory is that people have a general tendency to attribute their achievements to good inner qualities, whereas they attribute failure to adverse factors within the environment. A manager would thus attribute increased productivity to his or her leadership skills but blame low productivity on poor support from the organization.

How Do We Respond to Life Span Changes and Challenges?

◀ Learning Objective 4 ◀

At different stages in life we face different challenges, beginning with the embryo struggling for enough oxygen and ending with the 99-year-old fretting about physical well-being and passing on his or her estate. Here we overview the stages of the life cycle and challenges associated with adolescence and beyond.

STAGES OF THE LIFECYCLE

Several approaches have been developed over the years to explain the various stages of human development, or the tasks people face at different periods in life. Among the best known is the eight stages of human development formulated by psychiatrist Erik H. Erikson in the 1950s.[20] Figure 15-3 presents an outline of these stages and the associated primary crisis for each one. According to Erikson, the socialization process consists of the "eight stages of man," with each stage representing a psychosocial crisis. The crisis must be resolved at each stage before the next stage can be satisfactorily negotiated.

Satisfactory learning and resolution of each stage is necessary if the child is to manage the next and later stages successfully. The building of a skyscraper is an appropriate metaphor. Each floor, including the foundation and ground level, must

Stages and Ages	The Primary Crisis and Related Comment
1. Infancy (0–1 year)	*Learning basic trust versus basic mistrust (hope)* A well-nurtured child develops trust and security.
2. Toddler (1–2 years)	*Learning autonomy versus shame (will)* The well-parented child emerges from this stage proud rather than feeling shamed.
3. Preschool (3–5 years)	*Learning initiative versus guilt (purpose)* Healthy children broaden their skills at this stage through active play.
4. Elementary school (6–12 years)	*Learning industry versus inferiority (competence)* Here the child learns the more formal life skills such as mastering reading and arithmetic, and some self-discipline.
5. Adolescence (13–19 years)	*Learning identity versus identity diffusion (fidelity)* The adolescent can now answer satisfactorily and happily the question, "Who am I?"
6. Young adulthood (20–40 years)	*Learning intimacy versus isolation (love)* The successful young adult experiences the type of intimacy that makes possible a good marriage or a genuine or enduring friendship.
7. Middle adulthood (40–65 years)	*Learning generativity (building a generation) versus self-absorption* In adulthood, the successful adult engages in a partnership and raises children.
8. Late adulthood (65 and over)	*Learning integrity versus despair (wisdom)* The mature adult has integrity, is independent, and enjoys people and work. If the earlier psychosocial crises have not been resolved, he or she may have a self-view of disgust and despair.

FIGURE 15-3

ERIKSON'S EIGHT STAGES OF DEVELOPMENT AND ASSOCIATED CRISIS

Source: Erik H. Erikson, *Childhood and Society* (New York: Norton, 1963); Child Development Institute, "Stages of Social-Emotional Development in Children and Teenagers." Retrieved May 10, 2006, from: www.childdevelpmentinfo.com

be built correctly or the next floor will collapse. An example of this stage-by-stage development is that if the young adult cannot experience intimacy at stage 6, he or she will not be successful at the marriage or parenting that takes place at stage 7.

Erikson's stages of human development have prompted later investigation into how humans develop through different phases of their lives. Despite these analyses of life stages, there are huge cultural and individual differences in the successful development of an adult. For example, what about Russians, whose life expectancy is only about fifty-nine years old? Do Russians never deal with Stage 8, integrity versus despair? And is it not possible to be a successful, well-adjusted adult even if you are not in a committed relationship and have no children?

Next, we summarize briefly challenges people face in adolescence, adult life, and late life.[21] The first stage, infancy and childhood, is an important building block for later stages but lies outside the purview of our treatment of human relations.

RESPONDING TO CHALLENGES IN ADOLESCENCE

Adolescence

the period in life from approximately age thirteen to twenty; from a biological standpoint, adolescence begins with puberty

In its technical meaning **adolescence** is the period in life from approximately ages thirteen to twenty. From a biological standpoint, adolescence begins with puberty, the beginning of sexual maturation marked by rising levels of sex hormones and rapid growth. During adolescence many people start building work-related human skills, such as teamwork, and also engage in career choice and career preparation. Adolescents (or *teenagers*) vary considerably in their accomplishments, with some teenagers being successful entrepreneurs, information technology consultants, professional athletes, and movie stars. Industries such as retailing and food service depend on the adolescent workforce, suggesting that even average teenagers occupy an important work role in society.

Cognitive Challenges

Adolescents headed for a successful career must rise to the challenge of developing logic, abstract thought, and hypothetical reasoning. Many adolescents are studying five different subjects at once and feel compelled to think well enough to perform well in school and on college entrance exams. Adolescents must also deal with the development of moral reasoning in which they attempt to learn acceptable versus unacceptable codes of conduct. According to Lawrence Kohlberg, former moral education professor at Harvard University, adolescents begin to development three levels of moral thought:[22]

■ At the *preconventional level* moral dilemmas are resolved in a self-centered way. An act is moral if it enables someone to avoid punishment or obtain reward. Obeying safety rules or returning a lost wallet might fit this category of moral development.

■ At the *conventional level* moral dilemmas are resolved in ways that reflect laws or norms set by parents and other influential adults. Making a complete stop at a stop sign on a country road when no one else is watching would fit the conventional level of moral development.

■ At the *postconventional level* moral dilemmas are resolved by relating to abstract principles such as equality, justice, and the value of life. An adolescent at this level of moral development might start a food-and-clothing campaign for homeless people in the community.

One reason offered for the unethical behavior of many adults in executive positions in business is that they did not advance to the postconventional level of moral development.

Personality and Social Challenges

As an adolescent struggles to establish a reliable self-concept, or personal identity, he or she faces an **identity crisis.** In a multicultural world, the adolescent may need to establish an ethnic identity. Adolescents often struggle with whether to retain close ties with the family or invest more energy in developing peer relations. Adolescents struggle with sexuality, with some happily engaging in sex and others facing unintended negative consequences such as parenthood, paternity suits, dropping out of school, and sexually transmitted diseases. Another conflict many adolescents face is one of body image, with discontent possibly leading to anorexia and excessive body piercing.

Successfully Managing the Teenage Brain

A cognitive challenge of the adolescent years meriting separate mention is dealing successfully with the **teenage brain,** a stage of brain development in which people are easily influenced by their environment and more prone to impulsive behavior. Based on several research findings, the teenage brain differs from the adult brain in four primary ways:[23]

- Overproduction of dendrites, which leads to a greater propensity for learning new concepts and skills.

- Pruning, or loss of dendrites not being used, taking place more rapidly.

- Decision-making processes governed by the amygdala, leading to the propensity for teenagers being more emotionally driven in an impulsive sense.

- The medial prefrontal cortex, located in the front of the brain, is not used to the same extent as by adults. As a result, the teenager will often have less empathy and guilt than adults.

- The frontal lobe, responsible for cognitive processes such as reasoning, planning, and judgment, is only about 80 percent developed in teenagers. The frontal lobe finally connects with the rest of the brain between ages 25 and 30.

The heavy reliance on the amygdala often causes misunderstandings, incendiary language, and faulty decision making despite high cognitive capacity. This helps explain why a teenager might engage in such activity as mastering a complex calculus problem in class or building a robot and then run a red light after class "just for the excitement."

Another characteristic of teenage thinking governed by brain differences is that a teenager's judgment of what he or she would do in a given situation is driven by the question, "What would I do?" In contrast, adults tend to ask, "What would I do, given how I would feel and given how the people around me would feel as a result of my actions?"[24]

RESPONDING TO ADULT LIFE CHALLENGES

Adulthood is not marked by the same more predictable milestones as childhood and adolescence. Assuming that a person lives until about age eighty, he or she spends more than half of life in the adult stage, so adults face an enormous number of challenges, including managing social life, work, and finances; raising children; keeping a blended family working together; staying current with technology; and investing for retirement.

Cognitive Challenges

Adults face the unique challenge of applying the many cognitive skills they have acquired during study. For example, some people who performed well in math exams have no clue how to calculate miles per gallon on a vehicle or balance a checkbook. To prosper in a career, the adult must often learn creative-thinking skills and apply wisdom. For example, the self-employed adult must find a way to convince bankers or venture capitalists on the merits of investing in his or her idea for the launch of a new product or service. An adult faces the challenge of learning to think more flexibly rather than finding the "correct" answer to a problem—the essence of creative thinking.

Personality and Social Challenges

Midlife crisis
time that adults in their forties face when they feel unfulfilled and search for a major shift in career or lifestyle

Midlife transition
adults taking stock of their lives and formulating new goals; among dozens of other personality and social challenges facing adults are the loss of a youthful appearance and a decreased reproductive or sexual capacity

Adults must learn to become less self-centered and refine their interpersonal skills, including developing business etiquette. For some young people a major adjustment is to learn to take off their sports cap when eating at a restaurant or being interviewed for a job. Many adults in their forties face a **midlife crisis,** when they feel unfulfilled and search for a major shift in career or lifestyle. Adults facing a midlife crisis often wonder whether their choice of career or life partner was the right decision. During the more common **midlife transition,** adults may take stock of their life and formulate new goals, such as an engineer working for IBM deciding to teach high school math. (IBM encourages such transitions to foster math and science knowledge and skills.) Among the dozens of other personality and social challenges facing adults are the loss of a youthful appearance and a decreased reproductive or sexual capacity. Such challenges have spurred the development of plastic surgery, youth-enhancing cosmetics, and lifestyle drugs such as those designed to enhance sexual performance.

The Sandwich Generation Challenge

Sandwich generation
those placed in the middle between the needs of their own children and their aging relatives

During the adult stage of life many people face the difficult challenge of being part of the **sandwich generation**—those placed in the middle between the needs of their own children and their aging relatives. According to one estimate, nearly two-thirds of baby boomers will be taking care of an elderly parent during the next ten years. Taking care of the parent sometimes translates into having an older relative live with the couple or person, along with the children, resulting in an intergenerational household. Such an arrangement was common in the United States in years past, and is now common throughout the world. During economic downturns intergenerational living increases in frequency. The sandwich generation challenge might be faced by a couple, or a single parent, and is often complicated by the person or couple needing to plan for their own retirement.[25]

A survey was conducted with social workers who assisted sandwich generation women, defined as those between thirty-five and sixty-four who are a parent to at least one child and have at least one living parent. A sampling of major findings about the sandwich generation women is as follows:[26]

- Unhappiness among these women can be attributed to being overwhelmed with too many responsibilities.

- Sandwich generation women underestimate the toll caring for an aging relative will take on their own health.

- Many sandwich generation women are not prepared for the cost of paying for care of an aging relative.

Successfully managing the challenge of being a member of the sandwich generation includes such steps as taking the time for oneself or each other to avoid neglecting marriage or personal life. Avoiding emotional, physical, and financial overload is also important. Getting help from community and government resources is another way of coping with the sandwich-generation challenge.[27]

RESPONDING TO LATE LIFE CHALLENGES

The challenges of late life have increased because more people live longer beyond the traditional retirement age, and many remain active and in good health. Yet still many other people in late life are infirmed, impoverished, and dependent on family and government to maintain their well-being.

Cognitive Challenges

Many people in late adulthood face cognitive decline, whereas many others do not. The ability to learn rapidly and reason abstractly and logically may decline through adulthood, starting as early as age thirty. Part of the problem is that there is a normal slowing down in cognitive functioning starting in the fifties and sixties. Neurotransmitters, the chemicals that enable nerve cells to communicate, diminish.[28] Another problem is that older people have some difficulty in concentrating when interrupted by extraneous sounds.[29] But wisdom and judgment based on the accumulation of knowledge may increase up into the 80s. The issue of the cognitive skills of late-life adults has been the subject of much opinion and research in recent years because the life span of people has increased, and so many old people hold responsible positions, drive cars, and even fly airplanes solo.

Common wisdom suggests that staying in shape mentally by such activities as doing crossword puzzles, surfing the Internet, or studying a foreign language can slow the decline of an aging brain. Brain-imaging studies support the idea that mental workouts help preserve **cognitive fitness,** a state of optimized ability to remember, learn, plan, and adapt to changing circumstances. Acquiring expertise in such diverse areas as playing a cello, juggling, speaking a foreign language, and driving a taxicab expands your neural systems and helps them communicate with one another. This means that learning new skills can alter the physical makeup of the brain even in later life. Engaging in play also enhances brain functioning, which helps explain the link between creativity and play.[30]

A long-term study called Active, trained 2,832 adults sixty-five to ninety-four years old in memory, reasoning, or visual attention and perception. The study is slightly less optimistic about the results of mental workouts. Although the trainees performed better on the skill they practiced, that training did not translate to improvement in the other skills. Many mentally active, late-life adults show smaller cognitive decline than their less mentally active counterparts. Yet, the mentally active people most likely had a stronger cognitive reserve (mental capacity) that led them to stay mentally active.[31] Although this study did not support the "use it or lose it" hypothesis, it demonstrates that older adults can still master specific cognitive tasks with practice. So your grandmother who studies Mandarin Chinese may not then be able to decipher a manual for a digital camera easily, but at least she now knows Mandarin.

Staying physically healthy in general has a positive impact on preserving cognitive functioning. Part of staying healthy is obtaining physical exercise and managing stress. One reason that physical exercise helps brain functioning is that the exercise increases the amount of blood flow to the brain.

The accompanying Human Relations in Practice illustrates what many people are doing to stay mentally sharp in during adult life and late life.

Personality and Social Challenges

A change noted in late adulthood is that people begin to value the present more because they correctly perceive that they have a shorter future than do younger adults. As a result, late-life adults are less concerned about activities that may have a payoff in the long run, such as networking. Instead, they look to spend times with good friends and family already available. Practical problems for those in the most

Cognitive fitness
a state of optimized ability to remember, learn, plan, and adapt to changing circumstances

Human Relations in Practice

Writer Linda Hale Bucklin Works Out at Brain Gym

Linda Hale Bucklin, a 63-year-old writer, signed up on the spot when she saw a new "gym for the brain" in her San Francisco neighborhood. She now works out three times a week and credits a computer "visual processing program" for helping her find her car keys faster and sharpen her tennis skills. On the court, "my game is just at a different level," says Bucklin. "I'm playing with 40-year-olds, and I'm holding my own really well."

Vibrant Brains, the business that drew her in, attracted 200 members in less than two years. Patrons pay $60 a month to work out on 20 computer stations loaded with "mental fitness" software, including a "neurobics circuit" that purports to stretch the brain. Bucklin says she's addicted to an art-auction game that displays a dozen Monets for purchase. "Then they'll intersperse them with other Monets, and you have to tell them apart," she says. "I minored in art history, and I still find it difficult."

The workouts at Vibrant Brains are based on the theory that people engaged in greater degrees of mental stimulation increase their brain mass and neural pathways, protecting them if a brain injury or dementia starts chipping away at brain connections.

Source: Kelly Greene, "The Latest in Mental Health: Working Out at the 'Brain Gym,'" *Wall Street Journal*, March 28–29, 2009, pp. A1, A5.

advanced years are that many friends die and family members move away. Thus, the late-life adult may have to seek out new friends. Retirement communities, including assisted living, provide an opportunity for affluent older people to make new social contacts, to help compensate for the loss of friends and family members.

A challenge for some late-life adults is to engage in fulfilling physical activities to replace favored activities of previous years. For example, a 75-year-old with a hip and knee replacement may not be able to play tennis or golf any longer and may have to find satisfaction in a replacement activity such as light hiking.

LIFE AND JOB SATISFACTION THROUGHOUT THE LIFE SPAN

People at various stages of their life span often wonder what type of satisfaction and happiness awaits them at later stages. Typical self-questions are these: "Will I enjoy my work more in late career?" "Will I be more (or less) happy in my later years?" Although the research evidence about life and job satisfaction throughout the life span is not entirely consistent, some trends are notable.

Life Satisfaction and Age

Life satisfaction tends to increase throughout adulthood, partially because many of the major challenges in life are met as one reaches the fifties and sixties. For example, by middle age most people have completed their formal education, chosen a career, and reared children. According to a study by Daniel Mroczek, a psychology professor at Fordham University, life satisfaction for men tends to peak at age sixty-five. His study synthesized more than twenty years of data from almost two thousand men in the Veterans Affairs Normative Aging Study. The life satisfaction and personal traits of the subjects were measured over almost a thirty-year span.

After life satisfaction peaking around sixty-five, the men around age ninety-five were about as happy as they were in their mid-forties. Nevertheless, there was considerable variation among individuals, with some people peaking in satisfaction early and then experiencing a permanent decline in happiness. In contrast, some of the men in the study continued to gain in happiness. Personality factors influenced the happiness and satisfaction curve. Highly extroverted people were more likely to have high levels of life satisfaction and more stability in life satisfaction. (One interpretation of these findings is that extroversion helps a person develop friends, and positive human contact contributes to life satisfaction.) Another finding was that life satisfaction dropped considerably during the last year of life—often because a person has poor physical health during his or her final year.[32]

Women also tend to gain in life satisfaction as they become older. Psychology students Brian Scott Ehrlich and Derek Isaacowitz, guided by their professors at the University of Pennsylvania, conducted a study of subjective well-being, including life satisfaction, among young, middle-aged, and older people. The sample consisted of 190 women and 90 men, ranging in age from eighteen to ninety-three years old. Young adults and middle-aged adults showed relatively the same degree of life satisfaction, and older adults tended to be the most satisfied with life. The findings about older people having higher life satisfaction were of modest magnitude, but they did support similar evidence from other studies.[33]

Not all researchers have found that life satisfaction increases with age. Yet the bulk of evidence is at least that the ratings of life satisfaction do not *decline* with age. Apparently, as long as people have a reasonable amount of love and satisfying work, they tend to stay happy.[34]

Job Satisfaction and Age

Job satisfaction also tends to increase with age, as would be predicted, because work satisfaction is such a major component of life satisfaction. Business cycles exert a strong influence on the link between job satisfaction and age. When jobs are scarce, people are more likely to be satisfied with their jobs because there is a short supply of more exciting jobs available elsewhere. As age brings about more financial responsibilities, workers are all the more appreciative of having a job during a period of job shortages. Furthermore, it is possible that still being part of the workforce during an era of so many downsizings would add to an older person's appreciation and job satisfaction.

A general explanation for the many studies indicating the increase in job satisfaction during a person's career is that with more work experience older workers understand better which needs work can and cannot satisfy. In addition, they have a more realistic view of life and work.[35] Experience also contributes to income, and a higher income in turn contributes to job satisfaction for many workers.

What Are Some Basic Concepts about Changing Careers?

◀ Learning Objective 5 ◀

The new type of career emphasizes doing work that fits your major values in life, so many people switch careers to find work that fits their values. And these values could include earning enough money to support a family well and pursue preferred leisure activities. A major reason for switching careers is to find better opportunities after a job loss.

FACTORS INFLUENCING A CAREER CHANGE

A major principle of career switching is to *be thorough*. Go through the same kind of thinking and planning that is recommended for finding a first career. Obtaining valid career information is essential, such as consulting www.bls.gov/oco/home.htm, the online edition of the *Occupational Outlook Handbook*. The advantage for the career switcher, however, is that the experienced person often has a better understanding of the type of work he or she does not want to do. *Finding a mentor* who can help guide you through a career change is also helpful.

One of the first steps in making a career change is to *assess your likes and dislikes*. Career coach Randall S. Hansen advises that many people change careers because their dislike their job, their boss, and their company. Yet you also need to examine your likes. What work-related activities excite and energize you?[36] Many people learn more about their career preferences by taking a career assessment instrument combined with the guidance of a career counselor. Three of the most scientifically developed career inventories are as follows:

- Campbell Interest and Skill Survey (http://pearsonassess.com/HAIWEB/Cultures/en-us/Productdetail.htm?Pid=PAg115&Mode=summary)
- Myers-Briggs Type Indicator Career Report (www.cpp.com)
- 16PF Personal Career Development Profile Plus (www.careers-by-design.com)

A new career should be *built gradually*. Few people are able to leave one career abruptly and step into another. For most people who switch careers successfully, the switch is more of a transition than an abrupt change. A constructive approach would be to take on a few minor assignments in the proposed new field and then search for full-time work in that field after building skill. An electronics technician, for example, might request to visit customers with sales representatives to facilitate a switch to industrial selling. To prepare for your new career, you may need to acquire the necessary education and training, as illustrated in the following representative example.

Frank Harrington was a manager at a semiconductor maker in California. Eventually he began to dislike the political battles involved in his work. Harrington wanted to become a nurse, but he found that he recognized some prerequisites for admission, so he enrolled in night classes. He eventually obtained a nursing degree, but arranging the financing for his career switch was difficult because his stock investments declined in value. To help with finances, his wife returned to work. Upon graduation, Harrington received four job offers in three days. He now works in the trauma intensive-care unit of a hospital in Silicon Valley.[37]

Sometimes an interim assignment can offer a person useful ideas for a complete career change or at least a different emphasis. One such possibility is to fill in for a person who is on a company-paid leave of absence, referred to as a *sabbatical*. Another possibility for an interim assignment is filling in for someone who is on family leave because of the birth or adoption of a child. Filling in for the boss, for example, can give a person a firsthand sense of managerial work.

CHANGING CAREERS WITHOUT CHANGING EMPLOYERS

A major concern many people have about changing careers is the loss of job security that they have already established with a large employer. If you stay with the same employer after a career switch, you are able to retain the same benefits, including retirement contribution. Your familiarity with the corporate culture will still be an asset. However, if the employee switches careers into a lower-rated position, a salary cut might occur. Only a select number of large employers offer the opportunity for a career change, yet it can happen, as follows:

> Christine Murphy had been a consultant for Accenture Ltd. for eight years. She then became a human resources professional without leaving the professional-services firm. Murphy arranged the move with the help of an Accenture program that supports internal career changes.
>
> Jill B. Smart, Accenture's chief human resources officer, says she developed the career-change initiative after reviewing exit interviews showing that many employees leave the company because they want to work in different fields. These employees almost always thought they had to look outside the company for a career switch.[38]

From the employer perspective, programs of internal career changes improve retention rates. From the standpoint of the employee, the same program satisfies his or her need to develop new skills and make a career change.

SELF-EMPLOYMENT AS A CAREER CHANGE

A major reason that many employees consider a new career is that they crave more independence. As a consequence, an increasingly popular path for the career switcher is to move from salaried employment to self-employment. The prospective self-employed person needs to decide on which particular business to enter. For many people, self-employment means continuing to perform similar work, such as the company cafeteria manager entering the food catering business. Other formerly employed workers go into competition with their former employers, such as a restaurant manager opening a restaurant of her own. Another approach to self-employment is to choose an enterprise that fits a passion of yours, such as a wine connoisseur opening a wine store or operating a wine-store franchise.

For those who lack specific plans of their own, prepackaged plans can be purchased. A sampling of these is as follows:

- Cartridge printing, recharging, and repair
- Check-cashing service
- Damage restoration
- Language translations services
- Bed-and-breakfast
- Liquidated goods broker
- Self-storage center

Anyone contemplating self-employment should recognize that it offers potentially high rewards as well as risks. An editor of *Entrepreneur* magazine explains the downside of being a business owner in these terms:

> Any business owner knows what deep corrections in the stock market mean for young companies. Venture capital dries up. Frustrated sellers, unable to unload shares, stop buying stock in companies like yours. Consumers resist the urge to pull the old Visas out of their wallets and buy your products. Inventories pile up, cash gets tight and pink slips appear on staffers' desks. At times like these, owning a business ranks right up there with root canals and tax audits on the list of life's undesirables.[39]

Another self-employment possibility is to purchase a franchise, thus lowering the risk of a start-up business. Currently, franchises account for about one-third of retail sales in the United States and Canada. Yet franchises require a substantial financial investment, ranging from about $6,000 to $600,000. Furthermore, some of the big name franchisors, such as Dunkin' Donuts, require that the franchisee purchase multiple stores simply to get started. Another caution is that some franchise operators may work about seventy hours per week to earn about $18,000 per year.

▶ Learning Objective 6 ▶

What Are Some Tactics for Coping with Change?

We have all heard that adapting to change is necessary for career success, and even survival. At the same time, a well-accepted proposition is that change is scary.[40] A fitting conclusion to this chapter is therefore to present a few tactics for coping with change. To begin, *look for the personal value that could be embedded in a forced change.*[41] If you are downsized, take the opportunity to assume responsibility for your own career rather than being dependent on the organization. Many downsizing victims find a new career for themselves that better fits their interests or try self-employment in search of more job security. Whether or not self-employment is truly more secure than working for a large employer, many people fear that a big company will lay them off during a corporate downsizing.

When faced with a significant change, *ask "What if?" questions*, such as "What if my company is sold tomorrow?" "What if I went back to school for more education?" and "What if I did accept that one-year assignment in China?" When confronting major change, *force yourself to enjoy at least some small aspect of the change.* Suppose the edict comes through the organization that purchases can now only be made over the Internet. This means you will no longer be able to interact with a few of the sales reps you considered to be buddies. With the time you save, however, you will have spare hours each week for leisure activities.

You are less likely to resist change if you *recognize that change is inevitable.* Dealing with change is an integral part of life, so why fight it? Keep in mind also to *change before you have to, which can lead to a better deal.* If your manager announces a new plan, get on board as a volunteer before you are forced to accept a lesser role. If your company has made the decision to start a Six Sigma (company-wide quality improvement) program, study the subject early and ask for a role as a facilitator or team leader. Stop trying to be in control all the time, because you cannot control everything. Many changes will occur that you cannot control, so relax and enjoy the ride. Finally, recognize that change has an emotional impact, which will most likely cause some inner turmoil and discomfort. Even if the change is for the better, you might remain emotionally attached to your old system—or neighborhood, car, or PC.

Continuing to acquire useful knowledge is also helpful in dealing with change because you have the new knowledge at hand to get past the change.[42] When digital photography became dominant, the operators of many portrait studios felt threatened and were too slow to offer digital services to their customers. Many of these photographers who waited too long to offer digital services were forced out of business. In contrast, many other portrait photographers were early learners of digital technology and survived the transition well.

The bestseller *The World Is Flat: A Brief History of the Twenty-First Century* (2005) by Thomas L. Friedman has made thousands of educators and individuals aware of the potential changes imposed on us by globalization and outsourcing. One key point of the book is that the global economic playing field has been leveled by information technology that enables people to collaborate regardless of their location. Another key point is that the success of individual workers will depend on the development of specialized skills. Furthermore, to cope with these changes workers must constantly upgrade their skills. At the same time, they should search for jobs that cannot be outsourced or that are anchored because they must be done at a specific location, such as calling on an industrial customer.[43]

Many personal service jobs cannot be outsourced or sent offshore, including hairdressers, massage therapists, custodial technicians, and auto mechanics. Yet even here, some personal service workers in North America complain that residents from lower-wage countries are willing to perform these services at lower wages than the North American workers are. Some corporate professional jobs are more difficult to outsource than others. The positions less likely to be outsourced are those requiring the combination of technical (or discipline skills) plus connections with people.[44] A real estate agent with hundreds of personal contacts cannot be replaced by a Web site. An information systems specialist who performs hands-on work with internal clients cannot be replaced by an information technology specialist working eight thousand miles away in another country. The change-management lesson here is that building relationships with work associates helps ward off some of the threats of the "flat world."

Concept Review and Reinforcement

Key Terms

Learning, 434
Classical conditioning, 434
Operant conditioning, 435
Negative reinforcement, 435
Punishment, 435
Extinction, 436
Modeling, 436
Informal learning, 436

Implicit learning, 436
E-learning, 437
Group learning, 438
Learning style, 438
Perception, 444
Selective attention, 445
Perceptual congruence, 446
Attribution theory, 446

Adolescence, 448
Identity crisis, 449
Teenage brain, 449
Midlife crisis, 450
Midlife transition, 450
Sandwich generation, 450
Cognitive fitness, 451

Summary and Review

In this chapter we have studied additional knowledge that helps a person attain career thrust.

- Classical conditioning is the most elementary form of learning. It occurs when a previously neutral stimulus is associated with a natural (unconditioned) stimulus. Eventually, the neutral stimulus brings forth the unconditioned response. For example, a factory whistle blown just prior to the lunch break induces employees to salivate and experience hunger pangs.

- Operant conditioning (or instrumental learning) occurs when a person's spontaneous actions are rewarded or punished, which results in an increase or a decrease in the behavior. Much of human learning occurs through operant conditioning. The four reinforcement strategies involved in such conditioning are positive reinforcement, negative reinforcement, punishment, and extinction. A continuous reinforcement schedule rewards behavior each time it occurs, whereas an intermittent schedule delivers rewards periodically.

- Two important processes that help in learning complicated skills are modeling and informal learning. Modeling occurs when you learn a skill by observing another person perform that skill. Informal learning is unplanned and occurs in a setting without a formal classroom, lesson plan, instructor, or examination. Informal learning can be spontaneous, or the company might organize the work area to encourage such learning. Informal learning can be regarded as a form of implicit learning.

- E-learning is a Web-based form of computer-based training. The geographical dispersion of employees makes e-learning more important. Self-motivation and self-discipline are essential for the e-learner. Most companies continue to use blended learning (Web and classroom) to capitalize on the efficiencies of e-learning yet still rely on human contact.

- Groups can learn in that members come to adapt their behavior collectively in response to experience. Group learning has the three basic features of sharing, storage (in the brain), and retrieval.

- People learn best in different ways—for example, some people acquire information best through passive learning. A preference for working alone versus cooperatively is another difference in learning style. A useful classification of learning styles is the preference of visual, auditory, or kinesthetic learning. Most learners use a combination of the three styles.

- According to the Golden Personality Type Profier, two dimensions of psychlogical functioning are the basis for the relationship between personality and learning style. We judge through thinking (T) and feeling (F). We perceive through sensing (S) and intuition (N). The four mental processes of thinking, feeling, sensing, and intuition results in four learning styles as shown in Figure 15-1.

- In general, people with higher mental ability and personality traits that allow them to concentrate better (e.g., conscientiousness) acquire knowledge and skills more readily.

- A reality of almost all professional, technical, and sales occupations is that career success and survival depend on continuous learning.
- Perception, the organization of sensory information into meaningful experiences, influences job behavior. Perceptual problems stem from both a stimulus with an emotional meaning and the mental processes of people. These mental processes, or shortcuts, include selective attention, denial, stereotyping, the halo effect, and projection.
- Perceptual congruence refers to the degree to which people perceive things the same way. High congruence generally leads to more positive consequences for the organization than does low congruence.
- Attribution theory explains how people attribute the causes of behavior. People have a general tendency to attribute their achievements to good inner qualities, whereas they attribute failure to adverse factors within the environment.
- According to Erickson, the socialization process consists of the "eight stages of man," with each state representing a psychosocial crisis. The crisis must be resolved at each stage before the next stage can be successfully negotiated.
- The challenges of adolescence include the cognitive challenge of developing logic and abstract thought as well as developing moral reasoning. A key personality and social challenge is the identity crisis. Successfully managing the teenage brain is another challenge, with the brain being quite adept at new learning yet tending toward impulsiveness and lack of empathy.
- The challenges of adulthood include applying cognitive skills to real-life problems. Adults must also learn to become less self-centered and refine their interpersonal skills. Adults may also face a midlife crisis and a midlife transition, as well as being part of the sandwich generation.
- The challenges of late adulthood include cognitive decline, even though older people can be trained to learn new, complex tasks. A change facing late-life adults is more of a focus on the present.
- Life satisfaction tends to increase throughout adulthood but may peak for men at about age sixty-five. Job satisfaction also tends to increase with age, partially because older adults understand better which needs work can and cannot satisfy.
- A major principle of career switching is to be thorough. Obtain valid career information, and assess your likes and dislikes. A new career should be built gradually, often by phasing into the new career part-time. An increasingly popular path for the career switcher is to move from salaried employment to self-employment.
- Suggestions for managing change well include searching for the personal value that could be embedded in forced change, asking "What if," forcing yourself to enjoy at least some small aspect of the change, recognizing that change is inevitable, and understanding that change has an emotional impact. To help cope with possible changes caused by outsourcing and off shoring of one's job is to incorporate building relationships into one's job.

Check Your Understanding

1. Why is it that so many employers believe that a valuable skill for their employees is to "learn how to learn"?
2. Give an example of a valuable skill you have learned in life through modeling. Did you intend to learn it at the time?
3. Provide an example of knowledge that you have acquired without a conscious intention to learn.
4. What steps can a company take to encourage informal learning among employees?
5. If e-learning is so effective, why haven't most schools of higher education converted completely to distance learning?
6. Give an example of where it *is* true that perception is more important than reality.
7. What evidence can you present that you now have, or ever had, a *teenage brain*? Or what evidence can you present that you do not have, or never have had, a *teenage brain*?
8. How would you know if your brain were actually improving after having engaged in brain-strengthening exercises such as doing crossword puzzles, learning new software, or learning another language?
9. How reasonable is it to establish minimum and maximum ages for commercial airline pilots?
10. What is your strategy for dealing with the biggest change you will have to face during the next twelve months?

Web Corner

Changing a bad habit:
www.changeonehabit.com

Insight into your Myers-Briggs Personality Type:
www.cpp.com

Quiz about whether to change careers:
www.quintcareers.com

INTERNET SKILL BUILDER

Although opinions vary as to the precise meaning of a *millennial,* the term generally refers to the last generation born in the twentieth century. Search the Internet to identify about ten life span challenges facing the millennials—in other words, challenges facing members of this generation attributed to their stage in life. You can probably supplement the list with reading you have done or personal observations. Did you find the World Wide Web useful for this type of search, or did you have better luck with a library database?

Developing Your
Human Relations Skills

Applying Human Relations Exercise 15-1

Developing Your Brain and Learning Ability

The belief is widespread that the human brain can be developed through mental exercise. We found about 76 million entries using the Yahoo! search engine entry "exercising the brain." Even when a given brain builder may work for many other people, you do not know if the technique will help you specifically. Here is an opportunity to try a brain exercise and see what the positive consequences might be for you. You will need a few minutes a day for at least ten days to determine whether the technique works. First, do one or both of the following exercises for ten to fourteen days:

1. Recite the alphabet backward until you are proficient. Perform the exercise a few times a day until can do the backward version almost as easily as the forward version.
2. Learn a new word in your native language or your second language every day. Visualize the new words that you have learned during this time span.

After the ten days or two weeks are completed, reflect on your learning ability and memory. Compare your learning on new tasks today with your learning in the past. Is it easier for you to study? Do you grasp the meaning of news stories more quickly? Can you remember telephone numbers or e-mail addresses more readily? If other classmates have done this exercise, ask them about their experiences. Have these exercises resulted in more brain power for them?

If these straightforward exercises really improve brain power, what are some of the implications for human relations?

Source: The core idea for the two games is credited to http://me.essortment.com/brainexercises_rcas.htm.

Applying Human Relations Exercise 15-2

Life Span Challenges Facing Seniors

The life span challenges described in this chapter that seniors face are certainly valid. Your role in this exercise is to find out directly what challenges advanced seniors face. We refer to people seventy years old and beyond. The older the people you can find for this study, the better. Conduct interviews with parents (if they qualify), grandparents, nursing home residents, friends, and neighbors. Obtain a sample of at least four people. Ask your interviewees about the challenges and problems they face now, those in the recent past, and those they anticipate in the future. After you have collected your interview data, answer these questions:

1. What are the physical and health problems facing these seniors?
2. What are the emotional and human relations problems facing these seniors?
3. What could other people do to help these seniors with some of their most pressing concerns?

Capitalizing on the Halo Effect

The halo effect can work to a person's advantage or disadvantage in terms of job finding and career advancement, depending on how a person is perceived. The class assignment is to investigate which characteristics or behaviors of a professional or future professional will help or hurt him or her. Each student in the class communicates with an experienced worker in speaking or writing to obtain answers to the following two questions:

1. Give me an example of a characteristic or action of a worker that would make you think he or she is either worthy of hiring or has good potential to advance in his or her career.
2. Give me an example of a characteristic or action of a worker that would make you think he or she is either not worthy of hiring or has limited potential to advance in his or her career.

Next, individual students enter their survey findings into a shared database or class Web site or e-mail their findings to all other students. After looking through all the results, reach a conclusion about positive and negative halos held by participants in the survey. For example, two results might be (1) "It looks like having good oral communication skills creates a positive halo" and (2) "It looks like being rude creates a negative halo."

After students have reached their conclusions, a brief class discussion is held about frequent reasons for creating a positive or negative halo and how useful this information might be.

Human Relations Case Study 15-1

Julie's Bad Habit

Julie works as a market research analyst at a large business communications firm, a position she has held for close to one year. Her primary responsibility is to conduct research via the Internet on a variety of topics. Sometimes her research assignments are to provide information to be used in an advertising or public relations campaign conducted by her employer. At other times, she conducts research needed by a client instead of tracking down information to be used for an advertising or public relations campaign.

Julie's recent Internet researches have included finding answers to the following: (a) What percent of subcompact cars are bought by Latinos? (b) How much per year do people under thirty spend on vitamins and food supplements? (c) How many people sixty-five and over purchase single-use cameras?

Julie's boss is satisfied with most of the results of Julie's Internet research but not with her speed. Julie has explained her predicament to her manager in these terms:

I'm sorry that I don't get my Internet researches done faster. My problem is that I've developed some bad habits that have become part of how I work. About every ten minutes I check my e-mail. And on days the stock exchange is open, I check how the market is doing about every fifteen minutes. About six times a day I check to see if I have a LinkedIn message. Also, I sometimes take a quick peek at my cell phone to see if anybody has left me a Tweet.

My habit is that I check my e-mail, the stock market results, LinkedIn, or Twitter right after I've accomplished something, like having found a Web site that seems to have the information I need. When I do not to check my e-mail or the Web sites, I become so nervous that I cannot concentrate on my work. But I don't go outside for a cigarette like some of my coworkers do.

One more than one occasion, Julie's boss has explained to her that if she can't break her bad habit, she will have to find another job.

Questions

1. What do you recommend Julie do to break her "bad habit"?

2. What might Julie's manager do to help her get her Internet research accomplished more quickly?

3. How might Julie continue with her checking habit yet still get her work accomplished on time?

Human Relations Role-Playing Exercise

Julie's Boss Attempts to Break Her Bad Habit

The case study about Julie serves as the background and the story line for this role-play. One person plays the role of Julie, who feels that if she does not break, or lessen, her habit of checking her e-mail and Internet sites, she could lose her job. Her boss, Kim, will be visiting her cubicle right after lunch to see is she can help Julie.

Another person plays the role of Kim, who wants to help Julie but also recognizes that research has to get accomplished quickly to be most useful to the firm. Kim is not very sympathetic toward the idea that a bad habit is a valid excuse for not getting work accomplished on time. Kim attended parochial school, where the teachers were quite strict about students paying full attention to their work. She remembers clearly how laptop computers and cell phones were not allowed in the classroom unless they were needed for a class assignment.

Observers rate the role-players on two dimensions, using a 1 to 5 scale from very poor to very good. One dimension is "effective use of human relations techniques." For Kim, focus on how effective she is in helping Julie correct her bad habit. The second dimension is "acting ability." A few observers might voluntarily provide feedback to the role-players in terms of sharing their ratings and observations. The course instructor might also provide feedback.

"I Know I Can Make a Contribution Somewhere"

Brad Martinez, age forty-three, is a senior account manager for Western Office Supply, a company that sells a wide range of products to business firms, hospitals, and schools. Western does not manufacture any products of its own but resells the products of several hundred manufacturers, much like being a department store for other firms. His company typically sells supplies in much larger quantities than sold by giant office-supply stores such as Staples and OfficeMax. Western also sells office furniture and decorations, such as lamps and wall hangings.

Although Brad's job title is account manager, he is essentially an outside sales representative who reports to the sales manager of Western Office Supply. Brad personally calls on about fifty established accounts and solicits new business regularly. After Brad opens an account, replacement sales for smaller items are usually made through the company Web site or telephone. However, he periodically makes in-person visits and telephone solicitations to sell office equipment such as small photocopiers, desktop computers, printers, fax machines, and office telephones.

After graduating from a career school with a major in business administration with a marketing concentration, Brad thought he would explore the world before settling on a career. He joined the U.S. Army and worked in the medical service field as a medic in several Army hospitals. Because Brad was not in the service during armed combat, he assisted in treating injuries and injuries to dependents of Army personnel. Brad served admirably in the Army and worked his way up to the rank of sergeant.

In Brad's words, "I left the Army proud of my service but looking for a more promising career. No matter how much the Army liked me, they weren't going to make me the Surgeon General. I thought it was time to get started in the business field."

After the Army, Brad worked six years in the purchasing department at a machine-tool company, working his way up to a position as purchasing supervisor. After that he joined Western as a sales trainee and progressed up to his present position.

During the past several years, Brad's sales commissions have begun to decline. One problem he has faced is that many of his customers are now purchasing their supplies directly from both distributors and manufacturers over the Internet. Another problem is Western's own e-commerce initiative. Brad and the other sales representatives receive a very small commission when a new customer makes an Internet purchase or an established customer orders more supplies.

Brad has recently become discouraged with the diminishing direct people contact in his work. As he explains, "Three times during the past month I have been turned down by purchasing agents or business owners when I asked them out to lunch. Until a few years ago, I made some of my largest sales during lunch. I'm hearing more now that my customers simply want to buy over the Internet. I guess they would rather sit at the keyboard eating yogurt for lunch than discuss business in a restaurant.

"The phone has become a major headache for me also. Instead of talking to a manager or a purchasing agent, I have to conduct my business with a voice mail message. A woman told me outright the other day that when she wanted to order something from Western, she would use our Web site. She told me that phone conversations take up too much of her time."

During the past six-month period, Brad's commissions declined 45 percent from the previous six months. For Brad, this was the last straw. He decided to change careers, as soon as he could figure out what else he could do to earn the same kind of living he did previously. For three consecutive years, Brad had even earned a six-figure income.

One Saturday morning Brad was looking at the job search site Monster.com. He murmured to himself, "Let's see, Brad. The world no longer needs a good sales rep with a personal touch. You have no more talent with the computer than most nineteen-year-olds. Being an astronaut is out because you get motion sickness. The NFL doesn't want any 43-year-old quarterbacks without experience. My few years as an Army medic don't qualify me to be the chief of surgery at the Mayo Clinic.

"Oops, here's an opening for a chief financial officer for a $50-million-dollar company, but they do want experience as a controller. Here's another one I like, an international marketing specialist. Except that the successful candidate must speak English, Spanish, and Italian. All I have is English, and about twenty words of Spanish I know from listening to salsa music.

"Maybe, I should start by updating my résumé. I know I can make a contribution somewhere, but I'm not sure where to start."

Questions

1. To what extent do you think Brad Martinez really needs a career switch?

2. What approach should Brad take to finding a new career?

3. What improvements do you think Brad needs to make in his attitude before he gets down to the serious business of finding a new career?

4. What criticisms do you have of Brad's career direction so far?

REFERENCES

1. Excerpted from Joann S. Lublin, "One Man's Switch from Factory Floor to a New Desk Job," *Wall Street Journal*, April 1, 2008, p. B1.

2. John W. Donahoe and David C. Palmer, *Learning and Complex Behavior* (Boston: Allyn & Bacon, 1994), p. 2.

3. Research reported in Charles Duhigg, "Warning: Habits May Be Good for You," *New York Times* (www.nytimes.com), July 13, 2008, p. 3.

4. Nancy Day, "Informal Learning Gets Results," *Workforce*, June 1998, p. 31.

5. Michael A. Stadler and Peter A. Frensch, eds., *Handbook of Implicit Learning* (Thousand Oaks, CA: Sage, 1998).

6. Karen Frankola, "Why Online Learners Drop Out," *Workforce*, October 2001, p. 54.

7. "Assessing Online Learning: Defining the Efficacy of Online Learning," *Keying In*, March 2001, p. 3.

8. "The Business Value of E-Learning," *Elearning!* (www.2elearning.com), December 18, 2007.

9. Nic Paton, "E-Learning Is a Boring Distraction," *Management Issues* (www.management-issues.com), December 5, 2007.

10. Joe Mullich, "A Second Act for E-Learning," *Workforce Management*, February 2004, p. 52.

11. Jeanne M. Wilson, Paul S. Goodman, and Matthew A. Cronin, "Group Learning." *Academy of Management Review*, October 2007, pp. 1041–1059.

12. Wanda L. Stitt-Gohdes, "Chapter 1—Teaching and Learning Styles: Implications for Business Teacher Education," in *The Twenty-First Century: Meeting the Challenges to Business Education* (Reston, VA: National Business Education Association, 1999), p. 10.

13. "Learning Styles." Retrieved April 13, 2009, from: http://www.nwlink.com/~donclark/hrd/styles.html, pp. 4–6.

14. Isabel Briggs Myers, *Introduction to Type,* 6th ed. (Mountain View, CA: CPP, Inc., 1998), p. 10. (Revised by Linda K. Kirby and Katharine D. Myers.)

15. John Patrick Golden, *Golden Personality Type Profiler Technical Manual* (San Antonio, TX: Pearson TalentLens, 2005).

16. Golden, *Golden Personality Type Profiler,* p. 27.

17. Golden, *Golden Personality Type Profiler,* p. 24.

18. The quote and the content in this section are from Mark Greer, "Strengthen Your Brain by Resting It," *Monitor on Psychology*, July/August 2004, p. 60.

19. Ricky W. Griffin, "Effects of Work Redesign on Employee Perceptions, Attitudes, and Behavior: A Long-Term Investigation," *Academy of Management Journal*, June 1991, p. 42.

20. Erik H. Erikson, *Childhood and Society* (New York: Norton, 1963); Child Development Institute, "Stages of Social-Emotional Development In Children and Teenagers." Retrieved May 6, 2006, from: www.childdevelpmentinfo.com.

21. Our discussion of the challenges of adolescence and adulthood follows closely Saul Kassin, *Psychology*, 3rd ed. (Upper Saddle River, NJ: Prentice Hall, 2001), pp. 406–440; and Charles G. Morris and Albert A. Maisto, *Psychology: An Introduction*, 11th ed. (Upper Saddle River, NJ: Prentice Hall, 2002), pp. 418–441.

22. Lawrence Kohlberg, *Essays on Moral Development: Vol. 2. The Psychology of Moral Development* (New York: Harper & Row, 1984).

23. Debra Bradley Ruder, "A Work in Progress: The Teen Brain," *Harvard Magazine* (http://harvardmagazine.com/2008/09/the-teen-brain.html); "Teaching the At-Risk Teenage Brain," *ASCD Inservice* (http://ascd.typepad.com/blog/2009/03/teaching-the-atrisk-teenage-brain-.html).

24. Sara Goudarzi, "Study: Teenage Brain Lacks Empathy: Area of Brain Associated with Higher-Level Thinking Underused in Youths," *LiveScience*, September 8, 2006 (www.msnbc.msn.com/id/14738243).

25. Sheri Stritof and Bob Stritof, "Sandwich Generation: The Cluttered Nest Syndrome." Retrieved April 7, 2009, from: www.about.com.marriage.

26. "Not Ready for Prime Time: The Needs of Sandwich Generation Women, A National Survey of Social Workers & a Window into the Lives of Sandwich Generation Women, an Online Journaling Project," HelpStartsHere.org, March 2008.

27. Stritof and Stritof, "Sandwich Generation."

28. Melinda Beck, "The Science Behind 'Senior Moments,'" *Wall Street Journal*, May 27, 2008.

29. Robert Lee Hotz, "Surveying the Brain for Origins of the Senior Moment," *Wall Street Journal*, December 2, 2008, p. A14.

30. Roderick Gilkey and Clint Kilts, "Cognitive Fitness," *Harvard Business Review*, November 2007, pp. 53–66.

31. Research from the *New England Journal of Medicine* summarized in Sharon Begley, "Oops! Mental Training, Crosswords Fail to Slow Decline of Aging Brain," *Wall Street Journal*, April 21, 2006, p. B1; Begley, "Studies on Dementia Often Confuse Causes with Consequences," *Wall Street Journal*, April 28, 2006, p. B1.

32. Research summarized in Karen Kersting, "Happiness in Men Usually Drops after Age 65, Study Finds," *Monitor on Psychology*, March 2005, p. 10.

33. Brian Scott Ehrlich and Derek Isaacowitz, "Does Subjective Well-Being Increase with Age?" *Perspectives in Psychology*, Spring 2002, pp. 20–26.

34. Kassin, *Psychology*, p. 435.

35. Michael Drafke, *The Human Side of Organizations*, 9th ed. (Upper Saddle River, NJ: Pearson Prentice Hall, 2006), p. 335.

36. Randall S. Hansen, "Quintessential Careers: The 10-Step Plan to Career Change." Retrieved April 13, 2006, from: www.quintcareers.com.

37. Based on facts in Erin White, "Profession Changes Take Time but May Be Worth Wait," *Wall Street Journal*, November 27, 2007, p. B6.

38. Sarah E. Needleman, "New Career, Same Employer," *Wall Street Journal*, April 21, 2008, p. B9.

39. "The End of Entrepreneurship as We Know It?" *Entrepreneur*, September 2000, p. 18.

40. Angel Jennings, "Book Brings Penguins into Boardrooms," *New York Times* (www.nytimes.com), July 16, 2007.

41. The first two items noted are from Fred Pryor, "What Have You Learned from Change?" *Manager's Edge*, September 1998, p. 2.

42. Al Siebert, *The Resiliency Advantage* (San Francisco: Berrett-Koehler, 2005).

43. Thomas L. Friedman, *The World Is Flat: A Brief History of the Twenty-First Century* (New York: FSG, 2005).

44. Peter Svensson, "Hands-On Jobs May Be the Safest," Associated Press, July 4, 2004.

16

Developing Good Work Habits

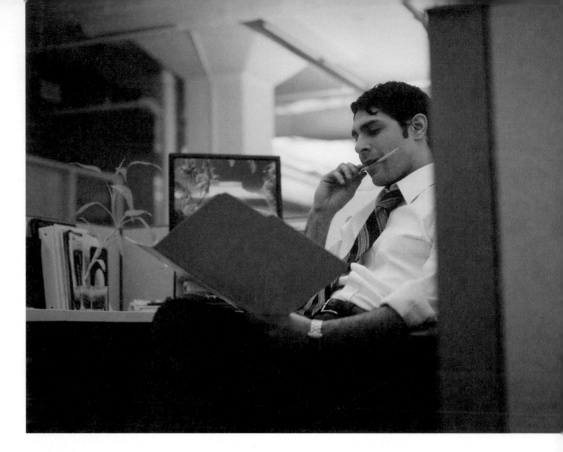

Outline

1 How Does a Person Deal with Procrastination?
Why People Procrastinate
Techniques for Reducing Procrastination

2 What Are Some Proper Attitudes and Values to Develop?
Develop a Mission, Goals, and a Strong Work Ethic
Value Good Attendance and Punctuality
Value Your Time
Value Neatness, Orderliness, and Speed
Work Smarter, Not Harder
Become Self-Employed Psychologically
Appreciate the Importance of Rest and Relaxation

3 What Are Some Effective Time-Management Techniques?
Clean Up and Get Organized
Plan Your Activities
Get off to a Good Start
Make Good Use of Office Technology
Concentrate on One Key Task at a Time
Streamline Your Work, and Emphasize Important Tasks
Work at a Steady Pace
Create Some Quiet, Uninterrupted Time
Make Use of Bits of Time, and Use Multitasking for Routine Work
Stay in Control of Paperwork, the Inbox, and E-mail

4 How Does One Overcome Time Wasters?
Minimize Daydreaming
Prepare a Time Log to Evaluate Your Use of Time
Avoid Unproductive Use of Computers
Keep Track of Important Names, Places, and Things
Set a Time Limit for Certain Tasks and Projects
Schedule Similar Tasks Together (Clustering)
Bounce Quickly from Task to Task

After studying the information and doing the exercises in this chapter, you should be able to:

1 Appreciate the importance of good work habits and time management.

2 Decrease any tendencies you might have toward procrastination.

3 Develop attitudes and values that will help you become more productive.

4 Develop skills and techniques that will help you become more productive.

5 Overcome time-wasting practices.

C omputer giant Intel is studying the importance of uninterrupted time for creative thinking. In a six-month project dubbed "Quiet Time," workers shut out all distractions and wait for a creative thought. Quiet Time happens each Tuesday at two U.S. sites. From 8 a.m. to noon, the 300 engineers and managers in the test group set email and instant messaging in the off-line mode, forward all calls to voice mail, and hang "do not disturb" signs at their cubicle entrances.

They're then free to do "thinking work," says Intel IT principal engineer Nathan Zeldes, the man behind the project. "These guys are designing products, so I would hope they'd devote it to that," he says. "Although I'm sure some of them are tempted to clean out their inboxes.

"Today's rapid flow and exchange of information, and the consequent tasks they impose, are overwhelming," notes a report co-authored by Zeldes. "The barrage of communication exacts a toll on workers' productivity, as well as on their personal well-being." It also costs a typical knowledge-intensive company of 50,000 employees an estimated US$1 billion each year. Intel employees receive about 350 emails a week (a third of which they deem unnecessary) and spend 20 hours managing them.[1]

The story about reserving quiet time for heavy thinking illustrates the importance companies place on individual productivity and concentrating on work with a big potential payoff. The story also illustrates how important it is to use office technology tools wisely instead of allowing them to interfere with accomplishing the major purpose of your job.

Work habits
a person's characteristic approach to work, including such things as organization, priority setting, and handling of paperwork and e-mail

Productivity
the amount of quality work accomplished in relation to the resources consumed

Because good work habits and time management (including concentrating carefully on a major task) improve productivity, they contribute to success in business. **Work habits** refer to a person's characteristic approach to work, including such things as organization, priority setting, and handling of e-mail and intranets. Good work habits and time management are more important than ever because of today's emphasis on **productivity,** which is the amount of quality work accomplished in relation to the resources consumed. On the job, being more productive often translates into eliminating unnecessary steps and finding ways to get more accomplished in less time.[2]

Also, because so many workers are expected to be productive without close supervision, including the telecommuter, good work habits increase in importance. Furthermore, a person is more likely to be fired from a job or flunk out of school because of poor work habits than because of poor aptitude.

People with good work habits tend to achieve higher career success and have more time to invest in their personal lives. They also enjoy their personal lives more because they are not preoccupied with unfinished tasks. Effective work habits are also beneficial because they eliminate a major stressor—the feeling of having very little or no control over your life. Being in control also leads to a relaxed, confident approach to work.

The goal of this chapter is to help you become a more productive person who is still flexible. Someone who develops good work habits is not someone who becomes so obsessed with time and is so rigid that he or she makes other people feel uncomfortable. Ideally, a person should be well organized yet still flexible.

Information about becoming more productive is organized here into four related categories. One is overcoming procrastination, a problem that plagues almost everybody to some extent. The second is developing attitudes and values that foster productivity. The third category is the lengthiest: developing skills and techniques that lead to personal productivity. The fourth category is overcoming time wasters.

▶ Learning Objective 1 ▶

How Does a Person Deal with Procrastination?

Procrastination
delaying a task for an invalid or weak reason

The leading cause of poor productivity and career self-sabotage is **procrastination**—delaying a task for an invalid or weak reason. Procrastination is also the major work habit problem for most workers and students. The presence of computers in the cubicle or office increases the risk of procrastination because it so easy to check e-mail or a favorite Web site just before starting almost any task. Unproductive people are the biggest procrastinators, but even productive people have problems with procrastination at times. A business owner who does not ordinarily procrastinate might delay preparing taxes, knowing that she was behind in her taxes.

WHY PEOPLE PROCRASTINATE

People procrastinate for many different reasons, as described in the following list.

1. **Unpleasant task or overwhelming task.** When we perceive the task to be done (such as quitting a job) as unpleasant, we tend to procrastinate. Similarly, we tend to procrastinate when we perceive the job facing us to be overwhelming, such as assembling a computer console that arrives in a large box. To avoid an overwhelming or taxing task, some people flood their workday with small, easy-to-do tasks. As a result, these people do not appear to be procrastinators on the surface.[3]

2. **Fear of consequences.** Another major cause of procrastination is a fear of the consequences of our actions. One possible negative consequence is a negative evaluation of your work. For example, if you delay preparing a report for your boss or instructor, that person cannot criticize its quality. Bad news is another negative consequence that procrastination can sometimes delay. If you think your smart phone may need to be replaced because it no longer works well, delaying a trip to the electronics store will avoid the verdict of "replacement needed."

3. **Fear of success.** Another reason some people procrastinate is the **fear of success.** People sometimes believe that if they succeed at an important task they will be asked to take on more responsibility in the future. They dread this possibility. Some students have been known to procrastinate completing their degree requirements to avoid taking on the responsibility of a full-time position.

4. **Lack of meaningful reward.** People frequently put off tasks that do not appear to offer a meaningful reward. Suppose you decide that your computer files need a thorough updating, including deleting inactive files. Even if you know this task should be done, the accomplishment of updated files might not be a particularly meaningful reward.

5. **Rebelling against control.** Many people procrastinate as a way of rebelling against being controlled. Procrastination, used in this way, is a means of defying unwarranted authority.[4] Rather than submit to authority, a person might tell himself, "Nobody is going to tell me when I should get a report done. I'll do it when I'm good and ready." Such people might be referred to as "anti-control freaks."

6. **Enjoying the rush.** A curious reason for procrastination is to achieve the stimulation and excitement that stems from rushing to meet a deadline.[5] Some people, for example, enjoy fighting their way through traffic or running through an airline terminal so they can make an appointment or airplane flight barely on time. They appear to enjoy the rush of adrenaline, endorphins, and other hormones associated with hurrying.

7. **Perfectionism.** Finally, some people procrastinate because they are perfectionists. They attempt to perfect a project before being willing to admit the project is completed. As a result, the person procrastinates not about beginning a project but about letting go. When asked, "Have you finished that project?" the perfectionist replies, "No, there a few small details that still need to be worked out." Being a perfectionist can also block starting new projects because the perfectionist will often want to keep working on the present project. The perfectionist is often hesitant to take on the risk of a new project because trying something new is likely to result in mistakes. Also, perfectionists like order, and a new task may not be so easy to organize.[6] Perfectionism comes in degrees, with slight perfectionists simply being extremely conscientious and heavy-duty perfectionists almost stalled in their actions. Human Relations Self-Assessment Quiz 16-1 gives you an opportunity to measure your degree of perfectionism.

> **Fear of success**
> belief that if one succeeds at an important task, one will be asked to take on more responsibility in the future; reason some people procrastinate

TECHNIQUES FOR REDUCING PROCRASTINATION

To overcome or at least minimize procrastination, we recommend a number of specific tactics. A general approach, however, is simply to be aware that procrastination is a major drain on productivity. Being aware of the problem will remind you to take corrective action in many situations. When your accomplishment level is low, you might ask yourself, "Am I procrastinating on anything of significance?"

Calculate the cost of procrastination. You can reduce procrastination by calculating its cost.[7] One example is that you might lose out on obtaining a high-paying

Human Relations Self-Assessment Quiz   16-1

Tendencies toward Perfectionism

Many perfectionists hold some of the following behaviors and attitudes. To help understand your tendencies toward perfectionism, rate how strongly you agree with each of the statements below on a scale of 0 to 4: 0 = disagree strongly; 1 = disagree; 2 = neutral; 3 = agree; 4 = strongly agree.

1. Many people have told me that I am a perfectionist.	0	1	2	3	4
2. I often correct the speech of others.	0	1	2	3	4
3. It takes me a long time to write an e-mail because I keep checking and rechecking my writing.	0	1	2	3	4
4. I often criticize the color combinations my friends are wearing.	0	1	2	3	4
5. When I purchase food at a supermarket, I usually look at the expiration date so I can purchase the freshest.	0	1	2	3	4
6. I can't stand when people use the term *remote* instead of *remote control*.	0	1	2	3	4
7. If a company representative asked me, "What is your *social*?" I would reply something like, "Do you mean my *Social Security number*?"	0	1	2	3	4
8. Neatness is very important to me.	0	1	2	3	4
9. I like the Martha Stewart idea of having every decoration in the home just right.	0	1	2	3	4
10. I never put a map back in the glove compartment until it is folded just right.	0	1	2	3	4
11. Once an eraser on a pencil of mine becomes hard and useless, I throw the pencil away.	0	1	2	3	4
12. I adjust all my watches and clocks so they show exactly the same time.	0	1	2	3	4
13. It bothers me that all the clocks at an athletic club or college sometimes do not have the same exact time.	0	1	2	3	4
14. I clean the keyboard on my computer at least once a week.	0	1	2	3	4
15. I organize my e-mail messages and computer documents into many different, clearly labeled files.	0	1	2	3	4
16. You won't find old coffee cups or soft-drink containers on my desk.	0	1	2	3	4
17. I rarely start a new project or assignment until I have completed my present project or assignment.	0	1	2	3	4
18. It is very difficult for me to concentrate when my work area is disorganized.	0	1	2	3	4
19. Cobwebs in chandeliers and other lighting fixtures bug me.	0	1	2	3	4
20. It takes me a long time to make a purchase such as a digital camera because I keep studying the features on various models.	0	1	2	3	4
21. When I balance my checkbook, it usually comes out right within a few dollars.	0	1	2	3	4
22. I carry enough small coins and dollar bills with me so when I shop I can pay the exact amount without requiring change.	0	1	2	3	4
23. I throw out any underwear or T-shirts that have even the smallest holes or tears.	0	1	2	3	4
24. I become upset with myself if I make a mistake.	0	1	2	3	4
25. When a fingernail of mine is broken or chipped, I fix it as soon as possible.	0	1	2	3	4
26. I am carefully groomed whenever I leave my home.	0	1	2	3	4
27. When I notice packaged goods or cans on the floor in a supermarket, I will often place them back on the shelf.	0	1	2	3	4
28. I think that carrying around antibacterial cleaner for the hands is an excellent idea.	0	1	2	3	4
29. If I am with a friend, and he or she has a loose hair on the shoulder, I will remove it without asking.	0	1	2	3	4
30. I know that I am a perfectionist.	0	1	2	3	4

Scoring and Interpretation

91 or over You have strong perfectionist tendencies to the point that it could interfere with your taking quick action when necessary. Also, you may annoy many people with your perfectionism.

61–90 Moderate degree of perfectionism that could lead you to produce high-quality work and be a dependable person.

31–60 Mild degree of perfectionism. You might be a perfectionist in some situations quite important to you but not in others.

0–30 Not a perfectionist. You might be too casual about getting things done right, meeting deadlines, and being aware of details.

job you really want by not having your résumé and cover letter ready on time. Your cost of procrastination would include the difference in salary between the job you do find and the one you really wanted. Another cost would be the loss of potential job satisfaction.

Counterattack. Forcing yourself to do something overwhelming, frightening, or uncomfortable helps to prove that the task was not as bad as initially perceived. Assume that you have accepted a new position but have not yet resigned from your present one because resigning seems so uncomfortable. Set up a specific time to call your manager or send an e-mail to schedule an appointment. Force yourself further to show up for the resignation appointment. After you break the ice with the statement "I have something important to tell you," the task will be much easier.

Jump-start yourself. You can often get momentum going on a project by giving yourself a tiny assignment simply to get started. One way to get momentum going on an unpleasant or overwhelming task is to set aside a specific time to work on it. If you have to write a report on a subject you dislike, you might set aside Saturday from 3 p.m. to 4 p.m. as your time to first attack the project. If your procrastination problem is particularly intense, giving yourself even a five-minute task, such as starting a new file, might help you gain momentum. After five minutes, decide if you choose to continue for another five minutes. The five-minute chunks will help you focus your energy.

Peck away at an overwhelming task. Assume that you have a major project to do that does not have to be accomplished in a hurry. A good way of minimizing procrastination is to peck away at the project in fifteen- to thirty-minute bits of time. Bit by bit, the project will get down to manageable size and therefore not seem so overwhelming. A related way of pecking away at an overwhelming task is to subdivide it into smaller units. For instance, you might break down moving into a series of tasks, such as filing change-of-address notices, locating a mover, and packaging books. Pecking away can sometimes be achieved by setting aside as little as five minutes to work on a seemingly overwhelming task. When the five minutes are up, either work five more minutes on the task or reschedule the activity for sometime soon.

Motivate yourself with rewards and punishments. Give yourself a pleasant reward soon after you accomplish a task about which you would ordinarily procrastinate. You might, for example, jog through the woods after having completed a tough take-home exam. The second part of this tactic is to punish yourself if you have engaged in serious procrastination. How about not visiting your favorite social networking site for one week?

Follow the WIFO principle. Personal effectiveness coach Shale Paul recommends that you use the technique of **worst in, first out (WIFO)** for dealing with unpleasant tasks you would prefer to avoid. After you finally get the task done, Paul says, "Chances are, you'll find that you spent nearly as much time worrying and rescheduling it as you did actually doing it." If the task fits high enough on your priorities, simply get it done and out of the way.[8] A related motivational principle is that after completing the unpleasant task, moving on to a more pleasant (or less unpleasant) task functions as a reward.

Worst in, first out (WIFO)
dealing first with unpleasant tasks you would prefer to avoid; simply getting them done and out of the way

Make a commitment to other people. Put pressure on yourself to get something done on time by making it a commitment to one or more other people. You might announce to coworkers that you are going to get a project of mutual concern completed by a certain date. If you fail to meet this date, you may feel embarrassed.

Express a more positive attitude about your intentions. Expressing a more positive attitude can often lead to changes in behavior. If you choose words that express a serious intention to complete an activity, you are more likely to follow through than if you choose more uncertain words. Imagine that a coworker says, "I *might* get you the information you need by next Friday." You probably will not be surprised if you do not receive the information by Friday. In contrast, if your coworker says, "I *will* get you the information you need by next Friday," there is less likelihood the person will procrastinate. Psychologist Linda Sapadin believes that you are less likely to procrastinate if you change your "wish" to "will," your "like to" to "try to," and your "have to" to "want to."[9]

▶ Learning Objective 2 ▶

What Are Some Proper Attitudes and Values to Develop?

> "Effective time management has become an urgent priority for both workplace performance and personal sanity."
>
> —Fran Finn, organizational productivity expert, quoted in *Executive Focus*, February 2009, p. 17.

Developing good work habits and time-management practices is often a matter of developing proper attitudes toward work and time. For instance, if you think that your job is important and that time is valuable, you will be on your way toward developing good work habits. In this section we describe a group of attitudes and values that can help improve your productivity through better use of time and improved work habits.

DEVELOP A MISSION, GOALS, AND A STRONG WORK ETHIC

A mission, or general purpose in life, propels you toward being productive. Assume that a person says, "My mission is to become an outstanding professional in my career and a loving, constructive parent." The mission serves as a compass to direct your activities, such as being well organized in order to attain a favorable performance appraisal.

Goals to Support Mission Statement

Goals are more specific than a mission statement. The goals support the mission statement, but the effect is the same. Being committed to a goal also propels you toward good use of time. Imagine how efficient most employees would be if they were told, "Here is five days of work facing you. If you get finished in less than five days without sacrificing quality, you can have that time to yourself." If the saved time fit your mission, such as having more quality time with family members, the impact would be even stronger.

Stephen Covey, a popularizer of time-management techniques, expresses the importance of a mission of goals in his phrase, "Begin with the end in mind." He recommends you develop your mission statement by first thinking about what people who know you well would say at your funeral if you died three years from now. Also, list your various roles in life, such as spouse, child, family member, professional, and soccer player. For each role, think of one or two major lifetime goals you have in that area. Then develop a brief mission statement describing your life's purpose that incorporates these goals.[10]

A person might have the mission of becoming an outstanding professional person. Your goals to support that mission might include achieving advanced certification in your field, becoming an officer in a professional organization, and making large donations to charity. When you are deciding how to spend your time each day, give goals related to your mission top priority.

Work Ethic Contribution

Closely related to establishing a mission and goals is developing a strong work ethic. Developing a strong work ethic may lead to even higher productivity than goal setting alone. For example, one might set the goal of earning a high income. It might lead to some good work habits but not necessarily a high commitment to quality.

VALUE GOOD ATTENDANCE AND PUNCTUALITY

On the job, in school, or in personal life, good attendance and punctuality are essential for developing a good reputation. Also, you cannot contribute to a team effort unless you are present. Poor attendance and consistent lateness are the most frequent reasons for employee discipline. Furthermore, many managers interpret high absenteeism and lateness as signs of emotional immaturity. An important myth about attendance and punctuality—that a certain number of sick days are owed an employee—should be challenged early in a person's career. Some employees who have not used up their sick days will find reasons to be sick at the end of the year.

The causes of chronic lateness follow those of the causes of procrastination. Time management specialist Diane DeLonzor says that the motivations are often unconscious, related to personality characteristics such as lack of self-control and a desire for thrill seeking. Some people are drawn to the adrenaline rush of that last-minute sprint to the meeting (or class), while others receive an ego boost from overscheduling and filling each moment with activity. Trying to get one more thing done before leaving for an appointment will often lead to being late. Keeping a time log (as described later in the chapter) can help control lateness because the result can be a more accurate estimation of the amount of time necessary to complete various activities. For example, if it takes a person forty-five minutes to commute to work, he or she must leave the residence about fifty-five minutes before an important meeting.[11]

VALUE YOUR TIME

People who place a high value on their time are propelled into making good use of time. If a person believes that his or her time is valuable, it will be difficult to engage that person in idle conversation during working hours. Valuing your time can also apply to personal life. The yield from clipping or gathering grocery coupons is an average of $9 per hour—assuming that purchasing national brands is important to you. Would a busy professional person, therefore, be better off clipping and gathering coupons or engaging in self-development for the same amount of time? Being committed to a mission and goals is an automatic way of making good use of time.

VALUE NEATNESS, ORDERLINESS, AND SPEED

Neatness, orderliness, and speed are important contributors to workplace productivity and therefore should be valued. An orderly desk or work area does not inevitably signify an orderly mind. Yet orderliness does help most people become more productive. Less time is wasted and less energy is expended if you do not have to hunt for missing information. Knowing where information is and what information you have available is a way of being in control of your job. When your job gets out of control, you are probably working at less than peak efficiency. Being neat and orderly helps you achieve good performance. Frequently breaking your concentration for such matters as finding an e-mail message you printed a month ago inhibits high performance.

Neatness is linked to working rapidly because clutter and searching for misplaced items consume time. Employers emphasize speed today to remain competitive in such matters as serving customers promptly and bringing new products and services to the market. Speed is widely considered a competitive advantage, as in getting a product to market faster than others or delivering take-out lunches on time.

The best approach to maintaining a neat work area and to enhance speed is to convince yourself that neatness and speed are valuable. You will then search for ways to be neat and fast, such as putting back a reference book immediately after use or making phone conversations brief. The underlying principle is that an attitude leads to a change in behavior.

Although neatness and orderliness are usually an effective approach to accomplishing work, at times a little disorder can be beneficial. According to Eric Abrahamson and David H. Freedman, co-authors of *A Perfect Mess*, neatness has some disadvantages. A major disadvantage of being a *neat freak* is that so much time is spent on keeping a desk clutter-free that it takes time away from major activities such as dealing with customers or clients. Also, to get things done you may wind up making a mess, such as in painting or redecorating your work area. According to Abrahamson and Freedman, "Moderately disorganized people, institutions, and people turn out to be more efficient, more resilient, more creative, and in general more effective than highly organized ones.[12]

Keep in mind also that Albert Einstein had a messy work area, as do many successful scientists and professors.

WORK SMARTER, NOT HARDER

People caught up in trying to accomplish a job often wind up working hard but not in an imaginative way that leads to good results. Much time and energy, therefore, are wasted. A working-smart approach also requires that you spend a few minutes carefully planning how to implement your task. An example of working smarter, not harder, is to invest a few minutes of critical thinking before launching an Internet search. Think through carefully what might be the keywords that will lead you to the information you need. In this way, you will minimize conducting your search with words and phrases that will lead to irrelevant information. For example, suppose you want to conduct research on back-stabbing as negative office politics. If you simply use the term "back-stabbing," the search engine will direct you to such topics as street crime and medical treatment for wounds. Working smarter is to try "back-stabbing in the office" or "backstabbing and office politics."

An advanced approach to working smarter is to avoid doing work that is already being accomplished in another part of the organization by using information technology designed to foster collaboration. Some programs make it easier to find out what coworkers in other parts of a far-flung company are working on, thus avoiding duplication. Company blogs can also be helpful in identifying other workers who are engaged in a similar project. For example, you might be mining data attempting to discover which customers are likely to buy a variety of products from your employer.[13] A blog might tell you that Sally in Madison, Wisconsin, is working on the same project. If you then collaborate, you will save lots of time—and work smarter.

BECOME SELF-EMPLOYED PSYCHOLOGICALLY

A distinguishing characteristic of most self-employed people is that they care deeply about what they accomplish each day. Most of their job activities directly or indirectly affect their financial health. Additionally, many self-employed people enjoy high job satisfaction because they have chosen work that fits their interests. Because of the factors previously mentioned, the self-employed person is compelled to make good use of time.

If a person working for an employer regards his or her area of responsibility as self-employment, productivity may increase. To help regard employment by others as self-employment, keep this thought in mind. Every employee is given some assets to manage to achieve a good return on investment. If you managed the cafeteria for your company, you would be expected to manage that asset profitably.

APPRECIATE THE IMPORTANCE OF REST AND RELAXATION

A productive attitude to maintain is that overwork can be counterproductive and lead to negative stress and burnout. Proper physical rest contributes to mental alertness and improved ability to cope with frustration. Greg Belenky, the director of the Sleep and Performance Research Center at Washington State University says, "Even mild sleep loss, losing forty minutes a day for five to seven days, will degrade performance over time."[14]

Constant attention to work or study is often inefficient. It is a normal human requirement to take enough breaks to allow yourself to approach work or study with a fresh perspective. Napping during the day has gained in popularity as productivity booster. Workers who have private offices might nap under the desk, while cubicle dwellers often nap with their head on the desk. Each person has to establish the right balance between work and leisure within the bounds of freedom granted by the situation.

Neglecting the normal need for rest and relaxation can lead to **workaholism,** an addiction to work in which *not* working is an uncomfortable experience. (In some cases, therefore, workaholism leads the neglect of rest and relaxation.) Some types of workaholics are perfectionists who are never satisfied with their work and therefore find it difficult to leave work behind. Career counselor Janet Salyer notes, "Workaholics put the job before family, friends, and their own health. And even if they're spending time with their families, their minds are on work."[15] In addition, the workaholic who is a perfectionist may become heavily focused on control, leading to rigid behavior.

However, some people who work long and hard are classified as happy workaholics who thrive on hard work and are usually highly productive. As executives, they encourage others to work hard to achieve company goals and also pursue what matters to them in their personal lives.[16] Furthermore, many people who work long and hard to be successful in their careers also intensely enjoy other activities. Warren Buffet, the legendary investor who is one of the world's richest people, carries an enormous workload, although he is more than eighty years old. But he is also a fanatic about bridge and regularly interrupts his workday to play bridge on the computer.

Workaholism
neglecting the normal need for rest and relaxation that can lead to an addiction to work in which not working is an uncomfortable experience

What Are Some Effective Time-Management Techniques?

◀ Learning Objective 3 ◀

So far we have discussed improving productivity from the standpoints of dealing with procrastination and developing the right attitudes and values. Skills and techniques also contribute substantially to becoming more productive. Here we describe some well-established methods of work habit improvement along with several new ones. For these techniques to enhance productivity, most of them need to be incorporated into and practiced regularly in our daily lives. This is particularly true because many of these techniques are habits, and habits have to be programmed into the brain through repetition.

CLEAN UP AND GET ORGANIZED

An excellent starting point for improving work habits and time management is to clean up the work area and arrange things neatly. The starting point in the popular system of work habits and time management developed by David Allen is to unclutter your life. You begin by collecting everything you must do, or hope to do, or that is unfinished or undecided.[17] You are likely to find that many of these tasks can be thrown out right away. An example would be a throwing out an expired discount coupon from an office supply store.

Eliminate clutter by throwing out unnecessary paper and deleting computer files that will probably never be used again. The idea is to learn to simplify the work area so that there are fewer distractions and the brain can be more focused. In addition, finding important files becomes easier. Designate a specific time, such as one Saturday morning, for cleaning up your work area and getting rid of files that will not be needed again.

Desktop search software such as Google's Desktop Search or Apple's Spotlight can help you find many missing documents. But there is still a productivity advantage to having fewer obsolete documents and files in your computer, including a desktop with dozens of icons with similar-sounding names. Conducting an electronic search to find your expense report is one more task on your to-do list.

Getting organized includes sorting out which tasks need doing, including assignments and projects not yet completed. Getting organized can also mean sorting through the many small paper notes attached to the computer and on the wall. A major cleanup principle is therefore to discard anything that is no longer valuable. A suggestion worth considering is to throw out at least one item every day from the office and home—even if the item thrown out is as humble as a empty ballpoint pen. Because new items come into the office and home almost daily, you will always have possessions left.

PLAN YOUR ACTIVITIES

Planning

primary principle of effective time management; deciding what to accomplish and the actions needed to make it happen

The primary principle of effective time management is **planning**—deciding what you want to accomplish and the actions needed to make it happen. The most elementary—and the most important—planning tool is a list of tasks that need doing. Almost every successful person works from a to-do list. These lists are essentially daily goals. Before you can compose a useful list, you need to set aside a few moments each day to sort out the tasks at hand. A good starting point in using to-do lists is to prepare such a list on Sunday for the rest of the week. The list can then be modified on Monday through Saturday. A list used by a working parent is presented in Figure 16-1.

Where do you put your to-do lists? Many people dislike having small to-do lists stuck in different places. One reason is that these lists are readily lost among other papers. Many people, therefore, put lists on desk calendars or printed forms called *planners*, which are also available for computers. Planners give you an opportunity to record your activities in intervals as small as fifteen minutes. Day-Timer Planner Pads include the categories of weekly lists of activities by category, daily things to do, appointments, notes/calls, and expenses. Many people place their to-do list in an appropriate place on their desktop computer or personal digital assistant. Keep in mind that several information technology experts rely heavily on index cards to plan their lives.[18]

Another useful approach for organizing your lists is to use a notebook small enough to be portable. The notebook becomes your master list to keep track of work tasks, errands, social engagements, and shopping items. Anything else requiring action might also be recorded—even a reminder to clean up the work

FIGURE 16-1

A SAMPLE TO-DO LIST

Job

> Make 10 calls to prospects for new listings.
>
> Have "For Sale" signs put outside Hanover Blvd. house.
>
> Set up mortgage appointment at 1st Federal for the Calhouns.
>
> Update Web site listings.
>
> Upgrade antivirus software.
>
> Check for possible sales leads on Facebook, LinkedIn, and Twitter.
>
> Meet with the Guptas at 5 p.m.
>
> Set up time to show house to the Bowens.

Home

> Buy running shoes for Todd.
>
> Buy jeans for Linda.
>
> Get icemaker fixed on refrigerator.
>
> Write and send out monthly bills.
>
> Clip cat's nails.
>
> Check out problem with hot-water tank.
>
> Make appointment with dentist to have chipped filling replaced.
>
> Check Twitter and send out at least ten Tweets this evening.

FIRST REALTY CORPORATION

Jacksonville, Florida

jbartow@firstrealty.com

area again. Some people have such clear focus that they register their to-do lists in their brain, thereby skipping paper or a computer.

No matter where you place your to-do list, its usefulness diminishes if the list is not consulted regularly, perhaps twice per day.

How do you set priorities? Faced with multiple tasks to do at the same time, it is possible to feel overwhelmed and freeze as a result. The time-tested solution is to establish a priority to each item on the to-do list. A typical system is to use A to signify critical or essential items, B to signify important items, and C for the least important ones. Although an item might be regarded as a C (for example, refilling your stapler), it still has a contribution to make to your productivity and sense of well-being. Many people obtain a sense of satisfaction from crossing an item, however trivial, off their list. Furthermore, if you are conscientious, small undone items will interfere with concentration.

To effectively set priorities, you have to recognize which tasks are critical or important. In general, those activities that deal directly with the major purposes of your job are critical, such as dealing with a major customer or completing your portion of a budget. Tasks your manager perceives to be urgent should also be classified as critical tasks. Emergency items, such as dealing with the effects of a tornado or a product recall, are also essential tasks.

How do you plan when you have to interact with people from different time zones? The globalization of business has created challenges in planning work with people in other time zones. Even within the United States there are four time zones in the contiguous United States plus different time zones for Alaska and Hawaii. (And add the Atlantic time zone for Canada.) One way to take time zone differences into account is to consult the international calling section of the phone book and then calculate. For example, when you are in Chicago it is seven hours later in Italy, and fifteen hours later in Japan. So if your work associate in Italy wants to speak to you at 8:30 a.m. her time, phone her at 1:30 a.m. your time. Or, to speak to your Japanese work associate at 8:30 a.m. his time, make the call at 6:30 p.m. your time. Your understanding of time-zone differences can also be used to send work via the Internet so it arrives by a particular time for a work associate.

If you prefer to avoid the calculations, consult a time zone converter such as www.timeanddate.com. These sites will also help you choose a reasonable time for a phone call between two different time zones, or a conference call or videoconference that involves people from several different countries. In general, if the meeting is held often, people from different time zones will have to take turns being inconvenienced.

How do you schedule and follow through? To be effective, a to-do list must be an action tool. To convert your list into action, prepare a schedule of when you are going to do each of the items on the list. Follow through by doing things according to your schedule, checking them off as you go along.

Time-and-activity charts (also referred to as Gantt charts) have been used in factories and offices for over a hundred years to keep track of projects. Many people find these basic charts useful in scheduling their own activities and keeping track of progress. Time-and-activity charts also reinforce the reality that much of work is calendar driven. A calendar anticipates all the dates, deadlines, and seasons essential to running a successful business firm.[19] For example, many customers want shipments by a particular date, and bills are due at a specific time. Figure 16-2 presents a time-and-activity chart you might want to use as a personal productivity booster.

FIGURE 16-2

A TIME-AND-ACTIVITY CHART FOR SCHEDULING ACTIVITIES

Charting key tasks and their deadlines, along with your performance on the task, can often get you focused and organized.

Deadlines for Task Accomplishment

Task to Be Accomplished	Feb. 1	Feb. 28	Mar. 15	Mar. 31	Apr. 15	Apr. 30
Expense reports	Did it					
Antivirus treatment for PC		Two days late				
Web site updated			Blew it			
Plan office party				Did it		
File federal tax report					In the mail at midnight ☺ ☺	
Provide input to department budget						On time

GET OFF TO A GOOD START

Get off to a good beginning, and you are more likely to have a successful, productive day. Start poorly, and you will be behind most of the day. According to time management specialist Douglass Merrill, people who get going early tend to be in the right place at the right time more often, thus seeming to be lucky. "When you start early, you are lucky enough to get a good parking spot. You are lucky enough to avoid traffic jams. You are lucky enough to finish your job by the end of the day."[20] To get off to a good start regularly, it is important to start the day with the conscious intention of starting strong.

An effective way of getting off to a good start is to tackle the toughest task first because most people have their peak energy in the morning. (You will recall that a variation of this technique is useful in combating procrastination.) With a major task already completed, you are off to a running start on a busy workday.

MAKE GOOD USE OF OFFICE TECHNOLOGY

Companies now derive productivity increases from office automation. Used properly, most high-tech devices in the office improve productivity. Among the most productivity-enhancing devices are word processors, spreadsheets, voice mail, and personal digital assistants. How you use these ever-present devices is the key to increased productivity. A major consideration is that the time saved using office technology must be invested in productive activity to attain a true productivity advantage. Assume that you save two hours by ordering office equipment over the Internet. If you invest those two hours in activity such as finding ways to save the company money, you are more productive.

A helpful attitude about boosting personal productivity through office technology is to stay alert to new tools that would be useful in your situation. For example, a person who travels frequently for business might be able to use a product called NeatDesk, which scans receipts, business cards, and documents and organizes the information into a database.[21] This information saves time when submitting expense reports. The business owner could use this information for preparing income taxes.

A productivity error many workers make with respect to office technology is that they assume because they are using the technology they are being productive. Thus the worker who checks e-mail forty times per hour perceives himself or herself to be highly productive. Unless the person's job requires such frequent checking, he or she is being unproductive.

CONCENTRATE ON ONE KEY TASK AT A TIME

Effective people have a well-developed capacity to concentrate on the problem or person they face, however surrounded they are with potential distractions. Distractions are indeed a problem based on recent data that suggest that the average U.S. worker loses 28 percent of his or her day to interruptions such as responding to an instant message or checking out YouTube.[22] (Of course, the instant message is more likely to be work related.) The best results from concentration are achieved when you are so absorbed in your work that you are aware of virtually nothing else at the moment—referred to as the flow experience. Another useful byproduct of concentration is that it reduces absent-mindedness. If you really concentrate on what you are doing, the chances diminish that you will forget what you intended to do.

Conscious effort and self-discipline can strengthen concentration skills. An effective way to sharpen your concentration skills is to set aside ten minutes a day and focus on something repetitive, such as your breathing pattern or a small word. This is the same approach that is used in meditation to relieve stress. After practicing concentration in the manner just described, concentrate on an aspect of your work, such as preparing a report.

Some people have difficulty concentrating on important tasks, or almost any task, because they have attention deficit hyperactivity disorder (ADHD), formerly called attention deficit disorder (ADD). Workers with ADHD may find it difficult to focus, organize, and finish tasks and often forget to accomplish items on their to-do list. Before workers with ADHD can improve their concentration on important tasks, they may require professional help in terms of medicine, counseling, or cognitive behavior therapy.[23]

Note that the suggestion here is to concentrate on one *key* task at a time. As described later in this chapter, sometimes doing two or three minor tasks at the same time can help save time. In general, younger people are more effective at multitasking than much older people, yet being distracted can lower performance for both groups, as described in Chapter 8. The many electronic distractions in the office make it more difficult to concentrate on important tasks. Some of these distractions are self-imposed, such as the temptation to jump to e-mail, an instant message, or the Web site indicating today's stock market performance.

The key to concentrating on important tasks is to develop better self-discipline, following the model presented in Chapter 3. The self-disciplined person is, by definition, able to focus on the present without jumping to other tasks. According to Edward Hallowell, director of the Center for Cognitive and Emotional Health in Sudbury, Massachusetts, you need to set limits on the constant bombardment of information that surrounds you.[24] This could mean, for example, that while attempting to develop a new idea for reducing costs within your department, you eliminate any other activity for thirty minutes.

STREAMLINE YOUR WORK, AND EMPHASIZE IMPORTANT TASKS

As companies continue to operate with fewer workers than in the past even during good economic times, more nonproductive work must be eliminated. Getting rid of unproductive work is part of *reengineering*, in which work processes are radically redesigned and simplified. Every employee is expected to get rid of work that does not contribute to productivity or help customers. Another intent of work streamlining is to get rid of work that does not add value for customers. Here is a sampling of work that typically does not add value:

- E-mail or intranet messages that almost nobody reads

- Sending receipts and acknowledgments to people who do not need them

- Writing and sending reports that nobody reads or needs

- Holding meetings that do not accomplish work, exchange important information, or improve team spirit

- Checking up frequently on the work of competent people

In general, to streamline your work, look for duplication of effort and waste. An example of duplication of effort would be to routinely send people e-mail three times with the same question. An example of waste would be to call a meeting for disseminating information that could easily be communicated by e-mail.

Important (value-contributing) tasks are those in which superior performance could have a large payoff. No matter how quickly you took care of making sure that your store paid its bills on time, for example, this effort would not make your store an outstanding success. If, however, you concentrated your efforts on bringing unique and desirable merchandise into the store, this action could greatly affect your business success.

Many people respond to suggestions about emphasizing important tasks by saying, "I don't think concentrating on important tasks applies to me. My job is so filled with routine that I have no chance to work on the big breakthrough ideas." True, most jobs are filled with routine requirements. What a person *can* do is spend some time, perhaps even one hour a week, concentrating on tasks of potentially major significance.

WORK AT A STEADY PACE

In most jobs, working at a steady clip pays dividends in efficiency. The spurt worker creates many problems for management. Some employees take pride in working rapidly, even when the result is a high error rate.

Another advantage of the steady-pace approach is that you accomplish much more than someone who puts out extra effort only once in a while. The completely steady worker would accomplish just as much the day before a holiday as on a given Monday. That extra hour or so of productivity adds up substantially by the end of the year. Despite the advantages of maintaining a steady pace, some peaks and valleys in your work may be inevitable. Tax accounting firms, for example, have busy seasons.

Working at a steady pace throughout the day is difficult because it counters a natural tendency to slow down toward the end of a workday. The staffing firm Accountemps polled 150 senior executives on employee productivity. A third of the executives said that from 4 to 6 p.m. is the least productive time of the day; another third cited the post-lunch period from noon to 2 p.m. as being the least productive. Suggestions for combating the productivity dip include napping, getting fresh air, taking a short walk, and tackling the most challenging tasks early in the day.[25]

CREATE SOME QUIET, UNINTERRUPTED TIME

Many office workers find their days hectic, fragmented, and frustrating. Incessant interruptions make it difficult to get things done. The constant start–stop–restart pattern lengthens the time needed to get jobs done. Quiet time can reduce the type of productivity drain previously described. To achieve quiet time, create an uninterrupted block of time, enabling you to concentrate on your work. This could mean turning off the telephone, not accessing your e-mail, and blocking drop-in visitors during certain times of the workday.

As illustrated in the opening case to this chapter, quiet time is used for such essential activities as thinking, planning, getting organized, doing analytical work, writing reports, and doing creative tasks. One hour of quiet time might yield as much productive work as four hours of interrupted time.[26] Interruptions lower productivity more for mental than physical work. This is true because interruptions break the flow of thought, and it takes time to get back into a train of thought.

Quiet time is difficult to find in some jobs, such as those requiring customer contact. An agreement has to be worked out with the manager about when and where quiet time can be taken. Sometimes the quiet time can be taken at home early in the workday or in a vacated office or conference room.

MAKE USE OF BITS OF TIME, AND USE
MULTITASKING FOR ROUTINE WORK

A truly productive person makes good use of miscellaneous bits of time both on and off the job. While waiting in line at a post office, you might update your to-do list; while waiting for an elevator, you might be able to read a brief report; and if you have finished your day's work ten minutes before quitting time, you can use that time to clean out a file. When traveling for business, bring as much work as you can comfortably carry. Many business travelers carry a laptop, notepad, or netbook computer so they can perform work in transit. Spare time at airports because you arrive early or because of flight delays provides a good opportunity to perform routine work. By the end of the year, your productivity will have increased much more than if you had squandered these bits of time.

Some forms of making use of bits of time, such as reviewing your to-do list as you ride the elevator, are a form of constructive multitasking. Doing two or more routine chores simultaneously can sometimes enhance personal productivity. While exercising on a stationary bike, you might read work-related information; while commuting, listen to the radio for information of potential relevance for your job. Also, while reading e-mail, you might clean the outside of your computer; while waiting for a file to download, you might arrange your work area or read a brief report.

Despite searching for productivity gains through multitasking, it is important to avoid rude or dangerous acts or a combination of the two. A rude practice is doing paperwork while on the telephone or sitting in class. A dangerous practice is engaging in an intense conversation or sending and receiving text messages while driving. Checking out e-mail on a laptop or onboard computer is more dangerous because you are forced to lose full eye contact with the road.

STAY IN CONTROL OF PAPERWORK, THE INBOX, AND E-MAIL

Despite the major shift to the use of electronic messages, the workplace is still overflowing with printed messages, including computer printouts. Paperwork essentially involves taking care of administrative details, such as correspondence, expense account forms, and surveys. Responding to e-mail messages, instant messages, and text messages has created additional administrative details that require handling, even if they are actually *electronic work* rather than paperwork.

Unless you handle paperwork, e-mail, instant messages, and text messages efficiently, you may lose control of your job or home life, which could lead to substantial negative stress. Ideally, a small amount of time should be invested in paperwork and routine e-mail every day. Non–prime time (when you are at less-than-peak efficiency but not overly fatigued) is the best time to take care of administrative routine work.

A workable suggestion for most people intent on staying on top of e-mail and instant messages is to set aside some time to respond to every important message that you have not taken care of in the last two days. Move all other messages of potential future value to the archive folder. Whenever you receive a new e-mail or instant message, take action by responding, deleting, forwarding, or storing it. When an e-mail requires a complicated response, you are justified in leaving the e-mail in your inbox until you obtain the information necessary to respond intelligently.[27]

The accompanying Human Relations in Practice illustrates how a successful business firm familiar to you emphasizes high productivity from its frontline workers.

▶ **Learning Objective 4** ▶

How Does One Overcome Time Wasters?

Another basic thrust to improved personal productivity is to minimize wasting time. Workers wasting time is one of the most devastating problems facing work organizations of all types, probably far exceeding the cost from theft and fraud. According to a survey by America Online and Salary.com, the average worker admits to wasting 2.09 hours per 8-hour workday, aside from lunch and scheduled

Human Relations in Practice

Big Brown Squeezes Productivity from Its Drivers

By driving 2 billion miles a year to deliver packages, UPS has learned a lot about how to save fuel, thereby increasing productivity. The largest package delivery service in the world, UPS operates 93,637 vans, delivery trucks, tractor trailers, and motorcycles. Of those, only 1,629 use alternate fuels. With fuel having become the carrier's number one expense, conserving is a top priority for Big Brown. Here are three driving productivity tips from the pros, designed to save fuel and reduce operating costs as a result:

- **Avoid left turns.** UPS routes are designed to avoid left turns as much as possible. Idling while waiting to turn left wastes time and gas. This suggestion eliminated 29 million miles from its U.S. drivers' routes in one year, saving UPS more than 3 million gallons of gas. At the time gas was $4 a gallon, resulting in a $12 million savings.

- **Reduce idling.** UPS practices a strict policy of prohibiting idling—no matter how short a stop a UPS driver makes, the engine is turned off. By reducing idling time 24 minutes per driver shift, UPS can save $1,888 per driver per year.

- **Plan your route.** For errands or trips, UPS drivers plan a route that doesn't backtrack. The drivers find the quickest and most direct route with a map or Web site.

Source: Based on facts from Rachel Tobin Ramos, "Take It from UPS: Left Turn Wastes Gas," *Atlanta Journal Constitution* (www.ajc.com), July 4, 2008.

breaks.[28] One caution about this figure is that many employees who waste time during the day will speed up their work toward the end of the workday or work at home to catch up on unfinished tasks. Figure 16-3 presents an overall view of how employees waste time, based on a survey of 10,000 workers.

Many of the techniques already described in this chapter help save time. The tactics and strategies described next, however, are directly aimed at overcoming the problem of wasted time.

MINIMIZE DAYDREAMING

Allowing the mind to drift while on the job is a major productivity drain. Daydreaming is triggered when the individual perceives the task to be boring—such as reviewing another person's work for errors. Unresolved personal problems are an important source of daydreaming, thus blocking your productivity. This is especially true because effective time utilization requires good concentration. When you are preoccupied with a personal or business problem, it is difficult to give your full efforts to a task at hand.

The solution is to do something constructive about whatever problem is sapping your ability to concentrate. Sometimes a relatively minor problem, such as driving with an expired operator's license, can impair your work concentration. At other times, a major problem, such as how best to take care of a parent who has suffered a stroke, interferes with work. In either situation, your concentration will suffer until you take appropriate action.

FIGURE 16-3

TOP TIME-WASTING ACTIVITIES BY AMERICAN WORKERS

Source: Dan Malachowski, "Wasted Time at Work Costing Companies Billions." Retrieved, April 20, 2009, from: www.salary.com

Time-Wasting Activity	Percent
1. Surfing Internet (personal use)	44.7
2. Socializing with coworkers	23.4
3. Conducting personal business	6.8
4. Spacing out	3.9
5. Running errands off-premises	3.1
6. Making personal phone calls	2.3
7. Applying for other jobs	1.3
8. Planning personal events	1.0
9. Arriving late/leaving early	1.0
10. Other	12.5

PREPARE A TIME LOG TO EVALUATE YOUR USE OF TIME

An advanced tool for becoming a more efficient time manager is to prepare a time log of how you are currently investing your time. For five full workdays or school days, write down everything you do, including such activities as responding to e-mail and taking rest breaks. A daily planner is the tool of choice for a time log. Some people use a spreadsheet for the same purpose, including HP CEO Mark Hurd, who maintains a spreadsheet that tracks and analyzes his daily tasks.[29] Study your results, and look for patterns of lost time. A hospital administrative worker who used a log discovered that she was spending about twenty minutes at the start of each workday circling around the parking ramp look for a space. Her conclusion was that by arriving five minutes earlier to the hospital, she could find a space within a few minutes.

Time leak

anything you are doing or not doing that allows time to get away from you

One of the most important outputs of a time log is to uncover time leaks. A **time leak** is anything you are doing or not doing that allows time to get away from you. Among them are spending too much time for lunch by collecting people before finally leaving and walking to a coworker's cubicle rather than sending an e-mail. The process of streamlining your work will also identify time leaks.

AVOID UNPRODUCTIVE USE OF COMPUTERS

An unproductive use of computers is to tinker with them to the exclusion of useful work. Many people have become intrigued with computers to the point of diversion. They become habituated to creating new reports or exquisite graphics and making endless changes. It is easy to become diverted by the thousands of commands in a program such as Microsoft Word or PowerPoint. Some managers spend so much time with computers that they neglect leadership responsibilities, thus lowering their productivity.

In addition to these problems, Internet surfing for purposes not strictly related to the job has become a major productivity drain. According to an Accountemps survey, workers spend an average of fifty-six minutes per day with non-work-related Internet use.[30] For example, many Internet shopping sites and sports sites have found that their peak number of visits is during traditional working hours. Social networking sites are also visited frequently during typical working hours.

The message is straightforward: To plug one more potential productivity drain, avoid using the computer for nonproductive purposes. Many companies block the use of recreational Web sites on company equipment so that workers have to resort to authorized sites, such as those selling equipment and supplies!

KEEP TRACK OF IMPORTANT NAMES, PLACES, AND THINGS

How much time have you wasted lately searching for such items as a telephone number you jotted down somewhere, your keys, or an appointment book? Many managers and professionals store such information in a database, in their cell phones, or even in a word processing file. Such files are more difficult to misplace than a pocket directory, yet these files should be backed up to prevent lost data.

Two steps are recommended for remembering where you put things. First, have a parking place for everything. Put your keys, appointment book, or personal digital assistant in the same place after each use. (This tactic supports the strategy of being neat and orderly to minimize wasting time.) Second, make visual associations. To have something register in your mind at the moment you are doing it, make up a visual association about that act. Thus, you might say, "Here I am putting my auto insurance policy in the back section of my canvas bag."

SET A TIME LIMIT FOR CERTAIN TASKS AND PROJECTS

Spending too much time on a task or project wastes time. As a person becomes experienced with certain projects, he or she is able to make accurate estimates of how long a project will take to complete. A paralegal might say, "Getting this will drawn up for the lawyer's approval should take two hours." A good work habit to develop is to estimate how long a job should take and then proceed with strong determination to get that job completed within the estimated time period. A productive version of this technique is to decide that some low- and medium-priority items are worth only so much of your time. Invest that much time in the project but no more. Preparing a file on advertisements that come across your desk is one example.

SCHEDULE SIMILAR TASKS TOGETHER (CLUSTERING)

An efficient method of accomplishing small tasks is to group them together and perform them in one block of time. Clustering of this type has several applications. If you are visiting an office supply store, think of whatever you need there to avoid an unnecessary repeat visit. As long as you are visiting a particular search engine, look for some other information you will need soon. A basic way of scheduling similar tasks together is to make most of your telephone calls in relation to your job from 11:00 to 11:30 each workday morning. Or you might reserve the last hour of every workday for e-mail and other correspondence. By using this method, you develop the necessary pace and mental set to knock off chores in short order. In contrast, when you flit from one task to another, your efficiency may suffer.

BOUNCE QUICKLY FROM TASK TO TASK

Much time is lost when a person takes a break between tasks. After one task is completed, you might pause for ten minutes to clear your work area and adjust your to-do list. After the brief pause, dive into your next important task. A compliance officer at a mutual fund once said that he turns over an hourglass when he needs to decompress after handling an urgent situation. When the sand runs out, he moves to the next priority.[31]

Incorporating many of the ideas contained in this chapter will help you achieve peak performance or exceptional accomplishment.

Concept Review and Reinforcement

Key Terms

Work habits, 468
Productivity, 468
Procrastination, 468

Fear of success, 469
Worst in, first out (WIFO), 471
Workaholism, 475

Planning, 476
Time leak, 484

Summary and Review

People with good work habits tend to be more successful in their careers than poorly organized individuals, and they tend to have more time to spend on personal life. Good work habits are more important than ever because of today's emphasis on productivity.

Procrastination is the leading cause of poor productivity and career self-sabotage. People procrastinate for many reasons, including their perception that a task is unpleasant, is overwhelming, or may lead to negative consequences. Fear of success can also lead to procrastination. Awareness of procrastination can lead to its control.

Eight other techniques for reducing procrastination are the following:

- Calculating the cost of procrastination
- Counterattacking the burdensome task
- Jump-starting yourself
- Pecking away at an overwhelming task
- Motivating yourself with rewards and punishments
- Following the WIFO principle
- Making a commitment to other people
- Expressing a more positive attitude about your intentions

Developing good work habits and time management practices is often a matter of developing proper attitudes toward work and time. Seven such attitudes and values are these:

- Developing a mission, goals, and a strong work ethic
- Valuing good attendance and punctuality
- Valuing your time

- Valuing neatness, orderliness, and speed
- Working smarter, not harder
- Becoming self-employed psychologically
- Appreciating the importance of rest and relaxation

Ten skills and techniques to help you become more productive are these:

- Cleaning up and getting organized
- Planning your activities (including the use of time-and-activity charts)
- Getting off to a good start
- Making good use of office technology
- Concentrating on one key task at a time
- Streamlining your work and emphasizing important tasks
- Working at a steady pace
- Creating some quiet, uninterrupted time
- Making use of bits of time and using multitasking for routine work
- Staying in control of paperwork, the inbox, and e-mail

Time wasting is a major problem in the workplace. Seven suggestions for overcoming time wasting are as follows:

- Minimize daydreaming.
- Prepare a time log and evaluate your use of time.
- Avoid unproductive use of computers.
- Keep track of important names, places, and things.
- Set a time limit for certain tasks and projects.
- Schedule similar tasks together (clustering).
- Bounce quickly from task to task.

Check Your Understanding

1. In recent years, companies that sell desk planners and other time management devices have experienced all-time peak demands for their products. What factors do you think are creating this boom?

2. What have you observed to be two of the most important areas for improvement in work habits and time management for students?

3. Many tidy, well-organized workers never attain much in the way of career success. Which principle of work habits and time management described in this chapter might they be neglecting?

4. How can preparing a personal mission statement help a person become better organized?

5. Why might drastically reducing procrastination often increase a person's income substantially?

6. When people learn that a person is self-employed, they often comment, "Oh, that's wonderful, you don't have to worry about time. You can play golf (or engage in some other activity) whenever you want." In what way does this statement misunderstand the importance of time management for the self-employed?

7. Give an example of any work you have ever performed or heard of someone else performing that could be eliminated because it is unproductive.

8. Identify five bits of time you could put to better use.

9. How might reducing the amount of time wasted at work help stop the flow of outsourcing of jobs?

10. Give an example of how the principles and techniques of good work habits and personal productivity could be applied to a job search.

Web Corner

Procrastination test (must take within 48 hours):
www.queendom.com/. Search for the test measuring procrastination tendencies.

Prioritizing effectively:
www.time-management-guide.com/prioritizing.html

National Association of Professional Organizers:
www.napo.net

INTERNET SKILL BUILDER

What Are You Doing with Your Time?

Go to www.getmoredone.com/tabulator.html to find the Pace Productivity Tabulator. This interactive module enables you to enter the time you spend on eleven major activities (such as employment, eating, sleeping, and television watching) and compare your profile to others. You are also able to enter your ideal profile to see where you would like to be. Simply follow the straightforward instructions. After arriving at your personal pie chart, ask yourself, "What have I learned that will enhance my personal productivity?"

Developing Your Human Relations Skills

Applying Human Relations Exercise 16-1

Squeezing Productivity out of Social Networking Sites

The number of computer literate people using social networking sites continues to grow explosively, with some people even learning how to use the Internet so they can join a networking site such as Twitter or Facebook. We all know that these sites can be an enjoyable pastime and a distraction from work. The issue we want you to address in small brainstorming groups is how to use social networking sites to improve your work productivity.

After each group has completed its task of brainstorming ways to improve productivity by being a member of a social networking site, you might hold a class discussion of your major findings. See if the class can reach a consensus on whether social networking sites can be a productivity booster or simply a pleasant diversion.

Applying Human Relations Exercise 16-2

My Personal Procrastination Analysis

The purpose of this exercise is to give you practice in understanding why you might have procrastinated in the past and how you might overcome a similar episode of procrastination in the future. To begin, write a twenty-five-word or so description of some important activity on which you have procrastinated in the past. An *important* activity is one that could have a noticeable impact on your mental or financial well-being. Describe also any negative consequences that might have stemmed from the procrastination. Here is an example from an assistant manager at a health club who lives in New York state:

"I knew my vehicle inspection sticker was due in a month. But I was simply so busy with other things, I couldn't get to it. Also, I figured because it was wintertime, I could spread some snow over the dated sticker, and no police office would catch me. Well, it worked out that I was pulled over for the expired sticker. Unfortunately, the officer also found out I had not renewed my driver's license. My total fines were about $500 plus having to spend loads of time at the motor vehicle bureau straightening out the mess."

Use the following table (or copy the form on your computer) to record your procrastination episode and analyze the cause. After you have checked the most likely cause or causes, make a few notes in the third column as to how you might avoid procrastinating about that situation, or similar situation, in the future.

Procrastination Episode

Reason(s) for Procrastination	Check Each Reason That Applies	Technique I Might Use to Overcome the Procrastination Next Time I Am in That Situation
1. Unpleasant task		
2. Overwhelming task		
3. Possible negative evaluation of my work		
4. Fear of success		
5. Rebelled against being controlled		
6. No meaningful reward		
7. Liked the last-minute rush		
8. I'm a perfectionist		

The assistant manager of the health club admitted that reasons 5 and 6 applied to his situation. He noted that he regards inspection stickers as a form of control over him. He noted also that having the sticker may be important but that he doesn't feel any particular reward for complying with the law. On further reflection, he realizes that some control is necessary in a civilized society. Many uninspected vehicles are a menace on the road. So not getting a sticker has a cost to society as well as to him. He will therefore calculate the personal cost next time. He said, "Maybe I should use the WIFO next year. It takes a little time and money to get my car inspected, so I should do it first thing on the day set for the inspection."

Human Relations Class Activity

Personal Productivity Checklist

Each class member will use the following checklist to identify the two biggest mistakes per category he or she is making in work habits and time management. The mistakes could apply to work, school, or personal life. In addition to identifying the problems, each student will develop brief action plans about how to overcome them. For instance, "One of my biggest problems is that I tend to start a lot of projects but finish very few of them. Now that I am aware of this problem, I am going to post a sign over my desk that reads, *No one will give me credit for things I never completed.*"

Students then present their problems and action plans to the class. After each student has made his or her presentation, a class discussion is held to reach conclusions and interpretations about the problems revealed. For instance, it might be that one or two time management problems are quite frequent.

	Especially Applicable to Me
Overcoming Procrastination	
1. Increase awareness of the problem.	_____
2. Calculate cost of procrastination.	_____
3. Counterattack.	_____
4. Jump-start yourself.	_____
5. Peck away at an overwhelming task.	_____
6. Motive yourself with rewards and punishments.	_____
7. Follow the WIFO principle.	_____
8. Make a commitment to other people.	_____
9. Express a more positive attitude about your intentions.	_____

Developing Proper Attitudes and Values

1. Develop a mission, goals, and a strong work ethic.	_____
2. Value good attendance and punctuality.	_____
3. Value your time.	_____
4. Value neatness, orderliness, and speed.	_____
5. Work smarter, not harder.	_____
6. Become self-employed psychologically.	_____
7. Appreciate the importance of rest and relaxation.	_____

Time-Management Techniques

1. Clean up and get organized.	_____
2. Plan your activities (including a to-do list with priority setting).	_____
3. Get off to a good start.	_____
4. Make good use of office technology.	_____
5. Concentrate on one key task at a time.	_____
6. Streamline your work and emphasize important tasks.	_____
7. Work at a steady pace.	_____
8. Create some quiet, uninterrupted time.	_____
9. Make use of bits of time, and use multitasking for routine work.	_____
10. Stay in control of paperwork, the in-basket, and e-mail.	_____

Overcoming Time Wasters

1. Minimize daydreaming.	_____
2. Prepare a time log to evaluate your use of time.	_____
3. Avoid unproductive use of computers.	_____
4. Keep track of important names, places, and things.	_____
5. Set a time limit for certain tasks and projects.	_____
6. Schedule similar tasks together (clustering).	_____
7. Bounce quickly from task to task.	_____

Josie Struggles to Get It Done

Twenty-six-year-old Josie DiSalvo is intelligent and talented, yet not nearly as successful as she would like to be. In high school and college she too frequently waited too long before preparing papers or studying for exams. As a result, her grades were lower than when she took her time to research and write a paper or study for an exam. At college, she often asked to be given a grade of Incomplete so she could complete a course requirement. Josie's request for a grade of Incomplete was usually refused because she could not provide proof of an emergency to justify it.

After graduating from college, six month later than she planned, Josie embarked on a career in sports management. Being energetic, athletic, and personable, Josie soon found employment as a personal trainer at a fitness center. Her intent was to work her way up into a management position at an athletic club. Six months into the program, Josie was told that she was doing a fine job but that she would need to attend a two-week program for certification as a personal trainer in order to stay in her position.

One week later Josie went to the Web site containing the application for the personal trainer certification program. She began answering the easy biographical questions from memory, such as name, e-mail address, and postal address. But the online form also required that Josie track down information from outside sources, such as requesting that a transcript of her grades be sent to the certifying organization. In addition, Josie was asked to write a two-hundred-word essay explaining why she wanted to become a personal trainer.

Josie thought, "I'll just have to get to this later, maybe next week. I've got a lot on my plate already. It's such a bother sending for a transcript and writing a career essay." Two weeks passed, and Josie still had made no more progress with her application.

One morning Josie's supervisor, Lucy, said to her, "I noticed that you did not get your application in on time for the certification training program. This means that we will be taking you off personal trainer status and assigning you to the front desk, in a part-time position."

Josie replied, "Lucy, can you give me one more shot? I've had some personal issues to deal with. Maybe I could take the next program coming up in the fall."

Questions

1. If you were Josie's supervisor, would you grant her "one more shot"? Why or why not?

2. Why might Josie be procrastinating about becoming certified as a personal trainer?

3. What advice can you offer Josie to help her control her procrastination?

Josie's Boss Attempts to Help Her Overcome Procrastination

The case study about Josie serves as the background and the story line for this role-play. One person plays the role of Josie, who thinks she deserves another chance at attending the certification program for personal trainers. She does not like the idea of being demoted to a part-time front-desk clerk. Her boss, Lucy, will be meeting with Josie in her (Lucy's) office right after the club closes on Tuesday night.

Another person plays the role of Lucy, who wants to help Josie get certified but also recognizes that the club was quite clear with Josie about getting her application in to become certified as a personal trainer. Lucy has noticed that Josie has not been prompt in getting the few reports in on time that she has been requested to prepare.

Observers rate the role-players on two dimensions, using a 1 to 5 scale from very poor to very good. One dimension is "effective use of human relations techniques." For Lucy, focus on how effective she is in helping Josie be more prompt in getting a work obligation completed. For Josie, observe if she can overcome her defensiveness about being a procrastinator. The second dimension is "acting ability." A few observers might voluntarily provide feedback to the role-players in terms of sharing their ratings and observations. The course instructor might also provide feedback.

Human Relations Case Study 16-2

The Cubicle Blues

Paul Chen works as a design technician for Design-Trend, a furniture manufacturer in San Francisco. His major responsibility is to design support devices for home and office furniture, such as the arms, legs, and frames. His employer has configured the office into cubicles, with even the company executives being assigned to cubicles. When the creative staff needs more space, such as when laying out blueprints for an office, a common area with large drawing tables is available. Because most design work is computer aided, the creative staff does most of their work in the assigned cubicles.

Previous to the reconfiguration of the office, design engineers and technicians were assigned to small private offices with doors. In this way, the engineers and technicians could work relatively uninterrupted without colleagues frequently conversing with them. The offices also closed off most sounds so a creative worker could avoid hearing office chatter, including telephone conversations.

CEO Kenneth Yang decided to change from closed offices to cubicles to enhance communication and idea sharing among all staff members. Yang opined, "Unstructured communication leads to an exchange of ideas that is vital for creativity. I don't want the staff holed up in offices and minimizing communication with each other."

Chen became increasingly troubled by life in his cubicle. He grumbled to coworkers, friends, and family members about working in a cubicle farm. He disliked the distractions, and he was having difficulty concentrating on creative tasks. One day when his supervisor dropped by his cubicle, Chen explained his problem:

"How can Yang expect the creative staff to be creative when assigned to these cubicles? I hear every conversation that's going on up to two cubicles down. When I am working on a design, I need to concentrate. I need to reflect. I don't want to be interrupted by a neighbor telling her husband over the phone to pick up a pizza on the way home. I enjoy working for DesignTrend, but the cubicles have made my days insufferable."

The supervisor replied, "I'm in no position to assign you a private office. Even Ken Yang works out of a cubicle. Yet, I will give some thought to your problem."

Questions

1. Is Paul Chen offering a valid complaint that creative thought is difficult without privacy?

2. What advice can you offer Chen to help him manage interruptions better?

3. What should Chen's supervisor advise him to do?

Source: A few of the facts in this case are from Linda Tischler, "Death to the Cubicle," *Fast Company*, June 2005, pp. 29–32.

REFERENCES

1. Excerpted from Kate Lunau, "Sshh: Men at Work," *Macleans* (www.macleans.ca/business), January 9, 2008.
2. "Define 'Productivity,'" *Manager's Edge*, December 2007, p. 6.
3. Research of Timothy A. Psychl, reported in Danielle Kost, "Professor Says Putting Off Chores Is a Breakable Habit," *Rochester (NY) Democrat and Chronicle*, September 22, 2002, p. D3.
4. Theodore Kurtz, "Ten Reasons Why People Procrastinate," *Supervisory Management*, April 1990, pp. 1–2.
5. "When to Procrastinate and When to Get Going," *Working Smart*, March 1992, pp. 1–2.
6. Hara Estroff Marano, "The Making of a Perfectionist," *Psychology Today*, March/April 2008, pp. 80–86.
7. Alan Lakein, *How to Gain Control of Your Time and Your Life* (New York: Wyden Books, 1973), pp. 141–151.
8. Cited and quoted in "Get with It: Nip Your Procrastination Right in the Bud," *Entrepreneur*, September 1998, p. 94.
9. Linda Sapadin, *It's about Time! The Six Styles of Procrastination and How to Overcome Them* (New York: Viking, 1996).
10. Stephen R. Covey with Elaine Pofeldt, "Why Is This Man Smiling?" *Success*, January 2000, pp. 38–40.
11. Cited in Alfred A. Edmond, Jr., "Alone in Your Time Zone," *Black Enterprise*, December 2004, pp. 154–155.
12. Eric Abrahamson and David H. Freedman, *A Perfect Mess* (Boston: Little Brown, 2007).
13. Michael Mandel, "The Real Reasons You're Working So Hard . . . and What You Can Do about It," *Business Week*, October 3, 2005, p. 62.
14. Cited in Teresa Odie, "Sleep-Working," www.philly.com, July 26, 2008.
15. Quoted in Carrie Ferguson, "The Wages of a Workaholic," Gannett News Service, May 23, 2000; Brenda Goodman, "A Field Guide to the Workaholic," *Psychology Today*, May/June 2006, p. 40.
16. Stewart D. Friedman and Sharon Lobel, "The Happy Workaholic: A Role Model for Employees," *Academy of Management Executive*, August 2003, pp. 87–98.
17. Paul Keegan, "The Master of Getting Things Done," *Business 2.0*, July 2007, p. 77.
18. Jeremy Caplan, "Hacking toward Happiness," *Time*, July 2, 2007, p. 73.
19. Joyce R. Rosenberg, "Calendar Remains a Valuable Business Tool," Associated Press, June 20, 2005.
20. Merrill Douglass, "Timely Time Tips: Ideas to Help You Manage Your Time," *Executive Management Forum*, September 1989, p. 4.
21. Edward C. Baig, "Expense Receipt Overload? NeatDesk Can Help," *USA Today*, November 6, 2008, pp. 1B, 5B.
22. Maggie Jackson, "May We Have Your Attention Please?" *Business Week*, June 23, 2008, p. 56.
23. "Attention Deficit Hyperactivity Disorder: What It Is and Who Is Affected," www.health.com, January 12, 2009. Copyright © 2009 Time Inc.
24. "Avoid the Burden of 'Workplace ADD,'" *Manager's Edge*, May 2007, p. 7.
25. Survey cited in "Productivity Declines as the Workday Ends," *Democrat and Chronicle* (Rochester, NY), July 18, 2005, p. 10D.
26. Douglass, "Timely Time Tips," p. 4.
27. Farhad Manjoo, "An Empty Inbox, or with Just a Few E-mail Messages? Read On," *New York Times* (www.nytimes.com), March 5, 2009.
28. Dan Malachowski, "Wasted Time at Work Costing Companies Billions." Updated version retrieved April 20, 2009, from: www.salary.com.
29. Adam Lashinksy, "Mark Hurd's Moment," *Fortune*, March 16, 2009, p. 94.
30. Survey cited in "Workers Dawdle on Net an Hour a Day, Firm Says," *Democrat and Chronicle* (Rochester, NY), August 22, 2005, p. 10D.
31. "Beating the Clock: Time Management When You Are under the Gun," *Working Smart*, March 1999, p. 1.

17

Managing Stress and Personal Problems

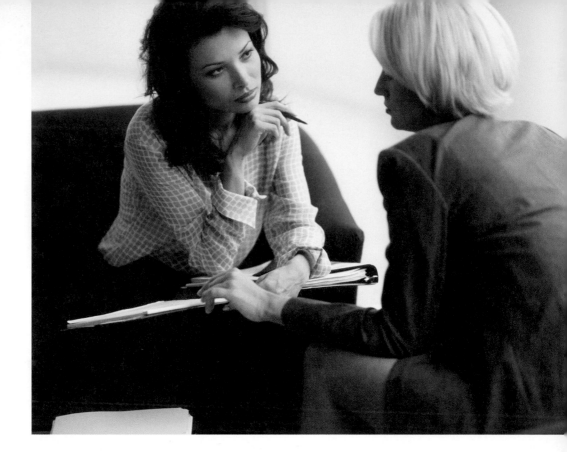

Outline

1 What Are the Physiology and Consequences of Stress?
Physiological Changes
Consequences and Symptoms

2 What Are Some Sources of Stress in Personal Life?
Personality Factors Contributing to Stress

3 What Are Some Key Sources of Work Stress?
Work Overload or Underload
Role Conflict and Role Ambiguity
Job Insecurity and Job Loss
Adverse Environmental Conditions
Adverse Customer Interaction and Emotional Labor

4 What Are Several Effective Approaches to Managing Stress?
Dealing with Stress by Attacking Its Source
Receiving Social and Organizational Support
Relaxation Techniques for Handling Stress
Managing Stress by Staying Well (Proper Exercise, Diet, and Rest)

5 What Are Two Key Perspectives on Understanding and Dealing with Personal Problems?
Self-Defeating Behavior
Developing Resilience

Max was having difficulty concentrating on his work as the supervisor of order fulfillment at the online department of a national retailer. He was frequently late in submitting sales and shipping data to his manager. When asked a question by one of his group members, Max would often ask the employee to repeat the question because he didn't listen carefully the first time.

Soon, Max's boss, Sara, approached him and explained that she was noticing that he seemed to be too preoccupied to pay full attention to his job. Sara explained to Max that his performance as a supervisor was slipping badly and that he had to improve. Max told Sara, "Yes, I've been facing some personal issues lately that are stressing me out. I'll be back on top of my game as soon as I get my problems under control."

Sara then offered Max the opportunity to visit an employee assistance program the company has to help employees deal with personal problems that interfere with work. Max followed up and asked to see a counselor specializing in financial problems. In speaking with the counselor, Max explained how he and his wife have become overwhelmed by credit card debt and that the associated stress was making it difficult for him to concentrate.

The financial counselor worked with Max to help him cope with the couple's financial problems. An immediate stress reliever for Max was the technique of tackling his smallest debt first—one that required a minimum payment of $55 per month. The counselor explained, "After you conquer this debt, it will seem like a salary increase of $55 per month after taxes." Based on the counseling, Max and his wife also cut way back on expenses by switching to the most basic packages for their cable television and cell phone services, and purchasing $4 lattes.

With a financial recovery plan in action, Max reduced his stress level enough to concentrate better on his work. Sara remarked how Max was back to his former self.

Learning Objectives ▸

After studying the information and doing the exercises in this chapter, you should be able to:

1 Describe the meaning of stress and its physiology.

2 Identify several positive and negative consequences of stress.

3 Pinpoint potential stressors in personal life.

4 Pinpoint potential stressors in the workplace.

5 Describe key methods for managing the potential adverse effects of stress.

6 Develop insight into dealing with personal problems through understanding self-defeating behavior and the importance of being resilient.

The story about the distracted supervisor illustrates how companies are concerned about preventing and reducing stress to boost productivity, including having employees overcome personal problems that interfere with work. In this chapter we describe the nature and cause of stress, managing personal and work stress, and the related topic of coping with personal problems.

▶ Learning Objective 1 ▶

What Are the Physiology and Consequences of Stress?

Stress
an internal reaction to any force that threatens to disturb a person's equilibrium; the internal reaction usually takes the form of emotional discomfort

Stressor
the external or internal force that brings about the stress

An important part of learning about stress is to understand its meaning, underlying physiology, and consequences to the person. **Stress** is an internal reaction to any force that threatens to disturb a person's equilibrium. The internal reaction usually takes the form of emotional discomfort. A **stressor** is the external or internal force that brings about the stress. Your perception of an event or thought influences whether a given event is stressful. Your confidence in your ability to handle difficult situations also influences the amount of stress you experience. If you believe you have the resources to conquer the potentially stressful event, you are much less likely to experience stress. A computer whiz, therefore, would not be stressed by the prospect of having to install a new computer operating system. Two key aspects of understanding stress are the accompanying physiological changes and the consequences—including symptoms—of stress.

PHYSIOLOGICAL CHANGES

Fight-or-flight response
the experience of stress prompts the adrenal glands to release a flood of hormones that prepare the body to fight or run when faced with a challenge

The physiological changes taking place within the body are almost identical for both positive and negative stressors. Riding a roller coaster, falling in love, or being fired, for example, make you feel about the same inside. The stress response begins in the brain, and a number of structures, including the pituitary gland, go on alert. The experience of stress prompts the adrenal glands to release a flood of hormones that prepare the body to fight or run when faced with a challenge. This battle against the stressor is referred to as the **fight-or-flight response.** (The "response" is really a conflict, because you are forced to choose between struggling with the stressor or fleeing from the scene.) It helps you deal with emergencies.

The activation of hormones when the body has to cope with a stressor produces a short-term physiological reaction. Among the most familiar reactions are increases in heart rate, blood pressure, and blood glucose as well as blood clotting. Digestion stops during the stress episode. To help you recognize these symptoms, try to recall the internal bodily sensations you felt if you ever were almost in an automobile accident or if you heard some wonderful news. Less familiar changes are a redirection of the blood flow toward the brain and large-muscle groups and a release of stored fluids from places throughout the body into the bloodstream.

CONSEQUENCES AND SYMPTOMS

If stress is continuous and accompanied by these short-term physiological changes, annoying and life-threatening conditions can occur. A stressful life event usually leads to a high cholesterol level (of the unhealthy type) and high blood pressure. Men who respond most intensely to mental stress run a higher risk of blocked blood vessels. The result is a higher risk of heart attack and stroke. A series of studies indicated that job stressors such as a hostile work environment or excessive hours can enhance a worker's risk for cardiovascular disease. One explanation of this problem is that mental stress, over time, may injure blood vessels and foster the buildup of arterial plaques.[1] Other conditions associated with stress are migraine headaches, ulcers, allergies, skin disorders, and cancer. Stress often results in memory problems, such as forgetting where you put your keys or not remembering an appointment.

Stress symptoms vary considerably from one person to another. A sampling of common stress symptoms is listed in Figure 17-1.

FIGURE 17-1

A VARIETY OF STRESS SYMPTOMS

Mostly Physical

Shaking or trembling	Upper- and lower-back pain
Dizziness	Frequent headaches
Heart palpitations	Low energy and stamina
Difficulty breathing	Stomach problems
Chronic fatigue	Constant cravings for sweets
Unexplained chest pains	Increased alcohol or cigarette consumption
Frequent teeth grinding	Frequent need to eliminate
Frequent nausea and dizziness	Skin eruptions and rashes
Premature aging, including a haggard appearance	

Mostly Emotional and Behavioral

Difficulty concentrating	Anxiety or depression
Nervousness	Forgetfulness
Crying	Restlessness
Anorexia	Frequent arguments with others
Declining interest in sex and romance	Feeling high strung much of the time
Feelings of hopelessness, despair, anger, and sadness	Withdrawal from people and listlessness
	Decrease in job performance, including increased tardiness and absenteeism

Note: Anxiety is a feeling of distress or uneasiness caused by fear of an imagined or unidentified problem. For example, you might be anxious about meeting your supervisor today, but you have no specific concern in mind.

A major consequence of stress is that it affects our ability to fight infection. Psychology professors Suzanne Segerstrom of the University of Kentucky and Gregory Miller of the University of British Columbia analyzed the results of 293 studies, involving 18,941 individuals, conducted over a thirty-year span. Three major findings emerged from this massive analysis. First, stress does alter immunity—as has been long theorized. Second, short-term stress boosts the immune system, functioning as an adaptive response preparing for injury or infection. Giving a public speech or class presentation are examples of short-term stress for most people. Yet long-term chronic stress causes too much wear and tear, breaking down the immune system. An example of a long-term chronic stress would be long-term unemployment. Third, the immune system of older people, or those who are ill, is more susceptible to stress-related change.[2]

Challenge versus Hindrance Stressors

A useful framework for understanding work-related stressors is that they can have positive or negative consequences. **Challenge stressors** are stressful events and thoughts that have a positive direct effect on motivation and performance. They include work-related stimuli or forces such as a reasonably high workload, times pressures, and a realistic level of responsibility. Workers perceive these stressors as relatively under their control. Challenge stressors also offer the opportunity for personal growth if they are overcome, such as learning a complex new skill.

Hindrance stressors are those stressful events and thoughts that have a negative effect on motivation and performance. They include work-related stimuli or forces such as negative organization politics, red tape, and confusion about responsibilities. Hindrance stressors encompass potentially stressful demands usually perceived as beyond the control of the worker and that might block the opportunity for personal growth.[3]

Challenge stressors
stressful events and thoughts that have a positive direct effect on motivation and performance

Hindrance stressors
stressful events and thoughts that have a negative effect on motivation and performance

The Consequences of Negative Stress

Stress has enormous consequences to employers as well as individuals. It has been estimated that American companies lose about $200 billion annually in absenteeism, below-standard performance, tardiness, and Workers' Compensation claims linked to stress disorders.[4] A research study involving 820 truck drivers in Holland illustrates the consequence of negative job stress to employers. The drivers who suffered the negative consequences of stress (strain) were more likely to quit than drivers who experienced less strain. Furthermore, the stressed truck drivers were more likely to find another occupation after they quit.[5] We emphasize again that positive stress is not associated with negative consequences to the employer.

Evidence suggests that alcohol and illicit drug use might increase when workers experience negative stress. Michael R. Frone, of the State University of New York at Buffalo, studied how the stressors of work overload and job insecurity affected drug use, based on a national sample of U.S. workers. Telephone interviews were the method of data collection. Frone found a positive relationship between these two work stressors to alcohol use before, during, and after work.[6]

The concept of challenge stressors indicates that stress can play a positive role in our lives. The right amount of stress prepares us for meeting difficult challenges and spurs us on to peak intellectual and physical performance. (The findings about the immune system support this conclusion.) An optimum amount of stress exists for most people and most tasks. In general, performance tends to be best under moderate amounts of stress. If stress is too great, people become temporarily ineffective because they may freeze or choke. Under too little stress, people may become lethargic and inattentive. Stress can lower job performance because the stressed person makes errors in concentration and judgment.

Overall Relationship between Stress and Job Performance

Figure 17-2 depicts the relationship between stress and performance, as already suggested by the difference between challenge versus hindrance stressors. An exception to this relationship is that certain negative forms of stress are likely to lower performance even if the stress is moderate. For example, the stress created by an intimidating boss or worrying about radiation poisoning—even in moderate amounts—will not improve performance.

FIGURE 17-2

THE RELATIONSHIP BETWEEN STRESS AND JOB PERFORMANCE

Performance is generally best at moderate levels of stress

Performance declines as stress becomes too intense

Multitasking contributes to the relationship between stress and performance, based on a study conducted by information technology professors Gloria Mark and Victor Gonzalez at the University of California at Irvine. The participants were thirty-six information technology workers at an investment firm. For most workers, as the number of tasks juggled increased, stress rose and performance decreased. However, a little multitasking raised the challenge bar and often led to enhanced performance.[7]

Burnout as a Consequence of Long-Term Stress

One of the major problems of prolonged stress is that it may lead to **burnout,** a condition of emotional, mental, and physical exhaustion in response to long-term job stressors. The exhaustion aspect of burnout can be triggered by such factors as a heavy physical workload, time pressures, and shift work.[8] Burnout is also associated with a poor congruence between the person's demands and what the job offers. A measure of poor congruence would be agreeing with the statement, "I have enough time to do what's important in my job."[9]

The burned-out person often becomes cynical. Burnout is most likely to occur among those whose jobs call for frequent and intense interactions with others, such as a social worker, teacher, or customer service representative. Yet people in other occupations also suffer from burnout, especially when not much support from others is present and the rewards are few.

Also, a hostile work environment, such as being harassed by coworkers and managers, is a major contributor to burnout.[10] Students can also experience burnout because studying and preparing reports is hard work. Conscientiousness and perfectionism also contribute to burnout because people with these characteristics feel stressed when they do not accomplish everything they would like. Similarly, being obsessed about what you are doing can trigger burnout.

Burnout can be treated in many ways, just as with the negative effects of stress. Showing gratitude for hard work by employees is particularly helpful in preventing and treating burnout because many cases of burnout are caused by intense feelings of being unappreciated.

> **Burnout**
> a condition of emotional, mental, and physical exhaustion in response to long-term job stressors

What Are Some Sources of Stress in Personal Life?

◀ Learning Objective 2 ◀

Almost any form of frustration, disappointment, setback, inconvenience, or crisis in your personal life can cause stress. The list is dynamic because new sources of stress emerge continuously. For example, a prolonged downturn in the stock and bond markets can be a stressor for investors who previously paid little attention to how well their investments were performing. Our life stage also helps determine which events are stressors. A person building his or her career is more likely to be more stressed by a limited supply of jobs than a person nearing retirement. Presented next are major categories of stressful events in personal life.

1. Significant life change. A general stressor that encompasses both work and personal life is having to cope with significant change. According the research of Thomas Holmes and Richard Rahe, the necessity of a significant change in an individual's life pattern creates stress. The more significant the change you have to cope with in a short period of time, the greater the probability of experiencing a stress disorder.[11] As shown in Figure 17-3, the maximum negative change is the death of a spouse. Twenty-four other stressors created by change are listed in the table in decreasing order of impact. The rank order shown in Figure 17-3 consists of

FIGURE 17-3

THE TOP 25 STRESSORS AS MEASURED BY LIFE-CHANGE UNITS

Source: These stressors have changed over time. This version is from Thomas H. Holmes and Richard H. Rahe, "The Social Adjustment Rating Scale," *Journal of Psychosomatic Research, 15,* 1971, pp. 210–223, with an interview updating from Sue MacDonald, "Battling Stress," *Cincinnati Enquirer,* October 23, 1995, p. C4.

1. Death of a spouse
2. Divorce
3. Marital separation
4. Jail term/imprisonment
5. Death of a family member
6. Personal injury or illness
7. Marriage
8. Fired from the job
9. Marital reconciliation
10. Retirement
11. Change in health of family member
12. Pregnancy
13. Sexual difficulties
14. Change in financial status
15. Number of arguments with spouse
16. Major mortgage
17. Foreclosure of a loan
18. Change in responsibilities at work
19. Son or daughter leaves home
20. Trouble with in-laws
21. Outstanding personal achievement
22. Spouse begins or stops work
23. Begin or end school
24. Change in living conditions
25. Revision of personal habits

averages and does not hold true for everybody. For example, a person who could fall back into working for a family business might not find being fired from the job (item 8 in the figure) so stressful.

2. Low self-esteem. A subtle cause of stress is low self-esteem. People who do not feel good about themselves often find it difficult to feel good about anything. Low self-esteem has several links to stress. One is that being in a bad mood continually functions as a stressor. People with low self-esteem drag themselves down into a funk, which creates stress. Another link between low self-esteem and stress proneness is that people with low self-esteem get hurt more by insults. Instead of questioning the source of the criticism, the person with self-doubt will accept the opinion as valid.[12] An insult accepted as valid acts as a stressor because it is a threat to our well-being.

Low self-esteem is linked to stress in yet another way. People with low self-esteem doubt their ability to work their way out of problems. As a result, minor challenges appear to be major problems. For example, a person with low self-esteem will often doubt he or she will be successful in conducting a job search. As a result, having to conduct a job search will represent a major stressor. A person with high self-esteem might feel better prepared mentally to accept the challenge. (As you will recall, your perception of an event influences whether it is stressful.)

3. Everyday annoyances. Managing everyday annoyances can have a greater impact on your health than major life catastrophes. Among these everyday annoyances are losing keys or a wallet, a hard drive crashing, being stuck in traffic, having your car break down, and being lost on the way to an important appointment. People who have the coping skills to deal with everyday annoyances are less likely to be stressed out over them. A major reason everyday annoyances act as stressors is because they are frustrating—they block your path to an important goal, such as getting your work accomplished.

4. Social and family problems. Friends and family are the main sources of love and affection in your life, but they can also be the main source of stress. Most physical acts of violence are committed among friends and family members. One of the many reasons we encounter so much conflict with friends and family is that we are emotionally involved with them.

5. Physical and mental health problems. Prolonged stress produces physical and mental health problems, and the reverse is also true. Physical and mental illness can act as stressors—the fact of being ill is stressful. Furthermore, thinking that you might soon contract a life-threatening illness is stressful. If you receive a serious injury, that too can create stress.

6. Financial problems. A major life stressor is financial problems. Although you may not be obsessed with money, not having enough money to take care of what you consider the necessities of life can lead to anxiety and tension. If you do not have enough money to replace or repair a broken or faulty personal computer or automobile, the result can be stressful. A major stressor for recent graduates who move to areas with high costs of living is being able to afford a comfortable place to live. Another indicator of the negative stress caused by financial problems is that during 2008, while the recession was in full swing, telephone calls to the National Suicide Prevention Lifeline (800-273-TALK) increased by 35 percent. Many of the callers expressed concerns about feeling hopeless and helpless because of the economic crisis. Also, many investors who are wiped out do commit suicide.[13] Figure 17-4 illustrates the impact of financial problems on the perceived stress among different generations.

7. School-related problems. The life of a student can be stressful. Among the stressors to cope with are exams in subjects you do not understand well, having to write papers on subjects unfamiliar to you, working your way through the

FIGURE 17-4

GENERATIONS AND STRESS

In percentage of respondents as of September 2008

Although older adults report less stress overall, more "matures" and boomers are reporting the economy as a source of stress than younger generations. Money is also a cause of stress for 79 percent of boomers and 73 percent of matures.

	Millennials Ages 21–32	Gen Xers Ages 33–46	Boomers Ages 47–65	Matures* 66+
Money	83	87	79	73
The economy	71	78	83	86
Work	74	73	66	39
Health problems in my family	58	58	70	79
Housing costs	67	68	62	49
Job stability	57	59	57	43

*Generation designations are accurate for 2011.

Source: *APA Stress in America* survey reprinted in Sara Martin, "Money Is the Top Stressor for Americans," *Monitor on Psychology*, December 2008, p. 29.

complexities of registration, and having to deal with instructors who do not see things your way. Another source of severe stress for some students is having too many competing demands on their time. On most campuses you will find someone who works full-time, goes to school full-time, and has a family.

PERSONALITY FACTORS CONTRIBUTING TO STRESS

Some people are more stress prone than others because of personality factors. Three key personality factors predisposing people to stress are type A behavior, a belief that external forces control their life, and negative affectivity.

Type A Behavior and Hostility

Type A behavior

personality characteristics that lead a person into stressful situations. Type A behavior has two main components: (1) the tendency to try to accomplish too many things in too little time and (2) free-floating hostility

People with **type A behavior** characteristics have basic personalities that lead them into stressful situations. Type A behavior has two main components. One is a tendency to try to accomplish too many things in too little time. This leads the type A individual to be impatient and demanding. The other component is free-floating hostility. Because of this combined sense of urgency and hostility, trivial things irritate these people. On the job, people with type A behavior are aggressive and hardworking. Off the job, they keep themselves preoccupied with all kinds of errands to run and things to do.

Certain features of the type A behavior pattern are related to coronary heart disease. Hostility, anger, cynicism, and suspiciousness lead to heart problems, whereas impatience, ambition, and being work driven are not associated with coronary disease. One study showed that men who received a high score on a personality test about hostility were much more likely to develop coronary heart disease several years later.[14] Many work-driven people who like what they are doing—including many business executives—are remarkably healthy and outlive less competitive people. In reference to heart disease, medical and clinical psychologist David Krantz concluded, "You can be ambitious. You can be time pressured. But if you're not hostile and angry, your risk is lower."[15]

Belief in External Locus of Control

External locus of control

individual's belief that external forces control their fate

Internal locus of control

individual's belief that fate is pretty much under a person's own control

If you believe that your fate is controlled more by external than internal forces, you are probably more susceptible to stress. People with an **external locus of control** believe that external forces control their fate. Conversely, people with an **internal locus of control** believe that fate is pretty much under their control. The link between locus of control and stress works in this manner: If people believe they can control adverse forces, they are less prone to the stressor of worrying about them. For example, if you believed that you can always find a job, you will worry less about unemployment. At the same time, the person who believes in an internal locus of control experiences a higher level of job satisfaction. Work is less stressful and more satisfying when you perceive it to be under your control.

The everyday problem of lost computer files illustrates the importance of an internal locus of control. When a hard drive crashes or a valuable file is lost in some other way, the "external" person blames the computer or the software for the stressful event. An "internal," in contrast, would most likely have created backup files along the way. So when a crash occurs, the person is less stressed because relatively little data have been lost.

What about your locus of control? Do you believe it to be internal? Or is it external?

Negative Affectivity

Negative affectivity

a tendency to experience aversive (intensely disliked) emotional states; predisposition to experience emotional stress that includes feelings of nervousness, tension, and worry

A major contributor to being stress prone is **negative affectivity,** a tendency to experience aversive (intensely disliked) emotional states. In more detail, negative affectivity is a predisposition to experience emotional stress that includes feelings of nervousness, tension, and worry. Furthermore, a person with negative affectivity is likely to experience emotional states such as anger, scorn, revulsion, guilt, and self-dissatisfaction.[16] Such negative personalities seem to search for discrepancies between what they would like and what exists. Instead of attempting to solve problems, they look for them. Although negative affectivity is a relatively stable personality characteristic, the circumstances a person faces can trigger such behavior.[17] For example, a four-hour wait in an airplane parked on the tarmac might trigger a person's mild tendencies toward negative affectivity.

What Are Some Key Sources of Work Stress?

◀ Learning Objective 3 ◀

No job is without potential stressors for some people. A survey indicated that work is the major source of stress for Americans, with 74 percent of respondents reporting that work is their top stressor.[18] But when work is lacking stressful elements it may not have enough challenge to prompt employees to achieve high performance. Figure 17-5 illustrates five major job stressors you might encounter or have already encountered .

WORK OVERLOAD OR UNDERLOAD

A heavy workload is a widely acknowledged source of job stress. **Role overload,** a burdensome workload, can create stress for a person in two ways. First, the person may become fatigued and thus be less able to tolerate annoyances and irritations. Think of how much easier it is to become provoked over a minor incident when you lack proper

Role overload
a burdensome workload that creates stress for a person in two ways: (1) the person may become fatigued and less able to tolerate annoyances and irritations and (2) a person subject to unreasonable work demands may feel perpetually behind schedule, a situation that itself creates an uncomfortable, stressful feeling

FIGURE 17-5
FIVE FREQUENT JOB STRESSORS

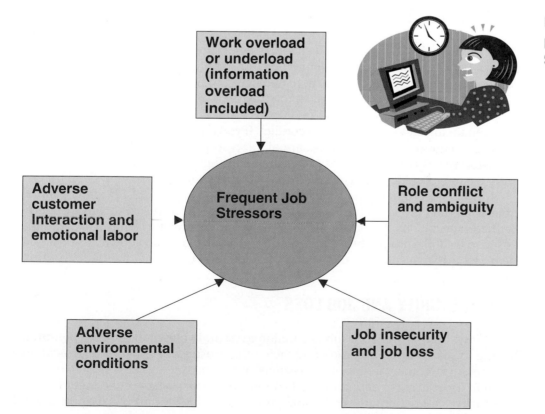

rest. Second, a person subject to unreasonable work demands may feel perpetually behind schedule, a situation that itself creates an uncomfortable, stressful feeling.

In extreme form, role overload can kill. For example, death from too much work is so common in Japan that the word *karoshi* has been coined to label the situation. In a celebrated case, a Toyota chief engineer worked up to 114 hours of overtime a month in the six months before he died of heart failure. For decades, the Japanese government has been attempting without much success to set limits on hours of work. The consequences of role overload show up in claims for death and disability from overwork and also in suicides attributed to work fatigue. Among 2,207 work-related suicides in Japanese companies in one year, the most frequent reason (672 suicides) was overwork.[19]

Another form of work overload is demanding higher and higher speed from workers. Speed is important to companies because delivering goods and services very quickly brings a competitive edge. The most stressful situation occurs when a company downsizes and the remaining workers are expected to carry a heavier work-load at a faster pace than previously. The combination of additional responsibility and high speed can be a major stressor. Among the problems are that hurried employees have very little time to ask for help or to carefully study what they are doing.

A powerful stressor for knowledge workers is information overload. Workers have to process so much information in the form of e-mail messages, text messages, Web sites, written reports, and job-related news that their brain circuits become overloaded, leading to stress and lowered concentration. Many workers encourage overload by multitasking while receiving information.

A disruptive amount of stress can also occur when people experience **role underload,** or too little to do. Some people find role underload frustrating because it is a normal human desire to want to work toward self-fulfillment. Also, making a contribution on the job is one way of gaining self-esteem. Some people, however, find it relaxing not to have much to do on the job. One direct benefit is that it preserves their energy for family and leisure activities.

Role underload
disruptive amount of stress that can occur when people experience too little to do

ROLE CONFLICT AND ROLE AMBIGUITY

Role conflict
having to choose between two competing demands or expectations

Being pulled in two directions is a classic stressor. **Role conflict** refers to having to choose between two competing demands or expectations. Many workers receive conflicting demands from two or more managers. Imagine being told by your manager to give top priority to one project. You then receive an e-mail message from your manager's manager, who tells you to drop everything and work on another project. It's often up to you to resolve such a conflict. If you don't, you will experience stress. Having to choose between taking care of job responsibilities versus personal responsibilities is another potent type of role conflict, such as having to work the night a good friend is getting married. Do you upset your boss or your good friend?

Role ambiguity
condition in which the job holder receives confusing or poorly defined expectations

Not being certain of what they should be doing is a stressor for many people. **Role ambiguity** is a condition in which the job holder receives confusing or poorly defined expectations. A typical complaint is, "I'm not really sure I know what I'm supposed to be doing around here." Role ambiguity is related to job control. If you lack a clear picture of what you should be doing, it is difficult to get your job under control.

JOB INSECURITY AND JOB LOSS

Worrying about losing your job is a major stressor. Even when jobs are plentiful, having to search for another job and facing the prospect of geographic relocation are stressors for many people. Downsizings and corporate mergers—which usually result in downsizing to eliminate duplication in positions—have contributed to job insecurity. The anticipation of layoffs among employees can increase negative stress and lower job performance. In addition, the survivors of a downsizing often experience pressure from the fear of future job cuts, loss of friends, and worry about a sudden increase in workload.[20]

Job loss is a more intense stressor than job insecurity because it is compounded by the stressors of financial problems, decreased status, and blows to the self-esteem. Negative confrontations with creditors might also add to the stress.

ADVERSE ENVIRONMENTAL CONDITIONS

A variety of adverse organizational conditions are stressors, as identified by the National Institute of Occupational Safety and Health. Among these adverse organizational conditions are unpleasant or dangerous physical conditions, such as crowding, noise, air pollution, or ergonomic problems. Enough polluted air within an office building can create a *sick building* in which a diverse range of airborne particles, vapors, molds, and gases pollute the indoor environment. The result can be headaches, nausea, and respiratory infections as well as the stress created by being physically ill. Dealing with constant informational overload might also be considered an adverse environmental condition.

Working at a computer monitor for prolonged periods of time can lead to adverse physical and psychological reactions. The symptoms include headaches and fatigue, along with eye problems. Common visual problems are dry eyes and blurred or double vision. An estimated one out of five visits to vision care professionals is for computer-related problems. Another vision-related problem is that people lean forward to scan the monitor, leading to physical problems such as back strain.

The neck pain, shoulder strain, and backaches so often associated with people working at computers might also be related to other forms of job stress. As such, working on the computer alone might not be the only cause of the symptoms. Having poor relationships with coworkers and the manager might also contribute to the physical problems. A study with call center workers in the United Kingdom found that 45 percent of participants reported upper-body strain, and 34 percent complained of lower-back problems. These same employees reported the most job strain in terms of job-related anxiety and depression.[21] (It is also conceivable that the physical problems could have led to anxiety and depression.)

A repetitive-motion disorder most frequently associated with keyboarding and the use of optical scanners is **carpal tunnel syndrome.** The syndrome occurs when repetitive flexing and extension of the wrist causes the tendons to swell, thus trapping and pinching the median nerve. Carpal tunnel syndrome creates stress because of the pain and misery. The thoughts of having to permanently leave a job requiring keyboarding is another potential stressor. Repetitive-motion disorders can be prevented somewhat by computer workers taking frequent rest breaks and using a well-designed combination of the worktable, chair, and monitor. Wearing elasticized wrist bands provides enough support to the wrist tendons to prevent many cases of repetitive motion disorders. Many people who blame their job for having caused carpal tunnel syndrome fail to recognize that they spend perhaps an additional four hours per evening on the keyboard for purposes such as e-mailing friends and visiting Web sites.

Being comfortable while working prevents much physical strain. Figure 17-6 presents the basics of a workstation designed on *ergonomic* principles. (Ergonomics has to do with making machines and equipment fit human capabilities and demands.)

Carpal tunnel syndrome
repetitive-motion disorder most frequently associated with keyboarding and the use of optical scanners; occurs when repetitive flexing and extension of the wrist causes the tendons to swell, thus trapping and pinching the median nerve

ADVERSE CUSTOMER INTERACTION AND EMOTIONAL LABOR

Interactions with customers can be a major stressor. Part of the problem is that the sales associate often feels helpless when placed in conflict with a customer. The

An Ergonomic Workstation

- Keep the screen below your eye level.
- Keep your elbows on the same level with home-key row, with your wrists and lower arms parallel to floor.
- Support your back and thighs with a well-constructed chair.
- Position your feet flat on the floor.
- Use lamp to supplement inadequate room lighting.

Emotional labor
process of regulating both feelings and expressions to meet organizational goals

sales associate is told that "the customer is always right." Furthermore, the store manager usually sides with the customer in a dispute with the sales associate. Related to adverse customer interaction is the stressor of having to control the expression of emotion to please or to avoid displeasing a customer. Imagine having to smile at a customer who belittles you or makes unwanted sexual advances.

Alicia A. Grandey, associate professor of psychology at Penn State University, defines **emotional labor** as the process of regulating both feelings and expressions to meet organizational goals.[22] The process involves both surface acting and deep acting. Surface acting means faking expressions, such as smiling, whereas deep acting involves controlling feelings, such as suppressing anger toward a customer you perceive to be annoying. Sales workers and customer service representatives often experience emotional labor because so often they have to fake facial expressions and feelings to please customers. Nevertheless, according to one study, the top five occupations in terms of emotional labor demands are (1) police and sheriff's patrol officers, (2) social workers, (3) psychiatrists, (4) supervisors of police and detectives, and (5) registered nurses. Bill and account collectors ranked 15![23]

Engaging in emotional labor for prolonged periods of time can lead to job dissatisfaction, stress, and burnout. A contributing cause is that faking expressions and emotions takes a physiological toll, such as the intestines churning. Workers who engage in emotional labor may also develop cardiovascular problems and weakened immune systems.

▶ Learning Objective 4 ▶

What Are Several Effective Approaches to Managing Stress?

Because potentially harmful stressors surround us in work and personal life, virtually everybody needs a program of stress management to stay well. Stress management techniques are placed here into four categories: attacking the source of the stress, receiving social support, relaxation techniques, and wellness through proper exercise, diet, and rest. Your challenge is to select those techniques that best fit your circumstances and preferences. At the same time you should be seeking the amount of stress that enables you to capitalize on the benefits of positive stress but not fall prey to the negative symptoms of stress.

DEALING WITH STRESS BY ATTACKING ITS SOURCE

Stress can be dealt with in the short range by indirect techniques such as exercise and relaxation. But to manage stress in the long range and stay well, you must also learn to deal directly with stressors. Several of these techniques are described in the next few paragraphs.

Eliminating or Modifying the Stressor

The most potent method of managing stress is to eliminate the stressor giving you trouble. For example, if your job is your primary stressor, your stress level would be reduced if you found a more comfortable job. At other times, modifying the stressful situation can be equally helpful. Using the problem-solving method, you search for an alternative that will change the stressor.

Placing the Stressful Situation in Perspective

Stress comes about because of our perception of the situation. If you can alter your perception of a threatening situation, you are attacking the source. A potentially stressful situation can be put into perspective by asking, "What is the worst thing that could happen to me if I fail in this activity?" The answer to this question is found by asking a series of questions, starting with the grimmest possibility. For instance, you are late with a report that is due this afternoon. Consider the following questions and answers:

■ Will my reputation be damaged permanently? (*No*)

■ Will I get fired? (*No*)

■ Will I get reprimanded? (*Perhaps, but not for sure*)

■ Will my boss think less of me? (*Perhaps, but not for sure*)

Only if the answer is yes to either of the first two questions is negative stress truly justified. This thought process allows stressful situations to be properly evaluated and kept in perspective. You therefore avoid the stress that comes from overreacting to a situation.

An analysis of many studies concludes that the most effective approaches to managing workplace stress are **cognitive–behavioral interventions**—essentially a way of thinking constructively about a problem that includes perspective setting. Cognitive–behavioral interventions teach individuals to recognize how their pessimistic and often distorted thoughts of gloom and doom become stressors. Next, they learn to replace their unrealistic and highly pessimistic thinking with more realistic or more optimistic thinking.[24]

Cognitive–behavioral interventions
a way of thinking constructively about a problem that includes perspective setting

Gaining Control of the Situation

Feeling that a bothersome situation is out of control is almost a universal stressor. A key method of stress management is therefore to attack the stressor by gaining control of the situation. A multipurpose way of gaining control is to improve your work habits and time management. By being "on top of things," you can make heavy work and school demands less stressful. A trend related to reducing stress by gaining control is to simplify your life by getting rid of unessential activities. Andrew Weil, the natural health guru, recommends that you downsize your life. He believes that significant stress stems from the complexity of our lives, a major contributor being our material possessions. Many people have too many physical objects that require attention and maintenance. Weil recommends that you get rid of what you can spare.[25] You will gain control of your life situation by having less clutter.

A note of caution is that an oversimplified life can also be an impoverished life, creating stress of its own. Throw out or give to charity those physical possessions that contribute virtually nothing to your life. Yet save the sources of an enriched life. For example, why give up a smart phone, wide-screen TV, and iPod if all three are major sources of pleasure and satisfaction?

RECEIVING SOCIAL AND ORGANIZATIONAL SUPPORT

Support system
a group of people on whom one can rely for encouragement and comfort

An ideal way to manage stress is one that provides side benefits. Getting close to people falls into this category. You will reduce some stress symptoms and form healthy relationships with others in the process. By getting close to others, you build a **support system,** a group of people on whom you can rely for encouragement and comfort. The trusting relationship you have with these people is critically important. People within your support network include family members, friends, coworkers, and fellow students. In addition, some people in turmoil reach out to strangers to discuss personal problems. According to neuroscientist Steven W. Porges, engaging socially with others triggers neural circuits that calm the heart, relax the intestines, and dampen fear.[26] (Interacting with friendly people is likely to be more beneficial than interacting with hostile individuals.)

The usual method of reducing stress is to talk over your problems while the other person listens. Switching roles can also help reduce stress. Listening to others will make you feel better because you have helped them. Another advantage to listening to the feelings and problems of others is that it helps you to get close to them.

A happy marriage is another support system that can help a worker cope with job stress. According to one study with dual-earner couples, happily married women rebounded quicker from daily stress than women with less blissful unions. Stress was measured by saliva samples of the stress-related hormone cortisol.[27]

Receiving organizational support refers here to using the organization as part of your support system when experiencing heavy stress. The support might come from a friendly supervisor who will listen to the problems you are experiencing and perhaps offer some advice. A widely used form of support is an employee assistance program that offers counseling services for a variety of personal problems that could be impairing performance. (Do you recall Max's situation in the opening case to the chapter?) A large employer might have a full-time employee assistance program, whereas small employers use an outside counseling group.

The accompanying Human Relations in Practice illustrates how an employer can provide the type of support helpful in managing stress.

RELAXATION TECHNIQUES FOR HANDLING STRESS

"Relax" is the advice many people have always offered the stressed individual. Stress experts give us similar advice but also offer specific techniques. Here we describe three techniques that can help you relax and, consequently, help you

Human Relations in Practice

A Stress Prevention Program at a Small Service Organization

A department head in a small public service organization sensed an escalating level of tension and deteriorating morale among her staff. Job dissatisfaction and health symptoms such as headaches also seemed to be on the rise. Suspecting that stress was a developing problem in the department, she decided to hold a series of all-hands meetings with employees in the different work units of the department to explore this concern further. These meetings could be best described as brainstorming sessions where individual employees freely expressed their views about the scope and sources of stress in their units and the measures that might be implemented to bring the problem under control.

Using the information collected in these meetings and in meetings with middle managers, she concluded that a serious problem probably existed and that quick action was needed. Because she was relatively unfamiliar with the job stress field, she decided to seek help from a faculty member at a local university who taught courses on job stress and organizational behavior.

The manager and the professor reviewed the information collected at the brainstorming sessions. They then decided it would be useful for the faculty member to conduct informal classes to raise awareness about job stress—its causes, effects, and prevention—for all workers and managers in the department. It was also decided that a survey would be useful to obtain a more reliable picture of problematic job conditions and stress-related health complaints in the department. The faculty member used information from the meetings with workers and managers to design the survey. The faculty member was also involved in the distribution and collection of the anonymous survey to ensure that workers felt free to respond honestly and openly about what was bothering them. He then helped the department head analyze and interpret the data.

Analysis of the survey data suggested that three types of job conditions were linked to stress complaints among workers:

- Unrealistic deadlines

- Low levels of support from supervisors

- Lack of worker involvement in decision making

Having pinpointed these problems, the department head developed and prioritized a list of corrective measures for implementation. Examples of these actions included (a) greater participation of employees in work scheduling to reduce unrealistic deadlines and (b) more frequent meetings between workers and managers to keep supervisors and workers updated on developing problems.

Source: Case reported in "Stress of Work," *National Institute for Occupational Safety and Health Publication*, No. 99-101.

reduce stress and its symptoms In addition, Figure 17-7 lists a variety of "stress busters," many of which are relaxation oriented. Recognize that many of these techniques contribute directly to wellness and that stress management is a major component of wellness. Pick and choose among stress management techniques until you find several that effectively reduce your stress.

FIGURE 17-7
STRESS BUSTERS

- Take a nap when facing heavy pressures. Napping is regarded as one of the most effective techniques for reducing and preventing stress.
- Give in to your emotions. If you are angry, disgusted, or confused, admit your feelings. Suppressing your emotions adds to stress.
- Take a brief break from the stressful situation and do something small and constructive, such as washing your car, emptying a wastebasket, or getting a haircut.
- Get a massage, because it can loosen tight muscles, improve your blood circulation, and calm you down.
- Get help with your stressful task from a coworker, boss, or friend.
- Concentrate intensely on reading, surfing the Internet, a sport, or a hobby. Contrary to common sense, concentration is at the heart of stress reduction.
- Have a quiet place at home and have a brief idle period there every day.
- Take a leisurely day off from your routine.
- Finish something you have started, however small. Accomplishing almost anything reduces some stress.
- Stop to smell the flowers, make friends with a young child or an elderly person, or play with a kitten or puppy.
- Strive to do a good job but not a perfect job.
- Work with your hands, doing a pleasant task.
- Hug somebody you like and who you think will hug you back.
- Become a rag doll by standing with your arms dangling loosely at your sides. Start to shake your hands, then start shaking your arms. Next, sit and repeat the same moves with your legs.
- Find something to laugh at—a cartoon, a movie, a television show, a Web site for jokes, even yourself.
- Minimize drinking caffeinated or alcoholic beverages, and drink fruit juice or water instead. Grab a piece of fruit rather than a can of beer.
- Sit in a man-made salt cave, a relatively recent approach to relaxation.

Relaxation Response

Relaxation response
a physical state of deep rest in which one experiences a slower respiration and heart rate, lowered blood pressure, and lowered metabolism; a standard technique for reducing stress

A standard technique for reducing stress is to achieve the relaxation response. The **relaxation response** is a physical state of deep rest in which you experience a slower respiration and heart rate and lowered metabolism. Scientists have shown that the relaxation response lowers the heart rate, blood pressure, and oxygen consumption. Also, the relaxation response alleviates symptoms associated with many disorders and conditions, including hypertension arthritis, insomnia, depression, infertility, cancer, anxiety, and even aging. By practicing the relaxation response, you can counteract the fight-or-flight response associated with stress.

According to cardiologist Herbert Benson, four things are necessary to practice the relaxation response: a quiet environment, an object to focus on, a passive attitude, and a comfortable position. You are supposed to practice the relaxation response for ten to twenty minutes, twice a day. To evoke the relaxation response, Benson advises you to close your eyes. Relax. Concentrate on one word or prayer. If other thoughts come to mind, be passive and return to the repetition.

The relaxation response can be released in many ways besides the ritual just described. Among these methods are participating in repetitive sports such as running, progressive muscular relaxation, practicing yoga, and playing a musical instrument.[28]

Similar to any other relaxation technique, the relaxation response is harmless and works for most people. However, some very impatient people find it annoying to disrupt their busy day to work through the relaxation response. Unfortunately, these may be the people who most urgently need to learn to relax.

Meditation

Perhaps the oldest stress management technique of all, mediation is back in vogue. An estimated 10 million American adults meditate regularly. **Meditation** is a systematic method of concentration, reflection, or concentrated thinking designed to suppress the activity of the sympathetic nervous system. The relaxation response is essentially a meditation technique, and napping provides some of the benefits of meditation. The meditator reaches a deep state of mental and physical calmness and relaxation, driving away accumulated stress. Meditation is also recommended as a way of preventing and slowing down and reducing the pain of chronic diseases such as heart disease, AIDS, and cancer. People who meditate learn to tolerate everyday annoyances better. Meditation has been widely researched, and its key benefits in relation to stress include calming the mind and eliminating anxiety.[29]

A very important benefit of mediation as well as other relaxation techniques is that they enhance mental alertness. It would therefore be beneficial to you to meditate shortly before you needed to perform at your best, such as giving a presentation to management about your project.

The usual approach to meditation involves four simple steps. First, find a quiet place with a minimum of distractions. Second, close your eyes so that you can close yourself off from the outside world. Third, pick a word whose sound is soothing when repeated. Fourth, say the word repeatedly. For most people, one fifteen-minute session daily will accomplish the benefits of meditation.

Meditation
a systematic method of concentration, reflection, or concentrated thinking designed to suppress the activity of the sympathetic nervous system

MANAGING STRESS BY STAYING WELL (PROPER EXERCISE, DIET, AND REST)

A far-reaching strategy for managing stress is to both prevent and reduce negative stress by leading a healthy lifestyle, or being well. Three major components to staying well are proper exercise, diet, and rest. The three components are interrelated because each component facilitates the other: For example, if you exercise enough you tend to prefer healthy food; if you diet properly, physical exercise is easier, and so is obtaining rest. Also, if you rest well you will be in a better frame of mind to exercise, and you will not crave so much caffeine and sugar to stay energized. Proper diet and exercise are also important in helping ward off physical illness that creates stress for the individual. Poor diet and lack of exercise are responsible for almost as many deaths in the United States as smoking.[30]

Exercising Properly, Including Yoga

The right amount and type of physical exercise contributes substantially to wellness. Part of the reason exercise is useful for managing stress is that it contributes to relaxation and being better able to cope with frustration. To achieve wellness it is important to select an exercise program that is physically challenging but that does not lead to overexertion and muscle injury. Competitive sports, if taken too seriously, can actually increase a person's stress level. The most beneficial exercises are classified as aerobic because they make you breathe faster and raise your heart rate. Most of a person's exercise requirements can be met through everyday techniques such as walking or running up stairs, vigorous housework, yard work, or walking several miles per day.

A major benefit is the euphoria that often occurs when brain chemicals called *endorphins* are released into the body. The same experience is referred to as "runner's high." Other mental benefits of exercise include increased self-confidence;

improved body image and self-esteem; improved mental functioning, alertness, and efficiency; release of accumulated tensions; and relief from mild depression.[31]

Millions of people seek to reduce and prevent stress though yoga, which is both physical exercise and a way of developing mental attitudes that calm the body and the mind. During yoga, blood pressure lowers and your heart works more efficiently. One of yoga's many worthwhile goals is to solder a union between the mind and body, thereby achieving harmony and tranquility. Another benefit of yoga is that it helps people place aside negative thoughts that act as stressors.[32] Yoga can therefore reduce anxiety, with the key being deep, slow breathing, as follows:

> Breathe through your nose, drawing air down into your lungs as you expand your diaphragm. As you relax and exhale, the diaphragm contracts. The process controls the pace of your breathing and creates a natural calmness.[33]

Unlike the relaxation response and mild exercise, yoga has some potentially severe negative consequences to the body. Yoga should be first practiced under the guidance of a certified professional to minimize torn muscles and ruptured blood vessels from extreme bending and twisting.[34]

Resting Sufficiently

Rest offers benefits similar to those of exercise, such as stress reduction, improved concentration, improved energy, and better tolerance for frustration. Achieving proper rest is closely linked to getting proper exercise. The current interest in adult napping reflects the awareness that proper rest makes a person less stress prone and enhances productivity. A growing number of firms have napping facilities for workers, and many workers nap at their desks or in their parked vehicles during lunch breaks. Naps of about twenty minutes taken during the workday are used both as energizers and as stress reducers. To keep the effectiveness of workday napping in perspective, workers who achieve sufficient rest during normal sleeping hours have less need for naps during working hours. But the meditation-like benefits of napping offer an advantage even for the person who sleeps adequately at night.

Maintaining a Healthy Diet

Eating nutritious foods is valuable for mental as well as physical health, making it easier to cope with frustrations that are potential stressors. Many nutritionists and physicians believe that eating fatty foods, such as red meat, contributes to colon cancer. Improper diet, such as consuming less than 1,300 calories per day, can weaken you physically. In turn, you become more susceptible to stress. Some non-nutritious foods, such as those laden with caffeine or sugar, tend to enhance stress levels. According to the Dietary Guidelines of the U.S. Department of Agriculture, a healthy diet is one that

- Emphasizes fruits, vegetables, whole grains, and fat-free or low-fat milk and milk products
- Includes lean meats, poultry, fish, beans, eggs, and nuts
- Is low in saturated fats, trans fats, cholesterol, salt (sodium), and added sugars

These recommendations are for the general public over two years of age. Using MyPyramid, the government personalizes a recommended diet, taking into account our age, sex, and amount of physical exercise. Consult http://www.mypyramid.gov.

What Are Two Key Perspectives on Understanding and Dealing with Personal Problems?

◀ Learning Objective 5 ◀

Our approach to understanding and overcoming personal problems will be to first describe self-defeating behavior in general and how to reverse the trend. We then emphasize the importance of resilience in dealing with personal problems.

SELF-DEFEATING BEHAVIOR

Many problems on the job and in personal life arise because of factors beyond our control. A boss may be intimidating and insensitive, an employer might lay you off, or your partner might abruptly terminate your relationship. Many personal problems, nevertheless, arise because of **self-defeating behavior.** A person with self-defeating tendencies intentionally or unintentionally engages in activities or harbors attitudes that work against his or her best interest.[35] A person who habitually is late for important meetings is engaging in self-defeating behavior. Dropping out of school for no reason other than being bored with studying is another of many possible examples. In short, self-defeating behavior means the same as being your own worst enemy.

A group of self-defeating behaviors that might escape your attention are **soft addictions,** or ordinary behavior that if done to excess can wreak havoc with your life. Soft addictions often take the form of habit or compulsions that drain your time and money, although they may seem harmless at first.[36] In our complex world, there are extensive opportunities for developing soft addictions. Here are a few samplers, and you could probably easily add more to the list:

■ Making a purchase from a soft-drink vending machine or carry-out café several times a day

■ Checking e-mail, instant messages, and text messages every few minutes although not required for work or because of an urgent personal problem

■ Watching television or playing video games for so many hours that interaction with people and getting household chores done or studying (or self-improvement) suffers

■ Engaging in physical exercise so frequently that you suffer frequent injuries and lack the time to get other things in life accomplished

■ Devoting endless hours to the Internet, including being in contacts with hundreds of "friends" and "followers" on social networking sites

■ Daydreaming excessively

To examine your present tendencies toward self-defeating behavior, take the self-sabotage quiz presented in Human Relations Self-Assessment Quiz 17-1. Taking the quiz will help alert you to many self-imposed behaviors and attitudes that could potentially harm your career and personal life.

Overcoming self-defeating behavior requires hard work and patience. Here we present four widely applicable strategies for overcoming and preventing self-defeating behavior. Pick and choose among them to fit your particular circumstance and personal style.

Self-defeating behavior
activities or attitudes that work against one's best interest

Soft addiction
ordinary behavior that if done to excess can wreak havoc with your life

Human Relations Self-Assessment Quiz   17-1

The Self-Sabotage Questionnaire

Indicate how accurately each of the following statements describes or characterizes you, using a 5-point scale: (0) very inaccurately, (1) inaccurately, (2) midway between inaccurately and accurately, (3) accurately, (4) very accurately. Consider discussing some of the questions with a family member, close friend, or work associate. Another person's feedback may prove helpful in providing accurate answers to some of the questions.

		Answer
1.	Other people have said that I am my own worst enemy.	_____
2.	If I don't do a perfect job, I feel worthless.	_____
3.	I am my own harshest critic.	_____
4.	When engaged in a sport or other competitive activity, I find a way to blow a substantial lead right near the end.	_____
5.	When I make a mistake, I can usually identify another person to blame.	_____
6.	I have a strong tendency to procrastinate.	_____
7.	I have trouble focusing on what is really important to me.	_____
8.	I have trouble taking criticism, even from friends.	_____
9.	My fear of seeming stupid often prevents me from asking questions or offering my opinion.	_____
10.	I tend to expect the worst in most situations.	_____
11.	Many times I have rejected people who treat me well.	_____
12.	When I have an important project to complete, I usually get sidetracked, and then miss the deadline.	_____
13.	I choose work assignments that lead to disappointments, even when better options are clearly available.	_____
14.	I frequently misplace things, such as my keys, and then get very angry at myself.	_____
15.	I am concerned that if I take on much more responsibility people will expect too much from me.	_____
16.	I avoid situations, such as competitive sports, where people can find out how good or bad I really am.	_____
17.	People describe me as the "office clown."	_____
18.	I have an insatiable demand for money and power.	_____
19.	When negotiating with others, I hate to grant any concessions.	_____
20.	I seek revenge for even the smallest hurts.	_____
21.	I have an overwhelming ego.	_____
22.	When I receive a compliment or other form of recognition, I usually feel I don't deserve it.	_____
23.	To be honest, I choose to suffer.	_____
24.	I regularly enter into conflict with people who try to help me.	_____
25.	I'm a loser.	_____

Total Score _____

Scoring and Interpretation:

Total your answers to all the questions to obtain your score.

0–25   You appear to have very few tendencies toward self-sabotage. If this interpretation is supported by your own positive feelings toward your life and yourself, you are in good shape with respect to self-defeating behavior tendencies. However, stay alert to potential self-sabotaging tendencies that could develop at later stages in your life.

26–50   You may have some mild tendencies toward self-sabotage. It could be that you do things occasionally that defeat your own purposes. Review actions you have taken during the past six months to decide if any of them have been self-sabotaging.

Continued

51–75 You show signs of engaging in self-sabotage. You probably have thoughts and carry out actions that could be blocking you from achieving important work and personal goals. People with scores in this category characteristically engage in negative self-talk that lowers their self-confidence and makes them appear weak and indecisive to others. People in this range frequently experience another problem. They sometimes sabotage their chances of succeeding on a project simply to prove that their negative self-assessment is correct. If you scored in this range, carefully study the suggestions offered in this chapter.

76–100 You most likely have a strong tendency toward self-sabotage. (Sometimes it is possible to obtain a high score on a test like this because you are going through an unusually stressful period in your life.) Study this section of the chapter carefully and look for useful hints for removing self-imposed barriers to your success. Equally important, you might discuss your tendencies toward undermining your own achievements with a mental health professional.

Solicit Feedback on Your Actions

Feedback is essential for monitoring whether you are sabotaging your career or personal life. A starting point is to listen carefully to any direct or indirect comments from your superiors, subordinates, coworkers, customers, and friends about how you are coming across to them. Consider the case of Bill, a technical writer:

> Bill heard three people in one week make comments about his appearance. It started innocently with, "Here, let me fix your collar." Next, an office assistant said, "Bill, are you coming down with something?" The third comment was, "You look pretty tired today. Have you been working extra hard?" Bill processed this feedback carefully. He used it as a signal that his steady late-night drinking episodes were adversely affecting his image. He then cut back his drinking enough to revert to his normal healthy appearance.

Take notes to show how serious you are about the feedback. When someone provides any feedback at all, say, "Please continue. This is very useful." Try not to react defensively when you hear something negative. You asked for it, and the person is truly doing you a favor.

Learn to Profit from Criticism

As the preceding example implies, learning to profit from criticism is necessary to benefit from feedback. Furthermore, to ignore valid criticism can be self-defeating. People who benefit from criticism are able to stand outside themselves while being criticized. It is as if they are watching the criticism from a distance and looking for its possible merits. People who take criticism personally experience anguish when receiving negative feedback.

Ask politely for more details about the negative behavior in question so that you can change if change is warranted. If your boss is criticizing you for being rude with customers, you might respond, "I certainly don't want to be rude. Can you give me a couple of examples of how I was rude? I need your help in working on this problem." After asking questions, you can better determine if the criticism is valid.

Stop Denying the Existence of Problems

Many people sabotage their careers because they deny the existence of a problem and therefore do not take appropriate action. Denial takes place as a defensive maneuver against a painful reality. An example of a self-sabotaging form of denial is to ignore the importance of upgrading one's credentials despite overwhelming evidence that it is necessary. Some people never quite complete a degree program that has become an informal qualification for promotion. Consequently, they sabotage their chances of receiving a promotion for which they are otherwise qualified.

Observe the Discrepancy between Your Ideal Life and What Exists Now

Motivational speaker Kevin Hogan recommends that you write a description of your ideal life. Describe in specific terms what you would like your life to be now or in the future. Use several senses, including touch, taste, and smell. (For example, what would your log cabin or condominium town home smell like?) Next, write a description of your current self and life. You have a reasonably clear idea of what discrepancies have to be closed to attain you goals.[37] It could be that the discrepancies involve some self-defeating behavior, such as having a low credit score.

Visualize Self-Enhancing Behavior

To apply visualization, program yourself to overcome self-defeating actions and thoughts. Imagine yourself engaging in self-enhancing, winning actions and thoughts. Picture yourself achieving peak performance when good results count the most. A starting point is to identify the next job situation you will be facing that is similar to ones you have flubbed in the past. You then imagine yourself mentally and physically projected into that situation. Imagine what the room looks like, who will be there, and the confident expression you will have on your face. Visualization is akin to watching a DVD or video of you doing something right.

DEVELOPING RESILIENCE

Resilience
the ability to withstand pressure and emerge stronger because of an experience; being challenged and not breaking down

A master strategy for dealing with personal problems, as well as stress, is to develop resilience. The ability to overcome setback is an important characteristic of successful people. **Resilience** is the ability to withstand pressure and emerge stronger because of the experience. Being resilient also refers to being challenged and not breaking down. The ability to bounce back from a setback, or resilience, is another aspect of emotional intelligence. In the context of emotional intelligence, resilience refers to being persistent and optimistic when faced with setbacks.[38] Learning how to manage stress is an important part of developing resilience. Being resilient also closely associated with self-confidence. Human Relations Self-Assessment Quiz 17-2 gives you an opportunity to examine your tendencies toward being resilient.

An important part of being resilient is to first overcome the emotional turmoil associated with the setback you have encountered, such as losing a job or being left by a spouse or good friend. Discussing your problem with a friend or counselor is a standard approach for overcoming the emotional turmoil that accompanies a setback. Selecting the right person with whom you can vent your problem is an asset in dealing with your problem. Ideally, you should find someone who can help you help yourself by listening carefully and not jumping in with advice immediately. Remember also to find a good time to discuss your problem with a confidant rather than springing it on him or her.[39]

"Failure is simply the opportunity to begin again, this time more intelligently."
—Henry Ford

After some of the emotional trauma from your problem has been reduced, it is time to use your creative problem-solving skills to find a solution—those that you have developed through experience and in your study of other subjects as well as human relations.

Human Relations Self-Assessment Quiz   17-2

The Resiliency Quiz

From 1 to 5, rate how much each of the following applies to you (1 = very little, 5 = very much)

1	2	3	4	5	If I have a bad day at work or school, it does not ruin my day.
1	2	3	4	5	After a vacation, I can usually get right back into work at my regular work pace.
1	2	3	4	5	Every "no" I encounter is one step closer to a "yes."
1	2	3	4	5	The popular saying "Get over it" has a lot of merit in guiding your life.
1	2	3	4	5	The last time I was rejected for a job (or assignment) I wanted, it had no particular impact on me.
1	2	3	4	5	I enjoy being the underdog once in awhile.
1	2	3	4	5	I enjoy taking risks because I believe that the biggest rewards stem from risk taking.
1	2	3	4	5	I rarely worry about, or keep thinking about, mistakes I have made in the past.
1	2	3	4	5	If I ran for political office and lost, I would be willing to run again.
1	2	3	4	5	When I encounter a major problem or setback, I will talk over the situation with a friend or confidant.
1	2	3	4	5	I am physically sick much less frequently than most people I know, including friends, coworkers, and other students.
1	2	3	4	5	The last time I lost my keys (or wallet or handbag or cell phone), I took care of the problem within a few days and was not particularly upset.
1	2	3	4	5	I get more than my share of good breaks.

Scoring and Interpretation:

Add numbers to get your total score.

60–70   You are highly resilient with an ability to bounce back from setbacks.

45–59   You have an average degree of resiliency when faced with problems.

30–44   Setbacks and disappointments are a struggle for you.

1–29   You may need help in dealing with setbacks.

Concept Review and Reinforcement

Key Terms

Stress, 496
Stressor, 496
Fight-or-flight response, 496
Challenge stressors, 497
Hindrance stressors, 497
Burnout, 499
Type A behavior, 502
External locus of control, 502

Internal locus of control, 502
Negative affectivity, 502
Role overload, 503
Role underload, 504
Role conflict, 504
Role ambiguity, 504
Carpal tunnel syndrome, 505
Emotional labor, 506

Cognitive–behavioral
  interventions, 507
Support system, 508
Relaxation response, 510
Meditation, 511
Self-defeating behavior, 513
Soft addiction, 513
Resilience, 516

Summary and Review

The body's battle against a stressor is the fight-or-flight response. Stress always involves physiological changes, such as an increase in heart rate, blood cholesterol, and blood pressure. Men who respond most intensely to mental stress run a higher risk of blocked blood vessels. Stress adversely affects our ability to fight infection.

- Challenge stressors have a positive effect on motivation and performance, whereas hindrance stressors have a negative effect. Negative stress has enormous consequences to individuals and organizations. Alcohol and illicit drug use might increase where workers experience negative stress.
- The existence of challenge stressors suggests that the right amount of stress can be beneficial, such as the right amount of multitasking. Performance tends to be best under moderate amounts of stress, yet certain negative forms of stress almost always decrease performance.
- Prolonged stress may lead to burnout, a condition of emotional, mental, and physical exhaustion in response to long-term job stressors, such as a heavy workload. Occupations that require frequent and intense interaction with others often lead to burnout.
- Almost any form of frustration, disappointment, setback, inconvenience, or crisis in your personal life can cause stress. The categories of situations that can produce stress include significant life changes, low self-esteem, everyday annoyances,

social and family problems, physical and mental health problems, financial problems, and school-related problems.

- Personality factors contribute to stress proneness. People with type A behavior are impatient and demanding and have free-floating hostility, all of which leads to stress. People with an external locus of control (believing that external forces control their fate) are more susceptible to stress. Negative affectivity (a predisposition to negative mental states) also contributes to stress.
- Sources of job stress are quite varied. Among them are work overload (including techno stress) or underload, role conflict and ambiguity, job insecurity and job loss, adverse environmental conditions including a sick building and carpal tunnel syndrome, and adverse customer interaction and emotional labor (faking expressions and feelings).

To successfully manage stress in the long range, you have to deal with the stressors directly. Three direct approaches are to do the following:

- Eliminate or modify the stressor.
- Place the situation in perspective (cognitive–behavioral approaches to managing stress help with perspective setting).
- Gain control of the situation.

Stress can also be reduced through social support from others, including the organization. Relaxation techniques for handling stress include the relaxation response and meditation. Managing stress by staying well includes proper exercise, diet, and rest. Exercising properly, including yoga, helps reduce and prevent stress. Sufficient rest also helps manage stress. Maintaining a healthy diet makes it easier to cope with frustrations that could be stressful.

Unless personal problems are kept under control, a person's chances of achieving career and personal success diminish. Many personal problems arise out of self-defeating behavior. Soft addictions can be self-defeating. Approaches to overcoming and preventing self-defeating behavior include the following:

- Solicit feedback on your actions.
- Learn to profit from criticism.
- Stop denying the existence of problems.
- Visualize self-enhancing behavior.

Developing resilience is a master strategy for dealing with personal problems as well as stress. To be resilient, it is helpful to get past the emotional turmoil by talking to a confidant and then working to solve the problem.

Check Your Understanding

1. An office manager in an emergency room, and a mother of young triplets, said she knew she was emotionally drained and stressed out because of all her responsibilities. She said she knew that she should manage her stress better, but she simply did not have the time. What advice can you offer this woman?
2. Identify several potential stressors created by commuting a long distance to work. What can be done to reduce these stressors?
3. In what way do many sales representatives at an automobile dealership experience role underload? How do they appear to deal with the problem?
4. Assume that a professional-level worker, such as a customer service representative, is convinced that napping during the workday is an excellent way of managing stress. Where should this person nap?
5. How can a person who becomes stressed from having to interact with coworkers several hours a day compete in the modern world?

6. Why does a simple act like emptying a wastebasket or cleaning out and washing one's car reduce stress for so many people?
7. What is the difference between making a bad mistake once and self-defeating behavior?
8. Give an example of self-defeating behavior engaged in by a professional athlete. What appear to be the negative consequences to that athlete's career stemming from the self-defeating behavior?
9. Give an example of self-defeating behavior engaged in by a business executive or public office holder. What appear to be the negative consequences to the person's career stemming from the self-defeating behavior?
10. Imagine that a student receives an F in a course. What can he or she do to be resilient?

Web Corner

The nature of stress and stress management:
www.stress.org

Burnout self-test:
www.mindtools.com/stress/brn/burnoutselftest.htm

Overcoming self-sabotage:
www.kevinhogan.com/selfsabotage.htm

INTERNET SKILL BUILDER

Use your favorite search engines to learn about employee assistance programs (EAPs). After visiting several sites, answer these questions: (1) What type of help can an employee expect to receive from an EAP? (2) How does an EAP help with stress management? (3) Does the EAP counselor typically tell the company the nature of the problem facing the employee who sought assistance? (4) What benefits do companies expect from offering an EAP to employees?

Developing Your
Human Relations Skills

Human Relations Application Exercises

Applying Human Relations Exercise 17-1

Personal Stress Management Action Plan

Most people face a few powerful stressors in their work and personal life, but few people take the time to clearly identify these stressors or develop an action plan for remedial action. The purpose of this exercise is to make you an exception. Here is an opportunity to inventory your stressors, think through the problems they may be causing you, and develop action plans you might take to remedy the situation. Use the accompanying form or create one with a word processing table or a spreadsheet program.

Work or School Stressor	Symptoms This Stressor Is Creating for Me	My Action Plan to Manage This Stressor
1.		
2.		
3.		

Personal Life Stressor	Symptoms This Stressor Is Creating for Me	My Action Plan to Manage This Stressor
1.		
2.		
3.		

Seven days after preparing this worksheet, observe if any of your stress symptoms have diminished. Also, identify those stressors for which only a long-term solution is possible. One student reported that a major work stressor he faced was that the wanted to work in international business that emphasized doing business with Italian fashion companies. Yet he was experiencing stress because he had almost zero knowledge of the Italian language or culture. (By the way, can you offer this man any suggestions?)

Applying Human Relations Exercise 17-2

Overcoming Self-Defeating Behavior

Most people engage in some behavior that could be self-defeating, even to a very minor degree. For example, hundreds of otherwise rational people are seriously injured every year because they climb on their roof to clean a gutter or replace a shingle. Also, many people walk out into traffic or bump into a lamppost or building while sending or receiving a text message. Another example is that some well-to-do people cannot resist the urge to shoplift occasionally. If you engage in no self-defeating behavior or behavior that is potentially self-defeating, you are exempt from this exercise. For all others, answer the following four questions:

1. What is my most self-defeating behavior, even if the behavior is infrequent or only has the potential to be self-defeating?
2. If this behavior continues or becomes exaggerated, what are the consequences to my career and personal life?
3. What action steps can I take to overcome this self-defeating behavior?
4. What help can I get to overcome my self-defeating behavior?

Human Relations Class Activity

The Stress-Buster Survey

Each class member thinks through carefully which techniques he or she uses to reduce work or personal stress. Class members then come to the front of the room individually to make brief presentations of their most effective stress-reduction techniques. After the presentations are completed, class members analyze and interpret what they heard. Among the issues to explore are the following:

1. Which are the most popular stress-reduction techniques?

2. How do the stress-reduction techniques used by the class compare to those recommended by experts?

3. For each technique mentioned by a class member, indicate whether you think the method of stress busting will be helpful in the long run or is simply a short-term expedient that might even have negative consequences in the long range. Two examples of the latter are (1) "I like to drink a six pack of beer when I'm stressed out" and (2) "If I'm really uptight, I ride my motorcycle about 75 miles per hour in the middle of the night."

4. Send e-mails to three class members today or tomorrow indicating what you thought of their methods of stress reduction. If everybody in the class sends e-mail messages to three class members, it is most likely that each student will receive some feedback.

Human Relations Case Study 17-1

The Overwhelmed Former Coworkers

The longer he waited, the more David worried. For weeks he had been plagued by aching muscles, loss of appetite, restless sleep, and a complete sense of exhaustion. At first he tried to ignore these problems, but eventually he became so short-tempered and irritable that his wife insisted he get a checkup. Now, sitting in the doctor's office and wondering what the verdict would be, he didn't even notice when Theresa took the seat beside him. They had been good friends when she worked in the front office at the plant, but he hadn't seen her since she left three years ago to take a job as a customer service representative. Her gentle poke in the ribs brought him around, and within minutes they were talking and gossiping as if she had never left.

"You got out just in time," he told her. "Since the reorganization, nobody feels safe. It used to be that as long as you did your work, you had a job. That's not for sure anymore. They expect the same production rates even though two guys are now doing the work of three. We're so backed up I'm working twelve-hour shifts six days a week. I swear I hear those machines humming in my sleep. Guys are calling in sick just to get a break. Morale is so bad they're talking about bringing in some consultants to figure out a better way to get the job done."

"Well, I really miss you guys," she said. "I'm afraid I jumped from the frying pan into the fire. In my new job, the computer routes the calls and they never stop. I even have to schedule my bathroom breaks. All I hear the whole day are complaints from unhappy customers. I try to be helpful and sympathetic, but I can't promise anything without getting my boss's approval. Most of the time I'm caught between what the customer wants and company policy. I'm not sure who I'm supposed to keep happy. The other reps are so uptight and tense they don't even talk to one another. We all go to our own little cubicles and stay there until quitting time.

"To make matters worse, my mother's health is deteriorating. If only I could use some of my sick time to look after her. No wonder I'm in here with migraine headaches and high blood pressure. A lot of the reps are seeing the employee assistance counselor and taking stress management classes, which seems to help. But sooner or later, someone will have to make some changes in the way the place is run."

Questions

1. How constructively are David and Theresa dealing with their work stress?

2. What recommendations can you make to David and Theresa to get their stress under control?

3. What recommendations would you make to the employers of David and Theresa in terms of helping them with their work stress?

Source: "Stress Prevention Programs: What Some Organizations Have Done," www.athealth.com, March 4, 2007. Retrieved April 22, 2009.

Human Relations Case Study 17-2

Geomania Naps

Geomania is a telecommunications firm based in the information technology section of New York City. Some of the several hundred employees live in Manhattan, but many have commutes of up to two hours from other cities. Having survived the downturn in the telecommunications business during the late 2000s, Geomania is understaffed. Many staff members in professional, technical, support, and managerial jobs are doing work that was once performed by two people.

A case researcher asked human resources manager Stephanie Cohen what impact the heavy workload was having on employees. She replied, "We've got a bunch of great soldiers here, but the overload problem is taking its toll. Some staff members are having many more fights at home. More people are having serious medical problems such as chest pains, migraine headaches, and stomach ulcers. I also think the error rate in work is going up. Manuel Gomez, the customer service manager, tells me Geomania is receiving more complaints about our systems not working."

The case researcher pointed out that Cohen's observations were to be expected when so many people are working so hard. She was asked if she noticed any other unusual behavior in the office in recent months. Cohen said that her assistant, Bonnie Boswell, had made some observations about unusual behavior and that Boswell should be asked to participate in the interview.

Boswell got right to the heart of the matter, explaining that she has observed behaviors that could be helping productivity, hurting productivity, or a combination of both. "What I've noticed," said Boswell, "is that our people are finding more and more creative ways to take naps on the job. The motto has become, 'You snooze, you win,' instead of 'You snooze, you lose.'"

"There certainly is a positive side to napping. According to one NASA survey, 71 percent of corporate aviation pilots, 80 percent of regional pilots, and 60 percent of hospital workers said they took naps on the job. Another NASA study found that airline pilots who fell asleep on average for twenty-six minutes had 34 percent improvement in performance and 54 percent improvement in alertness. In less than a half hour of napping, the pilots were able to increase their performance significantly. The effects of a short nap lasted between two and four hours. Of course, they were not sleeping while flying!

"But on the negative side, if you are sleeping you are not producing for the company. Besides that it looks so totally unprofessional to be sacked out in your cubicle, especially if you snore or scream because you are having a bad dream."

When asked where and how these workers were napping, both Boswell and Cohen had plenty of answers. Cohen said it has always been easy for executives to nap because they have private offices. Several keep their offices equipped with pillows so they can nap comfortably on a couch, at their desk, or on the floor under the desk. Cohen said that she had walked in on napping executives by mistake, and an office assistant told her about the pillows.

Boswell said that cubicle dwellers have to be more creative about napping because other workers can readily see them. She explained, "Quite often they catch a nap during meetings. At some meetings half the audience is listing to one side or nap jerking (falling asleep, then quickly jerking the head to awake). One napper closes his eyes at his desk and holds a bottle of eye drops to make it appear as though he is in the process of self-medication. Many nappers sleep in their cars during lunch break.

"Some of the most stressed-out workers catch a few winks in the office supply room by resting their head on a box," said Boswell.

Cohen said she was even wondering if Geomania should hire, as a consultant, psychologist Bill Anthony, who founded the Napping Company, to promote productive naps in the workplace. He contends that companies do not have to set up special sleeping rooms. Instead, they can institutionalize nap breaks the way they have the coffee break.

"My concern right now," concluded Cohen, "is what to recommend to top management. I think our CEO is opposed to napping on the job (except for his own little forty winks now and then), and napping does not look professional. Yet, a formal napping program could be a real productivity booster. Maybe we could even cut down on some medical problems."

Questions

1. If you worked for Geomania and were stationed in a cubicle, explain why you would or would not nap on the job.

2. Would it be a good idea for management simply to let workers decide for themselves whether to nap on the job? Explain your reasoning.

3. As the human resources director for Geomania, develop a written policy for napping on company time. (A policy is a general guideline to follow.) Include aspects of napping, such as when, where, under what circumstances, and for how long workers might nap. Mention whether Geomania should have a separate napping area. (To get a few ideas, see the information about a napping policy that follows this case.)

Source: Some of the facts in this case are from Jared Sandberg, "As Bosses Power Nap, Cubicle Dwellers Doze under Clever Disguise," *Wall Street Journal*, July 23, 2003, p. B1; Heather Hatfield, "The Power of Napping," *WebMD*. Retrieved April 22, 2009, from www.webmd.com

Portions of a Sample Company Napping Policy

Our company believes that the health, wellness, and productivity of every employee is an essential part of the company's success. Part of sustaining health, wellness, and productivity is to permit employees who have no critical need to interact with a customer at the time to take a maximum of a twenty-minute nap on company premises. Only one nap per eight-hour shift is permitted, except in cases of unusual fatigue. Discretion must be used as to where to take the nap, such as never napping in sight of customers or in any place that could be dangerous to the employee or other workers. This would include sleeping in an aisle or a stairwell. Bringing a blanket for napping to the workplace is discouraged, yet a small pillow is permissible. Employees must nap individually rather than in teams or with a friend, partner, or spouse. After awaking from a nap, employees are expected to ensure that their clothing is not rumpled and to not make loud, yawning noises.

Human Relations Role-Playing Exercise

Charlotte's Boss Finds Her Napping

The case study about Geomania serves as the background and the story line for this role-play. One person plays the role of Charlotte, who believes strongly that a twenty-minute nap during the workday is an effective productivity booster and stress reliever. Based on her beliefs, she often takes a nap under her desk in her cubicle. Her former supervisor regarded Charlotte's naps as acceptable, particularly because Charlotte is a superior performer.

Another person plays the role of Bert, Charlotte's new boss, who believes strongly that workers in his department must conduct themselves professionally at all times. He also expects subordinates to work at full speed during the day. One day Bert is walking down the hall. As he passes Charlotte's cubicle, he notices that she is sleeping under the desk. His first impulse is to call 911, but he decides to first see if Charlotte can be woken up. Charlotte jumps up when she feels Bert's shoe prodding her foot.

Run the role-play from the point at which Bert prompts Charlotte to awaken. Charlotte, of course, wants to quickly and rationally explain her behavior. Bert does not like what he sees but will at least listen to Charlotte.

Observers rate the role-players on two dimensions, using a 1 to 5 scale from very poor to very good. One dimension is "effective use of human relations techniques." For, Charlotte, see how well she presents her case for the productivity advantages of napping on the job. For Bert, see how well he communicates the message of the importance of workers appearing professional at all times. The second dimension is "acting ability." A few observers might voluntarily provide feedback to the role-players in terms of sharing their ratings and observations. The course instructor might also provide feedback.

REFERENCES

1. Research reviewed in Mark Greer, "Mental Stress Wreaks Physical Havoc on Workers," *Monitor on Psychology*, May 2005, pp. 28–29.

2. Suzanne C. Sergerstrom and Gregory E. Miller, "Psychological Stress and the Human Immune System: A Meta-Analytic Study of 30 Years of Inquiry," *Psychological Bulletin*, no. 4, 2004, pp. 601–630.

3. J. Craig Wallace et al., "Work Stressors, Role-Based Performance, and the Moderating Influence of Organizational Support," *Journal of Applied Psychology*, January 2009, p. 255; Nathan P. Podaskoff, Jeffrey A. LePine, and Marcie A. LePine, "Differential Challenge Stressor Relationships with Job Attitudes, Turnover Intentions, and Withdrawal Behavior: A Meta-Analysis," *Journal of Applied Psychology*, March 2007, pp. 438–454.

4. Michele Conlin, "Meditation: New Research Shows that It Changes the Brain in Ways That Alleviate Stress," *Business Week*, August 30, 2004, p. 137.

5. Einar M. de Croon et al., "Stressful Work, Psychological Job Strain, and Turnover: A Two-Year Prospective Cohort Study of Truck Drivers," *Journal of Applied Psychology*, June 2004, pp. 442–454.

6. Michael R. Frone, "Are Work Stressors Related to Employee Substance Abuse? The Importance of Temporal Context in Assessments of Alcohol and Illicit Drug Use," *Journal of Applied Psychology*, January 2008, pp. 199–206.

7. Unpublished research reported in Claudia Wallis and Sonja Steptoe, "Help! I've Lost My Focus," *Time*, January 16, 2006, p. 75.

8. Evangelia Demerouti et al., "The Job Demands–Resources Model of Burnout," *Journal of Applied Psychology*, June 2001, p. 502.

9. Christina Maslach and Michael P. Leiter, "Early Predictors of Job Burnout and Engagement," *Journal of Applied Psychology*, May 2008, p. 504.

10. Raymond T. Lee and Blake E. Ashforth, "A Meta-Analytic Examination of the Correlates of Three Dimensions of Job Burnout," *Journal of Applied Psychology*, April 1996, p. 123; Joanne Cole, "An Ounce of Prevention Beats Burnout," *HRfocus*, June 1999, pp. 1, 14–15.

11. Rabi S. Bhagat, "Effects of Stressful Life Events on Individual Performance and Work Adjustment Processes within Organizational Settings: A Research Model," *Academy of Management Review*, October 1983, pp. 660–670.

12. "Building Self-Esteem." Retrieved May 23, 2006, from: www.ashland.com/education/self-esteem/best_shot.html

13. David Lazarus, "Suicide Hotlines See Rise in Calls as Economy Tanks," *Los Angeles Times* (www.latimes.com), December 24, 2008.

14. Research reported in Etienne Benson, "Hostility Is among Best Predictors of Heart Disease in Men," *Monitor on Psychology*, January 2003, p. 15.

15. Quoted in Nadja Geipert, "Don't Be Mad: More Research Links Hostility to Coronary Risk," *Monitor on Psychology*, January 2007, pp. 50–51.

16. Peter Y. Chen and Paul E. Spector, "Negative Affectivity as the Underlying Cause of Correlations between Stressors and Strains," *Journal of Applied Psychology*, June 1991, p. 398.

17. Paul E. Spector, Peter Y. Chen, and Brian J. O'Connell, "A Longitudinal Study of Relations between Job Stressors and Job Strains while Controlling for Prior Negative Affectivity and Strains," *Journal of Applied Psychology*, April 2000, p. 216.

18. Norman B. Anderson, "Toward Reducing Work Stress," *Monitor on Psychology*, February 2008, p. 9.

19. Blaine Harden, "Japan's Overtime Proves to Be Killer," *Washington Post* syndicated story, July 16, 2008.

20. Richard S. DeFrank and John M. Ivancevich, "Stress on the Job: An Executive Update," *Academy of Management Executive*, August 1998, pp. 56–57.

21. Christine A. Spring et al., "Work Characteristics, Musculoskeletal Disorders, and the Mediating Role of Psychological Strain: A Study of Call Center Employees," *Journal of Applied Psychology*, September 2007, pp. 1456–1466.

22. Alicia A. Grandey, "Emotion Regulation in the Workplace: A New Way to Conceptualize Emotional Labor," *Journal of Occupational Health Psychology*, January 2000, pp. 95–110; Grandey, "When the 'Show Must Go On:' Surface Acting and Deep Acting as Determinants of Emotional Exhaustion and Peer-Related Service Delivery," *Academy of Management Journal*, February 2003, pp. 86–96.

23. Theresa M. Glomb, John D. Kammeyer-Mueller, and Maria Rotundo, "Emotional Labor Demands and Compensating Wage Differentials," *Journal of Applied Psychology*, August 2004, p. 707.

24. Katherine. M. Richardson and Hannah. R. Rothstein, "Effects of Occupational Stress Management Intervention Programs: A Meta-Analysis," *Journal of Occupational Health Psychology*, January 2008, pp. 69–93.

25. Andrew Weil, "Beating Stress," *USA Weekend*, December 26–28, 1997, p. 4.

26. Cited in Stephanie Gold, "A Higher Road to Relaxation," *Psychology Today*, July/August 2007, p. 57.

27. Amy Novotney, "Marital Bliss May Blunt Office Blues," *Monitor on Psychology*, March 2008, p. 11.

28. Herbert Benson (with William Proctor), *Beyond the Relaxation Response* (New York: Berkley Books, 1995), pp. 96–97; "Are You Working Too Hard? A Conversation with Mind/Body Researcher Herbert Benson," *Harvard Business Review*, November 2005, p. 54; Sara Martin, "The Power of the Relaxation Response," *Monitor on Psychology*, October 2008, p. 33.

29. Evidence reviewed in Roger Walsh and Shauna L. Shapiro, "The Meeting of Meditative Disciplines and Western Psychology," *American Psychologist*, April 2006, p. 228.

30. Research reviewed in "Unhealthy Behaviors Cause Approximately One Half of U.S. Deaths," *Monitor on Psychology*, May 2004, p. 15.

31. Philip L. Rice, *Stress and Health: Principles and Practices for Coping and Wellness* (Monterey, CA: Brooks/Cole Publishing Company, 1987), pp. 353–354.

32. Stacy Forster, "Companies Say Yoga Isn't a Stretch," *Wall Street Journal*, October 14, 2003, p. D4.

33. "Yoga Can Reduce Anxiety," *Personal Best Healthlines*, Special Report, 2007, p. 5.

34. Pamela Paul, "When Yoga Hurts," *Time,* October 15, 2007, p. 71.

35. Mark Goulston, *Get Out of Your Own Way at Work . . . and Help Others Do the Same* (New York: Putnam Adult, 2005); Andrew J. DuBrin, *Your Own Worst Enemy: How to Overcome Career Self-Sabotage* (New York: AMACOM, 1992).

36. Based on the work of Judith Wright, as reported in Julie Deardorff, "Soft Addictions: You Can Get Hooked in So Many Ways," *Chicago Tribune,* March 18, 2007.

37. Kevin Hogan, "Why Everything Goes to Hell . . . How to Stop Self-Sabotage, NOW and Forever!" www.kevinhogan.com/selfsabotage.htm, 2009.

38. Daniel Goleman, "Leadership That Gets Results," *Harvard Business Review*, March–April 2000, p. 80.

39. Robyn D. Clarke, "A Reason for Ranting," *Black Enterprise,* November 2005, p. 161.

Why Take the Golden Personality Type Profiler?

Self-awareness is the key to professional development and success. By taking the Golden Personality Type Profiler you will learn about your personality, which is the essence of who you are as a unique individual. It is reflected in what you say, how you feel about yourself, and how you act. Knowing about your personality will help you develop a deeper understanding of your strengths, a clearer picture of how your behavior affects others, and a better appreciation for the interpersonal style of others and how to interact with them more effectively.

The Golden takes about 15 to 20 minutes to complete and measures five core personality dimensions that describe how you:

- Focus your energy (extraversion/introversion)
- Gather information (sensing/intuition)
- Make decisions (thinking/feeling)
- Approach life (judging/perceiving)
- Respond to stress (tense/calm)

What Will You Learn?

After you complete the assessment, your will receive a personalized Student Feedback Report that explains your five personality scores, your overall personality type, and your preferred:

- Learning style
- Communication style
- Approach to teamwork
- Personal motivators
- Leadership style
- Ways to cope with stress

You will also receive a Student Guide to Interpreting Your Golden Results, which will give you a deeper understanding of your results. You will learn about the personality theory of the Golden, how to interpret your scores, and how to relate them to career planning and workplace effectiveness. You will also receive a snapshot description of the 16 major personality types, so that you can see how you are similar to and different from others.

Learning about your personality will better prepare you for success in school and in your career. You will know more about your strengths, areas to develop further, and what motivates you. You will also gain a better understanding of how to work most effectively with people whose styles are different than your own.

Summary of Global Results

Your global results provide insight to how the four different dimensions of your personality work together to form your personality type. The results indicate your level of preference for each of two opposite scales. A strong preference is not necessarily better than a slight preference, or vice versa - the preferences simply indicate how strongly you favor certain behaviors versus others. You may have relatively equal preference, but slightly favor one scale.

Your Type is   ESTZ

Where you focus your energy:	Extraverting
How you gather information:	Sensing
How you make decisions:	Thinking
How you approach life:	organiZing

Your test results do not reveal a clear preference.

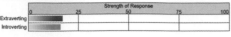

	Strength of Response			
	0	25	50	75	100
Extraverting				
Introverting				

Extraverting
- focuses attention externally toward people and things
- enjoys being sociable, talkative, and gregarious
- enjoys discussions more than reading
- active rather than reflective

Introverting
- focuses attention inward on thoughts and ideas
- prefers a few close friends to many acquaintances
- likes to reflect on ideas before sharing them
- needs quiet time away from action and noise

Summary of Global Results

You have a Slight preference for Thinking.

	Strength of Response			
	0	25	50	75	100
Thinking				
Feeling				

Thinking
- makes decisions based on logic and rationality
- prefers to deal in objective reason and logic
- does not get personally involved in his/her decisions

Feeling
- focuses on how a decision will impact others
- makes decisions based on person-centered values
- gets personally involved in his/her decisions

Your test results do not reveal a clear preference.

	Strength of Response			
	0	25	50	75	100
organiZing				
Adapting				

organiZing
- prefers an orderly, organized and planned lifestyle
- likes to make decisions and reach closure
- prefers systematic approaches

Adapting
- prefers a flexible, open-ended and emergent lifestyle
- holds off deciding until there is more information
- prefers spontaneity and limited structure

Access the Golden Personality Type Profiler

If your textbook was not packaged with an access code, you may purchase an access code for the Golden Personality Type Profiler Assessment online at www.pearsonhighered.com.

Action plan describes how you are going to reach your goal

Active listener person who listens intensely, with the goal of empathizing with the speaker

Adolescence the period in life from approximately age thirteen to twenty; from a biological standpoint, adolescence begins with puberty

Affective component (of attitude) the emotion connected with an object or a task

Affirmative action programs that comply with antidiscrimination laws and attempt to correct past discriminatory practices

Aggressive characteristic of people who are obnoxious and overbearing; they push for what they want with almost no regard for the feelings of others

Aggressive personalities people who verbally and sometimes physically attack others frequently

Assertive characteristic of people who state clearly what they want or how they feel in a given situation without being abusive, abrasive, or obnoxious; open, honest, and up-front people who believe that all people have an equal right to express themselves honestly

Attitude a predisposition to respond that exerts an influence on a person's response to a person, a thing, an idea, or a situation

Attribution theory the study of the process by which people ascribe causes to the behaviors they perceive

Autocratic leader leader who attempts to retain most of the authority granted to the group; autocratic leaders make all the major decisions and assume subordinates will comply without question

Backstabbing an attempt to discredit by underhanded means, such as innuendo or accusation

Barriers to communication (or **noise**) missteps that can occur between encoding and decoding a message; unwanted interference that can distort or block a message

Behavior modification system of motivation that emphasizes rewarding people for doing the right things and punishing them for doing the wrong things

Behavioral component (of attitude) how a person acts

Behavioral interview an interview during which a candidate is asked how he or she handled a particular problem in the past

Blind area pane of the Johari Window that contains information that others are aware of but we cannot see in ourselves in reference to both positive and negative qualities

Brainstorming technique by which group members think of multiple solutions to a problem

Brainwriting arriving at creative ideas by jotting them down

Buddy system the company assigns a new employee a coworker who looks out for his or her welfare, such as explaining company etiquette

Bully a cruel and aggressive boss who intimidates and verbally abuses subordinates

Burnout a condition of emotional, mental, and physical exhaustion in response to long-term job stressors

Business etiquette special code of behavior required in work situations

Career path sequence of positions necessary to achieve a goal

Carpal tunnel syndrome repetitive motion disorder most frequently associated with keyboarding and the use of optical scanners; occurs when repetitive flexing and extension of the wrist causes the tendons to swell, thus trapping and pinching the median nerve

Challenge stressors stressful events and thoughts that have a positive direct effect on motivation and performance

Character trait an enduring characteristic of a person that is related to moral and ethical behavior that shows up consistently

Charisma type of charm and magnetism that inspires others; important quality for leaders at all levels

Classical conditioning principles stemming from Ivan Pavlov's digestion experiments that help people understand the most elementary type of learning—how people acquire uncomplicated habits and reflexes

Cognitive component (of attitude) the knowledge or intellectual beliefs an individual might have about an object (an idea, a person, a thing, or a situation)

Cognitive dissonance situation in which the pieces of knowledge, information, attitudes, or beliefs held by an individual are contradictory

Cognitive fitness a state of optimized ability to remember, learn, plan, and adapt to changing circumstances

Cognitive–behavioral interventions a way of thinking constructively about a problem that includes perspective setting

Cognitive restructuring technique of mentally converting negative aspects into positive ones by looking for the positive elements in a situation

Cognitive skills problem-solving and intellectual skills

Communication the sending and receiving of messages

Communication overload phenomenon that occurs when people are so overloaded with information that they cannot respond effectively to messages

Conflict condition that exists when two sets of demands, goals, or motives are incompatible

Conflict of interest judgment or objectivity is compromised because of two competing ends that must be satisfied

Confrontation and problem solving the most highly recommended way of resolving conflict; method of identifying the true source of conflict and resolving it systematically

Consensus leader leader who encourages group discussion about an issue and then makes a decision that reflects the consensus of the group members

Consideration the degree to which the leader creates an environment of emotional support, warmth, friendliness, and trust

Consultative leader leader who solicits opinions from the group before making a decision yet does not feel obliged to accept the group's thinking; this type leader makes it clear that he or she alone has authority to make the final decisions

Creativity the ability to develop good ideas that can be put into action

Critical thinking solving problems and making decisions through a systematic evaluation of evidence

Cultural intelligence (CQ) an outsider's ability to interpret someone's unfamiliar and ambiguous behavior the same way that person's compatriots would

Cultural mosaic an individual's unique mixture of multiple cultural identities that yields a complex picture of the cultural influences on that person

Cultural sensitivity an awareness of and a willingness to investigate the reasons why people of another culture act as they do

Cultural training set of learning experiences designed to help employees understand the customs, traditions, and beliefs of another culture

Culture a learned and shared system of knowledge, beliefs, values, attitudes, and norms

Customer service orientation approach of employee whose thoughts and actions are geared toward helping customers

Decision making choosing one alternative from the various alternative solutions that can be pursued

Decoding the process of understanding a message; the receiver interprets the message and translates it into meaningful information

Defensive communication tendency to receive messages in such a way that one's self-esteem is protected

Democratic leader leader who confers final authority on the group; functions as a collector of opinion and takes a vote before making a decision (in extreme, referred to as a free-rein leader)

Denial the suppression of information one finds uncomfortable

Developmental opportunity teammates rating one another on performance dimensions, such as cooperation with other members of the team, customer service attitude, productivity, and contribution to meetings

Diagonal communication the transmission of messages to higher or lower organizational levels in different departments

Difficult people a coworker is classified as difficult if he or she is uncooperative, touchy, defensive, hostile, or even very unfriendly

Disarming the opposition method of conflict resolution in which you disarm the criticizer by agreeing with his or her criticism

Diversity training program that attempts to bring about workplace harmony by teaching people how to get along with diverse work associates; often aimed at minimizing open expressions of racism and sexism

Downward communication the transmission of messages from higher to lower levels in an organization

E-learning studying independently outside of a classroom setting and interacting with a computer in addition to studying course material; Web-based form of computer-based training

Emotional contagion the automatic and unconscious transfer of emotions between individuals based on cues the other person observes

Emotional intelligence the ability to accurately perceive emotions, to understand the signals that emotions send about relationships, and to manage emotions

Emotional labor process of regulating both feelings and expressions to meet organizational goals

Empathy understanding another person's point of view

Empowerment process by which a manager shares power with team members, thereby enhancing their feelings of self-efficacy

Encoding the process of organizing ideas into a series of symbols, such as words and gestures, designed to communicate with a receiver

Ethical screening running a contemplated decision or action through an ethics test, particularly when a contemplated action or decision is not clearly ethical or unethical

Ethics the moral choices a person makes

Ethnocentrism the assumption that the ways of one's culture are the *best* ways of doing things

Exit strategy determining in advance how to get out of a bad decision, such as having joined a failing family business

Expectancy theory of motivation people will be motivated if they believe that their efforts will lead to desired outcomes

External locus of control individual's belief that external forces control fate

Extinction the weakening or decreasing of the frequency of undesirable behavior by removing the reward for such behavior

Fear of success belief that if one succeeds at an important task, one will be asked to take on more responsibility in the future; reason some people procrastinate

Feedback information that tells one how well he or she has performed

Fight-or-flight response the experience of stress prompts the adrenal glands to release a flood of hormones that prepare the body to fight or run when faced with a challenge

Flow experience total absorption in work; when flow occurs, things seem to go just right

Formal communication channels the official pathways for sending information inside and outside an organization

Frame of reference model, viewpoint, or perspective

Galeta effect a type of self-fulfilling prophecy in which high expectations lead to high performance

Goal an event, circumstance, object, or condition a person strives to attain

Grapevine major informal communication channel in organizations; the grapevine refers to the tangled pathways that can distort information

Grievance procedure formal process of filing a complaint and resolving a dispute within an organization

Group dynamics the forces operating in groups that affect how members work together

Group norms unwritten set of expectations for group members—what people ought to do; basic principle to follow in getting along with coworkers

Groupthink a deterioration of mental efficiency, reality testing, and moral judgment in the interest of group solidarity; extreme form of consensus

Hawthorne effect applying research methods to investigate problems of employee productivity using the scientific method; in the study, employees reacted positively because management cared about them

Hedonic adaptation the tendency to adapt to or regard exciting new aspects of life as routine after a while

Hidden area part of Johari Window that contains information known to us about ourselves but is hidden from others

Hindrance stressors stressful events and thoughts that have a negative effect on motivation and performance

Horizontal communication the transmission of messages among people at the same organizational level

Human relations the art of using systematic knowledge about human behavior to improve personal, job, and career effectiveness

Human relations movement movement that began as a concentrated effort by some managers and their advisors to become more sensitive to the needs of employees or to treat them in a more humanistic manner

Identity crisis adolescent struggle to establish a reliable self-concept, or personal identity, including concerns over ethnic identity, the need to keep close ties with the family or develop peer relations, sexuality, and body image

Implicit learning learning that takes place unconsciously and without an intention to learn

Informal communication channels unofficial networks of channels that supplement the formal channels

Informal learning planned or unplanned learning that occurs without a formal classroom, lesson plan, instructor, or examination; a way of learning complex skills in the workplace

Ingratiating attempting to increase one's attractiveness to others to influence their behavior

Initiating structure organizing and defining relationships in the group by engaging in such activities as assigning specific tasks, specifying procedures to be followed, scheduling work, and making expectations clear

Insight an ability to know what information is relevant, to find connections between the old and the new, to combine facts that are unrelated, and to see the "big picture"

Intermittent rewards rewards that sustain desired behaviors longer and slowdown the process of behaviors fading away when they are not rewarded

Internal locus of control individual's belief that fate is pretty much under a person's own control

Intranet a company version of the Internet with the basic purpose of giving employees a central place to find what they need amidst a sea of digital information

Intrinsic motivation a person's beliefs about the extent to which an activity can satisfy his or her needs for competence and self-determination; instead of looking to somebody else for rewards, a person is motivated by the intrinsic, or internal, aspects of the task

Intuition an experience-based way of knowing or reasoning in which weighing and balancing of evidence are done automatically

Job enrichment making a job more motivating and satisfying by adding variety and responsibility

Johari Window a grid showing how much information you know about yourself as well as how much other people know about you

Jury of peers grievance procedure used in many firms without a union whereby unresolved grievances are submitted to a panel of coworkers

Keywords terms for skills, certifications, job activities, and other qualifications sought for a particular job

Lateral thinking process of spreading out to find many different alternative solutions to a problem

Leader–member exchange model (LMX) leadership model that focuses on the quality of leader–member relations; recognizes that leaders develop unique working relationships with each group member

Leadership the process of bringing about positive changes and influencing others to achieve worthwhile goals

Leadership effectiveness inner quality of a leader who helps the group accomplish its objectives without neglecting satisfaction and morale

Leadership style a leader's characteristic way of behaving in a variety of situations

Learning generally considered a lasting change in behavior based on practice and experience

Learning style method of coming to understand; different people learn best in different ways; some people acquire new material best through passive learning, such as acquiring information through studying texts, manuals, magazine articles, and Web sites; others learn best by doing rather than by studying alone or cooperatively

Management by walking around managers intermingle freely with workers on the shop floor or in the office, as well as with customers; enhances open communication

Maslow's hierarchy of needs the best-known categorization of needs; according to psychologist Abraham H. Maslow, people strive to satisfy the following groups of needs in step-by-step order: physiological needs, safety needs, social needs, esteem needs, and self-actualizing needs

Meditation a systematic method of concentration, reflection, or concentrated thinking designed to suppress the activity of the sympathetic nervous system

Mentor a more experienced person who guides, teaches, and coaches another individual

Micro-inequity small, semiconscious message sent with a powerful impact on the receiver

Micromanagement the close monitoring of most aspects of group member activities by the manager

Midlife crisis time adults in their forties face when they feel unfulfilled and search for a major shift in career or lifestyle

Midlife transition adults taking stock of their lives and formulating new goals; among dozens of other personality and social challenges facing adults are the loss of a youthful appearance and a decreased reproductive or sexual capacity

Mirroring form of nonverbal communication to overcoming communication barriers by subtly imitating another; used to improve rapport with another person

Mixed signals type of message in which the sender might recommend one thing to others yet behave in another way

Modeling learning a skill by observing another person perform the skill; considered a form of social learning because it is learned in the presence of others

Morals an individual's or a society's determination of what is right and wrong

Motivation concept with two widely used meanings: (1) an internal state that leads to effort expended toward objectives and (2) an activity performed by one person to get another to accomplish work

Motive an inner drive that moves a person to do something

Multicultural identities a state in which individuals incorporate the values of two or more cultures because they identify with both their primary culture and another culture or cultures

Multicultural worker one who can work effectively with people of different cultures

Multitasking doing two or more routine chores simultaneously, which can sometimes enhance personal productivity

Need an internal striving or urge to do something, such as a need to drink when thirsty

Need for achievement the desire to accomplish something difficult for its own sake

Negative affectivity a tendency to experience aversive (intensely disliked) emotional states; predisposition to experience emotional stress that includes feelings of nervousness, tension, and worry

Negative reinforcement taking away something unpleasant from a situation; being rewarded by being relieved of discomfort; form of avoidance learning or motivation

Negotiating and bargaining situation of conferring with another person to resolve a problem

Networking the process of establishing a group of contacts who can help you in your career; establishing contacts to find a better position, become a customer, become a valuable supplier, solve difficult problems, or find a mentor; people in a network also offer emotional support

Nonassertive characteristic of people who let things happen to them without letting their feelings be known

Nonverbal communication using the body, voice, or environment in numerous ways to help get a message across

Open-door policy communication channel that is structured upward that allows employees to bring a gripe to top management's attention without first checking with the employee's manager

Open area pane of Johari Window consisting of information that is known to use and others

Openness to experience personality characteristic of positive orientation toward learning; people with considerable openness to experience have well-developed intellects

Operant conditioning learning that takes place as a consequence of behavior; a person's actions are instrumental in determining whether learning takes place

Organizational citizenship behavior (OCB) the willingness to go beyond one's job description to help the company, even if such act does not lead to an immediate reward

Organizational culture values and beliefs of a firm that guide people's actions

Organizational effectiveness the extent to which an organization is productive and satisfies the demands of interested parties, such as employees, customers, and investors

Paraphrase repeating in one's own words what a sender says, feels, and means

Participative leader leader who shares decision-making authority with the group; motivates group members to work as a team toward high-level goals

Partnership the leader and group members are connected in such a way that the power between them is approximately balanced

Peak performance exceptional accomplishment in a given task

Peer evaluations system in which teammates contribute to an evaluation of a person's job performance

Perception the various ways in which people interpret things in the external world and how they act on the basis of these perceptions

Perceptual congruence the degree to which people perceive things the same way

Performance standard a statement of what constitutes acceptable performance

Personal communication style verbal and nonverbal communication style for a unique approach to sending and receiving information

Personal brand your distinctive set of strengths, including skills and values

Personal support assisting others in the workplace through the use of interpersonal skills

Personality clash antagonistic relationship between two people based on differences in personal attributes, preferences, interests, values, and styles

Personality disorder pervasive, persistent, inflexible, maladaptive pattern of behavior that deviates from expected cultural norms

Person–organization fit the compatibility of the individual and the organization

Person–role conflict the demands made by the organization or a superior clash with the basic values of the individual

Planning primary principle of effective time management; deciding what to accomplish and the actions needed to make it happen

Political skills an interpersonal style that combines awareness of others with the ability to communicate well; developing effective relationships with work associates, including customers

Positive psychological capital a state in which you have hope, self-efficacy, optimism, and resilience

Positive reinforcement increasing the probability that behavior will be repeated by rewarding people for making the desired response; improves learning and motivation

Positive self-talk saying positive things about yourself to yourself

Positive visual imagery picturing a positive outcome in your mind

Private self the actual person an individual may be

Proactive personality a person who is relatively unconstrained by forces in a situation and who brings about environmental change; highly proactive people identify opportunities and act on them, showing initiative, and keep trying until they bring about meaningful change

Problem gap between what exists and what you want to exist

Procrastination delaying a task for an invalid or weak reason

Productivity the amount of quality work accomplished in relation to the resources consumed

Prosocial motivation the desire to expend effort to help other people

Psychological hardiness mental state in which the individual experiences a high degree of commitment, control, and challenge

Public self what a person communicates about himself or herself and what others actually perceive about the person

Punishment the introduction of an unpleasant stimulus as a consequence of the learner having done something wrong

Pygmalion effect leader's ability to elevate worker performance by the simple method of expecting them to perform well; the manager's high expectations become a self-fulfilling prophecy

Recognition need the desire to be acknowledged for one's contributions and efforts and to feel important

Relationship management the interpersonal skills of being able to communicate clearly and convincingly, disarm conflicts, and build strong personal bonds

Relaxation response a physical state of deep rest in which one experiences a slower respiration and heart rate, lowered blood pressure, and lowered metabolism; a standard technique for reducing stress

Resilience the ability to withstand pressure and emerge stronger because of an experience; being challenged and not breaking down

Role particular way one tends to behave, contribute, and relate to others

Role ambiguity condition in which the job holder receives confusing or poorly defined expectations

Role conflict having to choose between two competing demands or expectations

Role overload a burdensome workload that creates stress for a person in two ways: (1) the person may become fatigued and less able to tolerate annoyances and irritations, and (2) a person subject to unreasonable work demands may feel perpetually behind schedule, a situation that itself creates an uncomfortable, stressful feeling

Role underload disruptive amount of stress that can occur when people experience too little to do; one benefit is the preservation of energy for family and leisure activities

Sandwich generation those placed in the middle between the needs of their own children and their aging relatives

Scientific management theory that focuses on the application of scientific methods to increase individual workers' productivity

Selective attention giving exclusive attention to something at the expense of other aspects of the environment

Self a complex idea generally referring to a person's total being or individuality

Self-awareness the ability to understand moods, emotions, and needs as well as their impact on others; self-awareness also includes using intuition to make decisions you can live with happily

Self-defeating behavior a person with self-defeating tendencies intentionally or unintentionally engages in activities or harbors attitudes that work against his or her best interest

Self-discipline the ability to work systematically and progressively toward a goal until it is achieved

Self-disclosure the process of revealing one's inner self to others

Self-efficacy confidence in your ability to carry out a specific task in contrast to generalized self-confidence

Self-esteem the trait of feeling competent to cope with the basic challenges in life and of being worthy of happiness

Self-leadership leading oneself; influencing oneself without waiting for an external leader to lead; all organizational members are capable of leading themselves to some extent

Self-management the ability to control one's emotions and act with honesty and integrity in a consistent and acceptable manner

Self-understanding possessing valid information about oneself; self-understanding refers to knowledge about oneself, particularly with respect to mental and emotional aspects

Semantics the study of the meaning and changes in the meaning of words or symbols

Servant leader one who serves group members by working on their behalf to help them achieve their goals, not the leader's goals

Sexual equity parity among heterosexual, gay, lesbian, bisexual, and transgender employees

Sexual harassment unwanted sexually oriented behavior in the workplace that results in discomfort or interference with the job

Shadow organizations where much of the real work gets accomplished, the shadow organization is revealed by network analysis, which traces who talks to whom

Shared leadership the leader granting group members authority to carry out some of the leadership activities

Skill–benefit statements brief explanations of how an individual's skills can benefit the company

Social awareness having empathy for others and having intuition about work problems

Social network analysis the mapping and measuring of relationships and links between and among people, groups, and organizations that reveals the shadow organization

Soft addiction ordinary behavior that if done to excess can wreak havoc on your life

Stress an internal reaction to any force that threatens to disturb a person's equilibrium; the internal reaction usually takes the form of emotional discomfort

Stressor the external or internal force that brings about stress

Success syndrome pattern in which the worker performs one assignment well and then has the confidence to take on an even more difficult assignment

Support system a group of people on whom one can rely for encouragement and comfort

Synergy a product of group effort whereby the output of the group exceeds the output possible if the members worked alone

Team player one who emphasizes group accomplishment and cooperation rather than individual achievement and not helping others

Teamwork work done with an understanding and commitment to group goals on the part of all team members

Teenage brain a stage of brain development in which people are easily influenced by their environment and more prone to impulsive behavior

Telecommuter employee who works at home, or other offsite location, full-time or part-time and sends output electronically to a central office

Time leak when time gets away from you because of anything you are doing or not doing

Traditional mental set fixed way of thinking about objects and activities

Trust a person's confidence in another individual's intentions and motives and in the sincerity of that individual's words

Two-factor theory of work motivation two different sets of job factors—one set, the motivators, or satisfiers, can motivate and satisfy workers; the other set, dissatisfiers, or hygiene factors, can only prevent dissatisfaction

Type A behavior personality characteristics that lead a person into stressful situations. Type A behavior has two main components: (1) the tendency to try to accomplish too many things in too little time and (2) free-floating hostility

Unknown area pane of Johari Window that contains information that you and others do not know about you

Upward communication the transmission of messages from lower to higher levels in an organization

Value the importance a person attaches to something; values are also tied to the enduring belief that one's mode of conduct is better than another mode of conduct

Variable pay incentive plan that intentionally pays good performers more money than poor performers

Vertical thinking analytical, logical process that results in few answers; the vertical thinker looks for the one best solution to a problem, much like solving an equation in algebra

Virtual office one in which employees work together as if they were part of a single office despite being physically separated

Webinar a Web-based method of holding a seminar

Win–win after conflict has been resolved, both sides gain something of value

Work ethic a firm belief in the dignity and value of work and therefore important for favorably impressing a manager

Work habits a person's characteristic approach to work, including such things as organization, priority setting, and handling of paperwork and e-mail

Workaholism neglecting the normal need for rest and relaxation that can lead to an addiction to work in which not working is an uncomfortable experience

Work–family conflict conflict that occurs when an individual has to perform multiple roles: worker, spouse or partner, and often parent

Worst-case scenario helpful decision-making aid that involves visualizing what you would do if the alternative chosen proved to be dreadful

Worst in, first out (WIFO) dealing first with unpleasant tasks you would prefer to avoid; simply getting them done and out of the way

Company Index

Accenture, Ltd., 455
Alliant Energy, 389
Alpine Access, 220
Aon Corporation, 222
Apple Computer (now Apple Corp.), 318
Cirque du Soleil, 167
Costco, 22
Crystal Icing, 177
DeCalo Fashion, 35
Detroit Police Dept., 63
Dixon Schwabl, 102
Dunkin' Donuts, 399
Federal Deposit Insurance Corp., 311
Genetech, 101

Goldman Sachs & Co., 4
Google Inc., 167
Gorbel Inc., 166
Intel Corp., 467
J. A. Frate Inc., 29–30
Jump Associates LLC, 5
KPMG, 403
McDonough, Bolyard Peck Inc., 78
Meetup, 349
Merck & Co., 21
Microsoft Corporation, 124
Monsanto Co., 217
NASA, 363
Novo Nordisk AS, 121

Pitney Bowes, 282
Principal Financial Group, 102
Skyline Construction, 352
Super Group Creative Omnimedia Inc., 151
Tata Motors, 20
3M, 157
UPS, 483
Urban Pathways, 411
Vibrant Brains, 452
Wells Fargo & Co., 139
W. L. Gore & Associates, 102
Yahoo!, 369–370
Yum Brands Inc., 69

Abrahamson, Eric, 474
Acceptance of power and authority, 374, 375
Achievement need, 66
Action plans for goals, 74, 75, 81
Active listening, 203–206
Adaptation to leader's style, 327, 328
ADHD (attention deficit hyperactivity disorder), 480
Adolescence challenges, 448–449
Adult life challenges, 449–450
Adverse customer interaction, 505, 506
Adverse environmental conditions, 505
Affiliation need, 66
Affirmative action, 395
Aggressive personalities, 281
Airitam, Scott, 134
Ajello, Andrew, 121
Allen, David, 476
Amabile, Teresa M., 165
Ameson, Steve, 254
Anger management, 299–301
   choosing technique, 300
   management of others, 300
   self-management, 301
Annoyances and stress, 500, 501
Anonymous conversations for shyness, 291
Appeal to a third party, 295
Appearance and communication, 190–191
Appearance and cross-cultural relations, 391
Appearance for career, 414
Armstrong, J. Scott, 299
Ash, Mary Kay, 39
Assertive, nonassertive, aggressive behaviors, 289–290
Assertiveness for conflict, 289
Assertiveness for leadership, 316
Attendance and punctuality, 473
Attention faking when listening, 206
Attitudes, 98–104, 198
   changing of, 101
   cognitive dissonance, 99
   communication and, 198
   company encouragement, 101–103
   components, 98–99
   formation of, 99, 100
   job satisfaction and, 101–102, 103
   optimism and, 100
   organizational citizenship behavior, 103–104
   positive attitude importance, 100

Attribution theory, 446
Autocratic leader, 327, 329

Backstabbing avoidance, 259
Bad news delivery, 251, 252
Bair, Sheila, 311, 312
Balanced life for career, 423
Barnes, Brenda C., 131
Barren, James, 63
Bartz, Carol, 369, 370
Behavior detection officer, 192
Behavior modification, 79
Behavioral interview, 409
Belbin, Meredith, 360, 362
Belensky, Greg, 475
Bennis, Warren G., 333
Benson, Herbert, 510
Bethume, Gordon, 356
Bezos, Jeff, 227
Bits of time, 481, 482
Biyani, Kishore, 379
Blake, Frank, 345
Block, Peter, 322
Blogs as formal communication channel, 218–219
Body piercing and appearance, 362
Bono, 183
Borelli, Rick, 384
Bouncing back from setbacks, 51
Brain functioning and rest, 443
Brainstorming, 169–170
Brainteasers for problem solving, 160–161
Brainwriting, 170
Brand called you, 416
Brewer, Miriam, 377
Broad experience for career, 333
Bronson, Po, 128
Brooks, Arthur C., 110
Brown, Michael E., 129
Brown, Tim, 236
Bucklin, Linda Hale, 452
Buddy system for career, 421
Buffet, Warren, 475
Bullies and conflict, 281
Bullying boss, 252
Burnout, 499
Burton, Jeremy, 220
Burton, Valorie, 45
Buscaglia, Leo, 43
Business meetings and communication, 234–236
Bypassing manager, 250

Callahan, Patricia, 139
Career advancement approaches, 412–424
   balanced life for, 423
   brand called you, 416
   broad experience for, 420, 421
   buddy system, 421
   career path for, 419, 420
   code of professional ethics for, 413
   continuous learning for, 416
   control of self, 412–418
   control over outside world, 418–423
   documenting accomplishments, 415, 416
   etiquette for, 416, 417, 418
   expertise, passion, and pride, 412–413
   favorable appearance for, 414, 415
   first impressions for, 414, 415
   flexible career path, 419–420
   horizontal career path, 419, 420
   interpersonal skills for, 414
   mentor for, 421
   networking skills for, 423–424
   older subordinate challenge, 422
   performance beyond job description, 413, 414
   personal appearance for, 414, 415
   personal branding, 416, 417
   proactive personality, 414
   self-development for, 416
   success syndrome, 414
   traditional career path, 419, 420
   visibility for, 416
   younger boss challenge, 422, 423
Career changing, 453–455, 456
   inventories for, 454
   reasons for, 454
   self-employment possibilities, 455
   staying with same employer, 454, 455
Career paths, 419–421
Career success and self-esteem, 39
Carlson, Richard, 110, 111
Carnegie, Andrew, 354
Carnegie, Dale, 100
Carpal tunnel syndrome, 505
Cause-and-effect diagram, 158
Cenderella, Marc, 407
Center for Business Ethics guide, 137
Challenge vs. hindrance stressors, 497
Chance encounters and communication, 225, 226
Chao, Georgia T., 376
Character attributes of leaders, 315

Character traits and ethics, 136
Charisma and its development, 316–319
Christakis, Nicholas, 106
Circles of intimacy and communication, 188
Civility with coworkers, 255, 256–264
Classical conditioning, 434, 435
Cleaning up and getting organized, 476
Clustering of tasks, 485
Code of professional ethics, 413
Codes of conduct for cross-cultural relations, 379
Codes of professional conduct, 140
Cognitive behavioral interventions, 507
Cognitive challenges of life span, 448, 449, 451
Cognitive dissonance, 99
Cognitive fitness, 451
Cognitive intelligence, 152–153
Cognitive problems and multitasking, 232, 233
Cognitive restructuring, 294
Cognitive skills of leaders, 315, 316
Cognitive styles and personality, 388–399
Coleman Mayes, Michele, 282
Communication in workplace, 216–243
    alternative technologies to e-mail, 194, 196
    blogs as formal channels, 218, 219
    business meetings, 234–236
    chance encounters, 225, 226
    communication technology challenges and, 226–234
    company blogs, 218, 219
    computer-generated data overconfidence, 234
    crisis channels, 221–222
    diagonal type, 223
    directions of, 222, 223
    downward type, 222
    e-mail alternatives, 228
    e-mail challenges, 226–228
    etiquette for e-mail and messaging, 229
    Facebook, 219, 220
    formal channels, 218–223
    gossip, 225
    grapevine, 225
    horizontal type, 222, 223
    informal channels, 223–225
    in-person reprimand avoidance, 228
    intranets, 221
    management by walking around, 226
    multitasking consequences, 232–233
    network of contacts, 223–224
    open-door policy, 222
    presentation technology, 228, 229
    rumors, 225
    shadow organization, 223
    social network analysis, 223–224
    social network Web sites, 219, 220

    telecommuting and remote workforce, 231, 232
    telephone, voice mail, and speakerphone skills, 230, 231
    upward type, 222
    webinars, 221
    wikis, 221
Communication network and coworker relationships, 254, 255
Communication overload, 195
Communication (personal), 182–215
    channel selection, 185
    credibility of sender, 194
    cultural and language barriers, 196
    decoding, 185
    defensive communication minimization, 200
    different perspectives and experiences, 195
    distortion of information, 194
    emotions and attitudes, 196
    empathy, 203
    empowered attitude for, 198
    encoding, 185
    feedback check, 198, 199
    frames of references, 198
    gender barriers, 201
    hand gestures, 189
    human needs appeal, 197
    improper timing, 195
    limited understanding of people, 193
    listening improvement, 203–206
    mirroring for rapport, 200, 201
    mixed signals, 194
    nonverbal type, 187–192
    one-way communication, 193
    overload problem, 195, 200
    personal communication style, 206–207
    persuasive type, 198, 199
    process of, 184–185
    relationship building and, 185–186
    repetition of message, 197
    roadblocks to, 192–197
    semantics problem, 193, 194
    skills problem, 196
    small talk and constructive gossip, 201
    timing of messages, 195
Communication skill problem, 196
Communication technology challenges, 226–234
Company blogs, 218, 219
Company recognition programs, 354
Company-sponsored social events, 259
Company values, 123, 124
Compartmentalization, 81
Competition for limited resources, 280
Complaint minimization, 249, 250
Complimenting others appropriately, 260–261

Compromise in negotiation, 298
Computer-generated data overconfidence, 234
Computers and ethical dilemmas, 135
Computers and time wasting, 484, 485
Concentration, 155, 168, 479, 480
    creativity and, 168
    problem solving and, 155
    productivity and, 479, 480
Confidential information and ethics, 134
Conflict of interest, 134
Conflict resolution techniques, 289–299, 358
    appeal to a third party, 295
    asking questions to reframe, 294
    assertiveness, 289–291, 292
    cognitive restructuring, 294
    confrontation and problem solving, 292, 293
    disarm the opposition, 293
    grievance procedure, 295–296, 297
    jury of peers, 296
    negotiation and bargaining tactics, 297–299
    tactic selection, 300–301
    team development and, 358
    win-win approach, 292, 293
Conflict with others, 167, 278–308
    advantages and disadvantages, 287–289
    aggressive personalities, 281
    bullies and, 281
    causes and contributors, 280–287
    competition for limited resources, 280
    creativity and, 167
    cross-generational conflict, 284
    cross-national differences, 283
    culturally diverse teams, 281
    differences of opinion and, 280, 281
    factional groups, 282
    micro-inequities, 284
    personality clashes, 281
    sexual harassment, 284–297
    work–family conflict, 282–283
    workplace violence, 289
    work-related issues and rights, 280–281
Confrontation and problem solving, 292, 293
Confronting manager, 253
Conscientiousness, 125
Consensus leaders, 326, 356
Consideration and initiating structure, 325
Consultative leaders, 326
Continuous learning in career, 416, 443
Coolidge, Calvin, 81
Cooper, Cecily D., 251
Coping with change, 456–457
    "flat world" challenge, 456
    knowledge acquisition for, 456
    outsourcing prevention, 457

Core self-evaluation, 39
Corporate culture and ethics, 139
Corporate ethics programs, 138–139
Corporate spiritualism, 124
Coué, Emile, 107
Courage and leadership, 313
Courtesy, 103, 104
Covey, Stephen, 423, 472
Covie, Bobby, 298
Coworker relationships, 138, 254–266
  backstabbing avoidance, 259
  civility for developing allies, 255, 256
  communication network center
    and, 254, 255
  complimenting others appropriately,
    260, 261
  difficult people dealing, 261–264
  emotional support in, 259
  ethics and, 138
  Golden Rule, 259
  group norms, 259, 260
  honest and open relationships,
    256, 257
  interest in others, 260
  making others feel important, 256
  office romance challenge, 264–266
  organizational culture and, 259
  positive reinforcement for, 260
  self-disclosure for, 256
  self-esteem for, 254, 255
  team player, 258–259
Creativity, 22, 52, 161–173, 383
  brainstorming, 169
  brainwriting, 170
  characteristics of creative workers,
    161–165
  concentration for, 168
  conditions necessary for, 165–167
  conflict and tension for, 167
  critical thinking and, 172–173
  cultural diversity advantage, 383
  encouragement and permissive
    atmosphere for, 167
  expertise for , 165
  explorer, artist, judge, and lawyer
    roles, 171, 172
  fluid vs. crystallized intelligence, 163
  humor and, 167
  idea quotas, 170
  improvement of, 167–172
  insight for, 163
  intellectual abilities, 163
  knowledge for, 163
  motivation and, 165
  multicultural experiences and,
    170, 171
  personality factors, 163
  physical exercise for, 171
  self-confidence and, 52
  time pressures and, 167
  traditional mental sets, 168

  vertical vs. lateral thinking, 168, 169
  workplace challenges and, 22
Creativity and innovativeness
    demands, 22
Credibility of communicator, 194
Credit sharing, 258
Crisis management, 323
Critical thinking, 172–173
Criticism profiting, 515
Cronin, Matthew, 438
Cross-cultural competence (see Diversity
    and cross-cultural competence)
Cross-cultural relations barriers, 377–380
Cross-generational conflict, 284
Cross-national differences and
    conflict, 283
Cultural and language barriers, 196
Cultural bloopers, 384–385
Cultural difference recognition, 388
Cultural intelligence, 381, 382
Cultural mosaic, 376
Cultural sensitivity, 380
Cultural training, 386
Culturally diverse teams, 281, 282
Customer complaints, 269
Customer relationships, 266–270
  care and concern for, 267, 268
  complaint handling, 269
  customer service orientation, 266
  ethics for, 268
  feel-good technique, 268
  goals for, 267
  helpfulness vs. defensiveness, 269
  invitation to return, 269
  needs of customers, 267
  organizational citizenship behavior
    and, 266
  positive attitude toward for, 268
  professional and polite
    communication, 269
  rudeness avoidance, 269
  "wow" experience, 268
Customer service orientation, 266

Dagit, Deborah, 21
Daydreaming problem, 483
De Bord, Grace, 185
Decision making, 152
Decisiveness, 155
DeCremer, David, 38
Defensive communication
    minimization, 200
Dekel, Eran, 35
DeLonzor, Diane, 473
Democratic leaders, 326
Denial in communication, 200
Denial in perception, 445
Denial of personal problems, 445, 515, 516
Dependability and honesty for
    manager, 248
Dependency relationship, 263, 264

Developmental opportunity, 12
DeVore, Jeevan, 408
Diagnosis of motivation, 346
Diagonal communication, 223
Diaz, Antonia, 373
Diet for stress, 512–513
Difficult people dealing, 261–264
  dependency relationship avoidance,
    263, 264
  feedback giving, 262
  humor and, 263
  listening and responding, 263
  personality disorders, 261, 262
  reinforce civil behavior and good
    moods, 264
  reverse gossip, 264
  tact and diplomacy for, 263
  take problems professionally, not
    personally, 262
  types, 261
Difficult times job hunt, 410–412
Digital lifestyle, 123
Direction setting for leadership, 321, 322
Disability legal protection, 395
Disarm the opposition, 293
Distortion of information, 194
Diversity and cross-cultural competence,
    21, 97, 252, 283, 330, 372–401
  acceptance of power and authority,
    374, 375
  affirmative action, 395
  appearance differences, 391
  application of value knowledge, 376
  barriers to good relations, 377–379, 380
  communication barrier overcoming,
    390, 392
  creativity advantage, 383
  cross-national differences in
    work–family conflict, 283
  cultural bloopers, 384–385
  cultural intelligence, 381, 382
  cultural mosaic, 376
  cultural sensitivity, 380
  cultural training, 386–387
  cultural values, 374–375
  disability legal protection, 395
  diversity training, 387–389
  diversity training concerns, 389
  diversity umbrella, 388
  emotional intelligence and, 97
  ethnocentrism, 377, 378
  etiquette differences across cultures,
    390, 391
  federal laws prohibiting job
    discrimination, 393–394
  foreign language training, 386–387
  formality vs. informality, 375
  gender differences in leadership
    style, 392, 393
  genetic discrimination protection, 395
  high-context vs. low-context culture, 375

Diversity and cross-cultural competence
  (*continued*)
  improvement approaches, 380–389
  individual rather than group focus, 382
  individualism vs. collectivism, 374
  job discrimination legislation, 393–395
  leadership adaptation to cultural
    values, 330
  legal aspects, 393–395
  manager relationships, 252
  materialism vs. concern for others, 375
  micro-inequities, 379, 380
  multicultural experiences, 170, 171
  multicultural identities, 376
  multicultural team meeting, 39
  multicultural worker, 383
  norms and codes of conduct, 379
  perceptual expectations, 377
  recognizing differences in cultures, 388
  religious values, 376
  respect for all workers and cultures,
    382, 383
  sexual equity, 383
  stereotypes in intergroup relations,
    378, 379
  time orientation, 375
  unconscious bias protection, 395
  value dimensions, 373–375
  valuing cultural differences, 383, 384
  work vs. leisure orientations, 375
  workplace challenges and, 21
Diversity and globalization as
    workplace challenge, 21
Diversity training, 387
Diversity umbrella, 388
Documenting accomplishments, 415, 416
Doucet, Lorna, 268
Downward communication, 222
Drew, Richard, 157

Eco-friendly jobs, 411
Edison, Thomas, 167
Ehrlich, Brian Scott, 453
Einstein, Albert, 474
E-learning, 437
Ellison. David, 404
E-mail, 226–228, 229
  alternative technologies for, 228
  business meetings and, 236
  communication and, 226–228
  etiquette for, 229
  negotiation and, 228
Emotion in communication, 196
Emotional contagion, 96
Emotional hurdle in job search, 411
Emotional intelligence, 94–97, 153,
    154, 248
  acquisition and development, 97
  concerns about, 97
  consequences of, 96
  cross-cultural considerations, 97

  emotional contagion in, 96
  leadership and, 314
  manager relation and, 248
  problem solving and, 153, 154
  relationship management, 94
  self-awareness, 94
  self-management, 94
  social awareness, 94
Emotional labor, 506
Emotional support to coworkers, 259
Emotional turmoil in setbacks, 51, 52
Empathy and listening, 203
Employment history and ethics, 134, 135
Empowered attitude, 198
Empowerment as motivation, 348–349
Endorphins, 511
Eneli, Aya Fubara, 335
Energy for leadership, 315
Engagement and self-motivation, 69
Envy of others, 40–41
Erikson, Erik H., 447, 448
Esteem needs, 68
Ethical screening of decisions, 136–138
Ethics, 128–141, 268, 321, 413
  career advancement and, 413
  challenges to being ethical, 129, 131
  character traits and development, 136
  codes of professional conduct, 140–141
  computers and information
    technology, 135
  confidential information, 134
  conflict of interest, 134
  corporate culture for, 139
  corporate programs for, 138–139
  create then fix problem, 136
  customer relationships and, 268
  dilemmas frequently faced, 132–135
  employment history, 134, 135
  extent of problems, 132
  guidelines for decisions, 136–137
  harm to people, 129
  hotlines, 139
  importance of, 128–129
  leadership and, 34
  relationship aspects, 138
  role model for, 140
  screening approach, 137–138
  sexual harassment and, 134
  software copying, 132, 133
  survey of problems, 132
  training programs for, 139
  unfair treatment of people, 134
Ethics hotlines, 139
Ethics training program, 139
Ethnocentrism, 377, 388
Etiquette, 195, 342, 363
  career advancement and, 416
  cross-cultural differences, 391
  e-mail and messaging, 229
Everyday annoyances and stress,
    500, 501

Excuse making and self-discipline, 83
Exit strategy in decision making, 160
Expectancy theory of motivation, 79
Expectations of managers, 249
Expertise for career, 412
Expertise for creativity, 165
Explorer artist, judge, and lawyer roles,
    171, 172
External locus of control, 502
Extinction in learning, 436
Extraversion vs. introversion, 439
Eye contact and listening, 206
Eye contact as nonverbal
    communication, 190

Facebook, 219
Face saving in negotiation, 299
Facial expressions, 190
Factional groups, 282
Favorable interactions with
    manager, 251
Fear of success, 460
Federal laws and job discrimination,
    393–394
Feedback
  business meetings and, 235
  communication barriers and, 198
  coworkers and, 12
  difficult people and, 262
  job enrichment and, 350
  leader and, 323
  learning and performing orientation
    toward goals and, 72
  negative type and self-esteem, 39
  peer evaluations and, 12
  personal problems and, 515
  positive reinforcement and, 351
  self-assessment quizzes and, 12
  self-defeating behavior and, 515
  self-motivation and, 79
  self-understanding and, 11
  superiors and, 11–12
Feel-good technique with customers, 268
Fight-or-flight response, 496
Financial incentives, 350–352
  linking compensation to
    performance, 352
  personal factors influence, 353
  problems created by, 353
  variable pay, 352
Financial problems as stressor, 501
Finn, Fran, 472
First impression for career, 414, 415
First-time leader challenges, 334–335
Fishbone diagram, 158
"Flat world" challenge, 456
Flexibility and adaptability for leadership,
    329, 330
Flexibility vs. rigidity in problem
    solving, 154
Flexible career path, 419

Flow experience, 107, 155
Fluid vs. crystallized intelligence, 163
Focus on interests, not positions, 298
Follett, Mary Parker, 17
Ford, Henry, 516
Ford, William C., 123
Foreign language training, 386, 387
Formal communication channels, 218–223
Formality vs. informality in culture, 375
Four-criteria ethics test, 137–138
Fowler, James, 106
Frame games, 160
Frames of reference in communication, 198
Frank, Robert H., 41
Franklin, Benjamin, 107
Freedman, David H., 474
Friedman, Thomas L., 456
Frone, Michael R., 498
Fuerstman, Alan J., 268

Galatea effect, 49, 50, 79
Galbraith, Tim, 69
Gardner, Howard, 321
Garner, Randy, 233
Gates, Bill, 291, 356
Gen Y stereotype overcoming, 126–127
Gender barriers in communication, 201–203
Gender differences in leadership style, 392, 393
Generational differences in values, 125
Gestures as nonverbal communication, 163
Gillespie, Elizabeth, 125
Gladwell, Malcolm, 413
Goals, 71–77, 81, 267, 322, 323, 419
    action plan for, 74, 75
    advantages, 71, 72
    career path and, 419
    customer satisfaction and, 267
    guidelines for setting, 75–76
    job and, 73
    leadership and, 322, 323
    learning and performance orientations, 72, 73
    personal life and, 73–74
    problems created by, 76–77
    realistic goals, 75–76
    relationship with supervisor and, 73
    self-discipline and, 81
    stretch type, 75, 76
    work habits and, 472
    work performance and, 72
Goldberg, Elkhonon, 97
Goldberg, Hal, 169
Golden, Gail, 50
Golden Personality Type Profiler, 439
Golden Rule, 108, 259, 321
Goldsmith, Marshall, 76, 206

Gonzalez, Victor, 499
Goodman, Paul S., 438
Good-start technique, 479
Gossip and small talk, 201, 225
Gottman, John M., 8
Graen, George, 331
Grandey, Alicia A., 506
Grapevine in workplace, 225
Green, Kesten, 299
Greenberg, David, 161
Greenleaf, Robert K., 324
Grievance procedure, 295–296, 297
Group development stages, 358–360
Group dynamics, 358–364
    effective work group characteristics, 364
    groupthink, 363
    stages of group development, 358–360
    team member roles, 360–362, 363
Group learning, 437, 438
Group norms (standards of conduct), 259, 260
Groupthink, 363
Gupta, Sangeeta, 391

Habits in everyday life, 435
Hall, Douglas T., 44
Halo effect, 446
Hamel, Gary, 159
Hand gestures as nonverbal communication, 189
Hansen, Randall S., 454
Happiness attainment, 104–111
    flow experience, 107
    hedonic adaptation, 107
    keys to happiness, 105–119
    meaningful life for, 110
    money and, 109, 110
    physical fitness for, 109
    principles of psychological functioning, 110–111
    recreational fun, 108, 109
    self-esteem and, 107
    spheres of life and happiness, 105
    values and, 109
Harrington, Frank, 454
Harvey, Eric, 134
Hawthorne effect, 16
Hawthorne studies, 16–17
Hayes, David, 352
Hazan, Cindy, 264
Healthy diet for stress, 512–513
Hedonic adaptation, 107
Henderson, Jerome, 413
Herzberg, Frederick, 347
Heyer, Stephen J., 314
High expectations for others, 323
High expectations for self, 49, 50
High- vs. low-context cultures, 375
Hitt, William D., 334
Hogan, Kevin, 516

Hollenbeck, George P., 44
Holmes, John G., 41
Holmes, Thomas, 499
Honest and open relationships, 256–257
Hope and self-confidence, 52
Horizontal career path, 419, 420
Horizontal communication, 222, 223
Huhman, Heather, 125
Human behavior information, 11
Human relations
    advantages of studying, 4–7
    major workplace challenges and, 19–23
    movement for, 15–19
    nature and importance of, 4
    self-understanding and, 10–15
    values link, 122
Human relations movement, 18–19
    Hawthorne studies, 16–17
    industrial humanism philosophy, 17
    relevance today, 18–19
    scientific management, 15–16
    Theory X and Theory Y, 18
    unionization threat, 17
Humble servant (leader), 324
Humor, 167, 251, 263, 318
    creativity and, 167
    difficult people and, 263
    leadership and, 318
    manager relations and, 251
Hurd, Mark, 325, 484

Iacocca, Lee, 317
Idea quotas, 170
Identity crisis, 449
Ilardie, Barbara, 43
Ilies, Remus, 7, 100
Immune system and stress, 497
Implicit learning, 436
Importance feelings for others, 256
Individualism and collectivism, 374
Industrial humanism philosophy, 17
Informal communication channels, 223–225
Informal learning, 436
Information technology and communication, 226–234
Ingram, Harry, 12
Ingratiating behavior, 251
Insight and creativity, 163
Integrated human being, 334
Intellectual ability and creativity, 163
Interest in others, 260
Intermittent rewards, 351
Internal locus of control, 502
Internet for job searches, 406, 407
Internet skill-building exercises
    charisma development, 337
    corporate values fit, 143
    creativity test, 175
    creativity training, 175

Internet skill-building exercises
(*continued*)
customer relationship skills, 272
employee assistance programs, 519
employee motivation, 366
happiness doses, 113
human relations importance, 27
job search, 426
life span challenges of the
millennials, 460
listening skills improvement 209
multicultural skill development, 397
negotiation skills, 303
personal goal setting, 86
self-confidence development, 55
self-esteem building, 55
telecommuting positions search, 238
time log and productivity, 487
values and priorities of a
workplace, 143
Interpersonal skills for success, 414
Intranets, 221
Intrinsic motivation, 77
Intuition and problem solving, 154, 155
Inventory of assets and
accomplishments, 46–48
Isaacowitz, Derek M., 245
Issac, Ray, 245

Jacobi, Jeffery, 190
Jennings, R. Douglas, 29
Job design and interesting work, 349–350
Job discrimination legislation, 393–395
Job enrichment, 350
Job insecurity and job loss as stressors,
504, 505
Job interviews, 409–410
Job performance and behavior factors,
23–25
Job performance and manager
relationship, 246, 247
Job performance for success, 413, 414
Job problem coping, 7
Job résumé, 357–358
Job satisfaction, 101–102, 103, 453
age and, 453
attitudes and, 101–102, 103
leadership and, 322
Job search, 404–412
bad habits to avoid, 412
behavioral interview, 409
difficult times hunt, 410–412
emotional hurdle in, 411
Internet and résumé database services,
406, 407
interviews, 409–410
Linkedin.com, 406
networking for, 405–406
networking sites, 406
online reputation, 409
person–organization fit, 405

résumé for, 407–409
skills-benefit statement, 410
targeted approach, 404
T-form cover letter, 407
Twitter.com, 406
Jobs, Steven, 318
Johari Window for self-understanding,
12–14
Jones, Tom E., 225
Judge, Timothy A., 7, 49, 100, 254, 414
Judging vs. perceiving, 441
Jung, Andrea, 319
Jung, Carl, 439
Jury of peers, 296

Kahneman, Daniel, 155
Kaplan, Bob, 330
Kayes, D. Christopher, 386
Kent, Steve, 4
Keys to happiness, 105–110
Klein, Gary, 154
Knowledge for creativity, 163
Kochan, Thomas A., 389
Koen, Deb, 292
Kohlberg, Lawrence, 448
Kotis, Marty, 225
Kotter, John P., 225
Krantz, David, 502
Krawcheck, Sallie, 280
Kruse, Tim, 421

Lafley, Alan, 222
Lagomasino, Marian Elen, 317
Laissez-faire leadership style, 329
Lamor, Daniel, 167
Lampert, Eddie, 51
Late life challenges, 451
Latham, Gary, 72
Leader–member exchange (LMX)
model, 331
Leader self-efficacy, 313
Leadership, 310–341, 348, 349, 392, 393
adaptation to leader's style, 327, 329
assertiveness, 316
autocratic style, 327, 329
behaviors and skills of effective
leaders, 319–324, 325
broad experience for, 333
character attributes, 315
charisma, 316–319
cognitive skills, 315, 316
consensus leaders, 326
consideration and initiating
structure, 325
consultative leaders, 326
courage, 313
crisis management, 323
cultural value adaptation, 330
democratic leaders, 326
development of potential, 332–334
development programs for, 333

direction setting, 321, 322
effectiveness, 312
emotional intelligence and, 314
ethics, 321
feedback on performance, 323
first-time leader challenges, 334–335
gender differences in style, 392, 393
goal attainment, 322, 323
group member assistance, 324, 325
high expectations for group
members, 323
humble servant, 324
humor and, 318
integrated human being for, 334
laissez-faire style, 329
leader–member exchange (LMX)
model, 331
leader self-efficacy, 313
"little leadership" practice, 334
modeling effective leaders, 333
motivation and energy, 315
openness to experience, 316
participative (team) style, 326–327, 329
partnership with people, 322
passion, enthusiasm, and
excitement, 317
Pygmalion effect, 323
recognition for subordinates, 332
right question asking, 324
satisfaction of members, 322
self-confidence, 312–313, 314
self-development of characteristics,
333, 334
self-efficacy and, 313
self-leadership, 334
servant type, 324, 325
shared leadership as motivation,
348, 349
style flexibility and adaptability,
329, 330
styles for, 325–327, 328
subordinate relationships, 331–332
traits and characteristics, 312–319
trustworthiness, 314, 315
vision for, 317
"walk the talk," 314
Leadership development
programs, 333
Leadership lopsidedness, 330
Learning from manager's mistakes, 254
Learning strategies and processes,
434–438
classical conditioning, 434, 435
continuous learning for, 443
e-learning, 437
extinction strategy, 436
Golden Personality Type Profiler, 439
group learning, 437–438
habits in everyday life, 435
implicit learning, 436
informal learning, 436

modeling, 436
negative reinforcement, 435
operant conditioning, 435–436
positive reinforcement, 435
punishment, 435
reinforcement strategies, 435, 436
rest for brain functioning, 443
schedules of reinforcement, 436
styles of learning, 438–442
traits and attributes of e-learners, 437
visual, auditory, and kinesthetic (VAC) learning styles, 439, 440–441
Learning styles, 438–452
Leary, Mark, 41
LeDoux, Joseph, 10
Lee, Kibeom, 285
Levels of moral thought, 448
Life cycle stages, 447
Life satisfaction and age, 452–453
Life span changes and challenges, 447–453
adolescence challenges, 448–449
adult-life challenges, 449–450
cognitive challenges, 448, 449, 451
cognitive fitness, 451
identity crisis, 449
job satisfaction and age, 453
late-life challenges, 451–452
levels of moral thought, 448
life satisfaction and age, 452–453
midlife crisis, 450
midlife transition, 450
personality and social challenges, 449, 450, 451
sandwich generation challenges, 450
stages of life cycle, 447
teenage brain, 449
Limited understanding of people, 193
Linkedin.com, 406
Listening, 203–204, 263, 298, 324
active listening, 203–206
attention faking, 206
cross-cultural barriers and, 391
difficult people and, 263
discussion shut-down avoidance, 206
empathy, 203
eye contact for, 206
feedback, 204
negotiations and, 298
paraphrasing, 204
sentence finishing, 206
servant leadership and, 324
"Little leadership" practice, 334
Lockwood, Gary, 48
Locus of control and stress, 502
Loft, Joseph, 12
LUNA (Listen for Understanding, Not Agreement), 391

Maas, James B., 443
Making others feel important, 256

Management by walking around, 226
Manager and team leader relationships, 246–254
bad-news delivering, 251, 252
bullying boss, 252
bypassing manager, 250
complaint minimization, 249, 250
confrontation about problem, 253
cross-cultural factors, 252
dependability and honesty for, 248
emotional intelligence and, 248
expectations of manager, 249
favorable interaction with, 251
job performance for, 246, 247
learning from manager's mistakes, 254
organizational citizenship and, 248
performance standards, 249
pet peeves of manager, 253
problem manager coping, 252–254
reevaluation of manager, 252, 253
strong presence and, 249
work ethic for, 247
Manz, Charles C., 334
Mark, Gloria, 499
Maslow, Abraham H., 68, 346
Maslow's need hierarchy, 68–69, 346
Materialism vs. concern for others, 375
Mayer, John D., 94
Mayer, Marissa, 167, 232
Mayo, Elton, 17
McDermott, Tom, 217
McGregor, Douglas, 18
McNatt, D. Brian, 49
Meaningful life, 110
Meaningful work, 78
Meditation for stress, 511
Melrose, Kendrick, 38
Mendes, Wendy Berry, 382
Mental health and self-esteem, 38–39
Mentoring, 421, 422
Merrill, Douglas, 479
Meyer, David E., 233
Micro-inequities, 284, 380, 381
Micromanagement, 356
Midlife crisis, 450
Midlife transition, 450
Miller, Gregory, 497
Mirroring for rapport, 200, 201
Mission and work habits, 472
Mission statement for self-motivation, 81
Mitchell, Pamela, 77
Mixed signals, 194
Modeling for learning, 436
Modeling for self-esteem, 44
Modeling leaders, 333
Money and happiness, 109, 110
Moon, Henry, 376
Moral thought levels, 448
Motivating others, 344–354
classic approaches, 346–347
company recognition programs, 354

diagnosis of motivation, 346
empowerment as motivation, 348–349
financial incentives, 352–353
intermittent rewards, 351
job design and interesting work, 349–350
job enrichment method, 350
leadership trait and, 315
Maslow's need hierarchy, 346
positive reinforcement, 350–352
prosocial motivation, 350
recognition and praise, 353–354
shared leadership and, 348, 349
two-factor theory, 347
visibility of rewards, 351, 352
Motives and motivation, 65
Mroczek, Daniel, 452
Multicultural experiences and creativity, 170, 171
Multicultural identities, 376
Multicultural team meeting, 391
Multicultural worker, 383
Multitasking, 232, 233, 481, 482, 499
benefits of, 232
bits of time, 481
cognitive problems and, 232, 233
communication challenges and, 232
interpersonal consequences, 233
productivity and, 482
stress and, 499
Murphy, Christine, 455
Myers-Briggs Type Indicator (MBTI®), 439

Nadler, Janet, 228
Napping for productivity, 475
Napping for stress, 512
Neatness and orderliness, 473
Needs and motivation, 64–69
Needs vs. wants, 64
Negative affectivity, 502, 503
Negative reinforcement and learning, 435
Negative self-talk, 49
Negotiating and bargaining, 297–299
compromise, 298
e-mail role, 228
face saving, 299
focus on interests, not positions, 298
last and final offer, 298
listening first, 298
plausible demand or offer, 372
positive climate for, 297
role play to predict other side, 299
Network of contacts, 223–224
Networking for career advancement, 423–424
Networking for job search, 405–406
Networking sites, 406
Newbold, Phillip A., 171

Nonverbal communication, 187–192
  airport security and, 191
  circles of intimacy, 188
  cross-cultural differences, 391
  distance from other persons,
    188, 189
  eye contact, 190
  facial expressions, 190
  hand gestures, 189
  personal appearance, 190
  voice quality, 190
Norms for cross-cultural relations, 379
Nutt, Paul C., 156

Office romance, 264–266
Office technology and productivity, 479
Offsite training, 357
Older subordinate challenge, 422
One-way communication, 193
Online reputation, 409
Open-door policy, 222
Openness to experience for
    leadership, 316
Operant conditioning, 435
Optimism and attitudes, 100
Optimism and self-confidence, 52
Order need, 66
Organizational citizenship behavior,
    101–104, 248, 266
  attitudes and, 101–104
  customers and, 266
  manager relations and, 248
Organizational culture, 259
Organizational effectiveness, 4
Organizational prosperity and
    self-esteem, 39
Overconfidence problem, 53

Pace, Peter, 327
Padworski, Brian, 403
Palmisano, Sam, 123, 324
Paraphrasing for listening, 204
Participative (team) leadership style,
    326–327, 329
Partnership for leadership, 322
Passion, enthusiasm, and excitement
    for charisma, 317
Passion for leadership, 317
Patnaik, Deve, 5
Paul, Shale, 471
Pavlov, Ivan, 434
Pawiak, Jim, 412
Peak performance, 50
Pearsall, Christopher, 433, 434
Pease, David C., 422
Peer evaluations, 12
Perception, 443–446
  attribution theory, 446
  congruence in, 446
  denial, 445
  halo effect, 446

  mental processes of people, 445–446
  problems possible, 444–446
  projection, 446
  selective attention, 445
  stereotyping, 445, 446
  stimulus characteristics, 445
Perceptual congruence, 446
Perceptual expectations and culture, 377
Perez, Antonio, 123
Perfectionism and procrastination, 469
Perfectionism in problem solving, 156
Performance standard, 249
Perkins, David, 170
Personal appearance, 190, 191, 414–415
Personal brand, 416, 418
Personal communication style, 206–207
Personal problems, 513–517
  criticism profiting, 515
  denial of problems, 515, 516
  discrepancy between ideal and real
    self, 516
  feedback on actions, 515
  resilience development, 516–517
  self-defeating behavior, 513–516
  self-enhancing behavior, 516
  soft addictions, 513
Personal productivity expectations, 20
Personality and creativity, 163
Personality clashes, 281
Personality and social challenges in life
    span, 449, 450, 451, 452
Personality and stress, 502–503
Personality disorders, 261, 262
Person–organization fit, 405
Person–role conflict, 128
Perspective setting for stress, 507
Persuasive communication, 198, 199
Pet peeves of manager, 253
Pfeffer, Jeffrey, 4
Physical and mental health
    problems, 501
Physical exercise benefits, 171, 511–512
Physical fitness, stress, and
    happiness, 109
Physiological needs, 68
Planning for productivity, 476–478
Political skills, 246
Porges, Steven V., 508
Positive attitude, 100, 101, 268
  customer service and, 268
  importance, 100
  job satisfaction and, 101
Positive reinforcement, 223, 303–307, 382
  coworkers and, 260
  learning and, 435
  motivation and, 350–352
  rules for, 351–352
Positive self-talk, 48
Positive visual imagery, 49
Posture and nonverbal communication,
  189

Power need, 66
Presence on the job, 248, 249
Presentation technology, 228, 229
Price, Alvin, 38
Principles of psychological functioning,
    110–111
Priority setting for productivity, 477
Private self, 10
Proactive personality, 414
Problem manager coping,
    252–254
Problem solving, 152–161
  brain teasers for, 160
  cause-and-effect diagram, 158
  cognitive intelligence, education,
    and experience, 152–153
  concentration, 155
  critical thinking and, 172–173
  decision making and, 152
  decisiveness and perfectionism, 155
  emotional intelligence, 153, 154
  exit strategy for, 160
  flexibility vs. rigidity, 154
  flow experience, 155
  influential factors, 152–156
  intuition, 154, 155
  risk taking and thrill seeking, 155, 156
  steps in, 156–158
  values of the decision maker, 156
  worst-case scenario, 160
Procrastination, 412–415, 416
  fear of success, 469
  perfectionism and, 469
  reasons for, 468–469
  techniques for reducing and
    overcoming, 468–471
  WIFO principle, 471
Productivity and work habits, 468
Projection and perception, 446
Prosocial motivation, 350
Psychological capital and
    self-confidence, 52
Psychological hardiness, 80
Psychological need, 64
Public self, 10
Punishment and learning, 435
Pygmalion effect in leadership, 323

Qi, Lui, 131
Question asking by leader, 324

Rahe, Richard, 494
Ramirez, Ida, 185
Raudsepp, Eugene, 38, 44
Recognition for subordinates, 332,
    353, 354
Recognition need, 66
Reengineering, 480
Reframing for conflict resolution, 294
Reframing with questions, 294
Reinforcement strategies, 351, 435, 436

Relationship building and
communication, 185–187
Relationship management, 94
Relationship with subordinates, 331–332
Relaxation response, 510
Relaxation techniques, 508–511
Religious values, 376
Resilience for problems, 516
Resilience for self-confidence, 51
Respect for others, 357, 382, 383
Rest and relaxation for productivity, 475
Rest for brain functioning, 443
Rest for stress, 511
Résumé for job, 407–409
Reverse gossip game, 264
Rewards in motivation, 351, 352
Rice, Derica W., 314
Risk taking and thrill seeking, 67,
155, 156
Roethlisberger, Fritz J., 17
Role ambiguity, 504
Role conflict, 504
Role model for ethics, 140
Role model for self-discipline, 81
Role overload, 503
Role-playing exercises
bad-habit breaking, 462
business ethics on ski slope, 146
career decision making, 178
charisma projection during
videoconference, 340
demographic match-ups for
customers, 400
empathy with another person, 116
ethical deviant confrontation, 147
getting a worker focused, 90
kindness and recognition for
others, 30
listening to problems of others, 213
management by walking around, 241
manager relationship building, 275
mentor seeking, 428
motivation diagnosis, 369
napping subordinate, 523
procrastination overcoming, 490
self-confidence display, 58
self-esteem boosting, 58
sexual harassment defense, 306
work–family conflict resolution, 207
Role playing for negotiation, 299
Role underload, 503
Rudeness with customers, 269
Rumors in organization, 225

Safety needs, 68
Saloey, Peter, 94
Salyer, Janet 474
Sandwich generation challenge, 450
Sapadin, Linda, 472
Schedules of reinforcement,
351, 436

School-related problems, 501, 502
Schwartz, Barry, 159
Scientific management, 15–16
Scott, Brent A., 254, 414
Scott, Sophronia, 205
Segerstrom, Suzanne, 497
Selective attention, 445
Self-actualizing needs, 68
Self-assessment quizzes
career development inventory, 404
conflict management styles, 290
core self-evaluation scale, 40, 108
creative personality test, 162
cross-cultural skills and attitudes, 378
emotional intelligence, 96
ethical reasoning inventory, 130
human relations skills, 9
leadership style, 328, 329
listening traps, 204
making others feel important, 257
manager interaction checklist, 251
need hierarchy standing, 70
ostracism scale, 201
perfectionism tendencies, 470
readiness for leadership role, 320
resiliency quiz, 517
rhyme and reason creativity test, 164
risk-taking scale, 67
rudeness with customers, 270
self-confidence measure, 46
self-discipline quiz, 82
self-esteem checklist, 37
self-portrait (written), 13
self-sabotage questionnaire, 514
team player roles, 360
visual, auditory, and kinesthetic
survey, 440–441
voice quality checkup, 191
Self-awareness and emotional
intelligence, 94
Self-confidence, 44–53, 312–314
behave confidently, 50
bouncing back for, 51
creative solutions for problems, 52
development and strengthening,
45–53
emotional arousal aspect, 45
emotional turmoil handling, 51
Galatea effect, 49
high expectations (Galatea effect),
49, 50
inventory of assets and
accomplishments, 46–48
knowledge base for, 48
leadership and, 312–314
negative self-talk, 49
optimism for, 52
overconfidence problem, 53
peak performance, 50
positive psychological capital for, 52
positive self-talk for, 48, 49

positive visual imagery for, 49
resiliency and, 51
self-efficacy and, 50
sources of, 44–45
Self-defeating behavior, 513–516
Self-development for career, 414
Self-discipline, 80–83, 437, 480
e-learning and, 437
goals and motivation, 80–83
self-motivation, 80–83
work habits and, 480
Self-disclosure, 12–14, 256
Self-efficacy and leadership, 313
Self-efficacy and self-confidence, 50
Self-employed attitude for productivity,
474, 475
Self-enhancing behavior, 516
Self-esteem, 36–44, 107, 254–255, 500
career and success, 39
consequences of, 38–41
coworker relationships and,
254–255
development of, 36, 38
enhancement of, 41–44
envy of others, 40–41
happiness and, 107
legitimate accomplishments and,
41–42
mental health and, 38–39
models for, 44
nature of, 36
negative feedback processing, 39
organizational prosperity, 39
people boosters, 43–44
personal strengths and, 42–43
settings and interactions, 43
stress relationships, 38, 500
Self-evaluation traps, 14–15
Self-expectation and motivation, 79
Self-leadership, 334
Self-management, 94
Self-motivation 64–71, 77, 471
creativity and, 165
engagement and, 69
goal contribution, 77
Maslow's need hierarchy, 68–69
need theory, 65
needs requiring satisfaction,
65–67
procrastination and, 79
Self-motivation techniques, 77–80
behavior modification, 79
expectancy theory for, 79
feedback for, 79
Galatea effect, 79
goals and, 79
intrinsic motivation, 77–78
psychological hardiness, 80
self-discipline and, 80–83
self-expectation level, 79
work ethic for, 79, 80

Self-understanding, 10–15
  coworkers and peer evaluations, 12
  feedback from superiors, 11–12
  general information about human
    behavior, 10
  informal feedback from people,
    11–12
  Johari Window and, 12–14
  self-assessment quizzes, 12
  self-evaluation traps, 14–15
Seligman, Martin, 38, 109, 110
Semantics, 193, 194
Sensation vs. intuition, 439
Servant leadership, 324–325
Sexual equity, 383
Sexual harassment, 134, 284–287
  effects of, 285
  ethics of, 134
  false accusation, 287
  guidelines for dealing with, 286, 287
  prevention of, 286–287
  types and frequency, 285–286
Shack, Frederick, 411
Shadow organization, 223
Shapiro, Cynthia, 413
Shared leadership as motivation,
    348, 349
Shepley, Michael, 230
Shyness, overcoming, 290–291, 292
Significant life changes, 499, 500
Sinegal, James, 22
Skill acquisition vs. upward mobility, 23
Skill-building exercises
  active listening, 210
  brain and learning ability
    development, 461
  business meeting evaluation, 239
  career pathing, 427
  charisma development, 338
  communication skills
    effectiveness, 211
  company message evaluation, 239, 240
  cultural gaffes, 398
  cultural mistakes avoidance, 398
  customer service providing, 273
  elevator 30-second speech, 273, 274
  emotional intelligence
    enhancement, 114
  empathy for differences, 398
  ethical challenges, 145
  ethical decision making, 144
  getting in good with the boss, 274
  goal setting and action plan
    worksheet, 87
  halo effect capitalizing, 461
  happiest person search, 115
  happiness achievement, 114
  human relations journal, 28
  human relations skills of others, 28
  hunting for advertising
    placements, 176

imagination stretching, 176
job enrichment squad, 367
leadership advice receiving, 339
leadership journal, 338
life span changes facing seniors, 461
need satisfaction for Generations
    X and Y, 87, 88
need satisfaction importance, 88
negotiating for bigger raise, 304
network building, 427
office design for virtual agent, 239
personal productivity checklist, 488
personal stress management action
    plan, 520
persuasive skills, 210
positive motivator survey, 368
problem-solving process, 176
procrastination analysis, 489
productivity from social networking
    sites, 499
reframing through cognitive
    restructuring, 304
self-confidence and self-efficacy
    building, 57
self-confidence for customer
    problem, 58
self-defeating behavior
    overcoming, 520
self-esteem and self-confidence
    survey, 57
self-esteem building club, 56
stress buster survey, 520, 521
stress management action plan, 520
team member roles, 367–368
uniqueness of others observations, 31
value clarification, 144
virtual office design, 239
win–win conflict management, 304
YouTube and Company Web site
    messages, 239, 240
Skills-benefit statements, 410
Skills in dealing with people, 7
Skinner, B. F., 435
Small talk, 201
Smart, Jill B., 455
Smith, Joanne, 322
Social and family problems, 501
Social and organizational support
    for stress, 508
Social awareness, 94
Social needs, 68
Social network analysis, 223–224
Social networking Web sites, 219, 220
Soft addiction, 513
Software piracy, 132, 133
Sorenson, Rich, 185
Sosa, Cesar, 423
Speed for productivity, 473–474
Spheres of influence and happiness, 105
Steady pace approach, 481
Steel, Piers, 285

Steiner, David, 131
Stereotypes and perception,
    445, 446
Stereotypes in intergroup relations,
    378, 379
Sternberg, Robert, 163
Stimulus characteristics in
    perception, 445
Stress, 109, 485–512
  burnout problem, 499
  challenge and hindrance
    stressors, 497
  consequences and symptoms,
    496–499
  fight-or-flight response, 496
  happiness and, 109
  immune system problem, 497
  management of, 506–512
  physiology of, 496
  sources of stress (stressors),
    499–506
Stress busters, 509
Stress management, 506–512
  attacking the source, 507–508
  cognitive behavior interventions, 507
  eliminating or modifying
    stressor, 507
  endorphins, 511
  exercise including yoga 511–512
  gaining control of the situation,
    507–508
  healthy diet, 512–513
  meditation, 511
  organizational support for, 508
  perspective setting, 507
  relaxation response, 510
  relaxation techniques, 508–511
  resting sufficiently, 511
  social support, 508
  stress busters, 509
  support system, 508
  wellness for, 511
Stress sources, 499–506
  adverse customer interaction,
    505, 506
  adverse environmental conditions, 505
  carpal tunnel syndrome, 505
  emotional labor, 505
  everyday annoyances, 500, 501
  external locus of control, 502
  financial problems, 501
  job insecurity and job loss, 504
  low self-esteem, 500
  negative affectivity, 502, 503
  personality factors, 502–503
  physical and mental health
    problems, 501
  role ambiguity, 504
  role conflict, 504
  role overload, 503
  school-related problems, 501, 502

significant life change, 499, 500
social and family problems, 501
type A behavior and hostility, 502
work overload or work underload, 503–504
Strong presence for manager relationship, 249
Style flexibility and adaptability, 329–330
Success syndrome, 414
Sudoku as problem-solving exercise, 160, 161
Sulkowicz, Kerry L., 53, 443
Sullenberger, Chesley "Sully," 153, 233
Support system, 508
Sutton, Robert, 166
Synergy in group, 259

Tact and diplomacy, 263
Takash, Joe, 206
Tannen, Deborah, 201
Tattoos and body piercing, 415
Taylor, Frederick W., 15
Team book for teamwork, 357
Team member roles, 360–362, 363
Team player tactics, 258–259
Teamwork and collaboration, 19, 20
Teamwork culture, 356
Teamwork development, 354–358
Teenage brain, 449
Telecommuting and remote workforce, 231, 232
Telecommuting as workplace challenge, 22–23
Telephone, voice-mail, and speakerphone skills, 230, 231
T-form cover letter, 407
Theory X and Theory Y, 18
Thinking vs. feeling, 439
Thompson, Jeffery A., 414
Time-and-activity (Gantt) chart, 478
Time leaks, 484
Time limit for tasks, 485
Time logs, 484
Time orientation in culture, 375
Time pressure and creativity, 167
Time valuing, 473
Time wasting control, 482–485
Time-zone adjustments, 477–478
To-do lists, 476
Traditional career paths, 419
Traditional mental sets, 168
Traits and attitudes of e-learners, 437
Treviño, Linda Klebe, 129
Trustworthiness and leadership, 314, 315
Turnaround managers, 327
Tversky, Amos, 155
Twitter.com, 406

Two-factor theory of work motivation, 347
Type A behavior and hostility, 502

Unfair treatment of people, 134
Unionization of workers, 17
Upward communication, 222
Useem, Michael, 327

Value clarification, 127
Values, 122–128
    career path and, 419
    clarification of, 127
    classification of, 124–125
    company values, 123, 124
    corporate spiritualism, 124
    cultural differences, 383, 384
    decision making and, 156
    ethics and, 122
    Gen Y stereotypes overcoming, 125–126
    generational differences, 125–127
    happiness and, 109
    individual and job fit, 128
    late-life influences, 123
    learning of, 122–124
    mesh between individual and job values, 128
    person–role conflict, 128
    religious types of values, 376
Valuing cultural differences, 383, 384
Valuing time, 473
Vance, Michael, 167
Variable pay, 352
Vertical vs. lateral thinking, 168, 169
Video résumé, 498
Violence in workplace, 289
Virtual office, 22
Virtual teams, 357
Visibility for career, 416
Vision and leadership, 317
Visual, auditory, and kinesthetic (VAK) learning styles, 439, 440–441
Visual and sensory stimulation, 82
Voice quality, 190

Wainright, Tony, 205
"Walk the talk," 314
Wallace, Chris, 151
Watson, John B., 435
Webinars, 221
Webster, E. Carol, 79
Weill, Andrew, 508
Welch, Jack, 44, 350
Welch, Suzy, 350
Wellness, 511
Whitman, Meg, 314, 315
WIFO (worst in, first out), 471
WIIFM (What's in it for me?), 65
Wikis in company, 221
Willness, Chelsea R., 285
Wilson, Jeanne M., 438

Winfrey, Oprah, 313
Win-win conflict resolution, 292, 293
Wooden, John, 332
Woolley, Linda, 422
Work and personal life interaction 7–8, 10
Work ethic, 42, 79, 80, 247, 472, 473
Work-family conflict, 282–283
Work group characteristics, 364
Work habits and time management, 20–21, 466–492
    ADHD (attention deficit hyperactivity disorder), 480
    attendance and punctuality, 473
    attitudes and values for, 472–475
    bits of time, 481, 482
    cleaning up and getting organized, 476
    clustering of tasks, 485
    computer misuse, 484, 485
    concentration on one task, 479, 480
    daydreaming problem, 483
    good start technique, 479
    important task emphasis, 480, 481
    keeping track, 485
    mission, goals, and work ethic, 472, 473
    multitasking, 482
    napping for productivity, 475
    neatness, orderliness, and speed, 473
    office technology use, 479
    paperwork, in-basket, and e-mail control, 482
    planning activities, 476–478
    priority setting, 477
    procrastination problem, 469–471, 472
    productivity link, 468
    quiet, uninterrupted time, 481
    rest and relaxation for, 475
    scheduling and follow through, 478
    self-discipline and, 480
    self-employed attitude, 474, 475
    similar task scheduling, 485
    speed factor, 473–474
    steady work pace, 481
    streamlining approach, 480
    task-to-task movement, 486
    techniques for, 475–482
    time-and-activity report, 478
    time leaks, 484
    time limits for task, 485
    time logs, 484
    time-wasting control, 482
    time-zone adjustments, 477–478
    to-do lists, 476–477
    valuing time, 473
    work smarter, not harder, 474
    workaholism problem, 475
    workplace challenges and, 20–21

Work overload and underload, 503, 504
Work smarter, not harder, 474
Work streamlining, 480
Work vs. leisure orientation, 375
Workaholism problem, 475
Workplace challenges, major, 19–23
   creativity and innovativeness
      emphasis, 22
   diversity and globalization, 21

personal productivity expectations,
   20–21
skill acquisition versus upward
   mobility, 23
teamwork and collaboration, 19–20
virtual workplace and telecommuting,
   22–23
Workplace violence, 289
Worst-case scenario, 160

"Wow" experience for customers, 268
Wozniak, Steve, 318

Yamazaki, Yoshitaka, 386
Yoga for stress, 512
Younger boss challenge, 422

Zeldes, Nathan, 467
Zimpleman, Larry, 102